Landmarks in
Print Collecting

Albrecht Dürer: *Nemesis*, c.1501–2 (cat. 74)

Landmarks in Print Collecting

Connoisseurs and Donors at the British Museum since 1753

Edited by Antony Griffiths

Published by
British Museum Press
for The Trustees of the British Museum
and by Parnassus Foundation
in association with
The Museum of Fine Arts, Houston

Published to accompany an exhibition to be shown at the
following venues:

31 March – 16 June 1996
The Museum of Fine Arts, Houston
Houston, Texas

12 July – 29 September 1996
Huntington Art Collections
San Marino, California

16 October 1996 – 5 January 1997
The Baltimore Museum of Art
Baltimore, Maryland

25 January – 6 April 1997
The Minneapolis Institute of Arts
Minneapolis, Minnesota

© 1996 The Trustees of the British Museum

Co-published by British Museum Press
A division of The British Museum Company Ltd
46 Bloomsbury Street, London WC1B 3QQ
and Parnassus Foundation
in association with
The Museum of Fine Arts, Houston

A catalogue record for this book is available from the British Library

ISBN 0–7141–2606–3 (cased)
ISBN 0–7141–2609–8 (paper)

Designed by James Shurmer

Typeset in Sabon by Southern Positives and Negatives (SPAN)

Printed and bound in Great Britain by Cambridge University Press

Contents

continued overleaf

Contents *continued*

Preface

This exhibition and the accompanying catalogue present, to the best of our knowledge, an entirely new approach to print scholarship. Previous literature has dealt with the graphic oeuvre of individual artists or the publications of professional engravers and publishers. Prints have been examined by nationality, school, century, or specific medium. Never before, however, has an exhibition been selected and organised around the collectors rather than the makers.

Because the show is structured around ten collections over a span of 250 years, it necessarily embodies a history of the evolution of taste within this discipline. The dominant concern of our own era is connoisseurship. Especially in old master prints, we are interested first and foremost in the quality of impression and its condition. Such an attitude is a relatively recent development within the history of the printed image and is, in many ways, a negation of the very quality for which prints have traditionally been valued: their ability to replicate exactly the same design.

The first section of this exhibition, the collection of Sir Hans Sloane, demonstrates that the majority of early collectors were concerned with the visual information that a print could convey and had little interest in its aesthetics. As William Ivins, founding Curator of Prints at the Metropolitan Museum of Art, pointed out: 'The principal function of the printed picture in western Europe and America has been obscured by the persistent habit of regarding prints as of interest and value only in so far as they can be regarded as works of art. Actually the various ways of making prints (including photography) are the only methods by which exactly repeatable pictorial statements can be made about anything. The importance of being able exactly to repeat pictorial statements is undoubtedly greater for science, technology, and general information than it is for art' (William M. Ivins, Jr., *Prints and Visual Communication*, Cambridge, MA, 1953, pp. 1, 2). The last sentence perfectly defines Sloane's attitudes and concerns.

Later sections of the exhibition deal with the collections of such connoisseurs as the Reverend Clayton Mordaunt Cracherode; the collecting of prints by subject, nationality, and period; the works of *peintres-graveurs* versus those of reproductive engravers; specialised collecting by medium, and the collecting goals of professional curators. Along the way, we learn how early collections were organised and housed, what prints cost at different times, and how a robbery led to new standards of professionalism in cataloguing and storage.

This is the first exhibition of prints drawn exclusively from the British Museum's collection ever to travel outside the United Kingdom. We are grateful to the Trustees of the British Museum for their willingness to lend the works that comprise this magnificent exhibition, and to the Director, Dr R. G. W. Anderson, for his support of the project. We also thank Emma Way of British Museum Publications for overseeing the editing and production of the catalogue, and Janice Reading for ably handling all the administrative details of the tour.

Our warm thanks go to Antony Griffiths, Keeper of Prints and Drawings, for supervising every aspect of the exhibition and catalogue, writing the Introduction as well as several chapters, and for his unfailing good humour and professional courtesy in replying to innumerable questions and requests. Like his previous publications, this catalogue sets new standards for scholarship and clarity of presentation. We also thank Frances Carey, Deputy Keeper, for her involvement in all areas of the project and for the chapters she has written. Equally remarkable research was contributed in chapters by Assistant Keepers Stephen Coppel, Sheila O'Connell and Martin Royalton-Kisch.

Barry Walker, Curator of Prints and Drawings, selected the works for the exhibition in conjunction with the staff of the British Museum, and coordinated the American organisation of the exhibition for the Museum of Fine Arts, Houston. His colleagues at San Marino, Baltimore and Minneapolis, Edward Nygren, Jay M. Fisher and Richard Campbell, together with the staffs of the four museums participating in the tour, have contributed their efforts to the realisation of the exhibition.

Our special thanks go to Raphael Bernstein and the Parnassus Foundation, co-publisher, with the British Museum Press, of the catalogue. It was Mr Bernstein who initiated this collaboration with the British Museum, and whose enthusiastic support throughout the entire process enabled its realisation.

Peter C. Marzio
Director, The Museum of Fine Arts, Houston

When we first received Peter Marzio's invitation to show a selection of prints from the British Museum in Houston and three other American institutions, we at first wondered what we could offer. There are many very fine collections of prints already in American museums and galleries, and there is no need to cross the Atlantic in order to find a selection of works that an American public will enjoy. But when we thought again, we realised that our collection was significantly different from all American ones in that it has been built up over nearly two hundred and fifty years; the oldest American public collections barely predate the middle of the nineteenth century. Our collection is probably larger than that of any American institution, and it covers a wider range of material.

These two facts are not unconnected. The British Museum was established in 1753, and was the first museum in the world to be founded by the public will – in the form of an Act of Parliament – for the benefit of a national and international public. The foundation collection was that of the physician and botanist Sir Hans Sloane, and the enormous range of his collection, both of objects and of books, was determined by his concept of its purpose. It was not an idle cabinet of curiosities; all the material in it was designed to be used, and the accumulation of information that it offered was seen as the only way to solve some of the great intellectual issues that vexed his age. This ideal of serving the advance of knowledge and the needs of an international public continues to inspire the British Museum. It is still maintained largely by public funds, and admission is still free to all.

Scholarship in recent years has begun to realise the value of studies of the history of collecting. But until now almost no work has been done on the history of the growth of the collection in the Department of Prints and Drawings. Yet, spanning two and a half centuries of fairly steady acquisition, it provides, as do few other institutions in the world,

a perfect case for studying the changing ideas of what a print collection might be, and what it might contain. So we have chosen ten collectors or significant episodes in the history of the development of our collection, and used them to present in microcosm a history of print collecting in this period. The story is of course incomplete, but it has never been told before even in part. Almost all the information contained in the following pages is presented for the first time, having been discovered in the course of research for this catalogue.

The exhibition itself contains a hundred prints, a very small number to represent a collection of nearly two million. Needless to say it cannot do this adequately, and many will lament the absence of some favourite. We take consolation in the words of one of the greatest of American print scholars, Hyatt Mayor: 'I never wanted to show very many prints at one time. A hundred is about all you can see at one go. Somebody once said that you can really *see* works of art for half an hour, then the next half-hour you check off the existence of things, after that you just wander about hoping for some indecency' (A. Hyatt Mayor, *Selected Writings and a Bibliography*, New York 1983, p. 174).

We are grateful to Peter Marzio, to Raphael Bernstein and the Parnassus Foundation, to Barry Walker and all who have enabled us to present this exhibition and catalogue to the public. We hope that it will present some very fine prints from the treasures that we are known to hold, and also introduce some surprises among completely unfamiliar material. The catalogue is the collaborative work of five members of the staff of the Department of Prints and Drawings, led by the Keeper, Antony Griffiths, and is the first study on such a scale of the history of any of the ten curatorial departments that now form the British Museum.

R. G. W. Anderson
Director, British Museum

Introduction: The Department of Prints and Drawings of the British Museum and the History of Print Collecting

Antony Griffiths

The ten essays in this book are devoted to individual print collectors, or to episodes in the growth of the British Museum collection. Each can be read independently of the others, and they form a series of studies in the history of print collecting. Most of them are not about the British Museum as such, and some say little about the institution in which the collections ended up. Others are very much about the Museum. The sections on William Smith, on Campbell Dodgson and on curatorial collecting in the twentieth century form part of an institutional history. But since they do not combine to give a coherent picture, the first part of this introduction gives a very brief account of the Department since its inception and a context into which all the essays can be placed. The second part considers the wider pattern in the history of print collecting into which they fit.

The British Museum in 1996 is an enormous establishment. It fills an entire block in Bloomsbury, employs over 1,000 staff, has a budget of £34 million a year, and has ten curatorial departments which cover all aspects of the material culture of mankind from the Stone Age to the present day. It has given birth to two other great institutions, the Natural History Museum in South Kensington and the British Library, both of which were in origin departments of the British Museum. Yet what remains still ranks among the greatest museums of the world, and its façade, designed by Sir Robert Smirke and built in the 1840s, has an appropriate grandeur (fig. 1). It is now visited by over six million people a year.

It is difficult to imagine how utterly different the Museum was in the eighteenth century. At that time it was the first national museum in the world founded as a public institution, and had no others to compare itself with. The collection was simply that of the physician Sir Hans Sloane (see section 1), and it was housed in a grand town house on the then outskirts of London which had been built seventy years earlier for Lord Montagu, and was completely inappropriate for a public museum. The staff was tiny, and visitors were only admitted in small parties for guided tours. A tour left every hour on the hour, for which tickets had to be collected from the porter's lodge in the morning. Once the day's supply had run out, there was no way to get in.

In these early days the Department of Prints and Drawings did not exist. Sloane owned many albums of drawings and many volumes of prints (see section 1), but they were

1. Charles Rivière,
*Smirke's Colonnade of the
British Museum*, colour
lithograph, c.1860.
178 × 263 mm.
Central Archives

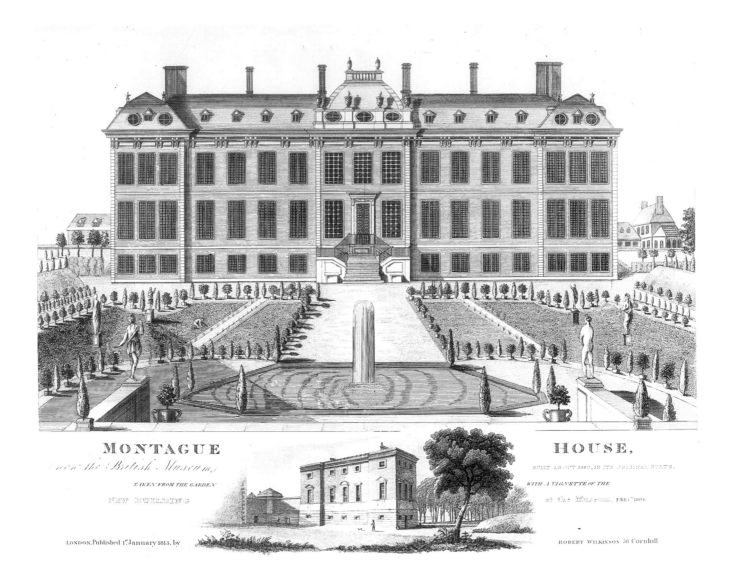

MONTAGUE HOUSE,

near the British Museum,

BUILT ABOUT 1680, IN ITS ORIGINAL STATE.

TAKEN FROM THE GARDEN

WITH A VIGNETTE OF THE

NEW BUILDING

of the Museum, ERECT^D 1804.

LONDON, Published 1st January 1813, by

ROBERT WILKINSON 58 Cornhill

2. Robert Wilkinson (publisher), *Montagu House*, engraving, 1813. Inset below is a vignette of the exterior of the Townley Galleries. 253 × 328 mm. 1936-5-11-100

housed in the Department of Manuscripts and the Department of Printed Books respectively. In these homes their identity was lost, and few visitors can ever have realised that there were any prints and drawings in the British Museum. This changed in 1799 with the arrival of the collection bequeathed by a former trustee, the Rev. C. M. Cracherode (see section 2). His prints and drawings were famous, and the Trustees decided to keep them together in a new room specially fitted up for the purpose. The key was given to a member of staff of Printed Books, William Beloe, and he was responsible for admitting visitors to it.

It took only seven years to bring home to the Trustees how unsatisfactory this was. A minor caricaturist called Robert Dighton had gained Beloe's confidence, and been given virtually unsupervised access to the room. He took advantage of this to begin stealing prints in a wholesale way, especially from Cracherode's famous group of etchings by Rembrandt. He was only discovered when he started selling his loot, by which time the damage was done. Since no inventory of the prints had ever been made, there was no way of telling what had been taken, and the Trustees had to agree to a messy compromise whereby Dighton was not prosecuted in return for making a full confession and helping to recover as many prints as he could lay his hands on. (See section 2; all the documents relating to this affair are here published in Appendix E.)

It was this sad event that led the Trustees belatedly to establish a separate section of Prints and Drawings in 1808. It was nominally a subsection of a new Department of Antiquities, but the newly appointed Keeper had virtually a free hand. Following the report of a Parliamentary Commission it was formally separated in 1837, and has remained an independent Department to the present day. Initially the Trustees' concerns were entirely to do with security. A room was fitted out to house the prints and drawings in the newly-constructed Townley Wing (fig. 3), and the Trustees themselves went round the shelves of the Departments of Printed Books and Manuscripts removing all the albums and volumes that they thought at risk. The new room had a fortified front door, which faced an equally strong door to a new Coins and Medals room, and was open to students only when the Keeper was in attendance.

This was not very often, because the first man appointed, William Alexander, was given a second job to draw the classical sculpture from the Townley collection so that it could be engraved for a luxury publication on which the Trustees had set their hearts. In was in fact his qualifications as a draughtsman that got Alexander the job, for he had no expertise in prints or drawings. He had made his name in 1792–4 when he accompanied Lord Macartney as official draughtsman on his famous expedition to the court of the Chinese Emperor in Peking, and the drawings he made there are still of great interest and charm. Alexander does indeed seem to have been a delightful man, and those who found their way to see the collection on the one or two afternoons a week that it was open all praised his affability.

The Trustees' concerns for security were furthered by employing an outside expert, the dealer and auctioneer Thomas Philipe, to rearrange all the prints that they had transferred from Printed Books in new albums, and to paste them down securely. (Philipe's paper explaining his new arrangement is published as Appendix F.) This operation caused considerable damage. Although Philipe was instructed to mark each print to record which of the foundation collections it had come from (Sloane, Cracherode, or the collection of William Fawkener, bequeathed in 1769), he either failed to do it, or did it so inaccurately that it is now extremely difficult to reconstruct these collections. As a result he wiped out most of their history; the essays in sections 1 and 2 are attempts to get behind this obliteration of information. In lifting the prints from the old albums he often skinned the versos or even tore the paper. Another problem was caused by the way in which he pasted the prints into their new albums. Very soon they began cockling, and then rubbing along the ridges. In the 1840s Josi had to begin to take them apart, and today not one of Philipe's albums survives.

After Philipe had finished, in 1810, the Trustees instructed William Alexander to draw up an inventory of what was in the albums. At this point, all the albums were placed flat on the shelves of a run of cabinets that were numbered from A to Z, and then Aa to Tt. So the inventory took the form of a number such as E 3–34, signifying the thirty-fourth print in the volume on the third shelf of case E. As can be imagined, such a system created insuperable problems in inserting new acquisitions in their proper places. The fact that it was adopted shows that the Trustees were not expecting the collection to grow. Alexander's inventory had not advanced very far when he died in 1816.

His successor was John Thomas Smith, the son of a print dealer, and a well-known figure in the London art world.

3. George Cruikshank, *The first Print Room in the Townley Galleries*, etching, 1828.
74 × 110 mm

He remains the most famous of all Keepers of the Department for his biography *Nollekens and His Times* of 1828, filled with scandalous gossip and a minor classic of English letters, and for *A Book for a Rainy Day*, published posthumously in 1845. Both books show his talent for story-telling, and accounts of the Department during his Keepership reveal that the Student Room was often occupied by his friends who had come to listen to his inexhaustible fund of amusing tales (fig. 3 shows precisely such a scene). Those who were not his friends received much shorter shrift, and the archives preserve a four-page diatribe to the Trustees from the painter Benjamin Robert Haydon, whom Smith had not let in on the pretext that the Room was full.

Smith was a typical figure of the Regency period, able, amusing and talented, but indolent. In the seventeen years of his Keepership he made no headway on the inventory that Alexander had begun, and did little to arrange unsorted parts of the collection. What he did do was supervise the transfer of the entire Department in 1828 out of the Townley Wing, which had proved utterly unsuitable for housing the collection. The walls often ran with damp, and Smith's reports to the Trustees include hair-raising accounts of his attempts to dry out the albums of mezzotints before an open fire, and to clean mildew off the Rembrandt etchings. The new home was in the south-east corner of the new building (the present British Museum) that Smirke was constructing on the site of Montagu House, which was gradually demolished to make room for it.

Smith was also responsible for the first programme of acquisitions for the collection. Throughout the eighteenth century not a single penny had been spent on adding to the collection of prints and drawings; the few additions, and they were very few, were all gifts or bequests. One very important and completely isolated purchase was made in 1806, of early engravings from the collection of Dr John Monro. Beyond the fact that they cost £50, the archives record nothing, but it can be shown that among them were prints of very great importance indeed (see p. 91). This was a unique event, and nothing further happened until 1820, when Smith bought George Cumberland's collection of prints by Giulio Bonasone. In 1823 followed the Hogarth collection of William Packer, a friend of Smith's, but it was not until 1827 that something like an annual allowance for purchases was allocated to the Department. This was initially fixed at £80, but was soon raised to £100. With this Smith, apparently following the Trustees' wishes, began to build up a collection of prints after Sir Joshua Reynolds, the founder of the English school of painting and the first President of the Royal Academy.

On Smith's death in 1833, his successor was William Young Ottley, undoubtedly the greatest living connoisseur of drawings and prints, but a man who was already aged sixty-two and in ill health. He lived only three more years, and so was unable to make much of a mark on the collec-

tion or its organisation. He did begin a new catalogue, but put more energy into a series of rows with the Director and the Trustees about his conditions of work. These clouded his time at the Museum. The purchases that he made were few, although very enterprising and original, and make one wonder what might have happened if he had joined when he was younger and if he had had more funds to spend. His own remarkable collection of prints, formed as working material for a projected dictionary of engravers, was auctioned after his death, when only a few lots were purchased for the Museum.

The founder of the modern Department of Prints and Drawings was Smith's successor, Henry Josi. He was a young man, only thirty-four when he was appointed in 1836, and he already knew the print business well. His father had been a well-known collector, and Josi himself had been a dealer or agent of some sort. He moved into action at astonishing speed. He at once began to inventory the collection afresh, and by the end of 1837 had finished it: there were 9,302 drawings and 45,752 prints. To supplement it he began a register of new acquisitions, which were given date numbers of the style 1837-4-8-1, in which the first number is the year, the second the month, the third the day, and the last a sub-number. Josi also devised the system of arrangement of the collection that is still followed today (his paper on the subject is published as Appendix G). He supervised the transfer of the collection to a new Print Room (the third) in the north-west corner of the Smirke building, and made it accessible to students of all types. In 1844 he reported to the Trustees that the whole nature of the Department had been completely altered: 'Whereas formerly the Print Room was so closed as to be scarcely admissible to anybody, it has now become a national school of design, many clever artists having emanated from the Print Room and formed themselves solely from that collection.'

Josi also revolutionised the Department's acquisitions. A few months after he joined he engineered the purchase of the Sheepshanks collection for £5,000 (see section 3). This was the first major purchase that the Department had ever made, and required a special Government grant. It did a little to repair the damage caused by the major disaster of Smith's Keepership, when, despite his and the Trustees' enthusiastic recommendation, the collection of old master drawings of Sir Thomas Lawrence, perhaps the finest ever formed, had been lost when the Government refused to find the asking price of £18,000. Josi followed up this success with several other purchases of blocks of material with further Government grants. Each block was assembled by his friend and ally, the dealer William Smith, and the mechanisms by which this series of acquisitions was made are explored in section 4. It is impossible to overestimate the importance of these purchases. It was not simply that the Department acquired a series of prints of the greatest rarity and importance. They were a decisive statement of intent. The British Museum had stopped being a collection of merely national and thus provincial importance; it had raised its sights and intended to become of international stature. This new ambition infected the Trustees, and they began to raise the annual grant for the Department's bread-and-butter purchases. In 1836 it was £100 a year; by 1847 it had reached £1,200 a year, and this was in a period that saw no monetary inflation whatever and relatively little rise in the price of prints either. Indeed it was only after the Second World War that the grant again reached this figure, having been cut for many years beforehand.

Josi was only forty-three when he died in 1845, but his work was carried on without interruption by his successor William Hookham Carpenter, who had evidently been a friend of his, as he was also a close friend of William Smith. Carpenter's twenty-one years in office saw the consolidation of everything that Josi had begun. The collection was rearranged, and the best drawings and prints began to be extracted from portfolios and individually mounted. The collection was expanded dramatically, and began to include modern works as well as those from the past. Carpenter's most startling achievement to the modern observer was perhaps the purchase of four etchings by Edouard Manet in 1865. More important to the future of the Department were the excellent relations that he established with collectors. These were to lead to a great harvest after his death in 1866.

Since the Cracherode bequest in 1799 there had been no really important gift or bequest of prints. Almost every acquisition that mattered had been purchased from the funds provided by successive British governments. They had been spectacularly generous; in the thirty years between 1836 and 1866 well over £50,000 of public money had been spent on purchases for the Department. The arrival of the treasures of the Slade bequest in 1868 (see section 5) marks the beginning of the tilting of the balance away from public support and towards private generosity. Slade had known Carpenter well, and there can be no question but that this friendship had played a part in his decision. Slade was a man of great public spirit, with a burning desire to raise the standards of art education in Britain. To this end he left the endowments that were to establish the Slade professorships in the history of art at Oxford and Cambridge Universities, and the Slade School of Art at University College London. His bequest to the British Museum has to be seen in the same light: he wished his prints to raise public standards of artistic awareness, and to give others the pleasure that he himself had experienced.

Carpenter and Josi had both joined the Museum as Keeper, Josi with a great experience of prints gathered from his previous career in or on the edges of the print trade, Carpenter with a considerable reputation as a scholar. In 1844 he had published an important collection of documents, *Pictorial Notices ... of Sir Anthony van Dyck*, in

which he included one of the first catalogues of van Dyck's etchings. George William Reid, Carpenter's successor, was a man of a different type. He had joined the Department as an attendant in 1842, as his father had been before him, and worked his way up to become the first Assistant (that is Assistant Keeper) in 1865, and Keeper the following year. He had learned a great deal about prints, and continued the work of reorganising the collection and making indexes on blue slips of sections of it. He also made purchases on a great scale and of great variety. But he was not a scholar, and as the Trustees began to show a greater concern to publish a catalogue of the entire collection, he found himself in increasing difficulties.

Since he had only two assistants, no one expected him to write the volumes himself. Instead he commissioned a number of outside authors. The catalogue of early Italian engravings up to and including Marcantonio and his followers was given to Richard Fisher, who had been one of Slade's executors. The early German prints went to W. H. Willshire, another collector. The political and personal satires, most of which had been purchased in 1868 from the collection of Edward Hawkins, the former Keeper of the Department of Antiquities, were assigned to F. G. Stephens, who had in 1848 been one of the founding members of the Pre-Raphaelite Brotherhood. A fourth catalogue was prepared of the prints relating to British history.

Of these only two were ever published. Stephens's was the first to come out, and four volumes appeared between 1870 and 1883. They were not very satisfactory. Stephens was paid by the printed page, and this gave him every reason to write at length rather than in depth. Page after page consists of transcriptions of what can be seen on the prints, and in minute descriptions of their content. Their meaning and historical significance are often left obscure. Similar problems affected Willshire's *Catalogue of Early Prints in the British Museum: German and Flemish Schools* which came out in two volumes in 1879 and 1883.

These problems were as nothing to those with Fisher. He was evidently a very difficult man, who treated the staff of the Department as if they were his personal servants. It was not long before relations between him and Reid had collapsed. Reid accused him not only of rudeness, but of time-wasting, incompetence, and of using the opportunity and the fees he was charging to build up his personal print collection. At this point in 1883 Reid retired at the age of sixty-four, rather against his will, and the Trustees brought in as the new Keeper Sidney Colvin, the Slade professor and director of the Fitzwilliam Museum in Cambridge, to sort out the mess. He patched up relations with Fisher, but was forced to the conclusion that the catalogue was so poor that it could not be published, even though it had all been set in type and was in page proof. Eventually only the introduction came out under the Trustees' name. Stephens's catalogue of satires was discontinued, and the catalogue of

British historical prints, also set in type, was suppressed: only one copy seems to survive. Fisher's own collection never came to the Museum, being auctioned in 1892 after his death. Willshire bequeathed his early prints to the Guildhall Library in the City of London, where they still remain.

If Josi was the first founder of the Department, Colvin must unquestionably be seen as its refounder. In the thirty years of his long Keepership he made a series of changes setting the Department on a new course that has determined its history during the past century. He stopped the employment of outside authors, and instead recruited to the staff a new and brilliant young generation of university-trained historians. Governments were by now being much meaner, and it took him a long time to achieve his goals. In 1884 he managed to get a third post for an Assistant, which was given first to Lionel Cust, and, after his departure to the National Portrait Gallery in 1895, to Laurence Binyon, the famous poet. When Louis Fagan resigned in 1892, a vacancy arose which was filled by Campbell Dodgson. In 1904 a new fourth post was created which was given to A. M. Hind. Dodgson, Binyon and Hind, together with A. E. Popham who joined in 1912, dominated the history of the Department for the next half-century. None had any specialised knowledge of the field when they were recruited, but all were of such ability that they rapidly became authorities of world renown: Dodgson and Hind on western prints, Binyon on English watercolours and Chinese and Japanese art, Popham on Netherlandish and Italian art. Until the founding of the Department of Oriental Antiquities in 1933, all oriental works on paper formed a subsection of the Department of Prints and Drawings; one of Colvin's many achievements was to create collections of Japanese prints and Chinese paintings where none had previously existed.

The driving force behind Colvin's innovations was undoubtedly Germany and what was happening in Berlin. Rivalry with the French and the model of Napoleon's creation of the Louvre had in large part explained the willingness of governments to fund the enormous growth of the British Museum in the first half of the nineteenth century. The movement towards cataloguing and scholarship in the last decades of the century can equally be explained by an uneasy awareness of what the Germans were doing. The unification of the country in 1870 by Prussia had led the German government to decide to build up the Berlin museums on the Museumsinsel to rival those in London and Paris. What happened over the next forty-five years was one of the great feats in the history of museums. It was not just that the collections were transformed and expanded; what amazed and unnerved the rest of the world was the unprecedented learning and scholarship possessed by the staff that allowed them to pull off coup after coup. England, as the richest country in the world in private collections, suffered the most as one masterpiece after another turned up in Berlin. When Botticelli's marvellous drawings for Dante's *Divine Comedy* were acquired for Berlin as part of the Hamilton manuscripts in 1882, it

4. *The fourth Print Room in the White Wing, c.*1913. After a photograph by Donald Macbeth. Standing at the back left is Arthur Waley, with Laurence Binyon seated behind him; Campbell Dodgson is seated at the Supervisor's desk in the centre right. 1914-7-24-1

was embarrassingly evident that hardly anyone in England had ever known that they were there in the first place.

It is against this background that the first serious catalogue published by the Department must be seen: Dodgson's *Catalogue of Early German Woodcuts in the British Museum*, of which two volumes appeared in 1903 and 1911. These were among the first works of British art-historical scholarship that matched up to German standards, and were immediately recognised as standard works in Germany itself. They were followed by Hind's equally impressive *Catalogue of Early Italian Engravings* in 1910, a catalogue that he later worked up into a corpus of all known Italian prints of the period before Marcantonio.

Colvin must have been delighted with these successes. He was just as skilful in building up the collection. He was a man of very wide culture, and was himself a minor literary figure. He numbered the writer Robert Louis Stevenson among his closest friends, and served as his literary executor. In *The Colvins and their Friends* by E. V. Lucas, the official biography published in 1928 after his death, relatively little attention is given to his work at the British Museum; it was his literary friendships and works that were recorded. This wide culture and the ease with which he mingled in different circles of British society undoubtedly helped the Museum. It is Colvin who takes the credit for attracting the gift of the Mitchell and the virtual gift of the Malcolm collections (see section 7), as well as the prints and drawings in the Salting bequest (see section 8). Of a different and more specialised kind was the bequest of

the mezzotint collection of Lord Cheylesmore in 1902 (section 6 is built around this, and examines the development of the mezzotint collection from the early nineteenth century), and the gift of the collection of fans and playing cards by Lady Charlotte Schreiber in 1891 and 1895.

One of Colvin's first tasks had been to see the transfer of the entire Department into new quarters, its fourth home, in the newly-built White Wing, back in the south-east corner of the Bloomsbury site (fig. 4). By the time he had retired the growth of the collections forced yet another move, and it was his successor, Campbell Dodgson, who oversaw the transfer to the fifth home (the present Print Room, fig. 5) in another newly-constructed wing, the Edward VII building on the north side of the site, just before the outbreak of the First World War.

The move to the Edward VII building brought to an end the saga of the display of the collections, a problem that had long vexed successive Keepers. Any curator of a print room who wishes to attract gifts needs to be able to assure donors that the objects will be seen not only by students in the room itself, but by a wide public in an exhibition gallery. Carpenter, the first Keeper who wanted to build up relations with collectors, frequently lamented to the Trustees his lack of any display area, and it was not until 1858 that screens were erected in the King's Library on which a changing selection of works could be shown in frames (a photograph of prints from Slade's bequest hung on these screens in 1869 is reproduced on p. 117). The departure of the natural history collections to South Ken-

5. *The fifth Print Room in the Edward VII building*, 1934. After an official British Museum photograph. The Print Room still occupies this space in 1995

sington temporarily allowed four empty rooms to be used for the display of an extraordinary number of works (well over 600) from 1883 to 1892. With the move of the Department to the White Wing, a new gallery, specifically called 'The Print and Drawing Gallery', was allocated to it adjacent to the Student Room, and a similar space was also opened in 1914 when the Department moved again to the Edward VII wing. It is this space that is still in use today.

This brings us to the twentieth century and modern times. Dodgson's keepership, outstanding in so many ways, is the subject of a special essay (section 9), and another essay (section 10) takes the story of the print collection up to the present day.

A collection is only given meaning by the use that is made of it, and any collection always has more potential uses than the ones that any generation actually makes of it. Occasional references in the Department's archives show that these uses have changed in surprising ways through the years. In the diatribe that Benjamin Robert Haydon addressed to the Trustees in 1826 about J. T. Smith's refusal to let him in, he revealed why he had dashed along to the Print Room. He was in the middle of one of his large historical paintings, and needed to look at an old print to check that a detail of the costume of one of his principal characters was correct. This was evidently a perfectly normal demand. The Department preserves a series of fifteen large boxes of prints of costume, arranged by country and century and social class, and prints showing domestic furniture, tools, tombs, architecture, and so on. This series still bears the label 'Authorities for Artists', which clearly reveals the reason why it was put together.

In 1844 Josi reported to the Trustees that the Print Room 'has now become a national academy of design, many clever artists having emanated from the Print Room and formed themselves solely from that collection. In fact after the Reading Room it is the Department most consulted for the purpose of study and for illustrations, as may be seen by the numerous artists making designs on blocks for the various publications of the day.' The requirement to copy prints on to blocks belongs to the era when the standard method of illustration in books and magazines was the wood-engraving. This was radically changed in the 1890s when the invention of the half-tone screen meant that a photograph could be successfully transferred to a relief printing block. From that moment the demand moved from the copyist to the photographer. That demand has constantly increased. The huge expansion of illustration in books since the 1960s, based on offset lithography and photocomposition that allow text and picture to be integrated easily and cheaply, has led to a situation where the Department is supplying over 7,000 photographs a year.

It is many years since artists were concerned to copy exact details of historic costume in their paintings, and the label 'Authorities for Artists' is now an historical anomaly. The series, however, has found a new use by historians of costume – a branch of historical study that was almost undreamed of in the 1820s. And art students still use the Print Room in large numbers. For centuries the practice of copying first two-dimensional drawings, and then three-dimensional objects or sculpture, led into the third stage of drawing directly from the nude. It was only when life drawing became deeply unfashionable in the 1960s that students stopped coming to the Print Room. Now they are coming back again. It is not even beyond the bounds of imagination to think that artists in future centuries will again wish to consult the 'Authorities for Artists'.

Would any of the collectors who gave or bequeathed their prints to the British Museum have expected such uses to be made of them? Some would, such as F. W. Fairholt (1818–66), a pioneer historian of costume. He bequeathed three albums he had assembled which he called 'A collection of prints and literary scraps illustrating costume'. Many others, including many of those studied in the essays in this book, would not. There is no telling on what collectors may decide to concentrate their attention. Sarah Sophia Banks, the sister of Sir Joseph Banks and a famous eccentric, left the Museum in 1818 her 'books relative to tournaments, chivalry, the orders of knighthood, ceremonials, processions, funerals, etc.' as well as her enormous collection of visiting cards, admission tickets, trade cards and suchlike ephemera. In 1931 Miss F. L. Cannan presented her collection of 600 prints relating to skating. In 1935 the seventh Marquis of Sligo presented his father's collection of 200 portraits from altered plates, showing both the first state and, after the plate had been altered, the new portrait head that had been substituted for the first in order to save the bother of making a new plate. Most recently Mr Edward Wharton-Tigar has offered his astonishing and well-nigh definitive collection of nearly a million cigarette and other trade cards of the past century, which will in due course join the collection of Sarah Sophia Banks.

All these collections would probably have surprised Cracherode. They would have astonished Malcolm or Salting. Slade would have wondered how they would improve public taste. Sir Hans Sloane would have taken them in his stride. This takes us back to 1750. If we could go back two generations further, to Samuel Pepys, whose prints, definitively assembled by him in albums in 1700, are now with the rest of his library at Magdalene College, Cambridge, we would find yet another response. He would wonder why we had not collected popular prints, the woodcuts at the top of street ballads, the skulls that undertakers pasted to coffins.

Generalisations are always dangerous, but one that might perhaps be true is that the scope of the mainstream of print collecting has progressively narrowed through the centuries. The further we look back into history, the more widely we find that people collected. One of the earliest collections about which we know much was that of the Roman scholar and antiquarian Cassiano dal Pozzo, who died in 1657. He was interested in visual information of all kinds, and so his albums contained not only portraits, architecture and sculpture, but also catafalques, historical events such as battles and executions, and costume. One surviving album is full of the most extraordinary prints of buffoons, beggars, Dutch peasant customs, heads assembled out of vegetables in the manner of Arcimboldo, and so on.

By the end of the seventeenth century, and the generation of Hans Sloane, the areas of interest were becoming narrower. Sloane still collected very widely, and his prints, like Cassiano's, covered the areas of learned enquiry of his day. But those areas of enquiry had themselves become more focused. Monsters were included, as they might have something to teach anatomy and medicine, but fanciful heads composed of vegetables and fruit were not. Other collectors, such as Sloane's friend William Courten, were more concentrated still. They were interested in those prints that were documents in the history of art, and recorded the designs of the great masters; those prints whose information lay outside the field of art history fell outside their range of interest. Such collectors in the first half of the eighteenth century assembled enormous collections of prints arranged by 'masters' – that is according to the artist responsible for the design. No collection of this type ever reached the British Museum.

By the second half of the century interest had concentrated further. Prints were further categorised according to whether they themselves were the designs by the masters, or whether they were simply recording those designs. In other words, engravings after the drawings or paintings of Rubens, being done by the hands of others, were different – and usually inferior – to the prints of a Dürer or Rembrandt, made by the hand of the artist himself. Such an approach can be seen in the collection of Cracherode, and was codified shortly after his death by the twenty-one-volume catalogue of Adam Bartsch, *Le Peintre-Graveur*, from which the reproductive print was deliberately excluded.

The nineteenth century introduced its own preoccupation with the earliest engravings and the origins of the medium, but its tendency was to restrict the field even more. If some had the ambition to collect the prints that Bartsch listed, they restricted it to a certain area; Sheepshanks, for example, confined himself to the Dutch school. Most, however, formed specimen collections that contained a handful of prints by the acknowledged masters of European engraving, and very little else. Felix Slade in the first half of the century had a particularly large collection of this kind; Malcolm and Salting in the second half had much smaller ones. All went for the best prints by the best masters in the best impressions. Quantity and completeness were of no importance at all. If there has been any definable tendency in twentieth-century collecting, it has been to narrow the field still further. The number of the great printmakers has become smaller, and the canon of the great prints has become very limited.

In this rapid survey of several hundred years of collecting history, some points have remained constant. Some names of the great printmakers of European art have never changed. There has never been a time in which the etchings of Rembrandt were not valued very highly. The prints of Dürer, Lucas van Leyden and Callot have always been appreciated. For almost the whole period Marcantonio has been ranked at the top. His fall from grace, such as it is, is something that has only happened in the twentieth century. Equally it is the late twentieth century that has rediscovered such eccentrics as Jacques Bellange, and begun to appreciate Mannerism again.

One of the earliest books on print collecting, published in London in 1752, included an appendix on 'the usefulness and use of prints'. The author concluded this section by stating that

for those that to be more happy, and more Gentleman-like, would form their Gout by the study of good Things, and have a reasonable Tincture of the *fine arts*, nothing is more necessary than good prints. Their Sight, with a little Reflection, will readily and agreeably inform them of every Thing that may exercise their Reason, and Strengthen their Judgment. They may fill their memory with the most curious things of all times ... They will Judge readily, by the facility with which they may open a few leaves, and compare the Productions of one Master with those of Another, and by this means, in sparing their time, they will spare their expense also; ... by means of Prints, one may easily see the Works of several Masters on a Table, one may form an idea of them, judge by comparing them with another, know which to chuse, and by practising it often, contract a habit of a good Taste, and a good Manner, especially if we do it in the Company of any body, that has Discernment in these Things, and can distinguish what is good, from what is but indifferent.

(*The Art of Painting in Miniature ... to Which is now Added the Usefulness and Benefit of Prints*, London 1752, quoted in Levis p. 43)

The availability of modern art books has altered the conditions since the eighteenth century, but nothing can and will remove the immediacy of prints and the enormous range they cover. They are the very objects by which our predecessors informed themselves about the appearance of things, and remain prime sources of information as well as being objects of great beauty. We hope that the selection shown here from a collection that has been formed over two hundred and fifty years will give some inkling of how wide a range of curiosity prints can satisfy.

Note

This introduction is based on the few books and articles that have so far been written on the subject:

Writings on the history of the Department of Prints and Drawings

Louis Fagan, *A Handbook to the Department of Prints and Drawings*, London 1876

Anon, *The Print Room of the British Museum. An Enquiry by the Ghost of a Departed Collector*, London 1876

A. E. Popham, *A Handbook to the Drawings and Watercolours in the Department of Prints and Drawings*, London 1939

Edward Miller, *That Noble Cabinet, a history of the British Museum*, London 1973

Antony Griffiths and Reginald Williams, *The Department of Prints and Drawings in the British Museum, User's Guide*, London 1987

Nicholas Turner, *The Study of Italian Drawings: the Contribution of Philip Pouncey*, London 1993

Antony Griffiths, 'The Department of Prints and Drawings during the first century of the British Museum', *The Burlington Magazine*, cxxxvi 1994, pp. 531–44

To these should be added the published writings by and obituaries of members of staff, and the very large quantity of unpublished information in the British Museum's archives.

Writings on the history of print collecting (a selection)

H. C. Levis, *A Descriptive Bibliography of the Most Important Books in the English Language Relating to the Art and History of Engraving and the Collecting of Prints*, London 1912

William Robinson, 'The Passion for Prints: collecting and connoisseurship in northern Europe during the seventeenth century' in Clifford S. Ackley, *Printmaking in the Age of Rembrandt*, Boston 1981, pp. xxvii–xlviii

Michael Bury, 'The taste for prints in Italy to 1600', *Print Quarterly*, ii 1985, pp. 12–26

Jan van der Waals, *De Prentschat van Michiel Hinloopen 1619–1708*, Amsterdam 1988

Antony Griffiths, 'The Print Collection of Cassiano dal Pozzo', *Print Quarterly*, vi 1989, pp. 2–10

Jan van der Waals and others, *Een Wereldreiziger op papier: Das Atlas van Laurens van der Hem 1621–78*, Amsterdam 1992

Antony Griffiths, 'Print collecting in Rome, Paris and London in the early eighteenth century', *Harvard University Art Museums Bulletin*, Spring 1994, pp. 37–59

Peter Parshall, 'Art and the theatre of knowledge: the origins of print collecting in northern Europe', *Harvard University Art Museums Bulletin*, Spring 1994, pp. 7–36

A List of the Keepers of the Department of Prints and Drawings

William Alexander (1767–1816)	Keeper	1808–16
John Thomas Smith (1766–1833)		1816–33
William Young Ottley (1771–1836)		1833–6
Henry Josi (1802–45)		1836–45
William Hookham Carpenter (1792–1866)		1845–66
George William Reid (1819–87)		1866–83
Sidney Colvin (1845–1927), knighted 1911		1883–1912
Campbell Dodgson (1867–1948)		1912–32
Laurence Binyon (1869–1943)		1932–3
Arthur Mayger Hind (1880–1957)		1933–45
Arthur Ewart Popham (1889–1970)		1945–54
Edward Croft-Murray (1907–80)		1954–73
John Arthur Giles Gere (1921–95)		1973–81
John Kendall Rowlands (b.1931)		1981–91
Antony Vaughan Griffiths (b.1951)		1991–

Glossary of Printmaking Terms

For fuller explanations see Antony Griffiths, *Prints and Printmaking, an Introduction to the History and Techniques*, British Museum Publications, London 1980 (revised edition 1996); and Paul Goldman, *Looking at Prints, Drawings and Watercolours, A Guide to Technical Terms*, British Museum Publications, London 1988.

Aquatint A variety of etching in which tone is created by fusing grains of rosin to the plate and etching it. The acid bites in pools around each grain; these hold sufficient ink to print a light grainy tone.

Counterproof A reversed impression of a print, made by placing an impression while the ink is still wet against another sheet of paper, and running both through a press.

Drypoint A process similar to etching except that the line is not bitten into the plate by acid, but is directly scratched in with a sharp needle.

Engraving Lines are cut into a metal plate (usually copper) using a V-shaped metal tool called a burin. Since this is pushed in front of the hand, it produces a clean and controlled incision. The plate is inked and printed in the same way as an etching.

Etching The artist draws his design through a hard ground of wax laid on a metal plate. The lines of metal thus exposed are eaten away in an acid bath. After cleaning off the ground, the plate is inked so that the ink lies only in the bitten lines and the surface is wiped clean. The plate is printed by laying a sheet of dampened paper over it and running both through a roller press under considerable pressure.

Lithography A method of printing from stone or zinc. It relies on the fact that grease repels water. The design is drawn on the surface in some greasy medium. This is printed from in the following way: the surface is dampened with water, which only settles on the unmarked areas since it is repelled by the grease in the drawing. The surface is then rolled over with greasy printing ink, which adheres only to the drawing, the water repelling it from the rest of the surface. Finally the ink is transferred to a sheet of paper by running paper and printing surface together through a scraper press.

Mezzotint A metal-plate process. The plate is worked over ('grounded') using a curved toothed tool (a 'rocker') so that the entire surface is roughened. In this state, the plate once inked will print a solid black. The lighter parts of the design are created by scraping and polishing down areas of the plate so that they hold less ink for printing.

Monotype The two most common processes involve:

(a) printing from any flat surface (usually a glass or metal plate) on which a design has previously been drawn using printing ink. The ink normally permits no more than one strong and one weak impression.

(b) using a carbon to transfer a design from one sheet to another during the process of drawing.

Silkscreen This is a variety of stencil printing. A mesh is attached to a frame, and a design is either drawn on it in some impermeable medium or on a stencil which is attached to it. Ink is forced through the screen on to a sheet of paper with a squeegee.

Stipple A way of creating tone by using a pointed metal tool to build up a mass of dots on an etching ground. Like aquatint, it was normally applied to plates on which the design had already been etched in outline.

Soft-ground etching A variety of etching which uses a soft etching ground. By laying a sheet of paper on top of the grounded plate and drawing on the paper, a precise facsimile of the drawing can be left on the ground when the paper is pulled away. This can be etched into the plate in the usual way.

Woodcut Having drawn a design on a block of soft-grained wood, the artist cuts away the background using knives and gouges, leaving the lines standing in relief. Ink is then rolled over the surface of the block, which is printed under pressure on to a sheet of dampened paper. A relief press is in principle the same as that used for traditional letterpress printing.

Wood-engraving A variety of woodcut which uses a hard-grained wood, such as boxwood, which is too hard to be cut with a knife. Instead, a V-shaped burin, similar to that used in copper engraving, is used to incise lines into the block. When printed (in the same way as a woodcut), the lines stand out as white against a black background.

Notes to Catalogue

The following essays have been written in close collaboration, and each author wishes to acknowledge debts to colleagues for information and advice in addition to the specific debts mentioned in each essay. A general debt is also owed to the Museum Archivist, Janet Wallace, and her colleague Christopher Date, for their help in research into the Museum's Central Archives. The photographs have been taken by Graham Javes and Lisa Bliss.

In order to save space, references to papers in the Department's or the Central archives are only given in a generalised way; the context should make it clear in which series the original may be found.

Abbreviations to standard *catalogues raisonnés* of the works of printmakers are given in the catalogue entries. The full references can be found in the bibliography of books cited on p. 256.

References to L. or Lugt in both catalogue and essays are to Frits Lugt, *Les Marques de Collection*, Amsterdam 1921, with a supplementary volume, Amsterdam 1956.

Many prices are given in pre-decimal British currency. Twelve pence (d) = one shilling (s). Twenty shillings = one pound (£). A guinea was £1 1s od. A price written as 12-6 or 12/6 stands for 12 shillings and 6 pence; £3. 2. 6 means 3 pounds, 2 shillings and 6 pence. 5 shillings is equivalent to 25 pence of the new decimal currency; 15 shillings to 75 new pence.

1. Sir Hans Sloane (1660–1753)

Antony Griffiths

Sloane was born in Ireland.[1] His father, who came from a family of Scottish immigrants, was receiver-general of taxes from County Down for the Earl of Clanbrassill. Sloane came to London to train as a doctor in 1679, and in 1683 went for a year to study in Paris, Orange and Montpellier. On his return he set up practice in London, and his competence, intelligence and charm soon attracted a fashionable clientele. In 1687 he was invited to go to Jamaica to act as the personal physician to the newly appointed governor, the Duke of Albemarle, and while there he compiled materials for his famous book *A Voyage to the Islands Madera, Barbados, Nieves, S. Christopher and Jamaica, with the natural history of the herbs and trees, four-footed beasts, fishes, birds, insects, reptiles etc. of the last of those islands … illustrated with the figures of the things described which have not been heretofore engraved, in large copper-plates as big as the life*, which was published in two volumes in 1707 and 1725. The title is given in full, as it gives an idea of the range of subject-matter Sloane covered and the way in which he had structured it as a contribution to the advancement of knowledge. The respect he gained among his peers helped him in 1693 to become one of the secretaries of the Royal Society, the premier learned body of England, where for many years he edited its transactions. In 1727 he became its president.

Sloane was not a man of inherited wealth, and the considerable fortune that he gained from his medical practice was spent in building up his collections. These were open to all interested parties, and his correspondence is full of letters from Englishmen and foreigners seeking admission to his home in Bloomsbury (very close to the present British Museum) where the collections were kept for most of his life. Thus in 1727 the widely travelled Scottish virtuoso Sir John Clerk of Penicuik recorded in his diary of a visit to London that he had seen at Sloane's 'the greatest collection of things that ever I had seen in my life; not the treasures of any forreign prince can equal them'.[2] By the time Sloane died in 1753, they were recognised by everyone, including Sloane himself, as the finest in the country, and he took great care in his will that they should be kept together and 'visited and seen by all persons desirous of seeing and viewing the same … that the same may be rendered as useful as possible, as well towards the satisfying the desire of the curious, as for the improvement of knowledge and information of all purposes'.[3] His efforts succeeded, and the distinctive character of the British

Museum among the great museums of the world was entirely determined by the extraordinary range in breadth and in depth of Sloane's collections and by his desire that they should be used to increase knowledge.

Sloane had the perfect temperament for a museum curator or librarian, and was an assiduous compiler of catalogues of his possessions, which he wrote in his own bold handwriting, occasionally with the help of a secretary. Merely to enumerate each category, with a note of the number of objects in each, gives an idea of his achievement. These were gems (232), cameos (290), rings (115), miscellanies (2,111), antiquities (1,129), seals (268), pictures and drawings (471), mathematical instruments (57), agates (542), plants (3,000), vegetables (3,000),

1. John Faber junior, *Sir Hans Sloane*, mezzotint after Sir Godfrey Kneller, 1728. 331 × 240 mm. I 8-160

insects (5,447), precious stones (2,256), metals (2,727), ambers (399), earths (1,037), crystals (1,868), fossils and flints (1,280), shells (5,846), fishes (1,563), birds (907), eggs (272) and quadrupeds (1,903).[4]

But all these categories were put into the shade by the catalogue of his library, which fell into two parts. The first consisted of his copy of G. A. Mercklin's standard bibliography of medical books, *Lindenus renovatus*, published in 1686, which he had bound interleaved with blank sheets. Since Sloane was a doctor himself, he set out to acquire all the books listed in it. As each arrived, he ticked it off and marked in the margin the press-mark assigned to each. These took the form of a letter of the alphabet followed by a number (e.g. A.578).[5] On the interleaved pages he added in full the titles of books omitted or published after 1686. Expanded in this way, this catalogue filled eight volumes. A further eight large hand-written folio volumes contained all the other books in his library, into which Sloane entered each book as he acquired it in chronological order. Two additional volumes of index by the name of the author enabled him to locate each title. By the time of his death, Sloane had filled 3,944 pages with between twenty and forty titles on each page.[6]

It was unquestionably the greatest library in England in its day, and anyone who reads through the catalogue today must be amazed at the variety of material that Sloane's curiosity embraced. On p. 3739, for example, is listed the contents of c.278, a volume in which Sloane had bound together over 100 miscellaneous items, mostly ephemera that he had been sent. Among them he described the following: 'Garrus's elixir, a bill for it; Advertisement of a rattlesnake; Mons. de Launois's mathematical statues; a model of a school for the better education of youth; Benj. Brooke sells china ware; Wm Shaftoe's proposal for a print of an antique piece of plate found at Corbridge; M. Crozat Avis aux souscripteurs des estampes'.[7] Among the subjects of interest to him was the history of printing itself, for he acquired some remarkable examples of books printed before 1500, as well as fine printing of later periods.

Sloane's collection included prints and drawings, and when the Print Room of the British Museum was set up after 1806, parts of the collection served as one of its foundations. Some of his drawings, in particular his album of drawings by Dürer, have always been recognised as among the Museum's greatest treasures, and the study that has so far been devoted to Sloane's collection has concentrated on these.[8] But what reached the Print Room after 1806 was only part of the whole of Sloane's collection, and the collection as a whole has so far resisted analysis. One of Sloane's manuscript catalogues is devoted to his paintings and drawings, and those who have enquired into this subject have not unnaturally paid close attention to it. But they have been disappointed because it contains none of the most important items that are known to have come from Sloane's collection. The reason for this is simply that

this catalogue was devoted to the framed or mounted items kept individually, and Sloane possessed little of interest in this line. He was no art collector, and did not buy to decorate his walls. Everything that he acquired was intended to serve his scholarly and scientific interests. So inevitably the great bulk of his prints and drawings were kept in volumes, and, as books, they were listed in the catalogue of his library. But it is only in the past decade that M. A. E. Nickson has drawn attention to Sloane's books and his catalogue of them.[9] Sloane wrote the press-mark he assigned to each book on the front flyleaf, but it was only in 1942 that these (which can still be found on thousands of books in the British Library) were associated with Sloane's library catalogue, and their provenance thereby recognised.[10] It was not until 1988 that the existence of a classification of prints within that catalogue was noted.[11] The result is the strange paradox that Sloane's print collection is probably the best documented collection of its period, yet no serious attention has ever been given to it. Much work remains to be done, and this essay can only report the conclusions of a preliminary investigation into the subject.

Sloane began collecting books while still a student. But it was only in about 1694, after his return from Jamaica, that he decided to begin his book catalogue. So the first pages clear the backlog of all the items that he had acquired up to that time. From then on he entered every item as he acquired it for his library. From the beginning Sloane distinguished books from manuscripts by giving them different types of number.[12] As the collection expanded and became more complicated, he created new categories. The first was a numbering in Roman capitals, which initially covered maps and large volumes of miscellaneous prints. He then separated out the prints, using a 'Pr.' prefix to a Roman number (e.g. Pr.CLXII), henceforth reserving the Roman sequence for maps alone. At the same time he added a category of miniatures (abbreviated 'Min.'), in which he included any drawings or coloured prints, and finally, towards the end of his life, rolls and 'prints oriental', which covered his Japanese and Chinese material. Sloane owned some famous and important Chinese coloured woodcuts, but he extended the category to include oriental books since they were printed from blocks rather than movable type. Because Sloane entered books in his catalogue as he acquired them, it is possible to date their arrival with fair precision by looking at the publication dates of the printed books on nearby pages. Thus we know that Sloane created his 'Print' classification in 1705.

In one burst in that year he listed seventy-four volumes (see fig. 2), and during the next five years added further entries in a single block every year. During this period he must have put volumes aside as they came in so that they could be entered together and thus found more easily. All the entries are in his own handwriting up to number 228, after which he usually passed the task to his various amanuenses. In 1711 he decided to reclassify in the 'Pr.' number sequence any volumes of prints that had been entered as books before 1705. In this year he left four pages blank (pp. 1162–5). On these his secretaries added titles of new acquisitions as they arrived, but the sequence of numbers is no longer continuous, since the missing numbers had been assigned to pre-1705 volumes. After these four pages had been filled up in about 1712, Sloane henceforth incorporated print volumes into the main sequence of book entries, either singly or in groups, as and when they were acquired. In the second volume of his book on Jamaica in 1725 he described his collection briefly, and gave the number of volumes of prints as 580.

The next development took place in 1726, when the numbering had reached 613. At this time Sloane had a

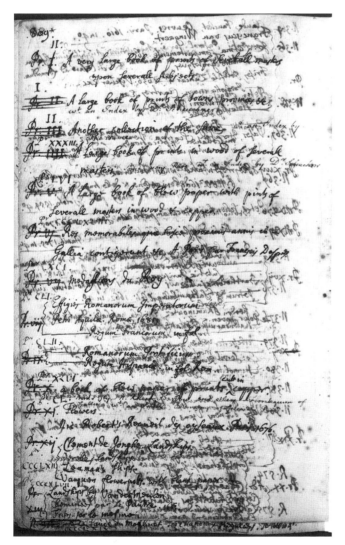

2. The first page of Sloane's autograph catalogue of his albums of prints in 1705. British Library, Sloane MS.3972C, f.191v (=p. 809*)

particularly expert and trustworthy helper, Johann Gaspar Scheuchzer (1702–29), the son of an old friend and correspondent, the Swiss doctor and geologist Johann Jacob Scheuchzer. Sloane entrusted him not only with the compilation of indexes to the volumes of miscellaneous prints, but also with a complete rearrangement of the order of the volumes on the shelves. Thus far they had been placed in little more than random order, and Scheuchzer devised a logical thematic sequence depending on the subject-matter.[13] He then crossed out the old press-mark and entered the new one both on the books themselves and in the catalogue. He added a few more pre-1705 titles, and so the numbering of new titles after 1726 began at 720. The next landmark was in 1734. In that year Sloane was given by Louis XV a complete set in twenty-three volumes of the *Cabinet du Roi*, the great series of prints made for the kings of France since the 1660s to record all aspects of royal affairs and interests – victories, palaces, sculptures, gardens, ceremonies and so on. These volumes were usually reserved for gifts to royalty, ambassadors and suchlike, and it was an extraordinary honour for a private individual to be given one.[14] Sloane was deeply flattered, and decided to use the occasion to rearrange and renumber his print albums yet again. The reorganisation seems to have been confined mainly to the arrivals since 1726, and this time plenty of gaps were left in the sequence of numbers so that new arrivals could be inserted in their proper places. The last number used seems to have been about 1150. A few items were later tacked on to the end, with the result that the highest number used before Sloane's death was 1182. But there were still many gaps in the number sequence, and so the total number of volumes that comprised Sloane's print collection was about 1,000.[15]

It is not certain what led Sloane to decide to create a print classification in 1705. Firm evidence may well lie awaiting discovery in one of the dozens of volumes of Sloane's correspondence in the British Library – for as Sloane could never throw away a piece of printed material, however ephemeral, so he never threw away a letter. But in the interim, one hypothesis is eminently plausible. We know that in 1702 Sloane received as a bequest the entire collection of his old friend and patient William Courten (1642–1702), who often used the name Charleton. Courten owned a significant collection of prints and drawings (see p. 26), and when the Leeds antiquary Ralph Thoresby visited Sloane in 1702, he noted that 'Mr Charleton's collection, which Dr Sloane now has, lies all in confusion as yet, and will require some time to put them in order'.[16] Many of the prints were loose, and Sloane had to arrange them and paste them in albums. This process doubtless turned Sloane's thoughts to prints, which he had so far neglected. Courten was an assiduous compiler of lists, and many of his lists of prints survive in Sloane Ms.3961 (see Appendix C). Thus we know very precisely, though very incompletely, what he owned, and can

3. Anonymous, *Portrait of William Courten as a Young Man*, painting. 698 × 559 mm. British Museum

compare this information with Sloane's catalogue. They prove to match very neatly many of the volumes numbered between 99 and 120, which Sloane entered in 1707. To all of these Sloane uniquely gave a prefix 'C', and in his descriptions he actually states that two of them (99 and 115) came from Courten. Moreover Courten's list in Sloane 3961 headed 'Georg Pentz' bears an annotation in Sloane's handwriting 'Pr.cxiii'; and Pr.cxiii is entered in Sloane's library catalogue as 'Severall pieces of the old & best masters George Pentz, Virgilius Solis' and so on. It therefore seems reasonable to guess that the prefix 'C' stands for Courten, and was applied to the volumes that derived from his collection.[17]

What then of volumes 1 to 98, which Sloane entered two years earlier in 1705? They have no prefix, and might have come from some other source or sources, such as a London dealer or auction. But it is quite possible that they also came from Courten. Courten's surviving lists are only of loose prints, but they include references to albums that contained his main collection. These albums are nowhere described, and so we cannot know what was in them. But it is very likely that Sloane first entered in 1705 the complete volumes that Courten had bequeathed to him, and only two years later, after he had himself assembled

the loose prints into albums, entered those as well. In this case most of Sloane's albums of prints up to number 120 may have come from Courten.

One very important implication of Sloane's methods of classification is that they define precisely which volumes Sloane himself regarded as part of his print collection. Thus we can view it through his own eyes, and not through the expectations and assumptions of the late twentieth century. The easiest way to get some idea of its nature is to look at the titles of the first 325 entries, given in Appendix A. The first surprise is how many refer to what we would now classify as printed books. Sloane seems to have regarded any heavily illustrated book, such as a treatise on botany or architecture, in which the prime information was carried by the plates on which the text served as a commentary, as part of the print collection. Books that contained mainly text, perhaps with the occasional plate, were entered as part of the main library.

After the illustrated books, the next largest category of Sloane's print volumes consisted of sets of prints bound together. From the mid-sixteenth century, publishers, initially in the Netherlands and later elsewhere, had begun to issue series of numbered prints in small sets. They would usually contain between six and twelve plates, though numbers could go much higher. They were initially sold unbound, possibly in paper wrappers, with a stitched thread holding them together at the left margin. The purchaser usually assembled a selection of such sets, and then had them bound between covers in whichever order he wished. Such sets covered a wide range of subjects. Favourites were religious or moral exemplars; topographical and landscape series; ornament prints and designs for the decorative arts; and sets of birds, fruit, fishes and other natural specimens. Sloane had many collections of sets of this kind in his library, and he carefully listed the titles or content of each set in his catalogue. Many of them were fifty to a hundred years old by the time that he acquired them, and he probably found most of them on the second-hand market, already bound together by previous owners.

From analysing the content of these two categories of print volume, we can get an overall impression of what subjects interested Sloane. In the first place, as might be expected from the author of a natural history of Jamaica, came anything to do with animal and plant life, together with shells, fossils and the other subjects that were so comprehensively covered by actual specimens in the rest of his collection. For the same reason his volumes on coins and medals, cameos, gems, classical sculpture and architecture are not a surprise. Nor perhaps are his many volumes of topography and geography that complemented his map collection. But what of his collection of portraits? He collected an astonishing number of sets of heads of famous men of all kinds, but with a preference for pictures of those who had distinguished themselves in some field of scholarship or what we would now call the arts. In a letter of 1698 he wrote to a friend: 'You cannot err in buying any books of voyages, elogia, icones of learned men, lives, or odd physick books.'[18] He owned festival and costume books; volumes on heraldry; drawing books and sets of emblems; and a surprising number of sets of engraved ornament. He also collected illustrations to the Bible, although not devotional prints, and had some surprising oddments, such as sets of political and geographical playing cards kept in bound form.[19]

The third type of print volume consisted of albums of blank paper on to which individual prints were pasted.[20] Sloane had a significant number of these. Most will be found listed in Appendix A under numbers 1–5, 37–46, 99–101, 109–21, 129, 154, 195–204 and 205–13. It was these albums that contained all his single-sheet prints, that is those that did not form part of any set. These include

4. William Courten's autograph catalogue of his prints by Callot in 1687. British Library, Sloane MS.3961, f.165

most of what the twentieth century would regard as his most important prints, including works by Dürer, Lucas van Leyden, the Little Masters, Marcantonio, Rembrandt and many others. All these albums were taken apart in the British Museum after 1806 by Thomas Philipe, and he made no record of their content, nor did he mark them properly.[21] So it is unfortunate that Sloane himself noted in only a summary fashion the contents of these volumes. According to annotations made against these entries by Thomas Stack, Sloane's last librarian, Scheuchzer had in the 1720s made indexes of the contents of each volume, but only two or three of these have survived. The longest gives two tables, one by name of the engraver, the other by subject. There is no list of prints as such, though something can be inferred by combining the two tables. It is therefore far more difficult to find information about these albums than about the rest of the print collection. Despite this, a surprising amount can be discovered from various sources.

The first point to note is that, besides these sixty or so volumes, all listed between 1705 and 1709, only eight other miscellaneous albums entered Sloane's collection, either earlier or later. The most interesting of these can briefly be described. The earliest, in the late 1690s, was LVI, later reclassified as Pr.CCCXL, which contained 'Prints & sculpt. of sevl. sorts' with an index added by Dr Massey. In 1701 he acquired a more exciting volume, later classified as Pr.LXXVI: 'A large volume pasted full of copper cuts, all etched by Mr Wenceslaus Hollar.' Added some time later is a note: 'His own proof prints bought of his widow'.[22] Later in 1711 came Titian's famous woodcut of the *Crossing of the Red Sea* on separate sheets: 'Severall sheets of wooden prints containing Pharaoh's Persecution of the Israelites through the Red Sea &c., pasted in a book of purple paper. In Venet.1549 in fol.' Later these prints were taken out of the album (Pr.CCCL) and pasted on to a large roll (p.3279); they are still in the Department. In 1715 Sloane added 'Several prints by Albert Dürer &c in fol.' as Pr.CCCCXXXXVIII. Finally in about 1726 he listed as Pr.DCIX 'A book of prints, ancient and modern, by Albert Dürer [crossed out and 'Lucas van Leyden' substituted], AG [i.e. Aldegrever] and several different masters'. A note added later reads 'A copy of Albert Dürer by Dr R. M. Massey; without an index, with room for more'.[23]

The final comment shows that Sloane used blank pages at the end of albums to add later acquisitions. Other albums were put together by Sloane himself out of individual prints or sets that he bought as they were published, and later had bound together. So Pr.DCCCLXI, listed in 1732, contained John Alexander's prints after Raphael's frescoes in the Vatican, six prints of the castles of the King of Poland by Alexander Thiele, the six plates of the *Harlot's Progress* by Hogarth, and the arms or common seals of all the cities and borough towns in England and Wales by William Jackson. Sloane made a point of binding together related sheets of ephemera, pamphlets and miscellaneous material of all kinds. One interesting example in the main library is a.2320, entered in 1726, in which he had put a portrait of the celebrated impostor Mary Toft, together with several prints concerning her pretended giving birth to rabbits, and a number of pamphlets on the topic. In 1739 a rhinoceros came to London, and this inspired Sloane to collect together in an album, given the number Pr.LVIII, a drawing of it supplied to him by James Parsons MD with the print after it made by Gerard Vandergucht, and several other prints of the animal, including Dürer's (for which he already owned the original drawing), a copy of the Dürer, and one of a rhinoceros that had visited London in the 1680s. Since there was space left he added a print of the great oak in the lane near Welbeck in Nottinghamshire, four views in Holland, and a plan of the solar system representing the sun and the planets in their natural proportions by William Barlow. But the rarity of such miscellaneous albums in the catalogue shows that Sloane did not habitually buy individual prints or sets. He usually bought on a larger scale, adding complete albums formed by earlier owners, and not worrying too much whether some of the contents duplicated sets that he already had bound in other volumes.[24]

Much information on the formation of the collection could undoubtedly be found by a thorough search of Sloane's vast correspondence, conducted across the world in French, Latin, Dutch, German and occasionally Italian. Until this can be done, all that can be offered are a few fragments. One correspondent and supplier was the eccentric bookseller John Bagford, whose great project to write a history of printing never went beyond a vast and indigestible assemblage of raw material.[25] One account book of his survives for the years 1703–8, and it includes several sales of books, maps and prints to Sloane. Bagford's spelling was atrocious, and the following extract gives the flavour of one such sale: 'Ye marterdome of St John in wood; a pese of triumphe one wood; horses fiting on wood by Baldung 1534; one of ye 12 month one wood; a German camp by HB; a wooden cut of ye citey of Norimberga; a large ship in wood finley don; a see schape [seascape] eched in a shete 1500; a larrge pese of hunting of a stag by Brusselles in 4 shetes eched one copper'. The total cost of these nine items was 8s 4d. In 1708 another large sale included the following: 'A parsell of prints, insects etc.; a Bolonian wooman pissing by Carache; night and day graved by Sandrant; Winser Cassell; ye story of ye goulden Appell, a print very ould' and 'ye sackrefising to Priapus'.[26]

An even stranger supplier was the Dutchman Adrian Beverland (1653–1712). This learned eccentric had had to leave Holland after causing a scandal writing a book that was judged to be obscene. He came to London, and blew an inheritance of £2,000 on purchasing a large collection of paintings, prints and other virtuoso objects. The rest of his life was spent in pitiful conditions, a prey to poverty, desperation and a severe persecution mania. One of his acquaintances was Sloane, who kept the extraordinary letters with which Beverland bombarded him. Beverland's English was terrible, and the letters are usually written in dog Latin, in execrable handwriting on odd sheets of paper. They are often addressed from a tavern, and read as if they were written by one far gone under the influence of alcohol. But Beverland knew everyone, and his letters are full of references to all the leading London connoisseurs of the day, with remarks about what they had been buying. He kept offering Sloane coins, and occasionally prints, but the replies are not preserved, and it is impossible to know what, if anything, was bought.[27]

The largest group of prints, as has been mentioned, and many of the albums of drawings, came to Sloane in 1702 by bequest from William Courten, alias Charleton. Courten's collection was well known to the curious of the day, and was described by John Evelyn in his diary on 16 December 1686:

I carried the Countesse of Sunderland to see the rarities of one Mr Charleton at the Middle Temple, who shewed us such a collection of miniatures, drawings, shells, insects, medailes & natural things, animals whereoff divers were kept in glasses of sp[irits] of wine, I think an hundred, besids, minerals, precious stones, vessells & curiosities in amber, achat, chrystal, etc; as I had never in all my travells abroad seene either of private Gent. or Princes exceede it; all being very perfect & rare in their kind, especially his booke of birds, fish, flowers, shells etc. drawn & miniatured to the life, he told us that one book stood him in 300 pounds; it was painted by that excellent workman whom the late Gastion duke of Orleans employed.[28] This gent.'s whole collection (gathered by himselfe travelling most parte of Europe) is estimated at 8000 pounds. He seem'd a modest and obliging person.[29]

Evelyn had himself a great interest in prints, and it is strange that he does not mention Courten's collection of them – there was probably no time to see them.

Courten compiled extensive lists of his prints in 1687, and these are now bound in some confusion in Sloane 3961. The lists are headed 'My best stamps that are out of my books', and describe individual prints that had been extracted from the albums of his main collection. The purpose of the extraction and the listing was to sell them, and Courten gives the price of each print in the right column. Other sheets and occasional annotations list the items actually sold, which seem to have been very few. Occasionally we are given the name of the purchasers, who included Talman, Gibson, Cromer, Bateman, Baker, Sir Godfrey Copley, Lord P (?Pembroke) and Adrian Beverland. It was Beverland who supplied valuations in 1700 for some of Courten's best prints. The lists are arranged by engraver, with separate sheets for Dürer (50 entries), Lucas van Leyden (44), Aldegrever (38), Baldung (18), Etienne Delaune (12 sets), Sebald Beham (43), Pencz (10),

Virgil Solis (5), de Bry (5) and others. A sheet dated May 1687 lists over twenty etchings he had by Rembrandt, valued at a total of 12s 7d. Courten also collected portrait prints, and there are several dozen pages of these, all arranged according to the profession of the sitter. Finally there are some sheets on which he recorded his purchases between 1688 and his death. Almost all these items are natural history specimens, and this suggests that after 1687 Courten's interests had moved away from his art collection. But there are a few prints: in 1688 he purchased from William Sherwin his mezzotint portrait of the Duchess of Albemarle, and in 1689 he was buying unspecified prints from Mr Tempest, Mr Floyd (John Lloyd) of Salisbury Exchange, Mr Thomson of the Sun in Bedfordbury, and Mr Baker.[30] (A fuller account and transcript of some of the Courten papers is given in Appendix C.)

The importance of Courten's papers is considerable. They are the earliest priced lists of individually identified prints so far discovered in the history of English print collecting, and reveal the interests of a collector at a very ill documented period, as well as the relative values given to different types of work. By far the most valuable items were Italian prints of the Renaissance. The best of these were given astonishing valuations of between £1 and £4 each. Agostino Veneziano's *Riders* was £3, and his *Martyrdom of St Lawrence* after Bandinelli was £3 3s.[31] The next most expensive artist was Dürer. His *Adam and Eve* was given the very high valuation of £2, and the rest fell in the range between a few and ten shillings. No Lucas van Leyden was valued above ten shillings, while no print of the Little Masters was above one shilling.

Courten had a very distinctive handwriting, and used a light brown ink. In his lists he put after each print a price code, which seems to represent the price he paid for the item. Exactly the same codes in Courten's handwriting and light brown ink can be found on the backs of many prints that are registered in the 1837 inventory of the British Museum. This discovery is doubly exciting. As is explained in the introduction (p. 11), the rearrangement of the collection in 1808 was done very carelessly, and the blindstamps recording the provenance which were then put on cannot be trusted. But any print which carries the mark that can now be recognised as Courten's has a certain provenance not just from Sloane, but further back from Courten himself. Since Courten seems to have written on the backs of his prints in a fairly systematic way, apparently giving in code the price that he paid for them, we now have a method of recognising most of the prints that he bequeathed to Sloane that are still in the British Museum. This task will take many years. But included in this exhibition are several prints that we can now state are the identical impressions that Courten listed, and we can say what he valued them for in 1687.

Other parts of Sloane's collection can be also be identified with absolute certainty. Many of his sets of prints and illustrated books that have remained bound carry Sloane's press-marks on the front flyleaf in the handwriting of Sloane, Scheuchzer, or one of his other assistants. Appendix B lists all the volumes that have so far been identified in the Department of Prints and Drawings. These volumes, with few exceptions, are unlikely to have come from Courten, and therefore represent Sloane's personal selection and taste. Many more volumes on the shelves of the British Library await discovery, but enough are in the Department of Prints and Drawings to allow some generalisations to be made.[32] Sloane was not noticeably concerned about quality of impression, or about whether his prints were from the first editions or later copies. Thus of his sets of ornament prints designed by Le Pautre, it is pure chance whether his impressions come from the first editions published in Paris, from later reissues, or from the piracies produced in Amsterdam or Augsburg. His sets of birds and fishes are sometimes late printings from worn plates.

Although Courten's collection was of quite a different type and standard, the overall impression that the Sloane volumes gave was probably unimpressive to anyone hoping to find a collection of fine prints. This must have been the reason that Sloane's collection was so neglected and slighted when parts of it came to be incorporated into the Department of Prints and Drawings at the beginning of the nineteenth century. The curators then had a very different idea of what a print collection should contain, and this ideal was exemplified by the Cracherode collection that had just arrived (see section 2).

Sloane had his own particular idea of what his collection was. He regarded it as working material. It contained visual information of all kinds that complemented the written information in his books and the specimens that he had collected. To understand how all these elements were used together, one has to understand the nature of scholarly and scientific enquiry at the end of the seventeenth and beginning of the eighteenth centuries.[33] The lesson of Francis Bacon had been thoroughly taken to heart, and it was realised that the increase of knowledge could not come from consulting earlier authorities, but only from the examination of particulars, and the compilation of vast quantities of primary evidence from which valid deductions could be drawn. In the late twentieth century, after three hundred years of investigation and discovery, we take all this knowledge for granted. But Sloane and his contemporaries did not have the books in which to look it up. They were the generation that had to begin the task of writing them, and their collections were the essential raw material for their work. The enormous scale of Sloane's collection gives the measure of his generation's ambition, and many of Sloane's friends are among the great names of the scientific and intellectual revolution of the late seventeenth century. Among his close associates were Isaac Newton, Robert Boyle, Robert Hooke and John Locke.

Although Sloane himself was no original thinker, his library and collections were an heroic attempt to provide the data which his colleagues could use. And for this reason he and they were so concerned that they should be kept together after his death.

Although he succeeded, and they all passed to the British Museum, they were not used in the way he expected. By the second half of the eighteenth century, science and the growth of knowledge was progressing into areas that he could not have foreseen. New questions were arising, and increasing specialisation meant that researchers were having to work within a narrower compass. The ultimate consequence of this growth and restriction was the division of the old British Museum into three: the Natural History Museum opened its doors in 1881, and the British Library was set up in 1973. And so the 1,000 titles of his print and the 350 titles of his 'Miniature' (drawing) classification must now be sought in three institutions. However, at no point were they ever kept together in the British Museum. The early librarians paid no heed to Sloane's classifications, and reorganised his books into new ones of their own. Only the albums with prints pasted in, and a few bound sets of sheets without letterpress, were ever transferred to the new Department of Prints and Drawings after 1806, and now barely more than 80 of Sloane's volumes can be identified in it.

Sloane would have been astonished by what was kept in the Department of Printed Books. His greatest treasure, the *Cabinet du Roi*, twenty-three volumes consisting entirely of prints, and the work that anyone of his generation would have regarded as the foundation of a print collection, never left the library.[34] Not even the bound series were transferred in any systematic way. Many of Sloane's sets of prints remained in the library because it never occurred to anyone that they might be better placed in the Print Room. And by the nineteenth century, it might well have been true to say that such works found a better place in a library than a Print Room. The idea of what a print collection should contain had changed dramatically since Sloane's day.

This different concept of a Print Room was based on the concept of the print as a work of art and as an example of human craftsmanship. This concept was as old as the idea of the print as containing visual information – perhaps older. Over the centuries these two ideas have competed for supremacy. In the High Renaissance the generation of Dürer, Lucas van Leyden and Marcantonio certainly saw themselves as producing works of art for aesthetic pleasure. But the rise of the large workshops in the second half of the sixteenth century, and the mass production of images in them, enabled the classificatory urge of the seventeenth century to rearrange prints according to their subjects. The two ways of looking at prints were often held by the same person at the same time. Some always continued to prefer to see prints as objects of art. By the end of the eighteenth century this approach was again dominant, and the print became a tool of the new subject of the history of art. So when the Department of Prints and Drawings was established in 1808 it was inevitable that the items from Sloane's collection that were transferred to it were those that were regarded as works of art or documents of art history. If the Department had been established in 1753, and had used Sloane's own classifications to determine its holdings, it would have contained an entirely different sort of collection and its subsequent history might have been very different.

I owe thanks for help of various kinds to many members of staff of the British Museum and Library, and especially to Margaret Nickson. She and John Rowlands kindly allowed me to read their articles on Sloane's library and on his collection of prints and drawings before they were published in the collection of essays edited by Arthur MacGregor (see n. 1). Ian Jenkins gave me the reference to the lists of prints in the Courten papers, and helped me with the decipherment of their code.

1. The standard biographies of Sloane are G. R. de Beer, *Sir Hans Sloane and the British Museum*, London 1953, and E. St John Brooks, *Sir Hans Sloane, the Great Collector and his Circle*, London 1954. An important recent publication is *Sir Hans Sloane, Collector, Scientist, Antiquary, Founding Father of the British Museum*, edited by Arthur MacGregor, London 1994, which contains eighteen essays on many different aspects of Sloane's collecting, including one on his prints and drawings by John Rowlands.

2. Quoted from Joseph M. Levine, *Dr Woodward's Shield: History, Science and Satire in Augustan England*, Berkeley 1977, p. 265.

3. de Beer, pp. 138–9.

4. These figures are derived from Peter Murray Jones, 'A preliminary check-list of Sir Hans Sloane's catalogues', *British Library Journal*, XIV 1988, pp. 38–51. According to the minutes of the Trustees Committee of 22 January 1754, Sloane left 89 folio and 10 quarto catalogues of his collection.

5. The term press-mark is derived from the old term book-press, for a cabinet with book-shelves. A traditional press-mark of the form still used in the Department of Prints and Drawings is 159 b.7, which signifies the seventh book along the second shelf of the press numbered 159. Sloane's marks must have begun in this way (so A.578 would be the 578th book in press A), but as the library expanded and he used numbers in the thousands, the relationship between the mark and the placing must have become less direct.

6. The copy of Mercklin is in the Department of Printed Books, 878 n. 8; the manuscript catalogue is Sloane 3972B-D. See M. A. E. Nickson, 'Hans Sloane, book collector and cataloguer, 1682–98', *British Library Journal*, XIV 1988, pp. 52–89, and the essay by the same author on Sloane's books and manuscripts in the 1994 collection of essays on Sloane (note 1).

7. The Corbridge Lanx, a famous late Roman silver dish, was acquired by the British Museum in 1993; the engraving by Gerard Vandergucht was published in 1736. The Recueil Crozat was a celebrated collection of prints after paintings and drawings in French collections: see Francis Haskell, *The Painful Birth of the Art Book*, London 1987.

8. The pioneering studies were begun by A. E. Popham in 1928, and

the Department holds many notes he made then. He only published a summary of them later: 'Sir Hans Sloane's collections in the Print Room', *British Museum Quarterly*, XVIII 1953, pp. 10–14. More recently John Rowlands has also concentrated on the drawings in his article on the prints and drawings in the 1994 volume of essays on Sloane (note 1).

9. Popham unfortunately never looked at the library catalogue, and so never realised that Sloane had catalogued all his albums of drawings in it. The 'Min.' (for Miniature) section was first created at the same time as the prints in 1705, and was completely recatalogued in 1726 on pp. 2489 to 2522 in 348 entries. This description must form the basis of any future catalogue of Sloane's drawings. It sometimes gives the provenance; for example, Sloane's five famous albums stamped 1637 (four with drawings and papers of Dürer, the fifth with drawings by Arent van Bolten of Zwolle) were acquired in Holland in 1724. (Cf. J. G. van Gelder, *Jan de Bisschop and his Icones and Paradigmata*, Doornspijk 1985, pp. 201–2; van Gelder discovered that the albums had originally been put together by Pieter Spiering Silfercrona.)

10. J. S. Finch, 'Sir Hans Sloane's printed books', *The Library*, XXII 1942, pp. 67–72.

11. By Nickson, art. cit. in n. 6, p. 54.

12. The Sloane manuscripts were numbered on arrival in the British Museum from 1 to 4100. The volumes of drawings were kept separately, and were added later as 5018–27 and 5214–308. No proper catalogue of the manuscripts has ever been published, but Edward J. L. Scott compiled a very useful *Index to the Sloane Manuscripts in the British Museum*, London 1904.

13. Scheuchzer's subject order could readily be worked out by reconstructing the sequence of press-marks.

14. I am not certain why Sloane was presented with it. He had close links with French scholars, and for years corresponded with the Abbé Bignon, Louis XV's librarian.

15. At the end of the first volume of the library catalogue (Sl.3972C, vol. 1, f. 209) is a list of missing numbers, as well as a list of all the albums that contained loose prints.

16. de Beer, op. cit. in note 1, p. 120.

17. A problem concerns the significance of the suffix 'b' or 'w' which Sloane added in lower case after the 'C'. Courten's lists are headed 'Best prints', and so the 'b' may stand for 'best' and refer to the listed prints. The 'w' would then be 'worst', and refer to prints not on the lists. I stress that this is only a guess.

18. Quoted by de Beer, op. cit. p. 114.

19. Under Pr.CCCLXV are listed 'Cards expressing various mathematical instruments etc.' and 'Cards having the twelve figures of the Zodiack with several other figures engraved thereupon etc.'. In a later hand is added 'Mathematical cards by Tho. Tuttell' and 'an entire pack of astronomical cards'.

20. Sloane also had two folio albums of specimens of paper, kept as Ms A.796 and 797: 'A large volum of the several sorts of papers made in the East Indies, China, Germany etc.' and 'A volum of the several sorts of ancient paper & parchment used in Europe'.

21. Sloane never marked his prints. Lugt 1363, his initials in black chalk, were put on by Philipe as a guide to his later stamping. This was a variety of the blindstamp Lugt 298, with the initials HS in place of CMC; Philipe added HS in pen in the centre. The oval stamp, Lugt 2292, was added after 1840. The large octagonal MUSEUM BRITANNICUM stamp Lugt 296, in black ink, is very early, and was put on the Sloane (and other) volumes in the late 1750s or 1760s.

22. Page 423 of his catalogue. This is the famous album whose existence was recorded by George Vertue. See *Walpole Society*, XX (Vertue Papers II), 1931–2, p. 12. This passage in Sloane's catalogue confirms Vertue. Sloane had other albums of the works of Hollar at Pr.LXIV, LXXXVII, LXXVIIII, CI and DCCCXX.

23. The other miscellaneous albums are Pr.335, 336 and 423.

24. One such album is Pr.CIC, 'A collection of miscellaneous old prints by Albert Dürer, Lucas van Leyden etc. gathered by Jacobus Colius Ortelianus 1599 in fol.' John Rowlands had established that Ortelianus was the nephew of the famous cartographer Abraham Ortelius (in footnote 43 of his essay in MacGregor, 1994: cited note 1).

25. See M. McC. Gatch, 'John Bagford, bookseller and antiquary', *British Library Journal*, XII 1986, pp. 150–71.

26. See Harley 5988, f. 11v and f. 79. I owe this reference to Margaret Nickson: see her article 'Bagford and Sloane', *British Library Journal*, IX 1983, pp. 51–5. Other material from Bagford's collection reached the Department of Prints and Drawings via the Harley manuscripts; some such items are listed in Gg.4 of the 1837 inventory. Some of these prints have a 'B' in brown ink, which seems to be an unrecorded mark put on by Bagford.

27. See Sloane 3963 for the letters. Sl.3395 contains copies of testimonials to his honesty from Courten dated 16 November 1695 and Peter Lely dated 25 July 1700. Sl.1985 contains a long autobiographical tract in Beverland's hand.

28. These are the 144 drawings on vellum by Nicolas Robert, Sloane 5277 and 5278, now in the Department of Prints and Drawings.

29. E. S. de Beer (ed.), *The Diary of John Evelyn*, Oxford 1955, vol. IV, pp. 531–2.

30. These were some of the main print dealers in late seventeenth-century London. See Antony Griffiths, 'Early mezzotint publishing in England', *Print Quarterly*, VII 1990, pp. 130–45.

31. Charle Beale recorded that Peter Lely had told him that 'several prints after Raphael Urbin in his collection had cost him 7 and 8 pounds a print' (Oliver Miller, *Sir Peter Lely*, London (National Portrait Gallery) 1978, p. 25). Passages in the Beverland papers show the developed standard of connoisseurship of the period. He praises the ten-year-old daughter of a collector who 'recognises soft and clear impressions of Marc Antonio from hard and reworked ones.' (Sl.Ms.3963, f. 51).

32. The staff of the British Library has for some years been recording volumes bearing a Sloane press-mark. I am told by Edmund King and Alison Walker that over 4,000 Sloane titles have so far been located.

33. I have found the monograph by Joseph M. Levine, *Dr Woodward's Shield: history, science, and satire in Augustan England*, Berkeley 1977, a most stimulating guide to the intellectual methods and horizons of the period.

34. To be precise one of the twenty-three volumes was transferred to Prints and Drawings, the one containing the famous prints by Audran after Le Brun's *Battles of Alexander* (Pr.DCCII). This is twice the size of the rest of the set, and for this reason was shelved separately and thus became separated from the rest and transferred. It is symptomatic of the neglect of the prints in Sloane's collection that no one has so far realised that it formed part of the set, or that the set was incomplete.

1a

1b

1c

2a

2b

1 Monogrammist PRK (active Netherlands)
Three blackwork jewellery designs, 1609

Engravings. 130 × 90 mm (average)

Berlin 735

This set of designs for jewellery pendants is the only known work by a designer who signs himself with the initials PRK. The complete set consists of eight prints, of which the last bears his initials and is dated 1609. The central element was probably intended as a locket, with pierced metalwork surrounds. The small hunting scenes in the bottom corners of the plates are purely decorative, and intended to make the print more attractive to the purchaser. Prints such as these were primarily made by specialist jewellers for sale to fellow-workers; the 'blackwork' effect seen in the centre is made by scoring the copper plate, in exactly the same way as an enamel worker 'keys' his plate before pouring on molten enamel.

Hans Sloane possessed a number of albums of metalwork designs. The most famous was an album of drawings by Hans Holbein made in England, but he also had some volumes of prints. These ones came from a small album

that has now been taken apart, but was originally shelved in the British Museum at the press-mark 2AA*a.29, which now serves as its inventory number. The album began with six of the set of eight prints by PRK; then followed a rubbing taken from a piece of metalwork; the title plate of Jean Vauquer's *Livre de fleurs*, and three plates from a set of ceiling designs by Jean Le Pautre. Finally came another 'blackwork' print by Jean Mignot. Such a mixture is typical of the few books of this kind that still survive intact. They were put together by individual craftsmen out of whatever came to hand and interested them, and served to inspire their own work. Sloane's interest in them probably arose from his concern, which he shared with fellow members of the Royal Society, for the history of technology, and the development of the various crafts.

2AA*a.29.1, 3, 4. Sloane collection

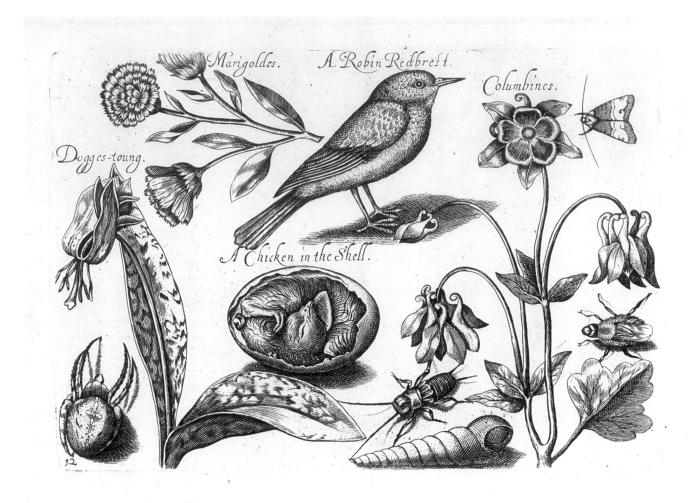

3a

2 Henri Le Roy (1579–1652)

Plates 12 to 15 from *Le Jardin des sauterelles et papillons, ensemble la diversité des mouches, recueilli au servisee d'un chacun* (The garden of grasshoppers and butterflies, together with flies of all kinds, gathered for the use of everyone), about 1650 [*Plates 12 and 13 illus.*]

Engravings. 120 × 74 mm (average)

These are the last four plates of a set of fifteen engravings. They are still on the large sheets of paper on which they were printed. Originally they were bound into an oblong album in Sloane's collection. The sheets have numbers in the top corners in the handwriting of Scheuchzer, Sloane's librarian, and Sloane himself wrote at the top of the first plate 'Pr.LXXIII'. His catalogue entry for this album (see Appendix A) shows that it also included flowers by Adrian Collaert, and Barlow's series *Diversae avium species* of

1658, as well as some unspecified insects. The prints by Collaert are now bound by themselves as 157 c.33, and the Barlows are almost certainly the set of birds mostly etched by Hollar, registered as Q.5–545 to 567, and described in Pennington's catalogue as nos. 2124 to 2143. It would have been because of the importance attached to assembling a complete collection of Hollar's work that Sloane's volume was taken apart by Thomas Philipe in 1808. The unspecified insects were pasted to the backs of the first seven plates of Le Roy's set, from which they have now been crudely torn.

Le Roy was a Parisian engraver and publisher. He came from Rotterdam, and is recorded in Paris when he married a Frenchwoman in 1604. His publications consist of series of animals and ornaments of various types. One set of butterflies he made in 1651 is copied from Hollar's set of *Muscarum, scarabeorum vermiumque varie figure* of 1646 (Sloane's set of these copies was Q.275 and is now at 157 b.7). The prints exhibited here are far too decorative to be of any value to a naturalist, and, despite the hopeful

Stock Gillflower.   A Dragon Fly.   Aenemonie   Single

Larke heele

Medlers.

A Ratt.'

A Parſnip.

·13

3b

statement on the title-plate that they were of use to every-one, the buyers must have been those who thought they could use the designs in the decorative arts. The subject of insects had been popularised in 1630 when Jacob Hoefnagel made sixteen plates of them after the drawings of his famous father Joris (1542–1600). Sloane owned two sets of the 1630 series, one at 157 b.25 (formerly Pr.CCCLXXXI), the other at 157 b.21 (formerly Pr.DXIII). The latter set had belonged to Sloane's friend, the natural-ist James Petiver, who numbered and indexed in pen each insect depicted on the plates.

Z.1–19 to 22. Sloane collection

3 John Payne (active *c.*1600 to 1640)

Plates 12 and 13 from *Flora. Flowers fruicts beastes birds and flies exactly drawne, with their true colours lively described*, about 1640

Engravings. 140 × 202 and 135 × 201 mm

Hind III p. 27; Globe 520

Sets of oblong engravings with miscellanies of flora and fauna were immensely popular in the seventeenth century. This set, which consists of a frontispiece and twelve plates, is one of the earliest to have been made in England. It was probably originally published by Payne himself (a rather obscure figure), and after his death was reissued by Peter Stent, who advertised it in 1653. Payne lifted each figure of his plates from similar sets, either from the earliest of the genre, Jacob Hoefnagel's *Archetypa Studiaque*, of 1592, a set of forty-eight plates after designs by his father, or from Crispin de Passe's *Hortus Floridus* of 1615. Payne added

33

the homely identifications that lend such charm to the series; they are not in the Dutch originals. Presumably the unnamed flowers and insects were ones he could not recognise.

Sloane's set is complete. In the 1837 register it was listed with seven other sets of loose decorative prints in a solander box at Gg.6 (i.e. cupboard Gg, shelf 6). It can be identified as part of H.66 in Sloane's inventory, a volume he acquired in about 1704 that also contained a set of Hoefnagel's 1630 insects, two sets of birds (one by Barlow), and two other English sets, one anonymous, and one by William Vaughan. This album was divided by Sloane himself in about 1712, and he re-entered the Payne and three other sets as Pr.CCCLXXX (later renumbered as Pr.CCCCLXII). Part of the remainder seems to survive at 166* d.21.

Gg.6.6.12 and 13. Sloane collection

4 Wenceslaus Hollar (1607–77)
Six plates from his series of thirty-eight shells, probably 1640s [*Two plates illus.*]

Etchings. Varying sizes, average 100 × 135 mm

Pennington 2187, 2188, 2193, 2194, 2195, 2196

Hollar was born in Prague, into the minor Czech Protestant gentry. After the victory of the Catholic armies and the repression of Protestantism, Hollar left for exile in Germany in 1627, where he supported himself as a topographical draughtsman and etcher. He came to England in 1636, and spent most of the rest of his life in London. Sloane was a great admirer of Hollar's work, and its meticulous precision must have appealed to his scientific mind. He possessed many bound sets of prints by him, as well as a large volume of miscellaneous work that he purchased from Hollar's widow in 1701 (see p. 29, n. 22).

The famous thirty-eight etchings of shells by Hollar (Pennington 2187–2224) are untitled and unnumbered, and their history and dating are completely obscure. They soon became notoriously difficult to find. In Courten's list of 1687 (see Appendix C), they are described as rare and given the exceptionally high valuation of 18s 6d. Courten bequeathed his set to Sloane, who entered it, with other Hollar etchings, as Pr.CI. Sloane later extracted the shells, for the entry is crossed out, and the set is re-entered as Pr.DCCCXX in 1730, when it is described as 'Icones conchyliorum ex collectione Arundeliana' (Pictures of shells from the Arundel collection). It was the great connoisseur the Earl of Arundel who brought Hollar to England; like many others at the time, he collected shells avidly. The prints were never published, and this suggests that they were intended as illustrations to a treatise on the subject that was never completed. Dimly visible in the

upper margins of this set are Latin identifications of each shell by a seventeenth-century hand that have been washed off by a later restorer.

Q.5–445, 446, 453, 447, 452, 470. Sloane collection

5 Jakob von der Heyden (1573–1645)
Pourtraict au naturel d'un raisin, ayant une triple barbe comme de poil (Accurate view of a bunch of grapes with a triple beard like hair), 1615

Engraving. 185 × 134 mm

Hollstein XIIIa p. 76

From the earliest days of printmaking, the medium was used to record the appearance of prodigies of nature of every kind. William Courten had six such prints, which he listed on one sheet under the rubric *Monsters* in 1687 (see Appendix C). All of these came to Sloane, and at least three of them (including this print) can be identified in the 1837 register as part of the volume Z.1. Heyden was a prolific engraver and publisher of Netherlandish origins. Like many other Flemings, he emigrated to Germany as a result of the religious wars, and worked in Strasbourg until 1635, when he returned to Brussels.

Z.1–146. Sloane collection

6 Anon publisher, London (Blackfriars), 1607
The Good Hows-holder, before 1607

Woodcut. 482 × 366 mm

This remarkable and apparently unique woodcut is recorded in the 1837 inventory, and almost certainly came from one of the miscellaneous volumes in Sloane's collection. Sloane possessed an album described as wood prints; many Luca Cambiaso woodcuts that turn up in the 1837 inventory may have come from this.

We have no idea who might have printed or designed this woodcut, besides the fact that it was printed in Blackfriars, London. It has been connected with two printers who worked in London in the sixteenth century, Giles Boulenger (active 1573–94), and Giles Godet (active 1547–68), but the evidence to link them with this print is entirely circumstantial, resting simply on documents that record their publishing broadsheets of the same title. All that can certainly be said is that the wood block is very likely to be earlier than 1607, and that similar heads to that of the Householder can be found in Dutch woodcuts of the mid-sixteenth century (see Wouter Nijhoff, *Nederlansche Houtsneden, 1500–1550*, The Hague 1931–9, plates 358–60). It is entirely possible that the block was

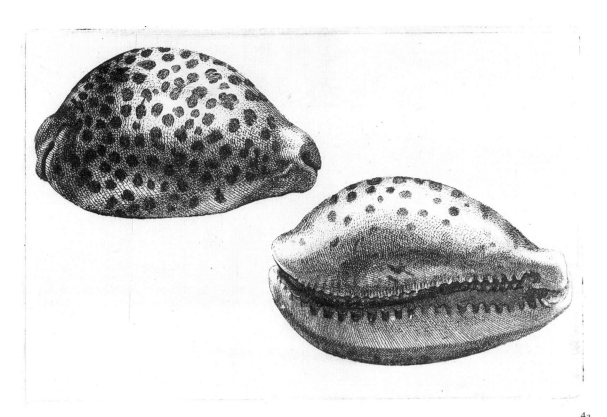

4a

4b

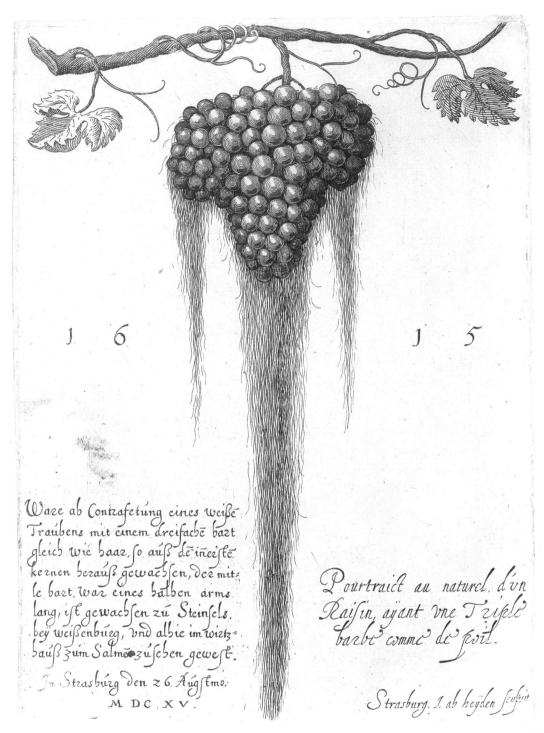

J 6   J 5

Ware ab Contrafetung eines weiße
Traubens mit einem dreifache bart
gleich wie haar, so auß dē ineeste
kernen berauß gewachsen, der mit=
le bart. War eines halben arms
lang, ist gewachsen zü Steinsels.
bey weißenbüeg, vnd albie im wietz=
bauß zum Salmē zusehen gewest.

In Strasbürg den z 6. Augstmo.
M DC XV.

Pourtraict au naturel. d'vn
Raisin, ayant vne Triple
barbe comme de poil.

Strasburg. I. ab heyden sculpsit

5

The good Howf-holder.

The good Howf-holder, that his Howfe may hold,
Firft builds it on the Rock, not on the Sand,
Then, with a warie head and charie hand
Prouides (in tyme) for Hunger and for Cold:
Not daintie Fare and Furniture of Gold,
But handfom-holfom (as with Health dooth ftand),
Not for the Rich that can as much command
But the poor Stranger, th'Orfan & the Old.

And (thus) to thefe to ftand ftill open wide,
  Hee neither wrings with Wrongs, nor racks his Rents;
  But faues the charge of wanton Wafte & Pride:

For, Thrift's right Fuel of Magnificence:
  'As Protean Fafhions of new Prodigalitie
  Haue quight worn-out all ancient Hofpitalitie.

PRINTED AT LONDON IN THE BLACKE FRIERS.

1607.

6

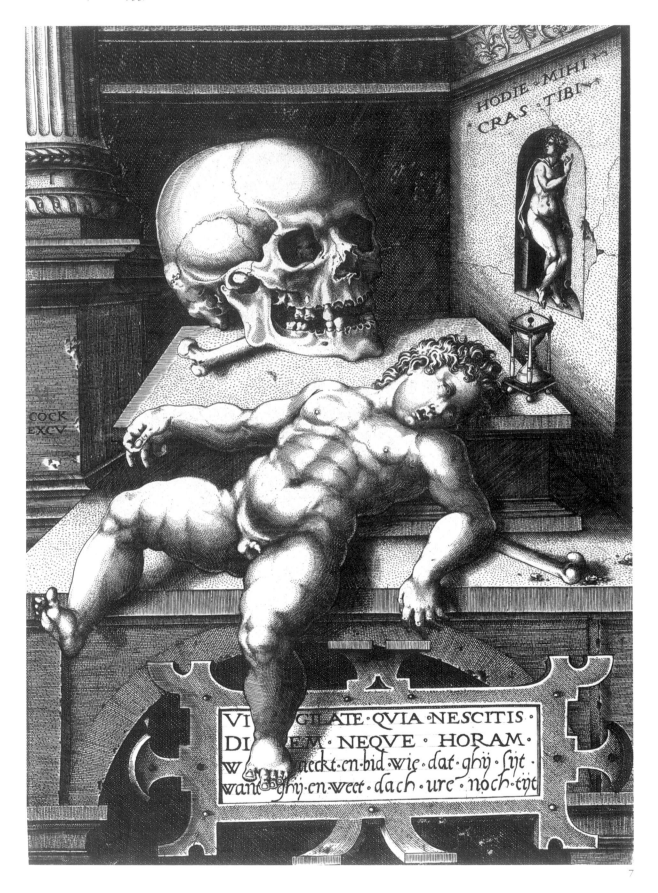

Nuncüs Eterna pandens mysteria Vita   Tuq: inquit sechi felix materona re ludes
Virgineum miro mulcet dulcedine pectus   Gaudia, quæ Dominum orbi sis paritura salutis. Blud.

Luke chap: 1 v. 28.   Crispin de pas Inuntor. et ex.   Madalena Van de pas fecit.

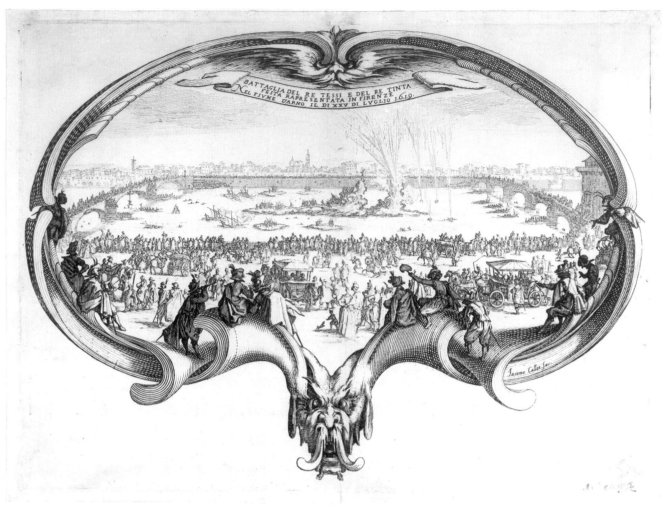

9

cut in the Netherlands, and imported into England. In the text the good householder is seen as an example of prudence and charity.

E.6–38. Sloane collection

7 Hieronymus Cock (1507/10–70, publisher)

A Putto Sleeping in Front of a Skull, probably 1550s

Engraving. 237 × 168 mm

Riggs 257

The subject of a putto with a skull is frequently found in sixteenth-century printmaking. The Latin text (with a Dutch translation) in the foreground points the moral: 'Be vigilant since you know neither the day nor the hour of your death'. On the wall at the top right is a similar text: 'Today for me, tomorrow for you'. At the base of the

column on the left is the name of Cock as the publisher of the print. An early owner has added the monogram ML, implying that he thought (wrongly) that the designer was the Danish artist Melchior Lorch (1527–after 1583). The engraver is unknown. It is highly unlikely to be by Cock himself, who is known to have worked only in etching, and was doubtless by one of the many engravers he employed.

This is one of the many prints that are stamped as coming from the Sloane collection, without there being any way of telling which volume they were taken from. Sloane was doubtless more interested by the subject than by the designer or engraver, both of whom are unknown.

F.1–265. Sloane collection

40

E Collectione prænobilis viri Thomæ Cook, Vice-Camerarij.

Printed & Sold by E. Kirkall in Wine Office Court, Fleet street

10

8 Magdalena de Passe (1600–before 1640)
The Annunciation, about 1630

Engraving. 229 × 182 mm

Hollstein 1

Magdalena de Passe was one of the finest female engravers in a profession dominated by men. She was a member of a large family of engravers of Antwerp origin, which, as a result of the religious wars, had to move to other cities. She herself was born in Cologne, and later moved with her father, Crispin, to Utrecht. She was trained and collaborated with him, as in this print which her father both designed and published. She married in 1634, but her husband died two years later. Some twenty-five prints by her are known.

Inscribed in light brown ink at the bottom left corner is 'Luke chap:12.28' – the reference in the Bible to this event. It is in the handwriting of William Courten, who bequeathed his print collection to Hans Sloane in 1702. Another inscription in Courten's price code is on the back.

D.5–138. Sloane collection

9 Jacques Callot (1592–1635)
Battaglia del Re Tessi e del Re Tinta, festa rapresentata in Firenze nel fiume d'Arno il di XXV di Luglio 1619 (The battle between King Weaver and King Dyer on the Arno in Florence on 25 July 1619)

Etching. 225 × 302 mm

Lieure 302

This famous print was designed to be cut out and mounted on wood to be used as a fan; it has traditionally been known to print collectors simply as 'The Fan'. The scene is the annual festival of the guild of weavers and dyers on the river Arno in Florence; an artificial hill was built in the river, and teams from the two guilds fought for its possession. The print was made at the expense of the Grand Duke of Florence before the event, and the fans were distributed to the spectators. Callot was at that time much employed in making prints related to the festivities at the court of Cosimo II; only after his return to his home town of Nancy after Cosimo's death in 1621 did he begin to publish prints mainly on his account.

The handwriting in code on the back of the print is that of William Courten. In his list of his Callot collection in 1687 this impression is given the highest valuation at 10 shillings. The British Museum also possesses a unique impression of this print before all letters. This formed part of an outstanding collection of 1,695 prints by Callot

purchased by the Museum in 1861 for £180. It had been formed by Thomas Wilson (see p. 94), and later belonged to Baron Verstolk and Charles Scarisbrick.

X.4–175. Sloane collection

10 Elisha Kirkall (c.1682–1742) after Willem Van de Velde II (1633–1707)
Plate 5 of a set of views of shipping, c.1725/30

Mezzotint printed in colours. 441 × 310 mm

Kirkall was one of the most interesting, though still very little studied, printmakers working in England in the early eighteenth century. He experimented with various ways of introducing colour into his prints. The earliest were chiaroscuro prints after old master and modern drawings that were printed from one wood block and a mezzotint tone plate. This print comes from a later series of sixteen mezzotints of shipping after paintings by van de Velde in British collections. They were printed from a single mezzotint plate, which was sometimes inked in several colours.

Sir Hans Sloane bought few contemporary prints, but among them was a set of the six plates of Hogarth's *The Harlot's Progress* in 1732 (Pr.DCCCLXI) and various prints by Kirkall. Most of these were bound together in 1728 in Pr.DCCLXXXI, which contained 'E. Kirkall's prints in claro obscuro in imitation of drawings in soot 1722 with his sea-pieces in a greenish ink etc.' Still in the British Museum is a subscription ticket dated 1722 and signed by Kirkall for the '12 prints in claro obscuro' with Sloane's name filled in. With it is an unsigned subscription ticket with a printed date '172_' (the last figure was meant to be filled in by hand) for the '16 prints of shipping', also from Sloane's collection.

X.6–128. Sloane collection

2. The Reverend Clayton Mordaunt Cracherode (1730–99)

Antony Griffiths

The second great benefactor of the Department of Prints and Drawings was a man of a very different kind to Sir Hans Sloane. Whereas Sloane, the President of the Royal Society, an author, and a physician with a wide practice, was always a public figure, Cracherode was retiring in the extreme. He received a thorough classical education at Christ Church, Oxford, and inherited a comfortable fortune from his father, a general in the British army, who died in 1768. After his mother died in 1784, he had an income of about £3,100 a year, partly from land, but mostly from government stocks. Although he took holy orders in the Church of England, he never practised as a clergyman, and spent his life at his home in Queen Square, London, or his country house at Clapham, cultivating his acquaintance with a small group of friends, and building up his collections. In 1784 Cracherode was appointed a Trustee of the British Museum, a duty that he filled conscientiously. When he died in 1799 it was found that he had bequeathed his entire collections to the Trustees – the first such comprehensive bequest since the foundation of the Museum in 1753 and one valued at the time at £23,500.

In his will Cracherode directed that all his personal papers should be destroyed. He even specified that his remarks on his interleaved copies of the Bible and of Walpole's catalogue of engravers should be cut out and burnt unread (this was done). The only published work from his pen was a short Latin poem. He allowed no portrait to be made of himself, and the print that is reproduced here (fig. 1) was made after his death from a drawing done for his friend and fellow-bibliophile Lord Spencer. As a result it is extremely difficult to discover anything about Cracherode as a man. The only exception is the anonymous obituary that was published in the *Gentleman's Magazine* a few months after his death on 6 April 1799.[1] It was evidently written by someone who knew him well. As the unique source for Cracherode's personality, and as a splendid specimen of the art of the obituary, it is worth quoting in full.

At his house in Queen Square, Westminster, the Rev. Clayton Mordaunt Cracherode, M.A. 1753, Student of Christ Church, Oxford, one of the Trustees of the British Museum, and fellow of the Royal and Antiquarian Societies, to which last he was chosen in 1787. He expired, after a severe struggle, in great pain. His death was probably brought on by a cold he caught in going out after a long confinement, being evidently much recovered, and having returned to his old haunts and habits. His disease, which it is not easy to define, was apparently an atrophy, but, finally, a constipation of the bowels. He had completed his seventieth year, and yet his look was that of a man of sixty till within this twelvemonth. Among his other habits, in which he was extremely regular, he was accustomed, for forty years of his life, to go every day first to Mr Elmsly's in the Strand, and thence to Mr Payne's at the Mew's Gate, to meet his literary friends; and punctually called every Saturday at the late Mr Mudge's, now Mr Dutton's, the ingenious mechanick in Fleet Street, to have his watch exactly regulated. For the last fortnight of his life he was dreadfully emaciated, and, on the Monday before his death, seemed to take a last farewell of the parlour at the Mew's Gate in a manner that could not escape the observation of its owner, to whom, as to his father, he had been so liberal a customer, and by his energetic recommendation engaged so many literati to follow his example. Soon after he got home it was found

1. W. H. Worthington, *Portrait of Clayton Mordaunt Cracherode*, engraving after Henry Edridge (made for T. F. Dibdin, *Bibliographical Decameron*, 1817). 149 × 119 mm. 1853-12-10-636

necessary to call in Sir George Baker, who paid the most unremitting attention, and revived him from the momentary effects of a fit in which he fell down, but could not protract life beyond the Friday following.

The principal features of his face, which was a very fine one, were mildness, kindness and goodness; and though they could not be well described in one line, yet they might be expressed by the single epithet of *il benevolo*. Mr C. was perhaps the most amiable man that ever went from Westminster to Christ Church. He was a universal favourite because he possessed those qualities of which mankind are seldom jealous, and which they are ever ready to commend. His judgement was sound and his taste excellent; he was eager to learn and modest to decide. His general manner of life, though he occasionally mixed with the world and lived with the first people, was quiet and recluse; and his excursions from Queen Square were, for the most part, terminated at Clapham. The greatest journey of his life was from London to Oxford, and he was never on horseback. He had an estate in Hertfordshire on which grew a remarkable chestnut tree, which he never saw but in an etching. This property of Great Wimondly, held of the Crown in grand serjeantry by the service of presenting to the King the first cup he drinks at his coronation, the cup to be of silver gilt, and the King returns it as the fee of office, Col. Cracherode purchased this manor of the Grosvenor family, and officiated at the coronation of his present Majesty. The apprehension of being called to perform this service occasioned no small uneasiness to his son. His fortune was large, which he received from his father, who sailed with Lord Anson round the world. Possessing about 600l. a year in landed property and nearly 100,000l. in three per cents, he was *dives agris, dives positis in faenore nummis*, of which he made the best use, for his charities were ample as his income, but secret.

His attainments were various and considerable. He wrote elegantly in Latin verse, as may be seen in the *Carmina Quadrigesimalia* for the year 1748, which is the only thing he was ever known to have published. He employed a considerable part of a large revenue in making collections of what was best and most curious in literature and certain branches of the arts. His library is unrivalled in its kind; and his cabinet of prints, drawings and medals, is considered as among the most select and valuable in a country that possesses so many of them. He was an exquisite judge of art, both ancient and modern, particularly of sculpture, painting and music, and collected the choicest of early printed books, drawings, coins and gems, of which a complete catalogue raisonné would require a volume. But thus much may be said in this short sketch of his character, that many of his articles were unique for their beauty, their preservation, or the rarity of their occurrence: such, for instance, as his cameo of a lion on a sardonyx, and intaglio of the discobolos; his Tyndale's New Testament on vellum that belonged formerly to Anne Boleyn; his Lord Finch with wings on his head by Marshall; his Olbiopolis and his Dichalcos, the first and smallest coin, being the fourth part of an obolus. Of these and every other curiosity in his possession he was at all times most obligingly communicative. His books, which he used modestly to call a specimen collection, particu-

larly the fourteen-hundreds, form perhaps the most perfect *collana* or necklace ever strung by one man. His passion for collecting was strong in death; and whilst at the last extremity, Thane was buying prints for him at Richardson's.[2] In his farewell visit to Payne's shop he put an Edinburgh Terence in one pocket, and a large-paper Cebes in another, and expressed an earnest desire to carry away Triveti Annales, and Henry Stephens's Pindar in old binding, both beautiful copies, and, as he thought, finer than his own, which Mr Payne had destined for Lord Spencer. There is a drawing in black lead of this elegant and amiable man by Eardesley, an ingenious artist in Dufour Court, made by order of Lady Spencer, but by himself expressly forbidden to be engraved.

It will not be easy to write in terms that are adequate to the merits of his character, but he will live as long as ever man lived in the affection of surviving friends. He was eminent for his erudition, and his taste for a liberality of sentiment and amiable manners. His learning he decorated with a superior knowledge of the Fine Arts; and to whatever objects he directed his attention, whether in the way of profound enquiry or elegant improvement, he was equally admired by the scholar, the critic and the connoisseur. But to his extensive knowledge and pre-eminent taste must be added the more solid qualities of candour, of liberality, of benevolence; and he presented them all to the world in which he lived at large in the form of an accomplished gentleman, heightened by the unaffected piety of a sincere Christian. He entered into the Church in the early part of his life, but accepted no preferment in it. At the same time he maintained that simplicity and purity in his appearance, manners and sentiments, which belong to the character he professed, though without any official claim upon the exertion of its practical duties. He was beloved and admired by all who knew him, and among them were the first and best men of the times in which he lived, and the country which he adorned. Though he was advancing fast to that period beyond which the Wise Man has announced to our unhappy species a sad detail of labour and sorrow, he might still have continued a blessing to his friends and an example to the world, if a sensibility that he could not resist had not led him to look on the convulsed and altered state of Europe with a degree of pain and apprehension that intruded upon his comforts, depressed his spirits and shortened his life. To say that he was a fellow of any of our public societies is rather to bestow an eulogium upon them than to afford honour to him. If indeed, as Demosthenes Taylor (and since him Mr Malone) has expressed himself, to be elected a trustee of the British Museum is to obtain the blue ribband of literature, Mr C. possessed that honourable distinction.

History too seldom records the quiet excellencies of private life. The memory of those indeed who have illumined the age in which they lived by their conversations and have added to its splendour by their various collections is too frequently doomed, after their short existence is terminated, to survive only in the recollection of their friends. Let not such be the lot of the late Mr Cracherode; let his name be registered in the annals of the eighteenth century, and let it be told for the instruction and emulation of posterity, that while his library was celebrated for the scarceness of its books and the beauty and splendour of their condition, it was also highly estimated for the intrinsic value of the authors. His collection of medals also, and specimens of minerals, were objects of admiration from their exquisite beauty and uncommon rarity; and his assemblage of prints and drawings was so choice and curious as to claim a conspicuous place in the list of private cabinets in this or any other country. Let it be told that Mr Cracherode, though possessed of an ample fortune, and eminent for those qualities and talents which render society estimable, carefully avoided the bustle and grandeur of a public life, and divided his time between the formation of those matchless collections, and the studies which were best calculated to enable him to render them complete. Some portion of each day was also allotted to the company and conversation of a small circle, composed of friends, who were remarkable for their taste, their abilities and their learning; and among them were numbered some who were not less ennobled by their talents and their virtues than by their exalted rank and well-supported dignities. To these his house was always open, and every scholar and man of genius found, on all occasions, the readiest and most grateful access to the examination of the books, prints and medals in his collections. Let it be told also that while he was employed in those researches which conduce so eminently to the improvement of taste and to the advancement of learning, his charities were large and extensive.

Mr C. vested in his bankers a power of receiving his rents and dividends and increasing his funded property to the best advantage, always reserving a surplus of 10,000l. in their hands. In his last illness he is said to have desired that no person should be allowed to visit a particular quarter of his library, which in consequence was first inspected after his decease by the Bishop of Durham and Mr Lambe, the family attorney. They found in some of the books banknotes to a large amount, and, on touching by accident a secret spring, a reservoir was disclosed containing upwards of 4,000 guineas and some jewelry.

Mr Cracherode has left no formal will. As he was never married his fortune devolves by inheritance to his sister, a maiden lady near eighty. He left however detached memoranda bequeathing his immense collection of books, medals, drawings etc. to the British Museum.

Every friend to literature must rejoice to hear that his unparalleled library (with the exception of the Polyglot Bible, which he has left to the Bishop of Durham, and his copy of the first edition of Homer, formerly belonging to the celebrated historian Thuanus, which he gives to the Dean of Christ Church) goes entire to this excellent repository, where they are intended to occupy a distinct room under the title of Museum Cracherodeanum; and for a distinct keeper of which he intended, had not the apprehension of invasion preyed upon his mind, to have provided a handsome establishment. All Mr C.'s copies are exquisitely fine. He was particularly attached to books which had formerly belonged to Grolier; and is also supposed to have possessed more books bound by the late unrivalled artist, Roger Payne, than any other person.

Besides this magnificent and invaluable present, which

secures the collection unbroken for ever to the learned world, he has bequeathed a considerable sum to benevolent purposes, and a few legacies to private friends; among which we must not forget the Dean of Christ Church and his brother. He was interred in Westminster Abbey, Lord Spencer and the Bishop of Durham attending in a single coach on the mournful occasion.

This impression of an amiable but crabbed Englishman, who was so introverted as to be almost eccentric, is supported by the other evidence that survives. Cracherode's handwriting is painfully slow and deliberate, with every letter beautifully formed, and the one manuscript in his hand that survived the destruction of 1799, his notebook record as a Trustee of the British Museum, is almost comically meticulous.[3] Every year from 1784 to his death he began a new section by listing all the forty-one Trustees, and the eight officers in full – despite the fact that there were usually only one or two changes from the year before. He then noted any change of personnel, any gifts, bequests, purchases or other item of business; but the record is entirely impersonal and factual. There is no record of discussion, opinion or division. The only occasions that he mentions himself are in 1786, when he and Robert Tyrwhitt, as fellow-executors of his great friend and fellow-Trustee Thomas Tyrwhitt, clerk of the House of Commons, selected 800 books from his library to give to the Museum, and twice when he himself gave a book to the Museum: in 1785 the first edition of the Greek Anthology, and in 1796 a copy of the Comte de Caylus, *Numismata aurea imperatorum Romanorum e cimelio Regis Christianissimi*. The same is true with his various records of his collection. They contain no expression of opinion or enthusiasm. These can now only be deduced from carefully examining what it was that Cracherode did collect.

Cracherode collected in five areas precisely. In order of importance they were books (but not manuscripts); coins and medals; prints and drawings; cameos and intaglios; and shells and minerals. At his death they were valued respectively at £10,000, £6,000, £5,000, £2,000 and £500. Since he devoted his entire life to building up these collections, and since he was a man of very refined, indeed exquisite, taste, these collections are of very high quality. Of most of them he made careful catalogues in beautiful handwriting; he never had a secretary. He wrote an author catalogue of his library in a blank volume prepared for the purpose in 1790 (fig. 2). There must have been a previous catalogue that had become disorganised through the years, and Cracherode carefully copied out every title into its replacement.[4] On the rare occasions that he wrote something incorrectly, the offending passage was carefully scratched out into the paper, and the correction written in its place.

Cracherode's library was never very large. It contained some 4,500 books, no more than would fit comfortably in

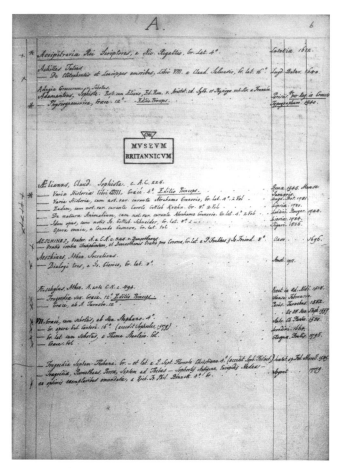

2. A page of Cracherode's autograph catalogue of his library, showing classical authors beginning Æ. British Library, Add.MS.11360, f.6

his house in London.[5] He had been trained as a classicist and churchman, and the library was that of a classical and Biblical scholar. He divided the pages for each letter of the alphabet in his catalogue into two parts: the section in upper case was reserved for classical authors, the lower case for the modern. He had all the first (which he underlined in red) and all the best modern editions of every author known from antiquity, and his editions of the Bible occupied four pages. His modern books were works of classical and Biblical scholarship, with a smattering of history, travel, literature and some architecture. It also of course included all the reference books he needed to build up his collections. It did not contain anything too modern; there was no Rousseau, and only one book by Voltaire, and he showed no interest in illustrated books as such. Cracherode chose every copy with great care, trading up whenever he found a better one. All his books are in immaculate condition, and in excellent – often superb – bindings; he owned, for example, no less than twenty-five bindings made for the great French bibliophile Jean Grolier.[6] He loved copies on vellum, with

large margins, and association copies that had belonged to great men and collectors of the past. Thus he owned the copy of Foxe's *Book of Martyrs* dedicated by the author to Queen Elizabeth I. For all this his library was talked about with due reverence by bibliophiles at the time – and Cracherode lived in a great age of bibliophily.[7] When his books and prints arrived at the British Museum, the Trustees were so impressed that they converted their Committee Room to hold them, erecting wire-fronted bookcases with six cabinets in the centre to hold the prints and drawings.[8]

Cracherode also wrote a complete catalogue of his coins and medals (the two categories were not distinguished at the time). This (together with Hans Sloane's catalogue of his medal collection) was destroyed by bombing in the Second World War, and since the coins themselves have long since been distributed through the British Museum's collection, it is now no longer possible to identify them or get much of an idea about the whole. All that can be said is that when they came to the Museum, they were valued at £6,000, and that the Trustees paid John Thane £20 for packing and transporting them and the prints to Bloomsbury. The few marked surviving copies of coin auction catalogues in Cracherode's library show how extensively and expensively he collected.[9] The catalogues of his mineral/fossil and shell collections have survived. These collections were put together for him by the leading London dealer of the day, George Humphrey, and it was Humphrey who began a catalogue which Cracherode continued. This lists 789 species or varieties of shell, in 897 specimens, and this part of his collection was valued in 1799 at £2,000 (including some minerals that came with them).[10] Of his gems and cameos there is no surviving autograph list, but there were eighty-three of them, including no less than six by Nathaniel Marchant.[11]

Our concern in this essay is with Cracherode's collection of prints and drawings. Unfortunately Cracherode never made a catalogue of these. He never went further than marking off in pencil in the margins the lists of prints he found in the standard catalogues that were published in his day and which he had in his library. Those copies that have been identified are the following, together with their pressmarks in the British Museum or Library:

1. C. H. von Heinecken, *Dictionnaire des Artistes dont nous avons des Estampes*, Leipzig, 4 vols, A-DIZ, 1778, 1788, 1789 and 1790 (BL 679 d.12–15), extensively marked; to be noted in vol. I are Marcantonio, Agostino Veneziano and Marco da Ravenna; in II Baillie, Bandinelli, Barocci, Bartolozzi, Beatrizet, Beccafumi, Della Bella, Berchem and Biscaino; in III Bonasone, Botticelli, Bourdon, Carpioni and the Carracci; in IV Cort, Antoine Coypel and van Dalen.

2. P. F. Basan, *Dictionnaire des Graveurs Anciens et Modernes*, Paris 1767 (BL 680 a.20–22, acquired by Cracherode in 1789), extensively marked, including lists of Dürer's engravings (almost complete), Marcantonio (almost complete), Rembrandt, Strange, Woollett, Jordaens (8), Rubens (93) and Visscher (26).

3. Page 293 of Cracherode's copy of Henry Bromley, *A Catalogue of Engraved British Portraits*, London 1793, showing (left) his annotations in pen, and (right) his pencil markings. Some of the marks are later additions. P & D, Desk E 3 6

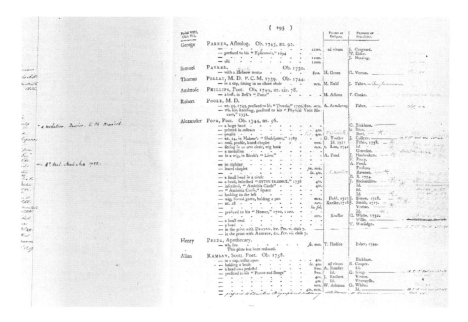

3. Florent Le Comte, *Cabinet des Singularitez*, Paris 1699 (BL 678 b.27–9), only Raphael and van Dyck marked; of the latter the portraits are almost complete, but there are no devotional subjects.

4. Henry Bromley, *A Catalogue of Engraved British Portraits*, London 1793 (P&D Desk E 3 6, 7) (see fig. 3).

5. E. F. Gersaint, *Catalogue Raisonné de Toutes les Pièces qui forment l'Oeuvre de Rembrandt*, Paris 1751; and the supplement by Yver, Amsterdam 1756 (BL 683 c.27–8).

6. George Vertue, *A Description of the Works of ... Wenceslaus Hollar*, London 1759 (BL 679 e.30(2)).

7. George Cumberland, *Some Anecdotes of the Life of Julio Bonasoni ... Followed by a Catalogue of the Engravings*, London 1793 (BL 674 b.9, the dedication copy from the author to Cracherode).

To these can be added information from two auction catalogues of prints in which Cracherode marked off the lots he had bought and the prices he had paid. These are:

8. *A catalogue of a most curious and valuable collection ... collected ... by the late Jonathan Blackburne Esq. of Liverpool*, 20 March 1786 (BL 679 e.31).

9. *A catalogue of the superb and entire collection of prints ... of John Barnard*, 16 April 1798 (BL 679 c.29).[12]

The last source of information is provided by the prints and drawings themselves. Cracherode's drawings were kept together until 1845, when a complete listing was made of them. So it can be said with reasonable precision that he possessed 662 drawings, as well as an album he had kept intact containing 130 drawings by Giovanni Francesco Grimaldi. The Museum never listed the prints, and this became a matter of great significance when a large number of them were (as will be seen) stolen in 1806. No one then could find out what the collection was supposed to contain. Unlike the books, none of them had been stamped on arrival in the British Museum, and so it was

not even possible to be sure that a recovered print had come from his collection in the first place. Occasionally Cracherode had written his initials in a monogram on the backs of his prints, together with the date of acquisition. But he never did this consistently, seeming to have reserved such a mark as a sign of special approval or attachment. So many prints had no mark at all. The only document that had been drawn up in the Museum was a small finding-list, made apparently for William Beloe in 1804, that described how the collection was stored in six cabinets that had been made for them (see Appendix D). This explains how many portfolios there were, and gives some idea what type of material was in them, but it is not a catalogue. It simply reveals how badly the collection was arranged: works by the Carracci are listed in albums N, O, R, Gg, Ii and Kk.

Fortunately, although these problems proved insuperable for the needs of the Trustees in 1806, they do not prevent us 188 years later from forming a good idea of the nature of Cracherode's print collection. By piecing all the sources together we can learn a surprising amount about it and its development.

Although Cracherode probably began print collecting in the 1760s,[13] he does not seem to have made many acquisitions before the 1780s, and most of his prints were purchased in the 1790s. The greatest sale of the 1770s was that of the collection of Pierre-Jean Mariette in Paris in 1775. Cracherode had a copy of the auction catalogue, which he signed and dated 1775, and priced in his own hand, but not a single purchase from it is marked.[14] The first sale at which we can be certain that he bought prints was that of the Liverpool collector Jonathan Blackburne in 1786.[15] Here he bought eighty lots for a total of £216.12.6; included among them were four drawings for £16.17.0 and an empty portfolio for £2.13.0. He was here interested above all in acquiring Italian prints, firstly of the sixteenth century, relating to Raphael, Michelangelo, Parmigianino and the other great figures of the High Renaissance. Secondly he was building up a collection of the Carracci, and in particular of the engravings of Agostino. As Heinecken was to remark of them three years later, 'C'est la collection la plus capitale et la plus rare de l'école italienne, recherchée par tous les vrais amateurs de la peinture et de la gravure'.[16] He was also interested in the etchers of the seventeenth century, such as Ribera and Schedoni.

Besides the Italians, Cracherode bought a group of etchings by Rembrandt, by Claude (including an extraordinary working proof), one print (the boy with the dog) that has always been considered Goltzius's masterpiece (cat. 14), a complete set of Count Goudt's engravings after Elsheimer, three engravings each by Dürer and Schongauer, and some of the French line-engravings by Drevet and others that were then so highly regarded. The most expensive single print was Marcantonio's strange engraving known as '*The Dream of Raphael*' at £6.0.0 (cat. 11). Then followed two French engravings at £4.10.0 each. Four shillings cheaper, at £4.6.0, came what would now be thought the most extraordinary item in the sale, an unfinished working proof of Agostino Veneziano's engraving after Bandinelli's *Massacre of the Innocents*.

Twelve years later came an even more remarkable sale, that of the prints from the collection of John Barnard. Barnard was one of the greatest of English collectors; in 1921 the Dutch collector and scholar Frits Lugt remarked that of all British collectors' marks that of Barnard was the most revered as the guarantee of exceptional quality.[17] Cracherode had already spent £167.18.0 on thirty-three lots at the sale of Barnard's drawings in 1787. At the print sale he excelled himself, buying 129 lots for a total of £450.19.6 (nearly 10% of the sale by value), according to Thane's invoice bound into his copy of the sale catalogue. His strategy on this occasion was quite different from that in 1786. Only eighteen lots among his purchases were of miscellaneous items, all Italian except for two rare portraits and one set of eight etchings by Cuyp. All the remaining 111 lots were by four artists.

The first was Hollar, of whom he bought eighteen lots, all but two being portraits. Then came twenty-three lots with prints by or after Parmigianino, to whose work Cracherode, like so many English collectors, was devoted (he also owned a number of his drawings). The third was Marcantonio, with no less than thirty-four lots. Finally came Rembrandt, with thirty-one lots.[18] Whereas most of the engravings by Marcantonio cost between £2 and £3, the normal Rembrandt lot cost between £1 and £2. Thus an impression of the *Three Crosses* printed on both sides of the sheet was only £1.16.0. But to this rule there were some startling exceptions. Sixteen prints in the sale (excluding the books) fetched £15 or more, and Cracherode

bought four of them. The two large early etchings of the *Ecce Homo* (unfinished proof) and the *Descent from the Cross* (with the arched top) cost him £15 and £20.5.0 respectively. The *Coach Landscape*, which is now attributed to Philips Koninck and was later to feature so prominently in Dighton's thefts (cat. 18), cost £19.8.6. But these extraordinary prices were completely cast into the shadow by the truly amazing price of £57.15.0, which Cracherode had to pay for an early impression of the portrait of the writing-master Coppenol, on Japanese paper (cat. 19). This was the highest price of the sale and very probably the world record price for a print at the time.[19] The second highest price was £36.15.0 paid for Rembrandt's *Arnold Tholinx*, a famous rarity of which Cracherode already owned an impression. The fact that Cracherode was willing to pay such a record price shows both his passion for Rembrandt and his willingness to spare nothing to get what he really wanted. He was used to having to pay prices like this for his best books and this may have inured him to the shock.

Unlike many collectors of the period, Cracherode never purchased in his own name at auctions, but always used an agent, John Thane (1748–1818). Thane was by far the biggest dealer of his day in old master prints, and regularly bought up to a quarter of the lots in any large print sale. An anonymous contemporary biographical sketch of him states that he was of a higher social class than other dealers, and this must have helped him in his dealings with collectors such as Cracherode.[20] He had started life in a different profession, and had entered the art world through a connection by marriage with Thomas Snelling (1712–73), who was by far the largest dealer in coins and medals, and the author of some standard works on the subject. Thane inherited his business in this field; it was almost certainly he who bought coins and medals for Cracherode, as is shown by the fact that the Trustees employed him to pack and transport the collection to Bloomsbury in 1799. By 1772 he had expanded the business to include prints and drawings, of which he was credited with a knowledge 'inferior to none'.[21] Thane also pioneered a new branch of collecting – the autograph. His publication of *British Autography* in parts from 1793 was the first ever devoted to the subject.[22] Cracherode was no fanatic for autographs, but did acquire in 1796 (the date he put on the fly-leaf) a bound volume containing a collection of letters or other documents with the signatures of every English monarch from Edward VI to George III.[23] The majority of the sheets carry Thane's signature with dates from between 1775 and 1785.[24]

Several bills bound into Cracherode's marked auction catalogues show that Thane charged Cracherode no commission when he bid for him. This shows that Cracherode must have been a very good customer, and he must have purchased many items directly from Thane's stock. There is of course no means of telling which these were. The obituary in the *Gentleman's Magazine* states that almost all Cracherode's books came from two dealers, Elmsly and Payne, and the same thing must have happened with Thane. In the evidence given after Dighton's thefts in 1806, it is recorded that 'Mr Thane in Spur Street was principally employed in making the collection of Mr Cracherode's prints, and Mr Philipe of Warwick Street sold the Burgomaster Six to Mr Cracherode' (see Appendix E). Cracherode also maintained friendly relations with some fellow-collectors. George Cumberland dedicated to him a copy of his book on Bonasone in 1793, in which he refers to his 'exquisite' collection. Richard Payne Knight, another future benefactor of the British Museum, sent him a copy of his didactic poem *The Landscape* in 1794, and Cracherode marked Knight's purchases in his auction catalogues.[25]

We are now in a position to summarise the nature of Cracherode's print collection. It is not clear how large it was; the best guess is somewhere between 5,000 and 10,000 impressions. It goes without saying that he bought nothing but the best, both in impression and in condition. He always sought fewer and better rather than more and worse. There were few fifteenth-century prints, only a handful of Schongauers though more Dürers, one of which (an *Adam and Eve*) was valued at £21 in 1806. Against this there were extraordinary strengths in Marcantonios and sixteenth-century Italian prints in general. He tried to collect the designs of Raphael and Parmigianino as completely as possible. He had a fondness for etchings by painters, and had good groups of all the major Italian etchers of the seventeenth century. His collection of Biscaino was noted as being 'very fine and almost complete'. But he had few of the main run of engravings after Italian paintings, such as the Rossi firm stocked in abundance, unless the prints were themselves outstanding works of the art of the engraver.

Of the northern schools, he had very little German material; there were very few Little Masters, and nothing later, and no modern German etchers such as Dietrich. He had very little French, no School of Fontainebleau, very few Callot and no Le Clerc, although he did have some prints after Poussin, and some very fine engravings by Edelinck, Masson and the great line-engravers of their generation. He had little by Goltzius and nothing by the other Mannerist engravers. There were good examples of the engravings after paintings by Rubens, van Dyck and Jordaens. His main interest in the Netherlands was in Dutch prints, preeminently the etchings of Rembrandt. Of these he had an almost complete collection. This was recognised at his death to be the best in England. With them went etchings by other Dutch artists, such as Waterloo and Berchem, and engravings by Cornelis Visscher (cat. 46), then highly regarded and now almost forgotten. Of more modern printmakers he possessed some classic line-engravings by Woollett, Strange and Hall, but seems never to have acquired mezzotints of any importance, and not to have collected modern innovations such as aquatints, stipples or colour prints.

After the engravings and etchings, the third great section of Cracherode's print collection was his portraits. Portrait print collecting, especially of English sitters, was enormously popular in England in the second half of the eighteenth century, and many collectors acquired only in this area.[26] Cracherode was inevitably affected by the vogue. For him Hollar was important in the first place for his portraits and secondarily for his prints after old masters. He seems never to have bought the muffs, butterflies and the other works of this type for which Hollar is now so highly prized. The portraits must have cost Cracherode at least as much as his other prints, and there is reason to think that this was the part of his collection that he regarded as of most importance. He catalogued it most carefully, and his annotations to his interleaved copy of Bromley are far more extensive than the rare notes that he made in his other print catalogues.

The reason for this may have been the destination he intended for his collection. He was made a Trustee of the British Museum in 1784 together with his close friend Thomas Tyrwhitt, who bequeathed his books to the Museum in 1786. Other Trustees were also directing their collecting activities with the Museum in mind. The outstanding examples were Sir William Hamilton, sending back Greek vases and specimens of lava from Naples, and Sir Joseph Banks, who accompanied Captain Cook's second expedition to the South Seas. Less well-known, but equally notable, was Sir William Musgrave, who devoted his life to collecting the materials for British biographical history, and bequeathed all his books and manuscripts to the Museum.[27] In this context Cracherode must have early decided that his collections should come to the Museum. He wrote a will to this effect in April 1792, and from that point onwards he was as much collecting for the public as for himself. Musgrave certainly saw Cracherode's portraits as the complement to his own manuscripts, and after Dighton's thefts it was the portraits that most concerned the Trustees.

According to his obituarist, Cracherode had even thought of endowing a post for a curator to look after them. If so, he must almost certainly have intended that curator to specialise in the prints and drawings, for there were already expert bibliographers, numismatists and antiquarians on the staff. He never in fact did this, and the reason, according to his obituary, was that the thought of a French invasion preyed on his mind. If this was so, his decision to leave everything to the British Museum, an obvious target for Napoleon's plundering armies, was indeed heroic.

But it was not the French who stole his collection. It was a minor caricaturist and amateur dealer, Robert Dighton, who managed to remove so much that the precise contents of Cracherode's print collection will remain unclear for ever. Dighton had insinuated himself into the good books of the Rev. William Beloe, appointed Keeper of the Department of Printed Books in 1803, and managed so to gain his

BOOK 112.

Published by Bowles & Carver, N.º 69 St Pauls Church Yard London, 9 Nov.ʳ 1795.

4. Robert Dighton, *Self-Portrait*, etching. The frontispiece to a drawing book published by Bowles and Carver in 1795. 158 × 125 mm. 1862-12-13-27

confidence that he was able to extract any print he wanted from Cracherode's portfolios and take them with him out of the Museum. He seems to have done this with impunity for two years, before finally being caught when he tried to sell one of the prints that he had stolen. This was a celebrated print, nothing less than the impression of Rembrandt's *Coach Landscape* on which Cracherode had spent £19.8.6 at the Barnard sale. The dealer Woodburn was suspicious that it might be a fake, and took it to the Museum to compare with Cracherode's impression. Failing to find it, he reported his suspicions, which were evidently already shared by many in the trade – for how did an impecunious caricaturist have such valuable rarities in his possession?

Within a few days the story was in the press,[28] and the Trustees were trying to repair the damage. Fortunately they took very detailed minutes of evidence from many collectors and dealers, and these fascinating and important documents are here printed for the first time (see Appendix E). From them we discover that Dighton had so comprehensively erased all distinguishing marks that no prosecution was possible. Not even he was certain which of the prints in his possession had come from the Museum. So at the end of the day, the Trustees had to strike a deal with

him by which, in return for his co-operation, he was left alone. In practice this meant that the Trustees kept all the prints in his possession, and purchased others back from the dealers and collectors to whom he had sold them. The only good that came of this sad affair was that Cracherode's abandoned intention to establish a curatorial position was realised, and a separate Department of Prints and Drawings was at last established.

I owe thanks to Chris Michaelides for his help in examining the books in Cracherode's library.

1. *The Gentleman's Magazine*, LXIX 1799, part I, pp. 354–6. The paragraph beginning 'History too seldom records' and ending 'his charities were large and extensive' had previously been used for his obituary in *The Times* of 8 April 1799. The obituary was later adapted, with no new information, for *The General Biographical Dictionary*, new ed. by Alexander Chalmers, London 1813, vol. X pp. 444–6.

2. This was the sale of the prints of Charles Rogers, which lasted from 18 March to 11 April 1799. See A. Griffiths, 'The Rogers collection in the Cottonian Library, Plymouth', *Print Quarterly*, X 1993, pp. 19–36.

3. British Library, Add.Ms.47611.

4. BL Add.Ms.11360. It is dated at the end of January 1790; subsequent additions are easily distinguished by the colour of the ink or other such signs.

5. See A. Davis, 'Portrait of a bibliophile XVIII: Clayton Mordaunt Cracherode', *Book Collector*, 23 (1974), pp. 339–54, 489–505.

6. See H. M. Nixon, *Bookbindings from the Library of Jean Grolier*, exhibition catalogue, British Museum, 1965. This contained all Grolier bindings then in British collections, a total of 133.

7. See T. F. Dibdin, *The Bibliographical Decameron*, 1817, vol. III pp. 326–36 for a general account of his library. Vol. II pp. 479–81 discusses his bindings from the library of de Thou; ibid. pp. 326–71 his copies on vellum.

8. See the minutes of the General Meetings for 11 May and 13 July 1799.

9. The surviving marked coin catalogues are for the Charles Lindgren sale of 21 May 1784 (BL 679 d.22(2)), and of Matthew Duane in 1785 (both parts, BL 679 c.27). It was from the Duane sale that he bought Marchant's intaglio of *Bacchus and Ariadne* for the enormous sum of £24.3.6, and a woman's head by Birch for £3.13.6.

10. See the excellent study by G. L. Wilkins, 'The Cracherode shell collection', *Bulletin of the British Museum (Natural History)*, Historical Series 1 no. 4, London 1957. Many were purchased at the Calonne sale in 1797.

11. See G. Seidman, 'Nathaniel Marchant, gem-engraver', *Walpole Society*, LIII 1987, p. 39, in which it is stated on information from G. Vaughan that Cracherode and Marchant saw the collector Charles Townley almost every day. This would have been after Marchant's return from Rome in 1788.

12. Cracherode also owned a copy of the catalogue of Richardson's sale of portrait engravings on 18 February 1799, but the markings in this are difficult to interpret, and may not signify purchases he made. The British Library also contains Cracherode's copies of two auction catalogues of drawings, marked with his purchases: the 1787 Barnard sale (679 e.27(2)) and the 1798 Duke of Argyll sale (679 c.28(2)).

13. The earliest date on a printed book is 1753 (Davis, op. cit. p. 348).

14. Now in the Department of Prints and Drawings, Sc.D 1 37. Cracherode might of course have bought at the sale, and may simply have failed to annotate his catalogue, but I have not yet seen any print with a Mariette signature that bears Cracherode's monogram and the date of acquisition 1775.

15. Very little is known about Blackburne (see Lugt 262). The survival of Cracherode's purchases enables the identification of Blackburne's distinctive handwriting (see *Print Quarterly*, XII 1995, p. 76), in which he wrote on the backs of his prints when and where he acquired them. They show that he had been collecting since the Mead sale in 1755, and had bought from dealers as well as from auctions.

16. Heinecken, op. cit. III p. 607.

17. F. Lugt, *Les marques de collections*, Amsterdam 1921, p. 256.

18. The British Museum owns Barnard's own copies of the 1751 Gersaint catalogue of Rembrandt's etchings, as well as its 1752 English translation, both marked off with his holdings (Ac 1 3,4).

19. According to the printed price list the highest price was in fact £59.17.0 for Hollar's portrait of Sir Thomas Chaloner, paid by John Towneley (a relation of Charles Townley). But I owe to Nicholas Stogdon the information that this was a false price and the print had simply been bid out. The story is in J. Caulfield, *Calcographiana*, London 1814, p. 47–8 footnote: 'Mr Townley, wishing to possess most of the rare portraits, made an overture after he had seen the catalogue, to purchase such as he had marked by private contract, which succeeded to his wish, and it was understood that those so distinguished were to be bought in at any price. Sir Mark Sykes, at the time beginning to collect, bid for the portrait of Chaloner to the amount of 56 guineas, when he ceased in disgust, and has since purchased one equally good for thirty pounds, which is the extent of its worth.'

20. *Portraits of characters who were constant attendants at Hutchins auctions*, c.1784 (P&D 210* c.4).

21. Thane's first published catalogue of prints is dated 1772; Thomas Snelling junior also published print catalogues between 1770 and 1773.

22. See A. N. L. Munby, *The Cult of the Autograph Letter in England*, London 1962.

23. BL. Add.Ms.5716.

24. The significance of these signatures is not entirely clear. Thane also sometimes initialled drawings that passed through his hands. The most plausible explanation is that Thane put his name to those items that he was particularly proud to have handled. It need not imply that they formed part of his personal collection. The British Museum possesses a large number of auction catalogues annotated by Thane during the course of the sales, all given by William Smith in 1850.

25. Knight became a Trustee in April 1814, and two months later changed his will in order to leave his collections to the Museum. He said he wished them to join those of his late friends Townley and Cracherode (M. Clarke and N. Penny, *The Arrogant Connoisseur, Richard Payne Knight 1751–1824*, Manchester 1982, p. 7).

26. This vogue was stimulated by the publication in 1769 of the Rev. J. Granger's *Biographical History of England*. Cracherode acquired his copy on publication, and sent his congratulations to the author via the publisher.

27. See A. Griffiths, 'Sir William Musgrave and British biography', *British Library Journal*, XVIII 1992, pp. 171–89.

28. See *The Courier*, 28 June 1806, where the stolen prints were valued at £1,500 and the thefts were said to have gone on for over a year.

11 Marcantonio Raimondi
(*c.*1480–before 1534)
*'The Dream of Raphael', c.*1508

Engraving. 235 × 332 mm (irregularly cut at top edge)

Bartsch XIV 274.359

This famous and mysterious engraving was already familiarly referred to as 'The dream of Raphael' by Florent Le Comte in his *Cabinet des Singularitez*, Paris 1700, III p. 268. Ottley in 1816 correctly remarked that 'the design was certainly not of that artist'. The engraving is by Marcantonio Raimondi, whose monogram can be seen at the bottom of the wall at the centre left. Before Marcantonio moved to Rome and began his collaboration with Raphael, he worked in Venice, and this print must have been made there, since both monster and nude are to be found in prints by the Venetian Giulio Campagnola (see cat. 40). The most plausible modern interpretation of the subject follows the traditional title, and sees it as an image of dreaming. Lucian talks of monsters that inhabit the island of dreams and Statius of true and false dreams being mixed like smoke and flames (see Marzia Faietti in *Bologna e l'Umanesimo*, Bologna 1988, p. 158). But the learned sources and the mixture of disparate elements – moonlight, a burning city, sleeping nudes and grotesque monsters – are typical of the imaginative subjects that Giorgione had made popular in Venetian art.

From at least the seventeenth century (see p. 269) Marcantonio's prints held a position of pre-eminent prestige among print collectors on account of his close association with Raphael and the achievements of the High Renaissance in Rome. It was only in the eighteenth century that his position was challenged by Rembrandt, and towards the end of the century Rembrandt took the lead. Cracherode collected both, but his Rembrandts were better, and cost him more. He bought this impression at the Blackburne sale in 1786, where it cost him £6 – his most expensive purchase at the sale. It is interesting that the impression of Marcantonio's more famous *Judgement of Paris* after Raphael at the same sale, where it was described (rightly) as 'extraordinarily fine', cost Cracherode only £3.15.0.

H.3–6. Cracherode collection

12 Federico Barocci (*c.*1535–1612)
*The Annunciation, c.*1584

Etching. 437 × 316 mm

Bartsch XVII 2.1

Barocci, perhaps the greatest Italian painter of the second half of the sixteenth century, made only four etchings, but these have always been highly valued by print collectors. Cracherode owned all four among his remarkable group

12a

12b

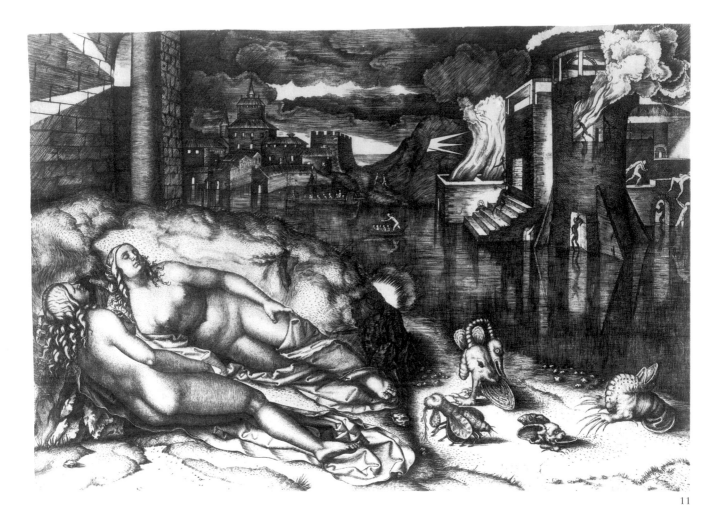

11

of etchings by Italian painters. Of the *Annunciation* he possessed two impressions, of which one is a unique proof of the first state before the addition of the lettering in the bottom right corner. On the back he wrote his initials and the date 1792, but it is not known where he got it from. It is an extraordinary impression, printed with much ink left on the surface: the printer's thumb-print is in the bottom right corner. When the ground has been cleaned off an etched plate, it is often necessary to print several impressions before the ink works fully into the lines. This had not yet been done and the background in several places prints unevenly. This proves that this impression was one of the very first taken off the plate. The second impression is shown for comparison as a good but typical example of the standard edition of the second state.

The etching follows the composition of a large altarpiece that Barocci had been commissioned to paint in 1582 by Duke Francesco Maria della Rovere of Urbino for the ducal chapel in the basilica in Loreto; it was removed to the Vatican picture gallery in the eighteenth century, and replaced by a copy in mosaic. Through the window behind the Virgin is a view of the palace at Urbino. The painting

was completed and installed in 1584, and this etching was probably made then.

Two impressions:

(a) V.8–152. First state. Cracherode collection

(b) V.8–151. Second state. Cracherode collection

13 Giovanni Benedetto Castiglione (1609–65)
The Raising of Lazarus, c.1650

Etching. 223 × 316mm

Bartsch XXI 12.6

Castiglione was a Genoese artist, whose career was spent moving restlessly between different cities in Italy. He spent two periods in Rome, the first between 1632 and 1635, the second from about 1647 to 1651. His etchings, of which Bartsch catalogued sixty-seven, seem to have been made at sporadic intervals throughout his career, and frequently relate to the compositions of his monotypes, drawings and paintings. This print is an example of his mature work

13

made in his second period in Rome, and is related to a monotype in the Albertina, Vienna, as well as to several brush drawings.

Cracherode's collection of etchings by seventeenth-century Italian painters was very complete. He had all Castiglione's prints, with the exception of a few rarities, a particularly fine group by his follower Biscaino, and everything by Salvator Rosa.

W.6–28. Cracherode collection

14 Hendrik Goltzius (1558–1617)
The Boy with the Dog, 1597

Engraving. 358 × 263 mm

Bartsch III 59.190

Goltzius was the greatest master of Netherlandish art of the late sixteenth century, and was renowned equally for his skill as an engraver and as a draughtsman and painter. His most famous feat of virtuosity was a set of prints on the Life of Christ, each one of which imitated the style of a different master from the past. The dog in this print belonged to Goltzius, and the boy is Frederick de Vries, whose father, Dirck, the painter of still lifes, lived in Venice from 1590 to 1609. He had sent both Frederick and his brother back to the Netherlands to be apprenticed to Goltzius, who was an old friend of his, and they are recorded as living in his house as late as 1606. The print is dedicated to Dirck 'as a mark of friendship and for the sake of showing him his absent son'.

This famous print has always been a rarity, and much sought after by collectors, so much so that a deceptive copy was made at an early date. Cracherode had only a limited number of Goltzius's prints, but they included some of his best works. This one was purchased at the Blackburne sale in 1786 for £3.17.0.

F.3–132. Cracherode collection

15

15 Rembrandt Harmensz. van Rijn (1606–69)

The Three Crosses, 1653

Drypoint. 387 × 452 mm

Bartsch 78; Hind 270, third state with signature and date

The *Three Crosses* is executed entirely in drypoint, which, for a plate of this size, is almost unparalleled. It exhibits perhaps the most extraordinary of all the transformations that Rembrandt made in his plates. The first to third states show relatively few changes, as Rembrandt refined the composition and signed and dated it. He seems then to have laid it aside for some years, and then returned to change it completely. The strong light that illuminates the centre of the first version is replaced by an overall dark-

ness. The thief at the right is almost eliminated, and most of the figures in the foreground are changed. At the left a figure on horseback is introduced wearing a mysterious hat, taken from a famous Renaissance medal of John Palaeologus by Pisanello. Rembrandt frequently altered the effect of this state by variant inking and wiping of the plate.

Such bravura and dramatic imagination have ensured that this plate has in modern times come to be regarded as Rembrandt's masterpiece. But this was not the case in the eighteenth century. It was admired, but it never fetched as much in auctions as more finished works.

Cracherode owned no less than five impressions of this print, which were inventoried in 1837 as F.4–171 to 175. Unfortunately, when they were lifted from their albums in

16

1842 prior to remounting no note was made of the inventory numbers, and for this reason they had to be given new numbers in 1973. Another separate problem is that the entire Rembrandt collection was laid down on mounts earlier this century, and no note was made of any annotations on the backs. So it is usually impossible to say where they might have come from. This impression is one of the rare exceptions, as it was window-mounted to reveal the verso. This reveals one stamp JD, and two pencil annotations, 'had of J. Vivian JD 1766' and 'A:V:1772-'. These initials cannot be identified (but see cat. 18).

1973 U.941. Cracherode collection

16 Rembrandt Harmensz. van Rijn (1606–69)

The Three Crosses, c.1661

Drypoint. 379 × 438 mm (cut irregularly)
Bartsch 78; Hind 270, fourth state

See previous entry.

1973 U.942. Cracherode collection

14

17

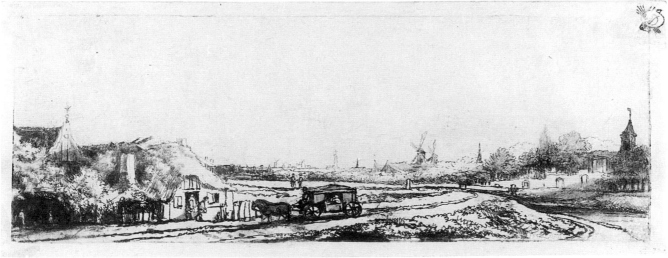

18

17 Rembrandt Harmensz. van Rijn (1606–69)
The Three Trees, 1643

Etching. 213 × 280 mm

Bartsch 212; Hind 205, only state

This highly worked masterpiece greatly appealed to the taste of the eighteenth century: in 1751 Gersaint called it the 'best and most finished' of all Rembrandt's landscapes. At the Barnard sale in 1798 an impression was sold for 8 guineas to Hibbert, more than any other landscape with the exception of the *Coach Landscape* (see cat. 18). The view is thought to have been taken near Amsterdam, near the Diemerdijk, but is given a heightened significance. It includes all kinds of easily overlooked detail such as the two lovers, barely visible, snuggling in the bushes in the right foreground.

Cracherode possessed only one impression of this print, which enables it to be identified in the 1837 inventory as F.5–164. At the left can be seen the stamp of Robert Dighton (L.727) who stole it in 1806 (see p. 49). In his letter to the Trustees dated 10 July 1806 (see Appendix E) Philipe thought that Dighton had substituted impressions: 'The three Trees landscape is very ordinary at the Museum, while that at Mr Conant's [i.e. the one recovered from Dighton] is a jewel of the first water. This is a celebrated print, and certain I am that Mr Cracherode would not have been satisfied with an ordinary impression when he had opportunities of procuring the best.'

1973 U.967 (=F.5–164). Cracherode collection

18 formerly attributed to Rembrandt Harmensz. van Rijn (1606–69)
The Coach Landscape, c.1645

Etching, on Japan paper with black ink wash. 63 × 178 mm

Bartsch 215; Hollstein 4 (as Koninck)

Throughout the eighteenth century this print was regarded as the rarest of Rembrandt's landscapes and for this reason was one of the most sought-after. It was accepted without question by all writers up to Thomas Wilson in 1836, and only rejected by Charles Blanc in 1861. It is now usually thought to be by Rembrandt's pupil Philips Koninck (1619–88). The most recent catalogue, by Hollstein, lists ten prints by him, all of great rarity. Many share the characteristic of being overworked in black wash. According to modern thinking this was something that Rembrandt never did; he experimented with films of ink on the plate, but he never altered his impressions after they had been printed. Koninck seems to have worked differently, and impressions of his prints are not uncommonly overworked.

Cracherode purchased this impression at the Barnard sale in 1798 for £19. 18. 6, by far the highest price for any

landscape. It was stolen from the British Museum by Dighton, who put his own collector's mark (L.727) in the top right corner. It was when Woodburn came to look for this print in 1806 that Dighton's thefts were first discovered. The reports of the investigators stated that Dighton had erased distinguishing marks, and this seems to have happened with this print. There are signs of rubbing on the verso, and the initials of Barnard which one would expect to find are not there. Instead there are two annotations in pen and black ink in what seems to be the same hand. One reads 'JV: 1760', the other 'JM 1761'. The JM is similar to Lugt 1488, the initials of Jean Mariette, but he died in 1742. Lugt has nothing like the JV. The most plausible explanation is that Dighton made up false marks to put investigators off the scent.

F.5–172. Cracherode collection

19 Rembrandt Harmensz. van Rijn (1606–69)
The Great Coppenol, 1658

Etching, drypoint and burin. 340 × 337 mm

Bartsch 283; Hind 300, first state

This is one of only seven known impressions of the first state of this print, before the background was filled in with a curtain. All are on Japanese paper. This impression fetched the highest price for any print in the Barnard sale of 1798, £57. 15. 0, and probably the world record price for a print at the time. The catalogue described it in capital letters: 'A MAGNIFICENT IMPRESSION, UPON INDIA PAPER – RARISS.'. It is indeed an extraordinary impression, both on account of the beautiful tone imparted by the interaction of the light film of ink left on the surface of the plate with the Japanese paper, and of the most unusually wide margins. The sheet of paper measures no less than 457 × 337 mm.

The portraits by Rembrandt that most appealed to eighteenth-century taste were those with a careful finish with an almost mezzotint-like chiaroscuro. The most famous example is the *Hundred-Guilder* print, which was always extremely expensive. Another highly-worked portrait of this type is of Jan Six standing at a window (Bartsch 285). In 1756 an impression of this fetched £34. 13. 0 at a London auction, a record price for a print that was not exceeded for many years (see Ellen D'Oench in *Rembrandt in 18th-century England*, Yale Center for British Art, 1983, p. 97).

Lieven van Coppenol (1599–after 1667) was a schoolmaster, whose hobby was calligraphy, of which he used to give displays in different towns in Holland. He commissioned this etched portrait – as well as another one showing him with his son – from Rembrandt, and some impressions have lines of calligraphy written in the bottom margin. These were doubtless made for presentation at

19

20a

GENEROSISS. HENRICUS RICHIUS EQVES AURATUS ET CUSTODIE REGIS PRÆFECTUS.

The generous and mosʒ Noble
HENRY RICH: Knight Caʃtaine of the
Guarde To his Royall Majeʃtic.

Are to be ʃould by *Thomas Ienner in Cornhill* .

Wilh:Paʃs:ʃculp:.

20b

one of his displays, and the texts were verses in praise of the portrait that he had solicited from poets of his acquaintance (see C. White, *Rembrandt as an Etcher*, London 1969, pp. 146–7). This is probably the reason why this impression has exceptionally wide margins.

1973 U.1132 (=F.6–63). Cracherode collection

20 Willem de Passe (1598–c.1637)
Portrait of Henry Rich, c.1620

Engraving. 200 × 130 mm

(a) Counterproof of unfinished state, overdrawn in black and red chalk

(b) Published state

Hind (Engraving in Britain, II 290.8); Hollstein 43

A very large and important part of Cracherode's collection comprised his portrait prints. In the 1804 list of the volumes of his prints in the British Museum, they occupy one entire case of a total of eight, and they cost him as much as his other prints. The vogue for collecting English portraits, which now seems so strange, lasted from the 1760s through to the end of the nineteenth century. Cracherode's impressions were always of high quality, and often, as in this case, included exceptional rarities.

Willem de Passe was the third son of the better-known engraver Crispin, and came to work for London publishers shortly before 1620 and stayed until his death around 1637. This print, made for Thomas Jenner in Cornhill, must be before 1624, since in that year Henry Rich was created first Earl of Holland. Rich was an ardent royalist, captain of the Royal Guard, and was executed in the Civil War in 1649.

The first impression is a most unusual example of a working proof from such an early period. Passe took a counterproof of an impression from the unfinished plate, and designed a border around it. The counterproof being in the same direction as the plate, the lines of the design were scored with a sharp blade to transfer them, and the design so indicated was engraved into the plate, and the lettering added.

(a) P.2–240. Cracherode collection

(b) P.2–239. Cracherode collection

3. John Sheepshanks (1787–1863) and his Dutch and Flemish Etchings

Martin Royalton-Kisch

The acquisition in 1836 by the British Museum of the collection of Dutch and Flemish etchings and drawings formed by John Sheepshanks was a significant landmark in the history of the Department of Prints and Drawings. It was the first substantial purchase made by the Museum for the Department, the first to attract a special grant from the Treasury, and its acquisition was marked by an unprecedented campaign of support for the Department from outside the Museum. Bowing to this external pressure, and encouraged by Henry Josi, the Acting Keeper of the Department at the time, the Trustees rallied to acquire, for £5,000, the 7,666 prints and 812 drawings that the collection contained. The episode also contributed to the recognition of the Department's importance within the Museum, and in the following year, 1837, it won its independence from the Department of Antiquities, of which it had previously formed a subsection.

The first part of this essay will relate the story of the acquisition of the Sheepshanks collection, quoting extensively from documents in the British Museum's own archives. They shed a great deal of light on the way the Museum operated, its relationship with the Treasury, and on the lines of communication within the Museum. The story will then continue with a biography of John Sheepshanks, focusing on the information that has been gleaned about his activities as a print collector. Finally, the context of Sheepshanks's activities as a collector, both of prints and of modern British art, will be examined.

Probably in February or very early March 1836, Sheepshanks sold his collection, to which he had devoted some fifteen years of his life and on which he had lavished considerable expense, to the dealer William Smith of Lisle Street. It was an unexpected act by a collector who had spared no effort in trying to complete his portfolios of Dutch and Flemish etchings as described in the first five volumes of Bartsch's catalogue, as well as assembling important holdings of prints by Rembrandt and van Dyck. The two last-named were not included by Smith in the package sold to the British Museum as the existing holdings were considered adequate. However, the Museum did purchase fourteen years later his most unusual collection of etchings by English seventeenth-century artists (see n. 6).

John Sheepshanks had no direct dealings concerning these sales with the British Museum, and negotiations for their purchase were conducted exclusively with the dealer William Smith. At the time of the purchase of the Dutch and Flemish prints, Henry Josi was the Acting Keeper of the Department, as William Young Ottley was already gravely ill (he died on 26 May). It was therefore Josi who alerted the Museum authorities to the presence of the Sheepshanks collection on the market, reporting to the Secretary of the Trustees, the Rev. Josiah Forshall, on 5 March 1836:

My dear Sir,

Permit me to call your attention to the Cabinet of Dutch Etchings lately belonging to Mr Sheepshanks, and now offered for sale by Mr Smith of Lisle St. The collection consists of the whole first five volumes of Bartsch, in many cases more than complete, and has long been acknowledged as unrivalled by any other collection. I take the liberty to press this subject for your consideration, as I consider it of such importance that whatever country becomes the possessor, will have a collection never to be matched. I believe I am correct in stating that an offer has been made from abroad regarding the purchase. Mr Smith's estimate of the value amounts to about £5,000.

I remain, My dear Sir, your most obedient and humble Servant

Henry Josi.[1]

Josi's submission was supported over the next two and a half weeks by a number of letters from outside the Museum and by a petition, which together suggest that a campaign was orchestrated in favour of the acquisition. As the extracts that follow demonstrate, patriotic pride and the potential usefulness of the prints to modern British artists were the reasons most often cited in support of the purchase. Indeed, it was pointed out that many artists had already benefited from studying them.

On 9 March, the dealer and collector Joseph Harding (see p.96 and p.98) wrote to Forshall one of the most informative of these letters. He had

learned from Colnaghi's house that an offer has been made by M. Brondgeest, the printseller of Amsterdam, to purchase Mr Sheepshanks' collection ... M. Brondgeest, as you probably know, ran away with nearly all the fine Rembrandts last year at Carew's Sale for Dutch Collections, and his present offer is in all likelihood either for the King of Holland or for the Baron Verstolk, who would most likely present it to the Country. Allow me to suggest the extreme importance of retaining the Collection in England. If it could be secured, I think I am justified in saying that such an acquisition would render the Print Room of the British Museum the richest in the world in this particular Class of Art, which is the most difficult to obtain, but in which this Collection abounds, not only in specimens of the utmost rarity, but also in specimens which are unknown even in Holland and which the Dutchmen are very anxious to possess. It has been Mr Sheepshanks's passion for years to travel for the express object of forming this Collection, and either from Caprice or from having exhausted every source by which it could be Increased, has sold it to Smith the Printseller …

That Sheepshanks travelled abroad in pursuit of the prints is again mentioned in a letter to Josi of 22 March from one Mr Burnet or Barnet (possibly the engraver John Burnet, a friend of John Sheepshanks who will be mentioned again), in which he states that the collector went to Germany, Holland and France to enrich his collection.

Austin Manson, of Christie's and Manson in King Street, wrote on 10 March stating that Sheepshanks, before selling the collection to Mr Smith, had offered it to a foreigner, although he may have inadvertently muddled the chronology of Brondgeest's offer. Frances Graves, proprietor of the firm Messrs Graves founded by her late husband, Henry, on 11 March thought that the collection would be 'an invaluable addition to the National Collection'. In a further letter of 21 March to Edward Hawkins, Keeper of the Department of Antiquities, she noted that 'with the exception of a few prints he [i.e. Sheepshanks] has the Whole of the first five Volumes of Bartsch's Catalogue Complete' as well as 'some hundred' others unknown to Bartsch; 'this collection … has more the appearance of a dream than a reality … the Dutch are after them – the Baron Verstolk and M. Six will do what they did last year at the sale of Pole Carew's Rembrandts – beat out our collectors and deprive the English artist of the opportunity of making these delightful works their study.' Graves thought the collection worth £10,000, twice the sum demanded for it. The purchase was also recommended by the dealer Walter Benjamin Tiffin, who wrote on 22 March stating that he did so on the basis of 'my perfect acquaintance with the collection, from having arranged the chief portion of it'. As we shall see, Tiffin had acted as Sheepshanks's agent for some of his most significant purchases.

On 17 March, Dominic Colnaghi stated that 'the Dutch Government having made an offer for them … it would be a stain on the reputation of England to allow any other country to possess such a treasure'. On 21 March he wrote again, this time to Edward Hawkins, noting that 'the entire Collection cost Mr Sheepshanks nearly Thirteen Thousand Pounds, and many of the Articles of the greatest rarity I know he picked up most reasonably'. From Colnaghi we learn not only that many of Sheepshanks's purchases were from the collection of the Count von Fries, but also that he bought 'likewise the choice of the Josi, the Baring and other collections besides'. He also stressed that the Cabinets of Vienna, Dresden and Paris would find many of the prints particularly desirable.

A collector, Colonel Durrant,[2] recommended the prints to the Trustees on 20 March 'as such choice and unique specimens can rarely be obtained, and must be considered a great acquisition to the National Collection'. And the opinion was sought of Samuel Woodburn (cf. p. 92), who on 21 March informed Hawkins: 'I certainly must consider the acquisition of these for the British Museum as highly desirable and having sold many of the most curious of them to Mr Sheepshanks and being perfectly well acquainted with the Collection as well as with the Cabinets on the Continent I am of [the] opinion that it is the finest existing.' This was a generous response from a dealer who had found it hard to sell works to the British Museum, not least his own stock of drawings from the collection of Sir Thomas Lawrence; as will be seen later, funds for them were being sought from the Treasury at this time.

The Trustees met routinely on 12 March 1836 and were shown Josi's recommendation and the supporting letters that had been received by that date. They instructed Josi to make a detailed report. As so often in the Museum's history, its financial resources were limited and under competing pressures, and the only possibility of acquiring the prints would be by applying to the Treasury for a special grant. Josi campaigned effectively for the acquisition, which was the first of five made from William Smith for which such a grant had to be requested (see p. 97).

Smith himself wrote to Forshall on 14 March to draw the Trustees' attention to the prints. As is to be expected, his letter promoted the quality of the collection and confirmed that it had already aroused interest in the market-place, especially from abroad. Smith even puts some pressure on the Trustees to respond within days:

Dear Sir,

I beg to address you with regard to a most extraordinary collection of etchings and drawings by the most eminent Dutch masters now in my possession, and which it is my most earnest wish should become National property.

The collection was formed by John Sheepshanks, Esqre, without any regard to cost, at the same time with the utmost judgment, and contains the whole of the best prints in this school, submitted to public or private sale during the last 15 years. It consists of above seven thousand prints, a large proportion of which being entirely unique, cannot of course be again procured, and the whole of which are in the most extraordinary state as to brilliancy of impression and perfection of preservation; and also of nearly eight hundred drawings. I would fearlessly challenge the whole of Europe to produce from all the collections combined, one equal either in extent or curiosity to this, and as I consider it of great importance to the British Museum to possess such an unrivalled assemblage, I beg, through you, to make an offer of it to the Trustees. The price I have fixed upon the whole is five thousand pounds, a sum far below what I am convinced it would bring by public auction, and much lower than what I would ask on any other account than my wish that the British Museum should possess it. At the same time I beg to observe that having several applications from abroad, I am unwilling to give offence by procrastination, and shall feel obliged by an answer as to whether the Trustees would feel disposed to become purchasers, as in the event of my receiving no answer by Thursday night, I shall consider myself at liberty to dispose of it elsewhere.

Smith's letter seems to have been timed to arrive the day before Henry Josi produced his own, full report dated 15 March, in response to the Trustees' request. The report is a well-argued document that sets out the special desirability of representing the Dutch and Flemish schools in the collection, despite their reputation as an 'inferior walk of the art', and Josi quoted extensively from Bartsch's own description of their character. His report also provides some leads for tracing the provenances of the prints in the collection:

Mr Sheepshanks, many years ago being intimately acquainted with the works of the Dutch Masters, formed a design of possessing an unrivalled collection of etchings from that School; in the accomplishment of this design he was greatly assisted by Mr Samuel Woodburn of St Martin's Lane, who was employed upon every occasion to secure the choicest specimens that could be procured. Not long after this plan was formed, the Count Fries at Vienna, in consequence of the failure of his bank, was compelled to sell his collection of prints, which had long stood pre eminent in Europe. At the Count's sale which took place at Amsterdam Mr Woodburn bought nearly all the rarest and most valuable etchings for Mr Sheepshanks, and subsequently Mr Sheepshanks several times travelled on the continent of Europe for the purpose of completing his collection and spared no expense whatever with a view to that object. Mr Sheepshanks made also very considerable acquisitions from the well known collections of Vindé, Claussin, etc.

... to the artist they must ever furnish important matter for Study. ... The productions of the other Schools with some few exceptions being from pictures, or designs, by the other artists, and however favoured a Raffaelle may have been in a Marc Antonio in his feeling of beauty and grace, worthy to perpetuate the works of that exquisite painter, still they are but translations from the great originals. ... The Dutch School has equally been allowed to be the great representative of nature, especially in landscape scenery and sea-views, and to the practicing [sic] this branch of art, their works have been looked up to as the criterion of excellence, and their etchings so delicately touched, so accurate and true to nature, have always been greedily sought after as models of Study. ... This explains why artists in this branch of art always endeavour to study the etchings of the Dutch School, and certainly we may look at them as drawings or sketches on copper in many instances being actually the faithful representation of nature, drawn with the etching needle on the copper by the artist out of doors, thus transferring the scene to the plate.[3]

Josi also pointed out that many of the prints were worked at least in part in drypoint, a fugitive medium that allowed only a few impressions to be taken from a plate, and that while other 'great National Cabinets on the Continent possess large collections of these etchings and are continually purchasing and adding to the store, the Print Room of the British Museum, however rich it may be in the productions of the other Schools, is especially poor in these works' and that while 'the Student of Historical Art possesses such a rich and liberal store for his use, the other branch has comparatively nothing from which to study'.

Lauding the quality of the collection itself, Josi states that 'a richer assemblage than this has never yet been collected together', and that it 'has constantly been visited by Foreigners as the most perfect standard of excellence as to quality and State'. He reiterates that should the Museum fail to purchase it, it would be acquired by collections abroad, that it could never again be formed, 'to the disadvantage and injury of those artists who make this Branch their Study'. This was particularly pertinent at the present time, 'for our present system of engraving being only a modification of etching, and the old method of engraving by cutting into the copper immediately with the graver entirely exploded .... The utility of the collection to the Print Room can well be attested by the engravers of the present day, who for some years have enjoyed an unlimited access to this cabinet and have constantly made it a principal object of their Studies'.

To prove Josi's point, a petition, signed by no less than thirty-five artists, urging on the Trustees the importance of acquiring the collection, was forwarded to the Museum on the same day. Someone had clearly been working behind the scenes. The signatories included Henry Courbould, Daniel Maclise, John Sell Cotman, David Cox jnr, William Hunt, Thomas Creswick, Henry Bright, Thomas Landseer and Miles E. Cotman.[4] They noted that 'From their extreme value to engravers and artists in general to study from, the opportunity ought not to be lost of securing them for this Country, rather than allowing them to be carried to any Foreign Museum. The Cabinet which contains these gems will always be the resort of artists and amateurs both native and foreign'.

These various sources of pressure clearly had an effect on the senior officers of the Museum. Edward Hawkins, the Keeper of the Department of Antiquities mentioned above, reported on 17 March that he favoured the acquisition and that 'Doo and Burnett among our best engravers hold it in the highest estimation'.[5] The Trustees were also active: R. H. Inglis, Tory MP and Trustee, wrote to Forshall from the House of Commons at 6.45 p.m. on 18 March to report on his visit to the Chancellor of the Exchequer (in Lord Melbourne's second administration), Thomas Spring-Rice, to whom he had written earlier that day to press the case for the purchase of the prints. He had enclosed other letters of recommendation, explaining that 'from their existing funds, the Trustees can do nothing'. Spring-Rice, who as Chancellor of the Exchequer was an *ex-officio* Trustee of the Museum, had reacted positively to the suggestion that Parliament be asked for a special Treasury grant to purchase the collection. Both Sir Robert Peel and Lord Stanley (as patronage secretary to the Treasury) had seen this response and 'both concur in the necessity of an immediate summons of all the Trustees to meet tomorrow at 3 p.m. I should rather say, that it was Sir R. Peel's own suggestion.' One reason for calling the special meeting was that the Trustees had not yet seen the collection. Peel had also suggested that Sir Martin Archer Shee, as the President of the Royal Academy also a Trustee, be asked to attend the meeting (he in fact sent his apologies), as well as the vendor, William Smith, bringing with him the collection itself.

The Chancellor's letter to Sir Henry Ellis to which Peel and Stanley referred is valuable in explaining the Treasury's relationship to the Museum as a whole, and sheds some light on the nation's failure to acquire Sir Thomas Lawrence's collection of drawings (see p. 12). The Treasury had turned the drawings down in 1830, and the negotiations in hand in 1836 were in fact with the National Gallery:

I have read all the papers. I can only say that, so long as I have had the opportunity of deciding upon any question of the kind, the Trustees have never asked anything which I have refused. I do not like to go further and to originate a special grant. Many of the Trustees are men who have great taste, and first knowledge in the arts and, if they will submit the matter to me, I will entertain it in the spirit which I have always manifested. My only doubt is, how far any such a purchase might hazard my being able to purchase the Lawrence drawings – a subject which is now also before me.

The drawings are alluded to again in a letter the following day from Spring-Rice to Sir Robert Inglis, but are not mentioned in the minutes or memoranda circulating within the Museum at this period.

Another opinion that arrived in time for consideration at the special general meeting of the Trustees held on 19 March was that of the ailing Keeper, William Young Ottley. From his sick-bed at 31 Devonshire Street, he wrote on 15 March to say that he had only seen parts of the Sheepshanks collection of prints but that 'from all that I have heard I should think them a most desirable acquisition for the Museum Colln., which, if we except the Rembrandts, is particularly weak in this Dept'.

The special general meeting of 19 March was chaired by Lord Stanley and attended by Peel, Inglis and four other Trustees. The minutes provide an account of the arguments found most persuasive by the Trustees. All the letters of recommendation and other documentation received to date were produced, and the portfolios examined (these would have been Sheepshanks's own portfolios, the appearance of which is now uncertain beyond their description as being bound in red morocco). Edward Hawkins was then summoned, as head of the Department of Antiquities, to express his view on the desirability of the acquisition. He was enthusiastic, stressing its utility to British engravers. Josi was then called, and stated that he had examined some of the portfolios and compared their contents with Bartsch's catalogue and found that 'not above ten or a dozen Prints mentioned by Bartsch were wanting in Mr Sheepshanks' Collection while it contained many not described by him'. Josi valued Sheepshanks's Rembrandts and van Dycks, which Smith had also purchased, at not more than six or seven hundred pounds, and stated 'that of the etchings of Rembrandt the Museum had already a very fine collection, and a good one of the works of Vandyck; while of the Masters now submitted to the Trustees the Museum had two portfolios only and these containing Prints of scarcely any value, being of very common occurrence and in bad condition'. Surprisingly, Josi also claimed that the Sheepshanks collection 'did not contain etchings of the Flemish Masters, and that in truth of that school few Painters had etched'. This is a somewhat astonishing claim, given that the *oeuvres* of some fifteen Flemish artists were almost complete in Sheepshanks's albums, which also contained Rubens's *St Catherine* (see cat. 21). The *oeuvres* of Gilles Neyts, Abraham Genoels, Lucas van Uden, Jan Fyt, Albert Flamen and Adriaen Brouwer were all present.[6] Perhaps returning to more secure ground, the minutes record that Josi stressed the frequency with which requests to see such material occurred, and that

Mr Sheepshanks' collection had been the resort for years of artists of all countries, and that if removed to the Hague or Amsterdam, our own artists would frequently be induced to visit those places for the purpose of consulting it. Mr Josi expressed his confident belief that the collection had cost Mr Sheepshanks more than double the sum required for it; that three times this sum would not now purchase it, and that in fact it would be impossible to procure many of the Prints at any price, some of them being unique, and the only known copies of the others being locked up in the National Cabinets of Amsterdam, Munich, Vienna and St Petersburgh [*sic*]: that he was acquainted with all the principal collections of the Continent and that none of them were equal to the one now offered to the Trustees, so that if it were purchased, the Museum would at once possess in this branch of art the finest Cabinet in the World. Mr Josi also mentioned a rumour to which he gave credit, that Messrs Woodburn had offered £2,000 for the selection of One Hundred Pieces from the Collection.

After Josi, Smith was called before the Trustees and stated that

the Engravings and Drawings offered by him corresponded in number with the list laid before the Board; that the Collection comprised all those described in the first five vols of Bartsch, with the exception of not more than twenty prints, and many unknown to that writer, and that it included the chief curiosities of the celebrated Cabinet of Count Fries. Mr Smith likewise stated that the collection when purchased from Mr Sheepshanks, was contained in 41 Portfolios of which one was appropriated to the works of Rembrandt, eight to etchings and engravings by and after Vandyck, and the remaining 32 were now offered to the Trustees. Mr Smith represented that he could not conveniently wait for the decision of the Trustees beyond Saturday next.

The Trustees then considered all the evidence, and resolved that it was their duty

strongly to urge upon the Lords of the Treasury the expediency of securing to the Country a Collection which appears to be universally acknowledged to be unrivalled in extent and excellence, which approaches so nearly to perfection that it would be quite impossible to obtain one equal to it at any future time, and which by the best judges is believed to have so important a bearing upon Art, and particularly to comprehend within its Portfolios so ample and choice materials for the improvement of our National School of Engraving in a branch, where the Collections of the Museum can at present afford little if any assistance.

On 24 March, Josi produced a final report to assure Forshall (and thus the Trustees) that the prints were worth the price demanded: 'I can confidently express my opinion, that if sold at a public auction, they would produce a sum far beyond this valuation, and it is the opinion of others acquainted with the subject. I consider the Collection very cheap'. At this point the Museum's archives include a general estimate, possibly produced by Smith, of the value of the works of each artist represented in the collection, which together totalled £5,565.10.0, including £200 for the portfolios.

A successful conclusion was reached within days. A grant of £5,000 was included in the estimates laid before Parliament and Smith was informed on 25 March that he could expect payment some three weeks after the end of the parliamentary session. In the meantime, the prints were kept at the Museum in a sealed cupboard, a list of the number of prints and drawings by each artist having been made.[7]

Although the Chancellor had warned the Trustees that the acquisition might end all chances of obtaining a Parliamentary grant for the Lawrence drawings, their fate was not considered at the special meeting. Parliament could have been urged through the Chancellor to purchase both the Sheepshanks and Lawrence collections, although it would probably have been politically impossible. But the special pleading that had been made for the Sheepshanks collection may finally have scuppered any possibility of acquiring the drawings. If so, it was a reflection, not just of the different order of sums involved, but also of the priorities held by most institutions in the first half of the nineteenth century and many collectors before: prints were preferred to drawings, as being more useful to visitors to the Print Room and to artists in particular.

When Josi gave evidence before the Select Committee of the House of Commons on the British Museum on 14 July 1836, he anticipated that it would take two years to complete the catalogue of the Sheepshanks collection. In fact the inventory of the entire collection on which he was then working seems to have delayed him, and it took him more than four. His reports to the Trustees in the succeeding period reveal that he was occupied in arranging the newly purchased prints into the red albums where most still remain from April 1836 until 6 October 1840, when he had finished marking them up in Bartsch's catalogue. These albums, many of them stamped 'W. & G. Smith, Lisle Street', were presumably acquired from Smith for the £200 already referred to, and they were subsequently blocked in gold with the standard royal coat-of-arms borne by most of the nineteenth-century albums in the British Museum.

The registering and arranging of the collection was a considerable task, and one which, to judge from the inventories drawn up at the time, somewhat defeated Josi. The drawings seem to have posed less of a problem than the prints, and in the section devoted to the drawings the Register seems complete and accurate. Although a consideration of the drawings in the Sheepshanks collection cannot form a significant part of this essay, a brief description of its contents illuminates Sheepshanks's taste. In general, they are by the Dutch *Kleinmeister* of the seventeenth century, and in many cases there are direct links between the artists represented as draughtsmen and those as printmakers. Thus Backhuizen, Jan Both, Breenbergh, Dusart, Everdingen, Flamen, Saftleven, de Vlieger, Waterloo and Zeeman are all well represented, some by important groups of drawings. There are no studies by the most celebrated masters – Rembrandt, Rubens or van Dyck – but there are works by Ruisdael and Adriaen van Ostade. Less expected are the many sheets by Anthonie van Borssum and Aelbert Cuyp, neither renowned as etchers, and the albums by Cornelis de Wael and Gillis Neyts. But all the drawings have one important characteristic in common with the prints in that they are in good condition, and they are usually fine examples of their type.

On 8 December 1836, Josi was able to report that he had 'completed the mounting of the drawings purchased with the Collection of Dutch etchings', although he had yet to make the inventory itself. But many pages of the inventory of the *prints* simply list the Sheepshanks inventory number without any description or note of location, making it impossible (until the collection is recorded on a computer database) to know precisely what the collection contained without ploughing through all the portfolios (into which many prints without a Sheepshanks provenance have also been pasted). Yet perhaps the most surprising feature of the collection in the light of Josi's submission to the Trustees is that it contains a considerable number of duplicates. Many of these, as the collection was sold rather than given or bequeathed to the Museum, have in the past been disposed of in exchange for other material.

From Josi's report of 4 June 1838, we know that the 'greatest part' of the prints was 'unmounted and un-arranged', presumably loose in the portfolios that the Trustees had been shown a year before. More than two years later, he was finally able to inform the Trustees on 6 October 1840 that he had completed cataloguing the prints in the first five volumes of Bartsch, 'comprising the Dutch and Flemish Schools'. By then they had doubtless been pasted into the albums along three sides, leaving the lower right corner loose – the way most remain mounted today.

John Sheepshanks is best remembered for his benefaction to the South Kensington Museum, now the Victoria and Albert Museum, to which he presented a collection of modern British paintings (and some drawings and prints) in 1857, with a view to establishing a National Gallery of British Art. Despite the later foundation of the Tate Gallery specifically for this purpose, the Sheepshanks gift has remained at South Kensington.

Apart from the visual arts, Sheepshanks's wide-ranging interests embraced book-collecting and horticulture. Yet a detailed study of his life has not previously been made, although the main outlines have often been rehearsed. They can now be elaborated to some degree, although the present essay will concentrate on his years to 1836, the date of the sale of his print collection.

Born in Leeds in 1787, he followed his father, Joseph, into a successful cloth-manufacturing business, the firm of York and Sheepshanks. His mother, Anne Wilson, came from a Westmorland family. The Leeds years have yet to be investigated in depth, but by around 1820 he had begun to exhibit a taste for the arts. In his mid-thirties he retired from business and devoted himself to his overriding passions as a collector.[8] It seems possible that his early retirement was partly prompted by ill-health, to which frequent references occur in his correspondence. Yet although he remained in contact with the Leeds industrial scene, he never seems to have regretted leaving it.

His collecting activities began modestly, with the purchase of copies of Italian old masters, but by the 1820s he had focused on the two fields for which he is now remembered, Dutch old master prints and modern British painting and printmaking. Thus in 1822 he purchased in Leeds, at the annual exhibition organised by the Northern Society for the Encouragement of the Fine Arts, a painting by Joseph Rhodes, the *Wash House*, for ten guineas, and a painting by Edwin Landseer, *The Twa Dogs*, for thirty-five.[9]

By 1826 Sheepshanks had met the Scottish artist Andrew Geddes (1783–1844), whose prints he collected

1. Andrew Geddes, *Portrait of John Sheepshanks*, etching. 200 × 145 mm. 1876-12-9-589 (Dodgson 13, iii, trimmed)

assiduously and who etched his portrait (fig. 1). On 10 January of that year Geddes wrote to Sheepshanks, asking him for permission to view his collection of mezzo-tints by Cornelis Dusart, together with a certain Mr Hodgetts. From Geddes, Sheepshanks commissioned a view of Claude Lorrain's house in Rome, which he was thinking of using to illustrate a new catalogue of Claude's etchings.[10] In the same year he became the lifelong friend and patron of William Mulready, the artist with whom he was to become most closely associated – not least because Mulready, a well-built individual, had rescued him from an attempted street robbery by hooligans.[11]

From around this time Sheepshanks also knew John Constable, six of whose paintings he was to acquire with the encouragement of C. R. Leslie, another artist whom Sheepshanks patronised.[12] Of particular interest in the present context is the fact that in 1828 Sheepshanks lent Constable, as a fellow-enthusiast of Dutch etchings, a rare print by Herman van Swanevelt (c. 1600–55) so that he could draw a copy of it (now in the British Museum; see figs. 2 and 3).[13]

In the same period, the 1820s, Sheepshanks probably

devoted equal or even larger sums to his rapidly growing collection of Dutch old master prints and drawings. In Appendix H is the extraordinary list of his purchases in June 1824 at the sale in Amsterdam of the collection of Count Moritz von Fries. Von Fries had assembled a collection of some 100,000 prints and drawings, one of the most important private collections ever formed, containing a wealth of desiderata for any print room, public or private. Before the 1824 sale, parts were sold privately, not least to the Archduke Charles of Sachsen-Teschen whose collections are now in the Albertina in Vienna, a fact that makes the extent and depth of what was sold in Amsterdam all the more astonishing. Sheepshanks spent an awesome fl.6,512 (before any commission) at the sale, acquiring many of the rarest – indeed unique – pieces that the collection contained, as well as the complete *oeuvres* of Adriaen van Ostade, Cornelis Dusart, Gillis Neyts, Cornelis Saftleven and other significant figures. Thence, too, came important additions to his holdings of Nicolaes Berchem's etched work, which was to become especially well known, together with rarities then deemed eminently desirable, not least the proof of a print by Philips Wouwermans for which he paid fl.505, one of the highest prices in the whole von Fries sale. Two of Sheepshanks's exceptional collection of eighteen etchings by Hercules Seghers also came from this source (see cat. 23), and he could be satisfied that he had taken every possible advantage of the opportunity that the von Fries sale had provided.

According to Henry Josi's report to the Trustees, quoted above, Sheepshanks's purchases from the von Fries sale were made at around the time that he began to collect Dutch prints in earnest. There is some evidence to suppose that he had already begun to collect a few years before, not least the letter from William Smith to Forshall of 14 March 1836 in which he states that the collection had been formed during the past fifteen, rather than twelve, years. In addition, among the papers still in the Sheepshanks family's possession, there is a receipt in French, dated 16 July 1821, for import duty of F.43.74 paid by Sheepshanks in France for bringing into that country 4½ kilograms of engravings and some other *objets de collection*, including *bas-reliefs*. This document suggests that much remains to be discovered about Sheepshanks's early collecting activities and his French contacts.

Later in the 1820s, Sheepshanks travelled to the Continent at least twice specifically in order to add to his collection of prints, in spite of his indifferent health.[14] He intended to be present at the Denon sale in Paris on 12 February 1827, but put this off because of an illness, as we know from a letter to his fellow Leeds industrialist William Gott. Writing on 4 December 1826, he explained to Gott that Holland and Germany were his chief objects; and on 14 January 1828, he records in a letter to the same correspondent that he had recently returned from Germany and elsewhere, and intended to travel again in a year's time.[15] On his travels he seems to have met Rudolph Weigel in Leipzig, and F. W. Fink and the artist Friedrich Gauermann in Vienna, from both of whom correspondence with Sheepshanks survives, and they no doubt supplied him with prints and information about Continental collections.

By the end of the 1820s, Sheepshanks seems to have found that there was little left for him to collect. No records of further travels to the Continent exist. In 1828, at the Dowdeswell sale (see Appendix H), his acquisitions – apart from some etchings by Everdingen – were mostly of English prints. They are not individually described in the

(*Right, above*) 2. Herman van Swanevelt, *Satyr Playing the Pipes*, etching. 63 × 83 mm. s.2147 (Bartsch 25)

(*Right*) 3. John Constable, *Satyr Playing the Pipes, after Swanevelt*, pen and black ink with grey wash. 89 × 111 mm. 1842-12-10-23

catalogue but may have been among the works that came to the British Museum in 1850 (see n. 6). No other collection of early English etchings had previously been made, and Sheepshanks's interest in them stands as an indicator of his independence of mind.

The main gaps among Sheepshanks's Netherlandish prints at the time of the Dowdeswell sale seem to have been in his Rembrandt *oeuvre*. This he had been assembling probably since at least 1826, the year in which he, Geddes, Tiffin and Steward took four modern impressions from the plate of Rembrandt's etched *Portrait of Cornelis Claesz. Anslo*, each in turn signing his name.[16] Sheepshanks's quest for Rembrandts continued until within months of the sale of his prints to William Smith. Near the time of the disposal, Sheepshanks bought substantially at the auction of Reginald Pole Carew's celebrated collection of Rembrandt's etchings on 13–15 May 1835; and his acquisitions from the Chevalier de Claussin, who sold works only reluctantly, could also have been made at this period, as other sources had run dry (see Appendix H).

Earlier, at the sale of prints from the collection of the *amateur* Thomas Wilson in March 1830, Sheepshanks had acquired only a modest spread of material, including six views by Jan van Brosterhuisen (*c.*1596–1650) that are hard to come by. But some of the lots marked with Sheepshanks's initials, with W. B. Tiffin acting as his agent, must have contained duplicates of material that he had already acquired from the von Fries sale and other sources (see Appendix H). Just two months later, in a letter to Andrew Geddes of 17 May 1830, one can detect that his enthusiasm for print collecting was becoming tinged with a certain *langueur*, not least because of a recent hike in prices:

Very little turns up, and it is now only a chance which brings me anything; articles of the first class, or of particular reputation, bring incredible prices. A few lots were sold last week which belonged to Mr Wilson and another gentleman; many of them sold considerably higher than they were marked when exposed for private sale in Tiffin's hands, who had them for this purpose months previously, and bought too by the very persons who declined buying them before the sale for less money.[17]

These difficulties were doubtless compounded by Sheepshanks's perfectionist attitude when it came to choosing impressions to buy. This is clearly revealed not only by the prints themselves, which are generally immaculate, but also by remarks he made in his letter to William Gott of 4 December 1826 now in the Brotherton Library. Of some prints he had been offered from the *Antiquarian Society's Cathedrals* he writes that 'they are loose & uncut, but the extreme edge has got soiled in places, with the dust, & two or three of the plates have a few spots acquired from the Tissue paper which communicates damp'.

If his enthusiasm for collecting Dutch old masters was

on the wane, his involvement with modern British painters and engravers was only increasing in the 1830s. Symptomatic of this is his request, in the same letter to Geddes of 1830, that Charles Eastlake (whom Sheepshanks had clearly met by this time) be informed that the picture he had commissioned from him could be of any size or subject, 'provided the latter is an agreeable one, and provided it is calculated for engraving … a large picture would be objectionable, as I am not likely to settle in a house soon'.

Nevertheless Sheepshanks continued to try to add to his portfolios of Dutch prints. This is difficult to prove on the basis of particular purchases, which are hard to trace, but in June 1835, less than a year before he sold his collection, he received a letter from Rudolph Weigel in Leipzig in which he thanks Sheepshanks for sending him a list of desiderata.[18] But Weigel had found none, although he listed a few prints in his stock which he hoped might still be required. It therefore seems that Sheepshanks's disposal of his collection was inspired partly by the lack of quarry to chase and rising prices, together with the pressure placed on his finances by his support for modern art. He had, after all, set himself – and many other print collectors have done the same – a specific task, in his case that of trying to collect all the etchings described in the first five volumes of Bartsch's catalogue, and his sources were running dry. There can be no clearer demonstration of the power catalogues had, and continue to have, in defining the scope of the interests of print collectors and scholars.

The sale of Sheepshanks's collection in 1836 was greeted with surprise. John Constable, in a letter to C. R. Leslie of March 1836 (not more precisely dated), exclaimed: 'have you heard of Sheepshanks disposal of his prints and laying out the amount in flower pots?'[19] He was referring to another of Sheepshanks's enthusiasms, horticulture, for which Sheepshanks is still remembered in the form of the geranium he engendered, *Sheepshanksiana grandiflora*. The artist John Calcott Horsley reminisced that Sheepshanks was a 'noted contributor to horticultural exhibitions at Chiswick and South Kensington, and distinguished as a prizewinner'.[20]

A necessary expense for this pursuit was the purchase of a house with a suitably large garden, which Sheepshanks found at Blackheath, where he settled in 1835. He had previously taken rooms on the first floor of 172 Bond Street, where he was depicted by Mulready in 1832, leafing through his collection of prints and attended by a maid (see fig. 4).[21] Thus the move to Blackheath, with the simultaneous sale of the prints, marked something of a watershed in his life.

He remained at Blackheath until the first half of the 1850s, and his house (Park House) was known as a meeting-point for the artists and engravers he patronised. He enjoyed the informality of a 'country' existence, as may be deduced from the way he greeted the painter J. C. Horsley,

4. William Mulready, *An Interior, including a Portrait of Mr Sheepshanks*, oil on panel. 500 × 400 mm. Trustees of the Victoria and Albert Museum, London

who found Sheepshanks in his garden wearing a shabby coat and a hat with a broken rim. An obituary notice in the *Art Journal* records an occasion when Sheepshanks was refused permission to board a first-class train from Blackheath to London Bridge because he was wearing his gardening clothes, an anecdote related 'to show the simple mind and unostentatious character of the man who must be numbered among the nation's greatest benefactors'. As a member of the Royal Horticultural Society, Sheepshanks also corresponded with other gardening enthusiasts, including the medallist William Wyon and his wife.[22]

At Blackheath he gave 'plain, but good' dinners (assisted by his 'wonderful' servant, Elizabeth – perhaps the maid in the Mulready portrait, see fig. 4). These were attended regularly by the likes of E. W. Cooke, Charles West Cope, J. C. Horsley, Edwin Landseer, C. R. Leslie, Mulready and the engravers John Henry Robinson, Charles Fox, B. P. Gibbon and John Burnet.[23] Generally regarded as a generous patron, who prided himself on having always paid what he was asked for a picture, his broad northern accent (Constable transcribed a reference that Sheepshanks had made to the painter E. W. *Cooooke*) seems to

have been one of several characteristics that marked him out in the metropolitan art world.[24] Sir Henry Cole, a regular visitor from 1843 (on 9 February 1845 he visited Sheepshanks with Turner), found him generally amenable and affable, though his collaborator Richard Redgrave and the artist William Powell Frith were somewhat less complimentary, finding him 'irascible' and 'difficult of approach by strangers'.[25] But these reminiscences were probably from late in Sheepshanks's life, by which time he had moved from Blackheath to 24 Rutland Gate, where he spent the last years of his life.[26]

This last home, which he built himself, 'being of limited dimensions, and only a very small establishment of servants kept', was one reason he gave for discouraging visitors from viewing his collection. The *Art Journal* found that the light was 'subdued and indifferently distributed' and that 'the visitor was in some degree embarrassed by a sense of intrusion'.[27] Nonetheless, he was always engaged, in a selfless fashion, in the promotion of modern British painting by purchasing works regularly, whether from the artists themselves or from the trade, creating a collection that he believed could form the nucleus of a National Gallery of British Art, and as the *Art Journal* reported, the prospects for this venture looked promising: 'What a gallery of British Art shall we possess when this collection, the Turner and the Vernon pictures, are all located under the same roof!' Sheepshanks also initiated projects to support engravers – indeed he 'was full of the ill usage & disgrace the engravers received at the hands of the Royal Academy', to quote Constable, who in 1833 sent Sheepshanks a copy of his *English Landscape Scenery*.[28] Not only did Sheepshanks regularly commission reproductive engravings after works in his own collection, but he backed a project coordinated by John Pye to reproduce the paintings in the National Gallery, and encouraged several engravers to copy and learn from the prints in his possession.[29]

Clearly, then, there were links between Sheepshanks's interests in old master and modern printmaking, and even in contemporary painting, as the majority of the pictures in his gift of 1857 to South Kensington were of subjects that would have been familiar to a seventeenth-century Dutchman: *genre* scenes, interiors (some with women receiving or reading letters), landscapes (some naturalistic, some idyllic), seascapes, and some portraits and illustrations of mythological or literary themes.

A catalogue of the collection was produced by Richard Redgrave soon after the gift was announced, and published in 1857.[30] One aspect of it is worthy of remark in the present context, for in the Introduction, Redgrave attacks Dutch art with a Ruskinian fervour. After noting that the gallery of modern British paintings shown in Paris at the exhibition of 1855 showed a marked preference for domestic subjects as opposed to the heroic and passionate scenes produced by the French, Redgrave continued:

The subjects chosen by British painters have been disparagingly classed with those of the Dutch school, but they are of a far higher character, and appeal to more educated and intellectual minds. Thus, if we examine the works of Teniers, Terberg [*sic*], Ostade, Jan Steen, De Hooghe, Dow, Mieris, and others of that school, they will be found to consist of music-meetings, tavern-scenes, conversations, feasts, games, revels, and drinking-bouts; often very doubtful in their subject, and frequently of the very lowest taste and character. They seem to be the productions of men who never read, since the subjects chosen rarely or ever have any connexion with the literature, or have been derived from the poets or writers, of their own or any other country; but represent, certainly with admirable truth and force, the scenes they daily saw, and among which they daily lived, embodying generally only the lowest sentiments and instincts of our common nature.

What are we to deduce from this? Although the denigration of the Dutch school was nothing new (and was mentioned in Josi's submission to the Trustees for the acquisition of the Sheepshanks prints in 1836), Redgrave must have known that Sheepshanks had devoted more than a decade of his life to building up a collection of Dutch etchings, many of them by the very artists he names. He may also have submitted his text to Sheepshanks before it was published in this first catalogue of his collection of paintings. Is it possible that in the 1830s, Sheepshanks's taste developed away from Dutch art, and that this was a factor in his decision to dispose of the collection? The answer remains elusive, but this may have been one of several factors, not simply financial ones, that led to the sale.

Another factor may have been the disparaging comments about his prints made by the artists Sheepshanks supported, which may have reached his ears. Apart perhaps from Constable and Geddes, fellow-collectors of Dutch etchings (Constable in fact not only borrowed them from Sheepshanks, but lent them to him as well), some of the painters in his entourage seem to have found his pursuit of so many multiple states of prints wearisome. John Calcott Horsley wrote that Sheepshanks 'used to boast that he possessed a proof of one of Isaac Ostade's famous etchings, in which the pig had three more scratches on its back than in any other known copy'.[31] Charles West Cope wrote that

he seemed to me to value them more for their rarity than for their merit; *e.g.*, an early impression which was scarce was to him worth much more than the finished production, and on my venturing one evening to say so, he was disconcerted; and to show me how wrong I was, he made me count, with a magnifier, the number of dots on a sheep's tail; and the impression with twenty dots he considered much better than that with fifty. I used to get very sleepy in dwelling so long on each impression.[32]

Such attitudes among some of the artists that Sheepshanks patronised, even if they were not shared by the print-makers among them, may gradually have taken their toll on his enthusiasm for his collection of Dutch and Flemish etchings.

John Sheepshanks's achievements as a collector were highly unusual. No other individual of his period in England approached collecting in a truly comparable manner, and achieved so much in two distinct fields of the visual arts. Yet his background in Leeds must have contained the spark that set him on the path of his many acquisitions, and an attempt is here made to reconstruct some of the forces that drove him to collect in the way he did.

He belonged, like Robert Vernon (1774–1849), to a generation that profited from the extraordinary boom in trade that occurred in the north of England in the second half of the eighteenth century, and which continued for much of the nineteenth. Sheepshanks and Vernon were already seen as comparable types in the nineteenth century, as for example when Frith reminisced that they were among the collectors who bought works of art out of a genuine passion from them, rather than as an investment.[33] To begin with, these beneficiaries of the industrial revolution, if they displayed a taste for art at all, tended to follow the lead of the landed aristocracy, acquiring old master paintings and family portraits (the latter whether sculpted or painted), of the type favoured by the 'old guard' – represented most notably in the Leeds area by Lord Harewood at Harewood House.

Sheepshanks himself began by collecting Italian old master paintings (or copies after them), as is recorded by the *Dictionary of National Biography*. In 1824, we find that he lent two such works to one of the exhibitions held in the Music Hall, Albion Street, in Leeds by the Northern Society for the Encouragement of the Fine Arts: the pictures were *A Sibyl* by Simone da Pesaro (i.e. Simone Cantarini) and a *Hagar and Ishmael* by Guercino.[34] The Society was formed in 1808 and from the following year regularly held art exhibitions in Leeds.

One of its chief early supporters was Benjamin Gott, whose fortune had been made as a textile manufacturer through the Bean Ing mills, powered by a modern steam engine designed by James Watt. Gott seems to have been a pivotal figure on the Leeds art scene of the period. He was a patron of the sculptors John Flaxman and Joseph Gott (his first cousin once removed), as also of the landscape painters Hugh William ('Grecian') Williams and Julius Caesar Ibbetson, and of two local artists, Joseph Rhodes and C. H. Schwanfelder. Rhodes, as we have seen, was an artist who also interested Sheepshanks, to whom Schwanfelder's animal genre pieces in the manner of Landseer would also have appealed.[35] A droll subject was clearly to the taste of Leeds businessmen, as can be deduced from Sheepshanks's letter to Benjamin Gott's son William of 4 December 1826. He informs him that Landseer had completed a companion to the *Rat Catchers*, and that 'it is a better plate, & a very comic subject. Two young puppies stealing a monkey's breakfast'.

Benjamin Gott also sat to Sir Thomas Lawrence, and from 1810 to 1822 built his home at Armley Hall to the design of the young Robert Smirke (later the architect of the British Museum). It was in the latest style, that of the Greek Revival, and was studied with profit by the German architect Karl Friedrich Schinkel during his journey around Britain in 1826.

To Gott's circle belonged, apart from Sheepshanks himself, John and Thomas Bischoff, John Marshall (the patron of William Collins), George Banks (another patron of the sculptor Joseph Gott), Thomas and George Walker and William Beckett, a banker. These were the kind of individuals who created the conditions in which a society devoted to the arts could thrive in Leeds, men with the power (Gott himself was a mayor of Leeds) and the capital to foster a cultural life in the city.[36]

Gott was also one of the first Leeds townsmen to collect old master prints, which he did in the form of an extra-illustrated (or 'Grangerised') edition of Bryan's *Dictionary of Painters and Engravers*, now in the Manchester City Art Gallery.[37] His lead was followed not only by Sheepshanks, but also by the Banks family and by his own son, William Gott (1797–1863), Sheepshanks's correspondent. William Gott seems to have heeded Sheepshanks's advice. Thus on 4 December 1826, Sheepshanks told him not to buy the Houbraken prints collected by Colonel Durrant (on whom see n. 2), and on 22 January 1827 Sheepshanks recommended the purchase of some prints after Wouwermans, a transaction that went ahead according to a later, undated letter between them.

It is therefore clear that Sheepshanks emerged from a lively and growing artistic scene in Leeds, without which he might never have embarked on his collecting activities.[38] In Leeds he also began to collect books, an interest that he seems to have sustained throughout his life, although details are scarce. Charles West Cope, who was born in Leeds and grew up there, reminisced that when he was a schoolboy he used to visit Sheepshanks, who was a friend of his father's. Sheepshanks 'was a collector of rare and costly books, in which, at that time, I had no interest, but I listened to their discussions about them'.[39] Much later, in the 1850s, William Cotton wrote to ask whether the Rev. J. Mitford, editor of Horace Walpole's correspondence, could study his 'valuable and interesting collection of Academy catalogues'.[40] And from the same period some letters from a book dealer, Joseph Robinson, reveal that he was interested in books related to various topics including travel, while another former dealer, John Martin (who became librarian to the Duke of Bedford at Woburn Abbey), received a letter from Sheepshanks written on 27 December 1852 listing several publications (including Lady Nugent's Journals and a pamphlet by Sir John

Franklin), and putting that eminent bibliographer right on a number of points of detail on which Sheepshanks felt that he had erred in his *Bibliographical Catalogue of Books Privately Printed*.[41] Clearly Sheepshanks brought to his pursuit of books the same fastidiousness that he applied to his prints, and this interest led him to another unusual act: in 1855 he published a facsimile, in an edition of just twelve copies, of a rare pamphlet of 1737 by Jonathan Hulls describing a form of steamboat tug that had intrigued him: *A description and draught of a new-invented machine for carrying vessels or ships out of, or into any harbour, etc.*[42]

After Sheepshanks had left Leeds he continued to lend to the exhibitions held at the Leeds Polytechnic and remained in contact with William Gott and others: on one occasion (letter of 14 January 1828), he asked Gott to forward an impression of a print after his painting by Landseer, *The Twa Dogs*, to a certain 'Mr Kinnear'. But from the environment of Leeds it was above all Sheepshanks who came to form collections of national and indeed international renown. His paintings were seen at exhibitions abroad as well as in England, and his prints were known not only to his suppliers in Vienna, Leipzig and other European centres, but are noticed by J. D. Passavant, who described Sheepshanks's holdings as 'the finest collection of etchings' in the country. The collector he describes as a man 'whose ardour in research has been almost unequalled; and who has taken several journeys, expressly, to the continent. He possesses many of unknown origin; the publication of which would considerably enrich the "Peintre Graveur" of Bartsch'.[43] Other writers to mention the Sheepshanks collection included the Keeper of the Bibliothèque Royale in Paris, Pierre Defer, as well as Sheepshanks's Leipzig contact Rudolph Weigel in a footnote to C. F. von Rumohr's and J. M. Thiele's history of the Copenhagen print room, published in 1835.[44]

His reputation as a collector who seemed to lack nothing in his chosen field of print collecting is exemplified by an anecdote with which he regaled Richard Redgrave late in 1856:

He was, he said, asked by a friend to go with him to see a very choice collection (all collections are choice and rare) of prints, etchings and drawings in the possession of Mr ---. He expressed his willingness, and even desire, to go, if the gentleman who invited him would allow his name to be withheld, and permit him merely to be introduced as an amateur of etchings.

This was agreed to, and the visit was arranged. When it came off, each successive specimen was shown with great empressement, as 'Very choice', 'Extremely fine state of the plate', and a direct appeal made to the visitor for an opinion on it – perhaps as a consequence of that opinion having as yet been charily given. 'Now, I think you will say that this is a unique specimen.' 'Nay,' said Mr. Sheepshanks, 'it is only the fourth state of the plate, and I have impressions of each of the three earlier states.' The collector looked at his guest with mixed wonder and incredulity. At length, a light seemed to break upon him. 'Impressions of the three earlier states!' said he. 'May I ask if you are Mr. Sheepshanks?' And on a reply in the affirmative, the folio was at once closed with the remark, 'Had I known that before, I would not have given you the trouble to look over them'.[45]

One aspect of Sheepshanks's collecting of prints that we have touched on is the degree to which it was informed by a 'philatelic' mentality – a desire to complete a series taken from a particular catalogue. There can be no doubt that the publication of Bartsch's twenty-one-volume corpus of prints, *Le Peintre-Graveur*, between 1803 and 1821 exerted a considerable influence on collectors. Here was a catalogue of prints, drawn up from some of the most prestigious collections in Europe, that collectors could use somewhat like a shopping-list. Sheepshanks probably realised, when he purchased so many etchings at the Count von Fries sale, that he was often buying the very impressions that Bartsch had described. What marks him out as a collector with few rivals – the Baron Verstolk the most obvious among them – was his determination to buy works so rare that Bartsch himself had not seen them. Not only did he assemble an astonishing number of unique proofs and rare states unknown to Bartsch but, as already mentioned, he also managed to create the most impressive group formed in the nineteenth century of the rare etchings of Hercules Seghers, an artist whom Bartsch never attempted to catalogue.

This is the characteristic which has led to the continued renown of his collection of prints, and for which we must remain grateful today. There can be no doubt that his ability to memorise and file notes about impressions that he had seen throughout Europe was fostered by an exceptional amount of hard work. As a collector, his standards were entirely professional. Thus when in 1848 the Keeper of Prints and Drawings at the British Museum, William Hookham Carpenter, asked his advice about the rarity of the etchings of Abraham Begeyn, the reply he sent on 24 June was extraordinarily complete: 'I find that the Amsterdam Colln. contains 4 pieces and all of which have his name – two are the same as mine, only that the larger one, is an uncut, perfect impression – being of the length of 11 3/8 inches – The other two are similar dimensions to the smaller one'.

Sheepshanks goes on to describe two further particular impressions in Amsterdam and Dresden, and notes that

Mr Weighl, a dealer at Leipsic, and who has printed a descriptive catalogue of etchings, where I remember noticing several references to my prints, has another print, patched and in bad condition, and which appeared to be cropped, although being a little larger than the Farrier, possibly it may be perfect in that respect – it represents a ford, which a woman is walking across, a back figure & near the centre – on the left side, a man, two oxen, a goat and a sheep, all in the water, and on the right, two sheep & a dog – the latter stands upon a bank, or

small island – in the background, a man is talking to a woman sitting on an ass – she appears advancing before a flock of sheep – on the water, in the right corner, at bottom of the plate ABegeijn fe 1665. L 11 5/8 H 9 in. ... All Begeijn's prints are scarce, as I found none at Vienna, either in the Imperial Colln or that of the Archduke Charles.[46] The farrier shoeing a horse, Josi notices he had only seen two impressions, and I think does not mention any other work by him – the same print appears in the catalogue of Vander Dussen's Colln. No 5424 sold for 4 florins & 10 stivers – and I have a notice of it in the Catalogue of a Picture dealer, of the name of Vernon, who supplied Dr. Peart with his Colln. and is priced £1.11.6 The Amsterdam prints were most probably Van Leydens, but I have omitted taking a note where they came from. Marcus's & Vander Dussens are probably the same print.[47]

Perhaps no one else in Europe could have written such a reply, and it reveals something of the extraordinary labour that led to the creation of one of the finest collections of Dutch prints ever assembled.

1. The quotations from letters and memoranda in this section of the essay are taken from the originals in the Central Archives of the British Museum, from the volume of *Original Letters and Papers*, vol. XIV, Jan.–April 1836. I have also been fortunate to study some of the Sheepshanks archive still in the possession of his descendants. My particular thanks must be expressed to William and Alice Sheepshanks, as also to Richard Godfrey and Belinda Hargreaves in the Print Department at Sotheby's, where I was able to study this material. Richard Godfrey also contributed freely of his knowledge (of Constable and Hollar in particular). Of the many people who offered me help at the Victoria and Albert Museum, I am especially indebted to Elizabeth Miller, Ronald Parkinson, Clive Wainwright and the unfailingly helpful staff of the National Art Library. In Leeds, I was fortunate in contacting and learning much from Dr Terry Friedman, and from Ann Farr (see further n. 10), as well as Alexander Robertson and Corinne Miller (both of Leeds City Art Gallery).

2. Durrant is mentioned in Sheepshanks's letter to William Gott of 4 December 1826 (see below). He is not in Lugt but his name appears in annotated sale catalogues of the period as a purchaser (e.g. the Department's copy of the Sir Thomas Baring sale, Christie's, 23 May, etc., 1831).

3. Recently, it has been argued that Dutch artists may never have taken plates out of doors. There is no written evidence to suggest that they did, and often the preparatory drawings for the prints have survived.

4. The other signatories were J. C. Hofland (for the Society of British Artists), J. H. Watt, R. W. Buss, T. Webster, E. Cotterell, W. H. Watts, G. B. Potts, F. Rawlston, Alfred Priest, Paul Fisher, C. Steedman, R. R. Macjan, J. Lilley, J. M. Leigh, Edward Printis, John Boaden, G. Smis, C. H. Seaforth, T. Fielding, Lambert, F. C. Lewis, J. G. Middleton, G. Stevens, L. J. Wood and John Bridges. Many of these artists must have known Sheepshanks personally, and it is possible that he was involved in the campaign to make the British Museum buy the collection. The mark eventually placed by the Museum on its acquisitions from the Sheepshanks collection (L.2333) imitates the 'S' of Sheepshanks's own handwriting, an act of homage that would be unusual had he played no part. The British Museum collection of Dutch and Flemish etchings was certainly poor prior to the acquisition of Sheepshanks's collection, apart from the holdings of Rem

brandt and van Dyck. William Alexander's *General Catalogue of Prints in the Museum Collection* lists only a few works by Dutch and Flemish artists. In volume O:2 could be found prints by or after Asselijn, Bamboccio, Berchem, Both, Cuyp, Ruisdael, Teniers, van de Velde, van der Veen, Wynants, Waterloo and Wouwerman; in P:1 were prints by or after Both, Brouwer, Brueghel, Cuyp, van Goyen, Jordaens, Ostade, Rubens and Teniers; elsewhere were works by or after Berchem, Diepenbeeck, Jordaens, Ostade, Rubens, van Sichem, van Dyck and Cornelis Visscher.

5. George Thomas Doo (1800–86) and John Burnett (1784–1868), reproductive engravers. The latter may have been responsible for the letter to Josi of 22 March mentioned above.

6. The other Flemish artists in the collection are P. Rysbrack, J.-F. Millet, Jan Miel, J. van den Hoecke and P. Boel. It might be argued that some of these artists were considered to be French, and there are also etchings by the French artist Dominique Barrière, as well as some proofs by Andrew Geddes of his *Portrait of Pieter van Laer* and a few copies of Dutch prints and around a hundred portraits of Dutch artists. The few other oddments include some woodcuts by or after Jan Lievens and Giuseppe Caletti's etching *Noi siamo sette* (S.6595), which in subject has much in common with Dutch 'drolleries'. In 1848, the British Museum purchased from W. B. Tiffin another unexpected print with a Sheepshanks provenance, Hans Sebald Beham's *Death and the Sleeping Woman* (Bartsch 146; 1848-7-8-120). As noted at the start of this essay, Sheepshanks's collection of seventeenth-century English etchings, many of them extremely rare (Gaywood, John Evelyn, Lodge, Place and Josiah English), was offered the Museum on 7 June 1844 by William Smith. The prints were bought in 1850 (1850-2-23-786 to 974) but Smith stated that the collection had by then been *greatly added to*, perhaps by Smith himself, since it was in Sheepshanks's possession (Central Archives, Misc. Papers I, items 232–515). Smith must have acquired these prints in 1836 with the rest of Sheepshanks's collection, but they do not appear to have been mentioned to the Museum at that time and Smith may have found another buyer for them or held on to them. Sheepshanks acquired some of the English etchings at the Dowdeswell sale (see Appendix H, II).

7. The minutes of the extraordinary general meeting of the Trustees on 19 March 1836 specify that the British Museum was not buying Sheepshanks's etchings by Rembrandt and van Dyck. Yet it has since emerged that at least one print by Rembrandt was included, Register no. S.6150, the *Bust of an Old Man with a Fur Cap and Flowing Beard*, Bartsch 312, Hind 49 (exchanged as a duplicate on 8 September 1982 and therefore no longer in the collection). William Coningham (on whom see p. 96) told the Parliamentary Select Committee on the National Gallery in 1853 (para. 6853) that the British Museum had been offered Sheepshanks's prints before they were sold to Smith, and at a much lower price, but there is no evidence whatever to support this story.

8. His retirement is usually dated to around 1833, based on the statement in the *Dictionary of National Biography* that 'on retiring from business Sheepshanks settled in London, moving to Hastings about 1833, and then to Blackheath [...]'. This clearly does not necessarily mean that he retired in 1833, and in a letter to William Gott of 14 January 1828, he announces that he is about to quit Leeds, although whether this was when he retired is not stated.

9. Information kindly provided by Alexander Robertson. The Landseer later formed part of Sheepshanks's gift to South Kensington, but not the Rhodes, which was presumably a topographical view by this local Leeds artist.

10. The letter is published by David Laing, *Etchings by Sir David*

Wilkie, RA, and by Andrew Geddes, ARA*, Edinburgh 1875, p. 17 and Campbell Dodgson, 'The etchings of Andrew Geddes', *Walpole Society*, V 1917, p. 22. I am grateful to Mungo Campbell (National Gallery of Scotland) for drawing my attention to Sheepshanks's unrivalled collection of Geddes's prints, part of his gift to the Victoria and Albert Museum. Nothing seems to have come of the project to write a catalogue of Claude's etchings. The first, by Robert-Dumesnil, was published in 1833, but does not contain the Geddes print. Sheepshanks was also a particular admirer of Wilkie, whom he praises in his letter to William Gott of 4 December 1826 now in the Brotherton Library. I am grateful to Ann Farr for arranging to send me copies and providing information about the Gott Papers held there. I was alerted to them by Dr Terry Friedman, who refers to this archive in his articles on the Gott family published in the *Leeds Art Calendar* (no. 63, 1968, pp. 21–4, and no. 70, 1972, pp. 18–25).

11. Ronald Parkinson, *Victoria and Albert Museum. Catalogue of British Oil Paintings, 1820–1860*, London 1990, p. xv. Marcia Pointon, *Mulready*, London 1986, p. 71, dates their association from 1833, but Kathryn Moore Heleniak, *William Mulready*, New Haven and London 1980, p. 171, dates Mulready's *Portrait of John Sheepshanks* (fig. 4) to around 1832–3, and this was perhaps not the cause of their first acquaintance (Richard Redgrave, *Catalogue of the Pictures ... deposited in the New Gallery at South Kensington; being for the most part the gift of John Sheepshanks, Esq.*, 1857, no. 152, dates the painting to 1832). The anecdote about the robbery is also mentioned by R. B. Beckett (ed.), *John Constable's Correspondence III. The Correspondence with C. R. Leslie, R.A.*, Ipswich 1965, p. 144.

12. Most of Sheepshanks's Constables were bought in the trade rather than from the artist. The purchases may have been in response to C. R. Leslie's enthusiasm. Leslie invited Sheepshanks, in an undated letter in the possession of Sheepshanks' descendants, to tea, 'and bring any others of your friends who might like to look at those studies I have by Constable, whom I appreciate and you do not'.

13. Register no. 1842.12.10.23 (LB 2); inscribed by the artist on the verso: *copy from the scarce Swanevelt lent to me by Mr Sheepshanks Hampstead 1828. 1829 May 17. John Constable RA* (see Graham Reynolds, *The Later Paintings and Drawings of John Constable*, 2 vols, New Haven and London 1984, p. 202, no. 29.11). It is after Swanevelt's *Satyr Playing the Pipes*, Bartsch 25, of which two impressions are in the Sheepshanks collection (S.2146–7). The collection contains impressions of an etched copy after the same print by another friend of Sheepshanks', the engraver B. P. Gibbon (S.2148–9). In 1951, the British Museum was presented by Colnaghi's with an album of prints made by B. P. Gibbon, J. Burnett and G. Lamberts after prints that Sheepshanks owned (*Copies by amateurs of Dutch etchings of the 17th cent & originally in the possession of J. Sheepshanks*, presented by Colnaghi, 1951-7-23-1 to 15).

14. J. D. Passavant, *Tour of a German Artist in England*, 2 vols, London 1836, vol. I, pp. 242–3, noted that Sheepshanks 'has taken several journeys, expressly, to the continent', as did several of the correspondents who urged the purchase of the collection on the Trustees, as noted above.

15. For the letters to William Gott, see n. 10 above. In the Sheepshanks family archive is a letter from Denon, dated only *17 March*, in which he agrees to see Sheepshanks with a woman and a certain Thomas Baker.

16. See Hollstein, XVIII 1969, p. 124, under no. B.271.

17. The letter is published by Laing, op. cit. n. 11, pp. 24–5.

18. Sheepshanks family archive. The letter is dated 14 June 1835.

19. Beckett, op. cit., p.139.

20. John Calcott Horsley, *Recollections of a Royal Academician*, ed. Mrs Edmund Helps, London 1903, p.49.

21. See n.11 above. According to the *Dictionary of National Biography*, Sheepshanks first lived in Hastings after he left Leeds. He was in the Bond Street rooms by 4 December 1826, the date of one of the letters to William Gott. The *Reminiscences of Charles West Cope*, published by his son Charles Henry Cope, London 1891, p.121, states that Sheepshanks 'left Bond Street, and took a house with a large garden at Blackheath'. In a letter of 5 December 1835, Constable mentions to Leslie a visit to Sheepshanks at Blackheath, so that he was certainly settled there by then, and perhaps before, as E.W.Cooke painted his *Windmills, Blackheath* as a gift to Sheepshanks on 4 September 1835 (Parkinson 1990, p.43). On 8 December, Constable states that Sheepshanks 'intends to buy Glebe Farm, or Green Lane'. See further n.8 above.

22. *Art Journal*, 1863, p.241; letter to Wyon, 13 May 1841 in Victoria and Albert Museum library (ref: 86.WW.1). Sheepshanks also kept a low public profile at the time of the gift to South Kensington. Cole recorded that Sheepshanks 'objected to all kind of recognition by the Crown' and that he 'rather flinched' from mounting the tablet in his honour in the New Kensington Museum, 'but as it was unostentatiously done, consented' (Cole Diaries, Victoria and Albert Museum Library, 13 and 20 February 1857). I must pay tribute to the index to these diaries prepared by Elizabeth Bonython.

23. Horsley, op. cit., pp.51–5; Cope, 1891, p.121. In what appears to have been Sheepshanks's only gift to the British Museum, he presented a few engravings by these and other friends (1837-7-15-8 to 14).

24. For Constable's reference (in a letter to Leslie of 5 November 1836) see Beckett, op. cit., p.142. An unpublished letter from Constable in the Sheepshanks family archive shows the artist keen to acknowledge Sheepshanks's generosity. But Beckett (IV, p.118, without giving a source) states that Sheepshanks has been described as a 'funny little man with a broad Yorkshire accent; a great oddity, with very little judgment, impressed by titles' – yet also as a 'capital fellow' and an enthusiast.

25. See F.M.Redgrave, *Richard Redgrave, a Memoir*, London, Paris and Melbourne 1891, p.171; W.P.Frith, *My Autobiography and Reminiscences*, London 1889, pp.136 and 216. Despite these more negative assessments, both writers have positive things to say about Sheepshanks, and it probably took a particularly snobbish wag, one E.W.Forster, to quip some years after Sheepshanks's death that 'all Sheepshanks' virtues were concentrated in his one act of giving his pictures to the nation', as recorded in Sir Henry Cole's diaries (15 April 1869). Leslie, Fink and others seem to have found Sheepshanks congenial, to judge from their letters (in the Sheepshanks family archive). Sheepshanks's diffident character is apparent from his behaviour at the time of the opening of the gallery of his pictures at South Kensington (see n.22 above).

26. According to the *Dictionary of National Biography*, Sheepshanks built the house at Rutland Gate. He was living there by 5 April 1845, when he gave a £500 bond as surety for Carpenter on his appointment as Keeper of the Department. Sheepshanks seems to have retained the Blackheath house simultaneously for a time, but to have left it for good some time between 17 August 1851, when Henry Cole visited him there, and 1857, when it was described as Sheepshanks's 'former home' by Redgrave in the Sheepshanks catalogue, 1857, p.87. He seems also latterly to have kept a house in Brighton, where Cole saw him on 9 November 1860. Redgrave 1891, p.215, also mentions that he had a house there.

27. See David Robertson, *Sir Charles Eastlake and the Victorian Art World*, Princeton 1978, p.256, quoting a letter from Sheepshanks to George Godwin of 19 July 1851 in his own collection. The anonymous article in the *Art Journal* appears in the volume for 1857, pp.239–40. Sheepshanks's house, coincidentally, was on the property market in September 1994, when it was described by the agents as a forty-room mansion and as one of the largest houses in London.

28. Letter to C.R.Leslie, 8 December 1836 (Beckett, op. cit., pp.144–5). The gift to Sheepshanks is recorded in the letter from Constable to Sheepshanks in the possession of the latter's descendants. Sheepshanks had been interested in a project to found a national collection of British art at least since 21 February 1847, when Henry Cole called on him 'to hear his suggestions abt British Art Scheme' (Cole Diaries). In 1848 he lent six paintings to a Mulready exhibition organised by the Society of Arts at the Adelphi 'in aid of the formation of a National Gallery of British Art'. G.F.Waagen (*Treasures of Art in Great Britain*, II, London 1854, pp.299ff.), describes Sheepshanks's paintings, which he had seen on a visit in 1851, noting that 'I understand that it is the patriotic intention of Mr Sheepshanks, in the event of a fitting gallery being provided, to bequeath this fine collection to the nation. This is an additional inducement for the Government to lose no time in providing a new National Gallery' (p.307). On 4 April 1852, Sheepshanks told Cole that he thought that the Crystal Palace should be used for his and Vernon's pictures. He also at one time thought of asking Mulready (or after his death, Redgrave) to be the curator of his collection. His gift went finally to South Kensington for several reasons, not least that he preferred to see the works kept outside the metropolis, and he was adamant that they should not be vested in the National Gallery's Trustees (which perhaps explains why they were not later transferred to the Tate Gallery).

29. Sheepshanks's correspondence with Pye is in the Victoria and Albert Museum Library (86.FF.73). Sheepshanks's involvement with the Etching Club also brought him into regular contact with printmakers.

30. *A Catalogue of the Pictures, Drawings, & Etchings in the British Fine Art Collections Deposited in the New Gallery, at South Kensington; being for the most part the gift of John Sheepshanks, Esq.*, London 1857 (with an introduction by Richard Redgrave).

31. Horsley, op. cit., n.20, p.49. The print was perhaps the first state of Adriaen van Ostade's *Woman Spinning*, Hollstein 31 (reg. no. S.1484), in which the pig's back is incomplete.

32. Cope, op. cit., n.21, pp.120–1.

33. Frith, op. cit., p.76. See also Beckett, IV, p.6, who also compares the two men. On Vernon see Robin Hamlyn, *Robert Vernon's Gift*, Tate Gallery, 1993.

34. Nos.117 and 120 of the exhibition respectively. I am most grateful to Alexander Robinson for providing this and other information about the Society's exhibitions.

35. Schwanfelder's painting of *Two Dogs Mauling a Cat* of 1825, on loan to the Leeds City Art Gallery from the Leeds City Museum, was published by Adrian Bridge, 'C.H.Schwanfelder – Animal Painter to the Prince Regent', *Leeds Art Calendar*, 85, 1979, repr. p.17, fig.5.

36. I am grateful for Dr Terry Friedman's time in discussing the Leeds art scene, as also to his two articles, 'John Flaxman and Benjamin Gott of Armley House', and 'Aspects of Nineteenth Century Sculpture in Leeds. 2. Patronage of the Benjamin Gott Family', in the *Leeds Art Calendar* (see n.10 above). I have also found useful for the background R.G.Wilson, *Gentlemen Merchants. The Merchant Community in Leeds, 1700–1830*, Manchester and New York 1971,

Trevor Fawcett, *The Rise of English Provincial Art*, Oxford 1974 (especially pp. 85ff.), and the thought-provoking essays in Janet Wolff and John Seed (eds), *The Culture of Capital*, Manchester 1988.

37. Bills for Gott from Colnaghi's survive among the family papers in the Brotherton Library at Leeds University. See M. Royalton-Kisch, *From Dürer to Boucher. Old Master Prints and Drawings from the Collection of the City of Manchester Art Gallery*, Manchester 1982, p. 8.

38. Caroline Arscott, in her essay entitled 'Without Distinction of Party: the Polytechnic Exhibitions in Leeds, 1839–45', in Wolff and Seed (eds), op. cit., p. 155, notes that the catalogues of the exhibitions held at Leeds show that a far wider range of picture-owners existed in Leeds than is generally realised. She argues that such exhibitions were a vehicle to assist in the establishment of the hegemony of the bourgeoisie.

39. Cope, op. cit., p. 12.

40. The letter of 2 July 1853 (?) is in the Sheepshanks family archives. In the same location is a letter from Mitford in which he asks to see notes by Gray in Sheepshanks's possession.

41. The letters from Robinson are in the Sheepshanks family's possession; that from Martin is in the British Library (Department of MSS, Add.MS 37967.f.119). Martin's book was first published in 1834.

42. Sheepshanks sent a copy to William Gott on 27 November 1855, stating that he had heard that a Hollar print shows a steamboat some eighty years before Hull's publication (he was perhaps referring to Hollar's print of a submarine described by Richard Pennington, *A Descriptive Catalogue of the Etched Work of Wenceslaus Hollar 1607–1677*, Cambridge 1982, no. 1283).

43. See Passavant, 1836, vol. I, pp. 242–3 (the first edition dates from 1833). Sheepshanks's Viennese contact, F. W. Fink, remained in touch with him as late as 27 April 1851, when he wrote and presented him with the etching by Johann Pasini after Friedrich Gauermann (an artist known personally to Sheepshanks) dedicated to him and entitled *Sheepshanks Schaf*, complete with verses composed by Fink himself (two impressions are in the Department, a first state before letters, 1851-4-12-69, and the complete print, 1867-3-9-1826). The British Museum's collection of Gauermann prints was almost all acquired in two *tranches*. The first, 1838-3-10-43 to 63, was purchased from Smith and might have been owned by Sheepshanks before; the second, 1851-11-8-145 to 213, was bought directly from Fink.

44. P. Defer, *Catalogue général des ventes publiques de tableaux et estampes depuis 1737 jusqu'à nos jours [...]*, 2 vols, Paris 1863, pp. 264 and 269. (Defer states that Sheepshanks had prepared a catalogue of Berchem's prints, but I have found no mention of this elsewhere.) C. F. von Rumohr and J. M. Thiele, *Geschichte der königlichen Kupferstichsammlung zu Copenhagen*, Leipzig 1835, p. 85 (on Sheepshanks's holding of prints by Jan Lagoor).

45. Redgrave, op. cit. n. 25, pp. 166–7.

46. Sheepshanks seems to have met Archduke Charles, who presented him with some drawings by Austrian artists (sold 5–7 March 1888, lot 49, see Appendix H). Charles inherited and added to the collections formed by Albert, which are now in the Albertina in Vienna.

47. The letter is in the archives of the Department of Prints and Drawings.

21 Peter Paul Rubens (1577–1640)
St Catherine in the Clouds, c.1625–30

Etching, second state. 296 × 198 mm

Hollstein 1, second state

In the third state, the etching is signed *P. Paul Rubens fecit*. Yet opinion remains divided over the reliability of this inscription. The design is based on a painted *modello* produced by Rubens as a sketch for a section of the ceiling of the Jesuit Church in Antwerp (See J. R. Martin, *Corpus Rubenianum I, The Ceiling Paintings of the Jesuit Church in Antwerp*, 1968, pp. 145–7). Yet the format is changed from a horizontal to an upright one, and on the unique impression of the print in its first state in New York, Rubens himself made corrections in pen and brown ink. While some commentators have retained the attribution to Rubens, the names of Pieter Soutman and Lucas Vorsterman the Elder – who may have produced the engraved elaborations of the print in its later states – have also been proposed.

Impressions in the first and second states, both unlettered, are exceedingly rare, and Sheepshanks also owned an impression of the third state, with the inscription containing Rubens's name.

S.5379. Sheepshanks collection

22 Jan van de Velde the Younger (1593–1641)
The Sorceress, 1626

Etching and engraving. 216 × 290 mm

Hollstein 152, second state

Jan van de Velde the Younger worked mostly in the city of Haarlem, where he achieved renown as a prolific printmaker and book-illustrator. The present work is unusual in his *oeuvre*, not so much because it is a nocturne – he produced several others – but because of its iconography, with its echoes of the fantastic inventions of Hieronymus Bosch and Pieter Bruegel the Elder. The inscription in Latin below is a moralising one, warning the beholder not to be diverted by sensual pleasures (represented by the monsters on the left), but to remember the afterlife and death, symbolised by the skull and other items on the right: *How many evils desire leads to, when checked by no limit; and how, with its sweet song, it leads even the purest minds of mortals into every fury. But how quickly we are deceived. Death takes over the brief pleasure of a brief life, and the small moment of laughter gives way to an eternity of grief.*

S.5774. Sheepshanks collection

21

Quantum malorum clausa nullo limite
Cogit libido, quamque dulci Carmine
Purissimas mortalium mentes rapit,
Furias in omnes: sed citoquam fallimur.
Vitam brevem breve gaudium Mors occupat;
Momentulum quod videt, æternum dolet.
I.A.B.

22

23 Hercules Seghers (c.1589/90–c.1638)

Country Road with Trees and a Farmhouse, c.1625

Illustrated in colour between pages 112 and 113

Etching with some drypoint, printed in black and brown inks on yellowish-brown paper; a ruled framing line in pen and brown ink down right edge. 230 × 275 mm

Springer 43; Hollstein 37

Seghers was one of the most interesting and eccentric artists in the history of printmaking; his work strongly influenced his younger countryman, Rembrandt, who owned some of his rare paintings.

He etched mostly landscapes, using an unprecedented variety of inks, techniques, hand-colouring and supports, including canvas rather than paper. At times the effect resembles that of a painting, and later in the century Rembrandt's pupil Samuel van Hoogstraten referred to Seghers' etchings as 'printing paintings'.

The exhibited print is unique – the only known impression of this composition, a not unusual occurrence in Seghers' *oeuvre* – and the techniques employed are unorthodox. Not only has the paper been given an unusual preparatory colour, but the drypoint seems also to have been printed in a slightly browner ink than the etched lines, which are black.

Seghers' imagery fluctuates between the fantastical and the naturalistic in landscape. When working in his more naturalistic mode, as here, the mood is often eerily silent, with no sign of human activity beyond abandoned roads and dwellings.

S.5532. Sheepshanks collection

24

25a

24 Jan Lievens (1607–74)

Bust of a Man wearing a Turban, c.1630

Etching. 160 × 143 mm

Hollstein 35, second state, from the collection of E. Astley (L.2775)

One of a series of seven oriental heads etched by Jan Lievens probably in around 1630. At this period in his career, he worked closely with Rembrandt in their native town, Leiden. In 1635, Rembrandt made free copies after four of the prints in the set, including the present one (Hollstein 288). But by this time, Lievens had abandoned the Rembrandtesque style that he himself had helped to formulate in favour of a more courtly manner, inspired by Anthony van Dyck.

S.56. Sheepshanks collection

25 Nicolaes Berchem (1620–83)

The Resting Cows, c.1670

Etching. 177 × 242 mm

Hollstein 3, first and second states

Berchem was a highly influential painter, etcher and draughtsman, who concentrated on idyllic pastoral landscapes with an Italian flavour. Karel Dujardin (see cat. 26) was one of his pupils. Yet for all the Mediterranean qualities of Berchem's imagery, he may never have visited Italy and depended on secondary sources for inspiration, including works brought back to the Netherlands by his compatriots.

The exhibited composition, with its focus on the animals in the foreground, resembles the work of his exact contemporary, Aelbert Cuyp (1620–91), but the vista to an Italian tower in the distance and the dissolving light are typical for Berchem and his followers. Sheepshanks assembled a rich collection of his etchings, with the present print represented in three further states.

26

27

Two impressions are exhibited, the second state being from the collection of the dealer Yver, sold in 1816 (see p. 290):

(a) S.3831. Sheepshanks collection

(b) S.3832. Sheepshanks collection. Inscribed on the verso in graphite: *du Cabinet Yver/ vendu 1816*

26 Karel Dujardin (*c.*1622–78)
Portrait of Jan Vos, 1662

Etching. 166 × 127 mm
Hollstein 52a, second state

The only formal portrait etched by Karel Dujardin, who worked primarily as a landscape and animal painter in the manner of his master, Nicolaes Berchem (see cat. 25). The print represents the Dutch poet Jan Vos (d.1667), whose reputation was considerable in his own day. In later states, the lower margin is occupied by a eulogistic poem written by his contemporary and fellow-writer Joost van den Vondel, and in this form the print was used as an illustration in an edition of Vos's poems published in 1662 (Jan Vos, *Gedichten*, published by J.Lescaille, Amsterdam, 1662).

S.934. Sheepshanks collection

27 Jacob van Ruisdael (*c.*1628/9–82)
*The Cottage on the Hill, c.*1660

Etching. 194 × 279 mm
Hollstein 3, first state

Only three other impressions are recorded of this masterpiece among Jacob van Ruisdael's etchings in this, the first state, before clouds were added in the sky.

Ruisdael is celebrated as one of the most overtly poetic of all landscape artists, whose magisterial sense of composition is well exemplified by this famous print. He made about a dozen etchings, and the earliest among them, dating from the 1640s, are executed in a tight, disciplined style. This later gave way, as here, to a broader and more confident technique.

S.1133. Sheepshanks collection

28

29

28 Claes van Beresteijn (1629–84)

Landscape with a Group of Oaks and a Peasant Resting, c.1650

Etching. 199 × 217 mm

Hollstein 9

Signed on the plate *C v Beresteyn. f. 1650* [?]. Inscribed verso, in graphite: *du Cabinet J. Yver 1816* and in pen and black ink: *F Rechberger 1816*

A characteristic example of the work of Claes van Beresteijn. He was one of a group of amateur printmakers active in Holland in the seventeenth century. Greatly influenced by Jacob van Ruisdael, van Beresteijn nonetheless evolved a personal vision of sprawling, uncontrolled undergrowth. The landscape dominates the composition and the lone figure dissolves into the vegetation.

Beresteijn's etchings are hard to come by, and their presence in Sheepshanks's collection is indicative of his determination to acquire Dutch etchings of great scarcity and recondite interest. The inscriptions on the verso show that this example was owned by the dealer Jean Yver (see Appendix H, 4), at whose sale in 1816 it passed to Franz Rechberger of Vienna (on whom see Appendix H, 1).

S.4778. Sheepshanks collection

29 Adriaen van Ostade (1610–85)

The Painter, c.1663

Etching. 238 × 181 mm

Hollstein 32, fourth state

Adriaen van Ostade has always been regarded as one of the most gifted artists to concentrate on everyday, genre scenes. Together with another specialist in these subjects, Adriaen Brouwer – who was much admired by Rubens – van Ostade was a pupil of Frans Hals in Haarlem, where he remained throughout his career.

While many of his compositions, whether painted, drawn or etched, teem with peasant life, in the present work he focuses on the isolated activity of the painter, one of many trades he depicted in his prints. He shows the artist in an untidy, humble studio, with two young apprentices grinding his colours in the background. Yet the open space below the image was later occupied by a Latin text, comparing his work with that of Apelles, the most famous artist of antiquity. A related painting, dated 1663, is in Dresden.

Cornelis Bega (see cat. 30) was one of Ostade's pupils.

S.1486. Sheepshanks collection

30 Cornelis Bega (c.1631/2–64)

The Inn, c.1660

Etching. 225 × 172 mm

Hollstein 35, first state

A characteristic late work by this short-lived master. Bega was a grandson of the Mannerist painter Cornelis van Haarlem and a pupil of Adriaen van Ostade (see cat. 29), and like the latter he concentrated on depicting scenes of everyday peasant life. He produced some thirty-five etchings of this type of subject-matter and, especially in his last years, these have an unsettling, slightly threatening atmosphere, heightened by the stark illumination against a dark background. Like his master, he worked mostly in the city of Haarlem, where subjects of this type were a particular speciality.

S.3710. Sheepshanks collection

30

4. William Smith (1808–76) and the Rise of Interest in Early Engraving

Antony Griffiths

In October 1844 William Smith, of the London print dealers W. & G. Smith, made an extraordinary offer to the Trustees of the British Museum. His letter ran:

We beg to submit to the notice of the Trustees of the British Museum a collection of prints we have recently purchased, which exceeds both in interest and importance every other that has as yet passed through our hands. It consists of the works of the early German engravers and is particularly rich in those of the 15th century, indeed far exceeding in number and consequence every other collection whether public or private in Europe. To prove this, it will be sufficient to mention that of the excessively rare works of the Master of 1466 and of his period, the Munich collection contains about 80 prints, the Imperial library at Vienna 51, the Archduke Charles's collection at Vienna 83, the Dresden collection 105, that of Berlin 44, of Amsterdam 10, of Paris about 70, of the British Museum 17, while this collection contains the most extraordinary number of 154 ...

Under these circumstances, and for the additional reason that the British Museum is excessively deficient in prints of this school, we consider it an object of some national importance that this collection should be secured for the country. If this opportunity be now lost, it can never occur again. The purchase of it would at once place the British Museum in the same high position with regard to the German school as the purchase of the Sheepshanks collection placed it with regard to the Dutch and Flemish, that of being the first in Europe ... It now contains 1807 prints and the price we ask for it is £3,000.[1]

The offer was warmly supported by the Keeper of the Department, Henry Josi, and the Trustees apparently had no difficulty in deciding that it was one that they should accept. So an application was made to the Treasury for a special grant, and this was granted in February the following year.[2] This acquisition is the foundation, and by far the largest element, of the British Museum's outstanding collection of early northern engraving. Three months later, in May 1845, Messrs Smith wrote another, even longer, letter to the Trustees:

We beg to offer to the consideration of the Trustees of the British Museum a collection far surpassing in interest and importance any that has ever passed through our hands. It consists, almost entirely, of the works of the Italian designers and engravers of the fifteenth century, and contains an extraordinary, and indeed almost incredible, number of the very earliest specimens of these arts. It forms an admirable and perfect series illustrative of the art of engraving from what may fairly be called its discovery by Maso Finiguerra, to the period when Marc Antonio in Italy, and Albert Dürer in Germany, brought it at once to perfection ...

The collection commences with the extraordinary number of 103 silver plates engraved by the most celebrated workers in niello of the fifteenth century. Among these is the celebrated Pax, an undoubted work by Maso Finiguerra, the inventor of the art of taking impressions from metallic plates, which even at Sir Mark Sykes's sale in 1824 produced no less than 300 guineas ... The silver plates are followed by fifteen impressions on sulphur which are objects of perhaps even greater curiosity and interest. ... No public collection on the Continent contains even a single specimen, and only 24 altogether are known ... Following the progress of the art, our collection next includes 63 impressions on paper from works of the same description as the preceding. Among them is the unique impression of another magnificent Pax also by Maso Finiguerra ...

Having now arrived at the period when the art of printing was invented, our collection contains nearly 650 specimens of the works of the earliest engravers, of a large proportion of which no other impressions are known ... It also contains many specimens, and in some instances nearly complete works of Pollaiuolo, Fogolino, Mocetto, Andrea Mantegna, Nicoletto da Modena, Zoan Andrea, the Di Brescias, Benedetto Montagna, the rare master of the Monogram P.P., the Campagnolas, Robetta, and other not less interesting artists, including a vast number of prints that have escaped the researches of Bartsch, Ottley and Duchesne.

The collection consists of 848 articles and the price we ask for it is £5,000, a sum we are firmly persuaded very much below what it is worth, but as we purchased the collection at a very reasonable price, we are willing to sell it as a whole accordingly ... We would beg most earnestly and respectfully to impress upon the Trustees of the British Museum the necessity of adding this magnificent assemblage to the national collection. The purchase of it will at once terminate and complete the series of the works of the early masters, and it will be positively the last time that any large sum will be required for these purposes. This will at once be evident when it is considered that the Museum contains the most complete collections in Europe of the Flemish, Dutch and German schools. Now the only one remaining is that of Italy, and we do hope that the only opportunity that can ever occur of securing a near perfect collection, more than half the articles contained in which are absolutely unique, will not be missed.

This offer was again supported by a warm recommendation from the new Keeper, William Hookham Carpenter, who had recently succeeded Josi, and the Trustees again had no hesitation in submitting a request for the money to the Treasury. This was granted with astonishing promptness, and three months later, in August, both collections were entered in the acquisitions register.[3] Smith's description has to be taken with a certain pinch of salt, but there can be little doubt that this was the finest group of early Italian prints that had been collected together up to that date. It remains the foundation of the astonishing collection of early Italian engraving in the British Museum, the single area in the history of printmaking in which the Museum can fairly boast that its collection is the best in the world.

The question that now arises is where all these prints came from, and how it was that in 1845 so many major examples of this period were in England. Smith's two letters, the complete texts of which are published for the first time in Appendix J, give important information on this subject. To them can be added evidence from sale catalogues, letters and publications during the first half of the nineteenth century. Much remains unclear, and much remains to be discovered, and the following essay is only a first attempt at a history of the rise in taste for early printmaking in England.

The story begins in the British Museum in 1806, with the first purchase ever made for the print collection. In February 1806 £50 was paid to James Monro Esq for 'a collection of ancient prints'. This had been put together by Dr John Monro (1715–91), the second of the well-known family of doctors at the Bethlehem Hospital. The Museum's record of the purchase says nothing about its contents, and it is only Joseph Strutt's *Dictionary of Engravers* of 1786 that reveals that it contained no less a print than the famous church interior engraved by Prevedari after Bramante, as well as a set of the Planets, forty plates of the so-called 'Tarocchi of Mantegna', and at least ten early German engravings.[4] This purchase remains one of the most brilliant and far-sighted in the history of the British Museum, but the records reveal nothing of who proposed it and how it came about. Monro himself is recorded as a purchaser at the sale in 1773 of the collection of James West, where he bought all the lots of early prints, which were sold in bundles. The main part of Monro's collection was auctioned after his death in 1792,[5] but the early prints must have been reserved by his son James, who may even have added to the collection.[6] The fact that the collection was sold to the British Museum is also significant. The British Museum had never bought prints, and there was no one on the staff who knew anything about them. The purchase could not have happened unless Monro or another enthusiast had forced his collection to the Trustees' attention.

The Monro collection, and the attention paid to it in Strutt's dictionary, stand at the head of the interest in early

engraving that was soon to become a marked feature of British print collecting. It is not difficult to find ancestors earlier in the eighteenth century, or even in the seventeenth. From the days of Vasari, writing in 1568, the subject of the discovery of engraving by the Florentine goldsmith Maso Finiguerra had been part of scholarly enquiry into the history of printmaking. John Evelyn's *Sculptura* of 1662 had talked about the origins of engraving, and the collection formed by his friend Thomas, eighth Earl of Pembroke, even had an album arranged to show 'a history of the rise and progress of prints'.[7]

The subject to which more attention was paid in the eighteenth century was the origins of book printing. Books, of course, are printed in the same way as woodcuts – and quite differently from engravings – and so the great controversy as to whether Gutenberg in Germany or Coster in Haarlem had invented printing attracted attention to the woodcuts that were frequently used to illustrate the books, and to blockbooks, in which text and illustration were cut and printed from a single block. This was an argument that by-passed Italy, as it was abundantly clear that no Italian could claim any particular role in the invention of printing.

Through most of the eighteenth century the Finiguerra problem remained a matter of concern to only a few. The great French connoisseur Pierre-Jean Mariette was interested in this matter and in 1732 asked his Florentine correspondent Francesco Maria Niccolo Gabburri to find him a print by Finiguerra. Gabburri replied: 'I have rummaged all Florence, hoping to have the good fortune to discover at least one print bearing the name or the cypher of that artist. But after having in vain searched the museums of the Gaddi, the Niccolini, the Giraldi and Covoni families, besides many other smaller collections belonging to private persons ... I have at last given the matter up in despair.'[8] Mariette himself had announced his intention to publish a treatise on this subject, and for decades the scholarly world waited in eager anticipation for his conclusions. But nothing ever came out.[9]

By the end of the century the matter had become of more general significance. Vasari had claimed the invention for Finiguerra, but German scholars were now asserting that the Germans had invented it before him – correctly, as modern scholarship has decided. So it became a matter of great importance to Italian scholars to demonstrate the accuracy of Vasari's report. Vasari had said that Finiguerra was a niellist – that is, he specialised in engraving decorative designs on to pieces of metalwork, and then filling these lines with 'niello', a black substance that made them stand out against the silver background. One day Finiguerra had thought of filling the lines with ink rather than niello, and by rubbing, transferring the design to paper. Hence the invention of engraving as an art of printing rather than simply metal-decorating. Vasari had identified as Finiguerra's work a pax of *The Coronation of the Virgin* in Florence that still survived. So if an impression on paper could be found from this pax before the lines had been filled with niello, Vasari's report could be confirmed.

The momentous discovery of just such an impression was made by an Italian scholar, the Abbé Zani, in 1797, in a volume in the Bibliothèque Nationale in Paris, and he published his find in 1802.[10] Zani knew a number of Italian collectors who were interested in these precious documents of Italian ingenuity. Their interest embraced not only nielli (the term used for prints from such plates), but the plates themselves, the sulphur casts that were very occasionally made from them as an alternative to paper impressions, and the printed engravings from plates made specifically for that purpose. Information on these early collectors is hard to find. One was Count Seratti, an official in Livorno, who owned a sulphur of Finiguerra's *Coronation*.[11] Another was Count Jacopo Durazzo, a Genoese who was closely associated with Archduke Albert in Vienna (the founder of the Albertina), and whose vast collection remained together until 1872.[12] Adam Bartsch, writing his great twenty-one-volume series on *Le Peintre-Graveur* in Vienna, was fascinated by nielli, but, when volume XIII on the early Italian engravers came out, he had never seen one. All he could include in his catalogue was a set of thirty-two facsimiles that Durazzo had made of the nielli in his collection, and had sent as a gift to Archduke Albert.[13]

The beginning of the nineteenth century was a terrible time for Italy. The country was full of French soldiers, looting officially for the Musée Napoléon and unofficially for themselves. One who profited was the great Milanese dealer of German origin, Giuseppe Storck.[14] According to Smith, writing in 1845:

That gentleman, one of the most ardent amateurs that ever existed, began to form his collection at a time when greater facilities existed for procuring specimens of early art than can ever again occur. At the latter end of the last and the beginning of the present century, owing to the troubles in Italy consequent upon the French revolution, a vast number of churches, convents and the palaces of noble and ancient families were destroyed, and their contents dispersed. For such places, it is well known, the finest works of art were originally executed, and, up to this period, had been carefully and religiously preserved. Signor Storck's agents secured for him, regardless of price, everything it was possible to obtain, and by degrees his collection became of the greatest importance. Unfortunately his circumstances became embarrassed, and he was compelled to deposit the whole of his treasures with the Bankers Carli of Milan as a security for a large sum of money advanced by them. Failing to redeem them, these bankers sold them in 1818 to Mr Woodburn, by whom they were brought over to England.

Samuel Woodburn (1786–1853), who plays a large part in this story, was by far the greatest English dealer in works

of art on paper in this period. His role in the formation and dispersal of the drawings collection of Sir Thomas Lawrence – probably the greatest that has ever been made – is well known.[15] But his role as a print dealer has never been studied. He first appears in the records of auctions in about 1803 when he dealt in many of the most expensive lots of portrait engravings, then at the height of their fashionability.[16] This would have introduced him to some of his major clients. One such was Viscount Fitzwilliam, whose collection remains in his eponymous museum in Cambridge. Another was Sir Mark Masterman Sykes, who gathered at Sledmere, his Yorkshire country seat, an astonishing collection of early printed books, portrait engravings and Italian prints – with a few exceptions he never touched northern prints. A third was the Duke of Buckingham, who was forming his enormous collection at Stowe, for whom Woodburn was already bidding at the Hibbert sale in 1809.[17]

In the years of peace after 1815, Woodburn carried out a series of astonishing coups. His purchases of collections of drawings have been described by Frits Lugt.[18] Of those that involved prints, the first was the purchase in Paris in 1816 of the entire Paignon-Dijonval collection, large parts of which he sold to the Duke of Buckingham. In 1823 he purchased Thomas Dimsdale's superb cabinet of drawings and prints. In 1824 he and two other London dealers, Hurst and Colnaghi, bought up most of the collection of the bankrupt Viennese banker Count Moritz von Fries, when it was auctioned by his creditors in Amsterdam. In this sale, the early Italian prints were omitted, as they had previously been sold privately *en bloc*. Certain evidence suggests that the purchaser had been Woodburn. In 1828 he bought the entire Rembrandt collection of Vivant Denon in Paris, half of a collection that had been formed at the beginning of the eighteenth century by the Dutch dealer Zomer.[19] His purchase of Storck's Italian prints in 1818 was simply one of these coups.

But we have to ask to whom Woodburn thought he could sell them in England. This leads us back to eighteenth-century London and the few collectors and scholars interested in the field. In 1799 two events occurred, both significant in different ways. The first was the sale of the collection of Charles Rogers.[20] Rogers had no particular interest in early prints, but had acquired by chance in 1745 two extraordinary albums of early German engravings, mostly by Israhel van Meckenem, that had been formed at the beginning of the seventeenth century. These were broken up at his sale, when the catalogue rightly described them as the 'most extensive as well as the most choice in point of impression ever offered to the public in this kingdom'. But the prices were low, with few lots going above one pound, and the sale made so little impact that it was forgotten and never mentioned by any writer in the nineteenth century.

The other event of 1799 was the return to England after

eight years in Italy of William Young Ottley (1771–1836). If Woodburn can be credited with bringing the prints to England, it was Ottley who created the interest in them. Excellent studies have been written on Ottley's role as the pioneer collector of early Italian paintings, and as collector-expert-dealer in Italian drawings[21] – he was one of Lawrence's closest friends, and rushed back from Holland at the news of his death in order to attend the funeral. But nothing has been written about his role in print scholarship, even though he assembled a vast collection in order to furnish materials for his *Notices of engravers and their works*, a dictionary of engravers of which he published only part, from the letters A to BAL, in 1831. This is an excellent work, though now quite unjustly ignored and hardly ever cited, probably on account of its extreme scarcity.

The great monument that Ottley published in the field of early prints was his ambitious *An Inquiry into the Origin and Early History of Engraving* of 1816. These two large and handsomely printed quartos were far in advance of anything published up to that time in any language, and, even if over the heads of almost every English critic of the time, must have had a considerable impact. Ottley must also have exerted a considerable influence by his own personality and enthusiasm. His obituary in the *Gentleman's Magazine* remarked: 'It is well known that Mr Ottley was not easily deterred when bidding for a scarce specimen or a choice impression, which he always did in person, and not by commission; and his presence on such occasions, together with that of a few of his brother collectors, used to give a zest and stimulus to the business of the auction-room, which subsequently it has often wanted.'[22]

The impact of Ottley can be dramatically shown in the sale-room. On 12 December 1816 Mr Stewart auctioned in Piccadilly the Seratti collection which he had just imported from Italy; he had acquired it in Malta whence it had come via Tunis following the unfortunate Seratti's capture by pirates.[23] Stewart had already sold the prize piece, a sulphur cast of the same plaque by Finiguerra of which Zani had found the paper impression, to Colnaghi for £150. Colnaghi sold it to Thomas Grenville, the great book collector who was to bequeath his library to the British Museum in 1846, and he in turn passed it on to his nephew, the Duke of Buckingham, as being more appropriate for his collection. For the prints that were included in the auction, prices were remarkably high. Two lots, one a print from a plaque of the *Procession to Calvary* thought to be by Finiguerra, the other an engraving of the *Adoration of the Magi*, sold for £46.4.0 each – more than any Marcantonio, even though the sale included a 'most brilliant impression' of the *Parnassus*.[24]

One of the principal purchasers in this sale was a passionate amateur, and intimate friend of Ottley, Thomas Lloyd (*c.*1757–1843). A letter from Sir Thomas Lawrence of 1827 reveals that he was a wine-merchant whose 'attachment to the arts and some untoward commercial circumstances' had bankrupted his business.[25] This helps to explain why no less than seven sales from his collection were held at fairly regular intervals during his life, and why he kept on buying until his death. The first of these sales, and, for our purposes, the most important, was held on 10 April 1817, and was advertised as 'containing the chefs-d'oeuvres and rarest specimens from the earliest periods of chalcography'. Its timing, and the frequent references in it to Ottley's two volumes, suggest that it was intended to capitalise on the interest raised by its publication the previous year. Lloyd's collection did indeed contain many remarkable early Italian prints, acquired in London auctions and possibly from Ottley himself.[26]

Lloyd's sale was an enormous success. The *Procession to Calvary* which he had bought four months before for £46.4.0 now made £84. The self-portrait of Israhel van Meckenem that had made 15s in 1799 now fetched £9.19.6. Of the Italians, most items fetched between £2 and £6. An engraving of *The Death of Orpheus* made £54.12.0. The great majority of the lots of early prints was bought by Ottley, who seems to have been acting as agent for Sir Mark Sykes. The remainder mostly went to Woodburn, and a few others were bought by individuals, among them Francis Douce. When Woodburn imported the Storck collection in 1818, it was again Sykes who bought it *en bloc*.

In 1823 Sykes died unexpectedly at the age of fifty-two, and the following year his entire collection was sold at auction. The catalogue of the third part, of the Italian school, was written by Ottley. The early prints occupied lots 848 to 1282. Ottley arranged them according to Bartsch XIII, but hived off all those omitted by Bartsch into a separate section, from lots 1035 to the end. This had the effect of emphasising the amazing number of rarities that Sykes had acquired.

The prices were still mentioned with awe decades later. The really extraordinary prices were made by the nielli and the prints related to them. A paper impression of *The Virgin Enthroned*, lot 1211, which, according to Maberly, Ottley had bought for a trifle in Rome and passed on to Sykes for about £70, sold to Woodburn for £315. For the same price he acquired the silver pax of the same subject, lot 1244 (fig. 1). Twenty-one small sulphur casts fetched an average of about £40 each. By comparison, the prices for fifteenth-century engravings seemed almost modest. They showed a less dramatic advance on 1817; *The Death of Orpheus*, for example, resold for £63. The majority of the lots were again bought by Ottley and Woodburn.

The sale provided the impetus for a luxury volume published for an unnamed proprietor, who may have been Woodburn: *A Collection of One Hundred and Twenty-Five Facsimiles of Scarce and Curious Prints by the Early Masters of the Italian, German and Flemish Schools, illus-*

1. Florentine between 1450 and 1475, *The Virgin and Child Enthroned with Angels and Saints*, silver inlaid with niello, set in a chased and enamelled frame. 205 × 182 mm (including frame). From the Storck, Sykes and Woodburn collections. 1845-8-25-8

trative of the history of engraving from the invention of the art by Maso Finiguerra in the middle of the fifteenth century, with introductory remarks and a catalogue of the plates, which came out in 1826. The text was by Ottley, although Maberly noted that 'Mr Ottley had nothing to do with this book beyond the writing of the preface and the lending of his name'.[27] The reproductions were excellent, and are still often mistaken for originals. The publisher evidently believed that there were many who would wish to buy this expensive production.

Another purchaser of early prints at the Sykes sale was Henry Smedley, a friend of J. T. Smith, the Keeper at the British Museum since 1816.[28] Smedley was a public-spirited small-scale collector of prints who had made it his business to stir the British Museum into action. He wrote a long letter to the Trustees pointing out that they lacked a single specimen of a niello, and told them why they needed one:

But while sensible of the value of what you possess, foreigners have also remarked, possibly not without a secret self complacency, the chasms, if I may so term them, which exist in your series, and which until they are filled up, detract materially from the value of the collection when considered as a whole. Of the six great collections in Europe, Paris, Vienna, Munich, Dresden, Amsterdam, London, the last is the only one which

is unable to show a single niello print ... I cannot too strongly impress upon you the duty, as I feel it, of becoming the purchaser of some of the nielli and especially the Finiguerra. If our leading artists and most curious amateurs are desirous of knowing the nature of the performance of those goldsmiths of Florence to whom engraving owes its use, is it not disgraceful in a national point of view that the National Cabinet should be without the means of exhibiting a single specimen, and that they must be indebted for the gratification of their curiosity to the liberality of private collectors. You need not be told that the choicest treasures of the Durazzo cabinet at Genoa were acquired by Sir M. Sykes,[29] and that I am urging you not to the purchase of one or two prints which according to the caprice of amateurs may be esteemed or otherwise, but to the acquisition of that which is absolutely essential to the right understanding of the history of the art.

In the face of this the Trustees authorised him to spend up to £300 at the auction 'for a Finiguerra and two or three of the niello prints'. In the event he succeeded in acquiring one sulphur and five prints for £153.16.0, and was the underbidder at £300 on the Finiguerra plate that Woodburn bought for £315.

A much bigger buyer than Smedley was the London firm of Hurst, Robinson & Co. who were acting for the wealthy collector Thomas Wilson. Wilson himself wrote a privately printed catalogue of his collection in 1828, under the title *A Catalogue Raisonné of a Select Collection of Engravings of an Amateur*. It covered classic prints of all periods, with great strengths in Ostade and Rembrandt, the latter being Denon's collection which he had purchased in its entirety from Woodburn. As a collection its only eccentricity was the inclusion of a print by the eighteenth-century engraver Thomas Major, but this is explained by the fact that he was Wilson's grandfather on his mother's side. It is very significant that a collector of this kind, who thirty years before would have shown no interest at all in early prints (Cracherode seems to have had none apart from Schongauer), not only included them in his select cabinet of only 1160 items, but was so proud of his early engravings that he devoted more space in his catalogue to them than to any section of his collection. In 1830 Wilson 'experienced a total reverse of circumstances from the failure of a large speculation'.[30] Part of his collection was sold through W. B. Tiffin, who had run the old master print section of Hurst, Robinson & Co. and, since their bankruptcy in 1825, was dealing on his own account. Almost all the early Italians, though many fewer of the Germans, had been sold privately before the remainder was auctioned on 8 March 1830.

The next landmark was the Stowe sale of 1834. The Duke of Buckingham (1776–1839) had been collecting prints, books and manuscripts on the most extravagant scale, and the 1834 print auction was the first sign of the financial difficulties that were to cloud his last years.[31] Buckingham's prize piece, the sulphur from the Seratti collection, was not included in the 1834 sale, but was sold directly to the Trustees of the British Museum in July the following year for £270, the price that the Duke had paid for it in 1818. The sale included twenty-three lots of early Italians and seven nielli. This time Woodburn bought nothing. The chief buyers were Tiffin, Smith, Molteno, the French dealer Pieri-Benard, and Ottley. Ottley was by this time Keeper of Prints and Drawings himself, and the nineteen lots of early German prints and twenty-four lots of early Italian prints bought in his name were all for the British Museum. The Museum also succeeded in acquiring certain lots three years later in 1837 at the sale of Ottley's own collection following his death the previous year. Josi, his successor, made a special effort to buy nielli, and carried off nineteen of them, although he bought no other early Italians.

The prices at the Stowe and Ottley sales were not high. Prints that Ottley had bought at the Sykes sale were selling for much less than he had paid thirteen years before. The two-sheet *Assumption of the Virgin*, which had fetched £33.12.0 at the Lloyd sale and £42 at the Sykes sale, now only made £22. Indeed the entire proceeds of the twenty days of the sale of Ottley's prints came to only £3,517.14.6. This slump was part of a wider phenomenon. The extraordinary rage for collecting early printed books, that had led to the foundation of the Roxburghe Club, and is exhaustively chronicled in the writings of Thomas Frognal Dibdin, had passed its peak. The aristocratic plutocrats, for one reason or another, had scaled down or stopped collecting, and the art market in general had entered a recession that lasted until the end of the 1840s. This was bound to affect a dealer like Woodburn, who had huge sums tied up in stock that was fast diminishing in value. To add to his concerns, he had in 1835 bought the whole of Sir Thomas Lawrence's collection of drawings for £16,000, and selling them was not proving easy. The result was that he withdrew from the print market. The lower prices provided an opening from which many new dealers and collectors profited, and the list of buyers at the Ottley sale included many new names of enthusiastic amateurs. Among them were Henry Munn, the Rev. Davenport-Bromley (on whom see later), as well as the German collector and dealer Ernst Harzen, who bequeathed his collection to the Hamburg Kunsthalle in 1863.[32]

Woodburn clearly had considerable difficulty in adjusting to the new market. In 1840 the collection of William Esdaile appeared at auction. Esdaile had been collecting constantly from the 1790s until his death in 1837, and had built up a tremendous collection of prints and drawings of a traditional kind, one that is still well-known, since he wrote his initials in the bottom right corner of every sheet. The two parts of the sale of prints together fetched £3,309.9.6. The British Museum copy of the catalogue is annotated by William Smith: 'Mr Smith had offered

£4,200 for these prints, which offer Mr Esdaile's Trustees rejected by Mr Woodburn's advice.' Three years later, in April 1843, Woodburn wrote a letter to Lord Ashburton, of which a copy is now in the British Museum (published here in Appendix J). In it he described his entire collection of prints, and offered to sell it to the Trustees for £12,000, or, if the Trustees preferred, to sell his entire collection of drawings for the same price, but, he went on, 'I find that both collections is rather too much on my hands'. Accompanying the letter was a memorandum in which its content was described. The Trustees asked Josi for his opinion. He reported that he had only had time for a cursory inspection, but that the collection included a very large number of duplicates of items already in the Museum. As a result, the offer was declined.

Woodburn then sold the entire section of early German and early Italian prints to William Coningham (on whom see later). In August 1844 Coningham resold the German section complete to William Smith, who offered it directly to the British Museum two months later. Woodburn's memorandum explains where this part of his collection had come from:

This department contains so large a portion of the splendid collection made by the Count Fries that there are probably upwards of 200 engravings which are the identical ones described by Bartsch and which are probably unique; particularly the celebrated set of engraved playing-cards described at length in that work. The entire work by the Hopfers are here and is that from which Bartsch made his catalogue. The work of J. van Meck, Schongauer and others are numerous and fine.

This is confirmed by the 1824 Fries auction catalogue, where Woodburn's name is against the majority of the early German lots.

The Treasury's agreement to purchase the German collection came through in February 1845. A month later Smith bought the other section of Coningham's collection, the Italian. By May he had catalogued it, and offered it too to the Trustees of the British Museum. On 24 May the Trustees, having been given an enthusiastic report by Carpenter, had decided to apply for another Treasury grant. Less than four weeks later, on 17 June, Sir Charles Trevelyan agreed to put a vote for the sum before Parliament. Never did a purchase go through more quickly or more smoothly.

One reason for this was that the importance of early prints was by now firmly built into general consciousness. It was not only Ottley who had written about them. Duchesne, the Keeper of the French national collection, had published his *Essai sur les Nielles* in 1826, at the end of which he included tables to show that Paris had more of them than any other collection, with the single exception of that which had formerly belonged to Sir Mark Sykes. Thanks to the enormous prices realised at that sale, they had been forced on everyone's attention. It was not only Thomas Wilson who felt that they formed part of his select cabinet; the taste for collecting them had spread so far that they had become part of any collection.

One example is the 'choice and valuable collection of the late Mrs Lattin of Bath' which was auctioned in London in February 1841. Among the 334 lots were four anonymous early Germans, one anonymous Italian, one Baldini, one F. von Bocholt, two Master ES and one Vellert. Another such example was the bookseller Joseph Harding of Bond Street, who had warmly recommended the purchase of the Sheepshanks collection in 1836 (see p.65), and whose print collection in part was purchased by the British Museum through Smith in 1841.[33] By far the greater part of this consisted of the modern reproductive engravings by Raphael Morghen and others that were then among the most expensive prints that money could buy. But the first thirty-three items were all fifteenth-century Italian engravings. The collection of Mr Munn, who had bought at the Ottley sale, was auctioned in July 1856. His early Italians were simply included alphabetically among his other prints, which covered the whole history of engraving. It is interesting that the impression of the *Assumption of the Virgin*, now ascribed in the catalogue to Botticelli, made £25, only £3 more than in 1837. But it would be a great mistake to think that such (relatively) low prices meant little interest. Many were interested; they simply happened not to be millionaires.

Lattin, Harding and Munn are unknown to history. But two other collectors were more significant. William Coningham (1815–84), through whose hands Woodburn's collection had passed, is a figure of great importance in the history of English collecting. It was he who in 1848 presented the first gold-back paintings to enter the collection of the National Gallery (two panels by Lorenzo Monaco), and he was a pioneer in collecting Italian paintings of the Gothic period.[34] Another such pioneer was the Rev. William Davenport-Bromley (1787–1863), whose collection of Italian gold-back paintings has furnished the National Gallery with a number of masterpieces. In May 1844 (that is, when he had just begun buying paintings)[35] Christie's sold for him his print collection which included no less than 138 lots of early German engravings and 70 lots of early Italian.[36] Most were bought by Smith, and were added to the Coningham group for sale to the British Museum.[37]

This phenomenon is of some interest in the chronology of the growing taste for primitives in the nineteenth century. Francis Haskell has determined that the great period for the formation of the pioneering collections of early Italian painting in England was during the 1840s, helped by the dispersal of great numbers of such pictures from the Fesch collection between 1841 and 1845.[38] Plenty was available, and prices were reasonable. Just the same process had occurred with the spread of collecting of

engravings in the 1830s; thanks to an earlier generation of enthusiasts, the prints were to hand and the prices were encouragingly low compared with what they had been. Given the recurrence of the same names, it seems that the collecting of early engravings may have been a powerful stimulus to the collecting of early paintings.

The two British Museum purchases of 1845 covered both Italian and northern engraving. But the tradition and pattern of collecting in the two fields was not always identical. Italian art always had a prestige that northern art lacked, and a few collectors, and in particular Sykes, never collected northern prints at all. German prints never in this period fetched anything like as much as Italian ones, and this is reflected in the prices that the British Museum had to pay in 1845. The German prints averaged a little over £1.10.0 each, while the Italian ones came out at just under £6. In his two letters Smith used very different arguments in favour of the acquisitions. The need for the Italian series is self-evident: 'These works of art form the finest studies in the world for the young artist'. The utility of the German one is more limited and specific:

Forming objects of the highest importance for the studies of painters on glass, goldsmiths, carvers in ivory and wood, designers of ornamental metal work, and the large class of artists employed in architectural decoration generally, these prints have always been most eagerly sought after, and more especially during the last few years, when the public taste not only of England but of the whole of Europe has been so much directed to these objects. In the course of our business we have had occasionally opportunities of meeting with small collections or detached prints of this description, which have been immediately purchased from us for the before mentioned purposes, principally by foreign artists and dealers, and particularly by those of Paris, where a publication of very mediocre copies from such of these prints as were attainable for that purpose has met with a most extensive sale.[39]

Whatever the motives, the British Museum had moved in time. In the 1850s prices began to rise, and in the 1870s the competition became intense. Two new and extremely wealthy buyers had entered the market: the Berlin Museum and Baron Edmond de Rothschild (whose collection is now in the Louvre). Both sought early Italian prints with great zeal, and the reason for this was the revolution in taste that had begun to elevate such works above all other prints. The prophet and promoter of this revolution was John Ruskin, whose *Ariadne Florentina*, based on lectures given at Oxford, was first published in 1872 – only twenty-seven years after the Museum's purchase. In it he pronounced views that are startling now, and must have seemed quite extraordinary at the time. He began by pronouncing an anathema on modern engraving: 'And, in sum, I know no cause more direct or fatal in the destruction of the great schools of European art, than the perfectness of modern line-engraving.' Instead he turned to the early Italians: 'These apparently unfinished and certainly unfilled outlines of the Florentine ... are these good or bad engraving? ... And the answer is, they are the finest gravers' work ever done by human hand.'[40]

Before leaving this subject, it is interesting to enquire more closely into the dynamics of the 1845 purchases, and how two such great acquisitions were made so quickly and so easily. The Lawrence drawings had been rejected, and so had Woodburn's offer of 1843. Yet Smith managed to sell the Museum five groups of material that required special Treasury grants – the Sheepshanks collection for £5,000, the Harding collection for £2,300, the two 1845 collections, and another package from Woodburn's former stock in 1847 for £4,200 – as well as a mass of smaller lots that were bought from the annual purchase grant. How did this come about?

The key was William Smith himself (1808–76). His father, also named William, had founded the family busi-

2. William Hookham Carpenter, *Portrait of William Smith*, etching with retouchings in pencil *c.*1850. 229 × 152 mm. 1876-12-9-485

ness as a printseller in Lisle Street, just north of Leicester Square, at some point, it seems, in the first decade of the nineteenth century. His two sons, William and George, were given an education superior to most in their profession, and were at Cambridge University when their father's sudden death in 1835 disrupted their studies and brought them back to continue the business.[41] Of the two, it was William who wrote all the letters and provided the public face; George, who is described by one source as his inseparable friend, is by comparison a shadowy figure.

The first record of the British Museum buying from William Smith is in 1832, when he was twenty-four. By 1835 the brothers had enough capital to buy the Sheepshanks collection, and this seems to have launched their remarkable career. Annotations in their copies of auction catalogues show that by 1837 they were acting as agents for Baron Verstolk in London sales,[42] and that in 1840 they were buying for Beckford.[43] They were immensely energetic, attending all the major auctions in Paris and in Holland. By the 1840s they were the largest purchasers in the London auctions, and in 1847 they set the seal on their success by acquiring Woodburn's entire stock of prints – a large part of which they immediately sold on to the British Museum for £4,200.

The following year they decided to retire from business while still in their forties. The British Museum made selections of large parts of their stock for purchase, and a valuable collection of caricatures by Gillray and their outstanding archive of auction catalogues were presented. The rest was sold at four auctions, realising more than £4,500. Henceforth, as an obituary of William Smith put it, his labours were 'entirely honorary and patriotic'. He was one of the original Trustees of the National Portrait Gallery in 1856, and became its very conscientious Deputy Chairman in 1858: the Trustees' report in 1877, the year after his death, recorded that he had attended every meeting of the board since 1856 with only one exception.[44] He formed an excellent collection of English watercolours, which he partly presented and partly bequeathed to the Victoria and Albert Museum and the National Gallery of Ireland.[45] Three papers carried obituaries, which all stressed his public service. That in *The Times* said that he 'was universally respected and exercised for many years a remarkable influence on the development of the fine art collections in this country ... many of the most eminent judges and patrons of art were on terms of personal friendship with him.'[46]

One such close friend turns out to have been W. H. Carpenter, the Keeper in the British Museum. In 1864 Smith published a catalogue of the engravings of Cornelis Visscher, and dedicated it to Carpenter, 'not only as a slight acknowledgment of much assistance received during its compilation, but as a memorial of an uninterrupted friendship extending over many years'.[47] More evidence emerges from stray references in letters. They had

3. Margaret Carpenter, *Portrait of William Hookham Carpenter*, watercolour over pencil 1817. 305 × 226 mm. 1893-4-26-4

travelled to the Continent to see Verstolk's collection before 1846; in 1854 they must both have been in Venice together.[48] Both were among the founding Trustees of the National Portrait Gallery. Both Carpenter and his wife, the well-known painter Margaret Carpenter, made portraits of Smith.[49] Long after his retirement, he kept an eye open on Carpenter's behalf. A letter of 1863 from Dominic Colnaghi to Carpenter stated that he had just 'bought a very beautiful drawing in white and black chalks of Prince Rupert by W. Vaillant (life size). I have shown it to Mr W. Smith, who thinks it ought to be offered to the Museum.' This was duly bought.

Such a close friendship opens itself to suspicions of possible malpractice, and William Coningham, giving evidence to the House of Commons Select Committee on the National Gallery in 1853, made a malicious and, in view of the history of the sale of his own collection, disingenuous accusation: 'I know, for instance, with regard to the British Museum, that in the print department before Mr Carpenter's time (and I know nothing about it since his appointment), unless collections of prints got into particular hands they never found their way into the British

Museum; they might be ever so good, but they were not received.'[50] He was ostensibly referring to Josi, who had doubtless also been a friend of Smith, as he certainly had been of Carpenter, who made a portrait etching of him. But the real target was Smith.

At this distance of time it is impossible to discover the full story, but Coningham was an unpleasant character, and the testimony to Smith's honesty and public-spiritedness from other sources is overwhelming. What Coningham would not realise is that an offer such as Woodburn's in 1843 is of no use to any public institution. Woodburn offered his entire collection in a take-it-or-leave-it fashion. It is clear from Josi's report that he had never been consulted and so, inevitably, the group contained numerous prints that were not needed. So the offer was rejected. Publicly accountable institutions have to sort out exactly what they need, and need time to arrange approvals and payment. Smith offered the Harding prints in March 1841; he was paid only in July 1842. He had previously sorted out with Josi which of the Harding prints he wanted. Josi knew Harding well, for Joseph Harding, along with William Nichol, had given a bond for his surety on his appointment at the British Museum. Harding probably even bought some of his prints with the British Museum in mind: some early Italian prints he had bought at the Lattin sale in February 1841 were included in Smith's offer two months later. If so, Josi, Harding and Smith between them

4. William Hookham Carpenter, *Portrait of Henry Josi*, etching 1845. 211 × 188 mm. 1876-12-9-319

had worked out an extremely successful stratagem for overcoming the Trustees' lack of purchase funds, and of going directly to the Treasury.

Smith's friendship with Josi and Carpenter was one that benefited both the Museum and the firm. The packages that he offered the Trustees had been previously carefully put together in collaboration with them. When duplicates turned up in the packages Smith took them back without question, and made due allowance in the price. Smith prepared the ground carefully, found out what was wanted, and then found the goods.[51] It was both his and the Museum's good fortune that the prints were waiting to be bought, and that the slump in the art market in the 1840s made them cheaper than they had been for many years. There is very little that any collector and any museum can do without the help of someone in the trade, and any dealer who is prepared to go out of his way to favour an institution is entitled to the curator's thanks. At the same time there is little that any dealer, however excellent, can do without someone inside an institution to recognise the value of his stock and to support its acquisition.

1. The complete texts of this and other letters quoted in this article are given in Appendix J.

2. The German collection was registered in August, as 1845-8-9-1 to 1762. The number was reduced after eliminating duplicates, and the final price was £2,880.

3. The Italian collection was given the numbers 1845-8-25-1 to 829. The final price, after the elimination of duplicates, was £4,875.

4. See J. Strutt, *A Biographical Dictionary of Engravers*, London 1786, I, introduction pp. 17–29; and W. Y. Ottley, *An Inquiry into the Origin and Early History of Engraving*, London 1816, I, pp. 300, 361, 531. Given that there is little reason to think that Sloane and Fawkener owned early engravings, and good reason to think that Cracherode did not, it follows that most of the early engravings in the 1837 inventory are likely to have come from Monro. If so, he owned sixty-five early Italian engravings, and possibly as many as two hundred German ones.

5. The prints were sold on 30 April, preceded by his library on 23 April. This included many early books, with learned annotations by the doctor, and was praised much later by T. F. Dibdin in *The Bibliomania*, London, 3rd edition, 1842, pp. 417–19. Lots 1 to 17 of the fourth day of the print sale were variously described as 'curious ancient' or 'very ancient' prints. Two lots were sold 'with Dr Monro's remarks'. Unfortunately I have found no copy with the names of the purchasers. So whether James (who was presumably his son) reserved these prints or bought them in at the sale is uncertain.

6. The argument for this is entirely negative. A drawing, included as lot 83, day 14, of Charles Rogers's sale in 1799 (see later), was in the British Museum by the time of the publication of Ottley's *Inquiry* in 1816. Since the Monro acquisition was the only purchase of prints in the intervening years, and no gift of this drawing is recorded, James Monro may have bought it in 1799 to add to his inherited collection.

7. See A. Griffiths, 'Print collecting in Rome, Paris and London in the early 18th century', *Harvard University Art Museums Bulletin*, Spring 1994, pp. 50–2.

8. Quoted from Ottley, *An Inquiry*, op. cit. p. 296. The original letter

was published in G. Bottari, *Raccolta di lettere sulla pittura...*, enlarged ed. by S. Ticozzi, Milan 1822, II pp. 333–71.

9. An important unpublished letter, dated 19 November 1767, on this subject from Mariette to Rogers shows that he had still not abandoned his intention (in the Cottonian collection in Plymouth).

10. Zani, *Materiali per servire alla storia dell'origine e de'progressi dell'incisione in rame e in legno*, Parma 1802.

11. An essay on this by Seratti himself was published by Zani in his book, op. cit. pp. 215–21 (translated by Ottley, op. cit. pp. 270–8).

12. Ottley (op. cit. 1816, p. 301), on the authority of Lanzi, states that many of these came from the collection of the Gaddi family, formed in the sixteenth century by Niccolo Gaddi (c.1537–91). See also Richard Fisher, *Introduction to a Catalogue of the Early Italian Prints in the British Museum*, London 1886, p. 41.

13. From facsimiles to fakes is a short step, and later Italian collections, such as that of Count Leopoldo Cicognara, were bedevilled by them. A good account, naming the fakers, is in R. Fisher, op. cit. pp. 32–47. The problem of distinguishing genuine from fake nielli is far from solved today.

14. See Lugt 2319.

15. See K. T. Parker, *Catalogue of the Collection of Drawings in the Ashmolean Museum, Italian Schools*, I, Oxford 1956, pp. x–xviii.

16. The earliest record of Woodburn as a buyer that I have come across is at the Woodhouse sale on 24 November 1803. At this time he would have been only seventeen; it is possible that the purchaser was one of his brothers with whom he was in partnership (see Lugt 2584). By 1806 Woodburn, this time specified as Samuel, turns up in the story of Dighton's theft (see Appendix E).

17. This information is given in the annotated copy of the sale catalogue in the British Museum.

18. See Lugt 2584.

19. See M. Royalton-Kisch, 'Rembrandt, Zomer, Zanetti and Smith', *Print Quarterly*, X 1993, pp. 116–22.

20. See A. Griffiths, 'The Rogers collection in the Cottonian Library, Plymouth', *Print Quarterly*, X 1993, pp. 19–36.

21. J. A. Gere, 'William Young Ottley as a collector of drawings', *British Museum Quarterly*, XVIII 1953, pp. 44–53; and E. K. Waterhouse, 'Some notes on William Young Ottley's collection of Italian primitives', in *Italian Studies Presented to E. R. Vincent*, London 1962, pp. 272–80.

22. *Gentleman's Magazine*, VI August 1836, pp. 210–11.

23. This information is taken from a memorandum by Stewart dated 2 May 1829, printed in J. T. Smith, *A Book for a Rainy Day*, edited with notes by W. Whitten, London 1905, pp. 309–12. This reveals that two of the three consignments of the collection were lost in shipwrecks on the way to England. Stewart also owned a memorandum by Seratti himself, which stated that he had acquired the sulphur 'from a painter who had purchased it with a heap of other trinkets at the stall of a petty dealer in Florence' – information that is not in his essay that Zani published (see n. 11). Garbled versions of the history of the collection are to be found in other sources.

24. See lots 479 and 480. The prints are now both in the British Museum. The first is 294 in A. M. Hind, *Nielli in the British Museum*, London 1936 (and thought by him to be a fake); the second is A. M. Hind, *Early Italian Engraving* I 1938, cat. A II.8.

25. D. E. Williams, *The Life of Sir Thomas Lawrence*, London 1831, II pp. 465–6.

26. Lloyd is one of the few buyers named in the British Museum's marked copy of the auction of the collection of Marquis Riccardi of Florence, held by Stewart, the importer, on 13 April 1812. Annotations in the British Museum's copy of the catalogue suggest that he bought many of the early German prints in the sale, lots 440 to 455. There were few early Italian prints in this sale, and perhaps others had been sold separately. See Ottley's *Inquiry* of 1816, p. 403n.

27. Joseph Maberly, *The Print Collector*, London 1844, p. 66 and p. 200.

28. Smith's *A Book for a Rainy Day* describes a visit that he and Smedley made to see Esdaile's collection in 1829 (1905 edn pp. 273–80).

29. This was not correct. It was the Storck collection that Sykes had bought.

30. This statement is contained in a letter of 1836 soliciting the vacant position of Keeper of Prints and Drawings in the British Museum.

31. For the Stowe manuscripts, now in the British Library, see A. N. L. Munby, *Connoisseurs and Medieval Miniatures*, Oxford 1972, pp. 132–5. It was his son, the second Duke, whose even greater extravagance led to a spectacular bankruptcy and the sale of everything he owned in the famous Stowe auction of 1848.

32. The Hamburg collection of early Italian prints is perhaps the best in Germany, and includes the unique *Death of Orpheus* from the Lloyd, Sykes and Wilson collections (Hind 1938, E III.17). It is curious to discover that it was formed in London, where Harzen was an assiduous buyer at auctions throughout the 1830s and 1840s.

33. Smith's list of the prints from Harding's collection which he was selling to the British Museum, now in the Central Archives, gives the provenance of a good many of them.

34. See Francis Haskell, 'William Coningham and his collection of Old Masters', *Burlington Magazine*, CXXXIII 1991, pp. 676–81. Curiously Coningham sold his paintings, just like his prints, soon after he acquired them.

35. According to Francis Haskell, on whose *Rediscoveries in Art* I have relied in these paragraphs, Davenport-Bromley began his large-scale purchasing of early paintings at the Fesch sales between 1841 and 1845 (2nd edn 1980, p. 203, n. 64). His prints may have been sold to raise funds to pay for these.

36. According to the annotated copy of this catalogue in the British Museum, Smith had bought many of these prints for him at the Sykes, Buckingham and Esdaile sales.

37. An exception was lot 969, a print by Nicoletto da Modena. This turned up in the auction at Sotheby's on 4 March 1861, the property of George Smith (almost certainly William's brother), where it was bought by the British Museum. The preface to the catalogue stated that the collection had been formed over a considerable number of years from sales in London and Paris, and had been intended as the basis of a more extended cabinet covering the history of printmaking. This project having been abandoned, the collection was being sold. After William Smith's death in 1876, George presented the collection of engraved portraits of eminent persons connected with the Fine Arts that had been formed by William and his father before him (1876–12–9–1 to 617).

38. Ottley's exceptional collection of early Italian paintings had been formed much earlier, in the 1790s. When the German Museum director Waagen admired it in 1835, Ottley told him that no one in England had paid as much attention to them as he had done. They were sold for very low sums, many being bought in, in various

sales in 1837, 1847 and 1850 (see Waterhouse, op. cit. in n. 21, pp. 274–80).

39. Smith must be referring to the first fascicles of the three volumes of *Ornemens des anciens maîtres des XV, XVI, XVII et XVIII siècles, receuillis par Ovide Reynard et gravés sous sa direction par les meilleurs artistes, dédié à M. A. Vivenel, architecte*, Paris, A. Hauser, 1844–6. In 'A nineteenth-century forgery of a Woeiriot print', *Print Quarterly* VII 1990, pp. 282–5, Peter Fuhring shows that the copies were very soon used for making fakes.

40. 1890 edition, pp. 121 and 244.

41. So the entry on Smith in the *Dictionary of National Biography*, based on his obituary in *The Times*.

42. The copy of the catalogue of the Robert-Dumesnil sale in London of 12 April 1836 that Smith gave to the Department is annotated by him: 'All the lots which have the names of Smith & Son and Fuller attached to them as purchasers were bought for Baron Verstolk.' His copy of the catalogue of the second Robert-Dumesnil sale on 1 May 1837 is similarly annotated, but substitutes Heyman for Fuller as the second name. Smith was the biggest purchaser in both sales.

43. The Bodleian Library in Oxford preserves the correspondence between Smith and Beckford from 1841 to 1843, mostly concerning the sale of Horace Walpole's collection at Strawberry Hill (Ms Beckford c. 35, ff. 28–51).

44. I owe this information to the kind help of Jonathan Franklin at the National Portrait Gallery.

45. The Victoria and Albert Museum received 222 works, including seven Turners (see the 16-page pamphlet, *List of the collection of watercolour paintings, the gift and bequest of William Smith, Esq. FSA 1871 and 1876*, published in 1877). The V & A was also bequeathed his library of over 1,000 books on art and his catalogues, as well as various manuscripts, which, although interesting, do not throw light on the subjects discussed in this essay.

46. *The Times*, 16 September 1876 p. 10. See also the *Athenaeum*, 1876 II p. 377, and *Notes and Queries* (to which he was a regular contributor) 5th series, VI 1876, p. 259.

47. The catalogue was first published in the *Fine Arts Quarterly Review*; the dedication is on a reprint 'for private circulation only', of which Smith presented a copy to the British Museum.

48. See D. Robertson, *Sir Charles Eastlake and the Victorian Art World*, Princeton 1978, p. 159, quoting from letters in the Victoria and Albert Museum that are currently mislaid. Carpenter was in Venice in September 1854, negotiating for the purchase of the Bellini sketchbook for the British Museum, and it can be inferred that Smith was with him.

49. Her painting of 1856, which was etched by her husband two years later, was bequeathed to the National Portrait Gallery by George Smith, his brother, in 1886. See R. Ormond, *Early Victorian Portraits*, London (National Portrait Gallery) 1973, pp. 422–3. Three paintings by Margaret Carpenter were included in John Sheepshanks's gift to South Kensington (see p. 70).

50. Minutes of Evidence, paragraph 6853. Coningham proceeded to instance the Sheepshanks collection as just such a purchase.

51. One such act of support concerns the outstanding collection of engravings by Lucas van Leyden formed by Henry James Brooke, who presented from it every missing print or greatly superior impression to the British Museum in 1849 (see cat. 43). Smith's copy of the Brooke sale catalogue of 1853 (now in the Victoria and Albert Museum) is annotated with the original price that Brooke paid. In it Smith noted 'It is impossible to give the cost prices of the Lucas van

Leyden's as Mr Brooke bought the whole Denon collection of his works from W. Smith, and gave many of them to the British Museum'. This proves that Smith had formed the Brooke collection. He also acted as intermediary – and doubtless promoter – in the gift and wrote a long memorandum to the Trustees to accompany it. As late as 1868 Smith valued the collection of caricatures formed by Edward Hawkins when the Museum wished to purchase it from his widow. There are numerous letters from him in the Department's letter books until his death in 1876 on a wide variety of subjects. For example, in the early 1870s he was providing photographs of missing prints, and in 1874 wrote a letter supporting an increase in the Department's annual grant for purchases.

31 Master ES (active c.1450–70)
The Virgin and Child Enthroned with Two Angels, c.1466

Engraving. 207 × 136 mm
Bartsch VI 16.34; Lehrs II 151.82

The Master ES (traditionally also often called the Master of 1466) was the first early engraver to be given a reasonably firm identity, thanks to his habit of marking his late prints with his monogram and/or the date 1466 or 1467. Bartsch catalogued 113 prints by him in 1808, and included many unsigned prints, such as this one, which he attributed to him on stylistic grounds. Lehrs, writing in 1910, increased his oeuvre to 314 items. Master ES was not the earliest engraver, but he was the dominant figure of the second generation in the two decades after 1450, working in the upper Rhine, probably in the border region between Switzerland and Germany. This is one of only five known impressions of what Lehrs describes as one of the major plates of his last years.

1845-8-9-48. Smith collection

32 Wenzel von Olmütz (active 1475–1500)
Christ as Man of Sorrows between the Virgin and St John, c.1490

Engraving. 196 × 153 mm
Bartsch VI 325.17; Lehrs VI 209.21

The collection purchased from Smith was far from a select one. Its strength lay in its comprehensiveness, and impressions were of miscellaneous quality and by engravers of varied competence. This is a very fine impression of a print by a minor figure, Wenzel von Olmütz. As a sixteenth-century owner noted on another impression of this print in the Albertina: 'This engraver was called Wenzel; he was a goldsmith.' Not much more is known about him today. His full name is found on one print, with which those marked 'W' were first associated by a scholar in 1886. Olmütz (Olomouc) is in Bohemia, due east of Prague, but

he is recorded in no archival documents there. Most of his ninety-one known prints are copied from other masters. This one is faithfully copied from an engraving by Martin Schongauer (Lehrs 34). It is in the same direction as the original, and only diverges in that Schongauer's stone embrasure is replaced with two tree-trunks and Gothic scrollwork. This impression is almost certainly that purchased by Woodburn at the 1820 Lloyd sale (lot 853) for £1.11.6.

1845-8-9-395. Smith collection

33 Master W with the Key (active c.1465–90)
St Martin and the Beggar, 1470s

Engraving. 225 × 109 mm
Bartsch X 25.45; Lehrs VII 45.19

This print was included by Bartsch among the anonymous engravings of the fifteenth century which could not be attributed to any engraver. It was Bartsch's son, who followed him as curator of the Imperial collection in Vienna, who first attributed it to the artist known from his monogram as 'W with the key', an attribution that is now accepted. There is strong evidence that he was Netherlandish, and he perhaps worked in Bruges between the mid-1460s and the end of the 1480s. He was probably a goldsmith by training, and many of the eighty-one prints that Lehrs attributes to him are designs for ornamental motifs. Only five impressions are known of this print, of which this is the best. This impression is probably the one sold in the 1817 Lloyd sale (lot 648*) for 12s to Woodburn.

1845-8-9-131. Smith collection

34 Master IAM of Zwolle (active c.1470–90)
Christ on the Mount of Olives, c.1490

Engraving. 388 × 290 mm
Bartsch VI 91.3; Lehrs VII 182.3

This master was another Dutch engraver, working in Zwolle to the east of Amsterdam. Lehrs catalogued twenty-six prints by him, of which the most dramatic are three large plates showing incidents from the Passion of Christ. They were perhaps intended for a larger series that was never completed. All share the same format with Gothic architectural frames, and the same narrative manner by which several scenes are shown. Here we see Christ praying alone in the centre, and again awakening St Peter in the foreground. Behind are the soldiers being led by Judas into the garden.

This impression was purchased by Woodburn at the 1817 Lloyd sale (lot 587) for £5.5.0. The catalogue states:

31

32

33

34

35

'Mr Bartsch does not seem to have seen this plate entire, as he is incorrect in the measure of the height, which is here corrected. In the margin at the top is the engraved name Zwoll; in the margin at the bottom is his monogram, with the navette [shuttle].' Most of the nine surviving impressions listed by Lehrs are cut at top or bottom or both; this is one of the few that are not. The object at the bottom, which was thought by Bartsch to be a weaver's shuttle, is now recognised as a goldsmith's drill, and gives a clue as to this master's early training.

1845-8-9-230. Smith collection

35 Augustin Hirschvogel (1503–53)
View of the Northern Part of Passau, 1546

Etching. 138 × 210 mm

Bartsch IX 190.72; Hollstein 45

Etching was first applied to printmaking in Germany and Italy in the first decades of the sixteenth century. One of the first uses made of the new invention was for making landscapes, and a number are known by artists working in the Danube region, first Altdorfer in the 1520s, and later Hirschvogel and Lautensack. An early annotation on another impression of this print correctly identifies the scene as a view of the junction of the Ilz and the Danube, although it is reversed in the print (see N. G. Stogdon, *German Landscapes of the 16th Century: Catalogue 9*, 1993, cat. 20). Eleven of the rare landscape etchings by Hirschvogel came into the British Museum with the Smith purchase of 1845. There is as yet no evidence for their earlier provenance.

1845-8-9-1578. Smith collection

36

36 Anonymous Florentine

*Theseus and Ariadne beside the Cretan Labyrinth, c.*1475

Engraving. 198 × 262 mm

Hind A.ii.16

This charming re-creation of the classical legend of Theseus and Ariadne in Italian Renaissance clothing is known in only three impressions – one in the Bibliothèque Nationale in Paris, and two in the British Museum. Bartsch did not know it, and it is first described in England in the early nineteenth century. This impression was lot 1058 in the 1824 Sykes sale, where it was bought by Woodburn for £16.16.0. The second impression in the Museum came with the Slade bequest in 1868.

1845–8–25–487. Smith collection

37 Manner of Leonardo da Vinci (1452–1519)

Profile Bust of a Young Woman, about 1510

Engraving. 106 × 75 mm

Hind v 90.12

In the early nineteenth century this was one of the most celebrated prints in England. It was acquired by Sir Mark Sykes with the rest of the Storck collection from Woodburn in 1816, and was bought for Thomas Wilson at the Sykes sale (lot 1070) for £64.1.0, the highest price for any print apart from the nielli. Ottley in his catalogue entry in the Sykes sale cautiously described it as 'ascribed to Leonardo da Vinci, of whom the design certainly is', but Wilson had no such hesitation. He had an excellent facsimile made as the frontispiece of his catalogue, and asserted that 'the following interesting and probably unique specimen is confidently believed to be from his hand: it bears all his style and character' (*A Catalogue*

Raisonné of the Select Collecion of Engravings of an Amateur, 1828, p. 39). Wilson even got Ottley to write him a letter retracting his former hesitation, and this he printed in a footnote. Hind, in 1948, still entertained the possibility that Leonardo might be the engraver: he instanced the direction of the shading (which points to a left-handed artist), and noted that 'the unpractised engraver is betrayed by the slipped stroke above the fore-head'. Few if any today would maintain such an attribution. But the print is certainly Leonardesque, is very fine and remains unique.

1845–8–25–583. Smith collection

38 Girolamo Mocetto (c.1458–1531) after Andrea Mantegna (1431–1506)

Judith and her Maid with the Head of Holofernes, c.1500

Engraving. 292 × 203 mm

Hind V p. 164.10

37

The story of Judith is to be found in the Book of Judith in the Old Testament Apocrypha. She seduced Holofernes, the enemy general, and while he was asleep cut off his head. She and her maid are here seen putting the head into a sack to take back to the Israelites. Mantegna made a series of variations on the group of the two women and the head, some of which are known as paintings and grisailles, others as drawings and prints. The closest version to this print is a composition of which several copies survive, the best being in Chatsworth, dated 1482.

Mantegna himself engraved, and also supervised the production of engravings by his assistants. This print, however, is in a quite different style to the 'authorised' production, and was first attributed by Bartsch to the Venetian painter and engraver Mocetto, by whom a number of signed prints are known. He must have come across a drawing by or after Mantegna, and decided to engrave it. This is a very fine impression of one of six listed of the first state; in the second state, a background with a tree and landscape was added behind the two figures. The print has been cut well within the design on three sides, but has been reassembled from the original pieces. This may be the impression in the 1817 Lloyd sale, lot 736, sold to Roberts for £6.16.6.

1845–8–25–590. Smith collection

38

39

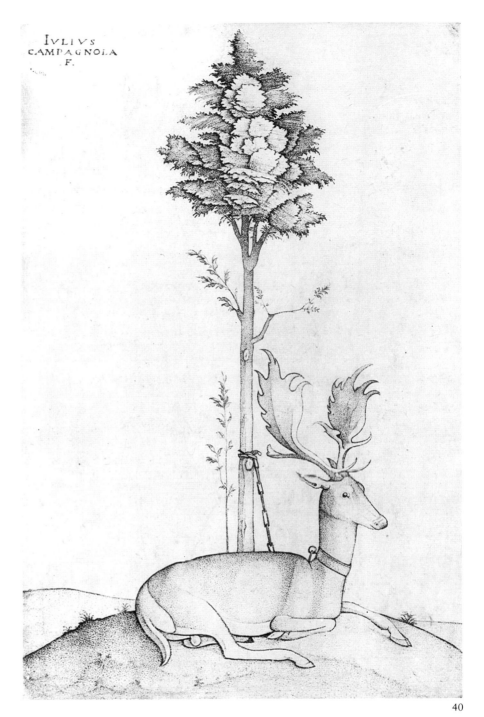

40

39 Jacopo de' Barbari (*c.*1470–1516)
Victory and Fame, late 1490s

Engraving. 180 × 123 mm
Hind V p.157.26

Barbari, as painter and engraver, links the worlds of the Italian and northern Renaissance. He knew Dürer, who refers to him in a letter of 1506. He was born in Venice, and was commissioned by the German merchant Anton Kolb to make a famous bird's-eye view of the city as a woodcut on six large sheets for the year 1500. Kolb then acted as his promoter in the courts of Germany, and the rest of his career was spent north of the Alps. He first worked for the Emperor Maximilian, then for Frederick the Wise of Saxony, and later for others; his final post was at the court of Margaret, Regent of the Netherlands, in Malines. He signed his prints simply with Mercury's caduceus, and for centuries his identity was lost. He was commonly thought to be German, and was called the Master of the Caduceus. It was only in 1832 that Brulliot published his real name, having found a painting in Munich signed with both his name and the caduceus.

Hind catalogued thirty engravings by him. None is dated and their chronology remains uncertain. Stylistically this is one of his first prints, and was presumably made in Venice. Barbari's prints are found relatively frequently, and he must have sold them in good numbers to the same sort of clients as were buying Dürer's engravings. This impression was part of lot 539 in the 1817 Lloyd sale, and of lot 1732 in the 1837 Ottley sale.

1845–8–9–1033. Smith collection

40 Giulio Campagnola (*c.*1482–*c.*1515/17)
A Stag Tied to a Tree, *c.*1515

Engraving. 182 × 118 mm
Hind V p.202.14

Contemporary documents show that Campagnola had considerable fame both as an artist and as a scholar and musician. He was born in Padua, and was employed in Mantua, Ferrara and Venice, where he was asked to cut Greek type for Aldus Manutius. His prints show his virtuosity in their employment of a manner of shading by stippling, a technique that he seems to have invented. Hind attributed nineteen plates to him. A few are known in twenty or more impressions, but most are extremely rare. This beautiful and enigmatic print was unknown to Bartsch, and no more than four impressions survive. Where Smith acquired this one from is not known.

1845–8–25–775. Smith collection

PLATE I

23 Hercules Seghers, *Country Road with Trees and a Farmhouse*

PLATE 2

61 Anonymous German, *The Virgin and Child Seated*

PLATE 3

69 Hans Wechtlin, *Alcon Slaying the Serpent*

PLATE 4

91 Charles-Melchior Descourtis after Frédéric-Jean Schall, *Les Espiègles (Mischiefmakers)*

PLATE 5

94 František Kupka, *The Way of Silence*

PLATE 6

70 Giuseppe di Cosimo Bianchino, *Sea Monster with Putti*

85 Paul Gauguin, *Auti te Pape* (*Women by the River* or *The Fresh Water in Motion*)

PLATE 7

97 Ernst Ludwig Kirchner, *Portrait of Otto Müller*

PLATE 8

86 Henri de Toulouse-Lautrec, *La Clownesse assise, Mlle Cha-U-Ka-O*

5. Felix Slade (1790–1868)

Antony Griffiths

Although Felix Slade's bequest only came to the British Museum thirty-two years after the collection of John Sheepshanks, the two men were almost contemporaries. Slade was born three years after Sheepshanks, and died five years after him. The two men had very different collections, but there are some striking parallels between them.

Slade's long and complicated will was drafted and signed four days before his death on 29 March 1868. He was a wealthy man, being the only survivor of his immediate family, and his estate was valued at no less than £160,000. Much of the will was devoted to apportioning it among his relatives. His personal and philanthropic bequests were put into seven codicils. It was the fourth of these that has preserved his name, if not his memory, to the present day. In it he bequeathed £45,000 to his executors, of which £35,000 was to be used 'to found and endow within two years after my decease three or more professorships for promoting the study of the Fine Arts to be termed the Slade Professorships of Fine Arts'. One was to be at Oxford, another at Cambridge, and the third in University College, London. The rest was to be used to endow at University College six scholarships in Fine Art 'to be given to students in the Fine Arts under nineteen years of age for proficiency in drawing, painting or sculpture'. He concluded: 'I have made the aforesaid disposition from a sincere wish and in the hope thereby to confer a benefit on society.' The annual professorships continue to the present day at Oxford and Cambridge, and the roll-call of the incumbents contains the names of almost every distinguished historian of art that this country has produced. At University College the bequest, supplemented by £5,000 of the College's own funds, was used to found the Slade School of Art, and the Slade Professor there has always been an artist. There can be no doubt that Slade's hopes have been more than met.

His bequest to the British Museum came in the first codicil. First to be mentioned was his famous collection of 944 pieces of ancient and more recent glass, 'of which a catalogue is now in the course of printing'. To this was to be added 'such specimens of pottery and such other works of art not specifically bequeathed by any other codicil as my friend Augustus Wollaston Franks out of my executors may select as desirable for the British Museum, and also my collection of Japanese carvings in ivory'. Next came 'all my unbound collection of engravings, woodcuts and

etchings at Walcot Place, and such of my bound collection of engravings, woodcuts and etchings and such of my manuscripts out of my books in ancient bindings, which my friends Augustus Wollaston Franks and Richard Fisher ... may think desirable for the British Museum'. He added a strong plea: 'I particularly request that none of the bound volumes of engravings and etchings hereby bequeathed shall be broken up or otherwise mutilated.' Finally he left a sum of £3,000 which Franks, at his absolute discretion, was empowered to spend on additions to the collection of glass in the British Museum. Franks, in a report to the Trustees on 20 May 1868, estimated the total value of the bequest at about £28,000, of which the glass accounted for £7,500 and the prints £16,000.

Of the remaining codicils, one provided for the completion and publication of the catalogue of the glass

1. Margaret Carpenter, *Portrait of Felix Slade*, coloured chalks 1851. 368 × 267 mm. 1874-3-14-1

collection. Another left £5,000 for the repair of the parish church of Thornton in Lonsdale in Yorkshire, near Slade's country estate at Halstead. The rest contained personal bequests to his relatives and friends. Franks himself was bequeathed a set of Apostle spoons in their box as well as a set of Samuel Rogers's *Poems* and *Italy* which had belonged to their mutual friend George Stewart Nicholson. Other relics of Nicholson went to Alexander Nesbitt. Small bequests of money went to fellow collectors, William Twopeny and John Henderson,[1] and the remaining parts of his collection went to his relative Mrs Margaret Tyers Weller Poley.

The will makes clear the dominant position of Franks among the four executors. Richard Fisher was only singled out in regard to the prints,[2] and the other two, a neighbour and one other, are never mentioned as having a role to play in disposing of the collection. In 1868 Franks was forty-two, and had been Keeper of the newly-formed Department of British and Medieval Antiquities in the British Museum for two years. The two men had certainly known each other since at least 1850, when Franks was the secretary to the Medieval Exhibition at the Royal Society of Arts; in 1857 Slade had supported him when he joined the Athenaeum, the gentlemen's club on Pall Mall. Franks had clearly deeply impressed Slade, thirty-six years his senior, as he was to impress so many others during his long and immensely distinguished career in the British Museum.[3] Slade, for some unknown reason, had very different feelings towards the South Kensington Museum (since 1899 retitled the Victoria and Albert Museum). The final clause of the codicil bequeathing his collection of glass contained a strict injunction: 'It is my particular desire that no article bequeathed by or purchased in pursuance of this codicil or which I may hereafter bequeath in like manner shall be at any time transferred to the South Kensington Museum.' His remarks that no one should cut up his books of prints suggest that he also had his reservations about the Department of Prints and Drawings in the British Museum. His request was entirely justified in the light of what was commonly done at the time,[4] and has, I am glad to say, been punctiliously observed by the Department.

Franks fulfilled his ambiguous role as discretionary executor and as servant of the Trustees of the British Museum with immense tact and efficiency, and without giving rise to any complaint from Slade's numerous relatives. He saw the catalogue of Slade's glass collection to its final publication in 1871, and added a preliminary notice before Slade's preface that contains the best of the very few biographical notices that we have of the collector.[5] Since none of Slade's own papers seems to survive, and very few of his letters can be found, his personality remains somewhat shadowy. But the outlines of his life are clear.

He was born in Lambeth in 1790, the younger of two sons of Robert Slade, who was a proctor in Doctors Commons in St Paul's Churchyard, a position roughly

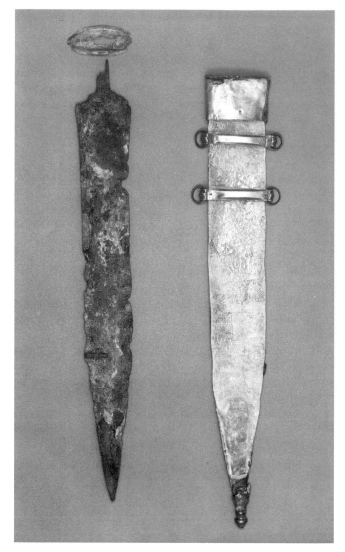

2. The 'Sword of Tiberius', the blade iron, the scabbard tinned bronze, Roman *c*.15 BC. Presented to the British Museum by Felix Slade in 1866. Department of Greek & Roman Antiquities, 1886.8-6.1

comparable to a modern solicitor. The father was a prominent figure in liberal circles: a volume of his papers left by his son to the British Museum reveals his close involvement with the cause of the exiled Spanish liberals in 1823.[6] For many years he was secretary of the Irish Society. His father was very successful, and after his death in 1835 and his elder brother's in 1858, Felix inherited not only his estate but the estate of Halstead from his mother's family. Felix followed his father into the law, and as late as 1857 wrote that he still attended at Doctors Commons every day. He never married, and a female cousin seems to have kept house for him.[7]

Passports among his father's papers show that as a twelve-year-old Felix was taken to see Paris during the peace of Amiens in 1802. A much longer visit in 1817 took him onwards to Italy and Rome. He doubtless travelled much in later life, but there is only one record of such journeys. His few letters show that he often went to Brighton, where he had relatives, as well as to the family estate in Yorkshire. They also reveal that he suffered increasingly poor health. Matthew Digby Wyatt, the first Slade Professor at Cambridge, recorded:

it was my pleasure to know him, and to have learned to recognise that consolation under many trials in his old age which he derived from his attachment to the studies and tastes of his manhood. The collections of glass, the prints, the books, and minor specimens of the art industries of the past by which he surrounded himself, became never-failing sources of happy relaxation when increasing infirmity rendered it difficult for him in later years to derive the pleasure his hospitable spirit once led him to enjoy in the society of his friends.[8]

There is no reason to doubt his convivial spirit and his wide circle of friends. Unlike his father, he moved always in a private rather than a public sphere. He seems never to have taken on any public position; he never engaged in public controversy; he never published anything under his own name. It was only in 1866 that he sought election as a Fellow of the Society of Antiquaries, although he had, through Franks, shown some of his books and antiquities there from 1861 onwards. He was public-spirited, as is shown by several gifts he made to the British Museum during his life. The most important of these was the so-called 'Sword of Tiberius', a famous Roman sword discovered in Mainz in 1848, which he bought for a large sum in order to give to the British Museum in 1866 (fig. 2).[9] Despite his own dire forebodings, he always agreed to lend his treasures – even his Venetian glass – to the exhibitions that began to be held from the mid-century: first the Medieval Exhibition of the Royal Society of Arts in 1850, then the Manchester Art Treasures exhibition of 1857, and the later ones in Ironmonger's Hall in 1861, at South Kensington in 1862, and at Leeds in 1868, the last of which only closed after his death.

Stray references and odd letters show that Slade stood in the centre of British collecting circles. In the preface to his glass catalogue he states that his collection began many years since, 'encouraged by the example and advice of my dear friends Mr George S. Nicholson and Sir Charles Price, both now departed.' Price was another print collector and bibliophile, whose collection was auctioned in 1867 (see p. 120), while Nicholson[10] is mentioned by Waagen, the Director of the Berlin Museums, when describing his visit to Slade in 1856, a visit that had been set up by W. H. Carpenter: 'These attractions [of the glass collection] are further set off by the taste with which these treasures are arranged in the different compartments of two cabinets, one of which is especially rich. This is the work of Mr Nichols[on], a friend of Mr Slade, who also possesses a fine collection of objects in glass.'[11] When in 1857 Slade

3. Part of a letter from Felix Slade to W. H. Carpenter, referring to his forthcoming visit to Slade with Gustav Waagen, 10 October 1855. P & D Archives

lent some book-bindings to the Manchester exhibition, it was again Price and Nicholson who collaborated with him in forming 'a pretty parterre' to fill a case.[12]

Slade's ill-health (he died in 1868) prevented him from becoming a member of the Burlington Fine Arts Club on its foundation in 1867 (see p. 163). But he was closely involved with its precursor, the Fine Arts Club and its conversazione. In a letter to his old friend, the Oxford antiquarian Philip Bliss, of 17 February 1857 he wrote: 'You may probably know that there is to be a meeting at the Baron Marochetti's studio on Wednesday with the view to establishing "a fine art conversazione". I shall be in Brighton ... Sir C. Price and Mr Nicholson have promised to attend, and I shall hear from them what suggestions are made. There have been two or three preliminary meetings. I rather think that it is to be confined to collectors, and perhaps, if well managed, may do good to the cause.' The letter also reveals his close association with another artistic and intellectual club, the Athenaeum, and his belief that the most important thing in it was its library; he complains that of the new members elected by ballot, 'only a small portion comes within the original object of the Club'.[13]

The same letter concludes with an attack on niggardly Government support for acquisitions. 'I cannot learn whether the Government has determined as to the purchase of the Soulages collection.[14] Is it not extraordinary that the great advantages of art education being admitted, there is such difficulty in obtaining the means from Government? Why, what addition would all the claims of art, in the most extended sense, make to the enormous amount of our expenditure, so much of it too carelessly spent? And what mistakes are made when a grant is squeezed out of them!' It was these views that explain the double-sided aspect of Slade's generosity a decade later, and what he did not include in his bequest.

For besides his 944 pieces of glass and 8,853 prints, which went to the British Museum, Slade possessed a wonderful bibliophile's library, full of specimens of fine printing and fine illustration in outstanding condition and superb bindings. Where he could not find good enough early bindings, he commissioned modern ones from the finest craftsmen of the day. He was in particular a patron of F. Bedford. Waagen in 1856 was full of admiration for what he called an 'embarras de richesses', and devoted more space to the library than he did to the glass and the prints. But from this library, housed in two rooms of his house in Walcot Place, Lambeth, the executors were only empowered to select books of prints and manuscripts in fine bindings; of these they passed thirty-three to the British Museum library and ten to the Department of Prints and Drawings.[15] The rest was sold at auction by Sotheby's on 3 August 1868. The 1,160 lots fetched £5,718, and the catalogue is now the only evidence that remains of its quality. Why did he not include this in his bequest? It could not be a question of money. His bequests

to the Museum were valued at £28,000, and his estate at £160,000; an extra £5,718 was small beer. It could be because the Museum had already been bequeathed two very fine bibliophile libraries, by C. M. Cracherode in 1799, and Thomas Grenville in 1846. But perhaps it was because Slade could not see how they were to be used to increase general knowledge and taste; they were essentially private objects for individual handling.

The prints on the other hand could be used by students and shown to the public, and Slade bequeathed them all to the British Museum, specifically including the duplicates. The acquisition register contains no less than 8,853 items, but this is misleading as the collection falls into two very different parts. Up to 2,163 the prints are individual items; the remainder are all sets of proofs of illustrations to nineteenth-century books, together with several hundred portrait, topographical and historical prints. The two parts of the collection are explained in a letter from the executors dated 23 July:

The prints in Mr Slade's collection consisted firstly of a collection of choice engravings and etchings, arranged in portfolios, and comprising many specimens duplicates of those in the Museum, but which will be useful for exhibition, and we are aware that Mr Slade desired they should be kept together; and secondly of a great mass of miscellaneous prints, acquired for the purpose of illustrating books, especially Shakespeare and the poets ... In some cases there are several sets in duplicate so that they do not form a collection, but rather a store intended to be applied to various purposes of illustration, and which, if carried out, would have removed them from the terms of Mr Slade's bequest.[16]

Setting apart for the moment the collection for illustration, let us examine more closely the 2,163 choice specimens which form the heart of Slade's print collection. The first point to note is what a small number this is, and how selective Slade had been in forming it. In his letter to Bliss on 1 April 1857, he reported amusingly and modestly, but accurately, that 'the vampyres' of the selection committee for the Manchester Art Treasures Exhibition had passed a morning in his print room in March, and that 'mine, being a sort of specimen collection, partaking a little of all shades, will be useful to them in filling up blanks and is reserved for that purpose'. So extensive were Slade's contributions that it would be truer to say that others filled blanks around his loans.[17]

The inventory made in the British Museum almost certainly follows Slade's own arrangement.[18] This is arranged by school, and the engravers are in a roughly chronological order within each school regardless of technique. The numbers of prints within each school vary considerably: 146 Italian, 456 German, 292 Dutch and Flemish, 183 French, and 1,086 British. The weight placed on the British school is noteworthy. Apart from a small group of early engravings and mezzotints, the great bulk of them is by five engravers: three are the classic late eighteenth-century line-engravers, William Woollett (cat. 49), Robert Strange and William Sharp. One is their contemporary Francesco Bartolozzi, the Italian stipple-engraver who made himself so at home in London as to become one of the founding members of the Royal Academy. The last was William Hogarth (cat. 48), by whom Slade had no less than 162 prints – almost his entire output. The only other group worth noticing is eighty prints after paintings by Reynolds.

With the other schools Slade was less focused, and collected a few examples each by most of the obvious names. But his selectivity within each artist is striking. For example in the Dutch school he owned only four engravings by Lucas van Leyden, but each was an outstanding example. He had one Vellert, ten Goltzius, twenty-three Wierix, two de Gheyn, two Suyderhoef, eight Dujardin, seven Swanevelt, nine Adriaen van Ostade, and so on. Had he wished to collect more by any of these men, he could very easily have done so. His restraint was deliberate and part of a conscious strategy.

The story is little different with the great names of print history. He had only forty-nine etchings by Rembrandt, nine engravings by Schongauer and thirty-six engravings by Dürer. He did not own any of Dürer's woodcuts, although he did possess a few by his contemporaries. Thus he had the equestrian portrait of *Emperor Maximilian* by Burgkmair, and *St John Chrysostom* by Cranach. He had a proof set of Holbein's *Dance of Death*, and Altdorfer's *St George*. But that is all. He had no Italian woodcuts, neither the large monochrome prints by Titian and his school, nor any of the chiaroscuro woodcuts by Ugo da Carpi and others working around Raphael and Parmigianino. This was despite his having collected thirty-two extremely fine engravings by Marcantonio, and about ten more by Agostino Veneziano, Bonasone, Caraglio and others of that period. His neglect of woodcuts extended to more modern times. No work by Bewick or his pupils was included in the print collection.

Slade's interests extended into the nineteenth century, and for each school he always included a few of the classic line-engravings of the late eighteenth and nineteenth

4. The display of prints from the Slade bequest in the King's Library of the British Museum in 1869. After an official British Museum photograph. Central Archives

centuries. He had fourteen prints by modern Germans: Schmidt, Müller and others. In the French school he had five prints by Bervic and twelve by Boucher-Desnoyers (cat. 50), to match the five he had by Drevet and four by Edelinck of the earlier generation. By the Italians, Raphael Morghen and his school, who had always been highly regarded, he had no less than sixty-two prints.

When we compare the 2,163 prints in Slade's specimen collection with the thousands of prints that Sloane and Cracherode had possessed, it is at once obvious that we have moved into a very different collecting world. The omnivorousness of one and the depth of the other have been laid aside in favour of obtaining nothing but the best impression of the best prints by the best engravers. As Franks described the collection:

The judgement and care bestowed upon its formation throughout a long series of years is especially evidenced by the purity and brilliancy of the impressions – mere rarity having been, in Mr Slade's estimation, a matter of secondary importance. Carrying out his intention of gathering together a typical series, whilst never missing an opportunity of adding important specimens of the works of the great masters, he did not attempt to form a complete illustration of their works, and one or more specimens of the less important engravers were deemed by him sufficient for the purpose.[19]

Even if Slade was exceptionally fussy, and exceptionally judicious, his type of collecting was typical of his period. If we examine auction catalogues of the 1860s, we can find many other collectors who had a limited number of prints by the same relatively small core of engravers, and which were of as good a quality as the collector's means permitted. Such collections were formed by many of those with whom Slade associated. An immediate parallel can be found in two sales of 1868, of the collections of the late Baron Marochetti and Sir J. S. Hippisley. Marochetti, one of the founders of the Fine Arts Club, was a successful sculptor, who had moved to England from Paris after 1848. The auction catalogue described his collection as 'very extensive and exceedingly choice' and as 'formed with great care and judgement during many years' research'. There were only 673 lots of prints in the sale on 23 March; a few were sold in bundles, but most lots were single prints. His collection therefore was little smaller than Slade's, and had similar strengths in works by Marcantonio, Rembrandt, Schongauer and Dürer. But the quality cannot have been so high: the total fetched was only £2,690. Two months later, on 23 May, followed the sale of Sir John Stuart Hippisley, who had been a fellow-exhibitor at the 1857 Manchester Art Treasures exhibition. His sale had only 357 lots, and, besides a sprinkling of works by the great masters of engraving, had extensive groups of prints by Rembrandt, Dürer, Marcantonio, prints after Reynolds and plates from Turner's *Liber Studiorum*. Hippisley also, unlike Slade or Marochetti,

had some old master and modern drawings. But it was the quality of his Rembrandts, Dürers and Marcantonios, many of which fetched over £100, that established a total of £5,162.

The great growth in this type of collecting seems to lie in the 1820s and 1830s. Lists of the finest works by the best engravers go back a long way in the literature of print collecting, but recommendations that a collection need only contain these works seem to be a new phenomenon. Some of the earliest books to take this approach are Italian. Giuseppe Longhi's *La Calcografia*, published in Milan in 1830, contains a section with advice to collectors, together with a list of the prints that would constitute an ideal collection. Another handbook of this type is Giulio Ferrario's *Le Classiche Stampe*, published in Milan in 1836. Its intention is given by its full title: 'The classic prints from the beginning of printmaking to the present, including living artists, described and adorned with historical and critical observations on the merit, the subject, on the quality of impression, on the size and on the prices of each one, selected and proposed as a delightful and instructive ornament of a collection by Giulio Ferrario'. Most of the book contains a dictionary of engravers, for each of whom is given their 'best' prints, together with notes on states, and prices reached at auction.

The earliest book to take such an approach in Britain is Joseph Maberly's treatise of 1844: *The Print Collector, an introduction to the knowledge necessary for forming a collection of ancient prints, containing suggestions as to the mode of commencing collector, the selection of specimens, the prices and care of prints*. His seventh chapter recommends just such a selective approach, and works through each school in turn, noting the best engravers. The Italian school, for example, is given seven pages, at the end of which 'it will be seen that we have not encumbered our young collector with above thirty names; yet no one artist of much importance is omitted'. Other chapters explained that collecting had a sound economical justification, as the prices for fine prints always went up. Maberly followed his own counsel in forming his own select collection, which was sold on 26 May 1851. William Smith, who somehow knew what Maberly had paid for each print, noted with suppressed pain or pleasure that on a total the sale realised of £3,799 Maberly had lost £304.[20]

Slade himself, as a man of the second quarter of the nineteenth century, belonged to this type of collector. The generation of collectors that followed him in the third quarter of the century was even more selective in forming their collections. Such choice cabinets as those of Brodhurst, Griffiths and St John Dent, which were all sold in the 1880s, contained only a few hundred prints. They still followed the traditional hierarchy in which engraving occupied the premier position, followed closely by etching, and with the woodcut coming at the bottom. None of these collections ever contained a lithograph, even though the medium had been flourishing for half a century, and had already produced many of what are now regarded as its masterpieces.

It would be desirable to find out when precisely Slade's collection was formed, but as yet there is too little evidence. The earliest date for an acquisition yet found is 1817, when he put his initials and the place of acquisition 'Roma' on a small booklet of etchings by Callot.[21] There is then a gap in the evidence. Slade never, until the very end of his life, seems to have bought in auctions under his own name, and prints he owned from specific collections (some, for example, from Maberly's or Brooke's collection)[22] may have been bought from dealers long after the sales of those collections. All that can be said for certain is that in December 1849 he gave a fine Hogarth engraving to the British Museum. In January 1850 he gave a set of proofs of Turner's *England and Wales* series, and in March 1852 followed this with the gift of some of Bartolozzi's engravings of the Marlborough gems. These were the only gifts he made to the Department in his lifetime. The next landmark is the 1857 Manchester exhibition; Slade lent so much to this that his collection was evidently very firmly established by then. The first occasion that I can find his name listed among the purchasers is at the Price and Goddard sales in 1867, the year before he died. So when did he decide to form a specimen collection? My own guess – and it is a pure guess – is after 1835, the year in which his father Robert died, and he inherited his position and fortune.

We must at this point return to Slade's 'second' print collection, those for illustration. In his preface to the catalogue of glass in 1871 Franks recorded that Slade's interest in artistic pursuits began at a young age, and developed with time. 'His interest was, in the first instance, directed to engravings and books relating to the Fine Arts, and he made a valuable series of illustrations for the works of Shakespeare, Byron and Dibdin. More recently he turned his attention to choice editions of books and ancient book bindings, as well as to Venetian glass.'

This 'series of illustrations' is to be found in the remaining 6,690 items in Slade's collection. They present a rather surprising aspect to anyone reading the inventory. A few sections are indeed subject series: there are groups of British and foreign portraits, historical prints and topography, as well as some satirical prints, but these do not exceed a thousand prints in all. The rest are all complete sets of plates taken from the many illustrated books published in London in the 1820s and 1830s. This is a semi-forgotten episode in the history of the British print, but one that at the period bulked very large in book and print publication. Typically the books were put together by the publisher. He would choose the title, commission an artist to make the drawings, find the team of engravers to engrave them, and select the printer and binder. The resulting books were not cheap, and were usually purchased as gifts. For this reason elegance of presentation was essential. They were usually

octavo in size, and so the plates were small. Frequently the area of the design was set within very wide empty margins, so that when the plates were bound into the book, the unsightly platemarks were cut away by the binder's knife, and the image floated in a sea of unblemished white paper.

The publishers usually chose for such treatment classic authors, such as Boccaccio, Defoe and Cervantes, and famous collections of essays, such as *The Spectator* or *The Tatler*. Sometimes there were anthologies, such as *British Poets*, and sometimes periodicals such as *The Novelist's Magazine* or *The Universal Magazine*. Since the decoration was the essential element in selling these books, no expense was spared in the choice of artist and engraver. Some excellent artists of the period, such as Thomas Stothard and Robert Smirke, did almost all their work in this field. Likewise there was an entire generation of specialist engravers, whose names were forgotten as this type of book fell out of fashion. They worked on a very small scale, usually on copper plates, but sometimes in later years on steel. In their day they were greatly admired, and collectors such as Slade not only purchased the books, but made a point of purchasing sets of proofs of their plates before they had been bound. This meant not only that they had the best impressions, but that they had them with complete platemarks before they had been cut by the binder.

Slade possessed thousands of prints of this type, and a letter that happens to have survived in the Department shows the care that he took in assembling them. He had purchased through Bohn a set of proofs of Finden's Byron and Bible illustrations. Slade had shown them to someone from the firm of Hodgson and Graves, who had pronounced them to be 'sham engravers' proofs', upon which he had at once returned them. The surviving letter is from Finden, indignantly sending 'the most positive and unequivocal denial' and explaining the source of the confusion.[23] Such a concern with contemporary engraving links Slade with John Sheepshanks (see p. 73). Although Slade does not seem to be mentioned in texts of the period as a *patron* of British engraving, his close interest in the subject has to be considered as a form of patronage.

Seen as they are housed today, as bundles of sheets in wrappers kept mostly under the name of the engraver, these prints appear as a natural part of a history of British engraving. And included among them are some prints that still form part of the standard accounts of the period, as for example a set of William Blake's illustrations to *Job*, and sets of J. M. W. Turner's *England and Wales* series.[24] But the evidence that Slade intended these prints to serve for extra-illustrating texts is unimpeachable. Besides Franks's obituary notice and the letter dated 23 July 1868 quoted above, there is interesting testimony in Slade's letter to Bliss of 15 February 1857, from which several extracts have already been quoted. The occasion of the letter was to thank Bliss for the gift of his newly published edition of extracts from the diary of the eighteenth-century antiquarian Thomas Hearne, *Reliquiae Hernianae.*

I am quite content with the book ... and certainly will in due course envelope it in a worthy mantle. I consider it capital for illustration, and although I have already too many such things on my hands, some of them deserted, to enter deeply into this, I had already made up my mind to insert some portraits which will I hope become it, and have a promise of Graves,[25] who is about to read it through, that he will make some notes to assist me.

This introduces a type of print collecting that has not so far been mentioned in these pages, but which was of great significance throughout the second half of the eighteenth and the entire nineteenth century.[26] It is often associated with the name of the Rev. James Granger, whose *Biographical History of England ... adapted to a methodical catalogue of engraved British heads* was first published in 1769. This for the first time associated a catalogue of known British portrait prints with short biographies of the sitters. It was an instant success, both on account of the quality of the catalogue and the excellence of the biographies. Owners and collectors at once began to bind up their prints and Granger's text into a single volume, and the verb 'to Grangerise' was later applied to extra-illustrated copies not only of this book but of any other text that lent itself to extra-illustration.[27] Favourite candidates were Pennant's *Survey of London*, Hume's *History of England* and Clarendon's *History of the Great Rebellion.*[28]

The origins of the fashion are still not clearly established, but they go back at least to the 1720s. In 1728 the London print publisher John Bowles included in his catalogue ten prints of the reign of Charles I, which could be framed or would 'serve to be bound up in my Lord Clarendon's folio history'. References to extra-illustrating seem to be rare through the first half of the century, but in its last three decades the practice became immensely fashionable, apparently very quickly. Quite why this happened is unclear. But one significant factor must have been the polarisation of mainstream print collecting. As collectors such as Cracherode concentrated more on prints as works of art and records of the development of the history of art, the many prints that had traditionally been collected for their subject-matter dropped out of sight. They were left to collectors outside the mainstream, who did not have print rooms and portfolios. It was probably these persons who seized on the idea of extra-illustrating books as both a good way to store their prints, and as an excellent method of giving some arrangement to material that in many cases might have lacked any organising principle.

Once the practice had become well-established, and indeed a tradition had come into existence, it generated its own momentum, and became an art form in its own right. Collectors began to sell completed volumes in order to raise the capital to start all over again. So it can easily be understood how a portfolio print collector and a bibliophile such as Slade might also have wished to extend his efforts into the extra-illustration of books. He certainly saw this part of his collection as separate from his 'specimen series', and the executors' letter of 23 July actually states that a portion of the illustrations was not at Walcot Place on Slade's death.

The catalogue of Slade's book sale includes only one extra-illustrated book, a copy of Thomas Frognal Dibdin's *Bibliographical Decameron*, lot 262, 'with 160 additional portraits and views'. This seems to have been the only time he actually got round to arranging and binding any of the prints he had bought for this purpose. This must have been the fate of many collections made with extra-illustration in mind. The moment that the prints were bound the collection was finished: nothing extra could be added without taking the binding apart. Doubtless the perfectionist Slade could never bring himself to say that he had acquired all that he might find to illustrate any title. Perhaps too, as time passed he found himself more and more interested in his glass, and so had less energy to devote to his prints, which Franks in his obituary states were the enthusiasm of his first years as a collector.

Nevertheless this argument cannot be taken too far. One of his closest friends was Sir Charles Rugge Price, whose collection was sold posthumously on 21 February 1867. The memory of this sale has survived because lot 395, Rembrandt's *Hundred Guilder* print, advertised as the finest known impression of the first state, fetched a world record price of 1,180 guineas, and remained a record for a print until 1883 when Dutuit paid £1,510 for Rembrandt's *Arnold Tholinx* at the Griffiths sale (see cat. 71).[29] Slade bought at the Price sale in his own name, something that he had done very rarely before, and so we know that he acquired eight lots for £34.8.0. Apart from one Hogarth (*The Distressed Poet*, 'first state with Pope assaulting Curll, brilliant impression with large margins' for 5 guineas: see cat. 48), all the lots were sets of illustrations for books. Thus, for example, he bought a set of proofs before letters by John Scott after Reinagle of illustrations to *The Sportsman's Cabinet*, 'very rare', for 7 guineas. Perhaps they were of sentimental value, as coming from an old friend who evidently shared his taste for 1820s and 1830s British book illustration. But the purchase certainly proves that this was not a part of his collection that Slade had rejected at the end of his life.[30]

The research into the British Museum archives and in the Probate Registry, Somerset House, that has been used in this essay was carried out by Stephen Coppel. Aileen Dawson kindly allowed me to consult the file on Slade held in the Department of Medieval and Later Antiquities, and read the text of a lecture she has given on Slade's glass.

1. Both Twopeny (1797–1873) and Henderson (1797–1878) left bequests to the British Museum. See Antony Griffiths and Reginald Williams, *The Department of Prints and Drawings in the British Museum, User's Guide*, London 1987, pp. 122 and 178. In 1886 the Director informed the Trustees that Henderson, like Slade, was one of the donors whose bequests were attributable almost entirely to their friendship with Franks (see E. Miller, *That Noble Cabinet*, London 1973, p. 314).

2. Richard Fisher (1809–90) was himself a serious collector of prints. In 1879 he published a catalogue of his collection, which was sold after his death in 1892 for a total of £8,088 (see Lugt 2204). Fisher was closely associated for many years with the British Museum, and the letter books preserve many letters from him to Reid. In 1881 Reid asked him to publish a catalogue of the Museum's early Italian engravings, but their collaboration ended in a furious row and very bad feeling (see Introduction p. 13).

3. See David M. Wilson, *The Forgotten Collector, Augustus Wollaston Franks of the British Museum*, London 1984.

4. One remarkable example of dismembering was Horace Walpole's historic two volumes containing 117 engraved portraits of British artists. These were sold at the 1848 Strawberry Hill sale, and purchased by the British Museum four years later (1852-2-14-265 to 381). They were then taken apart and the prints distributed among the wrappers of loose portraits. Fortunately Walpole's label was kept and bound (for some strange reason) in the volume of correspondence for 1802–47. It was only when the label was noticed in 1994 that the provenance of the prints was realised.

5. This privately printed and rare book is titled *Catalogue of the Collection of Glass Formed by Felix Slade, Esq. FSA, with Notes on the History of Glass Contributed by Alexander Nesbitt FSA*, London 1871. The catalogue was first written by W. Chaffers, then rewritten by W. A. Nicholls, and finally revised by A. W. Franks. An appendix contains an account of Slade's other gifts and bequests to the British Museum. The best recent account of Slade is the introduction to *Felix Slade, collector and benefactor*, being an eight-page pamphlet to the centenary exhibition held at the British Museum in 1968.

6. See BL.Add.Ms.27937.

7. This can be deduced from Add.Ms.34580 f. 540.

8. M. Digby Wyatt, *Fine Art, a Sketch of its History, Theory, Practice ... being a course of lectures delivered at Cambridge in 1870*, London 1870, p. 4.

9. Registered as G&R 1866.8-6.1, and no. 867 in H. B. Walters, *Catalogue of the Bronzes, Greek, Roman and Etruscan in the ... British Museum*, London 1899. Slade bought it at the sale of the collection of Henry Farrer, FSA, at Christie's on 12 June 1866. I thank Donald Bailey for his help in identification.

10. George Stewart Nicholson must have died late in 1857, as his collection was sold at Christie's on 19 February 1858. The sale contained forty lots of china and seventy-nine lots of German and Venetian glass.

11. G. F. Waagen, *Galleries and Cabinets of Art of Great Britain*, London 1857, p. 218. No photographs of the interior of Slade's house have been found. But some idea of its richness can be deduced from the catalogue of the sale of his household effects at Christie's on 30 April 1869, lots 157–85.

12. BL.Add.Ms.34580 f. 576.

13. BL.Add.Ms.34580 f. 540.

14. The Soulages collection was eventually purchased for South Kensington, after extraordinary manoeuvrings, briefly described by Anna Somers Cocks, *The Victoria and Albert Museum, the Making of the Collection*, London 1980, pp. 4–7.

15. The wording of the will seems to have posed a problem that is glossed over in the official documents. Strictly the executors could only select volumes of prints and manuscripts in fine bindings; but they extended their brief so far as to add twenty-two printed books in ancient bindings and one detached cover. Thomas Watts, the Keeper of Printed Books, certainly wanted many more. On 8 July 1868 he asked permission from the Trustees to spend up to £2,000 at the forthcoming auctions of the libraries of Slade and the Rev. Thomas Corser. Eight books were purchased at the Slade sale.

16. The letter continues to ask that Reid should weed out and return to them such duplicates, and this was done.

17. Edward Homes's introduction to the printed catalogue of the 1857 Manchester exhibition stated: 'This is the first time in the history of the art of engraving at which an attempt has been made to shew to the public generally at one view a complete chronological series of prints from the commencement of the art up to the present time [the catalogue in fact contains no less than 1,475 numbers lent by 29 individuals]. Fine specimens of various epochs are from time to time shown in glazed frames at the French Museum, and the officers in charge of the print department at the British Museum have long desired to adopt some such course, but the requisite facilities not being at their disposal, such a display has not as yet been accomplished there. We feel therefore that, independently of the excessive rarity and excellence of the engravings themselves, these galleries will be viewed with the utmost interest.' The first display in the British Museum, perhaps not coincidentally, took place the following year.

18. One of Slade's mounts still survives, and suggests that he hinged his prints to a thick card; the provenance and price paid were written underneath the print. Unfortunately all this information has been lost in remounting.

19. *Catalogue of the Collection of Glass ...* op. cit. n. 5, p. 177. A similar encomium is found in *The Art Journal*, VII 1868, pp. 217–18.

20. This information is given in Smith's marked copy of the catalogue in the Department's library (Sc A 3 11).

21. *Les Fantaisies* (161 a.20).

22. Almost all Slade's prints have long been laid down on mounts and so any collectors' marks on their versos cannot be seen. So the only evidence for earlier provenances is in *A Catalogue of the Antiquities and Works of Art Exhibited at Ironmonger's Hall in the Month of May 1861 ...*, published in parts, with a title-page dated 1869. Slade lent eighteen prints, and the catalogue gives the provenance for seven of them.

23. The problem was caused by some masked or uninked lettering underneath the plates, which Hodgson & Graves had thought were ordinary lettered impressions being passed off as proofs before letters. Finden's reply is of sufficient general interest to be worth publishing in full: 'An explanation of the stop'd out writing which appears in some of the proofs. It is necessary to inform you that the work was a monthly publication, and from the great sale of it (in order to insure punctuality) it was frequently found requisite from the short time we had to engrave them to have the *writing* put into some of them *immediately* after the etching, or whenever the plate could be spared for that purpose. So that when the plate was finished the writing so put in was oblig'd to be stop'd out for the sake of uniformity. They are however *the earliest proofs taken from the plates*, were never *intended* for sale, and have been in my possession ever since they were taken, until I parted with them to Mr Bohn. I should hold myself disgraced as an artist and a gentleman to have attempted a deception.' He cites the

printer, McQueen, as able to give confirmation. The letter is bound with other memoranda in a volume in the Department library (Pp 6.40).

24. Slade also possessed another copy of these prints in a spectacular binding by F. Bedford that had won a medal in the 1855 Paris exhibition, where it had been purchased by King Louis-Philippe. This was sold as lot 1134 with his books.

25. This must be the well-known printseller Henry Graves. Finding suitable prints for extra-illustrators was evidently a large part of a print dealer's business. William Smith's manuscripts in the Victoria and Albert Museum include several volumes with lists of portrait prints arranged according to the county in which the sitter lived. These can only have been of use to extra-illustrators of county histories.

26. The best available account of Grangerising is by Marcia Pointon, *Hanging the Head*, New Haven & London 1993, pp. 53–78.

27. The earliest citations for the verb given by the *Oxford English Dictionary* come from the 1880s. It would be interesting to find earlier ones.

28. Some excellent examples of such works are in the Department. J. C. Crowle bequeathed his famous Pennant in 1811, and the Duke of Gloucester his Clarendon in 1834.

29. This was a freak price. The buyer was Charles J. Palmer of Bedford Row, who was then a dying man, and was determined to possess this print, come what may; the underbidder was the French collector Dutuit, who had left an open bid with his agent. Price died later in 1867, and the print reappeared in his sale on 18 May 1868, when it was finally bought for Dutuit for £1,100. It is now with the rest of his collection in the Musée du Petit Palais in Paris (see Lugt 2946). A report in *The Times* for 25 February 1867 stated that the previous highest price for a print was 300 guineas given for Raphael Morghen's engraving of *The Last Supper* after Leonardo at Sotheby's 'about 10 years since'. This was corrected in a letter the following day from Henry Ottley, the son of W. Y. Ottley. He stated that an impression of the *Hundred Guilder* print had fetched £400 ten or twelve years before, and that Holford had paid £600 for Rembrandt's *Sabre Portrait*. An impression of the Finiguerra pax had cost its present possessor £400. He concluded his letter by stating that sixty years before £40 had been considered the maximum that any print might fetch.

30. On 4 March 1867 Slade was again in the rooms, buying in his own name five lots at the sale of the collection of the Rev. Edward Goddard at Sotheby's. He got a set of Cuyp's etchings of cows very cheaply for one shilling, but the Marcantonios and Agostino Venezianos in the other four lots cost him dear, no less than £55.5.0 in all.

41 Domenico Campagnola (1500–64)
Shepherd and Warrior, 1517

Engraving. 134 × 96 mm
Hind 9

Domenico was an adopted son of Giulio Campagnola. As a printmaker he is known from thirteen engravings, all of which are dated 1517 or 1518 and which were therefore done when he was still a teenager. He also designed (and probably cut) a small number of woodcuts. In later years he seems to have confined his activity to painting. This engraving, with its mysterious subject, shows him at his closest to the spirit of Giorgione. It is exactly the same size as another print of the same year, *Venus Reclining in a Landscape*, and Hind very plausibly suggested that the two were made on either side of a single copper plate.

This impression bears the collector's mark of Edmé Durand (L.741), a French diplomat of the Restoration years, who formed his collection before 1821. In that year he sold most of it at auction in Paris, and turned to collecting Greek vases instead. This collection was sold at auction in 1836, the year after he died, and the Louvre and the British Museum were among the largest purchasers. His remaining prints, mostly ones that had failed to sell in 1821, were sold in 1836.

1868-8-22-19. Slade collection

42 Marcantonio Raimondi (*c*.1480–before 1534)
The Virgin and Child with St Elizabeth and St John Baptist (known as '*The Virgin with the Palm Tree*'), *c*.1520/5

Engraving. 247 × 173 mm
Bartsch XIV 69.62

This is a fine impression of one of the group of engravings that Marcantonio made after designs supplied to him by Raphael or members of his studio. Like all the great engravings by Marcantonio, it remained among the most desirable of all prints to collectors from the sixteenth century right until the beginning of the twentieth. When Slade bequeathed it, the British Museum already possessed another equally fine impression, and in slightly better condition, from the Lely and Cracherode collections.

This was one of three engravings by Marcantonio among the eighteen prints that Slade selected in 1861 to exhibit at Ironmongers' Hall in London. The impression bears the stamp of the famous French collector and print scholar Robert-Dumesnil (L.2199), and was sold by him in London on 14 May 1838, lot 303, to the French dealer Pieri-Benard for £16.16.0. He took it back to France, and

41

sold it to the tailor François Debois, who formed a remark-able collection in a few years (see L.985) but had to sell after falling into financial difficulties. It reappeared with the rest of his superb group of Marcantonios (many of which had come from Denon) in his second sale in Paris on 26 November 1844, lot 515, where it was bought by William Smith for 800 f. (about £32). From Smith it went to Joseph Maberly for £42, and at his sale on 26 May 1851, lot 422, it was bought by the dealer Graves for £45 ('superb impression, very rare'). Graves must have sold it to Slade, but whether he was buying on commission is not known.

1868–8–22–32. Slade collection

43 Lucas van Leyden (*c.* 1489/94–1533)
Christ Being Presented to the People, 1510

Engraving. 285 × 451 mm
Bartsch VII 378.71

With Marcantonio and Dürer, Lucas forms the third of the three artists who dominated printmaking at the beginning of the sixteenth century. His plates seem to have worn quickly, for fine impressions of his prints have always been rare and sought after. This is one of the masterpieces of Lucas's early maturity, made when he was apparently only sixteen years old. In his catalogue Bartsch noted that 'it was sold for very high prices during the artist's lifetime, and since then the price has climbed enormously, espe-cially in Holland'. This impression was described in the appendix to the 1871 Slade glass catalogue as an 'excep-tionally bright and brilliant proof'. Its entry in the cata-logue of the 1861 Fishmongers' Hall exhibition reads: 'From the delicacy of his work, fine impressions of his

42

43

plates are excessively rare. This print was formerly in the possession of Mr Brooke and Prince Tufialkin and was on the point of leaving this country for a German court when it was secured by the exhibitor.'

This provenance is more interesting than at first glance appears. The Tufialkin sale was in Paris on 3 May 1845, lot 243, when it seems to have been sold to William Smith, who formed H. J. Brooke's collection (see p. 100), for 700 f. (£28). The remainder of Brooke's prints were sold on 23 May 1853, where it was described as 'a most superb impression, undoubtedly the finest known, of the greatest rarity' and was sold as lot 458 to Weber for £77. It was then that Slade bought it, saving it from export in the same way as he had purchased the Sword of Tiberius (see p. 115). But four years earlier, in 1849, Brooke had, through Smith, offered as a gift to the British Museum the choice of his Lucas collection, most of which had come via Vivant Denon and Antonio Maria Zanetti from the collection of Jan Pietersz. Zomer (1641–1724). Why this print was excluded from the gift is unclear, unless Brooke thought that the impression already in the Museum was not greatly inferior.

1868–8–22–603. Slade collection

44 Jean Duvet (*c.*1485–before 1570)
The Apocalypse, Chapters 4 and 5, 1555

Engraving. 300 × 215 mm (arched)
Robert-Dumesnil V 17.29

Duvet was a goldsmith by training, and held an appointment as royal goldsmith to two kings of France, François I and Henri II. He worked in Langres, and, apart from a number of single prints, produced two great series: six plates on the story of the unicorn, and a set of twenty-three illustrations to the *Apocalypse*, of which this is the third. Like all Duvet's prints, the dense composition, with no space left empty, makes for difficult reading. Besides this impression, the Department has a complete set of the *Apocalypse*, purchased in 1842 with the Harding collection.

In the history of French printmaking, Duvet plays the role of the great outsider. A surprisingly close parallel is William Blake, whose set of engravings to *Job* is an equally original departure from the conventions of his period. It is curious that Slade, who owned this single sheet by Duvet in his specimen group of French engravings, also owned a complete set of proofs of Blake's *Job*.

1868–8–22–1077. Slade collection

45

46

45 Anthony (Anthonie) van Dyck (1599–1641)

Self-Portrait, late 1620s

Etching. 236 × 158 mm

Mauquoy-Hendrickx 4, first state

This is one of the first plates from the series of portraits of distinguished contemporaries that van Dyck began soon after his return from Italy in 1627 and which was still incomplete at his death. The first collected edition was published by Gillis Hendricx in Antwerp in 1645, and it has always been known since as the *Iconography*. Eighteen plates were begun as etchings by van Dyck himself, and were later completed with the burin by others. These early etched states are rare, and have always been greatly sought after as one of the high points of the art of etching, and W. H. Carpenter published a catalogue of them in his *Pictorial Notices ... of Sir Anthony van Dyck* in 1844.

Twenty-one impressions of the first state of this *Self-Portrait* are recorded, before it was reworked by Jacques Neeffs to form the frontispiece of the series. Slade owned a total of seven early impressions, as well as two other unrelated etchings by van Dyck.

1868-8-22-806. Slade collection

46 Cornelis Visscher (1628/9–58)

The Large Cat, c.1657

Engraving. 139 × 184 mm

Hollstein 42, first state

Together with an etching by Hollar, this is the most famous of all prints of cats. Visscher himself was one of the rare professional engravers in seventeenth-century Holland, and made nearly 200 prints after his own designs or those of others during his short career. His original drawing for this print dated 1657 was sold in 1883 but has since been lost. Visscher's work was avidly collected in his own life-time, and remained popular right through the nineteenth century. William Smith sold a virtually complete collection to the British Museum in 1839; the 270 prints cost £300. Later in 1864 Smith wrote a *catalogue raisonné* of Visscher's work, the only thing he ever published. Visscher has now dropped completely out of fashion, and this print, on account of its subject, is one of the few still remembered. Slade's impression, one of seven Visschers he owned, is of the first state, before C. J. Visscher's address was added in the lower centre margin. The impudent mouse approaching from the safety of the bars in the background adds a touch of humour to the scene.

1868–8–22–881. Slade collection

47 Pierre-Imbert Drevet (1697–1739)

Bishop Jacques-Bénigne Bossuet, 1723

Engraving. 509 × 347 mm

Firmin-Didot 12, second state

From the middle of the seventeenth century, French engravers had a pre-eminent international reputation for their portraits. If mezzotint portraits were the British speciality, line-engraved portraits were the French. Pierre-Imbert was the greatest of three members of the Drevet family that specialised in this medium, and this engraving after a painting by Hyacinthe Rigaud has always been regarded as his masterpiece. His complete oeuvre was only thirty-three plates, in a career that abruptly finished in 1726 when he became mad. Writers have often assumed that it was the time and labour of engraving plates such as this that drove him out of his senses. Critics admired above all the way in which he captured the colour and textures of a wide range of materials and surfaces, as well as the vigour of the sitter's expression. Slade's impression is of the second state, which Firmin-Didot, writing in 1876, described as 'very rare' and priced at between 500 and 1000 f. (£20 to £40). It is not known where Slade acquired it.

1868–8–22–960. Slade collection

48 William Hogarth (1697–1764)

The Distressed Poet, 1737

Engraving. 357 × 406 mm

Paulson 145, second state (in fact first state)

Hogarth made his enormous reputation from the many prints that he engraved and published after paintings or drawings that he had made himself. Their blend of morality and topicality was something quite fresh in the history of printmaking. In this print the poet is a figure of fun, writing his poem titled *Poverty*, while his wife works to pay the milkmaid at the door. The caption is taken from Alexander Pope's *Dunciad* of 1729, and the picture hung in the window embrasure shows Pope thrashing the bookseller Edmund Curll, who had published pirate editions of his works. Later, when the reference to Curll was less topical, Hogarth changed this picture, and altered the poem's title to *Riches, a poem*.

Hogarth's prints were bought by an unusually wide public. Not only did the general public buy them to frame, but serious print collectors added them to their portfolios. This tradition lasted to Slade's day, and he owned 162 of his prints – almost the complete work – in excellent impressions. This one came from the sale of the collection of his close friend Sir Charles Rugge Price, at Sotheby's on 21 February 1867, lot 391, when it cost Slade £5.

1868–8–22–1541. Slade collection

49 William Woollett (1735–85) after Richard Wright (c.1720–c.1775)

The Fishery, 1768

Engraving. 435 × 550 mm

Fagan 61, fourth state

Woollett was the first English line-engraver to establish an international reputation, admired as much in France and Germany as in his home country. Most of the 123 plates he made were after landscape or historical paintings by his contemporaries, such as the little-known Liverpool artist Richard Wright, and in this way he was responsible for carrying their reputation abroad. His work used to be an essential element of every important cabinet, and the extraordinary collection of his prints in the British Museum is the outcome of putting together the treasures of many collectors.

In the case of this print, the Museum has impressions of all five states that precede the ordinary final published state. The first etched state came from Cracherode in 1799. The second state came with the Harding collection in 1842. The third, which is extensively overdrawn by Woollett himself, was purchased by G. W. Reid at the sale on 18 May 1868 of the collection of C. J. Palmer, whose Woollett collection was advertised as 'the most important that has ever been formed'; of the 197 lots, Colnaghi bought on behalf of the Museum no less than 89. The fourth state came from Slade, while the fifth was purchased from William Smith in 1842.

1868–8–22–1795. Slade collection

47

Studious he sate, with all his books around, ⟩⟩⟩⟩⟩⟩— | *Plung'd for his sense, but found no bottom there ;* ⟩⟩⟩⟩
Sinking from thought to thought, a vast profund : ⟩— | *Then writ, and flounder'd on, in mere dispair.* ⟩⟩⟩⟩

DUNCIAD. Book I. *line* III.

48

49

50 Auguste Boucher-Desnoyers (1779–1857) after François Gérard (1770–1837)

Napoleon as Emperor, 1808

Engraving. 687 × 513 mm

Boucher-Desnoyers was the outstanding French line-engraver of the first half of the nineteenth century. He first came to notice at the Salon of 1799, and in 1804 Napoleon personally chose him to engrave Gérard's portrait of himself as Emperor of France, a position to which he had appointed himself that year. The print took four years to complete, and was issued in three states. Slade's impression is a magnificent proof before the addition of the names of the artists.

The print and painting were modelled on a famous portrait of Louis XVI that had been painted by Callet and engraved by Bervic. Such imitation was deliberate as Napoleon tried to show himself as the legitimate successor to the Bourbons. At their Restoration in 1814, they did not hold this against Desnoyers, who was made a baron in 1828.

1868-8-22-943. Slade collection

NAPOLEON LE GRAND

50

6. William Second Baron Cheylesmore (1843–1902) and the Taste for Mezzotints

Sheila O'Connell

On 12 July 1902 Sidney Colvin, Keeper of the Department of Prints and Drawings, asked the Trustees of the British Museum for permission to exchange a group of duplicate prints with the dealer Colnaghi. The duplicates he wished to dispose of were a self-portrait etching by Rembrandt and eight mezzotints after portraits by Joshua Reynolds. The total value was £576.15.0. In exchange Colnaghi was to give an engraving by Maso Finiguerra, valued at £175, ten Italian old master drawings, a seventeenth-century English pastel portrait then attributed to Peter Lely, and an album of forty portrait drawings on vellum by Jonathan Richardson. Among the old master drawings was a self-portrait by Carlo Maratti, then valued at £7.10.0, which has been recently assessed for insurance purposes at £130,000, and a portrait of a man then thought to be by Andrea Solario and worth £60 which has since been attributed to Lorenzo Lotto and is valued at £600,000. None of the mezzotints given in exchange would fetch more than two or three hundred pounds today. This exchange provides a very clear demonstration of a revolution in taste over the period. While the value of Italian old master drawings has become enormously inflated, mezzotints – so eagerly sought after by collectors in the eighteenth and nineteenth centuries – are almost forgotten.

Mezzotint developed as a response to the seventeenth-century taste for striking contrasts of light and shade. The essentially linear techniques then available to printmakers were not best suited to working in broad areas of tone. The great innovation of the mezzotint was in avoiding line and allowing the printmaker to work in a much more painterly manner. This was achieved by reversing the normal convention, and working instead from dark to light: the copper plate is roughened uniformly ('grounded') – so that if inked it would print black – and the image is then created by scraping and burnishing areas that will print lighter.

The new technique emerged in the 1640s and 1650s, not from professional printmaking circles but from the experiments of two sophisticated amateurs: Ludwig von Siegen (1609–after 1676), an officer in the service of William of Hesse, and Prince Rupert (1619–82), the Bohemian nephew of King Charles I of England and commander-in-chief of the Royalist forces in the English Civil War. Siegen's prints are chiefly portraits, but Rupert's also include such striking images as *The Standard-Bearer* (see cat. 52) and *The Great Executioner* (after a painting then attributed to José de Ribera). Their interest in printmaking was not as surprising as it might seem today: etching, like drawing, was seen as a proper pursuit for a gentleman and there were many amateur printmakers. The initial concept of mezzotint was Siegen's but it seems to have been Rupert who perfected a fine-toothed tool (the 'rocker') that could be relied upon to produce an even ground. This problem-solving exercise would have appealed to Rupert's experimental turn of mind; among his other inventions were an alloy of copper and zinc, called 'Prince's metal', a type of gunpowder of ten times the normal strength, a prototype revolver, and a new method of boring cannon.[1]

In 1660 Rupert returned to England with the restoration of the monarchy and introduced the new technique to a group of like-minded amateurs, mostly members of the Royal Society.[2] Meanwhile his assistant, Wallerant Vaillant (1623–77; see cat. 53), set up in business in Amsterdam and by the end of the 1660s a market in mezzotints was flourishing in Germany, Holland and France. In England, however, commercial exploitation of the technique did not begin until the 1670s when Peter Lely (1618–80) – recognising that the new technique was particularly suited to reproducing the satiny surfaces of his fashionable court portraits – encouraged a number of Dutch mezzotinters to make prints after his work (see cat. 54). British printmakers soon followed their Dutch counterparts into what became an important market.[3]

Evidence of specialised collecting of mezzotints in the late seventeenth century appears in three albums which remained in the library of the Brownlow family at Belton, Lincolnshire, until 1984. One of these, now in the National Portrait Gallery, is lettered on the spine 'Brown collec. of Sr Antony van Dyc & Sr Peter Lelys' and contains excellent impressions of all the mezzotints known to have been published by Alexander Browne (c.1640–1706).[4] The prints, chiefly portraits – including one of Elizabeth Brownlow as a child by John Smith (1652–1743; see cat. 55) – were probably bought as a set by Sir John Brownlow who died in 1697. The other two albums contained more than a hundred fine impressions of mezzotints by Vaillant and other early Dutch mezzotinters, perhaps also collected by Sir John Brownlow, together with a similar quantity of British mezzotints of the first half of the eighteenth century, which would have been acquired by his nephew and heir, also Sir John Brownlow, later Viscount Tyrconnel (1691–1757).[5]

It was John Smith who was responsible for putting mezzotints firmly on the international map.[6] Three factors led to his success: he managed to achieve a virtual monopoly of mezzotints after Godfrey Kneller, the most promi-nent portrait painter of the decades after Lely; he published his own prints and so retained control over the quality of impressions;[7] and he sold his work in complete sets, an astute marketing strategy which helped his prints to find an important place in the major collections of the day. John, Lord Somers (1651–1716), Lord Chancellor, was said to be so fond of Smith's prints that he seldom travelled without them in the seat of his coach;[8] Somers's collection of mezzotints by Smith appeared in a sale in Paris in 1759[9] and included many proofs before letter with the mezzotinter's initials.[10]

Smith's prints also appeared in the great continental print collections, usually as a separate volume, or group of volumes, and often as part of a minority of select foreign prints. Thus the collection of Louis II de Rochechouart, Duc de Mortemart (1681–1746), which consisted of forty-two volumes, predominantly of French prints and with some by the great Dutch and Flemish masters, included a portfolio of 350 mezzotints by John Smith.[11] Among other collections assembled on the Continent which contained large groups of mezzotints by Smith were those of Prince Eugene of Savoy (now in the Albertina, Vienna), Consul Joseph Smith (c.1672–1770)[12] and Pierre-Jean Mariette (1694–1774), the last of the great print-dealing dynasty responsible for putting together many of the finest collec-tions. The sale of Mariette's enormous collection in 1775 included a group of 160 superb proofs of John Smith's mezzotints.

The second wave of concern with mezzotints in the mid-eighteenth century coincided with the fashion for large-scale collecting of portrait prints (see p. 49) and the tastes remained inextricably linked. This relationship with por-traiture was reinforced by the connection with the rise of British portrait painting. Like Lely and Kneller, the gener-ation of painters led by Joshua Reynolds (1723–92) knew that reproductive prints could play a vital role in promot-ing their work, and that the painterly chiaroscuro of mezzotint would serve their ambitions better than any other printmaking medium. A group of talented Irish mezzotinters, most notably James McArdell (see fig. 1), settled in London in the 1740s and dominated the market for the next twenty or so years.[13] They were followed in the 1770s by a younger group of mezzotinters – still concen-trating on prints after Reynolds – who took the portrait print to unforeseen heights: the mezzotints of Valentine Green (see fig. 2) or John Raphael Smith (see cat. 58) are often seen as the epitome of the technique. As the size of paintings increased and portraiture took on some of the pretensions of history painting, mezzotints became notice-ably larger – fitting better into a frame on the wall than into a connoisseur's, or portrait-hunter's, album.[14]

Mezzotinters shared the new status of the artist, marked by the foundation of the Royal Academy in 1769: in the 1770s Green held the office of Mezzotint Engraver to King

George III, and in 1800 his pupil John Young held the same office for the Prince of Wales. The effectiveness of mezzotints in reproducing ambitious paintings, and the relative speed with which they could be made, meant that the medium bulked large in print-publishing. In 1779 Georg Friedrich Brandes, writing in the Leipzig journal *Neue Bibliothek der schönen Wissenschaften und der freyen Künste*, remarked that line engraving was only used for landscapes, and the majority, and the best, of new British prints were in mezzotint.[15] Like contemporary painters, mezzotinters moved beyond portraiture to tackle subjects that were seen to have more intellectual sig-nificance. The mezzotints which Brandes particularly ad-mired were examples of complex historical compositions: Green's *Regulus* and *Hannibal Swearing Enmity to the Romans* after Benjamin West, 1773 (which Brandes con-sidered 'the most outstanding prints yet delivered by the

1. James McArdell, *Lady Charlotte Fitzwilliam*, mezzotint (proof before letter) after Joshua Reynolds 1754. 324 × 226 mm. This was the first mezzotint after Reynolds and was made at his own instigation; McArdell's fee would have been about fifteen guineas and is likely to have been as much as the young painter was paid for the portrait. 1868-8-22-2098*

2. Valentine Green, *Regulus*, mezzotint after Benjamin West 1771. 633 × 877 mm. 1841-12-11-163

English school'; fig. 2), *Ugolino* by John Dixon after Reynolds, and prints by Richard Earlom (see cat. 59) and William Pether after Rembrandt and Joseph Wright of Derby[16] (see cat. 57).

Prints after Reynolds and by Earlom found their way into important Continental collections, as John Smith's work had done a century earlier. There were major holdings of British mezzotints in, for instance, the collections of Count Moritz von Fries (see p. 71), Baron Jan Gijsbert Verstolk van Soelen (1776–1845),[17] and Fryderyk Józef Moszynski (1738–1817).[18]

Fine and rare impressions of earlier mezzotints also attracted collectors. In April 1776 the *Magasin des Estampes* in Cockspur Street, London, whose stock included many prints from Mariette's collection, offered *The Countess of Exeter* by William Faithorne II for 10 guineas and *The Earl of Shaftesbury* by Abraham Blooteling for 8 guineas; at the same time Rembrandt's *Hundred Guilder Print* was offered for 5 guineas. In 1798 John Barnard's sale[19] included an impression of Prince Rupert's *Great Executioner* which sold for £2. 15. 0.[20] In 1814 James Caulfield recorded that within the previous seven years two of Siegen's portraits had been sold at auction for 'very considerable sums, one I believe near forty pounds'. He listed prices between one and ten guineas for many other portrait mezzotints, and valued *The Bishops of Oxford and Rochester with Dr Allestry* after Lely at £20, and *The Ladies Anne and Mary Barrington* by R. Williams after St John Gascar at £30.[21] In 1816 Robert Morse's sale[22] included an impression of Siegen's *Princess Amelia of Hesse* which sold for £20. 10. 0. Sir Mark Masterman Sykes's collection, sold in

1824, contained mezzotints by Faithorne of *Mountague Bartie, Earl of Lindsey* after van Dyck, and *James, Earl of Perth* which fetched 16 guineas and 18 guineas.[23]

This was the situation of the London print world in the early days of the British Museum's Department of Prints and Drawings. Mezzotints were important both as a major part of current print production and as part of the history of printmaking. They were kept as a discrete group within the departmental collection – as they were within most private collections, and as they still are in the Museum – and appear as such in a number of reports to the Trustees from J. T. Smith about the lamentable state of the first Print Room (see Introduction, p. 12). Reports to the Trustees record that, as well as a number of mezzotints in the Sloane and Cracherode bequests, mezzotints had arrived in the Museum as gifts of portraits made by sitters and their families, and – frequently – as presentations by artists, engravers and publishers. The most important of these were presentations of mezzotints by James Ward and John Martin. In 1817 Ward gave up mezzotint to concentrate entirely on painting and he presented the British Museum with a set of 401 prints, 'in all their various states'.[24] In 1833 Martin gave ten proofs of his extremely popular Biblical subjects (see cat. 60); J. T. Smith made a point of reporting to the Trustees that 'Mr Martin's presents amount, according to the selling prices, to £101.18s.', about twenty times the average price of prints after Reynolds.

In 1827 the process of making acquisitions became easier when the Department was allowed its first annual purchase grant, initially of £80, soon to rise to £100. Additional funds for important purchases continued to be applied for to the Trustees. It surprises today's curators to learn that Smith spent the greater part of the grant in building up a collection of prints after Reynolds, but it was a logical – and patriotic – policy to begin a national collection with the great master of the British school and first President of the Royal Academy. Smith felt strongly about the importance of prints after Reynolds: 'Fortunate are those collectors who can boast of proof-impressions from the portraits of Sir Joshua: they of themselves form a brilliant school of Art, not only for the grace displayed in their attitudes, but also for the grandeur of their chiaroscuro …'.[25] Between 1830 and 1833 Smith and his successor, William Young Ottley, reported purchases of 604 prints after Reynolds at a cost of about £400 as well as a number of gifts from dealers and publishers.[26] In June 1833 Ottley reported that after the acquisition of two further groups (amounting to 163 prints in all)[27] the Department's collec-

3. James Ward, *Lady Heathcote as Hebe*, mezzotint after John Hoppner 1804. 652 × 453 mm. This proof was touched and annotated by Hoppner who then, according to Ward's note at the foot of the sheet, altered his painting to conform to variations which Ward had introduced in the print. It is one of six progress proofs from the plate included in Ward's gift to the Museum in 1817. Ii. 11-39

tion of prints after Reynolds would be 'not far from complete'. In July 1833 he bought another forty-five,[28] but thereafter the acquisition of prints after Reynolds slowed down.[29]

By April 1832 the collection of prints after Reynolds was so large that Smith had begun the task of arranging them, and in February 1833 he reported to the Trustees that they had been arranged in eleven portfolios. The bulk of the collection of prints after Reynolds remain in twelve 'portfolios' (which would now be termed albums) with leaves watermarked 1832, half-bound in gold-tooled brown leather with marbled boards. Portraits are arranged alphabetically; six volumes of men, four of ladies and two devoted to fancy, historical and miscellaneous subjects. The prints would originally have been inserted loosely between the leaves, but in the late nineteenth century the collection – by then further enlarged and including prints in a whole range of techniques – was guarded down along the edges.

The storage of the Department's print collection gives some indication of the relative importance attached to different sorts of prints over the years. The interest in prints after Reynolds, as a category, declined in the later nineteenth century and so they have never been moved from these far from satisfactory 150-year-old albums. Prints after Thomas Lawrence, Benjamin West and Richard Wilson, again chiefly mezzotints, are kept in similar volumes watermarked 1837, 1841 and 1842, the prints remaining loosely placed between the leaves.[30] Mezzotints dating from before the mid-eighteenth century were placed in a set of smaller volumes, where most of them remain, again loosely inserted between the leaves. The work of John Smith fills three of these volumes, but in the second half of the nineteenth century his mezzotints would have been regarded at least as highly as prints after Reynolds and they too were guarded down.

By the late 1830s the Department had entered a period of rapid growth: more than 100,000 prints were added to the collection between 1837 and 1853. Henry Josi, who had become Keeper in 1836, continued to acquire prints after Lawrence, West and other painters working in England,[31] but as far as mezzotints are concerned a broader approach was most clearly demonstrated by a purchase in April 1838 which definitively changed the shape of the Department's collection. On 1 December 1837 William Smith had written to Josi offering, for £210, a group of 221 mezzotints forming what he described as the most complete collection ever made on the history of mezzotint. Josi recommended to the Trustees that Smith's price was decidedly cheap and in April 1838 208 mezzotints were acquired.[32] There were examples by all the leading mezzotinters from Siegen to McArdell, including forty or fifty of the earliest mezzotints. Smith gave no provenance, but signatures on the versos of some prints indicate that the collection belonged to Hugh Welch Diamond (1809–86), who stated more than thirty years later that the British Museum had acquired his collection of early mezzotints.[33]

In December 1836 Diamond had presented his observations on early mezzotints to the Society of Antiquaries and had shown a mezzotint by Siegen after Honthorst of the Princess of Orange. The paper is one of the earliest essays on the origins of the technique.[34] Diamond pointed out that it was difficult to study the subject when Siegen's and Prince Rupert's prints were so rare that the early cataloguers had not seen examples of them; he remarked that 'not one of them is to be found in the fine collection of the British Museum'. The paper concludes with a catalogue of mezzotints by Siegen, Theodore Caspar von Furstenberg and Rupert, and of three etchings by Rupert. The prints purchased from Smith in April 1838 contained Rupert's etchings and all the mezzotints which Diamond listed as existing only in collections other than the British Museum's.[35]

Diamond had originally bought the mezzotints from William Smith for £40 (since Diamond was only twenty-eight years old when he sold the prints the purchase had presumably been made in the previous ten years); he had received enquiries about them 'from Vienna',[36] and then, 'having been offered a profit of £200', had passed them back to Smith.[37] A comparison with the prices for early mezzotints discussed above suggests that this great profit was partly due to the fact that Diamond had bought the mezzotints very cheaply. But it was also, doubtless, connected with the activities of Léon de Laborde, who was buying prints for the French national collection and had a particular interest in the earliest mezzotints. Laborde's *Histoire de la Gravure en Manière Noire* (1839) was the first substantial study of the origins of mezzotint. He provided a catalogue of mezzotints by printmakers living up to 1720 and, most significantly, published a letter by Siegen of 1642[38] in which he states that the new method of engraving used in his portrait of Princess Amelia of Hesse was his own recent discovery. The publication of the letter clarified the question of the invention of mezzotint with which Prince Rupert was previously – and often subsequently – credited. The first English translation of Siegen's letter to be published was by the Hamburg dealer and collector Ernst Harzen and appeared in 1868 in Diamond's note on *The Origin of Mezzotint Engraving*.[39]

Diamond, at the time a young surgeon, went on to become a specialist in mental diseases and Secretary of the Royal Photographic Society. He combined both interests in a series of photographs of his patients in the Female Department of the Surrey County Asylum which were exhibited by the Royal Society in 1852. Diamond was much respected at the time for applying his scientific knowledge to the new art of photography, and it is tempting to link Diamond's interest in the development of mezzotint with his role as a pioneer of photography where, again, light is used to create images. He was involved with the develop-

ment of the technique of photographic printing on paper, and from 1853 onwards was a regular contributor on photographic subjects, and occasionally on antiquarian and archaeological matters, to *Notes and Queries*.[40] He was an avid collector, and according to his obituarist the profit he made on his early mezzotints was not unique: 'with the exception of English pottery and old plate, which he bought with discretion and prudence almost to the last, he seldom cared to pick up things for which there were many hunters. It happened more than once that, on the rise of a "new rage" for collecting, Diamond parted with an assemblage of the coveted objects for a price greatly exceeding the sum he had spent upon it'.[41] The posthumous sale of his prints[42] included a group of 157 mezzotints of all periods and about a thousand portraits (including mezzotints), as well as over a thousand topographical prints, more than 300 trade cards and 'a large number' of woodcut capital letters.[43]

There was a general slump in the art market between about 1830 and the 1850s, but it was followed by another boom in mezzotint collecting in England. In 1868 Diamond remarked: 'I may note that the increase of the value of the early mezzotints is something fabulous; the more interesting of the early specimens scarcely ever occur for sale, and prints which formerly could have been bought for shillings would now be thought to be fairly purchased for as many pounds'.[44] This revival of interest in mezzotints of earlier periods, combined with a new demand for reproductive prints generated by an extremely successful exhibition of old master paintings at the Royal Academy in 1870, created a market for new work. The increase in trade was such as to bring Samuel Cousins out of retirement three years after giving up his business and presenting a huge collection of proofs to the British Museum.

Collectors of the period took prints very seriously. They were deeply concerned with variations between states, and scholarly catalogues gave precise details of proofs and differences in lettering as well as alterations to the image itself. Edward Hamilton in his *Catalogue Raisonné of the Engraved Works of Sir Joshua Reynolds* (1884) illustrated the preoccupation with states, recounting how a series of false proofs of mezzotints after Reynolds were sold in 1874 for sums up to 63 guineas.[45]

In 1878 John Chaloner Smith (1827–95), an Irish railway engineer, published the first part of his *British Mezzotinto Portraits ... from the Introduction of the Art to the Early Part of the Present Century*; this remains the definitive catalogue of the subject and provided a guide to collectors for the next fifty years. Chaloner Smith's arrangement was according to mezzotinters, so as to accord them the same respect as the continental printmakers whose work had been catalogued in the monumental publications of Adam Bartsch and A. P. F. Robert-Dumesnil earlier in the century.[46] But he retained the traditional British identification of the mezzotint with the portrait, harking back to the late eighteenth-century portrait print catalogues of Granger and Bromley[47] in his dedication to 'all who interest themselves in the Art of Mezzotinto Engraving, in the Study of Portraiture, or in Biographical Research'. Chaloner Smith's virtually complete omission of subject mezzotints has had the effect of marginalising any mezzotints that were not portraits. Even today the absence of any guide to non-portrait mezzotints makes it extremely difficult to assess how large their production was, and thus to write a balanced history of the subject.

Chaloner Smith built up a large collection to help with his study of the subject and it is illuminating – in view of the famously high prices of some mezzotints – to note that at first he spent no more than 6d per print.[48] The collection was dispersed in a series of sales between 1887 and 1896.[49] The British Museum bought 106 mezzotints,[50] and 300 portrait mezzotints – including many of the best-known of those made by McArdell and other Irish engravers between 1750 and 1775 – were purchased by the National Gallery of Ireland with funds provided by Sir Edward Guinness (later Lord Iveagh). Although the sale catalogues followed Chaloner Smith in arranging the prints by engraver, their prime interest to the National Gallery was as the foundation of a collection of 'Historical Portraits'.[51]

Among those whom Chaloner Smith named as having assisted in compiling his catalogue was the collector William Meriton Eaton, later second Baron Cheylesmore

4. William Meriton Eaton, second Baron Cheylesmore. After a photograph

(1843–1902). According to Alfred Whitman, writing in the year before Cheylesmore's death, 'all amateurs … associate Lord Cheylesmore's name with mezzotints'.[52] Cheylesmore inherited his title from his father, a prosperous silk broker and MP who was ennobled by Queen Victoria at her jubilee in 1887. His mother, Charlotte Gorham, was the daughter of Thomas Leader Harman of New Orleans. The first Baron was himself an art collector, his taste, typically for a Victorian man of commerce, being for contemporary paintings. His collection included *The Monarch of the Glen* by Edwin Landseer, one of the most popular paintings of the era, now in the possession of the whisky distillers John Dewar and Sons.[53]

Although the second Baron Cheylesmore was nominally a partner in the family business his role in it was small, and three attempts to follow his father into parliament were unsuccessful. A life-long batchelor, he appears from the 1870s onwards to have devoted himself to amassing a vast collection of mezzotints. In January 1902 Julia Frankau wrote an account of a visit to Cheylesmore's house, where the finest mezzotints were displayed in frames until there was 'no more hanging room … in the apartments set aside for them'; others were 'stacked in great heaps' or stored in 'great portfolios'.[54] She did not mention any paintings hanging in the house but they would presumably have included five that Cheylesmore bequeathed to the National Gallery: *A Rocky Landscape with an Ox-Cart* by Jan de Both; *The Execution of Lady Jane Grey* by Paul Delaroche; Edwin Landseer's *The Highland Flood* and *Dying Grouse*; and *Cromer Sands* by William Collins.[55] The last four paintings had belonged to Cheylesmore's father.[56]

Cheylesmore's fortune did not compare with those of contemporary collectors like John Malcolm and George Salting, who are discussed elsewhere in this catalogue, and at his death his total estate amounted to £51,475.17.0, even in 1902 not a very great sum. The catalogue of his collection[57] shows that, like Chaloner Smith, he spent remarkably small sums of money on his prints; the most expensive was *Charlotte, Countess of Cholmondeley and the Honourable Henry Cholmondeley* by Charles Turner after John Hoppner, purchased for £94.16.3 at the Huth sale, Christie's, 10–11 July 1895.[58] Cheylesmore spent more than £10 on only a few dozen prints and the vast majority were bought for shillings. He seems to have taken pride in buying at bargain prices: in his entry for *Louise, Duchess of Portsmouth* by Blooteling after Lely, for which he paid £2 at Christie's on 29 January 1884, he wrote 'Another sold at Dent's Sale No. 197 for £15 to Noseda',[59] and against a group of prints by Bernard Lens, for which he paid £19.2.0 at the Ellis sale at Sotheby's on 25 January 1886, that Ellis had bought the prints for £28 at the sale of Richard Bull's collection.[60] Julia Frankau also reported his pleasure in being offered a mezzotint for £650 when he had already bought a better impression for £40 – and had bought it from Henry Percy Horne, a rival collector.[61]

Although Cheylesmore occasionally bought continental mezzotints in Amsterdam and Paris, the vast majority of purchases were made from London dealers, especially Fawcett, and auction sales. He bought at all the great mezzotint sales from the 1870s until the last year of his life: Bull, Cheney, Ellis, Buccleuch[62], Huth, Ponsonby and Peel. He also took an interest in earlier collectors, noting, for instance, that his impression of *The Countess of Bridgwater* by Faithorne after Michael Dahl had belonged to Horace Walpole and was inscribed by him, and that *Elizabeth, Countess of Southampton* published after van Dyck by Richard Tompson (active 1656–d.1693)[63] had been in William Musgrave's collection.

There are references in the manuscript catalogue to Bromley ('B'), Chaloner Smith ('S') and other catalogues, such as J. E. Wessely's *Abraham Blooteling*.[64] Cheylesmore often noted additional states, or that prints do not appear in these published catalogues, and he clearly felt proud enough of such discoveries to mention to Julia Frankau that he had found many additions to Chaloner Smith's catalogue since its publication.[65] It is likely that there was a good deal of mutual encouragement between the two collectors: both Frankau and Colvin[66] mention Cheylesmore's initial dependence on Chaloner Smith's catalogue, but he had already bought large numbers of mezzotints before its publication and was, as has been said, acknowledged in Chaloner Smith's preface.

The low prices paid by Cheylesmore reflect the fact that the collection began as one of portraits; he was not searching for expensive rare states or prints in perfect condition. Eleven volumes of the catalogue are devoted to engraved portraits of British royalty in all techniques, but Cheylesmore appears to have disposed of many of these less important prints (some catalogue entries are annotated 'sold' and others are crossed through) and in his will of 1896 he referred only to 'my collection of Mezzotinto Portraits' which was to be left to the National Portrait Gallery.[67] He was well aware of the importance of his prints as examples of the technique of mezzotint, as distinct from their role as portraits, and insisted that different states of the same print were not to be disposed of, but were to be accessible to 'lovers of the Art of Mezzotinting'. By 1900 the balance of his interest had swung more decisively towards technique rather than subject, and in a codicil to his will he directed that his prints should be left to the British Museum rather than to the National Portrait Gallery and that they should be arranged as examples of printmaking under engravers' names, rather than as portraits under sitters' names.[68]

It is very likely that this change of heart was due to persuasion by Colvin, who was assiduous in luring gifts and bequests to the Museum (see p. 159), and, perhaps no less, to the efforts of Alfred Whitman, superintendent of the Print Room, whose *Masters of Mezzotint* had appeared two years earlier. A letter from Whitman to Cheylesmore, dated 14 March 1899, about mezzotints by S.W. Reynolds and Charles Turner is inserted in Volume 30 of Cheylesmore's catalogue. Cheylesmore would have known that great attention was being paid to the departmental collection of mezzotints, and that a number were being removed from albums for mounting. Annotations in the Smith albums record missing mezzotints as being 'with Mr Colvin', and notes by Alfred Whitman in the James Ward and Thomas Frye albums record that selections of mezzotints[69] were removed and mounted in 1900.

This shift in the way that Cheylesmore perceived his collection led to some uncertainty over whether the bequest to the British Museum was intended to include mezzotints other than portraits. On 26 August 1902 Colvin wrote to his heir (his brother, Major-General Herbert Francis Eaton, third Baron Cheylesmore)[70] that he thought prints other than portraits should be included, but, as the wording of the will was unclear, an entry in Chaloner Smith's catalogue might serve as the authority as to whether a print was a portrait or not; Mr Mackay of Colnaghi's might act as a referee for prints not listed by Chaloner Smith. No reply survives, but the prints finally received by the Museum include twenty-six that are not portraits, only two of which appear in Chaloner Smith.[71]

The collection arrived at the Museum on 27 November 1902 and by 6 February 1903 Colvin was able to report to the Trustees that it was the most extensive ever brought together. There were approximately 7,650 mezzotints and, in addition, 2,675 portraits of Queen Victoria and her family. The work of 284 British mezzotinters and seventy foreigners was represented with 'a large proportion of the rarest and a not inconsiderable proportion of the finest' mezzotints (Colvin pointed out that these qualities do not always coincide). A statement by Colvin that Cheylesmore had bought, 'for high prices', a number of the finest mezzotints in early or proof states and in very good condition, is at odds with the evidence of Cheylesmore's manuscript catalogue where prices are, on the whole, surprisingly low. These low prices are reflected in the ratio of fine to poor prints in the collection as a whole which Colvin reported as about one to six or seven, noting, however, that as far as the famous eighteenth-century prints after Reynolds, George Romney and their contemporaries were concerned almost half the prints were of the best quality. The whole collection was valued at approximately £30,000, including ten prints at £400, twenty at £250 and forty at £100 – an extraordinary testimony both to Cheylesmore's acumen and to the inflation in mezzotint prices during the last years of the nineteenth century.

Colvin was keen to exhibit the choicest prints in the collection, and he asked the Trustees' permission to repair and mount the 1,400 best mezzotints in the Cheylesmore bequest. This task was to be completed by William Walker,[72] who had worked for the Department on several occasions in recent years and was expected to produce sixty or seventy mounts a month at 5s each for the smaller ('royal' and 'imperial') sizes, and 10s 6d for the larger 'atlas' mounts. The 6,250 remaining, 'Ordinary' prints, valued at £1 or less, were to be dealt with by Museum staff. They were removed from the bulky mounts in which Cheylesmore had kept them, lettered in pencil with the names of artist and sitter and a reference to Chaloner Smith's catalogue, and 'guarded in a protecting wrapper of thin and very smooth, but strong, paper ... lettered in like manner'. The 'Ordinary' series of mezzotints remains in these wrappers today. 'Select' (mounted) mezzotints from the Cheylesmore collection and earlier sources remain, for the most part, in Walker's uniform mounts dating from the turn of the century.

The major exhibition of the Cheylesmore bequest had to be deferred until all this work was completed, but, in order to 'stay the curiosity of the numerous persons interested, and at the same time to whet their appetite for the full exhibition', a temporary display of fifty-nine mezzotints was put up in the King's Library in April 1903. The Director ordered six wainscot screens to be made, at a cost of £37.10.0 each, for use in this and future temporary exhibitions. In 1905 an exhibition of 641 mezzotints, chiefly from the Cheylesmore bequest, was shown in the Print and Drawing Gallery in the White Wing.

The rise in the prices of certain mezzotints in the years from the 1880s to the First World War was astonishing. In 1875 it was thought remarkable that *The Three Ladies Waldegrave* by Green after Reynolds had sold for 236 guineas,[73] but by the turn of the century prices had reached over £1,000. Among the most spectacular were 1,000 guineas for *Mary Isabella, Duchess of Rutland* by Green after Reynolds, and 1,160 guineas for *Mrs Carnac* by John Raphael Smith after Reynolds (see cat. 58), at the Blyth and Edgcumbe sales, both in 1901; 1,200 guineas for *Lady Bampfylde* by Thomas Watson after Reynolds at the Huth sale in 1905; and 1,150 guineas for *The Frankland Sisters* by William Ward after Hoppner at the Meinertzhagen sale in 1910.[74]

The market for portrait mezzotints became a specialist field separate from the main print trade. This extraordinary period in the taste for mezzotints was a spin-off from the tremendous vogue for eighteenth-century portraiture among the tycoons of the day – in particular the hugely wealthy American barons. These men were fascinated by the English aristocracy and, just as they were delighted to see their daughters married to dukes and earls, so they brought noble ancestors into their families in the form of paintings by Gainsborough, Reynolds and Romney. The attitude that saw ownership of portraits as forging a link with the subject is illustrated in Julia Frankau's description of Cheylesmore's collection as 'representing not only art, but society; not only history, but policy and the intrigues of State', and her description of the female portraits as if they were an assembly of court beauties present in person

at the house in Kensington.[75] The taste for British portraiture can still be seen in the painting collections founded by Henry Clay Frick, Andrew Mellon and, in Britain, Lord Iveagh, and an example of a contemporary mezzotint collection that remains intact is that of John Pierpont Morgan (1837–1913), now at the Yale Center for British Art.[76] Morgan built up a collection of nearly 1,500 grand late eighteenth-century mezzotints, buying from Thomas Agnew and Sons in London (the prints remain largely in the thin card mounts provided by Agnew's).

Prices for early mezzotints, or later mezzotints other than portraits, were a fraction of those reached by more fashionable prints. Whitman recorded in 1901 that a mezzotint by Prince Rupert had fetched £300 'and £40 has been reached more than once', but 'Richard Earlom's prints do not go at great prices, though £20 or more may be asked for a choice proof of one of his famous *Flower Pieces*, after van Huysum, before the motto in the coat of arms' (see cat. 59).[77] At the Theobald sale in 1910[78] two mezzotints by William Dickinson, *Mrs Mathew* after Reynolds and *Miss Ramus* after Romney, fetched £682.10.0 and £672 respectively, but even an exceptionally fine first state of *The Standard-Bearer* by Prince Rupert (see cat. 52) fetched only £252.

The great interest in mezzotint collecting led to demands for loan exhibitions which would reach wider audiences. The Burlington Fine Arts Club held two exhibitions of mezzotints: in 1881 198 mezzotints, lent by eighteen collectors, illustrating the history of the medium as far as the 1820s, and, in 1902 101 mezzotint portraits dating from the 1750s to the 1820s from the collections of King Edward VII, Lord Cheylesmore, John Pierpont Morgan and Henry Studdy Theobald. There were other loan exhibitions in New York in 1904 and Manchester in 1910.

There were also a number of publications on the subject, the most useful being those by Alfred Whitman. He published two general books for collectors, *The Masters of Mezzotint* (1898) and *The Print Collector's Handbook* (1901, and five further editions until 1912), and a series of monographs: *Valentine Green* (1902), *S.W. Reynolds* (1903), *Samuel Cousins* (1904) and *Charles Turner* (1907). A supplement to Chaloner Smith, Charles Russell's *English Mezzotint Portraits and their States*, appeared in 1926, too late for the height of the boom in collecting. Other monographs on mezzotinters were of less value: in *John Raphael Smith* (1902) and *William and James Ward* (1904) Julia Frankau introduced catalogues of prints with compilations of anecdotes recounted in flowery prose for 'that cultured, perceptive public to whom alone my subject makes appeal'.[79] In 1904 the subject also appeared in fiction as *The Mezzotint*, a ghost story by M.R. James.[80]

The Cheylesmore bequest had almost doubled the Museum's holdings of mezzotints and after more than seventy years of active collecting few gaps remained. In 1924 Campbell Dodgson made a major purchase, not of a fashionable portrait of a Georgian beauty but of an important early mezzotint: a unique impression of the head of a woman by Prince Rupert bought for £330 at Henry Percy Horne's sale.[81] Dodgson reported to the Trustees that the unexpectedly high price was 'owing to the competition of a New York dealer'. The Museum was only able to acquire the print because Horne's children contributed half of the cost and Agnew's, who had bid above the agreed price of £210, paid the £120 difference.

The crash of 1929 had a drastic effect on the collecting both of prints and of portraits; the taste for mezzotints never again reached such heights. In 1937 the important mezzotint collection of Martin Erdmann of New York had to be brought to London for sale.[82] Commenting on the sale, A. M. Hind summed up the falling market as follows: 'It is seldom that so large a collection of prints returns from America for sale in England, but though the vogue for English mezzotint portraits has dwindled in the last decade in England, it probably hardly exists in America. Their values had reached preposterous heights in the years before the War, to fall to absurdly low prices during the last few years.'[83] The sale was successful enough for Hind to hope that it might 'raise the interest of collectors at least to a reasonable appreciation of what is one of the most characteristic achievements of English art'. But an analysis of the prices fetched shows that there was no real cause for optimism. Although thirty-five years had passed since the Cheylesmore bequest, prices were similar to Colvin's valuations of 1902.

Subject-matter was still the chief interest: at the turn of the century collectors had been obsessed with aristocratic portraits; in the 1930s prints were chosen to fit a nostalgic view of Georgian England. Of 343 lots of mezzotints in the Erdmann sale only 29 reached prices over £100,[84] while four engravings of mail coaches after James Pollard (1797–1867) fetched between 200 and 260 guineas each. Some mezzotints of exceptional quality and rarity fetched high prices, but most of the expensive lots had some extrinsic interest: two portraits of Emma Hamilton went for 440 and 410 guineas; another of Joseph Tayadaneega, the Mohawk Sachem who came to England in 1785, for 240 guineas; a mezzotint after Romney's *Mrs Davenport*, the original of which was famous for having sold for 58,000 guineas in 1926, sold for 320 guineas; and William Ward's *Frankland Sisters* after the painting by Hoppner then in the collection of Andrew Mellon, now in the National Gallery of Art, Washington, sold for 420 guineas.

The Museum has acquired few mezzotints in the last fifty years. The reason that led to the significance of the medium in the early years of the century – its identification with portraiture – became its downfall as succeeding generations lost interest in portraits, and as the British aristocracy lost its selling power. Mezzotint has become the province of the print-historian and the interest is in prints that serve as landmarks in the history of the medium. The earliest examples now fetch far higher prices than prints by J. R. Smith or Valentine Green: Rupert's *The Standard-Bearer* appeared at Sotheby's in 1994[85] with an estimate of £30–40,000. The Museum's few recent acquisitions are historical documents that broaden the scope of the collection beyond the traditional British portrait mezzotint: in 1978 *L'Heureuse Famille* by Philibert Louis Debucourt (1755–1832),[86] in 1979 a portrait of the painter Christopher Weigel by Bernard Vogel (1683–1737) after Johannes Kupetzky,[87] and in 1984 an unrecorded first state of *Isabella Clara Eugenia, Infanta of Spain* by Vaillant, that shows how the tone on the plate was built up.[88]

I am grateful to David Alexander and Richard Godfrey for reading a draft of this essay, and for their helpful comments.

1. Rupert also introduced 'Rupert's drops' into England. These small glass drops with long slender tails – accidentally produced in the process of glass-blowing – cannot be damaged with a sledgehammer but explode when their tails are broken. As scientific phenomena they led to the invention of safety glass and as toys they still fascinate, appearing as the subject of a chapter in Peter Carey's magic-realist novel *Oscar and Lucinda* (1988), in which Rupert is dismissed, like the mezzotint, as long-forgotten: 'You need not ask me who Rupert is … because I do not know'.

2. Among these amateurs was John Evelyn who referred to mezzotint in his *Sculptura* (1662) in a manner that was deliberately enigmatic: 'I did not think it necessary that an *Art* so curious, and (as yet) so little vulgar (and which indeed does not succeed where the *Workman* is not an accomplished *Designer*, and has a competent talent in *painting* likewise) was to be prostituted at so cheap a rate, as the more naked describing of it here, would too soon have expos'd it to' (*Sculptura* [3rd edn C. F. Bell], Oxford, 1906, pp. 147–8).

3. Printmaking in Britain was at nowhere near the advanced stage that it had reached on the continent of Europe and the introduction of mezzotint was well timed to fill a vacuum. For a full account of the early development of professional mezzotint publication in England, see Antony Griffiths, 'Early mezzotint publishing in England – II Peter Lely, Tompson and Browne', in *Print Quarterly*, VII 1990, pp. 131–45.

4. Browne, one of the earliest mezzotint publishers in Britain, published the first description of the mezzotint technique in *Ars Pictoria*, London 1669. See also n. 3.

5. The albums were sold at Christie's, 27 June 1984, lots 438 to 481. Lot 438 was the album now in the National Portrait Gallery; the other two albums were broken up and sold as lots 439 to 481, lots 439 to 479 containing the early mezzotints and lots 480 and 481 the covers and the remaining eighteenth-century mezzotints.

6. For a full account of Smith's career see Antony Griffiths, 'Early mezzotint publishing in England – I John Smith, 1652–1743', in *Print Quarterly*, VI 1989, pp. 243–57.

7. The delicate surfaces of mezzotint plates wear down with the pressure of printing and need to be reworked after about two hundred impressions have been taken. Many publishers employed hacks for this work, but Smith reworked his own plates so that the quality remained consistently high and set a standard that encouraged collectors to appreciate fine impressions.

8. William Gilpin, *Essay on Prints*, 4th edn 1792, pp. 87–8.

9. Remy, 11 December 1759 (see Lugt 2981).

10. A substantial part of another great print collection of the period, that of the painter and connoisseur Hugh Howard (1675–1737/8), came to the British Museum in 1874. Of the 2,282 prints and 167 drawings purchased from Howard's descendant, Charles Howard, fifth Earl of Wicklow, 1,488 are seventeenth- or early eighteenth-century mezzotints (1874-8-8-1031 to 1360, 2282 to 2335; see cat. 53), but only forty-nine are by Smith.

11. See Antony Griffiths and Craig Hartley, 'The print collection of the duc de Mortemart', in *Print Quarterly*, XI 1994, pp. 107–116.

12. Antony Griffiths, 'The prints and drawings in the library of Consul Joseph Smith', in *Print Quarterly*, VIII 1991, p. 134.

13. Reynolds is famously recorded as having said that he would be 'immortalised' by McArdell. His informal portrait of the mezzotinter (c.1756–60) is now in the National Portrait Gallery.

14. As the merchant class became more prosperous many new buyers came into the market. Catalogues which had previously been mere lists of subjects began to provide guidance to less confident purchasers. John Bowles's catalogues of 1764 and 1768 contained 'capital prints' described as suitable 'for collections in the cabinets of the curious, or to be used as furniture to ornament rooms'. Robert Sayer's catalogues of 1766 and 1775 (the latter issued in partnership with John Bennett) included sets of prints 'proper to collect in the cabinets of the curious, and also [to] make furniture elegant and genteel when framed and glazed'.

15. Newly published British prints were reviewed in continental journals, especially in Germany where they received much more serious critical treatment than they did at home. See Timothy Clayton, 'English prints in German journals', in *Print Quarterly*, X 1993, pp. 123–37, for an account of Brandes's reviews of new prints in the *Neue Bibliothek*.

16. For mezzotints after Wright see Timothy Clayton, 'The engraving and publication of prints of Joseph Wright's paintings' and 'Catalogue of engraved works' in Judy Egerton (ed.), *Wright of Derby*, catalogue of an exhibition at the Tate Gallery, London, Grand Palais, Paris, and Metropolitan Museum of Art, New York, 1990, pp. 25–9, 231–58.

17. Verstolk's sale in Amsterdam on 28 June 1847 and successive days included his magnificent collection of prints by Dürer and other old masters as well as mezzotints by Earlom, Green, Pether and John Raphael Smith. See also pp. 299–300.

18. Moszynski's huge collection of contemporary prints included, among other British prints, fine impressions of mezzotints by Earlom, Green and John Raphael Smith, see Krzysztof Kruzel, 'The print collection of the Polish Academy of Sciences', *Print Quarterly*, XI 1994, pp. 158–66.

19. Philipe's, 16 April 1798 and twenty-five successive days; Barnard's collection was famous for his fine etchings by Rembrandt.

20. As much as forty years earlier three prints by Rupert had sold for £3.1.0 at George Vertue's sale (Ford's, 16 March 1756 and five successive days).

21. James Caulfield, *Calcographiana: the Printsellers' Chronicle and Collector's Guide to the Knowledge and Value of Engraved British Portraits*, London 1814, pp. 141–63. Although the book is devoted to portraits, mezzotints are, as is often the case, treated separately.

22. Dodd's, 15 May 1816 and twenty-seven following days.

23. Sotheby's, 6 December 1824 and seven successive days. For early Italian prints in Sykes's collection see p. 93; he also possessed a vast number of British portraits and mezzotints.

24. The majority of Ward's mezzotints remain as they were originally stored, loosely placed between the leaves of six large volumes, their surfaces protected by tissue fixed to the versos of the leaves. A manuscript list of prints in the first volume dated 8 February 1900 and signed by Alfred Whitman records a number of mezzotints removed for mounting. In 1821 Ward presented a further group of seventeen progress proofs for a portrait of the Rev. Johnson Atkinson Busfield.

25. J.T. Smith, *Nollekens and his Times*, ed. W. Whitten, London 1920, II p. 223.

26. These included, in November 1830, ninety-two prints after Reynolds from Thomas Thane, and, in January 1831, 'a truly magnificent present' of twenty brilliant proofs 'in the highest state of preservation' from Moon, Boys and Graves.

27. 1833-6-10-1 to 93, 1833-7-15-1 to 70.

28. 1834-2-12-1 to 45. Although Ottley reported the purchase at £36.4.6 in July 1833, Molteno and Graves were not paid until the following February and the price recorded in the departmental register is £43.19.6.

29. The next recorded purchase of prints after Reynolds was not until July 1835, when a group of seventy was acquired. In July 1838 a number of rarities were acquired from Lord Northwick's collection, and in April 1839 ten prints after Reynolds were purchased from Hodgson and Graves.

30. In 1845 George William Reid, then an attendant in the Department, later to become Keeper, was recorded as making a catalogue of the prints after Reynolds. This manuscript catalogue remains in the departmental library, together with Reid's catalogues of prints after Lawrence and West, and of the work of the great line-engravers William Sharp, Robert Strange and William Woollett.

31. In the years immediately after 1838 the majority of reproductive prints acquired were after Lawrence and West rather than Reynolds.

32. 1838-4-10-1 to 208. A collection of 486 prints by G.F. Schmidt (1838-12-15-12 to 497) was purchased at the same time and the total price amounted to £270.

33. *Notes and Queries*, 4 July 1868, 4th Series, II p. 3. In February 1838 Diamond presented eleven mezzotints (1838-2-18-7 to 17), presumably those in the group originally offered by Smith which were not bought by the Museum.

34. Published as 'On the Earliest Specimens of Mezzotinto Engraving', in *Archaeologia*, XXVII 1838, pp. 405–9. The copy in the departmental library contains an acknowledgement to Diamond by the Secretary of the Society of Antiquaries, and was presumably presented by Diamond.

35. 1838-4-20-1 to 22.

36. The enquiries would have been on behalf of Charles, Duke of Sachsen-Teschen, whose collection is now in the Albertina, Vienna.

37. John Chaloner Smith, *British Mezzotinto Portraits*, 1878–85, p. xxvi. Chaloner Smith recorded that Diamond himself had told him the story of his acquisition and subsequent sale of the prints.

38. The letter appears in facsimile (between pp. 70–1), transcription (pp. 44–5) and translated into French (pp. 69–71).

39. See n. 33.

40. On 22 December 1855 Diamond published a note reflecting his antiquarian interests: an 'Account of the Expenses for the Prince's Masque performed at Court in 1620', transcribed from 'one of the Exchequer documents ordered to be destroyed'. The masque concerned was *Pan's Anniversary* performed by Charles, Prince of Wales, to celebrate the birthday of King James I on 19 June 1620 (see

Stephen Orgel and Roy Strong, *Inigo Jones: The Theatre of the Stuart Court*, London and Los Angeles, 1973, I pp. 313–16).

41. *The Athenaeum*, 3 July 1886, p. 18. Diamond's collections of ceramics, glass, silver, miniatures and decorative arts were sold at Sotheby's on 18–20 April and 2–5 June 1887. Much of his glass and British pottery had been lost in a fire at Alexandra Palace.

42. Sotheby's, 8–10 August 1887. Diamond disposed of his large collection of engraved portraits of celebrated physicians and surgeons during his lifetime and it eventually became part of the Hope bequest to Oxford University.

43. The Department purchased a further group of ten early mezzotints from Diamond in 1851, together with 215 engravings by Claude Mellan (1851-12-13-440 to 664). He made at least two gifts of Egyptian artefacts to the British Museum: in 1836 a glazed scaraboid, and in 1858 a painted limestone shabti (EA 2047 and 8890). Several of his Chinese and British ceramic pieces and a silver medallion found their way to the Museum later in the nineteenth century via the collection of Sir Augustus Wollaston Franks (OA Franks 1537.a and Franks 91+; MLA 1879.XIII-1, 1887-3-7-H.76, 1887-3-7-II.19 and 1887-12-16-5).

44. *Notes and Queries*, 4 July 1868, 4th Series, II p. 4.

45. Edward Hamilton, *Catalogue Raisonné of the Engraved Works of Sir Joshua Reynolds*, 2nd edn, 1884, p. v.

46. John Chaloner Smith, *British Mezzotinto Portraits*, 1878, p. ix.

47. James Granger, *A Biographical History of England … adapted to a methodical catalogue of engraved British heads*, 1769, and Henry Bromley, *Catalogue of Engraved British Portraits*, 1795.

48. Alfred Whitman, *The Print-Collector's Handbook*, Oxford, 1901, p. 104.

49. Chaloner Smith's mezzotints were sold at Sotheby's on 21–30 March 1887 and 25 April–4 May 1888, and at Christie's on 3–6 February 1896. The highest price reached was 63 guineas for *Mrs Richards* by Spilsbury after Gainsborough in the final sale (Lugt 2295, 2295 bis).

50. 1887-4-6-41 to 147.

51. The series was to become the nucleus of the national print collection, see Adrian Le Harivel (ed.), *Illustrated Catalogue of Prints and Sculpture*, National Gallery of Ireland, Dublin, 1988, and review by David Alexander in *Print Quarterly*, VI 1989, pp. 431–3.

52. Alfred Whitman, *The Print-Collector's Handbook*, 1901, p. 4.

53. For the first Baron's collection see his posthumous sale at Christie, Manson and Woods, London, 7 May 1892.

54. Julia Frankau, 'Lord Cheylesmore's mezzotints', in *The Connoisseur*, II 1902, pp. 3–13.

55. The pictures by Both, Delaroche and Collins were accepted by the Trustees of the National Gallery, but the two Landseers were returned to the third Baron (National Gallery Board Minutes [NG/1/8], 16 December 1902; letter from George Ambrose, chief clerk, 22 June 1903). Collins's *Cromer Sands* was later transferred to the Tate Gallery. Landseer's *The Highland Flood* is now in the collection of Aberdeen Art Gallery. (I am grateful to David Carter, Archivist of the National Gallery, and Anne Lyles and Robin Hamlyn of the Tate Gallery for this information.)

56. They appear as lots 78, 60, 50 and 15 in the first Baron's sale, see n. 53.

57. The manuscript catalogue, consisting of thirty notebooks bound in red leather (Departmental library, Vv.1.11 to 40), was acquired as part of the Cheylesmore bequest. The first fifteen volumes list British

mezzotints according to printmaker (with the exception of volume 11 which lists prints after Reynolds by sitter). Volumes 16 to 18 list foreign mezzotints, volume 19 anonymous prints, and the remainder portraits of royalty from Henry VII to Queen Victoria, listed by sitter. Cheylesmore's signature appears inside the front cover of almost every volume with the year (from 1881 to 1885) in which it was first used. The names of mezzotinters included in each volume appear in an index on the first pages. In his initial listing Cheylesmore kept the work of each printmaker separately, but there was often not enough space to add later acquisitions and they had to be fitted into subsequent volumes. John Smith occupies two and a half volumes; Cheylesmore acquired his mezzotints individually or in small groups, not as one of the sets originally sold by Smith. Entries for mezzotints are arranged in columns: title, brief biography of sitter, price, where and when bought, catalogue reference, painter, publisher and date.

58. The cheapest prints in the collection were a group of twenty-eight mezzotint drolls by Carington Bowles and Bowles and Carver purchased at Sotheby's on 14 February 1882 for 3d each. On 5 July 1886 Cheylesmore bought sixty-nine similar prints, also at Sotheby's, for amounts up to 1s.

59. St John Dent's sale at Sotheby's on 28 March 1884 and six successive days.

60. Sotheby's, 23 May 1881 and six following days.

61. Frankau, op. cit., p. 4.

62. The Duke of Buccleuch's collection was famous for its great Rembrandts. It also contained many fine mezzotints after Reynolds, but prices at the sale (Christie's, 8–21 March 1887) were not extremely high. The largest sum fetched was £136, a number of fine mezzotints sold for between £30 and £100 and many for less (Lugt 402). The British Museum purchased forty prints (1887-4-6-1 to 40), the most expensive of which was *Mary Hale as Euphrosyne* by James Watson after Reynolds at 30 guineas.

63. Purchased at Andrew Fountaine's sale, Christie's, 4 July 1884.

64. J. E. Wessely, *Abraham Blooteling, Verzeichniss seiner Kupferstiche und Schabkunstblätter*, Leipzig 1867.

65. Frankau, op. cit., p. 13.

66. In a report to the Trustees in 1903.

67. Besides five paintings left to the National Gallery (see n. 54) Cheylesmore's other bequests were all of relatively small sums of money to members of his family and the clerks 'employed by me in my business'.

68. As well as mezzotints the bequest allowed Colvin to choose any of Cheylesmore's books on engraving. These would have been integrated into the departmental library, and, apart from the catalogue, the only book so far identified as being from the bequest is a copy of the catalogue of engraved British portraits published by the dealer Samuel Woodburn in 1815 which bears Cheylesmore's bookplate.

69. A few mezzotints by Frye remain placed loosely between the leaves of an early nineteenth-century volume similar to those housing the reproductive prints described above. A manuscript list of prints removed for mounting, compiled by Alfred Whitman and dated 3 May 1900, remains in the volume. See also n. 24.

70. According to the *Dictionary of National Biography* the third Baron Cheylesmore's main interests were rifle-shooting and the welfare of the Grenadier Guards, but he followed the family tradition of collecting and amassed a large collection of military medals.

71. A sale of prints belonging to Lord Cheylesmore's descendants at Christie's on 2 May 1932 included a number of portraits and subject mezzotints which may have been the remnant of his collection.

72. This was presumably the grandson of S.W. Reynolds whose help Alfred Whitman acknowledged in his monograph on the engraver (1903). He had contributed a chapter on English engraving to a translation of Henri Delaborde's *Engraving: Its Origin, Processes, and History*, published in 1886 (in which S.W. Reynolds is described as 'one of the most gifted men who ever applied themselves to the engraver's art', p. 317). He also acted as agent for the Museum at auctions, including the sale of Chaloner Smith's mezzotints in 1887.

73. Richmond sale, Christie's, 7 June 1875.

74. According to Whitman *The Frankland Sisters* was Ward's 'most celebrated achievement' and 'always commands a very high price for good impressions' (*The Print-Collector's Handbook*, Oxford, 1901, pp. 62–3). In 1895 it had fetched 380 guineas at the Huth sale. By 1937 the price (at the Erdmann sale, see below) had gone down to 420 guineas, and in 1983 an impression was offered by Boerner's, Düsseldorf, for DM6,000 (about £1,500), a considerable reduction when inflation is taken into account.

75. Frankau, op. cit., pp. 3, 5–8.

76. The Morgan collection of mezzotints became part of the Pierpont Morgan Library and in 1970 was purchased by Paul Mellon for the Yale Center for British Art. A selection of the earlier prints – most of which were added to the collection after Morgan's death – was shown at Yale in 1994–5 in an exhibition entitled *Fancy Pieces: Genre Mezzotints by Robert Robinson & His Contemporaries*, organised by James A. Ganz. I am grateful to James Ganz for information on the formation of the collection.

77. Alfred Whitman, *The Print-Collector's Handbook*, 1901, p. 126.

78. Christie's, 25–8 April 1910.

79. Julia Frankau, *John Raphael Smith*, 1902, p. iv.

80. *The Mezzotint* appeared in *Ghost Stories of an Antiquary*, 1904. M. R. James was a distinguished scholar, Director of the Fitzwilliam Museum, Cambridge, and a Trustee of the British Museum.

81. Sotheby's, 22–4 June 1926. The most expensive print in the sale was *Mrs Davenport* by Jones after Romney, which sold for £530.

82. Christie's, 15–16 November 1937.

83. A. M. Hind, 'The Erdmann collection of English mezzotints', in *British Museum Quarterly*, XII, 3, June 1938, pp. 99–101.

84. The Museum acquired nineteen mezzotints at the sale (1937-12-11-8 to 26): ten were purchased at prices between one and a half and fourteen guineas and nine were presented by the National Art Collections Fund, including a unique impression of *A Girl with a Shock Dog (Miss Vansittart)* after Joshua Reynolds, attributed to Giuseppe Marchi (1735–1808), which fetched 135 guineas at the sale.

85. 1–2 December 1994, lot 137.

86. 1978-6-24-17.

87. 1979-10-6-67.

88. 1984-6-9-2. The first state (illustrated in Hollstein, cat. 184) still lacks the background which prints white. This shows that in this exceptional case, the background was only rocked after the main design had been scraped down.

51 Ludwig von Siegen (1609–after 1676) after Annibale Carracci (1560–1609)

The Holy Family with St John the Baptist, before 1657

Mezzotint with etching. 332 × 272 mm (image)

Chaloner Smith 7, unfinished proof

Siegen invented mezzotint (see p. 134), and this early example of his work demonstrates the medium at an experimental stage. The surface of the plate was not rocked in the way which became conventional but was roughened in some other manner. The actual date of production is not recorded, but the second state (dedicated to Cardinal Mazarin) is dated 1657; the first state bears a dedication to Prince Leopold of Austria.

The print reproduces a lost painting formerly in the Salviati collection in Rome. It was much admired and several painted copies survive as well as a number of prints, including a mezzotint by Vaillant (Hollstein 24).

1838-4-20-1. Purchased from William Smith (Diamond collection)

52 Prince Rupert (1619–82) after Pietro della Vecchia (1605–c.1678)

The Standard-Bearer, 1658

Mezzotint with etching. 278 × 198 mm (image)

Hollstein 16, first state

Rupert developed the fine-toothed rocker which is used to roughen the surface of a copper plate for mezzotint (see p. 134), and in this early print he was investigating methods of creating different surface textures. The breast-plate and parts of the background have been rocked densely to produce a rich black while the texture of the sleeve is suggested by further light rocking on top of the scraped surface.

The final state of this print is lettered 'Giorgione', but the painting on which it is based (in the Schloss Schönborn, Pommersfelden, Germany) is now attributed to Pietro della Vecchia.

1838-4-20-13. Purchased from William Smith (Diamond collection)

51

52

53 Wallerant Vaillant (1623–77) after Michiel Sweerts (1624–64)

A Boy Drawing a Bust of the Emperor Vitellius, c.1665–75

Mezzotint. 333 × 269 mm

Hollstein 97, first state

Vaillant worked as an assistant to Prince Rupert and afterwards set up in business as a mezzotinter in Amsterdam. This print was made at a stage in the development of the technique where a uniform method of grounding the plate had not yet been established: the surface is much more consistent than that of the earliest mezzotints but it is clear that the rocker was still being applied in a fairly haphazard way.

The print is based on a painting in the Institute of Arts, Minneapolis. The subject of the young artist at work was a popular one and here a boy is shown surrounded by the paraphernalia of a draughtsman: three sticks of charcoal, a wing to dust off excess fragments, a knife and a dish to hold sharpenings, a discarded sheet of paper, and on his lap a portfolio which doubles as a drawing-board.

The mezzotint was one of twenty-six by Vaillant in the collection of Hugh Howard (see p. 143, n. 10).

1874-8-8-1051. Purchased from Charles Howard, fifth Earl of Wicklow

54 Abraham Blooteling (1640–90) after Peter Lely (1618–80)

James, Duke of Monmouth, c.1678

Mezzotint. 646 × 494 mm

Hollstein 186, first state

Blooteling was the most notable of a number of Dutch mezzotinters who worked in England in the 1670s (see p. 134). He developed a laborious system of closely spaced rocking in several directions which is visible here in the lighter areas of the sitter's face. The rich and finely grained ground allowed for subtle tonal gradation that could produce extraordinary surface effects such as the lustrous sheen of Monmouth's hair.

This is one of a group of three grand mezzotint portraits (the others are of King Charles II and the Duke of York, later King James II) by Blooteling which appear to have been sponsored by Peter Lely in order to publicise his work (see p. 134). It is based on a drawing by Lely in the Royal Collection.

James Scott, Duke of Monmouth and Buccleuch (1649–85), was the illegitimate son of Charles II by Lucy Walters. He laid claim to the throne and was executed at the Tower of London for leading a rebellion against James II, which came to a bloody end at the battle of Sedgemoor.

1844-5-11-2. Purchased from W. B. Tiffin

55 John Smith (1652–1743) after Willem Wissing (1656–87)

Madam Elizabeth Brownlowe, 1685

Mezzotint. 340 × 245 mm

Chaloner Smith 25, first state before letters

This impression is inscribed in a formal hand: 'Madam Elizabeth Brownlowe W. Wissing pinx.' and by Smith: 'J. Smith Fec 1685'.

Elizabeth Brownlow (c.1683–1723) was the daughter of Sir John Brownlow of Belton. In 1699 she married John Cecil, Lord Burghley, who later became sixth Earl of Exeter. This charming portrait of her as a small child would have been made for the family (see p. 134), but its Baroque setting – flowing drapery, lush foliage, an exotic bird and a classical vase – would have given it a far wider market as a decorative 'fancy' picture.

The plate was originally published by Alexander Browne, but most impressions bear the name of Edward Cooper, who seems to have had some sort of rights over the publication of prints after Wissing.

Wissing's painting is still at Belton House, Lincolnshire.

1902-10-11-4431. Cheylesmore bequest

53

Madam Elizabeth Brownlowe

W. Wysing pinx

55

56 Georges-François Blondel
(1730–after 1791)

A View of the Inside of the New Prison at Rome, 1765

Mezzotint. 565 × 407 mm

Blondel, the son of the French architect Jacques-François Blondel, travelled to Rome as a young man. He may have met Giovanni Battista Piranesi; there is certainly an echo of Piranesi's prison scenes in this mezzotint. He seems, like many foreign mezzotinters of the period, to have learnt the technique in London, where he published a number of prints between 1765 and 1767. He is known to have been in Amsterdam in 1777 and in Paris in 1791.

The method used in this plate was unconventional. Rather than scraping the image on a plate which had previously been systematically grounded, Blondel used the rocker in a largely additive manner, working from light to dark in many areas of the plate.

This impression is a first state before letters, signed in drypoint below the subject. In his catalogue of Blondel's prints (*The Print Collector's Quarterly*, IX 1922, pp. 302–14) Campbell Dodgson described a similar impression in the Albertina, Vienna, but he did not refer to the present example which then belonged to Fritz Reiss. Reiss's collection, renowned for the high quality of its proofs, was sold at Christie's on 18–19 May 1923 and, doubtless at Dodgson's instigation, the print was acquired for the British Museum by the National Art Collections Fund.

1924-3-8-335. Presented by the National Art Collections Fund (Reiss collection)

57 William Pether (1731–1821) after Joseph Wright of Derby (1734–97)

The Alchymist, 1775

Mezzotint (proof before letter). 577 × 455 mm

Clayton 15

Wright's paintings are primarily studies of the effect of light, and mezzotint was the perfect medium for reproducing his work. His relationship with mezzotinters was, however, a reciprocal one; certain figures in his compositions are taken more or less directly from mezzotints by Pether's master Thomas Frye.

The present example reproduces *The Alchymist, in Search of the Philosopher's Stone, Discovers Phosphorus, and prays for the successful Conclusion of his operation, as was the custom of the Ancient Chymical Astrologers* (Derby Art Gallery) exhibited by Wright at the Society of Artists in 1771. Wright's inspiration appears to have been Pierre Joseph Macquer's *Elements of the Theory and Practice of Chemistry* (English edition 1758) where Macquer

described how alchemists' experiments 'proved the occasion of several curious discoveries' and gave details of the twenty-four-hour-long process of producing phosphorus which finally emerges as a stream of light through a hole bored in a large glass balloon. Wright was very much concerned to depict the alchemist's apparatus accurately and a letter to him on the subject survives from his friend, the scientist and printmaker Peter Perez Burdett (for a full account see Judy Egerton, *Wright of Derby*, catalogue of an exhibition at the Tate Gallery, London and elsewhere, with 'A catalogue of the engraved works of Joseph Wright of Derby' by Tim Clayton, 1990, pp. 84–6, No. 39, and p. 243, No. 163. P15).

Proofs of the mezzotint originally sold for a guinea each, but in 1785 Pether sold the plate at auction, together with twenty impressions, for the same price. It was republished by Edward Orme in 1801. This example was one of a group of over 1,700 prints, chiefly portraits, bought from the dealer William Benoni White in 1868 at a period when British Museum purchases were frequently on such a scale.

1868-8-8-2648. Purchased from William Benoni White

58 John Raphael Smith (1752–1812) after Joshua Reynolds (1723–92)

Mrs Carnac, 1778

Mezzotint. 598 × 385 mm (cropped within plate-mark)

Chaloner Smith 31, first state before letters

Elizabeth Carnac (1751–80) was the daughter of Thomas Rivett MP. In 1769 she married John Carnac (1716–1800), a brigadier-general in the service of the East India Company, and after her premature death he made her brother his heir on condition that he adopted his name. The Rivett-Carnac family maintained the Indian connection for several generations and produced two governors of Bombay.

The varied surface of Smith's mezzotint is calculated to re-create the delicacy of Reynolds's portrait (now in the Wallace Collection, London), with its suggestion of flickering light falling through trees. Dark brown ink, rather than black, has been used to lighten the tone, but stronger notes are added with extra rocking in the shadows of leaves on the dress. *Mrs Carnac* was one of the most sought-after mezzotints at the turn of the century and in 1901 an impression reached the astonishing price of 1,160 guineas (see p. 141).

This proof before letters is inscribed in pen and ink with the artist's and mezzotinter's names and the date and address of publication. It also bears the collector's mark (L.2446) of Sir Thomas Lawrence and would have been one of a number of prints 'of Ladies' after Reynolds which appeared as lots 332–6 in his posthumous sale at Christie's, 10–14 May 1830. Reynolds's glamorous por-

56

Painted by S.t Joshua Reynolds Pt.
Engrav.ed by J. R. Smith

Dec. 12 d ... Done i Mch. ll N.o 15 Bateman Buildings Soho Square London

58

traits of society beauties were clearly an inspiration for Lawrence's own portraits, which were themselves reproduced in mezzotint to great success.

1830–6–12–2. Purchased from William Smith
(Lawrence collection)

59 Richard Earlom (1743–1822) after Jan van Huysum (1682–1749)

Flower-Piece, 1778

Mezzotint with etching, proof before letter. 557 × 420 mm

Earlom's *Flower-Piece* was one of the most famous prints of its day, described in William Chelsum's *History of Mezzotinto* (1786) as 'astonishing' and by M. Huber and C. G. Martini, in *Manuel des curieux et des amateurs de l'art* (1808), as one of the three finest and most agreeable of mezzotints ('La manière n'a rien produit de plus fin ni de plus ragoutant que ces trois pièces'). It was one of 162 prints issued by the print-publishing entrepreneur John Boydell between 1774 and 1788 in the series known as the *Houghton Gallery* reproducing the great collection of paintings assembled by Robert Walpole, the first Prime Minister of Britain. In 1779 the paintings were sold by a descendant to Catherine the Great of Russia, and van Huysum's *Flower-Piece* is now in the Hermitage Museum, St Petersburg. Earlom produced twenty-six mezzotints for the series (for a full account see Gregory M. Rubinstein, 'Richard Earlom (1743–1822) and Boydell's Houghton Gallery' in *Print Quarterly*, VIII 1991, pp. 2–27).

Earlom had a private income and freedom from commercial restraints enabled him to experiment. More than any of his contemporary mezzotinters he moved away from portraiture to a wide range of subjects, notably scenes from modern life after the paintings of Joseph Wright of Derby (see cat. 57). He also developed a virtuoso combination of etching and mezzotint which, as the present example shows, allowed him to create an extraordinary range of tone and texture. At the foot of the sheet, hidden by the mount, is a note signed by Earlom stating that this is the 'Very first Impression before ever touch'd upon'.

The print was acquired through William Smith from the Harding collection (see p. 96).

1842–8–6–207. Purchased from William Smith
(Harding collection)

60 John Martin (1789–1854)

The Fall of Babylon (Jeremiah L-LI), 1831

Mezzotint with etching. 464 × 719 mm
Campbell-Wees 88, proof before letter

Martin's huge and melodramatic paintings won him great acclaim. The mezzotint of *The Fall of Babylon* is based on the painting exhibited at the British Institution in 1819 about which William Beckford wrote to Chevalier Franchi: 'I have been three times running to the exhibition ... to admire *The Capture of Babylon* by Martin. He adds the greatest distinction to contemporary art, Oh, what a sublime thing', and C. R. Leslie wrote to Washington Allston (who, like another American painter, Thomas Cole, was a friend of Martin) that 'a magnificent picture of *The Fall of Babylon*, by Martin ... attracts admiration'. The picture was sold for 400 guineas to Henry Hope, and set Martin's career on a firm footing. It is now in an Italian private collection.

Like many painters Martin derived a large part of his income from prints after his work; in 1836 he gave evidence to a Select Committee of the House of Commons that he had taken up printmaking as a 'means which would enable the public to see my productions, and give me a chance of being remunerated for my labour'. It is clear, however, that Martin did not regard his prints merely as commercial reproductions but as independent works of art. His work relied to a great extent on dramatic contrasts of light and shade and mezzotint was the perfect print medium for creating such effects. He took personal responsibility for every stage of print production, even going so far as to ink his own plates, a task normally left to specialist artisan printers. Martin's extraordinary attention to detail was described by his son Leopold in a series of 'Reminiscences' in *The Newcastle Weekly Chronicle* in 1889.

The Fall of Babylon was the fifth large biblical subject published by Martin in five years and was shortly followed by a second version of his highly popular *Belshazzar's Feast*. There may have been some saturation of the market, for only 292 impressions sold (a small number if the plate was steel – as were most of Martin's plates) and Martin thereafter produced his large mezzotints at greater intervals. In 1848 he offered the plate for sale; there are many later impressions, often printed in colour and suffering from reworking in the background.

Mm.10–6. Presented by the artist, 1833

60

7. William Mitchell (1820–1908) and John Malcolm of Poltalloch (1805–93)

Stephen Coppel

Sidney Colvin's keepership (1883–1912) was marked by the arrival of three remarkable collections to the Department of Prints and Drawings. In January 1895, William Mitchell presented his comprehensive collection of early German woodcuts to the Museum. This gift was followed a few months later by John Malcolm of Poltalloch's celebrated collection of Renaissance drawings (almost 1,000) and prints (more than 400) which was sold to the Museum by his son John Wingfield Malcolm at the nominal price of £25,000, a figure well below its market value. The two collectors William Mitchell and John Malcolm were lifelong friends whose collections complemented each other. In February 1910, when Colvin was nearing retirement, there came the bequest of 291 old master drawings and 153 choice prints which had been made by the Australian George Salting as part of his munificent gift to the British nation. All three collectors were connoisseurs of the most discriminating kind, and all three were prominent members of the Burlington Fine Arts Club, London's most powerful academy of connoisseurship in the latter half of the nineteenth century. All three furthermore had connections with Australia, including substantial investments and landed interests there, that largely provided the income to support their pursuits. This essay focuses on William Mitchell and John Malcolm as collaborators in forming their respective collections. George Salting's activities as a professional collector are examined separately in the following essay.

On 4 February 1895, Colvin announced to the Trustees of the British Museum the gift of William Mitchell's collection of early German woodcuts which he described as 'one of the most important which has been made to the Department of Prints and Drawings for many years'.[1] In his report recommending the acceptance of the gift, Colvin estimated that Mitchell's woodcut collection amounted to approximately 1,200 prints; together with eight bound volumes, the woodcuts were housed in sixteen ordinary portfolios and in one large-size portfolio. In his summary of its contents, Colvin revealed the richness of this cabinet: 295 woodcuts by Albrecht Dürer, 273 by Hans Holbein, 43 by Lucas Cranach, 39 by Hans Burgkmair, 81 by Schäufelein and Springinklee, 36 by Hans Baldung Grien, 61 by Albrecht Altdorfer, 19 by Hans Sebald Beham, 30 by anonymous fifteenth-century German masters and 97 by those of the sixteenth century, including 16 heraldic designs; together with 96 Italian prints, mostly chiaroscuri, and 30 Dutch woodcuts.

What especially distinguished this extraordinary collection was William Mitchell's unusual decision to concentrate entirely on woodcuts, and within this field almost exclusively on early German woodcuts. In Germany by the mid-nineteenth century, there was a small but learned tradition of collecting early examples of printmaking which arose out of the bibliophilic interest in the history of the early printed book. The bibliophile tradition, however, was very much tied to the controversy over whether printing was invented in Germany or Haarlem; these collectors were fascinated by dated or datable woodcuts, and by blockbooks, but had little interest in art. Mainstream print collecting tended to ignore woodcuts as a genre. Exceptions to this were the works of Dürer, Cranach and the other acknowledged masters of the sixteenth century, whose paintings and engravings ensured that their woodcuts also found a place in Bartsch and later catalogues. But the woodcuts made prior to the arrival of Dürer were never included in Bartsch. It was these earliest woodcuts of the fifteenth century that presented the greatest difficulty for collectors; most were crudely executed and anonymous; at best an inscrutable monogram was the sole clue to an artistic personality. In England, most connoisseurs steered clear of obscure early German woodcuts and formed their print cabinets on the traditional lines of the masters of engraving and etching. By contrast, William Mitchell was most unusual for including pre-Dürer examples in his collection of German woodcuts of the late medieval and Renaissance periods.

Who was William Mitchell and how did he assemble his exceptional collection? A self-effacing and somewhat mysterious figure, he was born in 1820, although the place of his birth is still unknown. Without citing the source of his information, the print scholar Frits Lugt states that Mitchell made a tidy fortune from sheep farming in Australia.[2] For most of his life William Mitchell lived in London, where for many years he maintained a residence at 16 Grosvenor Street in the West End. This is the address at which he was living when he made his will on 19 June 1895. In his old age he appears to have moved a couple of times within St James's, then as now the heartland of the London art-collecting world: a codicil to his will written on 5 May 1902 shows him residing at 5 Bury Street while the probate note on his estate gives his final address as 91 Jermyn Street. He died unmarried in London on 2 December 1908 at the age of eighty-eight and was later buried outside the Episcopalian

Chapel at Poltalloch, Argyllshire, the Scottish estate of his close friend John Malcolm.[3] Unlike those of his fellow collectors Malcolm and George Salting, his death passed unnoticed and no obituary paid tribute to him as a national benefactor.

In the absence of personal papers, Mitchell's will provides the only information of practical value concerning his relationship to family and friends in later life.[4] Mitchell's closeness to the Malcolm family is confirmed by his appointment of John Malcolm's younger son, the banker William Rolle Malcolm, and of John Malcolm's brother-in-law, the Honourable Alfred Erskine Gathorne-Hardy, as executors of his will. A third executor, Ralph Palmer of Little Stanhope Street, was a former London neighbour of John Malcolm of Poltalloch. With the exception of the few legacies specified in his will, the executors were instructed to liquidate all his assets and to invest the money as trustees in stocks and shares. The income from these was to go to Mitchell's brother in Paris for life and then to pass in equal shares to the collector's four nieces, one of whom was married to Heinrich von Seckendorff, a major in the German army. After his 1895 gift to the British Museum, very little remained of Mitchell's collection. His 1902 codicil disposed of a few items as legacies to Mrs Gathorne-Hardy, wife of his executor, namely 'a head in French Chalks by Dumonstier' and 'a drawing by Hogarth in sepia representing Garrick in The Farmers Return', both of which hung in his sitting room, and 'three etchings by Seymour Haden in tortoiseshell frames' displayed in his bedroom. After Mitchell's death his executors sent to Christie's for sale on 24 February 1909 sixteen framed Dürer engravings, including *Adam and Eve* (B.1), *Melancholia* (B.74) and *The Great Fortune* (B.77), together with three framed Dürer woodcuts, which had a provenance from the collection of Bourduge (active around 1800, Lugt 70); among the remaining ten mixed lots of prints and drawings was the original woodblock for Baldung Grien's famous 1510 chiaroscuro *Witches Preparing for their Sabbath* (lot 60).[5] In the aftermath of his gift to the British Museum, these prints would have served as fond souvenirs of his collecting career.

Mitchell first comes to attention as a collector in 1849 when as a young man he disposed of his collection of autograph letters on 17 December at a sale held by Puttick and Simpson, the London literary auctioneers.[6] This collection, which Mitchell may have inherited, was arranged by categories of type – artists, authors, historians, poets, scientific men, political men and the like. It was particularly strong in autographs by the German poets and literati, including Goethe, as well as by Haydn and other German musicians, the artist Chodowiecki, philosophers and lawyers, all of which confirms Mitchell's attachment to German culture by his twenties. The separate class of autographs devoted to learned Scots and Scottish poets in Mitchell's collection

similarly reveals an interest in Scottish heritage. The only indication of his future interest in prints was lot 62, which offered a letter dated 15 June 1797 from the eighteenth-century physiognomist John Caspar Lavater to Professor Langer concerning the sale of Langer's collection of prints.

As Mitchell's next appearance as a collector occurs in the 1860s, when he had begun to assemble his cabinet of early German woodcuts, it is appropriate at this point to turn to his friend John Malcolm of Poltalloch (fig. 1), whose collection of Renaissance prints and drawings was also then being formed. In his recollections, Colvin later described Malcolm as 'a great highland laird, whose passion as a collector [was] to a large extent stimulated as well as directed by an inseparable *fidus Achates* in the person of a bachelor friend of education (and I believe origin) partly German, William Mitchell ...'.[7] Several years Mitchell's senior, John Malcolm was born in 1805, the surviving younger son of the twelfth Laird of Poltalloch, Neill Malcolm, who had extensive Highland holdings in Argyll and profitable sugar and rum interests in Jamaica. In keeping with the expectations of his landed class, John Malcolm was educated at Harrow and then Christ Church, Oxford, where he received his BA in 1827 and the MA in 1830. In 1832, he married Isabella

1. Thomas Lewis Atkinson after W.W. Ouless, *John Malcolm of Poltalloch*, mezzotint c.1860. 352 × 302 mm. 1931-5-8-2, presented by Sir Ian Malcolm, KCMG. The sheet displayed by Malcolm is either a print or a drawing from his collection

2. Michelangelo, *Epifania*, black chalk cartoon made up of 25 sheets, *c*.1550. 2327 × 1656 mm overall. 1895-9-15-518 Malcolm Collection, presented by John Wingfield Malcolm, executor and heir of John Malcolm of Poltalloch

and of his wife were commissioned and completed in Rome that year by the sculptor Laurence Macdonald.

Unlike his fellow collector Mitchell, whose probated wealth came to £20,386, John Malcolm of Poltalloch commanded a vast fortune which was valued at more than £413,046 at his death in 1893. While a measure of his wealth derived from his inherited estates in Scotland and the West Indies, it was the success of his landed ventures in the new colony of South Australia that consolidated his fortune and provided him with the purchasing power to form his collections. In 1839, his brother Neill Malcolm had taken a Special Survey of 4,000 acres in the district of Lake Alexandrina, near the mouth of the River Murray. The Special Survey was an opportunity for absentee landlords to invest in the young colony founded in 1836; on payment of £4,000 the purchaser selected an area of 15,000 acres outside the settled districts and once this had been fully surveyed could take 4,000 acres for himself and offer the remainder to other settlers at the set price of £1 per acre. In the late 1830s, when Scottish tenants on the Malcolm estates and elsewhere were enduring severe famines and poverty through forced enclosures, relief of their distress through resettlement in South Australia appeared an attractive scheme to landlords. When the Highlanders preferred hardship in Argyll to relocation at the other end of the world, the two Malcolm brothers decided to convert their newly acquired land into grazing property.[10]

Called 'Poltalloch' after the family seat, the cattle station in South Australia became a highly successful enterprise: it was controlled by Neill and then John Malcolm from London through Samuel Davenport, their conscientious agent in the colony who later became one of its most prominent politicians. John Malcolm acquired further holdings in the area of Lake Albert, near the original holding at Lake Alexandrina: in 1860, he made three separate purchases of land to form a second cattle station called 'Campbell House' of nearly 8,000 acres. In his account of his travels in Australia between 1871 and 1872, the Victorian novelist Anthony Trollope records a memorable visit to Poltalloch, 'a large cattle-station in the south of the colony, on the eastern side of the lakes. It belongs to a rich Scotch absentee landowner who sits in our parliament, and I will only say of it that I think I ate the best beef there that ever fell in my way.'[11] In June 1873, John Malcolm decided to liquidate his Australian holdings by selling the two properties 'Poltalloch' and 'Campbell House', together with 4,000 head of livestock, for the enormous sum of £175,000.[12]

It is not inconceivable that it was the business side of Malcolm and Mitchell's landed interests in Australia that brought the two collectors together.[13] Certainly from the 1860s we find their names linked together as collectors, and the person who was instrumental in helping to direct and influence their taste was the great Victorian connois-

Wingfield Stratford and lived as a country gentleman outside Maidstone, Kent, where he served as a magistrate. During this period he formed an extensive collection of ornithological specimens, which included the rare great auk and its egg, a bird extinct in the British Isles since the eighteenth century.[8]

On the death of his elder brother Neill in 1857, John Malcolm succeeded to the title of fourteenth Laird of Poltalloch at the age of fifty-two. He inherited the Poltalloch seat, a stately pile of more than a hundred rooms built by his brother near Lochgilphead, Argyll, in the early 1850s.[9] John Malcolm also inherited the family's grand London residence at 7 Great Stanhope Street, off Park Lane. It was here from the 1860s that the Highland laird entertained his connoisseur friends and enjoyed the pleasure of showing them the treasures of his cabinet; below the great staircase hung the celebrated life-size Michelangelo cartoon *Epifania* (fig. 2). A year after his succession, John Malcolm's wife died in 1858; companion marble busts of John Malcolm (now in the Manchester City Art Gallery)

seur John Charles Robinson (1824–1913), who was later knighted. Appointed in 1852 as superintendent of the art collections at the newly created South Kensington Museum (later renamed the Victoria and Albert Museum), Robinson matched his passion for objects with an unrivalled eye for quality.[14] In the fifteen years he held his post at the South Kensington Museum he was responsible for forming its superb holdings, notably in the area of Italian Renaissance decorative arts. A vast array of maiolica, bronzes, terracottas and marble sculptures was acquired by Robinson for the young museum, many of them procured on his frequent travels through Italy and Spain.

Aside from the purchases made in his official capacity for the South Kensington Museum, Robinson was a key figure in helping connoisseurs to form their own collections. In 1860, Robinson sold to Malcolm his outstanding collection of Renaissance drawings, thereby laying the solid foundation for Malcolm's old master drawings cabinet. Although no details of this transaction have survived,[15] the extent of the collection that Malcolm purchased can be reconstructed from the subsequent catalogue prepared by Robinson in 1869. Of the 870 Malcolm drawings catalogued in this volume, some 554, or two thirds, have a provenance note establishing that they had originally come from Robinson.[16] Although there was a number of Dutch drawings, Robinson's former collection concentrated on the works of the Italian Renaissance masters: for example, thirteen sheets attributed to the hand of Leonardo da Vinci, twenty-three to Michelangelo and thirteen to Raphael.

In the years immediately following this first purchase of 1860, Robinson continued to advise Malcolm on additions to his collection. At the Woodburn sale of June 1860 he bought on Malcolm's behalf, for as little as £11.0.6, Michelangelo's large cartoon which Woodburn had kept in an oak frame behind plate glass. [17] In March 1866, on Robinson's recommendation, Malcolm acquired some 135 lots, mostly seventeenth-century Dutch drawings, from the Leembruggen sale in Amsterdam. Three months later Robinson acted as one of Malcolm's two buyers at the posthumous sale of the Oxford divine Dr Wellesley, at which Malcolm purchased eighty-three lots, including twenty-four Claude drawings. According to a simple list Malcolm himself drew up in 1866, his collection by this time contained 708 old master drawings arranged in fifteen boxes. In addition there were ten framed works, including the Michelangelo cartoon, three unspecified drawings by Rubens and a Dürer.[18]

Robinson also promised Malcolm that he would keep an eye out for further purchases during his travels in Spain, adding in one letter written prior to his departure, 'I sincerely hope we shall both be long spared to continue a pursuit which has already during many years been an unfailing source of pleasurable occupation and instruction

to me.'[19] It was in Spain, in highly dramatic circumstances, that Robinson found the Sforza Book of Hours in 1871, one of the great treasures of Renaissance illumination, which Malcolm subsequently acquired.[20]

The rationale behind the formation of the Malcolm collection was unequivocally stated in Robinson's preface to the 1869 catalogue (reprinted also in the second augmented edition of 1876). Robinson distinguished between the choice specimens found in the Malcolm collection and those of eighteenth- and early nineteenth-century collectors, whose 'vast gatherings usually consisted of drawings of doubtful authenticity, or of little intrinsic value, such as academy studies, drawings by unknown and obscure masters, copies by engravers and young artists, etc'.[21] Robinson believed that the encyclopaedic collecting of drawings should properly be left to museums and public institutions, whose 'primary object [is] to illustrate in full detail the entire range of art'. The modern connoisseur, on the other hand, should be more disciplined and selective in approach. In this respect the Malcolm collection in 1869 was a model of the new connoisseur's cabinet. Robinson stipulated the four rules which he and Malcolm had tacitly observed when forming their collections, namely:

1. Irrespective of authorship, to collect only specimens of indisputable excellence as works of art.

2. To aim more particularly at the acquisition of authentic works of the *greatest* masters, and especially of drawings bearing the signatures of their respective authors.

3. In the case of less eminent masters to retain only exceptionally fine and well-preserved examples.

4. To select by preference works, the authenticity and relative importance of which were in a measure guaranteed by the fact of their having passed through celebrated collections of former times, as evidenced by the collectors' marks and written inscriptions upon them.

As we shall see, these criteria equally applied to Malcolm's print collecting, which he saw as supplementing his primary interest in drawings.

Robinson's activities on behalf of Malcolm should be seen in the context of the Burlington Fine Arts Club, the meeting place of like-minded connoisseurs, which Robinson had helped to found in 1866. The origins of this club go back ten years earlier when a select group of collector friends led by Robinson would gather informally in the evenings, initially at Marlborough House and then at the South Kensington Museum, but more frequently in private residences. From 1857 this association of gentlemen collectors became known as the Fine Arts Club; among its founding members were Robinson as Honorary Secretary, Baron Marochetti, Marchese d'Azeglio (the Sardinian Minister in London), John Ruskin, Felix Slade and Augustus Wollaston Franks of the British Museum.[22] The

German scholars Dr Waagen of Berlin and Professor Ludwig Grüner of Dresden were elected in 1857; the future Liberal Prime Minister W. E. Gladstone, who had developed a taste for blue-and-white porcelain, became a member in 1859. Among our collectors John Malcolm of Poltalloch was elected in 1862, William Mitchell in 1868 and George Salting in 1870. Membership of the Fine Arts Club stood at 200 by the end of 1860. Its purpose was to hold *conversazioni*, as these gatherings were called, in the houses of members whose private collections were made available for members and their guests to study and admire. For one of these grand receptions, Malcolm threw open his house at 7 Great Stanhope Street to members, who were also expected to bring examples from their collections to exhibit on these occasions.[23]

As the peripatetic Fine Arts Club grew in membership and as the *conversazioni* became socially more ambitious, several connoisseurs were concerned to establish a more permanent home for the serious pursuit of their interests. On 12 June 1866 the Burlington Fine Arts Club came into being when its first committee met at 177 Piccadilly, opposite the premises of the Royal Academy at Burlington House, from which the Club took its name.[24] Under the chair of the Marchese d'Azeglio, the inaugural committee comprised five members: J. C. Robinson, A. Barker, the Honorary Secretary Ralph Wornum, the print collector Richard Fisher, who was then closely associated with the Print Room of the British Museum, and C. J. Palmer, another print collector.[25] Also among the original members of the Burlington Fine Arts Club were Malcolm and Mitchell, Franks and the etcher and Rembrandt print connoisseur Seymour Haden. In 1870, the Burlington Fine Arts Club took out a lease on premises at 17 Savile Row, where it remained until 1943. It was here that the connoisseurs of the London art world met and discussed their collections, collaborated or competed for objects and exchanged the latest art world gossip over wines and cigars.[26] Most importantly, it was at the Burlington Fine Arts Club that regular exhibitions of objects from the private collections of members and their invited guests were mounted; these exhibitions were open to the public and were often accompanied by illustrated scholarly catalogues commissioned by the Club. Although several members of the Burlington Fine Arts Club still retained their membership of the Fine Arts Club, the latter was eventually disbanded in 1874 when it was resolved that the sum of just over £200 left in its account should be used to purchase books of art reference for the BFAC's Library.[27]

On 9 April 1867, John Malcolm of Poltalloch was proposed by Seymour Haden to become a member of the Committee, the organisational hub of the BFAC and its driving force. It was the Committee which decided the exhibitions proposed by its members as well as appointing new members to the Club after their election by ballot. As a new Committee member Malcolm soon found himself embroiled in a heroic feud between Haden and Whistler that ruptured the BFAC in its first year. In February 1867 the Committee had requested Haden 'to solicit from Mr Whistler the loan of some of his etchings' for an exhibition at the Burlington Fine Arts Club. The following month Whistler was elected a member of the Club, having been proposed by the Royal Academician William Boxall and seconded by Louis Huth, a friend of Whistler's and a collector of blue-and-white porcelain.[28] On 11 June Haden complained to his fellow committee members that 'he had, in a tavern in Paris, been grossly assaulted by Mr Whistler a member of the club'; although the exact nature of the outrage is not specified in the Minute Books of the General Committee, from other sources we know that Whistler had pushed his brother-in-law Haden through a plate-glass window during a brawl in a Paris café on 23 April 1867. While the attack was ostensibly provoked by Whistler's fury at Haden's burial of a mutual doctor friend without first notifying the deceased's family, it was the simmering professional jealousies of their respective reputations as etchers that finally brought about the eruption.[29]

Bent upon revenge, Haden used the General Committee of the Burlington Fine Arts Club first to air his grievance and then as the weapon to seek Whistler's ignominious expulsion from the Club by December 1867. As a Committee member Malcolm took part in all the painful deliberations on the Whistler débâcle, including the drafting of the final letter to Whistler on 2 December 1867. This demanded his withdrawal from the Club by the 10th of that month, with failure to comply being the official posting in the Club's reading room of a notice calling upon its members to hear and vote on the Committee's reasons for his expulsion. After a resolution passed at this extraordinary meeting on 13 December 1867 Whistler was expelled from the Club; his friends the Rossettis resigned in protest four days later. Charles Lutyens, the sporting artist and father of the architect Edwin, requested that the Committee read his letter recording his objections to the Committee's handling of the Whistler affair. On 19 December the Committee closed this shameful chapter with a report from the Honorary Secretary that 'he had struck the name of Mr J. A. Whistler from the list of the members of the club'.[30]

Despite the ramifications of the Whistler quarrel, the Burlington Fine Arts Club continued to expand its membership: on 21 May 1867 the Honorary Secretary recorded that George Salting and nine other gentlemen had recently been elected, raising the total number of members to 167; in the following month Malcolm and Robinson recommended the election of Waagen and Grüner as permanent honorary members of the Club, a British tribute to the important contributions to art-historical scholarship then being made by the Germans.[31] The day immediately after Whistler's expulsion from the

Burlington Fine Arts Club, Haden and Fisher respectively proposed and seconded to the Club's membership the name of George Reid, the Keeper of Prints and Drawings in the British Museum. A second signatory to Reid's nomination was the print connoisseur Julian Marshall. Reid was duly elected on 27 December 1867, but resigned seventeen years later after Fisher and Reid, longstanding friends in the print world, had a terrific row over Fisher's failure to deliver a print catalogue commissioned by the Trustees of the British Museum.[32]

Malcolm's business acumen made him a powerful and practical member of the Committee in securing the Club's financial fortunes. In 1871, to foot the bill of £2,500 for renovating the BFAC's newly acquired Savile Row premises, debentures were offered to Club members for £125, entitling the holder to an annual interest of four per cent. Robinson, Malcolm, Mitchell and Salting were among the thirty-six members who took out these debentures by 1876.[33] Year after year Malcolm was appointed to the Club's Finance Sub-Committee and throughout the 1870s and 1880s both he and Mitchell are regularly found serving on the General Committee, with Mitchell taking the chair on various occasions after his election to the Committee in May 1875. Gifts of books and reference material to the Club were gratefully accepted during Malcolm and Mitchell's tenure: in 1883 Reid presented the two-volume *Catalogue of Early Prints in the British Museum: German and Flemish Schools* prepared by W. H. Willshire under the Keeper's auspices, the final volume of which had just been published by the Trustees. The following year Robinson gave a set of Braun photographs of the Mantegna Cartoons at Hampton Court, the high technical quality of these facsimiles being then the most advanced tool for the comparative study of drawings by connoisseurs and artists.[34]

But the principal business of the Committee was the organisation of exhibitions. To some extent the collecting interests of Malcolm and Mitchell determined the type of exhibitions staged at the Burlington Fine Arts Club during the 1870s and early 1880s. The most ambitious of its earliest shows was one of Raphael and Michelangelo drawings arranged by Richard Fisher in 1870.[35] Of the fifty-seven Raphael drawings exhibited, twenty-three were lent by Malcolm while the second largest number of loans (eighteen) came from the Royal collection at Windsor; Malcolm also provided seventeen and Windsor fourteen of the forty-eight Michelangelos. Mitchell himself lent two Raphaels, including *The Ascension of Our Lord from the Tomb*, which he had acquired from under the nose of Fisher at the Hippisley sale two years earlier. This pen sketch, formerly in the Lawrence collection, showed preliminary ideas for figures found in several finished Raphael drawings at Windsor which had been catalogued recently by the German scholar Carl Ruland. On the day of the Hippisley sale, Fisher had scribbled an urgent note

to Reid at the British Museum, choking with regret at the missed Raphael opportunity:

I hope the mistake, if it be so, about the Raphael drawing, can be remedied. I called at Sotheby's on the way to the Station this afternoon and found that Mr Mitchell had just bought it for £15!! After the very important illustration of it in the Windsor Raphael Collection by Mr Ruland I had long regarded it as a most valuable drawing. And am so vexed I did not further talk to you about it.[36]

During the 1870s Malcolm continued to lend works from his collection to exhibitions at the Burlington Fine Arts Club: a number of Malcolm's Claude drawings acquired at the 1866 Wellesley sale and two examples from Salting's collection were shown at an 1872 exhibition of Claude drawings and etchings, Haden largely supplying the prints from his own collection. Malcolm's Sforza Book of Hours was the centrepiece of an exhibition of illuminated manuscripts in 1874, while his purchases from the 1866 Leembruggen sale found a new audience of admirers when he lent eighty-seven sheets to the BFAC's Dutch master drawings exhibition in 1878. For the latter, Mitchell only lent one drawing – an Everdingen (no. 55) – while Salting, whose taste for seventeenth-century Dutch art was then developing, provided six, including a van Goyen and two Cuyps.[37]

One of the most successful exhibitions was Haden's Rembrandt etching show of 1877, which attracted 3,379 public visitors, exclusive of members. It was the first time that Rembrandt's etchings had been arranged chronologically instead of according to subject, as hitherto had been the practice. Haden was responsible for this new schema and for the catalogue's introductory essay; the catalogue itself, which included many rare states, was written by the Rembrandt connoisseur, the Rev. C. H. Middleton, also a member of the BFAC.[38] Immediately following the success of the Rembrandt show came Mitchell's first exhibition (6 December 1877–5 January 1878) which was devoted to the early sixteenth-century German Little Masters, Sebald Beham and Bartel Beham. Compared to the appeal exerted by Rembrandt's etchings among connoisseurs and the public alike, the miniature woodcuts and engravings of the Beham brothers remained an esoteric interest, even with collectors. Only 196 public visitors ventured to see this exhibition of 370 prints and seven illustrated books. For the accompanying catalogue, Mitchell provided an unsigned introduction to the Nuremberg artists' career and work; he also lent nearly all the woodcuts, including those from *The Planet* series, while the engravings came from various collectors, including the Rev. W. J. Loftie and the ubiquitous Fisher.[39]

On 17 January 1882 Malcolm and Mitchell were again on the Committee when it resolved that the Club's next exhibition should comprise fifteenth- and sixteenth-century German woodcuts. Mitchell, Fisher and Julian

Marshall were appointed to put on the exhibition, which opened four months later. While Marshall supplied a brief introduction to the catalogue, the scholarship behind the entries was largely the work of Mitchell. Of the 161 works exhibited, some 111 came from Mitchell; many great rarities had entered his collection by this date. They included the remarkable colour woodcut, with gold heightening, of *St George* (B.65) by Cranach, which Mitchell remarked 'was discovered not long ago in Vienna'. Dürer's titles to *The Life of the Virgin* (B.4) and to *The Great Passion* (B.76), printed together on one sheet, were also shown. Mitchell included a trial proof of Dürer's portrait of the *Emperor Maximilian* (B.138), explaining that 'trial-proofs, such as this, are very rarely found, and are extremely interesting, as shewing the *modus operandi*'.[40]

It has already been described how Malcolm established the core of his collection of drawings by purchasing the Robinson corpus *en bloc*. No comparable single large purchase has yet been traced as the foundation of either Malcolm or Mitchell's print collection. Because so little documentation has survived, only a very incomplete account can be given of the stages by which Mitchell and Malcolm assembled their respective print collections. The most important extant document is a typescript copy of Malcolm's record of the drawings acquired from July 1865; the chronological listing breaks off on 24 June 1891 with the purchase of a Raphael bistre sketch from the Brooke collection. As Malcolm died two years later, this Raphael acquisition effectively concludes his collecting career.[41] Although it only specifies the drawings and the prices paid for them, this list does give the place and date of each sale and the lot numbers of each item purchased. As prints were often included in drawings sales, by using Malcolm's list it is possible to establish at which sales he may have purchased prints. By a painstaking process, it is possible to identify prints from particular sales by matching the provenance of the lot stated in the sale catalogue to the collectors' stamps on the Malcolm print itself (or as described in the Department's register of Malcolm acquisitions). Since Mitchell often accompanied his friend to the same salerooms, it is also possible to reconstruct, however impressionistically, the formation of his woodcut collection through the print purchases he made on these occasions.

In May 1875, we find Malcolm and Mitchell venturing to Paris to attend the celebrated sale of Emile Galichon (1829–75), the former editor of the *Gazette des Beaux-Arts* whose important collection of prints and drawings was being sold off following his recent death. Aside from a Leonardo da Vinci sketch and two Michelangelo black chalk drawings, Malcolm concentrated his buying upon Italian Renaissance prints at this sale.[42] He bought six Marcantonio prints, two of which – *Poetry* (B.382) after Raphael, being one of only three known proofs of the first state, and *Amadeus* (B.355), believed to be after Francia –

each fetched the very high sum of 2,500 f. (or £110 in 1875). In contrast, Malcolm secured the two Michelangelo drawings, one of which was a sketch for the *Last Judgement*, for 5,000 f. each (exactly double the price of the Marcantonio prints), which gives an indication of how high Marcantonio's reputation as a reproductive engraver stood in the last quarter of the nineteenth century and how it has sunk subsequently. Malcolm also bought engravings by Schongauer (B.100), an anonymous fifteenth-century Florentine master (B.XIII.95.20), and by Benedetto Montagna (B.XV.482.32) as well as three Jacopo de' Barbari engravings, including two (B.11 and B.12) which had once been in the collection of his Burlington Fine Arts Club friend, Julian Marshall. Also bought by Malcolm were two engravings (B.29 and B.33) to add to his very fine Dürer group, which provided a suitable foil to the Dürer woodcuts in Mitchell's own collection. The coup of the Galichon sale was Malcolm's purchase of the famous set of

3. School of Van Eyck, *Supposed Portrait of Philip the Good of Burgundy*, silverpoint on cream prepared paper *c.*1430. 215 × 144 mm. 1895-9-15-998 Malcolm Collection. This drawing was formerly owned by William Mitchell

fifteenth-century Italian Tarot engravings; divided into five suits, the anonymous set of fifty cards had been one of Galichon's most prized pieces and the subject of a lengthy article which he had written for his own journal.[43] The Tarot cards were clearly very important to Malcolm, who personally bid for them, paying the astonishing sum of 17,000 f. (about £750).

Not to be outshone as a connoisseur at the Galichon sale, Mitchell acquired for 6,000 f. a beautiful silverpoint drawing, believed to be a portrait of Philip the Good by Van Eyck (fig. 3), which had been the subject of a scholarly article by the Frenchman.[44] (The same drawing was later bought by Malcolm for Reichsmark 14,500 [or £725] at Mitchell's dispersal of his old master drawings in 1890, where it fetched the highest price in the sale.)[45] From the evidence of the Galichon sale we gain an insight, albeit a fragmentary one, of how the two connoisseur friends went about making their collections and of the importance they attached to objects distinguished by provenance, rarity and art-historical scholarship.

Mitchell was a regular figure in the German salerooms and the development of his woodcut collection can also be partially traced through the sale catalogues. In December 1876, for instance, he was in Leipzig for the sale of K.E. von Liphart (1808–91), the German connoisseur who spent his last years in Florence.[46] As George Redford, the remarkably well-informed sales correspondent for *The Times*, reported, the Liphart sale was 'an event of the highest interest to the world of print collectors'.[47] The collection of 2,000 prints had been assembled over forty years, with the 116 Dürer prints being 'one of the finest ever formed'. Redford commented on the conspicuous attendance of the leading Continental dealers holding commissions from their national institutions and the absence of any representation from the British Museum.[48] Mitchell bought some thirteen lots in person: they included Altdorfer's miniature woodcut series of the *Fall and Redemption of Man* (lot 67), Andreani's ten chiaroscuri making up *The Triumph of Julius Caesar*, after Mantegna (lot 79), and an early proof of Holbein's portrait of *Erasmus of Rotterdam* (lot 950, reproduced in the sale catalogue), which was Mitchell's most expensive purchase at Reichsmark 510 (or £25.10.0 in 1876). Referring to Mitchell's participation as a buyer at the Leipzig sale, Redford remarked that the London connoisseur's 'collection of wood engravings is one of the most complete of any private cabinets'; proof that Mitchell's international renown as a collector in this field was well established by the 1870s. Malcolm also attended this sale, but unlike his friend could always afford to pay more for his prints; for example, he acquired an engraving of the Master BM (B.1), which cost Reichsmark 1501 (or triple the highest price paid by Mitchell).[49]

With his superior purchasing power, it was Malcolm who created a national sensation at the 1884 St John Dent sale in London, when he used his agent Thibaudeau to bid

4. Anonymous fifteenth-century Florentine, *The Assumption of the Virgin* (B.XIII.86.4), broad-manner engraving from two plates once attributed to Botticelli, c.1490. 826 × 560 mm. 1895-9-15-66 Malcolm Collection

for *The Assumption of the Virgin* (B.XIII.86.4) (fig. 4), a Florentine broad-manner engraving attributed to Botticelli. The excitement of the room is conveyed in Redford's vivid description of the fierce contest between Malcolm's buyer and that of the implacable Frenchman Dutuit of Rouen:

When [the Botticelli print] came up to be contended for it was placed before the audience mounted upon a large cloth-covered board at the end of the long table, around which the anxious bidders were assembled in solemn admiration. The first bidding was £250 from M. Thibaudeau, who was at once opposed by M. Clément, and these two, who were the only bidders, kept advancing one against the other, M. Thibaudeau continuing to lead his Paris antagonist up to £800, at which there was a pause, after which M. Clément again advanced to his last bid of £850, but upon this M. Thibaudeau bid £860, and the hammer fell. The beautiful print has, we understand, passed now into a most worthy collection which has long held a high reputation among the best in England – that of Mr. Malcolm of Poltalloch, who is to be congratulated on his invaluable acquisition, and upon having retained this most covetable example among the art treasures of this country.[50]

It now remains to examine the stratagems by which the Keeper, Sidney Colvin, managed to steer the two complementary collections of Malcolm and Mitchell in the direction of the British Museum. In his reminiscences, written after he had long retired from museum life, Colvin reflected that 'it is a chief part of [the curator's] duty to win the regard and confidence of private collectors, to help and stimulate them in their pursuits, putting his knowledge at their disposal but making them feel the while that their prime, their binding, duty is to acknowledge such help by destining their collections in the long run to enrich the institution which he serves'.[51] An acquaintance of both men from his earliest days at the British Museum, Colvin was well aware of their stature as collectors; he encouraged their fields of collecting and attended the opening of the principal London sales in their company.[52] Like Reid before him, Colvin was elected in 1893 to the Burlington Fine Arts Club where he was assured of an opportunity of befriending the most prominent connoisseurs of the day.[53]

On 30 May 1893, at the age of eighty-eight, Malcolm died at his Poltalloch estate in Argyllshire. Only a week or so before he had presented to the British Museum the magnificent Sforza Book of Hours. This gift was the subject of a lengthy column in *The Times*, probably written by Colvin himself or E. M. Thompson, Principal Librarian of the British Museum, both of whom were close friends of Malcolm. The author of the unsigned piece was at pains to point out how Malcolm's munificence would repair the earlier failure by the British Museum to obtain the manuscript when it had been first offered to the Trustees by J. C. Robinson in 1871:

The price was, however, beyond their means, and the course of appeal to the Lords of the Treasury seldom runs smooth. The Chancellor of the Exchequer deemed the sum of £2,500 too large for even one of the most beautiful existing works of Italian art of the 15th century, and the chance was lost. Mr. Malcolm became the purchaser ... Were the Chancellor of the Exchequer of that day still among us, he might, and probably would, have cynically congratulated both himself and the public upon his foresight in trusting to the private enterprise and spirit which, from his point of view, have now justified his parsimony. But such venturesomeness does not always succeed, and a Malcolm is not always standing by.[54]

Shortly after Malcolm's death, speculation was rife among connoisseurs and museum officials as to the fate of his collections of prints and drawings. Malcolm, according to the terms of his will of 2 May 1888, had bequeathed 'my collection of drawings by the Old Masters and old prints' to his eldest son John Wingfield Malcolm, with the freedom to dispose of them should he so wish. But should his

son not be induced by 'special circumstance' to part with the collection, Malcolm expressed the wish that 'they might be kept together and remain in the family as they have for years afforded me much pleasure and are of themselves of very considerable value'.[55] Once again an article appeared in the columns of *The Times* arguing for the necessity of keeping Malcolm's collection intact for the benefit of the nation:

[S]ince the unfortunate refusal of the Treasury authorities half a century ago to acquire the unequalled collection of sketches and studies by old masters formed by Sir Thomas Lawrence, no second amateur had brought together a cabinet of equal importance with that formed during the last 30 years by Mr. Malcolm, buying at first under the advice of Sir Charles Robinson, and more recently on his own judgment.[56]

Colvin, it appears, had already prepared a plan to avert the danger of a possible dispersal by public sale. In all likelihood it was he or William Mitchell who persuaded Malcolm's heir to deposit the collection on loan in the Department of Prints and Drawings. On 15 June 1893, John Wingfield Malcolm wrote to the Principal Librarian of the British Museum offering the loan of his father's collection, on condition that 'I should wish them used for the benefit of students under such restrictions as the authorities of the Museum and Mr. Mitchell on my behalf may determine'. The same letter continued: 'I would also ask the Trustees to accept from me the cartoon by Michael Angelo which formed part of the collection'.[57] These arrangements were duly announced in *The Times* on 17 July 1893, when the spirit of public duty shown by Malcolm's heir was gratefully acknowledged.[58] By this manoeuvre not only was the collection preserved in one place, it was also available for amateurs to study in the Print Room like any other part of the permanent collection. Moreover the spectacular gift of the unique Michelangelo cartoon gave the Museum a powerful advantage when it later applied to the Treasury for a grant to purchase the Malcolm collection for the nation.

With the intention of drawing public attention to the richness of the Malcolm cabinet, Colvin mounted an extensive display of 450 old master prints and 500 drawings at the British Museum from March 1894. Almost two thirds of the total were selected from Malcolm's collection and these were readily distinguishable from the Museum's holdings by the special stamp of the collector's name and crest on the exhibition mounts. Colvin's specially written catalogue, which ran into a second edition by 1895, contained some 568 entries, with the Malcolm Collection prominently credited beneath each of the relevant items.[59]

Anxious to resolve the question of the collection's ultimate destination, Colvin in September 1894 sought the advice of Mitchell, who was then travelling in Italy. From the Grand Hotel in Venice, Mitchell forwarded Colvin's letter to the heir, adding in his reply to the Keeper that 'for

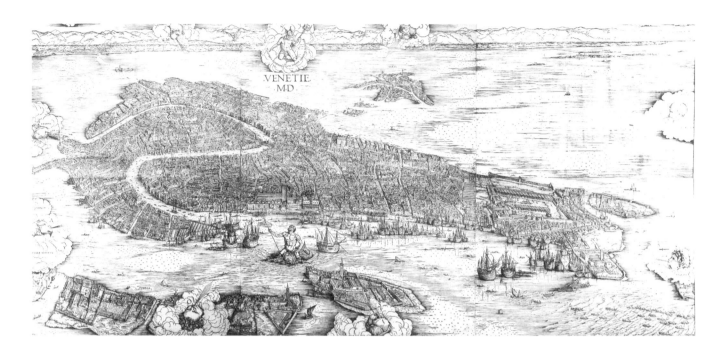

5. Jacopo de' Barbari, *View of Venice*, woodcut from six
blocks, 1500. 1390 × 2820 mm. 1895-1-22-1192 to 1197
Mitchell Collection

the present there is not, I think, any idea of selling, but
Harcourt's new succession laws may make it necessary or
expedient later on. I saw him last night in the Piazza with
Labouchere'.[60] On 19 October 1894 the Poltalloch heir
outlined to Colvin the dilemma he faced on entering his
inheritance:

Everyday I find something that must be redone, & now it is
much of the Home Farmsteading where walls & roofs are
giving way. Thus as things are I cannot afford to do what I
should like to do namely make it over to the nation as the
Malcolm collection in memory of my dear father. What am I
to do? If I sell it, it will be scattered abroad. If I let the
Museum pick what it wants, the rest will not sell at a fair
price. If it were possible for the Museum to purchase the
whole collection at a moderate price & then sell off what it did
not want that seems a way out of a difficulty but I believe that
is not possible. Sorely against my wish I only see a regular big
sale but I should like you & Thompson [the British Museum's
Principal Librarian] old friends of my fathers to give me your
advice.[61]

Prior to his departure early in December to supervise his
interests in the West Indies, John Wingfield Malcolm
sought an interview with Colvin in London to hear his
suggestions. Shortly after his return to England, he was
persuaded on 30 May 1895 'after our conversation today'
to inform Colvin of his decision 'that the collection of
Drawings & Prints made by my late father should become
the property of the nation at the price of £25,000 on the

condition that each drawing or print should be marked as
belonging to his collection'.[62] It is clear that William
Mitchell's advice to John Wingfield Malcolm was crucial
to the success of these negotiations with Colvin. On 17
January 1895, Mitchell had visited the Print Room,
presumably to see Colvin about giving his collection of
woodcuts to the British Museum, which the Trustees
accepted a few days later.[63] This munificent gesture may
well have forced John Wingfield Malcolm's hand in allowing his father's collection to join Mitchell's in the British
Museum, at a very favourable price.[64]

On 6 June 1895 Colvin recommended to the Trustees
the acceptance of the heir's offer and after the Trustees'
special application to the Treasury for a purchase grant,
Parliament eventually voted the sum of £25,000 to acquire
the Malcolm Collection for the nation.[65] Looking back
upon this achievement, Colvin later remarked: 'the
purchase of [Malcolm's] treasures for the British Museum
after his death almost doubled the importance of the
department I had the honour to serve'.[66] The decision of
Mitchell and Malcolm's heir to place the Mitchell and
Malcolm collections in the one institution was intended
both as a way of keeping them together and of preserving
the memory of the collectors' mutual passion for prints
and drawings. Today Malcolm's life-size Michelangelo
cartoon and Mitchell's equally large bird's-eye view woodcut of Venice by de' Barbari (fig. 5) hang on permanent
display facing each other in the Prints and Drawings
Department of the British Museum. By their impressive
scale, superlative quality and art-historical importance,
they epitomise the connoisseurship that forever binds the
two friends as collectors.

1. Sidney Colvin's Report to the Trustees, 4 February 1895.

2. Lugt 2638: 'William Mitchell fit une jolie fortune dans l'élevage des moutons, en Australie, puis passa le milieu et la fin de sa vie à Londres'. Although William Mitchell was the coeval of his namesake David Scott Mitchell (1836–1907) – the Australian bibliophile whose collection of early books on Australia was bequeathed to form Sydney's Mitchell Library – there is no evidence to suggest that the two were related, however tempting the supposition might be. I am grateful to Jim Andrighetti, Manuscripts Section, State Library of New South Wales, Sydney, for kindly checking the David Scott Mitchell papers in the Mitchell Library to confirm this point. I am also grateful to Professor John Ritchie, General Editor, Australian Dictionary of Biography, Australian National University, Canberra, and Irena Zdanowicz, Senior Curator of Prints and Drawings, National Gallery of Victoria, Melbourne, for their help in locating biographical information on Mitchell, Malcolm and Salting.

3. The epitaph on Mitchell's memorial stone at Poltalloch reads: 'He was for many years the intimate friend and companion of John Malcolm Esq. of Poltalloch'. It gives his age at death as eighty-eight and differs by one day from the death date of 2 December 1908 on Mitchell's probate note. I am grateful to Nicholas Turner (the J. Paul Getty Museum, Malibu) for informing me of the whereabouts of Mitchell's burial place.

4. Will of William Mitchell, 19 June 1895; probate granted 23 January 1909. Somerset House, Probate Registry, London.

5. Christie's, London, 24 February 1909, lots 33 to 60.

6. Puttick and Simpson, London, 17 December 1849, lots 1 to 107, which realised just under £60. Lugt 2638 is mistaken in assuming that the sale of an ornithological library belonging to one William Mitchell of Eastbourne at Sotheby's (10 November 1903) is the same Mitchell as our collector.

7. Sidney Colvin, *Memories and Notes of Persons and Places, 1852–1912*, London 1921, p. 207.

8. A privately distributed family memoir compiled by Dugald Malcolm, 'Neill Malcolm XIII Laird [and] John Malcolm XIV Laird of Poltalloch' (c.1992), has largely provided me with these biographical details. A copy of this document was kindly presented by its author, Malcolm's great-grandson, to the Department's library.

9. A century later Poltalloch was unroofed and abandoned by its heirs after a displenishment sale forced upon them by inheritance laws.

10. See Eric Richards, 'The Highland Scots of South Australia', *Journal of the Historical Society of South Australia*, 4, 1978, esp. pp. 33–9. The account of Malcolm's South Australian venture in the above and following paragraphs is derived from 'The Malcolms of the Lakes' in R. Cockburn, *Pastoral Pioneers of South Australia*, II, Adelaide 1927, pp. 192–3, and the more recent and more accurate archival research conducted in the Land Titles Office, Adelaide, by Necia Gilbert and presented in her fascinating unpublished 1981 paper, 'John Malcolm of Poltalloch (1805–1893): a great collector with South Australian connections', a copy of which the author has kindly given to the Prints and Drawings Department. I am also grateful to Julie Robinson, Art Gallery of South Australia, Adelaide, for providing references to George C. Morphett, 'The Malcolms', *Royal Geographical Society of Australasia*, South Australian Branch, 43, 1942, pp. 13–15, and J. D. Somerville, 'The Malcolms: a preliminary investigation', typescript, State Library of South Australia (Mortlock Library), Adelaide.

11. Anthony Trollope, *Australia and New Zealand*, II, London 1873, ch. 12, p. 216. On his royal visit to the Australian colonies in 1867, the Duke of Edinburgh (the future King Edward VII) was a guest in November at the two Malcolm properties in South Australia, where the royal party was welcomed by an Aboriginal corroboree and hunted kangaroos. John Malcolm appears not to have been in Australia during this royal visit, although when he renewed Davenport's power of attorney in April 1868 he is recorded as being temporarily resident in Adelaide. Gilbert, op. cit.

12. Malcolm's landed interests in Australia were sold to the Bowman brothers of Crystal Brook, South Australia, whose descendants still own Poltalloch.

13. Among the bequests made in his will, Malcolm left a legacy of £1,000 to 'my good friend' William Mitchell 'in remembrance of the kind assistance he has so often given me'. See n. 55.

14. For an outline of Robinson's career, see his obituary in *The Times*, 11 April 1913, p. 9, and the entry in the *Dictionary of National Biography, 1912–1921*, pp. 471–2. For a recent assessment of his influence as a connoisseur, see the unpublished D.Phil. dissertation by Helen Davies, 'Sir John Charles Robinson (1824–1913): his role as a connoisseur and creator of public and private collections', D.Phil. Oxford 1992. I am grateful to Dr Davies for allowing me to read her dissertation.

15. J. C. Robinson's Account Book, preserved amongst his papers in the Ashmolean, Oxford, only covers the later period, 1874–1907. See Davies, op. cit. pp. 377–8.

16. J. C. Robinson, *Descriptive Catalogue of the Drawings by the Old Masters, Forming the Collection of John Malcolm of Poltalloch, Esq.*, London, privately printed at the Chiswick Press, 1869. A second edition appeared in 1876, with additional drawings and some amendments of attribution prepared by Malcolm, who also added a new preface.

17. Samuel Woodburn sale, London (Christie's), 4 June 1860 and following days. *Epifania* (lot 160, £11.0.6.), 1895-9-15-518, Wilde 75.

18. John Malcolm, 'List of Drawings, 1866' is preserved in the Argyll and Bute District Archives, Kilmory, Lochgilphead; I am grateful to Murdo MacDonald, Senior Archivist, for providing me with a copy of this holograph MS. This document contains two separate listings of Malcolm's cabinet arranged by school in boxes. In both cases the artist and number of sheets are specified but not the drawings. The first list appears to be Malcolm's Robinson acquisitions made before 1866: this records 498 drawings kept in ten solander cases under the arrangement of early Flemish and German (box 1), Dutch and Flemish (boxes 2 and 3), early Italian (box 4), Italian (boxes 5 to 9), Spanish, French and English (box 10). The second list includes the Malcolm additions from the 1866 Leembruggen sale: the drawing collection has now expanded to 708 works housed in fifteen cases. Both lists antedate the acquisitions made by Malcolm at the Wellesley sale of June/July 1866, as the twenty-four Claudes are not included.

19. J. C. Robinson, letter to John Malcolm of Poltalloch, 1865, in the Robinson papers, the Ashmolean, Oxford; cited by Davies, op. cit. p. 386.

20. Malcolm's gift of this volume to the British Museum in 1893 is discussed later in this essay, see p. 167. With a collector's passion, Robinson, at the time of the Malcolm gift, related the story of how he had first acquired the Sforza Book of Hours in 1871: 'I forthwith engaged Don José [Robinson's Spanish agent who had already lost 20,000 pesetas by a theft from his pocket upon a previous attempt to buy the book] to get me sight of the ill-omened treasure; this he undertook to do, and the very same evening he brought the priest [the aristocratic owner's chaplain] to my room, when with much ceremony the little corpulent velvet-covered volume was put into my hands. The

very first page opened, disclosing two glorious illuminations, blazing with colours and gold, struck me dumb with admiration, but when every page of the book, and there were more than two hundred of them, was revealed equally enriched, the only thought was that it should not again for an instant leave my hands; and literally it did not, for luckily I had provided the funds in anticipation and so the bargain was instantly concluded. No entreaty could induce the vendor to give any information as to the previous ownership or history of the book, although I left no means of persuasion untried' (J. C. Robinson, 'The Sforza Book of Hours', *Bibliographica*, 1, 1895, pp. 433–4). For a recent short picture book, see Mark Evans, *The Sforza Hours*, British Library, London 1992.

21. Robinson, *Catalogue of the Drawings … of John Malcolm of Poltalloch*, op. cit. 1869, p.v, where Robinson's other remarks quoted in this paragraph are also found.

22. For a brief history of the Fine Arts Club, see Ann Eatwell, 'The Collector's or Fine Arts Club 1857–1874. The first society for collectors of the decorative arts', *The Decorative Arts Society*, 18, 1994, pp. 25–30.

23. Malcolm's reception, 8 June 1865, was attended by sixty-nine members and their forty-three guests, including Felix Slade and the British Museum officials W. H. Carpenter and Augustus Wollaston Franks. Among the twenty-four members who brought objects for discussion were J. C. Robinson, Richard Fisher and Louis Huth, the themes for the evening being 'Enamels of Limoges, Damascene Work in General, Art Bronzes, Carved Ivories and Sèvres Porcelain'. V & A National Art Library, London, Fine Arts Club, General Committee Minute Book, 2, 8 June 1865; FAC, Signature Books for the *Conversazioni*, 2, 8 June 1865. The elections of Malcolm, Mitchell and Salting are recorded in FAC, Candidates' Proposal Book (April 1857–20 June 1872), with Robinson and Richard Fisher being the proposer and seconder, respectively, for Mitchell and Salting's nominations.

24. For a brief history of the Burlington Fine Arts Club (hereafter BFAC), see the excellent editorial 'The Burlington Fine Arts Club', *The Burlington Magazine*, 94, April 1952, pp. 97–9. When the BFAC was finally wound up in 1951, the following documents belonging to the Club were deposited in the V & A National Art Library, London: the General Committee Minute Books (6 vols), 12 June 1866–2 February 1951; the less informative General Meeting Minute Books (2 vols), 27 April 1866–7 February 1951; the Candidates' Books (11 vols), 2 January 1867–27 May 1940; and Correspondence Relating to the BFAC's Debentures and Debenture Holders, 1871–1911. I have drawn heavily on the Club's records for the earlier years in the following account of Mitchell and Malcolm's role in the BFAC.

25. In February 1867, the terminally ill Palmer astonished the print world when he bought an excessively rare first state of Rembrandt's *Hundred Guilder Print* at the sale of Sir Charles Price for £1,180, then the highest price ever paid for any print.

26. Shortly after the Club was founded Fisher and Haden were entrusted 'to provide the supply of wines, refreshments, cigars etc'. BFAC, General Committee Minute Book, 1, 29 December 1866.

27. The only foreign newspaper to which the Club initially subscribed was the German *Wiener Zeitschrift*; General Committee Minute Book, 1, 17 December 1866. In 1877, when the BFAC was building up its art library, Fisher wrote to the Keeper at the British Museum asking for a list of 'good reference books, instead of showy picture books of modern publication'. R. Fisher, letter to G. W. Reid, 21 April 1877.

28. BFAC Candidates' Books, 1, Whistler proposed 22 February 1867, elected 12 March 1867. A portrait of Louis Huth's wife was later painted by Whistler in 1872–73; reproduced in Richard

Dorment and Margaret F. Macdonald, *James McNeill Whistler*, exhibition catalogue, Tate Gallery, London 1994, cat. 63. Huth was also a great friend of Salting who appointed him an executor of his will; see the following essay, p. 200, n. 5.

29. See Katharine A. Lochnan, *The Etchings of James McNeill Whistler*, New Haven and London 1984, pp. 145–6.

30. The events of the Whistler affair are recorded under 1867 in vol. 1 of the BFAC's General Committee Minute Books.

31. BFAC, General Committee Minute Book, 1, 25 June 1867. Fisher and Haden, by contrast, recommended the unremarkable Mr Goodale of New York for honorary membership.

32. BFAC Candidates' Books, 1, Reid proposed 14 December 1867, elected 27 December 1867. Mitchell and Marshall were present at the Committee meeting which reported and accepted Reid's resignation in 1884; BFAC General Committee Minute Book, 2, 12 February 1884. Complete sets of proofs for Fisher's 'Catalogue of Nielli and Italian Engravings of the XV Century in the British Museum' and his 'Catalogue of Engravings by Marcantonio and Agostino Veneziano', which were printed by order of the Trustees in 1883–4 but never published, are in the Department of Prints and Drawings library.

33. 'List of Debenture Holders and Interest', 31 December 1876, in Correspondence Relating to the BFAC's Debentures and Debenture Holders, 1871–1911.

34. For the use of Braun photographs and their appeal to nineteenth-century artists like Redon, see Ted Gott, 'Old Master Echoes: Odilon Redon, Photography and "La Vie Morale"', *Australian Journal of Art*, 5, 1986, pp. 46–72.

35. *Raphael Sanzio and Michel-Angelo Buonarroti*, exhibition catalogue, BFAC, London 1870.

36. R. Fisher, letter to [G. W. Reid], dated 'Monday' [Monday 25 May 1868]. Offered as lot 209 at the posthumous sale of Sir John Stuart Hippisley, 23–25 May 1868 (Sotheby's), the Raphael sketch was bought by Mitchell through his buyer Colnaghi's. It is listed as no. 32 in the catalogue for the 1870 BFAC exhibition. When Mitchell disposed of his old master drawings collection at the Frankfurt sale of 7 May 1890 (Prestel), it was Carl Ruland who wrote the catalogue introduction; on this occasion the Raphael sketch (lot 93) sold for Reichsmark 1,190. The drawing is now in the Musée Bonnat, Bayonne.

37. *Exhibition of Drawings and Etchings by Claude Le Lorrain*, exhibition catalogue, BFAC, 1872; *Illuminated Manuscripts Catalogue*, exhibition catalogue, BFAC, 1874; and *Exhibition of Drawings by the Dutch Masters*, exhibition catalogue, with an introductory essay on Dutch drawings by Frederick Wedmore, BFAC, 1878.

38. *Catalogue of the Etched Work of Rembrandt*, exhibition catalogue, with introductory remarks by Seymour Haden, BFAC, 1877. Middleton's contribution to the scholarly catalogue (which is nowhere mentioned in the publication) was acknowledged at the BFAC's Annual General Meeting as 'one of the most instructive and interesting of those that have been issued by the Club'; BFAC, General Meeting Minute Books, 1, 28 May 1878, which also gives the high visitor numbers.

39. *Exhibition of the Works of Hans Sebald Beham (born 1500 died 1550) and Barthel Beham (born 1502 died 1540)*, exhibition catalogue, with an unsigned introductory notice by William Mitchell, BFAC, 1877. Reid was on the exhibition sub-committee to plan this show with Mitchell, Fisher, Middleton, Loftie and J. J. Heywood; BFAC, General Committee Minute Books, 2, 13 November 1877. The minutes of the AGM note 'the Catalogue of which an Introductory Memoir of the artists by Mr. Mitchell was prefixed'; BFAC, General Meeting Minute Books, 1, 28 May 1878, where the number of public visitors is also recorded.

40. *Catalogue of a Collection of Woodcuts of the German School, Executed in the XVth and XVIth Centuries*, exhibition catalogue, with an introduction by J[ulian] M[arshall], BFAC, 1882. For Mitchell's primary responsibility for this exhibition, see BFAC, General Committee Minute Books, 2, 17 January, 9 and 27 June, 1 August 1882. Julian Marshall is noted in the BFAC, General Meeting Minute Books, 1, 29 May 1883, as the author of the catalogue introduction.

41. John Malcolm, 'Memorandum of the prices paid at different times for Drawings in my collection'(July 1865–24 June 1891); a typescript copy of this twenty-five-page document was given to the library of the British Museum's Prints and Drawings Department by Malcolm's son-in-law, the Hon. A. E. Gathorne-Hardy, in 1911. The running total of the prices paid (with those from foreign sales converted to English sterling) came to £9,422.4.5 for the period covered.

42. Emile Galichon sale, Paris (Hôtel Drouot, M. Clément), 10 May 1875 and the four days following; the copy in the library of the British Museum's Prints and Drawings Department is priced with the buyers' names. The drawings Malcolm purchased were Leonardo da Vinci, *Study of a Winged Figure; Allegory with Fortune* (lot 167, 2,025 f.), pen and brown ink and brown wash over sketches drawn with a stylus, 1895-9-15-482, Popham and Pouncey 104; Michelangelo, *The Fall of Phaeton* (lot 15, 5,000 f.), 1895-9-15-517, Wilde 55; and Michelangelo, *Studies for the 'Last Judgement'* (lot 16, 5,000 f.), 1895-9-15-518, Wilde 60.

43. Galichon sale, 10 May 1875, lot 331; with the exception of the Tarot cards for which Malcolm bid himself, the rest of his purchases were made through Colnaghi's, his commissioned buyer. Emile Galichon, 'Observations sur le recueil d'estampes du xve siècle impropremment appelé *Giuoco di Tarocchi*', *Gazette des Beaux-Arts*, 9, 1861, pp. 143–7.

44. Galichon sale, 10 May 1875, lot 49, through the commissioned buyer Colnaghi's. Emile Galichon, 'Des Dessins de Maîtres à propos d'un prétendu portrait de Philippe le Bon, attribué à Simon Marmion', *Gazette des Beaux-Arts*, 22, 1867, pp. 78–90.

45. William Mitchell sale, 7 May 1890, Frankfurt am Main (Prestel), lot 39. Five years later the Van Eyck drawing came into the British Museum with the purchase of the Malcolm Collection; 1895-9-15-998. Popham rejected the identification of the sitter as Philip the Good of Burgundy and relegated the drawing to School of Van Eyck (A. E. Popham, *Catalogue of Drawings by Dutch and Flemish Artists ... in the British Museum*, 5, London 1932, p. 17, cat. 1).

46. Karl Eduard von Liphart sale, 5 December 1876 and the days following, Leipzig (Boerner's). I am grateful to Dr Marianne Küffner of Boerner's, Düsseldorf, for kindly providing me with a list of the prints Mitchell purchased in his own name at this sale (from Boerner's priced and named copy of the sale catalogue). For further details on Liphart, see Lugt 1687–1689 and Lugt Suppl. 1687.

47. George Redford, 'The Liphart Collection', *The Times*, 19 December 1876, p. 5; reprinted in Redford, *Art Sales. A History of Sales of Pictures and Other Works of Art*, 1, London, 1888, p. 233. Redford's comments in this passage are quoted from this source.

48. The one English museum which did participate at the Liphart sale was the Fitzwilliam in Cambridge, whose university authorities had instructed its agents to spend upwards of £1,000 on the acquisition of fine and rare engravings for the collection, a step which Redford added 'will be viewed with great satisfaction, as evincing the determination of the University to make the splendid Fitzwilliam bequest fully efficient in promoting the influence of art'.

49. Other important sales at which Malcolm and Mitchell bought prints were the Firmin-Didot sale, 16 April–12 May 1877, Paris (Hôtel Drouot, M. Pawlowski and MM. Danlos et Delisle) and the Bale sale, 9–14 June 1881, London (Christie's); see cat. 67–70.

50. St John Dent sale, 28 March 1884 and the following six days, London (Sotheby's), lot 241; BM 1895-9-15-66 (Hind 1938, B.III.10). Redford, 'Sale of the Dent collection of prints', *The Times*, 31 March 1884, p. 8; reprinted in Redford, *Art Sales*, op. cit., p. 368.

51. Colvin, *Memories and Notes*, op. cit. p. 205.

52. For example, at the opening of the St John Dent sale which was reported in 'Sale of the Dent collection of prints', *The Times*, 29 March 1884, p. 12; reprinted in Redford, *Art Sales*, op. cit. p. 368.

53. BFAC Candidates' Books, 5, Colvin proposed 11 January 1893, elected 24 January 1893.

54. 'The Sforza Book of Hours', *The Times*, 24 May 1893, p. 3.

55. Will of John Malcolm of Poltalloch, 2 May 1888, item 9 (grant of probate 20 July 1893); Somerset House, Probate Registry, London.

56. 'The Malcolm Collection', *The Times*, 17 July 1893, p. 5.

57. J. W. Malcolm, letter to E. M. Thompson, 15 June 1893. British Museum, Central Archives, Book of Presents, Supplementary vol. II (January 1890–December 1896). The very day prior to the date of this letter, William Mitchell and friend visited the Print Room, presumably with the purpose of discussing the heir's intentions with Colvin. British Museum, Prints and Drawings Department, Visitors' Book, vol. x (14 June 1893).

58. See n. 56.

59. See Sidney Colvin, *Guide to an Exhibition of Drawings and Engravings by the Old Masters, Principally from the Malcolm Collection, in the Print and Drawing Gallery*, exhibition catalogue, British Museum, London, 2nd edition, 1895, p. 4.

60. W. Mitchell, letter to Sidney Colvin, 8 [October] 1894.

61. J. W. Malcolm, letter to Sidney Colvin, 19 October 1894.

62. J. W. Malcolm's letter of offer to Colvin on 30 May 1895 was written on official British Museum notepaper. British Museum, Central Archives, Original Papers, 1895, 2045/2.

63. Mitchell's collection of woodcuts bears the registration number 1895-1-22-1 to 1290. In 1904, Mitchell made the additional gift of his supplementary collection of early illustrated books of German origin (1904-2-6-1 to 170).

64. Mitchell's name is recorded with John Wingfield Malcolm in the Department's Visitors' Book, vol. XI, for 30 May 1895, the same day as the heir's letter to Colvin offering the Malcolm collection; see n. 62.

65. See 'The British Museum and the Malcolm Collection', *The Times*, 10 July 1895, p. 10. In his report to the Trustees of 6 June 1895, Colvin added that in the case of prints duplicating ones already held in the Museum's collection 'those of Mr. Malcolm are almost invariably the finer examples, so that their acquisition will not only raise the general quality of the Museum collections, but liberate a considerable number of duplicates, which can be utilised either by way of exchange for other examples required, or by way of loan to provincial museums' (British Museum, Central Archives, Original Papers, 1895, 2045/1). By a curious irony, because the Malcolm Collection was a purchase, it was the duplicate Malcolm prints, notably the superb Dürer engravings and the Rembrandt etchings, that Colvin's successors later exchanged or sold off to the trade for new acquisitions of prints and even drawings. Initiated with caution by Campbell Dodgson in 1931, this curatorial practice was continued

by Hind and Popham until 1947 when it virtually ceased. With the agreement of the Malcolm family, the new prints (but not the drawings) thus acquired were regarded as additions to the Malcolm Collection, being marked in the Department's register as 'Malcolm Additions'.

66. Colvin, *Memories and Notes*, op. cit. p. 207.

61 Anonymous German

The Virgin and Child Seated, c.1450–70

Illustrated in colour between pages 112 and 113

Coloured woodcut. 281 × 191 mm

Schreiber 1058; Dodgson A 54

Most fifteenth-century German woodcuts were made as purely devotional images and are usually of low quality; this print is unusual in that it reveals the work of an artistic personality. The Virgin is seated with the Infant Child on a tasselled cushion placed in the centre of the floor-tiled chamber; a large tapestry hanging from a rod provides a decorative backdrop to this intimate setting. The print was coloured at the time in washes of crimson, yellow ochre, viridian green and pale brown.

Mitchell acquired this print very late in his collecting career. It is catalogued in the first volume of Schreiber's monumental *Manuel* in 1891, where it is described as being in the collection of the Munich antiquarian book-dealer Ludwig Rosenthal. Rosenthal took advantage of the interest provoked by Schreiber's scholarship to issue *Incunabula xylographica et chalcographica* the following year. This lavishly produced publication in French and German served as an illustrated catalogue of his own collection of fifteenth-century woodcuts, illustrated books, metalcuts and engravings which he had put together over many years and which he was now offering for sale to discerning collectors of scholarly inclination. Mitchell bought this woodcut directly from Rosenthal himself, although it is not recorded in the latter's 1892 catalogue, and presented it three years later to the British Museum.

1895–1–22–12. Mitchell collection

62 Albrecht Dürer (1471–1528)

The Martyrdom of St Catherine, c.1498

Woodcut. 387 × 284 mm

Bartsch 120; Dodgson I 271.7

Whereas for engraving Dürer had predecessors in the work of Schongauer in the north and Mantegna in Italy, in woodcut he had no precursors to match his inventiveness and skill with the woodblock. This print belongs to Dürer's earliest group of woodcuts, made before 1500. Unlike those he executed for the Apocalypse and the Great

Passion series of this period, this woodcut was conceived as a single subject. It depicts the moment of St Catherine's execution: the heavens are torn apart by a sudden outburst of hail and thunder, the spiked wheel devised for her martyrdom lies blasted by lightning, while the Roman emperor's soldiers are thrown into confusion by these heavenly portents; indifferent to these signs, the executioner draws his sword to behead the saint, who kneels serenely in the confidence of her faith. Dürer's famous monogram is incised bottom left; the block survives in the Metropolitan Museum of Art, New York.

Mitchell's collection of early German woodcuts included 295 examples by Dürer, many acquired from print sales in Germany during the 1870s. Mitchell first exhibited this print in 1878 as no. 66 in the Liverpool Art Club's *Loan Collection of Wood Engravings*, to which he lent fifty-seven Dürer woodcuts from his collection.

1895–1–22–702. Mitchell collection

63 Albrecht Dürer (1471–1528)

The Mass of St Gregory, 1511

Woodcut. 298 × 206 mm

Bartsch 123; Dodgson I 304.117

The sophistication of Dürer's technique is exemplified by this woodcut of 1511. By this stage, Dürer had trained a team of specialist cutters to cut his blocks with an unprecedented fineness and skill. Spatial recession is suggested both by the Renaissance device of perspective and by the extremely fine cutting of the lines to create a half-tone effect in the shadowed background figures. The subject refers to a vision of the crucified Christ and the instruments of the Passion which, according to legend, appeared above the altar while Pope Gregory the Great, who formulated the Mass's liturgy and was one of the four Western doctors of the Church, was celebrating the Mass. The theme of the Mass of St Gregory often appears in prints of this period.

1895–1–22–705. Mitchell collection

64 Hans Baldung Grien (1484/5–1545)

Holy Family with St Anne, 1511

Woodcut. 375 × 250 mm

Hollstein 59

After six years working in Dürer's workshop in Nuremberg, Baldung returned to his boyhood town of Strassburg in 1509. He opened a workshop and for three years worked there as a painter, stained-glass designer and woodcut artist. This print dates from Baldung's Strassburg period (the year 1511 is incised into the upper left wall).

64

The informality of this family group, in which Joseph is seen from behind a rustic wall peering down upon the seated Virgin, Child and St Anne, is deceptively simple. Baldung introduces several motifs which refer to the passing of the Old Testament with the birth of Christ: the open book resting on the dilapidated wall implies that the New Testament has superseded the Old, while the clusters of grapes, symbolic of the Eucharist and entwined round the withered tree trunk at right, prefigure Christ's sacrifice. Most curious is the gesture of St Anne who touches the Infant Christ's genitals, a symbolic reference to the doctrine that Christ was made man. (See James H. Marrow and Alan Shestack, *Hans Baldung Grien: Prints and Drawings*, exhibition catalogue, New Haven, Yale University Art Gallery, 1981, cat. 21.)

Mitchell owned some thirty-six woodcuts by Baldung. This print must have been acquired before 1882, when Mitchell exhibited it as no. 101 in the Burlington Fine Arts Club's *Collection of Woodcuts of the German School, Executed in the XVth and XVIth Centuries*. Of the 161 woodcuts included in this loan exhibition, which had been put together by three amateurs, 111 prints came from Mitchell's collection.

1895-1-22-233. Mitchell collection

65 Lucas Cranach, the Elder (1472–1553)

The Judgement of Paris, 1508

Woodcut. 364 × 253 mm

Bartsch VII.291.114; Dodgson II 288.16

Together with Dürer in Nuremberg and Burgkmair in Augsburg, Lucas Cranach was responsible for raising the northern woodcut to the highest level of artistic expression in the first decade of the sixteenth century. After beginning his career in Vienna, Cranach moved in 1505 to the university town of Wittenberg where he became court painter to the Elector of Saxony, Friedrich the Wise. The Elector's insignia of crossed swords are shown here hanging from a branch; such woodcuts were instrumental in promoting the court's reputation for humanist learning and culture. Stylistically this print shows Cranach's familiarity with Dürer's early woodcuts, while the secular theme of the Judgement of Paris gave artists the opportunity to depict the *contrapposto* elegance of the nude from three viewpoints.

Mitchell had forty-three woodcuts by Cranach the Elder in his collection. This impression was once owned by the painter Sir Peter Lely (1618–80), whose stamp (L. 2092) is visible in the lower right. Lely formed one of the first great collections of drawings and prints to be made in England, and his stamp, put on by Roger North, one of his executors, is one of the first to be put on works of art on paper.

1895-1-22-269. Mitchell collection

66 Albrecht Altdorfer (c.1480–1538)

The Resurrection, 1512

Woodcut. 230 × 178 mm

Bartsch VIII 77.47; Dodgson II 227.48

In their minute execution and detail, Albrecht Altdorfer's woodcuts represent the next generation after Dürer. A citizen of Regensburg from 1505, Altdorfer began to design woodcuts around 1511–12, when this print was made. Although larger in format than the miniature woodcuts of the *Fall and Redemption of Man* series, which Mitchell also owned, this print shows the extraordinary precision of Altdorfer's design and the demands this must have imposed on the block-cutter's ingenuity. Altdorfer's miniaturisation of forms is evident in his depiction of the sleeping soldiers startled by the brilliant light of Christ's resurrection from the tomb; typical of Altdorfer's invention is the witty contrast between Christ's divine aureole and the redundant light emitted by the soldier's lamp.

This is one of sixty-one Altdorfer woodcuts in Mitchell's collection.

1895-1-22-357. Mitchell collection

67 Hans Burgkmair, the Elder (1473–1531)

Lovers Surprised by Death, 1510

Chiaroscuro woodcut from three blocks, with the outline block in dark grey, the tone-blocks in light grey and dull pink. 212 × 151 mm

Bartsch VII.215.40; Dodgson II 85.46

Hans Burgkmair is now credited with the development of the chiaroscuro woodcut in competition with Lucas Cranach (see cat. 68) around 1508. Burgkmair was born and worked as a painter and woodcut designer in Augsburg, a major centre of humanism, book production and woodcut printing. Burgkmair's invention of making a colour print from a line-block and one or more tone-blocks was taken up shortly after by Italian artists, who dispensed with the key-block altogether. This chiaroscuro woodcut is the earliest known example to be printed from three blocks. Its technical sophistication could not have been achieved without the practical support of the Augsburg block-cutter and printer Jost de Negker, whose name in letterpress is usually found on this third state. Burgkmair has created an extraordinary image in which a northern depiction of Death as a winged spectre attacking two lovers contrasts with a setting of Italian Renaissance architecture. The notion of death occurring as an unexpected chaotic event within a rational classical order would have appealed to Augsburg's humanist circles and is emphasised here by the presence of the *memento mori* set into the decorative architectural frieze.

65

66

67

Among the thirty-nine Burgkmair woodcuts in his collection, Mitchell owned this and two other chiaroscuri made in collaboration with Jost de Negker: *The Emperor Maximilian on Horseback*, B.32, which Mitchell bought at the 1877 Firmin-Didot sale in Paris, lot 1927, for the large sum of 1,025 f. (about £41), and *Johannes Paumgartner, Imperial Counsellor*, B.34. Possibly also acquired at the Firmin-Didot sale, *Lovers Surprised by Death* was certainly in Mitchell's possession by 1878. Listed as no. 122, it was shown that year, with eleven of his Burgkmair prints, including *The Emperor Maximilian on Horseback*, at the Liverpool Art Club's *Loan Collection of Wood Engravings*, where it was described as 'a most remarkable print, by far the finest work of this Master'.

1895-1-22-379. Mitchell collection

68 Lucas Cranach, the Elder (1472–1553)
Venus and Cupid, dated 1506 (in fact 1508)

Chiaroscuro woodcut from two blocks, with the tone-block printed in light brown. 277 × 189 mm

Bartsch VII.291.113; Dodgson II 297.62

In 1900 the German scholar Flechsig first pointed out that the date 1506 was not credible, since the print carries as part of the design Cranach's coat of arms which on historical grounds is known only to have been granted to him by the Elector of Saxony two years later, in 1508. The arms of a winged serpent with Cranach's initials can be seen here suspended from a tree branch. The pre-dating is clearly deliberate, and scholars have convincingly argued that Cranach's motive for pre-dating this print and another (B.58) to 1506 was to claim priority over Burgkmair for inventing the chiaroscuro colour print (see David Landau and Peter Parshall, *The Renaissance Print 1470–1550*, New Haven and London 1994, pp. 184–202). The rivalry between Cranach in Wittenberg and Burgkmair in Augsburg exemplifies the competitive exchange of ideas between the two humanist centres during the first decade of the sixteenth century. Visual conceits present in this print testify also to the learned audience to which it was addressed: here Venus stands on clouds, a tribute to her celestial status, but within the design lies the hidden image of a conch shell, the attribute of the seafoam-born goddess.

This print was acquired in Paris as lot 1967 at the Firmin-Didot sale of 1877 (see cat. 69), and cost Mitchell 720 f. It was included in the following year as no. 108 at the Liverpool loan show of woodcuts, where it was catalogued as 'the earliest Chiaro-scuro with a date'.

1895-1-22-268. Mitchell collection

69 Hans Wechtlin (1480/5–after 1526)
*Alcon Slaying the Serpent, c.*1512–15

Illustrated in colour between pages 112 and 113

Chiaroscuro woodcut from two blocks, with the tone-block printed in bluish grey. 270 × 182 mm

Bartsch VII 451.9

The identity of this master (whose monogram of crossed pilgrim's staffs appears in the tablet between Alcon's legs) as Hans Wechtlin was first recognised by the German scholar Loedel, whose researches were published by Rudolph Weigel in 1863. Wechtlin was a woodcut artist and designer for stained glass working in Strassburg, where he became a citizen in 1514. Although his birth and death dates are still unknown, his earliest woodcuts date from 1502 when they appear as book illustrations on the life of Christ published by J. Grüninger in Strassburg. Wechtlin is best known for the twelve chiaroscuro woodcuts he made in the second decade of the sixteenth century, many of which have unusual subjects. This print shows the dramatic moment when the Cretan archer Alcon rescues his son from the deadly coils of a serpent by firing an arrow through its head. Suspended from a tree is a tablet with a Latin inscription alluding to the scene below. The recondite subject exemplifies the interest in classical learning enjoyed by humanist circles in Strassburg.

One of three Wechtlin chiaroscuro woodcuts owned by Mitchell, this print and another (B.2) were bought by him at the sale of the celebrated collection of the French collector and publisher Ambroise Firmin-Didot in Paris (Drouot, 16 April-12 May 1877, lots 2013 and 2010 respectively). All five Wechtlin woodcuts offered in the 1877 sale were described as 'extremely rare' in the catalogue, but it was the two prints inscribed with the signature of Pierre Mariette (1634–1716), the famous Paris printseller and collector, that Mitchell wanted for his collection, paying 780 f. for this impression alone. Mitchell also owned a copy of Loedel's 1863 monograph on Wechtlin, which the publisher Weigel had dedicated to Firmin-Didot. Mitchell exhibited this print as no. 135 at the *Loan Collection of Wood Engravings* organised by the Liverpool Art Club in March 1878, where it was described as 'very rare and fine'.

1895-1-22-203. Mitchell collection

68

70 Giuseppe di Cosimo Bianchino
(active second half of the sixteenth century)

Sea Monster with Putti, c.1560–70

Illustrated in colour between pages 112 and 113

Chiaroscuro woodcut from three blocks printed in ochre, light brown and dark brown. 214 × 443 mm

Neither Bartsch nor his successor Passavant described this striking chiaroscuro woodcut. It shows a sea monster approaching the viewer at sea level, creating the illusion that both occupy the same space, although the putti playfully cavorting among the monster's fierce gills dispel all sense of danger.

Not much is known of the artist: a faded Latin inscription in the tablet at lower left of this print gives his name as Hieronymus Bianchini and says he came from Perugia. In all probability this is Giuseppe di Cosimo Bianchino, a painter and woodblock cutter who worked in the publishing house of his father Cosimo in Perugia, in the second half of the sixteenth century. Bianchino worked closely with Girolamo Cartolaio and belonged to the artists' guild of Perugia, where he served as its treasurer in 1559 and 1570. (I am most grateful to Jan Johnson, Montreal, for identifying the likely authorship of this print, and to Dr Peter Fuhring, Paris.)

Mitchell's interest in early German woodcuts also extended to the inclusion of a small number of Italian woodcuts in his collection. This print was bought by Mitchell for 10 guineas in 1881 at the posthumous sale of the connoisseur Charles Sackville Bale (Christie's, 10 June 1881, 15th day, lot 2515). This massive and wide-ranging collection of objects – pictures, Oriental and Western porcelain, medals, gems, etc. – provoked a sensation in the art world when offered for sale in some 3,500 lots; it produced the staggering sum of £72,523, of which more than £11,576 was raised by the sale of his old master prints and drawings alone. The Bale catalogue described this print, wrongly, as after Raphael.

1895-1-22-1265. Mitchell collection

71 Master of the Playing Cards
(active 1435–55)

Man of Sorrows, c.1450

Engraving, with hand-colouring. 198 × 129 mm

Lehrs I 85.28

The Master of the Playing Cards takes his name from a famous set of engraved cards most of which are known in only one or two impressions. He is the earliest engraver to emerge with a distinctive style in Western graphic art and it is believed he worked in the Upper Rhine area between Constance and Strassburg, where the first engravings in Europe are thought to have been made. Given the technical assurance of this print, in which the forms are meticulously built up in a series of very fine parallel strokes of the engraver's burin, it is most likely that the Master of the Playing Cards was preceded by other artists experimenting with the new technique from the early fifteenth century. (See Alan Shestack, *Fifteenth Century Engravings of Northern Europe*, exhibition catalogue, Washington, D.C., National Gallery of Art, 3 December 1967–7 January 1968, cat. 1.)

An aspect of late-medieval piety particularly widespread in Germany was the attachment to the five wounds of Christ. This engraving would have served such a devotional purpose: here Christ is shown as the Man of Sorrows displaying the five wounds of his Crucifixion and surrounded by the instruments of his Passion. The two gesticulating heads either side of Christ refer to those who spat at and mocked him; Caiaphas, Pilate and Herod who condemned him are at right; while the hands of betrayal (paying out thirty pieces of silver) and of torture (tearing out clumps of hair and slapping) are represented by the three isolated motifs at upper right. The addition of a light red wash to suggest the blood streaming from Christ's wounds intensifies the emotional impact of this image.

Malcolm paid £8.10.0 for this print at the sale of the Oxford divine, the Rev. John Griffiths (Sotheby's, 9–10 May 1883, lot 3), whose 'small but choice' collection of old master etchings and engravings attracted considerable interest from other connoisseurs. Griffiths decided to disperse his collection after his retirement in 1881 from university life, where he had latterly served as Warden of Wadham College. The sale of 258 lots produced a total sum of over £6,948; Malcolm (through Colnaghi's) also bought a print of Marcantonio (B.469), Schongauer (B.27), Benedetto Montagna (B.11) and Domenico Campagnola (B.3). Among the personal buyers at the Griffiths sale were Salting and Seymour Haden.

1895-9-15-184. Malcolm collection

71

/3

72 Martin Schongauer (*c.*1450–91)
*The Temptation of St Antony, c.*1470–5

Engraving. 314 × 230 mm
Bartsch VI.140.47; Lehrs V.243.54, second state

The son of a goldsmith from Colmar, Martin Schongauer is the first engraver whose name is known. Although he trained and practised as a painter, few of his paintings survive. Schongauer's importance therefore now rests on his 116 known engravings, which include this example made early in his career. This remarkable composition was one of the first engravings to be conceived as a work of art in its own right; earlier engravings had tended to be regarded as objects of functional value, for instance providing designs for goldsmiths. According to the medieval *Golden Legend*, St Antony, the third-century father of monasticism, was subjected to extreme hallucinations and temptations in the desert. Here Schongauer depicts St Antony attacked by an assortment of vicious demons whose spiky and scaled forms are part fantastic invention, part direct observation of bizarre species from the animal world. Vasari records that the young Michelangelo was so captivated by Schongauer's engraving that he bought fish

at the market with fantastic scales like those in the print in order to make a faithful copy in colour (Vasari's life of Michelangelo, *Lives* [2nd edn], 1568).

1895-9-15-261. Malcolm collection

73 Martin Schongauer (*c.*1450–91)
*Christ Bearing the Cross, c.*1480–5

Engraving. 290 × 434 mm
Bartsch VI.128.21; Lehrs V.69.9

This masterpiece from Schongauer's maturity shows his greater assurance with the burin, modelling form through a network of systematically organised lines. In this tumultuous scene on the road to Calvary, pathos is expressed by the weight and exaggerated proportions of the Cross being carried by Christ. Such complexity of composition and richness of detail found in this and other engravings by Schongauer exercised a profound influence on his northern successors, notably the young Dürer.

This and the preceding print were among sixty-four Schongauer engravings owned by Malcolm. They were

185

74

75

acquired individually at separate sales during his collecting career rather than *en bloc* from a single source. For instance, Malcolm bought three Schongauers at the Friedrich Kalle sale at Frankfurt in 1875, at which he paid DM8,000 (about £395 in 1875) for a brilliant impression of *The Death of the Virgin* (B.33), the highest price fetched in the entire sale.

1895–9–15–252. Malcolm collection

74 Albrecht Dürer (1471–1528)

Nemesis, c.1501–2

Engraving. 335 × 233 mm
Bartsch VII.91.77

It is not known where Dürer learned to engrave, but, as the son of a Nuremberg goldsmith, it is very probable that he acquired some instruction in his father's workshop. After his apprenticeship to the Nuremberg painter Wolgemut, Dürer travelled extensively in his youth. With the intention of becoming Schongauer's pupil, he visited Colmar only to find that he had died in 1491. Dürer's earliest engravings were made in Nuremberg shortly after returning from his first trip to Venice in 1495. This famous print demonstrates Dürer's complete mastery of engraving by the turn of the sixteenth century. Its unusual subject reveals Dürer's familiarity with the learned interests of the Nuremberg humanists led by his close friend Willibald Pirckheimer. Nemesis, the Greek goddess of retribution, appears here as a winged naked woman, who, turning the ball of fortune with her feet, with one hand offers a covered cup to the just and with the other grips a bridle to hold back human pride. The terrestial world is represented by the amazingly detailed bird's-eye view spread below the goddess's feet; this mountain landscape has been identified as a view of Klausen in the South Tyrol.

Like print connoisseurs of all periods, Malcolm, who owned sixty-five Dürer engravings, especially prized the brilliant clarity of the early impressions. This one is particularly choice because it was printed before a scratch below the bridge accidentally appeared on the plate shortly after the very first proofs were taken.

1895–9–15–346. Malcolm collection

75 Master MZ (Matthäus Zaisinger?)
(active *c.*1500–3)

Aristotle and Phyllis, c.1500–3

Engraving. 181 × 130 mm
Bartsch VI 379.18; Lehrs VIII 377.22

When in 1618 the Nuremberg collector Paul Behaim first listed as in his collection sixteen of the twenty-two engravings credited to this master, he identified the monogram MZ as Matthäus Zaisinger, a Munich goldsmith. In the absence of any more plausible theory, this identification is still largely accepted by twentieth-century scholars, although it has been questioned by Lehrs. Bartsch entitled this print *The Husband Subjugated by his Wife*, but the subject is the apocryphal medieval story of Aristotle's humiliation by Alexander the Great's mistress Phyllis, who reduced the wise philosopher to a fool when he agreed to carry her on all fours in return for her favours. Very popular in late-medieval art as an illustration of the power of women, this subject was first engraved by the Housebook Master in the 1480s. As the Housebook Master had earlier done, the Master MZ includes the two witnesses of Aristotle's folly. But the more modern influence of Dürer's recent engravings on the Master MZ is also shown by the prominence given to the protagonists in the composition and by the introduction of the landscape vista outside the garden wall. (See Ellen S. Jacobowitz and Stephanie Loeb Stepanek, *The Prints of Lucas van Leyden and His Contemporaries*, exhibition catalogue, Washington, D.C., National Gallery of Art, 1983, cat. 49.)

This is one of three Master MZ prints owned by Malcolm, who put together a representative group of early German engravings as part of his select collection covering the history of Renaissance engraving.

1895–9–15–232. Malcolm collection

8. George Salting (1835–1909)

Stephen Coppel

'The greatest English art collector of this age, perhaps of any age' was how the *The Times* described the Australian-born George Salting (fig. 1) in its announcement of his death on 12 December 1909.[1] He died at the age of seventy-four in his two rooms above the Thatched House Club, 86 St James's Street, London. Here for more than forty years he had lived very modestly as a bachelor, devoting his life and his immense wealth to forming his magnificent collections. These he left to the nation at his death: the paintings were bequeathed to the National Gallery, the prints and drawings to the British Museum, while the oriental porcelain, Renaissance bronzes, maiolica and the like, which comprised the main bulk of his collections, went to the Victoria and Albert Museum. The astonishing range of his collections and the high quality that invariably distinguished objects in each category drew acclaim from every quarter. In his tribute to George Salting in *The Burlington Magazine*, Charles Hercules Read, President of the Society of Antiquaries and Keeper of British and Medieval Antiquities and Ethnography at the British Museum, remarked: 'As a great collector of the most catholic sympathies he stood almost alone, and he has unquestionably left his mark on the connoisseurship of our day ... By his magnificent legacy he has made England's position in the art world immeasurably stronger ...'.[2] Unlike John Malcolm of Poltalloch and William Mitchell, who confined their collecting largely to prints and drawings, Salting was an art collector of great catholicity of taste and interest and his print collection should be viewed in the context of the many-sided character of his collections.

Little in Salting's background prepares us for the connoisseur of rarefied taste and discerning eye he was later to become. He was born of Danish parents in Sydney on 15 August 1835. His father Severin Kanute Salting had arrived in Australia in 1834, where he soon established himself as a successful marine merchant in Sydney. In 1842 Salting senior and Philip William Flower, son of a City of London merchant, formed a partnership called

Flower, Salting and Co. which had its premises in Hunter Street, Sydney. The firm invested the profits from Salting's merchant marine business in sheep stations and sugar plantations, which became the mainstay of the Salting fortune. The sons, George and his younger brother William, who was born in 1837, were both educated locally. In 1848 the two boys were taken by their parents to England where George was sent to Eton. Here he appears to have made little impression other than as 'a pale, lean, tall, eccentric person'. Owing to George's delicate constitution, the family returned to Sydney five years later. In March 1854 George and his brother entered the newly founded University of Sydney, where George achieved distinction in classics, winning several prizes for Latin, and graduated BA in 1857. In recognition of the education his sons had received, Salting senior established 'The Salting Exhibition' of £500 at the University of Sydney.[3]

1. *George Salting*, gum photograph by Dr Otto Rosenheim *c*.1900. 1905-2-13-1, presented by Max Rosenheim, F.S.A. The small bronze in Salting's hand remains unidentified; it is either classical or Renaissance, possibly of a centaur holding a club, and appears not to be in the Salting Collection of the Victoria and Albert Museum (information from Dr Clive Wainwright, Victoria and Albert Museum)

In 1858 his father retired from the Sydney firm and took the family to England, where shortly afterwards his wife died. After only a term at Oxford, George left Balliol to accompany his grief-stricken father to Rome, where they spent the autumn and winter of 1858/9 together. The sojourn in Rome was the turning point in George's life. Confronted with the rich artistic heritage of the city, he immersed himself in the first-hand study of its museums, churches and archaeological sites. His passionate interest in Rome's great treasures led him to take up photography, then a cumbersome and complicated exercise, which necessitated pushing a cart carrying his equipment and a black tent to develop the plates through the streets of Rome. In a letter written from Rome on 26 January 1859, his father expressed anxiety for his son's future to Edward Knox, a business associate and friend living in Sydney:

I was obliged to leave England at the approach of winter on account of George as it was thought that the inclement season there, might injure his health. He has been better here this year than last. But he is not strong; – far from it … George has taken to photography & Miss Donovan goes out with him almost every day when the weather permits. My plans for the future are quite unsettled still. I do not know what I may do or where to fix my abode. My greatest difficulty is to choose a pursuit for George.[4]

After a brief visit to Australia, Severin Salting decided to make the family home in England, where they settled at a house called Silverlands, near Chertsey, Surrey. He died there on 14 September 1865 and left his son George, at the age of thirty, in command of a fortune of £30,000 a year.

It was at this point that George Salting found his vocation as a professional collector of art. Inspired by the beautiful objects he had studied in Rome and encouraged in his pursuits by the advice offered by his friend Louis Huth, and by Charles Drury Fortnum and Augustus Wollaston Franks of the British Museum, George Salting embarked on his chosen career with single-minded determination. Chinese porcelain was the focus of his first serious collection. Many of the pieces he bought came from Dutch collections formed in the seventeenth and eighteenth centuries which were being broken up in a series of major sales in the late 1860s and early 1870s. In his acquisition of blue and white porcelain, the highly regarded *famille verte* and *famille rose* and the rare black enamelware, Salting received much encouragement from Louis Huth, himself a distinguished collector of Chinese porcelain.[5] From 1874 Salting began his practice of depositing on loan his oriental porcelain and other collections of *objets d'art* at the South Kensington Museum, where they were put on public display. Because he was frequently exchanging pieces from his collections for better examples there was no certainty that particular objects would always be on view. The Salting collections began to acquire an organic character as pieces were added or replaced before the eyes

of admiring visitors and collectors. When Salting died in 1909 his oriental porcelain filled twenty-nine glazed cases at the Victoria and Albert Museum. It was claimed to rank with that in the royal collection at Dresden and the Grandidier collection in the Louvre and to be surpassed only by that of Pierpont Morgan in New York.[6] In the informed opinion of Charles Hercules Read, Salting's Chinese porcelain was 'especially valuable and important as presenting, perhaps more satisfactorily than any other, a complete series of the strictly artistic productions of the Chinese in this material. He cared but little for the historical interest of the wares or for tracing their history; in his taste Chinese porcelain was confined to what he considered beautiful, without regard either to antiquity or to the evolution of the manufacture'.[7]

While he was forming his oriental collections Salting began to move into the area of Renaissance bronzes and maiolica. Although J. C. Robinson at the South Kensington Museum did much to change institutional neglect, art bronzes from the Renaissance were collected more avidly by connoisseurs like Charles Drury Fortnum and Salting than by public museums, which later became the recipients of these private collections. A year before Salting's death, Dr Wilhelm Bode, Director-General of the Berlin Museums and a great authority on small bronzes, recounted in his monumental three-volume study of the subject that 'there are still left in London and Paris some quite exquisite private collections. The choicest one in London belongs to George Salting'.[8] By 1896 Charles Drury Fortnum, in his authoritative book on maiolica, could describe Salting's maiolica collection as 'the richest private collection now in England … [he] kindly allows it to be exhibited, for the public benefit, at the South Kensington Museum'.[9] Many of his most important pieces were acquired at the famous Fountaine sale of 1884, where he spent thousands of pounds on well-known documented examples from Gubbio and Castel Durante. A few Urbino plates which had eluded him at the Fountaine sale were secured by Salting at later sales. By far the most important of these was the Frédéric Spitzer art sale in Paris held at the late collector's house in rue de Villejust from April 1893. Here Salting astounded the collecting world by his daily appearances in the saleroom over the course of seven weeks; he bid in person large sums of money for the Renaissance objects, to the fury of the dealers who, denied their commission, ensured that he paid a good price. Salting was reported to have spent more than £35,000 at the Spitzer sale. Amounting to just under one tenth of the 3,369 lots described and illustrated in the lavish two-volume catalogue of the Spitzer collection, Salting's purchases were conveyed in cases directly to the South Kensington Museum.[10] Many of the objects were of the highest art-historical importance; as one newspaper reported: 'The principle followed by Mr. Salting was to buy nothing but the best and rarest, whether in the class of enamels, or majolica, or metal work, or illuminated manuscripts, or what not; so that he disregarded a great number of the larger and more showy objects, and paid immense prices for quite small things, if they were rare and fine.'[11]

From *objets d'art* Salting turned his attention to pictures. Unlike the American millionaire collectors Frick and Carnegie, Salting was not attracted by the most expensive pictures on offer from dealers. With his preference for small highly finished works, he concentrated upon the early Flemish and Dutch masters, especially the genre paintings of Jan Steen and Adriaen Ostade. Among his greatest pictures were Memlinc's *A Young Man at Prayer*, Robert Campin's *Virgin and Child before a Fire Screen* and Vermeer's *A Young Woman Seated at a Virginal* (fig. 2). His Italian pictures on the whole were less distinguished, although they did include Cima da Conegliano's masterpiece *David and Jonathan*, with its finely delineated background of a Veneto hilltop town. He also owned three Canalettos of the Piazza San Marco and the Grand Canal, full of characteristic detail and minute observation of Venetian life. In his very last years Salting put together a group of landscapes by Corot, Daubigny and Théodore Rousseau, for which he paid the high prices commanded by the Barbizon School before the First World War. From 1900, he began to lend several of his more important pictures to the National Gallery for public view.[12]

While his prints and drawings were never as extensive as his collections of oriental porcelain and Renaissance decorative arts, the 291 drawings and 153 prints that came to the British Museum under Salting's bequest of 1910 reveal the collector's principles of high quality, fine condition and distinguished provenance. Like his pictures, the strength of his drawing collection lay in the Dutch school, particularly Rembrandt (sixteen examples; fig. 3) and several delicate Ostade watercolours. Among the German drawings were two important portraits by Dürer and Holbein.[13] The French school was noteworthy for an album of thirty-one finely executed portrait drawings of the sixteenth century from the circle of Clouet, a set of six Claudes and five Watteaus. One of the Watteaus was a lively study for the painting *La Toilette* in the Wallace Collection and another a study for two figures (fig. 4) in the Louvre's *Departure for the Island of Cythera*. Among the Italians were several vivacious Canaletto ink and wash drawings. The crowning glory of his English drawings, which included examples by Constable, Bonington and Stothard, were eighteen Turner landscapes, all finished presentation watercolours.

Salting's print collection was small but choice, with the emphasis on Rembrandt etchings (forty-nine), Dürer engravings (fifteen), and Marcantonios (twenty-four). The large number of Rembrandts was in keeping with the pre-eminence the Dutch master has always enjoyed among collectors. Salting's preference for rare early states and brilliant impressions likewise reflected the taste of Victorian print connoisseurship. Many of his beautiful impressions

2. Johannes Vermeer, *A Young Woman Seated at a Virginal*, oil on canvas 1674–5. 515 × 455 mm. National Gallery, London, NG 2568 Salting Collection. In Salting's collection by 1900, this Vermeer was among the 192 pictures selected by the National Gallery in 1910 under the terms of his will

were bought in person at the sales of the distinguished Rembrandt collectors Seymour Haden and Richard Fisher, both of whom Salting knew through the Burlington Fine Arts Club. With his penchant for the Dutch masters, it is not surprising to find etchings by Ostade and Waterloo included in his collection. Despite the late nineteenth-century etching revival and Salting's own purchases of paintings by the Barbizon artists, it is curious that no contemporary etchings were added to his print cabinet. Prints for Salting were an adjunct to his art collections; in this respect, he was no different from most nineteenth-century connoisseurs, for whom some well-chosen specimens by the received masters of etching and engraving were an integral part of a gentleman's collection.

The wealth that enabled Salting to assemble these great collections of art came out of Australia on the back of sheep.[14] By making further shrewd investments in Australian sheep stations, wool trading and Queensland sugar, George Salting greatly increased the capital of the fortune inherited from his father. His Australian investments included highly profitable shares in the Colonial Sugar Refining Company, goldmining interests in the Nintingbool estate, outside Ballarat, Victoria, and sheep stations at Mantuan Downs, in the Leichhardt district, Queensland, and at Cunningham Plains (fig. 5), an exten-

(*Left*) 3. Rembrandt, *Two Women Teaching a Child to Walk*, red chalk on rough grey paper *c*.1635–7. 103 × 128 mm. 1910-2-12-187 Salting Collection. Before coming into Salting's possession this intimate sketch had been owned by the great connoisseur J. C. Robinson, who sold it in 1868 at his sale in Paris

(*Left, below*) 4. Jean-Antoine Watteau, *A Cavalier Helping a Seated Lady to Rise*, a study for two of the principal figures in *Departure for the Island of Cythera*, red, black and white chalk on light brown paper, before 1717. 336 × 226 mm. 1910-2-12-98 Salting Collection

sive grazing property near Harden, NSW, owned jointly with his brother William. Some of these concerns were dealt with by Salting personally through regular correspondence with agents in Australia, including Edward Knox, his father's executor. Other business interests and shares were traded through the City of London firm P. W. Flower and Co. This had been set up by Salting's father's partner, who had returned to England around 1843 to run the London end of the business. Flower's brother Horace remained in Australia to supervise the Australian business ventures, including the shipping of wool. It was Arthur Flower, a nephew of Horace and a loyal friend of George Salting, who was entrusted with executing the collector's will.

By the time Salting died in 1909 he had amassed a colossal fortune: his property was assessed for probate at the gross value of £1,332,000 and his net personalty, that is, his art collections, valued at £1,287,906.[15] Although Salting was more than three times as wealthy as John Malcolm of Poltalloch, he chose not to live in baronial splendour in the Highlands nor to maintain a grand house in Mayfair. Instead the two rooms above the Thatched House Club, to which he moved shortly after his father's death, cost him only £52. 10. 0 per quarter, the rent remaining fixed at this amount for more than thirty years.[16] Although filled with objects, pictures and furniture, his bachelor chambers were furnished economically: a plain peacock blue felt covered the floors of his bedroom and sitting room, over which were placed old Persian and Daghestan rugs; plain dark linoleum, then a new flooring material, was put down in the small entrance lobby; and heavy maroon curtains

5. Salting's sheep station at Cunningham Plains, near Harden, New South Wales, showing a mob of prize merinos in front of the homestead, 1907 (Guildhall Library, Corporation of London, Guildhall Library MS 19,478, from a sale catalogue for the Cunningham Plains estate). Comprising an area of 52,624 acres, the property was traversed by the Great Southern Railway connecting Sydney with Melbourne. According to the 1907 sale prospectus, 'the pasture is superior, and the Wools grown have long been eagerly sought by English and Foreign buyers'

hung from the windows, which were fitted with Venetian blinds to keep out the light. Money was spent on display cabinets and mahogany showcases rather than on simple refurbishments: in 1873, for example, Salting ordered for his rooms a 'fine old English Satinwood Cabinet inlaid with tulipwood bands', with a cylindrical writing table in the centre and an 'upper compartment fitted up with shelves for China and enclosed by glass doors' for which he paid £65, plus the labour of three men to position it amidst the considerable shifting of other furniture and the taking down and re-hanging of several pictures. The entrance door to this Aladdin's cave was strengthened with new butts, a brass bolt and a patent mortice latch in 1887, presumably as an added precaution for security.[17] But during the day Salting himself preferred to live in the plusher surrounds of the Conservative Club, returning to the Thatched House Club to sleep.[18]

The simplicity of Salting's life gave rise to many anecdotes of his legendary meanness. In its obituary, *The Times* spoke of his 'queer personal miserliness which made

him deaf to appeals and yet allowed him to spend thousands on a picture or a Holbein miniature'.[19] One famous story relates how Salting was with connoisseur friends in his rooms when a porter from Christie's arrived with a Chinese vase, for which Salting had just paid 700 guineas in the sale room, whereupon the man was asked to unpack the piece in case he had cracked it en route from King Street; after scrutinising the object, Salting fished in his pockets for a tip and on finding half-a-crown promptly returned it; casting around, he opened a drawer and from a paper bag produced a left-over penny bun, which he offered to the standing porter.[20]

Salting's personal habits of extreme parsimony informed his approach to collecting. Every afternoon for more than forty years he called when in London on one dealer or the next in Bond Street, where he became proverbial in the trade for wasting their time as he slowly inspected the objects and haggled over price. In his reminiscences of the great collectors he had known, James Henry Duveen, who helped to run the famous Bond Street firm specialising in oriental porcelain, recalled:

Salting loved a deal, being almost Oriental in his love of protracted haggling. He would often spend half a day in a shop when he really wanted to buy something at his own price. As a youngster I have been present when he and my stepfather, Joseph M. Duveen, have sat down and talked about some beautiful and expensive *objet d'art*. Presently conversation would degenerate into desultory remarks, and at any given moment either or both of them might be seen asleep. But in the end the deal was always concluded, for Salting very rarely let go when he had set his heart on something.[21]

His other characteristic as a collector was to seek the advice of acknowledged connoisseurs in the field when unsure about an object he was considering. From his personal knowledge of the Australian millionaire, Charles Hercules Read provided this accurate account:

Where he felt uncertain of his own judgment, he would walk to one or other of the museums or to a fellow collector, to obtain an opinion. At times he bought objects that on examination did not prove to be of good enough quality for his taste, and he would cause dealers embarrassment by offering these, which he called 'marbles' in allusion to schoolboy usage, in part payment for something of higher quality.[22]

By this process of continually refining his collections, Salting became notorious among fellow connoisseurs as 'the prince of weeders'.[23]

Among the business papers belonging to Salting, which were recently deposited at the Guildhall Library, London, is a large bundle of receipts of his art purchases, including the prints.[24] Arranged alphabetically by dealer, the invoices are frequently annotated by Salting himself, with the prices he was asked set against those he finally paid and with the objects he part-exchanged enumerated beside the items he bought. These documents are crucial to our understanding of how he assembled some of his collections; they also provide important provenance details for a number of individual pieces. Although receipts clearly have not survived for all the objects he acquired, there is sufficient documentation to show the source and manner by which many of his prints and drawings and other items in his collections were acquired.

During his collecting career Salting seems to have relied on certain dealers for prints and drawings. In the early 1870s, he was buying prints from the dealer Holloway & Son, at 25 Bedford Street, off the Strand. An invoice for Christmas 1872 shows that Salting bought the Dürer engraving *The Four Witches* (B.75; 1910-2-12-304) for 8 guineas on 20 December; eight days later he returned to buy four more Dürer prints, including *The Sudarium Displayed by Two Angels* (B.25; V & A E.4629-1910), and two Rembrandt etchings, one of which – *The Marriage of Jason and Creusa* (B.112) – he later traded away after a better impression came up at the Haden sale in 1891. On 30 December Salting was back to collect another Dürer, *The Sea Monster* (B.71), and a Marcantonio, *Mars, Venus and Cupid* (B.345), both for 15 guineas. From the same dealer Salting bought three fine oriental crackle bottles on 27 November, and three large porcelain jars of blue, red and white with covers surmounted by kylins and a picture described as 'Landscape with St John seated by Herajuoli'(?) on 10 December. Salting corrected the Chinese attribution of the jars to Japanese on the invoice and later noted that these were 'sold long after at Xties [Christie's]' while the painting was 'sold to

Sedelmeier 1890'. The final amount invoiced for the prints and porcelain, after one 'Crackle Bottle [was] returned' on 28 December, came to £246.5.6, with Salting settling this sum by cheque a month later. This invoice[25] has been quoted at length because it exemplifies the way in which Salting went about forming his collections. The prints were bought piecemeal rather than as collections from dealers, who like Holloway might also carry porcelain and pictures in their stock and who could expect to see objects returned if Salting found them unsatisfactory on second examination. Salting's annotations on the invoice also show how ruthless he was in disposing of pieces that later failed to meet the discriminating standards he had set himself. Because he was constantly weeding out the 'marbles' from his collections, the status of his prints, like the other categories of objects, was constantly shifting. For this reason, he was more likely to have retained prints acquired later in his career; accordingly, it is the prints listed in the invoices from later years that can be identified more securely with those left in his bequest to the British Museum.

From the Paris print dealers Messrs Danlos fils et Delisle, Salting acquired five Marcantonios, including the so-called *Virgin of Foligno* (B.52; 1910-2-12-330) in 1883. These prints had come from the distinguished English connoisseur Henry Brodhurst, whose small cabinet of choice impressions had recently been bought by Danlos.[26] For three of the Marcantonios, *Parnassus* (B.247), 'Five Saints' (i.e. *St Cecilia* [B.101]) and *Two Fauns Carrying a Child* (B.230), Salting exchanged weaker impressions of these subjects that he had acquired at an earlier stage, thereby lopping off £50 from the sum of £185 asked by Danlos for the Brodhurst impressions.[27]

But it was the London-based German print dealer Gutekunst (later in partnership with Deprez) from whom Salting bought most of his prints. In 1889, Salting used the services of Otto Gutekunst to bid for him at the sale of J. C. Ritter von Klinkosch in Vienna, where he bought a silverpoint head of a young man attributed to Bellini, a Dujardin landscape, and a pen and ink Rembrandt landscape, for the sum of 1,336 florins, or just over £111.[28] The level at which Salting traded his 'marbles' could be quite staggering, with the stakes being raised each time another object was added to the deal. For example, in 1893, we find Salting offering Deprez & Gutekunst £160 in cash plus two Rembrandt etchings, *Rembrandt Drawing at a Window* (B.22) and a fifth state of *The Raising of Lazarus* (B.73), three unspecified van Goyen drawings, and five drawings attributed individually to Baroccio, Everdingen, Bakhuyzen, Titian and Bellini. These were exchanged for two engravings, one by Dürer, *The Nativity* (B.2; V & A E.4620-1910), the other by Lucas van Leyden, *The Return of the Prodigal Son* (B.78; V & A E.4614-1910), a second state of *Rembrandt Drawing at a Window* (B.22; 1910-2-12-357) (valued by Deprez & Gutekunst at

£140), an Ostade watercolour of a peasant interior, a Bonington oil of a Normandy coastal view and a red and black chalk drawing of figure studies by the same artist. The total value of this deal finally came to £380, with Salting noting on the invoice that the Boningtons were sold back to Deprez and Gutekunst at a later date![29]

For Salting the purification of his print collection was a never-ending process. In 1896, for the agreed value of £330 he bought from Richard Gutekunst three exemplary impressions: Rembrandt's *Old Haaring* (B.274; 1910-2-12-402), Dürer's *St Jerome in his Study* (B.60; V&A E.4624-1910) and Lucas van Leyden's *The Poet Virgil Suspended in a Basket* (B.136; V&A E.4613-1910). For these three items Salting exchanged a poorer impression of the Dürer *St Jerome in his Study* valued at £40, together with six other Dürers, two Schongauers (B.16 and B.17), Rembrandt's *The Goldweigher* (B.281), valued at £20, and a Seymour Haden etching, plus a cheque for £230 to make up the difference.[30] From this example, we can see how quality of impression replaced quantity in Salting's ceaseless quest to perfect his print collection, where only the finest examples by the greatest masters were admitted.

The receipts contain a mine of information on Salting's other purchases of works of art. A few examples will serve to indicate the dealers Salting relied upon in the different classes of his collection. Blue and white Chinese porcelain, the so-called Nankeen ware, in the form of beakers, vases and bottles, came from Murray Marks at 395 Oxford Street between 1876 and 1878 and a decade later from Charles Marks at 78 Wigmore Street, off Cavendish Square. From the early 1880s and all through the 1890s, the firm of J.J. Duveen (later the Duveen Brothers) became the principal supplier of Salting's *famille verte* and black enamel pieces. A receipt for one blue and white bottle bought from Duveen's in 1896 for £12. 10. 0 contains Salting's annotation that it was 'b[ought] orig[inal]ly by me for £20 or more some 20 years ago & exch[ange]d with L[ouis] Huth'[31] – a clear example of how closely he studied the art market and how keenly he remembered the pieces that had passed through his hands. Salting, with his love and understanding of objects, became the model connoisseur for young dealers, as Edward Fowles, first taken on as a thirteen-year-old assistant at Duveen's in 1898, later vividly recalled:

George Salting ... often walked over to the gallery from his bachelor flat in the Albany [*sic*] carrying a small work of art in his hands, which he would then proceed to sell in order to buy something finer. As he waited in the reception hall, he would stroke it lovingly, explaining to me all the while that one should not be satisfied by the mere look of a vase or a bronze,

but that one should fondle it, and thereby learn to appreciate its texture ...[32] [see fig. 1].

Salting seems to have started his famous collection of English miniatures in 1897, with the purchase of eleven examples, including two by Nicholas Hilliard and five by Samuel Cooper, from the Fine Art Society in New Bond Street for £1,300.[33] In the following year Salting turned to E.M. Hodgkins, who became his main supplier of miniatures until Salting's death. The weeding process continued unabated: in 1898, a miniature painted by the lesser-regarded Laurence Hilliard, son of the famous Nicholas, was part-exchanged for a better one by Samuel Cooper; Salting later scratched out Hodgkins's description of the sitter as Prince Rupert on the invoice and elevated it to a

(*Right*) 6. Nicholas Hilliard, *Young Man among Roses*, cabinet miniature, vellum stuck on card *c.*1587. 135 × 73 mm. Victoria and Albert Museum, London, P.163–1910 Salting Collection

portrait of 'Charles 2nd when quite young'.[34] The most important miniatures were acquired towards the very end of Salting's life as his eye became more discriminating and assured with this class of objects. In 1906, he entrusted Hodgkins with his commission at the Christie's sale of 27 June, when a pair of Nicholas Hilliard miniatures (lots 75 and 76) – one a portrait of Hilliard's father aged fifty-eight, the other a self-portrait aged thirty, both dated 1577 – were acquired for the fabulous sum of £3,050.[35] Only a few months before his death Salting bought through Frits Lugt, later to become the great authority on collectors of prints and drawings, the cabinet miniature that has now become the quintessential image of the Elizabethan age – Hilliard's *Young Man among Roses* (fig. 6), with its resonances of courtly love, chivalry and the cult of Elizabeth. The Amsterdam dealer Frederick Muller acknowledged on 14 July 1909 his 'receipt of £1,100 in payment of a miniature that Mr Frits Lugt sold for me'; in admiration of his collection, Muller expressed the hope of one day meeting Salting amidst his art-treasures.[36]

In the acquisition of pictures, Salting's familiar pattern of bartering objects for works of higher quality is also revealed in the invoices. In 1891, he acquired from Messrs Dowdeswell & Dowdeswell, the Bond Street printsellers and publishers, two pictures by Constable listed on the receipt as *Strand on the Green* and *Brighton* for which the initial asking price of 475 guineas was eventually bargained down to £375; but instead of paying this amount in cash, Salting settled the deal with the exchange of a John Crome wooded landscape, another landscape of gypsies by George Morland and a Bonington, all of which Salting haggled over as coming to £425, for which the exasperated dealer was compelled to make up the balance by writing out a cheque for £50.[37] Towards the end of his life, Salting bought several of his fashionable Barbizon pictures from Obach & Co., the New Bond Street picture dealers, who were also printsellers and publishers. In 1907, this distinguished firm sold him Corot's *Evening on the Lake* (National Gallery, London) for £475, but only after they had accepted in part-exchange Salting's 'marbles' of two drawings by William Collins and a Roman bronze traded in for £25.[38] Salting knew that his enormous wealth gave him the power to treat the trade as he wished, while the dealers recognised that this difficult eccentric would always return to drive another bargain.

Salting, the ambling figure on Bond Street, was also a familiar sight within the London sale-rooms, where he acquired a reputation as an implacable bidder (see fig. 7). Mention has already been made of his participation at the Fountaine and Spitzer sales. Less than a year after inheriting his fortune, we find Salting buying his first prints on 27 June 1866 at the Wellesley sale, which, as we have seen in the previous essay, was where John Malcolm of Poltalloch acquired his choice group of Claude drawings.

Salting's initial purchases reveal how uncertain was his taste for prints at this stage: on the third day of the sale he bought in person eight lots of reproductive prints, including two specified engravings after Landseer, which as proofs before letters had the appeal of scarcity but hardly the qualities of connoisseurship. None of these 113 reproductive prints was left in Salting's bequest and presumably all of them were swiftly swapped as his confidence and eye for prints improved. Likewise only two of the twenty-seven drawings Salting bought at the Wellesley sale appear to have been retained at his death: a Ter Borch, *The Music Master* (lot 1625; 1910-2-12-199, now described as only in the manner of Caspar Netscher, a pupil of Ter Borch) and an anonymous Venetian drawing of a courtly hunting party, then attributed to Titian (lot 1944; 1910-2-12-40).[39]

Salting gained his experience of prints by attending the heroic print sales of the 1880s and 1890s – those of the Reverend John Griffiths, the Oxford professor of divinity at Wadham (1883), John Webster, the late Member of Parliament of Aberdeen (1889), the surgeon-etcher Seymour Haden (1891) and the posthumous sale of the quarrelsome Richard Fisher (1892). These sales saw the rare, early states of Rembrandt etchings attain feverish prices as the etching revival and Rembrandt's position as its acknowledged father-figure escalated in prestige during the latter half of the nineteenth century.[40] Indeed Haden, an authority on Rembrandt prints and himself a leader of the etching revival in England, wrote in the catalogue introduction to his own sale:

The Connoisseur has only to run his eye along the long line of Catalogues professing to describe the etchings of Rembrandt, for instance, to see that there must be something wrong about them, since, in proportion as these etchings become fewer and rarer, the catalogues in question become more and more voluminous, and the "states" they describe more and more numerous. The reason of this is, that the Cataloguer being wholly uninformed as to the object and comparative value of the marks made upon his plate by the artist at the press side, and ferreting out more and more of such press-side marks every day, *makes them all into states* ... The portrait of Ephraim Bonus 'with the black ring', is another amusing proof of this form of manufacture, the only difference between the so called first and second states being that Rembrandt has taken the burr off the ring.[41]

Haden's Rembrandt etchings were the prize prints of the sale, producing more than £4,600. Meder of Berlin paid £1,000 alone for the first state on India paper of *Christ Presented to the People* (B.76), which in the great chain of provenance Haden had acquired from the Frenchman Galichon (see p. 165). Frederick Keppel and E. G. Kennedy, principal distributors of Whistler's etchings and others of the revival in New York, bought heavily at the sale, particularly the Rembrandts, which were later dispersed among American collections. Also among the

A GREAT PICTURE SALE AT CHRISTIE'S

7. Sydney P. Hall, *A Great Picture Sale at Christie's*, 1887, wood-engraving published in *The Graphic*, 10 September 1887. British Library, London. George Redford, the sales correspondent for *The Times*, wrote: 'The illustration represents a scene which may be witnessed any Saturday afternoon at the famous Rooms in King Street, St James's Square, during the London season, when some great collection of pictures is being sold ... Mr. Woods will be recognized in the rostrum ... The anxious moment of the last bid has come, as we see by the eager faces of the young ladies, and Mr. Agnew, sitting close by the side of the rostrum is about to take a telegram handed to him, which may tell him to buy the picture at any price ... Amongst the audience watching the contest we may recognize several well-known *habitués* of Christie's ... In the group standing behind the rostrum – a rather favourite place for the *cognoscenti* to compare notes – our artist seems to have seen Sir W. Gregory (Trustee of the National Gallery), with Lord Powerscourt and his friend Mr. Doyle (the Director of the National Gallery of Ireland) ... [and] we should be pretty sure to find [in the room] Sir F. Burton (the Director of the National Gallery), the Duke of St. Albans [and] Mr. Salting ...'

heavy buyers was Deprez who had been commissioned by Hubert Herkomer, in his capacity as adviser to the National Gallery of Victoria, Melbourne, to obtain the classic Rembrandt etchings *The Three Trees* (£148), *Jan Cornelius Sylvius* (£168) and *The Hundred Guilder Print* (£170) for the nascent print room in Australia.[42] Amidst this international competition from the dealers, Salting bought five Haden Rembrandts, the most expensive being *Jan Lutma* (see cat. 80) at £170. He also bought a number of etched views by Hollar, whom Haden in his foreword, somewhat caustically, described as 'an illustrator first and an artist afterwards'. All told Salting secured thirty-five prints (£248) and five drawings (£25) at the Haden sale, bidding as usual in person, to the chagrin of the dealers.

As Salting's connoisseurship of prints and drawings became more discriminating, so the care and conservation of his precious works began to demand increasing perfectionism.[43] During the 1870s Salting had used the services of J. Hogarth & Sons of Mayfair, who also sold and published prints, the costs of mounting mostly being set against the exchange of unwanted pictures, drawings and etchings. From the mid-1880s, when his print collection was becoming more refined, Salting engaged Robert Guéraut (Lugt 2210), who specialised in mounting the print cabinets of connoisseurs. Running his business, from 1891, from the print dealers Deprez & Gutekunst,

Guéraut applied a special stamp on the verso of his mounts with the inscription 'Mounted by R Guéraut' – an indication of how highly his professional mounting and conservation skills were held among fastidious collectors. From the invoices we gain a picture of the meticulous care Salting gave to his works on paper: for example, on 19 September 1885, he wanted his four new Rembrandt etchings mounted on toned Whatman simple mounts, with the edges gilded and the corners rounded; to preserve the uniformity of his print collection, he also took seventy-eight mounted Rembrandts and other Dutch prints and forty-eight mounted Dürers and other German Renaissance prints to Guéraut's workshop for cleaning, recutting and regilding of the old matts, and rounding of the corners.[44] A month later the drawing collection of eighty-eight mounts, of which eighteen had been put into sunk mounts, was conserved in a similar fashion. Shortly after the 1891 Haden sale Salting took round some of his new acquisitions, including three Rembrandt etchings for mounting on the more expensive variety of sunk Whatman mounts. Among his conservation requirements for the drawings were 're-sticking a piece on a drawing by Hollar, removing a fold from another drawing by Hollar on parchment [and] reviving discoloured white on an old drawing, by a special process'; the last, costing an expensive 7s 6d, was an early example of a chemical treatment of recovering white heightening that had oxidised on a drawing.[45] Salting persisted with the conservation of his collection up to the time of his death. Indeed, in February 1909, when E. Moreau-Nélaton was preparing his volume and presumably the photographic plates for *Crayons français du XVIe siècle conservés dans la collection de M. G. Salting à Londres* (Paris, Librairie Centrale des Beaux-Arts, [1909]), Salting paid £54 to a restorer to have the backs removed, the old paste cleaned away, all 'stains and smoke tint' removed, and the colours restored on all thirty-two sheets from his Clouet album of French portraits; the drawings and the title-page were individually mounted and placed in two specially built solander cases.[46]

It now remains to discuss Salting's will and the distribution of his gift to the nation. When Salting died on 12 December 1909, there was intense speculation in the national press over the fate of his great art collections. Not since the death of Lady Wallace a decade earlier in 1897, when the destiny of the treasures of Hertford House (shortly to be named the Wallace Collection) was still unknown, had so much attention been aroused. Salting had hinted to close friends that he intended to leave his collections to the British public, but it was feared he had not signed any of the wills he had drafted by dictation because of his habitual procrastination. The discovery of a not very recent will, written and signed on 14 October 1889, in which Salting disposed of his entire estate in less than 400 words, soon allayed public anxiety. The will was witnessed by a gardener and a coachman at Burnside,

Elgin, the country estate in Scotland where he sometimes spent some days shooting. After leaving legacies of money to relatives and friends amounting in all to £32,000, George Salting gave:

unto the Nation my Art Collections, namely my pictures or such as they, the Trustees may select for the National Gallery[,] and my other collections, whether in my chambers or at the South Kensington Museum, to be kept at the said Museum, and not distributed over the various sections but kept all together according to the various specialities of my exhibits ... And as regards my prints and Drawings, which I leave to the Nation, I desire that the Trustees of the British Museum shall select any that they deem worthy of being added to the National Collections.[47]

A sum of £10,000 was left for distribution among the London hospitals and another of £2,000 was given to the Prince Alfred Hospital, Sydney, the only bequest Salting made to the land of his birth and source of wealth.[48]

The executor Arthur Flower faced enormous difficulties in administering the will. First a complete inventory of the contents of his rooms at the Thatched House Club had to be drawn up, which was no small undertaking. 'These rooms are like the apartments of Balzac's Cousin Pons', wrote an astonished correspondent for *The Times*, 'for every corner is filled to congestion with masterpieces of the great artists of Italy, Holland and England stacked up in every available corner.'[49] Nearly two hundred paintings, together with forty-one framed watercolours and fifteen portfolios of prints and drawings, were discovered by his executor. On 1 January 1910, Flower wrote to the British Museum, as one of the beneficiary institutions, outlining his plan to the Principal Librarian:

I propose to deal first with the oil paintings and Drawings by Old Masters and to ask Mr. Lockett Agnew to make a list of all these – and having done this – to move the Oil Paintings to Messrs Agnew's Gallery at 43 Old Bond Street where the National Gallery Authorities might be asked to inspect them with a view to selection under the terms of the Will. And in similar manner the Drawings by Old Masters would be open to inspection by Authorities of the British Museum for the same purpose. The sooner these valuable collections can be removed from their present site with the attendant risks the better for all concerned.[50]

Under the executor's instructions an inventory of Salting's collection of pictures, drawings and prints was duly prepared and privately printed for circulation to the British Museum and the National Gallery.[51] This catalogue gave the artist and title of each work under two broad categories. The first comprised pictures (items 1–209) and framed watercolours (210–251, including eighteen Turners). The second itemised unframed drawings and prints (1–437) found in the portfolios and solanders at Salting's death. A second catalogue, just of the pictures and framed watercolours, was very shortly afterwards printed by

Agnew's with minor revisions and an addendum of fifteen previously overlooked paintings (252–266).[52] Charles Holroyd, the Director of the National Gallery, and Dr Wilhelm Bode, the Director of the Berlin Gallery, who had recently published some of Salting's art bronzes,[53] were invited to pick over the assembled pictures, annotating their catalogues with acceptance or rejection. A special meeting of the Trustees of the National Gallery was held at Agnew's on 25 January 1910, when the experts declared their decision to select 164 paintings of the 224 on the inventory. This, together with the twenty-eight Salting pictures already on loan to the National Gallery, brought the final number of paintings in the bequest to 192.[54]

With the paintings out of the way, the executor turned his attention to the prints and drawings destined under the terms of the will for the British Museum. Sidney Colvin was asked to inspect the Salting portfolios at Agnew's with a view to making a selection. Almost all the unframed drawings were chosen; with respect to the prints, the Keeper, in his report to the Trustees of the British Museum, wrote:

Few of these [prints] fill actual gaps in the Museum collection, but a considerable number will be useful additions, whether as being finer impressions than those already belonging to the Nation, or as providing duplicates or triplicates that can be either set aside for loans for Provincial Exhibitions or placed permanently on view in the public galleries of the Museum without breaking up the main series of any given master ... in the Print Room.[55]

As the Museum owned no drawings of Turner other than his early sketches, Colvin was determined to secure the finished framed watercolours (fig. 8) as well. Anxious that these should go to the British Museum as drawings and not to the National Gallery as pictures, Colvin wrote to the executor on 17 January to plead the Museum's case. On the eve of the National Gallery Trustees' special meeting at Agnew's, Colvin made further representations before Flower at his Princes Gate residence, pressing his claim 'that according to universal trade custom, as proved by sale catalogues, etc, works in water-colour are classed as drawings and separated from paintings in oil, which are classed as pictures'.[56] Flower, to whose authority as executor such decisions were referred, was keen to arrive at a settlement that would satisfy all three national museums. On 16 February Flower informed Colvin that, by mutual consent with the National Gallery, custody of the framed watercolours would pass to the British Museum, 'leaving untouched the crucial question "are the works of art in question pictures or drawings"? Solution of which would have found occupation I think for casuists and lawyers for a very considerable time to come.'[57]

The National Gallery did make a claim, however, for custody of Salting's collection of miniatures. Colvin had earlier expressed interest in these as well, but Flower was quick to reply: 'As to miniatures I must say at once that it seems to me under the terms of the will these must [go] to Victoria & Albert or (as I call it) S. Kensington Museum.'[58] A decision on the status of the miniatures was referred by the National Gallery and the Victoria and Albert Museum to the Law Officers of the Crown, who decided in South Kensington's favour.[59] The Victoria and Albert Museum was also the recipient of the residue of the prints and drawings not selected by the British Museum.

8. Joseph Mallord William Turner, *Richmond, Yorkshire*, watercolour *c.*1826. 275 × 397 mm. 1910-2-12-276 Salting Collection

These included a few leaves cut out from illuminated manuscripts, a handful of minor English drawings and fifty-one prints, nearly half of them Dürer engravings, several with distinguished provenance.[60]

Shunning all publicity during his life, George Salting was celebrated shortly after his death with three special exhibitions mounted by the National Gallery, the British Museum and the Victoria and Albert Museum in honour of his bequest to the nation. One of the rooms at the National Gallery was dismantled to display ninety-one pictures from the Salting gift, which opened to a curious public on 12 February 1910. Amid cheers of approval for the late benefactor the Director announced that 'his memory would be green as long as the National Art Gallery lasted. (Hear, hear.)'.[61] A month later, Colvin and his staff arranged a display of the Salting drawings in the cases and screens of the Exhibition Gallery at the British Museum. As one reviewer commented:

More attention has been paid, and perhaps will continue to be paid, to the pictures left to the National Gallery, for the public at large thinks more of the finished picture than of sketches and studies, however fine; but there can be little doubt that the collection of drawings is even more exceptional than the collection of pictures. In certain departments it surpasses everything that the Museum possessed already, whereas the same can hardly be said of the works gathered in the room at Trafalgar-square, good as many of them are.[62]

Because his extraordinary bequest of more than 2,500 objects to the Victoria and Albert Museum carried the stipulation that they should be preserved together according to their different classes, South Kensington was the last of the three museums to honour Salting with an exhibition. Three large rooms, with a further two on the floor above, were finally cleared for the Salting Collection in the south-east corner of the museum. For the grand opening on 22 March 1911, a large company of guests was invited, which, *The Times* in its coverage of the event reported:

seemed to include all the connoisseurs in London and many more besides. The opinion was unanimous that the bequest was a marvellous one, alike in the width of its range, in the number of the objects, and in the uniformly high quality of almost all. It would be difficult for the keenest eye to discover half a dozen among all these hundreds of objects which are not what they pretend to be ... Bronzes, majolica, Limoges enamels, Palissy ware, Renaissance furniture, Syrian and Persian pottery, Chinese porcelain and jade, Japanese lacquer – everything is wonderfully good of its kind, and in almost every class there are some objects which, in the strictest sense of the word, may be called masterpieces.[63]

By a strange twist, Arthur Flower, Salting's conscientious executor, was buried on the very day that the London art world at South Kensington was toasting the public possession of his old friend's magnificent bequest.

Like the collectors William Mitchell and John Malcolm

of Poltalloch, George Salting was always a generous lender to the Burlington Fine Arts Club, although he never appears to have sat on its Committee. He was by far the richest of the three collectors, but chose to live in the simplest circumstances. Possessed of the most discriminating eye for quality, Salting was a connoisseur for whom all fine objects were deserving of study. Unlike his fellow connoisseurs Augustus Franks of the British Museum or Charles Drury Fortnum, benefactor of the Ashmolean, Salting was not a scholar-connoisseur, for he never published or gave papers on the marvellous objects in his collections. Instead he drew on the learning of others to form his own aesthetic judgements. His life's work was making his collections, and it was this achievement that he left to the three national museums in London.

1. 'Mr. George Salting', *The Times*, 14 December 1909, p. 10.

2. C. H. Read, 'George Salting', *The Burlington Magazine*, 16, February 1910, p. 251.

3. Biographical details on George Salting are found in C. H. Read's entry in the *Dictionary of National Biography, Second Supplement*, III, London 1912, pp. 254–6. For more recent appraisals, see Frank Davis, *Victorian Patrons of the Arts: Twelve Famous Collections and Their Owners*, London 1963, pp. 80–4, and Paul Goldman, 'George Salting: A Professional Collector', *Antique Collector*, January 1987, pp. 61–8. An account of Severin Kanute Salting's life is given in A. F. Pike's entry in the *Australian Dictionary of Biography*, 2, Melbourne 1967, p. 415.

4. Severin Kanute Salting, letter to Edward Knox, 26 January 1859, in the Knox Family Papers ML MSS 98/3, pp. 479–85, Mitchell Library, State Library of New South Wales, Sydney. The letter continued with Salting senior's reservations about a permanent return to Australia: 'My friends in the Colony urge me to come back there. I own I should feel great reluctance to go back to that spot, where I lived so long in happiness. And what should I do there now? I have no wish to go back to the desk in Hunter Street. I would rather wish to withdraw altogether from business. For Colonial politics I have no taste; and to live in the Colony without any occupation seems to me very wretched.' Similar sentiments may have induced his son not to return to Australia either. I am most grateful to Jim Andrighetti, Manuscripts Section, State Library of New South Wales, Sydney, for providing me with a copy of this letter and other materials relating to George Salting from the Knox Family Papers. It is interesting to note that one of the three executors to Severin Kanute Salting's will (drafted on 16 March 1863, while on a brief visit to Sydney) was Sir Charles Nicholson, Bt (1808–1903), who formed the first notable collection of pictures and antiquities in the colony, which he presented to the University of Sydney in 1865, where he had served as its Chancellor. Through the family's business connections and his university career, George Salting would have been aware of Nicholson's taste in collecting. See Pamela Bell, 'Sir Charles Nicholson's Collection', *Australian Journal of Art*, 11, 1993, pp. 57–84. A copy of Severin Kanute Salting's will is in the Archives of P. W. Flower and Sons, MS 19,358, the Guildhall Library, London; see n. 14.

5. Louis Huth (1822–1905), merchant-banker and youngest son of Frederick Huth, founder of the City house of Frederick Huth and Co., was one of the first serious English collectors of oriental blue and white. For forty years he lived with his collections in a large house at Possingworth, Sussex, built for him by Digby Wyatt. A member of the

Burlington Fine Arts Club, he was a close friend of Whistler (see p. 163). He was brother of the famous bibliophile Henry Huth, who formed the Huth Library of rare and early printed books. See Louis Huth's obituary in *The Times*, 15 February 1905, p. 11. Although Huth was to predecease him, Salting left his friend the sum of £2,000 in his will of 1889. See n. 47.

6. For a lengthy, informative article on the different categories of objects in the Salting bequest to the Victoria and Albert Museum, see 'The Salting Collection', *The Times*, 25 December 1909, p. 6. I am most grateful to Dr Clive Wainwright, Research Department, the Victoria and Albert Museum, for discussing Salting's V & A bequest with me.

7. *DNB*, op. cit., p. 255.

8. Wilhelm Bode, *The Italian Bronze Statuettes of the Renaissance* (3 vols), assisted by Murray Marks, London and Berlin 1908–12, I, p. 6.

9. C. Drury E. Fortnum, *Maiolica. A Historical Treatise on the Glazed and Enamelled Earthenwares of Italy, with Marks and Monograms*, Oxford 1896, p. 77. Fortnum wrongly calls him 'Henry' Salting. For an interesting account of Fortnum's collecting career, see Nicholas Penny, *Catalogue of European Sculpture in the Ashmolean Museum, 1540 to the Present Day, 2: Italian*, Oxford 1992, pp. xvii–xxx. The Victorian pursuit of Renaissance maiolica by museum officials and collectors is discussed in Timothy Wilson, 'The Origins of the Maiolica Collections of the British Museum and the Victoria & Albert Museum 1851–55', *Faenza*, 71, nos. 1–3, 1985, pp. 68–80. See also Andrew Moore, 'The Fountaine Collection of Maiolica', *The Burlington Magazine*, 130, June 1988, pp. 435–47. Timothy Wilson, Keeper of Western Art, the Ashmolean, Oxford, kindly provided me with some of these references.

10. *Catalogue des objets d'art et de haute curiosité antiques, du moyen-âge & de la renaissance... collection Spitzer* (2 vols), Paris, 17 April–16 June 1893. An invoice in the Archives of P. W. Flower and Sons, MS 19,474, Guildhall Library, London, shows Salting had his copy of the Spitzer sale catalogue bound by Dulau & Co., Foreign & English Booksellers of Soho Square, for £1.14.6 on 9 February 1894. See n. 14.

11. 'Mr. Salting's Spitzer Purchases', *The Times*, 14 July 1893, p. 15.

12. For a detailed contemporary account of Salting's picture collection at his death, see 'The Salting Collection', *The Times*, 15 December 1909, p. 10. Salting's personal inventory of his pictures is recorded in a simple exercise book with blue boards (deposited among Papers relating to the Salting Collection, Box A1.6.31, Libraries and Archives Department, National Gallery, London). Begun in 'October 1900', this important document contains a list of 'Pictures at the National Gallery' and a list of 'Pictures in my rooms' at the Thatched House Club, with the prices he paid and their approximate market value. I am grateful to Jacki McComish of the National Gallery's Libraries and Archives Department for allowing me to consult this material.

13. Dürer, *Portrait of a Man*, charcoal, 1910-2-12-103, Rowlands 233, once mistakenly believed to be a portrait of Lucas van Leyden, and Holbein, *Portrait of an English Woman*, black and red chalk, with touches of white bodycolour, on pink prepared paper, 1910-2-12-105, Rowlands 323, long thought to be a likeness of Margaret Roper, daughter of Sir Thomas More.

14. Salting's business investments in Australia are contained in the vast Archives of P. W. Flower and Sons, MSS 19,338–489, the Guildhall Library, London. These records were deposited as a gift from the estate of P. W. Flower and Sons in September 1979. Documents concerning Salting's Australian landed interests and share income are

found in MSS 19,358–60, 19,374, 19,377, 19,470–89, many of which were organised by his executor Arthur Flower. I am particularly grateful to Stephen Freeth, Keeper of Manuscripts, Guildhall Library, for providing me with a list of these papers.

15. 'Mr. Salting's Estate', *The Times*, 26 January 1910, p. 11. According to this report, death duties payable on Salting's property were estimated under the new Budget scale at over £280,000, or under the old scale prior to the Budget change, at about £190,000.

16. Salting's rent payment for the Thatched House Club is regularly recorded in his Cash Books (January 1870–February 1903, 3 vols), MS 19,472, Archives of P. W. Flower and Sons, Guildhall Library, London.

17. This passage on the interior furnishings of Salting's rooms at the Thatched House Club has been pieced together from his receipted bills for personal expenses, etc. in the Archives of P. W. Flower and Sons, MS 19,474, Guildhall Library, London. In 1883, bills of refurbishment were sent in by Turberville Smith & Son, Carpet & Rug Manufacturers, 9 Great Marlborough Street (who in 1907 were called in to lay a new roll of plain blue felt in both rooms in exactly the same fashion as twenty-four years earlier); in 1883 and 1887, Wetherilt, Lee & Martin, the Mayfair firm of builders and decorators, undertook other renovations including the curtain fittings and new locks. The large satinwood display cabinet was supplied by Morant, Boyd & Blanford, the New Bond Street firm of painters, decorators, cabinet makers and upholsterers.

18. As Sir Charles Holroyd, Director of the National Gallery, London, commented on one public occasion after Salting's death: 'Mr. Salting enjoyed himself in his own way. He had a very happy life although he slept over one club and lived in another', 'The Late Mr. George Salting', *The Times*, 14 February 1910, p. 7.

19. *The Times*, 14 December 1909, p. 10. Several of Salting's close friends took exception to this and other comments on his character made in the Press at his death. Lindo Myers of Mayfair, who knew him well for many years, wrote to *The Times* (17 December 1909, p. 8) giving instances of his charity and added: 'His wit was great, and fulfilled an essential French qualification of being "surprising".'

20. This is related by Davis, *Victorian Patrons*, op. cit., p. 81.

21. James Henry Duveen, *Collections and Recollections: A Century and a Half of Art Deals*, London 1935, p. 114.

22. *DNB*, op. cit., p. 255.

23. This is the label given to Salting by the picture connoisseur R. H. Benson in the preface to his privately printed *Catalogue of Italian Pictures at 16, South Street, Park Lane, London and Buckhurst in Sussex Collected by Robert and Evelyn Benson*, Chiswick Press, 1914, p. vii.

24. George Salting's receipted bills for the purchase of works of art, 1872–1909, mostly from London and Paris dealers, in the Archives of P. W. Flower and Sons, MS 19,473, Guildhall Library, London. See n. 14.

25. Invoice from Holloway & Son, 25 Bedford Street, Strand, Christmas 1872, MS 19,473.

26. See Lugt 1296 and Lugt Suppl. 1296. In 1872, this collector had his *Catalogue of the Select Collection of Etchings and Engravings Formed by Henry Brodhurst* privately printed in twenty copies. He presented a copy (now in the Prints and Drawings Department's Library, 1890-1-7-6) to the collector H. J. Pfungst, with an accompanying letter of 17 December 1872 outlining his collecting principles: 'The Collection is a small one, as I have always been more anxious to obtain fine specimens, than to add unduly to the number –

an error, which I think many amateurs, are apt to fall into. It is however sufficient for enjoyment and has afforded me much pleasure during many years.' This copy contains Pfungst's annotations of some of the purchases made by Salting and John Malcolm of Poltalloch from Brodhurst's collection after it was sold *en bloc*, through the intermediary Colnaghi's, to the French dealer.

27. Invoice from Messrs Danlos fils et Delisle, Marchands d'Estampes, quai Malaquais 15, Paris, 29 May [1883], MS 19,473.

28. Invoice from O. Gutekunst, 20 Cockspur Street, Pall Mall, London, 27 April 1889, MS 19,473. The sale of the drawings and prints of Josef Carl Ritter von Klinkosch (L.577) was held on 15 April 1889 and the days following by Wawra of Vienna, with Salting buying lots 155 (Bellini), 365 (Dujardin) and 721 (Rembrandt).

29. Invoice from Deprez & Gutekunst, 18 Green Street, St Martin's Place, London, 26 September 1893, MS 19,473.

30. Invoice from R. Gutekunst, Old Prints and Drawings, 16 King Street, St James's Square, 2 December 1896, MS 19,473.

31. Invoice from Duveen Bros, Importers of Decorative Works of Art, 21 Old Bond Street, London, 22 January 1896, MS 19,473.

32. Edward Fowles, *Memories of Duveen Brothers*, introduction by Ellis Waterhouse, London 1976, p. 10.

33. Invoice from the Fine Art Society, 148 New Bond Street, 5 July 1897, MS 19,473.

34. Invoice from E. M. Hodgkins, Dealer in Works of Art & Valuer, 43 Old Bond Street, 4 August 1898, MS 19,473.

35. See cat. 48 and 49 in Roy Strong, *Artists of the Tudor Court: the Portrait Miniature Rediscovered 1520–1620*, exhibition catalogue, London, Victoria and Albert Museum, 9 July–6 November 1983.

36. Invoice from Frederick Muller & Cie, Ventes publiques de tableaux, dessins, estampes, antiquités, d'objets d'art, 10,16,18, Doelenstraat, Amsterdam, 14 July 1909, MS 19,473. For full details on Salting's most famous Hilliard, see Strong, op. cit., cat. 263.

37. Invoice from Messrs Dowdeswell & Dowdeswell Ltd, Printsellers and Publishers, at their Rooms, 160 New Bond Street, 4 February 1891, MS 19,473.

38. Invoice from Obach & Co., Dealers in Pictures & Other Works of Art, Printsellers & Publishers, 168 New Bond Street, 4 June 1907, MS 19,473. On 11 February 1908, Salting bought from them Daubigny's *River Scene with Ducks* (National Gallery, London) for £2,500.

39. Rev. Dr Wellesley sale, 25 June 1866 and the following thirteen days, London (Sotheby's); the prints acquired by Salting in person were lots 371, 379, 381, 387, 389, 406–7 (after Landseer) and 411. For the de-attribution of the Ter Borch brush and ink drawing, see A. M. Hind, *Catalogue of Drawings by Dutch and Flemish Artists … in the British Museum*, IV, London 1931, p. 7, cat. 6.

40. At the peak of the Rembrandt craze in 1883, the French collector Dutuit of Rouen paid the astonishing sum of £1,510 for the first state of Rembrandt's *Portrait of Doctor Arnoldus Tholinx* (B.284) at the Griffiths sale, 9 May 1883 and the following day, London (Sotheby's), lot 207. Extensive coverage of this sale is given in *The Times*, 14 May 1883, p. 3.

41. Seymour Haden sale, 15 June 1891 and the four days following, London (Sotheby's), 'Avant-Propos', pp. iii–iv.

42. The eleven Rembrandts, three Dürer engravings and a van Dyck etching bought at the Haden sale were the first important old master print acquisitions made by the National Gallery of Victoria, Australia. See Irena Zdanowicz, 'Prints of Fortune: Hubert Herkomer's 1891–92 Etching Purchases for the National Gallery of Victoria', *Art Bulletin of Victoria*, no. 33 (1993), pp. 1–17. Louis Fagan, Assistant Keeper in the Prints and Drawings Department of the British Museum, while on a visit to Melbourne was interviewed by the Trustees of the National Gallery of Victoria for advice on the formation of their print collection; Fagan's suggestions were printed and circulated for public perusal (Zdanowicz, op. cit., p. 3 and n. 10).

43. Receipts for the conservation of Salting's prints and drawings are found among Salting's receipted bills for personal expenses, Archives of P. W. Flower and Sons, MS 19,474. For the paintings, receipts are found in MS 19,473: F. Haines & Sons, located beside the station at South Kensington, were Salting's picture restorers for more than twenty-four years, 1883 to 1907, Mr Haines sometimes being asked to come up in person to remove the bloom from several pictures at the Thatched House Club, or, as on another occasion, 'coming up & touching [the] Velasquez' (attributed, National Gallery, London).

44. Invoice from R. Guéraut, Art Publisher, Framer and Mounter, 108 Devonport Road, Uxbridge Road, London, 19 September 1885, MS 19,474.

45. Invoice from R. Guéraut, 18 Green Street, St Martin's Place, London, [June 1891] MS 19,474.

46. Invoice from S. W. Littlejohn, 75 Arthur Road, North Brixton, London, 3 February 1909, MS 19,474. Louis Dimier's article on Salting's Clouet album appeared in *The Burlington Magazine*, XVI, January 1910, pp. 223–5, in which he complained that Moreau-Nélaton had taken many of the remarks Dimier had earlier made on Salting's mounts as his own.

47. Will of George Salting, 14 October 1889; probate granted 22 January 1910. Somerset House, Probate Registry, London. A copy of the will is in the British Museum, Central Archives, Book of Presents, 1910, item 183.

48. There was some reaction in the Australian press to Salting's failure to remember the country from which he had obtained his fortune. Judge Johnston of the Melbourne Bar suggested that the residue of the Salting bequest be given to one of the public art galleries in Australia. See his letter, 'Mr. Salting's Treasures and Australia', *The Times*, 31 December 1909, p. 11; and further Australian reports in *The Argus* (Melbourne), 1 January 1910, p. 13; 27 January 1910, p. 7; and 29 January 1910, p. 17.

49. 'The Salting Collection', *The Times*, 15 December 1909, p. 10.

50. A. Flower, letter to Sir George Murray, 1 January 1910. British Museum, Central Archives, Book of Presents, 1910, item 183.

51. *Catalogue of Mr. George Salting's Collection of Pictures*, printed by the Dryden Press, n.d. [early January 1910]. A copy is among the Papers relating to the Salting Collection Box AI.6.31, Libraries and Archives Department, National Gallery, London. From this catalogue, we can establish that the unframed drawings were preserved in several portfolios labelled 'English' (items 1–35), 'French' (36–72), 'Italian' (73–118), 'Dutch' (119–74), two portfolios of Clouet drawings (175), a portfolio of 51 lesser English mounted drawings (176), 'Flemish' (177–215), including a group of German drawings (216–220), and several drawings placed in the 'Miscellaneous engraving portfolio' (221–7). Japanese Ukiyo-e woodcuts, landscape etchings by Waterloo and Claude (228–56), were kept in the aforementioned miscellaneous portfolio; other unframed prints were stored in a small solander of Rembrandt etchings (257–80), a second portfolio of Rembrandt etchings (281–323), a small solander of Ostade, Sebald Beham, Lucas van Leyden and Dürer (324–61), a Dürer portfolio (362–97), and finally an Italian portfolio mostly of Marcantonios (398–437).

52. *Catalogue of the Collection of Pictures and Drawings of the late Mr. George Salting*, at the Galleries of Thos. Agnew & Sons, 43 Old Bond Street, London, January 1910. A copy is among the Papers relating to the Salting Collection Box A1.6.31, Libraries and Archives Department, National Gallery, London.

53. See n. 8.

54. The unwanted paintings were assigned to the residuary legatee, who, because Salting's brother William had predeceased him, became his niece Lady Katherine Binning, who had married the heir of Lord Haddington.

55. Sidney Colvin's Report to Trustees, 4 February 1910. In 1932, Campbell Dodgson prepared a *List of Duplicate Prints Available for Loan from the Department of Prints and Drawings*, which was circulated among the public museums and art galleries of Britain; among the 350 prints available for loan were several from the Salting bequest, including fourteen Rembrandts.

56. ibid.

57. A. Flower, letter to Sidney Colvin, 16 February 1910.

58. A. Flower, letter to Sidney Colvin, 19 January 1910.

59. See Copy *'of Report of the Director of the National Gallery, for the Year 1910, with Appendices'*, London, HMSO, 1911, p.8; Appendix 2, pp.11–32, contains a complete list of the pictures accepted by the National Gallery under the Salting Bequest, sometimes mentioning the provenance of the painting and its prior exhibition at the Burlington Fine Arts Club.

60. The Victoria and Albert Museum's residue of the Salting Bequest prints and drawings is recorded in the V&A, Prints, Drawings & Paintings Collection, MS Register of Acquisitions, 1909–1910, under the accession E.4575-1910 to E.4663-1910.

61. On the opening of the exhibition to the public, it was reported that 'from an early hour ... there was a constant stream of visitors to Room xv. at the National Gallery... There was hardly enough room to show the 91 pictures to the best advantage, and it is probable that the remainder of the Salting collection will not be seen until the gallery has been enlarged.' 'The Salting Bequest at the National Gallery', *The Times*, 14 February 1910, p.7.

62. 'The Salting Bequest to the British Museum', *The Times*, 18 March 1910, p.13. Colvin also prepared the accompanying catalogue *Exhibition of Drawings Bequeathed to the British Museum by the Late Mr. George Salting*, British Museum, Prints and Drawings Department, [1910]. The Keeper was one of four scholars who contributed an article for the series commissioned by *The Burlington Magazine* to celebrate the benefactor. See Sidney Colvin, 'The Salting Collection – IV. Drawings of the French School', *The Burlington Magazine*, XVII, August 1910, pp.277–83. The other contributors were G.F. Hill on the Italian bronze statuettes, March 1910, pp.311–18; Claude Phillips on the Italian Pictures, April 1910, pp.9–22; and C.J. Holmes on the French and English Pictures, May 1910, pp.79–86.

63. 'The Salting Bequest. The Display at South Kensington', *The Times*, 23 March 1911, p.7. To mark the opening in March 1911, the Victoria and Albert Museum published a special illustrated guide to *The Salting Collection*, London, HMSO, 1911; it quickly went out of print and another edition appeared in May 1911; a third edition was published in 1926.

76 Albrecht Dürer (1471–1528)
Hercules, c.1498

Engraving. 324 × 225 mm
Bartsch VII 86.73

In the diary of his trip to the Netherlands in 1520/1, Dürer simply referred to this print as 'Hercules'. Later commentators have greatly differed in their explanations of Dürer's perplexing subject. Bartsch called this print 'The Effect of Jealousy'. Panofsky argued that the subject derives from Xenophon's classical story of Hercules at the crossroads, when the hero must decide between vice or virtue, personified here by his encounter with two women, naked and clothed (Erwin Panofsky, *The Life and Art of Albrecht Dürer* [4th edn], Princeton, NJ, 1955, pp.73–6). Dürer's primary interest, however, was not so much with the Hercules story as with the opportunity it provided for depicting the nude in an antique manner. Although his first visit to Italy in 1494 had exposed him to the ruins of antiquity, it was the engravings of Mantegna and Pollaiuolo, with their overt interest in the classical nude taken from statuary and Roman sarcophagi, that exercised the strongest influence on Dürer.

Salting's bequest to the British Museum included fifteen Dürer engravings, which he had acquired with an eye to their distinguished provenance. This print had earlier been in the collection of the English connoisseur Robert Balmanno (1780–1866), whose signature and year of election to the Society of Antiquaries in 1828 (L.213) are inscribed on the verso.

1910-2-12-302. Salting collection

77 Lucas van Leyden (*c.*1489/94–1533)
Samson and Delilah, 1508 or earlier

Engraving. 284 × 203 mm
Bartsch VII 351.25

The chronology of Lucas van Leyden's life is still very unclear. According to Karel van Mander's published biographical account of 1604 (which was based on information from the artist's descendants), Lucas was born in Leyden in 1494, making him a boy of fourteen when he engraved this print. Although modern scholars have argued for an earlier birthdate of 1489, Lucas's precocious mastery of engraving remains undisputed. The compositional complexity of *Samson and Delilah* places it among the earliest masterpieces of engraving. Lucas demonstrates his understanding of Renaissance foreshortening in the supine figure of Samson whose locks, the source of his legendary strength, are being cut by the treacherous Delilah. The drama is intensified by the presence of the cowardly Philistines who creep towards the sleeping Samson ready

76

77

to capture him the moment Delilah has finished her deed. The structured composition and the rocky landscape in this engraving seem to owe a debt to the engravings of Mantegna, who also made a grisaille painting of this subject (National Gallery, London).

One of eight Lucas engravings bequeathed by Salting to the British nation, this print and two others – *Susanna and the Two Elders* (B.33) and *The Pilgrims* (B.149) – were accepted by the Trustees of the British Museum while the remainder went to the Victoria and Albert Museum.

1910-2-12-316. Salting collection

78 Marcantonio Raimondi (*c*.1480–before 1534)

Woman Watering a Plant, c.1510

Engraving. 189 × 116 mm

Bartsch XIV 292.383

Marcantonio Raimondi was the first engraver to collaborate with another designer in the production of prints. After an initial period in Venice where he copied some of Dürer's engravings, Marcantonio made his reputation in Rome from 1509 translating Raphael's drawings and designs into engravings. The popularity of the numerous engravings produced by this collaborative enterprise helped to spread Renaissance ideas and compositions throughout Europe. The elegantly twisted female nude in this print illustrates the Renaissance study of *contrapposto* and the general interest in secular subjects.

Salting greatly admired the engravings of Marcantonio. This example, which comes from the collection of Sir Peter Lely (see cat. 65), is one of twenty-four in his collection bequeathed to the British Museum.

1910-2-12-342. Salting collection

79 Rembrandt Harmensz. van Rijn (1606–69)

The Entombment, c.1654

Etching, drypoint, burin. 1st and 4th states. 210 × 161 mm
Bartsch 86; Hind 281

This print demonstrates Rembrandt's characteristic elaboration of a subject through successive workings of the plate. In the first state, the compositional grouping of the figures is established in etching; a few additional lines are lightly picked out in drypoint on the edge of the tomb and on the Virgin's left elbow. Through the progressive working over of the plate with a series of parallel and diagonal lines of shading, Rembrandt has plunged the scene in darkness by the time he has reached the fourth and final state.

In doing so, he creates a dramatic chiaroscuro effect appropriate to the subject of Christ's nocturnal entombment.

Salting formed a small but choice collection of Rembrandt's etchings. Of the forty-nine which were accepted by the Trustees in Salting's bequest, fifteen Rembrandt prints, including this rare impression of the first state, came from the collection of Ernst Theodor Rodenacher (L.2438), a wealthy shipowner from Danzig (now Gdansk). Shortly after Rodenacher's death in about 1894, many of his prize prints were acquired by Colnaghi's in London, who then sold them to Salting.

Two impressions:
(a) 1910-2-12-360. First state. Salting collection
(b) 1910-2-12-387. Fourth state. Salting collection

80 Rembrandt Harmensz. van Rijn (1606–69)

Jan Lutma, 1656

Etching and drypoint. 1st state. 196 × 150 mm

Bartsch 276; Hind 290

During the crisis of his bankruptcy in 1656, when his house and art collection were placed in the hands of receivers, Rembrandt etched this portrait of his friend Jan Lutma (1584–1669), a German silversmith who worked in Amsterdam. Lutma is shown holding an example of his fine workmanship; the tools of his profession, a hammer and a set of punches in a jar, rest on the table beside him, together with a shell-shaped drinking bowl skilfully chased in silver. (A documented silver bowl by Jan Lutma, very similar to the one depicted in this print, is now in the Rijksmuseum, Amsterdam; see *Face to Face with the Sitter for Rembrandt's Etched Portraits*, exhibition catalogue, Amsterdam, Rembrandt House Museum, 13 December 1986–22 February 1987, cat. 50–1.) In this first state Lutma is seated against an open backdrop; in the second state Rembrandt defines this space by adding a deep window niche which encloses the sitter.

This impression was bought by Salting himself for £170 at Seymour Haden's sale of 1891 (Sotheby's, 15–19 June 1891, lot 460). Haden, who ranked as one of the foremost collectors of Rembrandt etchings, had earlier mounted an important exhibition of his prints at the Burlington Fine Arts Club in London in 1877, which was the first attempt to arrange Rembrandt's etchings chronologically.

1910-2-12-403. Salting collection

78

79a

9. Campbell Dodgson (1867–1948)

Frances Carey

The figure who dominates much of the twentieth-century history of the British Museum's print collection is that of Campbell Dodgson (1867–1948), who succeeded Sir Sidney Colvin as Keeper from 1912 to 1932. Although he was the youngest of eight siblings, he inherited sufficient means to support the constant generosity, in money, and in kind, that he displayed throughout his life towards his department. The diffusive effects of his altruism were acknowledged in the preface to the exhibition held in 1933, of a selection from the nearly 4,000 prints and drawings acquired during Dodgson's Keepership: 'Apart from the many gifts which he made himself – hardly a week passed without some gift from him – the donations of the National Art Collections Fund and the Contemporary Art Society were made largely on his initiative. And many other gifts and bequests may in varying degrees have reflected Mr Dodgson's tastes and wishes, insofar as he was able to influence or encourage prospective donors.' The culmination of his years of dedication was the bequest of his entire private collection, which became effective in 1949; this, coupled with a further bequest of the sum of £3,000 to be administered by the National Art Collections Fund, made him the single most important modern benefactor to the Department of Prints and Drawings. The collection amounted to more than 5,000 items, almost all of them prints of the late nineteenth century onwards, with approximately 2,500 by British artists, another 1,500 by French artists and 1,000 by those of other nationalities including concentrations of work by German, Scandinavian and American artists. It has provided the point of departure for most aspects of the late twentieth-century acquisitions policy, yet in its totality represents a mode of collecting which has all but vanished from the post-Second World War art world.[1]

Campbell Dodgson embarked upon his museum career after attaining distinction as a classicist at Oxford, reflected in two of his earliest publications, reviews of Walter Pater's series of lectures on *Plato and Platonism* and R. C. Jebb's *The Growth and Influence of Classical Greek Poetry*.[2] While still an undergraduate he was drawn to the Anglo-Catholic movement centred at Pusey House, which inclined him towards a theological training. This did not long remain a fixed ambition. Throughout the period 1890–2

Dodgson wrestled with doubts about his suitability as a candidate for ordination, until he finally decided to submit himself to the Home Civil Service examinations with a view to entering the British Museum, despite advice to the contrary from his friends and mentors at the time; they feared that museum employment would involve too much drudgery and recommended a literary career instead, either teaching English at a university or attached to a respected publishing house such as John Murray.

He was one of a trio of a new breed of university-educated men appointed by Sidney Colvin, who imposed high standards of professionalism on the scholarship and organisation of the department, as well as demanding an equally high standard of written exposition from his staff.

(*Right*) 1. William Strang, *Portrait of Campbell Dodgson*, 1904. Photograph of a drawing in the Dresden Print Room

Dodgson's colleagues in this respect were Laurence Binyon (1869–1943), who moved to Prints and Drawings from the Library in 1895, after being superseded by Dodgson in the 1893 examination (they were again competitors in 1912 for the Keepership), and Arthur Mayger Hind (1880–1957), who came in 1904. Lincoln Kirstein, in his appreciation of the Metropolitan Museum's great print scholar Hyatt Mayor, remarked that when Mayor took over from William Ivins in 1946 as chief curator of the Print Department: 'He felt then he had entered something approaching a monastery – at least philosophically –. A stoic schedule precluded much free activity except with his mind ... he turned to the Museum's collections; their augmentation and exposition became his field of daring.'[3] The same could be said with even greater truth of Campbell Dodgson some fifty years earlier, who subsequently chose his family motto 'Diligence' for the bookplate executed for him in 1909 by the poet and wood-engraver Thomas Sturge Moore (fig. 2). He brought an almost religious sense of duty to bear upon his career; his private collection was to be but an extension of his public obligations, thereby reflecting the exhortation of Horace Walpole, one of Sir Hans Sloane's trustees, in 1757: 'Who that should destine his collection to the British Museum, would not purchase curiosities with redoubled spirit and pleasure, whenever he reflected that he was collecting for his country, and would have his name recorded as a benefactor to its arts and improvements?'[4]

Dodgson was by all accounts an austere man of retiring manner who shrank from even minor unconventionality, as when, for example, he had to abandon wearing stiff

2. Thomas Sturge Moore, *Campbell Dodgson's bookplate*, woodcut 1909. 100 × 100 mm. 1949-4-11-2053

collars in later life, on medical grounds; he was recalled at this stage by Sir John Pope-Hennessy as having been 'like an old tortoise – but then all the staff in the Print Room were rather pachydermitous in those days!'[5] The only real sign of expansiveness recorded by his contemporaries appeared when he conversed in French or German, of which he acquired a fluent command in both the written and the spoken language. His superior, Sidney Colvin, despite having a high regard for his general ability, felt that he lacked a natural aptitude or even inclination for aesthetic matters,[6] yet there is evidence to the contrary from Dodgson's early private life. He arrived at the British Museum immediately after an encounter with the bewitching figure of Oscar Wilde, whose effect upon the shy young scholar was instantaneous. Through the offices of the poet Lionel Johnson, who had been his contemporary schoolfellow at Winchester and a friend at university, Dodgson was engaged in February 1893 by Lady Queensberry as a tutor to her wayward son, Lord Alfred Douglas. In the event, the engagement lasted barely a week, cut short by Dodgson's impending examination for the British Museum, but his few days' contact with Oscar Wilde in Torquay, whence his pupil promptly bore him, proved to be an electrifying experience. To Lionel Johnson Dodgson confided on 8 February: 'I think him perfectly delightful with the firmest conviction that his morals are detestable. He professes to have discovered that mine are as bad. His command of language is extraordinary, so at least it seems to me who am inarticulate, and worship Irishmen who are not. I am going back on Saturday. I shall probably leave all that remains of my religion and morals behind me.'[7] Two days later, on the eve of his departure, Dodgson recorded Wilde's estimation of him based on a reading of his hand:

You have an extraordinarily sensuous and sensitive temperament, with a capacity for great passions and pleasures – the making of a hedonist, an artist. A strong imagination, memory, delight in colour, imagining worlds of beauty in a Greek phrase, or in some forms of Italian art. But this is restrained by your secretiveness, timidity, dread of action. Your best friends do not know you: you live intensely when you are quite alone: you can never be at your best, when expected to be. If you try to translate into words your intense delight in art, you will produce a dry string of names and dates. You cannot, or you dare not, assert yourself. Your one hope of winning your way to literary expression is to have the courage to yield to some powerful passion (for it takes more courage to yield, than to resist). Probably the chance will never come to you. Unlike — who has no remorse, no definite anticipation of the future, who makes the world afresh for himself every day, you are troubled and clogged by agonies of recollection, thoughts of duties neglected, ideals unrealised. If you would set yourself free, your effort should be to wash out this tyranny of duty in you. You are extraordinarily complex: you cannot decide on any one aim to which to devote yourself. Your hand is soft and warm, the sign of sensibility; your face mobile. You are condemned to an ascetic style of existence, because you have not tried life; you are young and do not *know* what you have divined by imagination.

Wilde was a controversial acquaintance for a young man on the brink of a public career in 1893. The publication of *A Picture of Dorian Gray* in April 1891 had caused a sensation, soon to be surpassed by that of his play *Salome* in the latter half of February 1893, whose performance had already been banned; two years later he was publicly disgraced as a result of his affair with Lord Alfred Douglas, and died in exile in Paris in 1900. As a character study Wilde's palm-reading reveals as much about Wilde as it does about his subject, for to quote Charles Ricketts: 'His was the typical literary temperament to whom words are realities and the sound of a sentence in itself convincing.'[8] Nonetheless, Wilde's observations were not without pertinacity; they illuminate some of the tendencies which inspired Dodgson's later activity as a collector and they balance the commonly-held view that it was largely duty which dictated his artistic interests rather than aesthetic response. That he did indeed experience the latter was independently borne out by the correspondence of a friend, who at the time of his greatest religious uncertainty in 1890 counselled Dodgson against becoming a priest, citing, among other factors, his keen artistic tastes and the value he attached to the world of sense. The episode with Wilde is of significance too because it locates Dodgson within a literary and artistic milieu of the 1890s which was a formative influence upon his taste. One of the many lithographs by Toulouse-Lautrec for which the British Museum is indebted to Dodgson was the portrait of Oscar Wilde with the French playwright Romain Coolus that he presented in 1922; this had been redrawn from a portrait Lautrec had made in 1895, and used for the theatre programme accompanying the production of *Salome* and Coolus's *Raphael* at the Théâtre de l'Oeuvre in February 1896.

Once Dodgson had joined the staff of the British Museum Print Room, Wilde, with typical hyperbole, imagined him in his new employment as 'either guarding marvellous Rembrandt etchings, or simply existing beautifully.'[9] The reality was rather more mundane and can best be described by analogy once again with Hyatt Mayor's reminiscences of his early days at the Metropolitan Museum in the 1930s:

I was simply turned loose with no instructions except that I was to learn the Collection. And the Collection was then several thousand boxes of prints. I would take the various catalogues and the books and I would open the boxes and try to remember what was in them. And then I had to man the study room, which is where the public comes in and asks questions and you get stuff out for them. It's the maid service for the Collection. Which teaches you an enormous amount, because just about every other question knocks you off your

perch and you have to go and look it up ... And of course there's an enormous amount of stock taking and inventory making.[10]

Dodgson, who was confronted by a far more extensive collection, perforce had to acquire a very general expertise but the direction of his career was almost immediately established for him by the British Museum's acquisition of the Mitchell Collection of German woodcuts in 1895. To him fell the task of cataloguing the material, and thereafter this dictated the main thrust of Dodgson's scholarly interests, the pattern of his travels and of his closest professional relationships. Within ten years of joining the British Museum, Dodgson had established himself internationally as a leading authority on early German and Flemish prints, publishing a critical bibliography on Lucas Cranach in 1900, the two volumes of the catalogue of the Museum's collection of early German woodcuts in 1903 and 1911, co-editing the Dürer Society publications from 1898 to 1911 and writing a catalogue of the intaglio prints of Dürer in 1926, among many other activities. Recognition abroad for his achievements in this field was such that after his retirement he was presented with the Goethe medal in July of 1933 by the German government, for his services to the history of German art.

There were many parallels between the development of the British Museum's collection and that of its great German counterparts, principally in Berlin, Dresden and Munich in the late nineteenth and early twentieth centuries. Friedrich Lippmann, Director of the Berlin Print Room from 1876 until his death in 1903, who was a frequent visitor to London and a great anglophile, reorganised the physical care of the Berlin collection according to the arrangements he had observed at the British Museum. At a personal level, Dodgson's taste was informed by that of his German colleagues who in turn came to esteem his judgement. The most notable influence came from Max Lehrs (1855–1938), the great authority on early German and Netherlandish engraving, who was director of the Dresden Print Room from 1896 to 1904, then again from 1908 to 1924, after a brief interregnum holding the same office in Berlin. Dodgson's obituary of Lehrs reads almost like a résumé of his own career:

Though he was first and foremost an expert in prints of the 15th century, Lehrs appreciated outstanding work of every period, and had the somewhat unusual distinction of being also a fine judge of modern prints. He was convinced that contemporary engravers could be best appreciated, with fullest knowledge and understanding, by their own generation, and he practised successfully, the art of interpreting them, verbally, by exhibitions in the Cabinet, and by articles in the press, to the public. Though he collected very completely modern German and especially Saxon prints, by such artists as Menzel and Richter, Klinger, and Greiner, Stauffer-Bern, Liebermann and Kollwitz, he realised also the importance of French 19th century graphic art and enriched the Dresden Cabinet by mag-

3. Hans Burgkmair, *St Radian*, woodcut *c.*1521. 205 × 156 mm. 1949-4-11-4051

into a public collection, Dodgson did so almost entirely in his private capacity because the British Museum's policy at that time precluded the use of public funds for the acquisition of material by living artists, a situation which remained substantially unchanged until the second half of the twentieth century. For this reason Dodgson was instrumental in setting up in 1919 a prints and drawings fund financed by private subscription, under the aegis of the Contemporary Art Society of which he had been a founder member ten years earlier, the express intention being to acquire contemporary work for presentation to the British Museum.

Dodgson's patronage of contemporary European artists developed at a time when 'artistic' or autographic printmaking was the focus of intense debate, a reaction engendered by the multiplication of reproductive techniques, especially the photo-mechanical ones; Camille Pissarro wrote to his son Lucien, in 1884, in a minatory letter attacking commercial wood-engraving practices: 'That's what we have to revive – lithography, etching, woodcut, every direct process...'[12] Dodgson was too good a museum curator and too wise a print scholar to despise reproductive printmaking *per se*; his researches into the division of labour effected in the execution of early German woodcuts and his admiration for eighteenth-century French line engraving were proof against such facile judgement, but when it came to his own collecting propensities, he did confess to a marked bias in favour of the so-called 'original' printmaker.

Though my museum training leads me to think that the reproductive engravers are now unduly depreciated, I own that as a collector I have let them alone. I confess my adherence to the generally prevalent belief that original engravers have the first claim on our interest, and in what follows I shall restrict myself to the consideration of prints designed as well as engraved by a single artist – the 'painter-engraver' as he has been called since the days of Bartsch.[13]

The character of his taste closely resembled that of Max Lehrs. It is familiar from many collections formed before the Second World War in Europe and America[14] where the means of execution and the evidential play of the printmaker's skill were frequently more important than the image itself. The American-born collector F. E. Bliss,[15] who settled in England, embarked in 1905 upon building one of the most substantial representations of contemporary French and British prints, some of which Dodgson was later to acquire. Another comparable group of work was that included in the print collection bequeathed by Harris Brisbane Dick to the Metropolitan Museum in 1917, as well as the early print acquisitions of Lessing Rosenwald in the mid-1920s, whose first purchase was D.Y. Cameron's *Royal Scottish Academy*, followed by the prints of Meryon, Muirhead Bone, Seymour Haden, Whistler, Forain, F. L. Griggs, Legros, Lepère, Brockhurst and Pennell.[16] The essential

nificent collections of Daumier, Toulouse-Lautrec, Manet, Carrière, Forain (whom he was the first to appreciate as an etcher) and others, before a great rise had taken place in their prices. Nor did he neglect the modern British school, with Whistler, Shannon, Strang and Bone.[11]

Dodgson did collect to some extent within his main scholarly field, and his bequest included a distinguished group of early sixteenth-century German printed books, as well as some important drawings and single-sheet prints such as the rare woodcut by Hans Burgkmair of *St Radian*, *c.*1521 (fig. 3), which he purchased for 500 Reichsmark at auction in Leipzig in 1933. Another subject on which he published was that of eighteenth-century French colour prints in 1924, prompting the acquisition a year later at the enormous price of £600 of P.L. Debucourt's colour print *La Promenade Publique* of 1792 from the London dealer Thomas Agnew (fig. 4). However, in both cases the purchase of this material was so closely related to his strategy of acquisition for the Museum's collection that its discussion more properly belongs with the final chapter. It was his patronage of contemporary artists that was the dominant factor in his activity as a collector; whereas Lehrs purchased examples of modern graphic art directly

features of such a taste remain encapsulated to this day by the Wiggin dioramas in the Boston Public Library, based on the collection of the same name which was given to the Library in 1941 (Wiggin had purchased Bliss's entire collection of prints by Alphonse Legros). Each scene depicts a print or an episode in the lives of the relevant artists which refers, with the exception of Rowlandson, to their activity as printmakers; the artists selected for this purpose were Forain, Whistler, Toulouse-Lautrec, F.L. Griggs, Félix Buhot, George Bellows, Rembrandt, Daumier, James Mc-Bey and Muirhead Bone, who is shown amidst the subject of one of his American etchings of 1923, *Manhattan Excavation* (see cat. 90).[17]

Dodgson's importance as a collector did not merely consist of reflecting contemporary taste; the conjunction of his public and private roles meant that he became one of the principal figures responsible for establishing the canon of that taste. Its influence was disseminated through his publications, through the annual *Fine Prints of the Year*, 1923–38, of which he was the editor after Malcolm Salaman, and above all, through the many articles devoted to contemporary printmaking in the periodical literature. Between 1905 and 1912, Dodgson and Hind contributed pieces to *Die graphischen Künste*, published in Vienna, on Frank Brangwyn, Charles Holroyd, Muirhead Bone, Camille Pissarro, Augustus John, Maurice and Edward Detmold and Donald Shaw MacLaughlan. This was eventually superseded by the *Print Collector's Quarterly*, established in 1911, to which Dodgson was a tireless

contributor; from 1921 to 1936 he edited it single-handedly, making it an indispensable guide for every serious or aspiring print collector.

The artistic tendencies in Britain with which Dodgson was most closely associated are best summarised by the membership of the Society of Twelve, which functioned as an exhibiting body from 1904 to 1915 to encourage drawing and the execution of original prints in all media. It began with George Clausen, Edward Gordon Craig, William Nicholson, William Strang, Thomas Sturge Moore, William Rothenstein, Charles Ricketts, D.Y. Cameron, Charles Shannon, Augustus John, Charles Conder and Muirhead Bone with Alphonse Legros as an honorary member, then expanded to admit Francis Dodd, William Orpen and W.R. Sickert among others. As a body they were overwhelmingly francophile in their artistic tastes, their choice of mentor, the Frenchman Alphonse Legros (1837–1911), and their friendships: Conder was a friend of Toulouse-Lautrec, Rothenstein of Rodin, and Sickert of Degas, for example. Legros's inculcation of the principles of composition in pure line as applied to drawing and etching exercised considerable influence both among and beyond his immediate circle of students at the Slade School of Art, which included William Strang and Charles Holroyd, a future Director of the National Gallery (1906–16). The Slade School had been opened as part of University College London in 1871 as a direct consequence of one of Felix Slade's many benefactions (see p. 113), and had from the outset been based on contemporary French art school

4. Philibert-Louis Debucourt, *The Public Promenade*, etching, colour engraving and aquatint 1792. 459 × 636 mm. 1949-3-11-3806

practice under the direction of the first Professor, Edward Poynter, who was succeeded by Legros in 1876. It was one of two central London art schools, the other being the Central School of Arts and Crafts, opened in 1896, whose proximity to the British Museum stimulated a close relationship with the Museum's collections that continues to this day. For their students, the members of the 'Twelve' and the artistic community as a whole, the collections and staff of the print rooms of the British Museum and the Victoria and Albert Museum in South Kensington were a natural source of ideas and information. The reciprocity of interest between curators and artists had been fostered by Sidney Colvin through his wide circle of acquaintance, and his successors, Dodgson, Binyon, Hind and A. E. Popham, were able to extend the network of relationships into virtually every society, advisory committee or periodical publication associated with the fine arts in the period prior to the Second World War. Dodgson did not have the ease of manner enjoyed by his almost exact contemporary and colleague, Laurence Binyon, who found particular favour in the milieu of Ricketts and Shannon because of his interests in poetry, the work of William Blake, the Pre-Raphaelites and Oriental art;[18] nevertheless, Dodgson's erudition and demonstrable commitment as a collector earned him immediate respect.

Dodgson wrote monographs, catalogues or essays on many contemporary British printmakers.[19] Two of the greatest importance to him were both artists associated with the 'Twelve': Muirhead Bone, whose *catalogue raisonné* he published in 1909,[20] and Augustus John (1920), by whom he acquired personal collections which were virtually co-extensive with the contents of the catalogues. John's activity as an etcher was almost over by the time Dodgson's catalogue appeared; the occasion for its publication was the 1919 exhibition at the Chenil Gallery in Chelsea, which achieved a phenomenal success, buoyed up by the artist's general reputation and a flourishing market for contemporary etching. Dodgson's catalogue was fully subscribed in advance, while the exhibition itself realised more than £7,000 in sales, according to a letter written by Dodgson in January 1920 to the collector Oskar Reinhart at Winterthur in Switzerland.[21] Dodgson had published an article on John's etchings in *Die graphischen Künste* as early as 1909, while his own unrivalled collection had already been launched with the purchase in 1905–6 of a large selection of early proofs from the artist himself. Notwithstanding his evident partiality for John's bravura as a printmaker, Dodgson was still able to provide a dispassionate appraisal of John's strengths and weaknesses in the preface to the *catalogue raisonné*; few would disagree that John's portrait studies, of which Dodgson singled out those of Jacob Epstein and Wyndham Lewis (fig. 5) for particular praise, were his real forte, but that 'Mr John, with all his intense interest in single types, and his power, unequalled among English etchers of to-day, of

5. Augustus John, *Portrait of Wyndham Lewis*, etching 1892. 178 × 140 mm (Dodgson 19 III). 1949-4-11-1178

expressing individual character, lacks the imaginative, constructive, or dramatic gift of showing several characters in action'.

In contrast with Augustus John's mercurial temperament and erratic practices was the methodical application of Muirhead Bone, whose activity as a printmaker extended from 1898 to 1939 with a production of some 478 etchings and drypoints. Campbell Dodgson's patronage covered almost precisely the same period, beginning in 1902 when Bone had just arrived in London from Glasgow to enjoy a highly successful exhibition at the Carfax Gallery. He published an article on Muirhead Bone in *Die graphischen Künste* in 1906, by which time Bone was well on his way to becoming one of the 'super-etchers', in contemporary parlance, along with his fellow Scots D.Y. Cameron and James McBey, and the Swede Anders Zorn, who had studied etching in London, 1882–4, with Axel Haig (1835–1921). Their steady and predictable output under the guidance of a small band of specialist dealers helped to expand and sustain the print-collecting market, which soared to new speculative heights in the decade after the First World War. Dodgson began by paying one and two guineas for Bone's etchings at his principal dealer Obach's (later to become Colnaghi), but by 1918 his outlay had increased steeply, to £51 for *Maryhill Canal* (CD59 I) for example, and £63. 15.0 for *Old Birch Hall, Manchester* (CD50 II). By 1916, when Bone was appointed an official war artist on Dodgson's recommendation, his annual income was in the region of £3–4,000; the profits from the prints he made on the basis of his wartime commission were sufficient to support a donation of £1,200 to the Belgian Relief Fund and the establishment at the end of 1918 of the 'Bone Fund' for acquisitions to the art collection of the newly created Imperial War Museum.[22]

In an article of 1925 Dodgson, with reference to the 'super-etchers', described the prevailing situation thus:

Many of their etchings have ascertainable values like stocks and shares, and are dealt in after the manner of such investments at prices out of all proportion to what they cost when first issued. It becomes a nice point of calculation for financial experts whether they are things to buy, to keep or to sell. They still remain works of art, and to those who wish to appreciate them as such, ignorance of these transactions may be recommended.[23]

He lived long enough to witness both the sudden collapse of the market in the general economic crisis of the early 1930s and the critical repudiation of the work which had been so highly favoured. Dodgson himself remained unswerving in his loyalty to Muirhead Bone, continuing to acquire his prints until the very end of his life at prices which had reverted to their former level of one and two guineas.

The American and British print markets were closely intertwined, with British artists' work supplied directly to subscribers in the United States or sold to American publishers as part-editions, while some of the American printmakers had similar arrangements with European publishers. Not surprisingly, Dodgson's choice among the American artists for his own collection tended to fall upon those who in their regularity of production and proficiency of technique most closely resembled the British etchers he admired. The monotonous talents of John Taylor Arms and the Canadian Donald Shaw Maclaughlan were the two principal examples, with lithography represented by Joseph Pennell (1857–1925), whom Dodgson knew well through the Senefelder Club in London, founded in 1909 to try to achieve for lithography a status comparable to that enjoyed by etching. Whistler, whose work Dodgson certainly admired, was given only a scant representation in his collection, probably because the British Museum already had a substantial body of his prints acquired through gift and purchase over a forty-year period, beginning with the purchase of a group of etchings from the artist himself in 1863. This holding was especially strong in the lithographs, of which 128 were given in 1905 by T. R. Way, son of the lithographic printer Thomas Way, who had assisted Whistler for fifteen years.

Apart from two etchings by Mary Cassatt, the one truly interesting purchase of American etchings was made by Dodgson in 1926 when he bought four prints by Edward Hopper, immediately presenting them to the Museum. The prints are identified in the artist's ledger books, now in the Whitney Museum in New York, as having been sold via an agent, E. P. Jennings; for *East Side Interior, Evening Wind, Night in the Park* and *Night on the El Train* (cat. 89), Dodgson paid $25.00, $22.00 twice over and $18.00 respectively.[24] By the time Dodgson made his purchases Hopper's career as a printmaker was already over, because the artist had made a conscious decision to abandon etching in favour of painting in oil and watercolour. How Dodgson became aware of Hopper's work is not known, for the first time his work was seen in Britain was in 1929 as part of an exhibition of contemporary American prints at the Victoria and Albert Museum, under the auspices of the American Federation of Arts. Carl Zigrosser, one of the leading American print scholars and a lifelong friend of Hopper's, accorded him due honour in an article he published in 1929 in the *Print Collector's Quarterly* on 'Modern American etching' (PCQ XVI), while James Laver of the V & A mentioned him in the same year in his *History of British and American Etching*, comparing Hopper in his choice of subject-matter to Sickert, 'but without Sickert's latent irony'.[25] George Bellows appears to have claimed Dodgson's attention at much the same time but no purchase took place; a letter from Mrs Bellows to Campbell Dodgson dated 16 September 1925 expresses her pleasure at receiving his inquiry via William Ivins at the Metropolitan Museum, as to whether some of her husband's lithographs might be available for the British Museum; she cites current prices for the work as ranging from $10 to as much as $800, offering for every print purchased to donate one of equivalent value. This was not pursued, unfortunately, and another fifty-three years were to elapse until the Department finally acquired its first print by Bellows.

The prestige of the main British printmakers was renowned not only among print collectors and public collections in the anglophone world but also in the German-speaking world, where the spate of international exhibitions at the turn of the century in Vienna, Berlin, Dresden and Munich encouraged a very cosmopolitan artistic awareness. By 1909, when Dodgson's *catalogue raisonné* appeared, Muirhead Bone's work was being widely collected by the Berlin, Dresden and Bremen print rooms, the Hofbibliothek in Vienna and two private collectors, Ludwig Guthier of Vienna and Oskar Reinhart in Winterthur. The latter eventually owned 152 prints and forty-two drawings by Bone, paying a record price of £250 as late as 1933 for the print Dodgson had described as Bone's masterpiece, *Ayr Prison* of 1905 (CD179). Many of the works were already in Reinhart's collection by 1912, when sixty-three of them were lent to be shown in conjunction with an exhibition of contemporary art at the Kunsthaus in Zurich; this otherwise contained some very different work, by Hans Arp, Robert Delaunay, Wassily Kandinsky, Gabriele Münter, Paul Klee and Franz Marc. By 1911 the Dresden and Berlin Print Rooms had complete collections of the lithographs of Charles Shannon (1863–1937), who had become a leading exponent of this medium in the 1890s. William Strang (1859–1921) was another etcher of Scottish extraction who enjoyed a notable success with the German collectors and with Dodgson; the latter's extensive holding of Strang's work was augmented in 1953 by the British Museum's purchase, with some of the money bequeathed by Dodgson, of a further 431 prints from the artist's family. Strang was the foremost pupil of Alphonse Legros at the Slade, where he developed a facility in portraiture, acknowledging the inspiration of Holbein's portrait drawings and van Dyck's series of etchings, the *Iconography*.

The success of the British artists in Germany attracted the wrath of the rebarbative Emil Nolde; in 1907 he wrote the following riposte to Max Lehrs, who in his capacity as Director of the Berlin Print Room had declined to acquire Nolde's series of eight etchings, *Phantasien*, of 1905:

It is well known among artists that you direct your particular enthusiasm to the technically 'clean' and temperamentally and apparently artistically empty English etchings, and that under your direction the Print Room in Dresden was filled with these prints and that the same thing is now happening in Berlin. People say that art which is really full of life and which looks to the future completely escapes your perception.[26]

Conversely, only three years earlier Charles Ricketts was complaining on behalf of his friend Shannon that while 'South Kensington' (i.e. the Victoria and Albert Museum) was buying 'German prints and engravings (modern), they have not bought Shannon's lithographs'.[27]

Dodgson's own purchases of prints by modern German artists and others of Central European or Scandinavian origin, such as Munch, who were associated with Germany, began well before and continued after the First World War. The pattern of their acquisition was often determined by the German auction sales in May at Gutekunst in Stuttgart before the war and in Leipzig at C. G. Boerner afterwards, which Dodgson used as a focus for periods of leave of up to six weeks, to allow time for visiting the German print rooms followed by a summer vacation. The surviving card index of his acquisitions in the Department of Prints and Drawings provides details of provenance for a disappointingly small proportion of his collection; however, it does show that of the eight prints he eventually owned by Munch, three were bought from the Graphisches Kabinett in Berlin in August 1911, another three from the dealer Ernst Arnold in Dresden in July 1921 (including a magnificent impression of the artist's *Self-Portrait with Skeleton Arm*) and the last two from the London Gallery in November 1936. Dodgson's bias towards etching manifested itself in his acquisition of the

work of the Viennese artist Ferdinand Schmutzer (1870–1928) and Emil Orlik from Prague (1870–1932), who frequented the British Museum's Print Room in the early part of the century. More interesting were the prints by Lovis Corinth and Max Liebermann, who in 1911 presented thirty-three of his etchings to the British Museum in association with his publisher, Bruno Cassirer. The two most unusual concentrations of work were by Nolde and Käthe Kollwitz; the British Museum acquired seven of Nolde's etchings in August 1909, three of them presented by Dodgson and the other four by the artist himself. These were comparatively conventional works, to which Dodgson's bequest in 1949 was to add a further six, including four of the famous Hamburg harbour scenes of 1910 (cat. 88).[28]

Dodgson's interest in Käthe Kollwitz was unquestionably the result of his friendship with Max Lehrs, who in 1898 was the first to acquire her prints for a public collection, and then in 1902 compiled a *catalogue raisonné* of the fifty subjects she had executed to that date.[29] The British Museum's first print by Kollwitz entered the collection in 1907 as part of a miscellaneous group of German prints purchased from the London dealer Dulau, but thereafter all further acquisition until 1979 was to be dependent on Campbell Dodgson's collecting on his own account, with the exception of a self-portrait lithograph of 1924 which was purchased and presented through his agency by the Contemporary Art Society in 1930. His bequest contained thirty-six of her prints, almost entirely from the period 1897–1910; it included some of the rarest of all her work, for example, the *Self-Portrait Looking Left* of 1901 and three states of *Woman with Dead Child* of 1903, a combination of etching and lithography, as well as the beautiful lithograph of 1903 in this catalogue (cat. 87). Kollwitz was the acceptable face of modernism to Dodgson and his German counterparts, whereas his interest in the early German woodcut style did not extend to its latter-day treatment at the hands of the Expressionist artists. He was not prompted to buy anything from the one exhibition of this type of material to be seen in London before the First World War, a travelling exhibition sent by Herwarth Walden from the Sturm Gallery in Berlin to the Twenty-One Gallery in 1914; it was enthusiastically reviewed by Wyndham Lewis together with the accompanying group of woodcuts by Edward Wadsworth, to whose work Dodgson was receptive. His antipathy for Expressionism endured; despite his admiration for many of the French wood-engravers, he did not urge upon the Society of Wood-Engravers, founded in 1920, the adventurous spirit of its French counterpart which at its third exhibition in 1928 included submissions from Barlach, Beckmann, Campendonk, Felixmüller, Heckel, Kirchner, Gerhard Marcks and Pechstein. It was on this basis that the even more conservative Hans Singer, Lehrs's colleague at the Dresden Print Room, made the following remarks in 1936 when he replied to an inquiry from Dodgson about contemporary woodcut artists who might be suitable for inclusion in a future exhibition. Singer's letter is expressed in terms which make uneasy reading in the light of the contemporary political climate in Germany and the Degenerate Art exhibition of the following year:

As to the German wood-cut artists, I shall look about and see what I can report to you: I suppose there is no hurry since the show is to be next year. Of course I wouldn't have recommended any of the terrible stuff perpetrated by the 'Brücke' and similar Expressionists, even if it were to be found nowadays still. But as a matter of fact that sort of 'art' has been completely wiped out since 1933. If you want to see any of it, you've got to go to America (and it seems, according to what you write) London, where· dealers of the type of Guthier still seem to try to launch it as 'German art': with us it has entirely disappeared.[30]

Stephen Coppel has already commented upon how the gift of the Mitchell Collection in 1895 came at a peculiarly apposite moment in terms of the contemporary interest in the woodcut medium. Dodgson contributed regular articles on early German woodcuts to *The Dome*, a quarterly, later monthly periodical covering all the arts that appeared between March 1897 and July 1900, published by the Unicorn Press. The Private Press movement in England of the period from 1890 to the First World War focused attention on the appreciation of early woodcuts as a vehicle for the artistic revival of the medium. Alongside the fifty books or pamphlets containing woodcuts mainly of the early sixteenth century in Dodgson's collection were sixty modern illustrated books, which included the work of the leading private presses in England: Kelmscott, the Vale, Eragny, Essex House and the Ashendene Press.

William Morris sought to emulate the achievements of German and Italian incunabula in the productions of the Kelmscott Press in the 1890s. One of the last of these in 1898, published after Morris's death, was on the subject of *Some German Woodcuts of the 15th Century*, while Morris, who was an avid collector of manuscripts and incunabula himself, had previously written an article in 1895 'On the Artistic Qualities of the Woodcut Books of Ulm and Augsburg in the 15th century'.[31] The executors of the William Morris estate presented to the Department of Prints and Drawings in 1897–8 the 422 woodblocks for the Kelmscott Chaucer of 1896, the Press's masterpiece. These blocks, however, were cut not by the artists responsible for the designs, but by W. H. Hooper who worked from drawings transferred photographically to the surface; in this respect they did not differ significantly from most nineteenth-century practice in this medium. Dodgson pointed out in his introduction to *Contemporary English Woodcuts* in 1922:

As in the days of Dürer and Holbein, so in the days of Northcote and W. M. Craig, of Menzel and Richter, of Gavarni and Gustave Doré, of Millais, Keene and Tenniel, of Rossetti, Burne-Jones and Walter Crane, the artist drew his design upon the block, or, at a later time, had it transferred to the surface of the block by photography, and took no further part in the production of the woodcut till a proof was submitted to him to be touched for alterations.

The figures to whom Dodgson gave the real credit for encouraging artists to make an original use of the woodcut medium were Ricketts and Shannon, and the work they printed in their occasional journal, *The Dial*, from 1889 to 1897 and at the Vale Press which they ran from 1894 to 1903. The first issue of *The Dial* brought them to the notice of Oscar Wilde, for whom Ricketts illustrated a number of books, but his most successful collaboration was perhaps that with Shannon for their edition of *Daphnis and Chloe* in 1893, for which Dodgson acquired a set of fourteen proofs in 1944 along with other material by the same artists which came from the Bliss collection. It was modelled on the *Hypnerotomachia Poliphili*, published in Venice in 1499, and according to Ricketts was 'the first book published in modern times with woodcuts by the artist in a page arranged by himself'.[32] Eventually 224 blocks employed in the publications of the Vale Press were bequeathed to the Department of Prints and Drawings in 1937 in the joint names of Ricketts and Shannon, to be followed in 1946 by an album of studies related to many of these illustrations.

The premises of the Vale Press, 'The Sign of the Dial', near Piccadilly, were also used for a series of small exhibitions designed to educate the public in a taste for woodcuts of the fifteenth and early sixteenth centuries and the work of the leading illustrators of the 1860s in the medium of wood-engraving, J. E. Millais and Arthur Boyd Houghton. Dodgson's copies of the beautifully printed pamphlets produced on these occasions are bound together with others they made for the dealer Van Wisselingh, who showed their work at the 'Dutch Gallery' in Hanover Square where in 1898 was held 'The First Exhibition of Original Wood Engraving'. This united the efforts of their coterie, among whom Sturge Moore and Lucien Pissarro were key figures in the revival of the woodcut. Sturge Moore (1870–1944), the brother of the philosopher G. E. Moore, was a friend of Yeats, much influenced by the woodcuts of the German Little Masters and William Blake's illustrations to Thornton's Virgil; between 1900 and 1910 he wrote a number of studies of earlier artists, which included Blake, Altdorfer (edited by Dodgson's colleague, Laurence Binyon, as part of 'The Artist's Library' series) and Dürer, published in 1905, for which Dodgson read the proofs.

Lucien Pissarro, after practising as a reproductive wood-engraver in France, returned to settle in England in 1890 because he had heard 'that a movement was afoot ... towards a revival of wood-engraving and printing'.[33] He was immediately struck by the belief Ricketts and Shannon had in the importance of grasping the intrinsic qualities of the medium and went frequently to consult what he described in January 1891 as 'the fabulous collection of woodcuts' which the British Museum already owned prior to the Mitchell Gift; these visits to the Print Room had a continual effect upon the evolution of his style and five years later he was remarking upon the impression made by the Italian chiaroscuro woodcuts in the collection, particularly those by Ugo da Carpi after Raphael and Andreani's *Triumph of Caesar* after Mantegna. The Print Room had the added advantage of providing a meeting place with his future wife, Esther Bensusan, whose father had forbidden their relationship for fear that Lucien would infect his daughter with Socialism.[34] In order to ensure a place for his own work within a great historical tradition of relief printing, Pissarro presented to the British Museum in 1901 forty-two of his wood-engravings together with his most famous portfolio, the *Travaux des Champs*, published in 1895, on which he had collaborated with his father over a period of nearly ten years. He published his work initially through the Vale Press, then established his own imprint of the Eragny Press from 1894 to 1914; his work increasingly departed from the linear style of his English mentors in his use of colour and the planar simplicity of his compositions, reflecting the influence of Japanese prints, which reached its zenith at this period. Dodgson himself did not collect Japanese prints, but he was abundantly aware of their impact, not only on some of the European artists whom he admired but through first-hand experience of this material in his own department which united European and oriental work on paper until 1933 when a separate Department of Oriental Antiquities was created. During the latter part of his career Sidney Colvin had acquired four important private collections of Japanese woodcuts for the Museum, an area which during Dodgson's Keepership was presided over by Laurence Binyon as part of a special subsection for Oriental art.

Dodgson's interest in contemporary wood-engraving long survived that of Ricketts and Shannon, whose focus shifted after the closure of the Vale Press. It continued into the post-First World War period to embrace the work of a new generation of artists, among whom were Edward Wadsworth, McKnight Kauffer, Edward Gordon Craig, Gwen Raverat, Robert Gibbings, Eric Gill and Paul Nash and the briefly interesting though technically somewhat inept experiments by some of the Bloomsbury artists under the auspices of the Omega Workshop and the Hogarth Press between 1915 and 1922.[35] Many of these artists were invited to exhibit in Paris by their French counterparts of the Société de la Gravure sur Bois Originale, founded in 1911 by the doyen of the woodcut revival in France, Auguste Lepère (1849–1918). Dodgson had frequent communications with the members of this body, such as Hermann-Paul and Tony Beltrand, while the woodcuts of Lepère himself amounted to just over sixty items among Dodgson's bequest.

Nowhere had the concept of the *peintre-graveur* been promulgated with greater persuasiveness than in Paris in the second half of the nineteenth century; this rose to a peak in the final decade with a series of exhibitions held at the Durand-Ruel Gallery and the appearance of a number of publications dedicated to the commission and dissemination of original prints, such as *L'Estampe Originale*, 1893–5, to which Charles Shannon was invited to contribute. Dodgson's representation of French prints was the crowning glory of the collection as a whole, from which the lithographs alone were able to furnish a substantial exhibition in 1978.[36] The lineaments of this part of his collection were already in place by 1919, when he held an exhibition of *Etchings and Lithographs by Modern French Artists* in his own home in London at 22 Montagu Square, to launch the prints and drawings fund of the Contemporary Art Society. Thereafter during the 1920s and early 1930s Dodgson used his home for further displays from his own collection, Forain's etchings in 1926 for example, and to show the acquisitions made through the Contemporary Art Society. The exhibition of 1919 was by far the most interesting in identifying the parameters of Dodgson's taste; it included etchings by Bracquemond, Legros, Rodin, Forain, Carrière, Manet, Degas and Pissarro; and lithographs by Redon, Manet, Forain, Carrière, Fantin-Latour, Steinlen and Toulouse-Lautrec, for which Dodgson provided the following justification in his preface to the brief catalogue:

There is nothing here by the pioneers of the [etching] revival, by Meryon, Millet, or, with trifling exceptions, by other masters of the Barbizon school. But they are well known, and their work has passed already through all the forms of canonisation known to Print Rooms. Such recognition has not been granted so promptly to the Impressionists, nor to the many painters and sculptors of modern France, less easily classified and labelled, who have practised etching and lithography, with more audacity and verve, as a rule, than is found in English artists, whether or no they are primarily and professionally etchers. French artists are more fearless, French collectors more immune to shocks, than their compeers 'd'Outre-Manche'.

This little exhibition itself may very likely be taxed with timidity and conservatism. It is certainly not ultra-modern. Of the artists represented in it, only four are living, though Rodin, Redon, Degas and Lepère have very recently joined the ranks of the illustrious dead. Neither M. Besnard, M. Helleu, M. Steinlen, nor M. Forain belong to the young generation, though the two last-named, at least, are still producing with all speed and vigour. Where are 'Les Jeunes', 'les Fauves', the Cubists and Expressionists and other exponents of revolutionary creeds and crazes passionately held to-day, and obsolete or orthodox – who shall say which? – to-morrow? In an ideal exhibition of modern French art they should undoubtedly make a display, but for that the time is not yet fully ripe. They are excluded now, not from prejudice, but from lack of space and lack of material to represent them properly. When travelling becomes easier, both for men and parcels, it may be possible for English collectors to study, and at least in some small degree to imitate, that wonderful gathering of modern French prints which the generosity of M. Doucet and the perspicacity of M. Clement-Janin and his collaborators have brought together at the Bibliothèque d'Art et d'Archéologie in the Rue Spontini. To form a similar collection, even on a much smaller scale, is one, and only one among many, of the objects which the Fund inaugurated by the present exhibition is intended to achieve.

Dodgson had plenty of opportunity to see modern French art in London in the first decade of the twentieth century, when a series of exhibitions from 1905 to 1913 introduced the more discerning public to all the major artists from Manet to Matisse, as well as through his extended travels on the Continent. Once again the formation of his taste was affected by his contacts and experience in Germany, where the reputation of the French Impressionists was mediated by an influential body of experts, prominent among whom were the critic Julius Meier-Graefe, the artist Max Liebermann, and the Director of the Berlin National Gallery, Hugo von Tschudi. Dodgson's purchases were made in London, Berlin, Dresden and Paris; one of the earliest recorded groups of material comprised thirteen prints by Redon, including the ten lithographs from the first of his famous series inspired by Flaubert's *Temptation of St Antony*, which Dodgson bought directly from the artist's successful one-man show in 1906 at the Durand-Ruel Gallery in Paris. Redon was one of the few modern French artists represented in the British Museum's own collection at this time, thanks to the gift of twenty-six of his lithographs in 1888 as part of a larger presentation of ninety-eight contemporary French lithographs made on behalf of the Société des Artistes Lithographes Français, and the gift of the second series of the *Temptation of St Antony* in 1905 from Archibald Russell. Further acquisitions of Redon lithographs were made by Dodgson at the Parsons Gallery in London, also in 1906, where he purchased the set of six plates known as *Songes* of 1892, at Ernst Arnold in Dresden in 1908, at a Perls auction in Berlin in 1912 and again at Durand-Ruel in 1913. The most prestigious purchase of all was transacted in 1920[37] between Dodgson and Dr A. E. Tebb, a London doctor who had become one of Redon's principal English patrons in the 1890s; Redon stayed with Tebb at his home in Hampstead in October 1895, when four of the artist's lithographs were being exhibited at Robert Dunthorne's Rembrandt Head Gallery, and the two men paid a joint visit to the British Museum's Print Room on the 23rd of that month. The material bought by Dodgson included two magnificent *fusains*, the pastel *La Cellule d'Or*, and one of only two known impressions of the first state of the lithograph *Cellule Auriculaire* (cat. 84), which had been obtained by Tebb directly from the artist in March 1895.[38]

Other relatively early French acquisitions included some of Manet's most important lithographs: *The Execution of Maximilian*, *The Racecourse* and *The Barricade* and a double set of *The Raven* of 1875, printed on laid and China paper, previously owned by Sidney Colvin, which Dodgson purchased from Colnaghi and Obach in 1912 for £7; he presented the volume on laid paper in the same year but retained the much rarer set on *Chine* until his death. Forain is a good example of an artist whose reputation has for a long time now been eclipsed by his contemporaries, but Dodgson shared Degas's high regard for his prints, giving Forain pride of place in both sections of his 1919 exhibition, which was swiftly followed by a major exhibition at Colnaghi's in 1920. In the April issue of the *Print Collector's Quarterly* for 1921 he published an article on Forain's etchings to coincide with an exhibition he had mounted in his department's new premises in the Edward VII Wing on the north side of the British Museum, where it had moved in 1914. Dodgson tried to allot space on a regular basis to the display of contemporary material of a fairly heterogeneous kind; alongside the Forain exhibition was one of First World War posters by French artists and, more improbably, of 'Bolshevist Posters' sent over from Riga which Dodgson showed for their topical interest, one of many instances of what Muirhead Bone was to describe in his obituary of Dodgson as 'his grand catholicity of taste'.[39]

By Degas himself Dodgson had a small collection, which nonetheless contained some outstanding examples, most notably the three monotypes, two landscapes and a sleeping nude (cat. 83) which Dodgson purchased at the beginning of 1926 from the heirs of the print publisher and dealer Gustave Pellet, for 4,000 f. and 9,000 f. respectively; in the same year too he appears to have acquired some of the Degas prints bought by Colnaghi's from the sale of Marcel Guérin, the authority on the graphic work of Gauguin, Toulouse-Lautrec, Forain and Degas.

Dodgson's French acquisitions gathered greater momentum after the First World War, when he paid frequent visits to Paris and evidently enjoyed the company of a number of artists, Forain, Dufy and Marie Laurencin among them. His collecting in this area was less trammelled by duty than his acquisitions closer to home, and more in keeping with the degree of spontaneity which Dodgson freely acknowledged as one of the advantages of many French artists' work compared with their British counterparts. He built extensive holdings of the line engravings of Emile Laboureur, the etchings of Dunoyer de Segonzac and Camille Pissarro, the lithographs of Pissarro, Toulouse-Lautrec, Steinlen, Bonnard and Vuillard and a much smaller but impressive body of work containing a monotype, woodcuts (cat. 85) and zincographs by Gauguin, who was particularly well received by British artists and critics from the moment of his initial impact in Roger Fry's first Post-Impressionist exhibition in 1910 at the Grafton

Galleries. At least two exhibitions in London after the war contained a good representation of Gauguin's prints, held at the Leicester Galleries in 1924 and 1931 (see cat. 85).

Dodgson's representation of Pissarro's work included many rarities inscribed by the artist which he purchased at the Pissarro sale on 8 December 1928. Pissarro's prints had their first real introduction to a British public in 1920 when the Leicester Galleries held a memorial exhibition, albeit some seventeen years after the artist's death, followed by an article by his son, Ludovic Rodo, in the *Print Collector's Quarterly* in 1922 (IX, pp. 275–301). So few of Pissarro's prints were printed in his lifetime that his work as a printmaker only became generally known from the mainly posthumous editions published by his family and from Loys Delteil's volume in the series *Le Peintre-Graveur illustré*, published in 1923. Charles Ricketts had, however, from the early 1890s shown an appreciation of Pissarro's graphic work, eventually presenting a group of his lithographs to the British Museum in 1920. In 1907 Lucien Pissarro and his wife presented the British Museum with a set of ten etchings posthumously printed in that year. Dodgson's colleague A. M. Hind had published an article on Camille as a printmaker in *Die graphischen Künste* in 1908, while Dodgson himself supplied a note on the prints for the Leicester Galleries catalogue which illuminates the rather different emphasis he adopted in determining the merits of some of the French artists' work.

Before the collector enters into possession of all the coveted details of date and provenance and state and relative rarity which are apt to warp, as much as they guide, his judgement, this is his last chance of looking at the etchings with a dispassionate and unbiassed eye, and judging them by merit on purely aesthetic grounds. If he is accustomed only to the kind of etching taught in the best schools by recipe and routine, he may find them at first sight baffling and, perhaps, unpleasant. Like other impressionist etchers, and notably Degas ... Pissarro forced the process to yield very personal and unconventional results, which presuppose a certain sympathy in the beholder ... Above all, they must be seen at the right distance. Look at them with a magnifying glass and you will make very little, except spots and splashes and scratches and untidiness in every possible shape, of the curious, apparently unmethodical blend of etching and aquatint and dry-point and 'vernismou', which will reveal, at the right stage of experience and at the due distance from a seeing and unprejudiced eye, the radiant light of 'L'Ile Lacroix à Rouen' or the more veiled atmospheric beauty of that long Pontoise landscape with one soaring poplar that interrupts on the left, so skilfully, the prevailing horizontal lines ... They are, in the strictest sense, painter's etchings, which produce by unconventional and incommunicable means, and not by rule, effects of light and colour similar to those of Pissarro's pictures. It is just this personal style, this individual and uncommon touch, that makes their value and distinguishes them from the average kind of impeccable, agreeable, but not exciting landscape etching that is produced in great quantities on both sides of the Channel.

The extensive holding of Toulouse-Lautrec lithographs, which rivalled that of Redon's work, was largely assembled after 1925, the year in which Dodgson purchased from the Haarlem dealer J. H. de Bois, for 600 florins, the complete set of the *Elles* series (cat. 86), originally published by Gustave Pellet in 1896. Lithographs by Bonnard and Vuillard were purchased in London from the Leicester and Redfern Galleries in the 1930s, when they devoted several exhibitions to modern French prints, and from the Parisian dealer Henri Petiet (1894–1980), whose own collection has recently been dispersed through a series of sales beginning in 1991.[40]

Dodgson continued to collect right up until the end of his life, but there was no particular deviation from the course he had mapped out some thirty years earlier, although he did add a number of the more conventionally tasteful prints by Picasso from the period 1904–6 and the 1920s, completing his Picasso purchases in 1946 with three plates from Buffon's *Histoire Naturelle* at eighteen guineas each from the Leicester Galleries. Matisse was less problematic for him; Dodgson represented his graphic work by a woodcut and a lithograph of 1906, followed by a group of lithographs of the mid-1920s, including the magnificent *Large Odalisque with the Culottes of an Indian Dancing Girl* of 1925, and three etchings of 1929. Dodgson had made no secret of the limitations of his taste in the introduction to the 1919 exhibition. If it does appear too polite by late twentieth-century standards, it was quite in keeping with the prevailing concept of modernism in Britain at the time, which had yet to come to terms with Cubism, Expressionism or any form of serious abstraction except in the modified form adapted for poster design by McKnight Kauffer. The painter John Piper, in writing an appreciation after the death of another remarkable collector and founder member of the Contemporary Art Society, Sir Michael Sadler (1861–1943), recalled how 'twenty years ago modern pictures really were modern. It was only a dozen years after the first post-Impressionist exhibition; Roger Fry's lectures had yet to fill the Queen's Hall; the seats of Underground trains had yet to grow their jazz-patterns, and Picasso had hardly become a music-hall joke, let alone an accepted master.'[41]

The erosion of traditional print-collecting patterns was hastened by the aftermath of the economic crisis of 1929 but the real threat came from the need to find recognisably modern subject-matter and forms of expression, to which intaglio printmaking, the mainstay of the market, was largely resistant. Edward Hopper summed up this dilemma in a 1926 review of *Fine Prints of the Year, 1925*:

We have had a long and weary familiarity with these 'true etchers' who spend their industrious lives weaving pleasing lines around old doorways, Venetian palaces, Gothic cathedrals, and English bridges on the copper ... One wanders through this desert of manual dexterity without much hope ... Of patient labor and skill there is in this book a plenty and more. Of technical experiment or strongly personal vision and contact with modern life, there is little or none.[42]

In Britain modernism in printmaking was associated with new media, linocut, woodcut or wood-engraving and lithography, and prints were increasingly aimed at a middle-class audience seeking interior decoration. In a combined review of *Six Centuries of Fine Prints* by Carl Zigrosser and *The English Print* by Basil Gray, Dodgson himself in 1939 pressed the claims of a literature that would satisfy the needs of 'the comparatively inarticulate collectors who would willingly let die the modern etching ...'[43] but his own habits remained unchanged. He was building a collection for the nation along traditional museological lines which valued a broadly comprehensive representation of as many different techniques as possible, with complete runs of the major printmakers' work documenting variant states and other details of execution. The language of print scholarship came easily to this man whose qualities 'did not include any great aptitude for generalisation' but 'was essentially a recorder of concrete facts which he was able to marshal with clarity and precision'.[44]

Such interest as there was in modern printmaking by the second half of the century differed markedly from the approach traditionally taken to old master print-collecting. Contemporary prints, if they were acquired at all, were bought for their imagery in the first instance, and not as fine examples of the artist's virtuosity. This if anything could be a handicap, hence the antithetical barb in Tom Stoppard's radio play of 1972, *Artist Descending a Staircase*: 'Skill without imagination is craftsmanship and gives us many useful objects such as wickerwork picnic-baskets. Imagination without skill gives us modern art.'[45]

1. For previously published accounts of the career and tastes of Campbell Dodgson, see the excellent obituary by A. E. Popham in the *Proceedings of the British Academy*, XXXVI 1950, pp. 290–7; James Byam Shaw's entry in the *Dictionary of National Biography*, 1941–50; his address at the opening of the Campbell Dodgson Memorial Exhibition at the British Museum, 14 December 1967, which was published in *J. B. S. Selected Writings*, London 1968, pp. 133–5; a short article by Peter Roth, 'Campbell Dodgson: 1867–1948' in *The Print Review*, 4, 1975, pp. 34–7; the introductory essay in Frances Carey and Antony Griffiths, *From Manet to Toulouse-Lautrec. French Lithographs 1860–1900*, London 1978, pp. 7–9, and the essay 'Painting a dream world from life' by Jenny Pery for the catalogue of an exhibition of paintings and drawings by John Dodgson (1890–1969), Campbell Dodgson's nephew, held at the Fine Art Society, London, in 1995, pp. 6–24. Mr Charles Potter, an artist with whom Campbell Dodgson corresponded in the 1930s, has been kind enough to pass on his material to the Department to assist this publication. I would also like to thank Dodgson's niece, Mrs Margaret Winkworth, for access to the letters she received from her uncle and for sharing her reminiscences of him with me.

2. Published in *The Academy* for 15 April 1893 and 19 May 1894 respectively. With the other reviews by Dodgson referred to in the main text, this is included in the bound volume of his cuttings from 1893 to 1943 in the library of the Department of Prints and Drawings.

3. Lincoln Kirstein, 'A. Hyatt Mayor' in *A. Hyatt Mayor: Selected Writings and a Bibliography*, New York 1983, p. 15.

4. 'Advertisement to a Catalogue and Description of King Charles the First's Collections' quoted by Mrs K. A. Esdaile in *The Life and Works of Louis François Roubiliac*, London 1928, p. 103. The original document is in the British Library, Department of Manuscripts, Add.MS.38,791 (see Edward Miller, *That Noble Cabinet*, London 1973, p. 73).

5. From a letter in the Department of Prints and Drawings addressed to Antony Griffiths, 23 April 1978.

6. Colvin never warmed to Dodgson as he did to Binyon, who shared his interests in literature and Oriental art, and he was greatly disappointed that Binyon was not appointed as his successor in 1912: 'I have just heard with extreme disappointment & regret that the choice this afternoon has not fallen on you. I have had a battle with myself all these months to do justice to Dodgson's claims against my strong personal preference which made me do more than justice to them. At the same time I thought in my heart that I had laid weight enough on your superiority in all personal distinction & power of handling men to ensure that you would be chosen. The enclosed is Kenyon's account of the consideration which turned the scales. Now that it has happened I know how deeply I regret it for your sake, and in many respects for the dept., and I blame myself for my own scrupulousness' (letter dated 12 June 1912 among the Binyon papers on deposit with the MS Department of the British Library).

7. *The Letters of Oscar Wilde*, ed. Rupert Hart-Davis, London 1962, appendix A, p. 868. This and the following quotations from Dodgson's correspondence concerning Oscar Wilde are taken from a collection of Dodgson's papers presented to the Department of Prints and Drawings by the late J. Byam Shaw. References are given where the material has been published.

8. *Self Portrait taken from the Letters and Journals of Charles Ricketts*, ed. Cecil Lewis, London 1939, p. 425.

9. Letter dated 23 February 1893, published in *The Letters of Oscar Wilde*, pp. 333–4.

10. Hyatt Mayor, op. cit. p. 165.

11. Published in *Maso Finiguerra*, III, 1938, pp. 351–3.

12. Jacquelynn Baas and Richard S. Field, *The Artistic Revival of the Woodcut in France 1850–1900*, The University of Michigan Museum of Art 1984, p. 55.

13. Campbell Dodgson, *The Classics*, New York 1938, pp. 3–4.

14. Reminiscences of printselling and collecting in America in the early decades of the twentieth century can be found among Carl Zigrosser's *A World of Art and Museums*, Philadelphia and London 1975. Zigrosser worked for the New York print dealers Keppel & Co., 1912–18, then for Erhard Weyhe, 1919–40, before becoming Curator of Prints and Drawings at the Philadelphia Museum of Art, 1941–63.

15. Lugt 265.

16. See Ruth Fine, *Lessing Rosenwald. Tribute to a Collector*, National Gallery of Art, Washington DC, 1982.

17. Although the Wiggin Collection was given to the Boston Public Library in 1941, prompting the foundation of both a department and an exhibition gallery devoted to prints, the dioramas were commissioned by the donor's family at a later date, opening in 1966.

18. For a biography of Binyon see John Hatcher, *Laurence Binyon: Poet, Scholar of East and West*, Oxford University Press, 1995.

19. For example on Charles Conder (1914), Edmund Blampied

(1926), Robert Austin (1931), Andrew Geddes (1936), F.L.Griggs (1941) and Stephen Gooden (1944).

20. A continuation up to 1938 was undertaken by Dodgson's close associate Harold Wright, who was a director of Colnaghi's, Muirhead Bone's principal dealer. This, however, was never published but a copy of the typescript exists in the library of the Department of Prints and Drawings. Wright's working papers were deposited by his widow with the University of Glasgow in 1962, where he had been awarded an honorary degree for his contribution to the study of etching and engraving.

21. I am indebted to Dr Peter Wegmann, Curator of the Museum Stiftung Oskar Reinhart, and the staff of the Reinhart Collection 'Am Romerholz' in Winterthur, for supplying me with copies of correspondence between Dodgson and Reinhart.

22. See Meirion and Susie Harries, *The War Artists*, London 1983, p.149 and p.293, nn126–7.

23. *Morning Post*, 21 March 1925, included in the bound volume of Campbell Dodgson's cuttings in the Department of Prints and Drawings. For a general account of the print market at this time, see the introduction to Frances Carey and Antony Griffiths, *Avant-Garde British Printmaking 1914–1960*, British Museum Publications, London 1990.

24. I would like to thank David Kiehl of the Whitney Museum for consulting the ledgers for me and providing the necessary reference.

25. op. cit. p.150.

26. See *Briefe aus den Jahren 1894–1926*, ed. Max Sauerlandt, revised edition Berlin 1967, p.56, quoted by Antony Griffiths in 'Acquiring an exhibition', *British Museum Society Bulletin*, Nov. 1984, p.17.

27. *Self-Portrait taken from the Letters and Journals of Charles Ricketts*, ed. Cecil Lewis, London 1939, p.105. Paul Delaney quotes the same remark in his article on 'Charles Shannon. Master of Lithography', *The Connoisseur*, March 1979, pp.200–5, but misunderstands it as applying to the British Museum.

28. See Frances Carey and Antony Griffiths, *The Print in Germany 1880–1933*, London 1984, pp.133–7.

29. For a discussion of Lehrs's patronage of Käthe Kollwitz see Werner Schmidt in *Die Kollwitz-Sammlung des Dresdner Kupferstich-Kabinettes*, Cologne 1988, pp.10–20, and Hildegard Bachert in 'Collecting the Art of Käthe Kollwitz' in *Käthe Kollwitz*, ed. Elizabeth Prelinger, New Haven and London 1992, pp.117–35.

30. The letter is among the Campbell Dodgson papers in the Department of Prints and Drawings.

31. *Bibliographica* I, 1895, p.452.

32. See Susan Ashbrook, *The Private Press Movement in Britain 1890–1914*, Boston University Ph.D. thesis 1991, printed by University Microfilms Int., Ann Arbor 1993, p.130. For further information about Ricketts and Shannon and their circle see the essay by J.G.P.Delaney in the exhibition catalogue *The Last Romantics*, ed. John Christian, London 1990. Their role as collectors is set out in the catalogue *All for Art*, ed. Joseph Darracott, Fitzwilliam Museum, Cambridge 1979.

33. Ashbrook, op. cit. p.189.

34. See the letter of January 1891 on p.173 of *The Letters of Lucien to Camille Pissarro 1883–1903*, ed. Anne Thorold, Cambridge 1993.

35. Carey and Griffiths, *Avant-Garde British Printmaking 1914–1960*, op. cit. pp.48–9.

36. Carey and Griffiths, *From Manet to Toulouse-Lautrec. French Lithographs 1860–1900*.

37. 1920 was also the year in which the Art Institute of Chicago acquired its holding of Redon's work from the artist's estate.

38. A third 'fusain', *Christ Crowned with Thorns* 1895, was purchased directly by the Department of Prints and Drawings in 1921. For information on Tebb and the sale of Redon's work see the two essays by Kevin Sharp, 'Redon in the Marketplace', in *Odilon Redon 1840–1916*, Art Institute of Chicago 1994, pp.237–57 and 258–80.

39. Another instance concerns the revolutionary Hungarian artist Béla Uitz (1887–1971), from whom Campbell Dodgson, without knowing anything of his work beforehand, purchased in 1924 a copy of his portfolio of etchings, *Ludditenbewegung* ('The Luddite Movement'), published in Vienna the previous year. The artist evoked his subject-matter of the handloom weavers' uprising in the north of England in the early nineteenth century with a vividly expressionist style which may well have taken Dodgson by surprise.

40. A total of eight sales has so far been held at the Hôtel Drouot in Paris between 1991 and 1995. Petiet combined an astonishing array of passions for Grand Prix car racing, railways and Wagnerian opera with his love of prints. His position as a dealer became all the more commanding after his acquisition in 1939 of the stock of Ambroise Vollard, including Picasso's *Vollard* suite. Through his agent in the United States, Jean Goriany, Petiet was closely involved with many American collections both public and private.

41. 'Sidelight. Michael Ernest Sadler: Friend and Encourager' in *Michael Ernest Sadler. A Memoir by his Son*, London 1949, p.396.

42. Quoted by David Kiehl in *Edward Hopper as Printmaker: Selections from the Whitney Museum of American Art*, Bremen 1994. David Kiehl kindly made available the English text which was translated for the catalogue.

43. *Apollo*, March 1939.

44. A.E.Popham's observation in his obituary, op. cit. n.1.

45. p.24 of the published text.

81 Edouard Manet (1832–83)
Le Ballon (The Balloon), 1862

Lithograph. 403 × 515 mm
Guérin 68; Harris 23

Le Ballon was the result of a short-lived attempt by Alfred Cadart, publisher for the Société des Aquafortistes founded in 1862, to promote the creative use of lithography by leading artists in the same way in which he hoped to encourage the original use of etching. Cadart accordingly despatched three stones to five different artists, Fantin-Latour, Bracquemond, Legros, Ribot and Manet, giving them *carte blanche* to draw what they chose with the promise that the work would be published as a portfolio. Manet, at only his second attempt at lithography, executed one of the finest prints of the nineteenth century. He chose a completely contemporary subject, one of the many popular balloon ascents of the period; in this case it is located on the esplanade of the Invalides where crowds would gather to watch balloon ascents and other entertainments on the national holiday declared by Napoleon III for 15 August as the *Fête de L'Empereur*, in celebration of

81

Napoleon I's birthday, which coincided with the Feast of the Assumption. (See Juliet Wilson Bareau in *Manet 1832–1883*, Grand Palais, Paris 1983, cat. 44, and Jay Fisher, *The Prints of Edouard Manet*, International Exhibitions Foundation, Washington 1985, cats. 22a & b.)

Cadart did not persist with his scheme, because of the disapproval expressed by the professional printer Lemercier towards the proofs pulled from Fantin-Latour's contribution. No more than five impressions are known to exist of *Le Ballon*, of which three are in American collections (the Fogg, the New York Public Library and the Mellon Collection, Virginia) and the fourth in the Bibliothèque Nationale. Manet used only one of the three stones he received from Cadart and did not return to lithography until the late 1860s when he was to prove equally adept in his manipulation of the medium.

1949–4–11–3334. Bequeathed by Campbell Dodgson

82 Camille Pissarro (1830–1903)
Paysage en Long (Horizontal Landscape), 1879

Etching and aquatint. 117 × 394 mm

Delteil 17, second state. Annotated in pencil 'no. 1–2 état, paysage en long, Zinc'

Pissarro was keenly interested in printmaking throughout much of his long career, making some 127 etchings in the years after 1863, a dozen lithographs in 1874 and a further fifty-five between 1894 and 1898. His reputation has rested largely on posthumous editions pulled by his family, for only eight subjects were published during his lifetime. He achieved little contemporary commercial recognition, although he exhibited at the Peintres-Graveurs exhibitions at Durand-Ruel in Paris in 1889 and 1890, and a number of dealers abroad, in Glasgow (Alexander Reid) and New York (Keppel and Kennedy), did buy his etchings in the

1890s; one of the best collections was formed by Samuel Avery (1822–1904), who presented them to the New York Public Library in 1900 with his print collection as a whole. At the beginning of the 1890s Pissarro was complaining that the public cared only for reproductions and the few serious collectors preferred to acquire complete runs of the etchings of Charles Jacques and Félix Buhot with some concession to Whistler, Seymour Haden or Legros perhaps. (See *Camille Pissarro. Letters to his son Lucien*, ed. John Rewald, London 1980, p. 143.)

The British Museum's unique second state of *Paysage en Long*, the only composition he etched in this format, is one of the few impressions pulled during Pissarro's lifetime; he had to rely largely upon fellow artists like Degas and Jacques or a professional printer like Delâtre for the printing of his plates, until he obtained his own press in 1894. This belongs to a group of seventeen prints executed in 1879–80 in which he explored the effects that could be achieved through a wholly unorthodox use of different etching techniques, drypoint, soft-ground etching and aquatint. Degas was the catalyst for this experimentation, giving Pissarro access to the printmaking equipment in his own studio, sending him detailed advice and introducing him to the American artist Mary Cassatt, with whom he proposed a collaboration on a journal of original prints to be called *Le Jour et la Nuit*; this however failed to materialise through lack of financial support. (See Barbara Shapiro, *Camille Pissarro. The Impressionist Printmaker*, Museum of Fine Arts, Boston, 1973, and 'Pissarro as print-maker' in *Pissarro*, Hayward Gallery, London 1980, pp. 191–234.)

1949-4-11-2594. Bequeathed by Campbell Dodgson

83 Edgar Degas (1834–1917)

Le Sommeil (Sleep), 1883–5

Monotype. 276 × 378 mm

Janis 135

Although Degas was by no means the first artist to experiment with monotype printing, the range of his invention has made him the exemplar for all subsequent practitioners. The number of monotypes he made far exceeded his etchings or lithographs (more than 250 subjects and 400 separate impressions), but they were a very private activity. He exhibited his efforts in this medium on only two occasions, at the third Impressionist exhibition in 1877 and at the Durand-Ruel gallery in 1892 where he showed twenty-one of his later, landscape monotypes, all executed between 1890 and 1892.

Sleep belongs to an earlier phase of Degas's monotype printing, when he found the medium ideally suited to capturing the secret, intimate quality of the life of his chosen subjects, which were predominantly of brothel scenes or of women engaged in their *toilette*. He worked on the surface of his plates in an additive and subtractive way to create both light-field and dark-field monotypes; *Sleep* is a particularly dramatic example of the latter technique which involved covering the entire surface of the plate with a film of ink, then creating the image by thinning or removing the ink in places. His customary practice, which he followed in the case of *Sleep*, was to pull two impressions, using the second one, which was always much paler, for reworking as a pastel composition.

1949-4-11-2425. Bequeathed by Campbell Dodgson

84 Odilon Redon (1840–1916)

Cellule Auriculaire (Auricular Cell), 1893

Lithograph. 312 × 251 mm

Mellerio 126; undescribed first state. A pencil inscription at the bottom, signed A.E.T(ebb), reads: 'This copy was given to me by Redon – only one other example in this state exists – viz. the one in his own collection. About 2 inches was cut off the top of the stone before the copies (100) were struck off for "L'Estampe Originale" – in which this & "Bouddha" appeared. This plate has not been reprinted – but the "Bouddha" has and the stone has been reworked considerably since the earlier copies were printed.'

Redon was encouraged to take up lithography in the late 1870s by Fantin-Latour, who introduced him to the workshop of Lemercier where all his lithographs were to be editioned from 1879 to 1887. Redon quickly perceived the process's possibilities, first as a means of reproducing his charcoal drawings or *fusains* and then as a medium with scope for original composition in its own right. His appreciation of the commercial role lithography could perform for his work as a whole was as acute as his artistic instincts. Redon acted with careful deliberation from the outset in the dedication, placing, promotion and display of his prints, nurturing a market among collectors, who by the 1890s were avidly purchasing new publications and advertising for earlier ones (see Ted Gott, *The Enchanted Stone: The Graphic Worlds of Odilon Redon*, National Gallery of Victoria, Melbourne 1990, pp. 57–65, and Kevin Sharp, 'Redon in the Marketplace' in *Odilon Redon*, Art Institute of Chicago 1994, pp. 237–80). Redon's connection with Dr A. E. Tebb, the original owner of *Auricular Cell*, is discussed on p. 221 together with the impressive body of work that Campbell Dodgson purchased from him in 1920.

Redon reduced the space between the upper curve of the 'auricular cell' and the edge of the composition as a whole before the edition was printed, thereby strengthening the dramatic impact of the subject, whose form is commonly encountered among Redon's occult and dream-like imagery.

1949-4-11-3525. Bequeathed by Campbell Dodgson

82

83

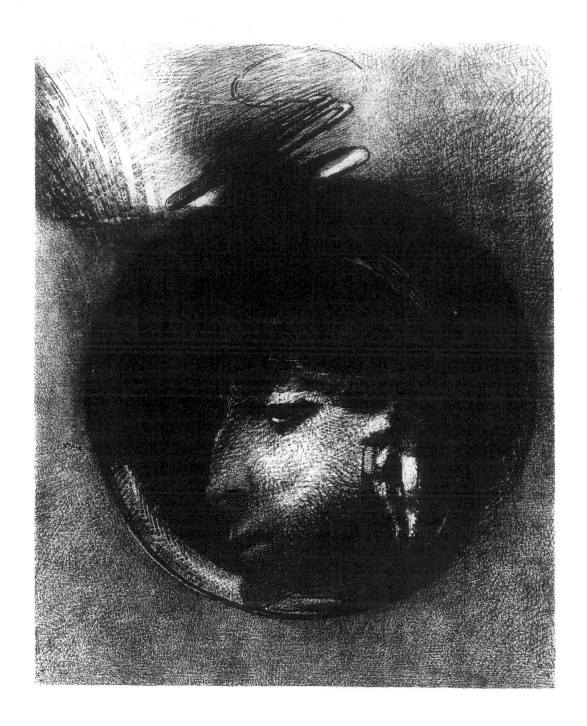

85

85 Paul Gauguin (1848–1903)

Auti te Pape (Women by the River or
The Fresh Water in Motion), 1893–4

Illustrated in colour between pages 112 and 113

Woodcut printed in black with three colours
on buff-coloured wove paper. 205 × 357 mm

Kornfeld 16:IIA

Gauguin returned from his first visit to Tahiti in August
1893; after the disappointing reception given to his paintings at the end of that year, he devoted his energy to the
composition of a written account and a series of dramatic
woodcuts to convey to a Parisian audience the transform-
ing nature of his encounter with a 'primitive' culture. By
April of 1894 all ten woodcuts of what became known as
the *Noa Noa* (Fragrant Scent) series were completed, including *Auti te Pape*, but without a clearly identifiable
sequence. After printing a few trial proofs himself, Gauguin
handed over the blocks to his friend Louis Roy to print sets
of twenty-five to thirty impressions each, although these
were never numbered. The final body of work was exhibited in his studio in December to a few mainly literary
friends, since the art world, with the exception of Degas,
had rejected his Tahitian paintings with such contumely. Six
months later he abandoned Europe for good, leaving eight

of the woodblocks and almost all the impressions pulled
from them in the care of his friends. Some of the blocks
were posthumously printed by the wood-engravers Tony
and Jacques Beltrand; finally an edition was published in
Copenhagen in 1921 by the artist's youngest son, Pola
Gauguin, who purchased the eight surviving blocks from
an exhibition of his father's work in Stockholm in 1919.

Campbell Dodgson assembled a range of impressions
from five of the *Noa Noa* subjects, representing several of
the variations in inking and colouring that the blocks
underwent during the course of their complicated history.
Auti te Pape is one of only two recorded impressions of
this subject printed by Gauguin himself, and it formerly
came from the collection of H. M. Petiet (see p. 222). The
second example belongs to the Art Institute in Chicago,
which acquired proofs printed by the artist for most of the
Noa Noa subjects (see Douglas Druick in *The Art of Paul
Gauguin*, National Gallery of Art, Washington, and the
Art Institute of Chicago, 1988, pp. 317ff); these were previously owned by a friend of Gauguin's, the Spanish sculptor Francisco Durrio, whose remarkable collection was
probably seen by Dodgson when it was exhibited at the
Leicester Galleries in 1931. In 1936 Dodgson bought
Louis Roy impressions of three *Noa Noa* subjects, including *Auti te Pape* (K.16:IIC), out of a group of seven offered
to him by Gutekunst and Klipstein in Bern. For *L'Univers*

est créé (The Creation of the Universe) he owned a unique trial proof printed in tangerine-orange by Louis Roy prior to the regular set (K.18:11C), and for *Manao Tupapau* (Watched by the Spirits of the Dead) he owned four separate impressions, proceeding from another rare artist's proof to the Roy version and then the posthumous ones by Beltrand and Pola Gauguin (K.20. B, D, E, F).

1949–4–11–3674. Bequeathed by Campbell Dodgson

86 Henri de Toulouse-Lautrec (1864–1901)
La Clownesse assise, Mlle Cha-U-Ka-O, 1896

Illustrated in colour between pages 112 and 113

Lithograph printed in five colours. 525 × 404 mm
Wittrock 156

La Clownesse assise, following a cover and frontispiece, opens the sequence of ten lithographs known as the *Elles* series, published by Gustave Pellet in 1896 in an edition of 100 and exhibited as a set in April of that year. The series was the outcome of Lautrec's observations of the more mundane moments of life in the Parisian brothels where he lived intermittently from 1890. Mlle Cha-U-Ka-O, who was a favourite subject of his, did not belong to the *maisons closes*, but serves as a link with another aspect of the *demi-monde* to which Lautrec was greatly attracted, that of the popular dance hall, epitomised by the Moulin Rouge where she was a regular performer (her name is a contraction of the name of a dance, 'Chahut-Chaos').

Most of the other plates from the same series are sparely executed in muted tones, demonstrating the artist's virtuosity as a draughtsman. *Mlle Cha-U-Ka-O* displays, by contrast, the full range of his chromatic brilliance, which by 1896 had given him a commanding position in the field of colour lithography.

The British Museum is almost entirely indebted to Campbell Dodgson for its collection of over ninety lithographs by Toulouse-Lautrec, including the complete set of *Elles* which he purchased in 1925 (see p. 222).

1949–4–11–3635. Bequeathed by Campbell Dodgson

87 Käthe Kollwitz (1867–1945)
Female Nude Seen from Behind, 1903

Lithograph printed in grey with a green tint-stone on grey-brown paper. 575 × 440 mm
Klipstein 69, second state; signed in pencil

The example of Max Klinger (1867–1920) as a writer, printmaker and creator of visual narratives was crucial to Käthe Kollwitz's decision to become a graphic artist.

Although etching was the predominant medium used for her early work, she was experimenting with lithography from the beginning of the 1890s and in 1901 she wrote to Max Lehrs of the Dresden Print Room: 'I devote myself to lithography next to etching, and promise myself great things from a mixing of the two techniques – I now have my own press to hand for experiments.' At this point in her career she used lithography as a technique for printing in colour, creating subtle, atmospheric images of which the *Female Nude Seen from Behind* is her masterpiece. The surface of the lithographic stone was subjected to careful manipulation and there are numerous variations between the different impressions. On some impressions of the first state, Kollwitz used an additional blue stone, while an impression of the second state in Berlin has blue wash added by hand in the background to the left of the figure.

1951–5–1–79. Bequeathed by Campbell Dodgson

88 Emil Nolde (1867–1956)
Hamburg, Landing-Stage, 1910

Etching with stipple and tonal effects. 311 × 411 mm
Schiefler-Mosel 139, third state; signed in pencil and annotated in bottom left corner '111 22'

Nolde was one of the first recruits to the Brücke movement in Dresden in 1906; this was a turning-point in his career as an artist, which had not seriously begun until he reached the age of thirty-five. Although his difficult temperament prevented him from ever sustaining an affiliation with particular artistic circles, he enjoyed the patronage of one of the most dedicated supporters of contemporary art, Gustav Schiefler, a Hamburg judge who went on to write catalogues of Nolde's and Kirchner's graphic work after publishing those for Max Liebermann and Munch in 1907. Nolde's prints were created in sporadic bursts between 1904 and 1926 with hardly any further production thereafter; he concentrated on etching at the beginning of his career, making almost 200 plates by 1911, the date of the *catalogue raisonné*.

After the opening of his successful exhibition, arranged by Schiefler at the Galerie Commeter in Hamburg in February 1910, Nolde disappeared to a cheap sailors' lodging-house on the waterfront of the Hamburg docks in order to immerse himself fully in the atmosphere of this district. The flurry of brooding, melancholy images that he produced over the next three weeks – nineteen etchings, four woodcuts and a large number of drawings in brush and black ink – belonged to a tradition of Hamburg views which the Director of the Hamburg Kunsthalle, Alfred Lichtwark, had encouraged from the 1890s onwards, by commissioning paintings for the collection from well-known artists of the day. Nolde's Hamburg etchings proved

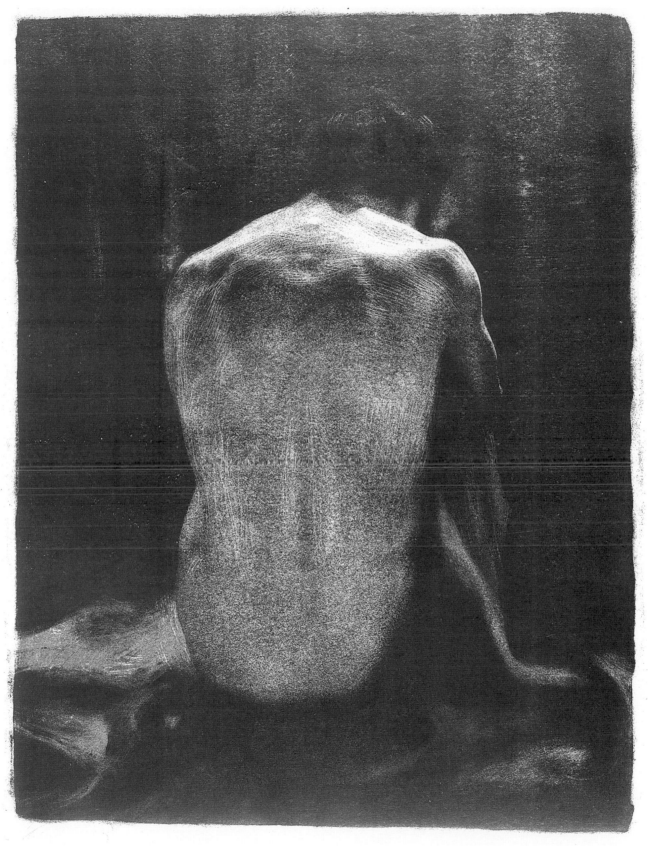

88

popular at the time; the initial proofing was done by a local printer followed by a proper edition printed at the Felsing workshop in Berlin. (See Clifford Ackley, Timothy Benson and Victor Carlson, *Nolde. The Painter's Prints*, Museum of Fine Arts, Boston, and Los Angeles County Art Museum, 1995, pp. 173–90.)

1949-4-11-3972. Bequeathed by Campbell Dodgson, together with three other subjects from the same series

89 Edward Hopper (1882–1967)
Night on the El Train, 1918

Etching. 185 × 200 mm

Zigrosser 21. Signed and annotated with the price of $18 in pencil on the recto, and the title 'On the L-Train' inscribed in ink on the verso

Hopper was a self-taught etcher; his prints, some seventy subjects done on fifty-seven plates (several were used on both sides), were virtually all executed between 1915 and the end of 1923. He benefited at the outset from the technical advice of his friend, the Australian-born printmaker Martin Lewis (1882–1962), and the example of John Sloan (1871–1951), whose ten etchings of 1905–6 entitled *New York City Life* introduced an informal narrative of plebeian subject-matter that Hopper greatly admired. His experience of original printmaking was instrumental in the development of his own distinctive vision, which quickly surpassed the anecdotal style that had been his and Sloan's point of departure as commercial illustrators. The subjects were carefully composed by Hopper in his studio; he often worked from pencil or charcoal drawings done in the same direction as the final prints. The plates might then progress through several different states as the artist added layers of shading or subtracted them through burnishing out, in order to achieve the lighting effects appropriate to the mood of his compositions.

Hopper's prints quickly gained admission to the principal exhibiting societies in New York and Chicago, but his interest in printmaking was superseded by the success of his watercolours at an exhibition in New York in November 1924, which encouraged him to concentrate on what he regarded as the more serious pursuit of painting in oils and watercolour.

The two seminal collections of Hopper's work are those held by the Print Department of the Philadelphia Museum of Art, through Carl Zigrosser's friendship with the artist, and at the Whitney Museum in New York, which owns the original plates as part of the estate bequeathed by the artist's widow, Josephine Hopper.

1926-6-24-15. Presented by Campbell Dodgson

90 Sir Muirhead Bone (1876–1953)
A Manhattan Excavation, 1923–8

Drypoint, signed and titled in pencil. 315 × 259 mm
Campbell Dodgson 390 XIII

Muirhead Bone sailed from Glasgow to New York on 21 April 1923, where he stayed until the end of July. Among the subjects he etched from life were portraits of the writer Joseph Conrad, who had been one of Bone's fellow passengers for the transatlantic crossing on board the *Tuscania*, the publisher Frank Doubleday, the playwright Don Marquis, and Frank Weitenkampf, curator of prints at the New York Public Library.

He embarked on the most ambitious of all his American subjects, *A Manhattan Excavation*, on 4 June, working directly on to the plate as he observed a site near the intersection of Broadway and Madison Avenue. Eventually there were to be 151 impressions pulled from as many as nineteen different states of this image. Seven impressions from the first two states only were actually printed in New York, the third state was completed in England before February 1924, while the remaining sixteen date from 1928; the printing from these was finished by March of that year. Bone used the other end of the same plate for an unfinished study of skyscrapers (CD391), whose spareness is rather more appealing to the modern eye than the plethora of detail characteristic of Bone's fully realised compositions; this portion of the plate he left alone after his return from New York, until he printed eight impressions from it in 1945, presenting one of them to Campbell Dodgson.

For *A Manhattan Excavation* the majority of the impressions were pulled from the thirteenth state catalogued here (eighteen), the seventeenth (forty) and the nineteenth and final state (forty-nine). The numerous states through which this subject progressed are partly attributable to the long pause in the artist's attention; however, the production of multiple states and numerous trial proofs was an essential feature of Muirhead Bone's practice, which Campbell Dodgson explained in the preface to his catalogue of the artist's etchings and drypoints 1898–1907, published in 1909: 'Since 1904, however, the great majority of Mr Bone's etchings have been issued through Messrs Obach and Co. and it has been his invariable practice to exclude trial proofs from the published issue. He has reserved them for his own collection and that of his publishers, or presented them, if further duplicates existed, to a friend.'

1949-4-11-1763. Bequeathed by Campbell Dodgson.
Purchased from Colnaghi in September 1928 for £18.18.0

Munhent zone.

90

10. Curatorial Collecting in the Twentieth Century

Frances Carey

The study of prints has always had a much wider application than that of drawings in so far as the material itself can embrace such a heterogeneous range of subject-matter and modes of representation from 'the most ephemeral of courtesies to the loftiest pictorial presentations of man's spiritual aspirations'.[1] The beginning of the twentieth century was a point at which many museums, particularly the nascent collections in North America, were prompted to examine the role of print acquisitions in terms of the educative function that could be fulfilled both by displays of this material and by the facilities of a properly constituted students' room. In 1912 the Director of the Kaiser Friedrich Museum in Berlin, Wilhelm Bode, wrote after a visit to the United States that in the interests of educating public taste: 'What the museums yonder should strive for are systematically assembled collections of engravings, wherein the Boston Museum alone has made a good beginning.'[2]

The Metropolitan Museum's Department of Prints was formally instituted in 1917, and William Ivins's address to the Trustees on this occasion is one of the most useful statements of purpose in relation to such a collection. Despite his initial assertion that collecting policy should be largely based on aesthetic criteria, he then went on to explain how in practice 'the print collection of a museum cannot be formed solely upon Yes or No answers to the question: is it a work of art? Rather must it be, like the library of a professor of literature, composed of a corpus of prints in themselves distinctly works of art, filled out and illustrated by many prints which have only a technical historical importance.'[3]

Of all the American collections, the Metropolitan's is most comparable to that of the British Museum which, by the time Ivins was making his declaration of intent, had been in existence as a distinct department for more than a hundred years, housing a collection of much longer antecedents. Throughout this history accidents of gift and bequest always played a part in the formation of the British Museum's print collection and have continued to do so in the twentieth century. Nonetheless, from the outset, it was a public not a private collection and by the mid-nineteenth century had developed a policy of acquisition or perhaps a 'pattern of universality achieved by purchase' which Hyatt Mayor described as the distinguishing feature of the new museological foundations of the nineteenth century.[4] A directed programme of acquisition in turn generated gifts to complement the department's perceived interests.

The emphasis had by and large been upon prints 'of importance for the manner in which they represent things, and not for the things they represent',[5] but the nature of the medium itself extended the range of material to encompass major holdings of trade cards, book-plates, extra-illustrated books, satirical, historical and topographical prints, and a vast portrait archive as well as prints by and after the leading fine artists. The diversity of the collection's use and content was summarised in the concluding chapter of A Print Collector's Handbook, first published in 1901 by Alfred Whitman, the superintendent of the Print Room:

The seven thousand or more visitors who annually pass some of their time in the Print Room comprise people in all walks of life – Cabinet Ministers as well as the hard-working artist who, perhaps, finds it difficult to make both ends meet. Authors go to seek materials for their books, publishers to find illustrations for the works they are about to issue, painters for authorities for the settings of their pictures, and theatrical managers and actors for hints as to the costumes they should use. It may almost be said that nothing of importance occurs in the country but it sends visitors to the Print Room, whether it be a Royal marriage, some historical controversy, a military tournament, or a jubilee.

... Besides the visitors just named, there are the bona fide students of prints who go to increase their knowledge of the world of engraving, to train themselves in judging the essential qualities of good prints and to examine specimens in a brilliant state of preservation. Among these are to be found many foreigners whose industry and studious habits are very noticeable. Many amateurs take prints of their own with them and ask permission to compare them with the specimens possessed by the department.

The superb resources of the Print Room, in terms of its secondary reference material as well as the main collection, were responsible for perhaps the most influential general guide ever written to the history of printmaking, A. M. Hind's A Short History of Engraving and Etching of 1908, which was immediately acclaimed as an indispensable handbook for all collectors and students: 'Mr Hind has produced a book of a scope and quality to which we are little accustomed in England. That so thorough an achievement should be the work of an official in the Print Room of the British Museum is a matter of congratulation to his department as well as to himself.'[6]

The Print Room's role as a great library of reference has been sustained throughout the present century with some modifications in the light of the development of other national collections, particularly that of the Victoria and Albert Museum, where a separate department of 'Engraving, Illustration and Design' was opened in 1908 with a special emphasis on the history of the various print media in relation to the decorative arts and the techniques of printmaking.

The first half of this century afforded opportunities for improving all aspects of the print collection which have never been equalled since. Despite the very limited acquisitions budget, the three Keepers of the years 1912–54, Campbell Dodgson, A. M. Hind and A. E. Popham, deployed these opportunities with great skill in relation to material from the pre-modern period, using their influence to secure further subventions from wealthy private collectors, such as Maurice Rosenheim,[7] Robert and Emile Mond, Viscount Bearsted, Sir Otto Beit, Sir Joseph Duveen, Sir Robert Witt, C. S. Gulbenkian and Count Seilern.

Duplicate prints formed another resource at their disposal which, with hindsight, was used rather too ruthlessly. However, precedents did exist, the most recent of them being the auction which took place in the British Museum itself on 21 April 1880, to provide the funds for the purchase of the Crace Collection of London topography. The incorporation of the prints from the Malcolm and Mitchell collections produced many more duplicates from the existing collection and Sidney Colvin recommended in March 1909 that they should be set aside as a 'stock for exchange' with the proviso that none of the material so exchanged should come from any gift or bequest. They became an increasing aid to acquisition during the 1920s and 1930s, when a welter of major print collections appeared on the market as a result of economic and political changes in Germany; the department would either trade in the duplicates with their invariable agent, Colnaghi's, to establish a credit reserve which could be set against the cost of the items secured at auction, or, on one occasion, authorise their outright sale as executed by the Leipzig auction house of C. G. Boerner, between November 1924 and May 1926, to whom more than 750 items were consigned. The Malcolm prints provided much of the 'stock for exchange' which moved Colvin, in retirement in 1924, to protest to Campbell Dodgson, because he felt that the very favourable price at which the original collection had been acquired rendered it comparable to a gift and therefore its integrity should be preserved.[8] Dodgson eventually addressed this question in 1930 to Sir Ian Malcolm, who gave his consent, provided prints of an equivalent value were purchased with the proceeds of the sale of duplicates from his grandfather's collection and the work registered as additions to the Malcolm Collection.[9]

The benefits reaped from the great Continental sales were undeniable and the feverish excitement of the auction rooms was conveyed even by the controlled prose of Campbell Dodgson in his reports to Colvin throughout the ten days of sales in May 1909, devoted to the collection of Baron Adalbert von Lanna of Prague,[10] at Gutekunst in Stuttgart. The keenest competition was for the early German material between Max Friedländer, buying for the Berlin Print Room, and the Viennese dealer Artaria, with the latter paying a record price of 8,100 Reichsmark for a Cranach woodcut after being bid up by the Berlin Print Room. Berlin secured the largest number of rarities, the other principal purchasers being Baron Edmond de Rothschild and 'a young Austrian millionaire, Herr Gutmann',[11] but the British Museum also managed to make important acquisitions. Dodgson gleefully relayed the various feints used to throw competitors off the scent in his pursuit of one particularly rare woodcut by the monogrammist DS (*fl.* 1503–15), whose corpus of prints he had been the first to identify in 1907;[12] this was a superior impression to the example already owned by the Museum.[13]

The British Museum was represented at all the major German sales after the First World War of collections such as that of Friedrich August II of Saxony (1797–1854), dispersed in eleven sales, 1927–37 (followed by a twelfth in 1943 of the nineteenth-century prints in which the Museum, for obvious reasons, did not participate), of von Passavant-Gontard and Julius Model, both auctioned by C. G. Boerner in May 1929, of Count Yorck von Wartenburg and the Duke of Saxe-Gotha sold together with duplicates from the Albertina in May 1932, and that from Northwick Park whose old master prints were sold in Leipzig in May 1933. The extraordinary quality of material available meant that the Museum not only added new images to the collection but could also improve on the quality of existing impressions or introduce examples of further states. The bulk of the purchasing took place within the northern European schools, especially from the fifteenth and early sixteenth centuries, where Dodgson and Hind, who had spent a year studying with Max Lehrs in Dresden before joining the Department in 1904, brought their scholarly expertise to bear upon the strategy for bidding. That focus was achieved through a comprehensive knowledge of the British Museum's holdings and those of the other major public collections in Europe, which often brought success, although the Museum's funds could not rival those of the Berlin and Munich Print Rooms, the Metropolitan Museum and a number of American private collectors. Dodgson, in reviewing the Leipzig auctions of May 1927, captured their flavour thus:

To attend such a sale in the character of a would-be buyer, doomed to many disappointments; to breathe for five days the heated atmosphere of rumour and anticipation; to speculate on the chances of this or that museum, on either side of the Atlantic, acquiring this or that rarity; to hear how much money the Munich print-room had begged from the rich brewers and to wonder whether it would all be spent before the last afternoon, and whether there was still any chance of making acquisitions under S or T or W; to have, just once or twice, the pleasure of finding that one knew a little more about some lot than the almost omniscient Mr Boerner; all this was a somewhat thrilling experience, rich in its alternations of pleasure and pain.[14]

As well as German and Netherlandish prints, Dodgson's acquisitions included early Italian material to add to the superb holding acquired with the Smith collection in 1845 (see section 4). It was an area to which Hind gave much of his attention, cataloguing the Museum's collection of early Italian engravings under the direction of Colvin in 1910, then later expanding the scope of publication to produce a comprehensive catalogue on the subject which appeared in four volumes in 1938 followed by a further three in 1948; the latter were published with the assistance of Lessing Rosenwald, to whom Hind sent his typescript for safekeeping during the Second World War.[15]

From the mid-1920s Dodgson also sought to improve the Department's representation of French eighteenth-century engraving and aquatint, which commanded high prices during the early decades of the twentieth century. In January 1925 the Department purchased from Agnew's,

for the considerable sum of £3,000 (£1,000 was raised by the sale of duplicates), forty-one proofs of one of the most important series of French eighteenth-century engravings, the *Monument du Costume* of 1774. These came from the residue of one of the finest collections of French eighteenth-century prints, formerly owned by the Comte de Greffulhe, which Dodgson had tried throughout 1924 to persuade the Museum's Trustees to purchase *en bloc*. During the course of 1925 it profited considerably from the sales at Sotheby's in April and December of the collection of the Earl of Crawford and Balcarres, which was especially strong in Napoleonic subjects (fig. 1) and French Revolutionary history; as well as the purchases made via Agnew's again, 123 prints from the collection were donated in July 1925 by Lord Crawford himself. Another great collection from this period was that of Julius Model (1838–1920) in Berlin;[16] with the help of privately donated funds, Dodgson obtained from the sale in Leipzig in 1929, prints by or after Baudouin, Boucher, Le Blon and Debucourt, a particular favourite of his.

Dodgson and his immediate successors were well aware

1. Claude Roy, *Calendar of Napoleonic Victories*, etching, engraving and colour aquatint 1806. 401 × 405 mm. 1925-12-15-7

that reproductive printmaking has been as important within the history of art as the work of the *peintres-graveurs* (see p. 214). When Colnaghi's acquired the great collection of the Prince of Lichtenstein after the Second World War, the British Museum purchased piecemeal, between 1949 and 1953, nearly 2,000 prints from the sixteenth to the eighteenth centuries after the acknowledged masters of all the main European schools. The then Keeper, A. E. Popham, who was more of a drawings than a print specialist, nonetheless realised it was a unique opportunity to round out the Museum's collection, describing the material to the Trustees as 'the largest and most representative general collection of prints existing outside the great European print rooms'.[17] He pursued the work with great tenacity, cajoling money out of Count Seilern towards the purchase of 250 eighteenth-century Venetian prints and refusing export licences on occasion to the Metropolitan Museum and the Rijksmuseum, from whom he withheld 206 prints after Martin van Heemskerck and sixty-seven after Frans Floris (fig. 2).[18] Popham remained on excellent terms, though, with his colleagues in those museums, van Regteren Altena and Hyatt Mayor, even selling a group of fifty-three British Museum duplicates to the latter as a way of financing further acquisitions from the Lichtenstein collection. Mayor, who was proud of what he did manage to secure, explained the significance of the material to any broadly based print collection such as those which the Rijksmuseum, the British Museum and the Metropolitan under his guidance sought to achieve:

I think the biggest purchased lot that ever came in was what I got out of the collection of Prince Lichtenstein, who lived in Vaduz – and had a collection which, I suppose, goes back to the early fifteen hundreds . . . It had been greatly augmented in the 18th century, all laid down on 18th century hardboard, which was very carefully sized and calendered on the back of each sheet so that the sheets wouldn't be rough against the prints facing them. These things were put in large red morocco portfolios with green linen flaps to keep the dust out. About 350 portfolios. What I got was all the unsaleable things. I got the reproductive prints of the Italian schools, of the German schools. It was a great purchase because they are not collector's prints. They are not prints you would ever show on the walls. They're not works of art, but they're the prints that answer questions.[19]

Beyond the prints classified according to artist or engraver in the British Museum's collection are the many series categorised by subject which were not neglected, either, during the first half of the twentieth century: sporting prints and drawings, to which important additions were made from the Schwerdt Collection, sold at Sotheby's in the summer of 1939, following on from two gifts of skating material in 1924 and 1931[20] and the portraits, to which, for example, 2,624 items were added in 1943 from the stock of Messrs Suckling, and another 600 in 1944 purchased from the Royal College of Music. In the field of

2. Hieronymus Cock (publisher), *Aristaeus the Discoverer of Honey*, engraving after Frans Floris 1563. 293 × 222 mm. 1950-5-20-446

single-sheet satirical prints, the Department had had an incomparable representation of British material since the purchase in 1868 of the collection of personal and political satires formerly owned by Edward Hawkins, Keeper of the Department of Antiquities in the British Museum, 1826–60; this was further augmented by the purchase of more than 1,000 items from the collection of the social historian of art F. D. Klingender in 1948, while some of the most unusual acquisitions from the Crawford Collection in 1925 were of French satires from the Revolutionary period. The collection remains of considerable importance to the Department and to the outside world at the latter end of the twentieth century; shifting aesthetic values and the increasing contextualisation of the study of material culture have thrown into relief the artistic achievement of many of these compositions as well as their historical significance. An exhibition on the British response to the French Revolution, *The Shadow of the Guillotine*, in 1989, focused attention on both British and foreign satires of the Revolutionary and Napoleonic eras in which a steady stream of acquisitions has continued to expand the collection's frame of reference (fig. 3). By association, popular printmaking has also come to the fore; although the acquisitions

(*Left*) 3. Anonymous French, *An English Family on its Travels*, hand-coloured etching *c.*1814. 1991-7-20-131

Famille Anglaise en Voyage

have been predominantly of British nineteenth-century examples, an exhibition held by the Museum's Department of Ethnography on the Mexican Day of the Dead prompted the purchase in 1992 and 1994 of sixteen of the original broadsheets or 'Calaveras' published between 1903 and 1913 on the occasion of this festival, with illustrations by J. G. Posada (1852–1913), the best-known of all the artists involved with this type of imagery (fig. 4).[21]

The most contentious issue for museum curators in the twentieth century has been their institutional relationship to the art of their contemporaries; it was a question guaranteed to be especially vexed in a collection as deeply rooted in the past as that of the British Museum, where as early as 1856 Nathaniel Hawthorne felt 'the present is burthened too much with the past. We have not time ... to appreciate what is warm with life, and immediately around us.'[22] Franz Marc expressed the same cultural predicament in the aphorisms he wrote in 1915 from the Western Front, where he was to be killed the following year:

The creative man honours the past by leaving it in peace and not by living in it. It was the tragedy of our fathers that they, like alchemists, wanted to make gold out of venerable dust. In doing so they lost their fortune. They ran the gamut of past cultures and lost the ability to create their own.[23]

As early as 1848, W. H. Carpenter was regretting the almost complete absence of any policy of acquiring modern prints for the collection; he proposed in his evidence to the Royal Commission on the British Museum to set aside the sum of £200 from his annual grant of £1,200 expressly for this purpose, subsequently using it to good effect in the acquisition of the early etchings of Manet and Whistler. Unfortu-

4. José Guadalupe Posada, *Calavera of the People's Editor Antonio Vanegas Arroyo*, type-metal engraving on off-white paper *c.*1907. 402 × 304 mm. 1992-4-4-90

nately his efforts were not continued; by the beginning of the next century it had become received wisdom that public funds should not be used for modern work although private funds might, and there was no restriction on accepting gifts. It was an attitude bred perhaps more of cowardice than prudence but it afforded some relief from the problems described by Max Lehrs, who did endeavour to modernise his collection in Dresden through purchase as well as gift (see p. 213):

It is more convenient for the administration, as in the case, for example, of the British Museum, to shelter behind the worthy principle that the work of a living artist should only be accepted as a gift, and I do not fail to recognise entirely the difficulty of consciously selecting only the best, without being influenced by personal connections with individual artists who though they may be good-hearted people are but poor performers, or diverted by the eternal sirensong of the local inhabitants who think that preference must be given to native talent. The majority of artists, and not usually the most talented, consider our public collections to be state-supported charitable institutions for the relief of the indigent.[24]

The British Museum did not enjoy the advantage of the Cabinet des Estampes of the Bibliothèque Nationale in Paris, where the *dépôt légal* had underpinned the print acquisitions of the royal and then the national collection since the mid-seventeenth century. Within the United Kingdom copyright legislation only applied to books, which in the case of volumes of prints benefited the library of the British Museum, not its Department of Prints and Drawings. Carpenter in 1848 advocated, without success, the extension of the existing Copyright Act to require publishers to deposit an additional proof of each print with the Museum. This proposal was revived in 1911, again to no avail. Sidney Colvin solicited the opinions of the leading printmakers and dealers of the day, of whom D. Y. Cameron was in favour but Sir Frank Short, Director of the School of Engraving at the Royal College of Art, was strongly opposed. He felt it would prove too onerous to the artists since as well as the British Museum there were four other copyright libraries in Cambridge, Oxford, Edinburgh and Dublin, and would probably be unenforceable too. His objections reflected what he regarded as a marked change in the whole pattern of print production:

I think it must be allowed that during the last thirty years the conditions of print publishing have changed, and that the majority of prints the Museum would probably desire, are made and issued by the artists themselves, or issued by them through dealers.

In most cases these prints are not registered for copyright, the now universal practice of the etcher or engraver of autographically signing each impression appearing sufficient to protect it from piracy, as no print without such a signature would now be considered authentic. Therefore I do not see how any claim in respect of these prints could be made effective, nor how the actual collection of them could be practicable.

It is now a general practice for the etcher to issue his work in limited editions, frequently of fifty copies or less, and I think that the compulsion to surrender one or more proofs of each edition would be considered a hardship by many artists. In these cases the Museum would certainly not get one of the best impressions.[25]

The British Museum's attitude to contemporary art was further complicated by the role of the Victoria and Albert Museum, which from its origins in the mid-nineteenth century had been enjoined to develop its collections as exemplars for the current practice of art. Its symbiotic relationship with the Royal College of Art gave it a particular sense of responsibility towards contemporary artists which made it seem a more natural repository for their work than the British Museum. This view was certainly fostered by Martin Hardie, Keeper of the Department of Engraving, Illustration and Design 1921–35, who was himself a practising artist.

The V & A and the British Museum were equally concerned to define their position concerning works on paper, vis-à-vis the third national collection to emerge with a responsibility to the twentieth century, the Tate Gallery, founded in 1897 as a subsidiary of the National Gallery. In response to the Royal Commission on Museums and Galleries of 1927–8 the three institutions drew up an agreement whereby the British Museum and the V & A promised to make available on loan such prints and drawings as the Tate might require for its displays, in return for the latter's resigning its claim to 'a Print Room System' and a government grant for the support of the same. It is clear from the correspondence at the time that their concern was to avoid further dilution of the meagre public funds available, rather than completely to prevent the Tate's acquisition of work on paper. No objection was raised to the occasional purchase by the Tate from private funds of important drawings, especially of modern foreign material.

It is perhaps typical of Campbell Dodgson's correctness as a public servant that he did not seek to question the inherited prejudice against using government funds for the purchase of contemporary art, but devised ways of circumventing it in order to prevent the Department from succumbing to a chronological delimitation which he believed to be detrimental to the good of the collection as a whole. From 1919 to 1945 the Contemporary Art Society's prints and drawings fund was the principal conduit for modern material into the collection, apart from Campbell Dodgson's own generosity and that of the many artists attracted by the status of the British Museum and Dodgson's personal commitment. It was not a purely chance means of acquisition, because the fund was administered *ex officio* by the successive Keepers of Prints and Drawings primarily for the benefit of the Department, which had first refusal on all material either purchased or donated once it had been toured to different venues around the country. The purchases inevitably reflected the taste of those Keepers, particularly Campbell Dodgson's, to the extent that the Contemporary Art Society's contributions became but another aspect of his own collecting proclivities. The tone of some of these acquisitions was thus of a cautiously modernist nature, exemplified at its most daring by the work of Edward Wadsworth, three of whose woodcuts were purchased from his exhibition at the Adelphi Gallery in 1919, including his *Illustration to 'Typhoon' by Conrad* (cat. 96); the artist, who was a subscriber to the fund himself, presented a further six woodcuts at the same time. They kept company with the prints of Paul Nash and C.R.W. Nevinson, first purchased in 1922; later, from 1928 to 1933, the linocut artists Claude Flight, Cyril Power, Sybil Andrews and Lill Tschudi somewhat expanded the range of interpretation of modern life.

Neither Dodgson nor Hind had a narrowly chauvinist approach towards contemporary material, and works by artists of every conceivable nationality continued to enter the collection; of the 243 prints acquired through the Contemporary Art Society in 1926–7, for example, 144 were by foreign artists. But there was individually, institutionally and nationally a real failure of nerve when it came to embracing Cubism, Expressionism or any form of abstraction, which inhibited most British public collections until well into the second half of the twentieth century. The acquisition of German avant-garde material proved particularly intractable. Michael Sadler, who has been previously mentioned, was almost the sole British private collector to take an interest in this area. Like Campbell Dodgson, he acquired Nolde's etchings and woodcuts directly from the artist before the First World War, but his taste also extended to work by Pechstein, Max Ernst and, above all, Kandinsky, with whom he corresponded from 1912 onwards. The only exhibition to focus on twentieth-century German art was that arranged at the New Burlington Galleries in July 1938 to act as a riposte to Hitler's 'Entartete Kunst' (Degenerate Art) exhibition of the previous year; the representation of living artists had to be confined to those outside Germany, the profits from the admission charges or any sales being designated for the relief of refugee artists. Max Beckmann came from Holland to lecture in conjunction with the exhibition, but its impact was of a political rather than an artistic nature and there were no profits to distribute to refugee artists. The difficulty of returning some of the works afterwards to lenders from abroad meant that, in at least one case, the artist had to endure the ignominy of having his material seized during the war and destroyed as the work of an enemy alien.[26]

One other audacious attempt to introduce modern German art to the British public was made in February 1944 by the Director of the Leicester Museums and Art Gallery, Trevor Thomas; his exhibition of this material from private sources, organised in conjunction with the local Free German League of Culture, had to be disguised

under the title of the *Mid-European Art Exhibition*. Thomas purchased three key works from the exhibition for Leicester, a Feininger painting of 1916, a Nolde watercolour of 1910 from the Hess family who, before the war, in Erfurt, had been among the most prominent patrons of the Expressionists, and, most striking of all, Franz Marc's painting of 1912, *Rote Frau*, which belonged to a Glasgow collector.[27] In 1942 Hind did accept for the British Museum a substantial gift of fifteen portfolios of prints from a German refugee, Erich Goeritz, who had been one of the lenders to the 1938 exhibition. Goeritz had been a textile manufacturer from Chemnitz and one of Lovis Corinth's most important patrons, so the gift included seven of Corinth's portfolios as well as others by Slevogt, Barlach, Kokoschka, and the first two Bauhaus portfolios, published in 1921–4.[28]

Hind's successor A.E. Popham did, however, materially harm the subsequent prospects for the British Museum of acquiring a reputation as a serious contender for twentieth-century material, by rejecting in the early 1950s the offer of the German émigré art historian Dr Rosa Schapire to present her virtually complete collection of the prints of Schmidt-Rottluff. Together with some paintings and drawings this was all she had brought with her when she arrived in London just two weeks before the outbreak of World War II. As a result the graphic work was eventually divided after her death in 1954 among fifteen museums, thirteen in Germany and only two in Britain, the Victoria and Albert Museum, and Leicester.[29] Popham, who was linked to the Bloomsbury artists through family connections and personal friendships, was not without a sense of responsibility towards modern acquisitions; indeed he petitioned the Trustees for an annual purchase grant to be used for this purpose immediately after the war, when the Department of Prints and Drawings ceased to have control over the purchasing of prints and drawings for the Contemporary Art Society.[30] But he recoiled from what Wyndham Lewis had once described as 'the surgery of the senses'[31] exemplified in the work of the German Expressionist woodcut artists, and, like so many of his peers, found it difficult to accommodate the more radical artistic movements within the historical continuum embraced by the Department's collections.

The Trustees only acceded to Popham's request in so far as they agreed, on 9 July 1949, that the existing purchase grant could be used for the purchase of contemporary prints, but the situation atrophied until 1967 when a survey of the collection, undertaken at their request by Ronald Alley of the Tate Gallery, made its weaknesses clear. The initial response was the cautious allocation of £1,000, far less in real value than the £200 proposed by Carpenter in 1848, to match an equivalent donation by the C.G. and S.L. Bernstein Trust for the purchase of prints and drawings executed after 1890. A more substantial commitment was made at the beginning of 1975 when the then Director of the Museum, Sir John Pope-Hennessy, appointed a curator (Frances Carey) with specific responsibility for developing a modern collection; this was followed by another new post in the summer of 1976 (Antony Griffiths) with a general brief for the print collection as a whole.

Although there was a sufficient foundation of good material to form a respectable collection, the omissions were nonetheless so great that the problem remained as to how to repair them in a period of high inflation, without dissipating the Museum's resources over too wide a field, or duplicating areas of acquisition which might be more appropriate to another of the national collections. Therefore it was determined to forgo any further development of the Department's limited holdings of photographs or posters in deference to the Victoria and Albert Museum's much stronger collections, and, with only occasional exceptions, to do the same for artists' books for which the National Art Library at the V & A and the British Library are the main repositories. Contemporary prints remain a difficult issue because the British Museum has neither the resources nor the storage space appropriate to cope with much of the material published since the early 1960s. At present it severely limits its acquisitions of prints (though not drawings) executed within the last twenty-five years to gifts or material acquired through private funds, often designated for the artists of nationalities largely unrepresented in the other public collections, for example artists from Scandinavia and Israel. There are few rigid lines of demarcation but a fluid set of relationships which reflect the different histories of the institutions and the consequent biases of their collecting. The Tate Gallery has generally concentrated on acquiring individually impressive items for exhibition purposes, while of the two great reference collections at the V & A and the British Museum, the former pursues its traditional function in relation to the applied arts, design and the development of new techniques in printmaking.

The Department's acquisitions policy has always been determined by its role as a study collection, a purpose which in the late twentieth century has expanded beyond catering for individual study to more communal teaching activity. However, a significant change wrought by the momentum of acquisition created for twentieth-century material since the late 1970s has been the importance given to the exhibitions programme. This provides a focus for collecting, a relatively swift means of publicising what has been achieved by the Museum, a permanent record, in the form of illustrated catalogues, of whole sections of the collection, and the basis for further acquisition. This policy has brought to fruition four major exhibitions between 1980 and 1990 on modern printmaking in America, Germany, Czechoslovakia and Britain, with two more concentrating on Scandinavia and printmaking in Paris planned for 1996–7. The two most decisive exhibitions which altered the whole emphasis of the collection were those on American prints from 1879 to 1979, held in 1980, and *The Print in Germany 1880–1933*, in 1984. Most of the work in the former case, dating from the 1920s or later, was acquired in two visits to New York in 1979. American prints, focusing on the years up to 1965, have since become one of the strongest aspects of the collection and another exhibition is planned for the end of the decade to display the very considerable additions made after 1979. The range of material has been extended to cover prints by artists working in Canada and Mexico and we would like to add further representation of artists from Latin America.

The *Print in Germany 1880–1933* involved a much greater expenditure, although some of the most important exhibits, such as the Käthe Kollwitz prints and the Bauhaus portfolios, were already in the collection. The starting-point was the purchase of two Expressionist lithographs in 1978 and 1979, Kirchner's *Hugo am Tisch* ('Hugo lying at table') of 1915 and a version of Nolde's *Junges Paar* ('Young Couple') of 1913, on which the Museum spent more money than on any modern print before, with the exception of Munch's *Vampyr* purchased in 1970. Although both these items were acquired from London dealers, London has not been the main market for modern prints since the late 1920s and thus much of our purchasing has been conducted elsewhere, subject to the vagaries of foreign exchange rates. It was no coincidence that the initial phase of vigorous buying for the American and German print exhibitions occurred at a time when the pound was relatively strong against the dollar. In more recent years the Department has acquired relatively little through the sale-rooms, needing the opportunity that dealers can afford for reflection and for mobilising the support which has been necessary for the modern material. Occasionally, it has been possible to take advantage of the fickle behaviour of auction prices, most notably at the Kornfeld auction in Berne in 1981 when the record price paid for one Kirchner lithograph of 1914 seemed momentarily to paralyse the bidders, so that the Museum was able to secure for almost a fifth of the price another Kirchner lithograph of the same date and comparable importance in the next lot, which had been its particular objective. Immediately after this sale came that of the collection of Reinhard Piper, Beckmann's publisher and patron in Munich, where the Museum was able to buy a range of items by adopting unusually flexible bidding tactics because the curator was there to confer with the agent throughout. This was a commonplace occurrence in Dodgson's day but the pressures of modern museum life do not usually allow the same sacrifice of time.[32]

Since 1984 rising prices and the static level of the Museum's purchase grant have made further acquisition of the work of the most famous German Expressionists well-nigh impossible, but there have been opportunities to obtain excellent examples by some of the less prominent names, Paul Gangolf, Bernhard Kretzschmar and Erich

Mueller-Kraus, for example. A fine collection of the prints of Rolf Nesch (1893–1975), who began his career in Hamburg then emigrated to Norway in 1933, has also been assembled over the past fifteen years, which reflects every aspect of his endlessly inventive imagery and technical experimentation, while in the late 1980s two major prizes were secured at auction in New York and in Hamburg: Heinrich Campendonk's hand-coloured woodcut of a *Half-Nude with Cat* of 1912, and Nolde's astonishing series of eight etchings from 1905, *Phantasien* (see p. 218), which were rejected with contumely by the thirteen print rooms in Germany to whom the artist sent them at the time.[33] Despite the financial constraints, the interest in German art remains important for the collection as a whole, and has led to acquisitions of drawings from the eighteenth century through to the work of contemporary artists. Within the field of prints, it has also focused attention on the German Romantic period, where a steady stream of acquisitions from 1975 onwards led to the exhibition in 1994 of *German Printmaking in the Age of Goethe*. The renewed importance of modern print acquisitions has attracted gifts of money and material from artists and private owners in Britain and abroad. A Swedish donor, for example, has provided a fund for the improvement of the Scandinavian holdings. Another collection, of twentieth-century Czechoslovak prints, was put together by the National Gallery in Prague in the mid-1980s for presentation to the British Museum, in exchange for a collection of British prints from Blake to Hockney, purchased by the Museum's curators with money donated by the friends' organisation, the British Museum Society.

Despite the 'strange faces, new images and incredible sounds' which have surrounded us in the twentieth century[34] and affected both private taste and public policy, the central purpose of the Museum's prints and drawings collection remains unaltered:

A leading characteristic of the present day is the unwholesome desire for knowledge to be served up and assimilated in essence form. The news of the day must be concentrated in a nutshell, the means for the study of a language must be arranged and tied into a parcel so that it can readily be 'picked up'. And there are even some amateurs who desire to gain a trained eye and to become expert in prints by some equally rapid and easy 'royal road', or by the help of some kind of ready-reckoner. Books are good and may be of the greatest value; but they can do little more than open the door and show the way; and the eye cannot be trained by any hot-house or artificial process. To become a real expert and to acquire a substantial knowledge of prints in their numerous styles and departments, the amateur must be willing to go through a steady course of study with the prints before him; and no one place in the country affords such a grand opportunity for the purpose as the Print Room of the British Museum. The room is large, a quiet pervades the place, and the surroundings encourage the student onwards in the pursuit of his hobby.[35]

1. 'A museum department of prints' in *Prints and Books. Informal Papers by William M. Ivins Jr.*, New York 1969, p. 5.

2. See the editor's note preceding the article by Francis Bullard on 'The Print Department of the Museum of Fine Arts, Boston', *Print Collector's Quarterly* II 1912, pp. 183–207.

3. Ivins, op. cit. p. 4.

4. 'Does your art collection express your community', 1964, in *A. Hyatt Mayor: Selected Writings and a Bibliography*, New York 1983, pp. 113–23.

5. Ivins, op. cit. p. 5.

6. From a review in *The Times*, 11 February 1909, quoted in H. C. Levis, *A Descriptive Bibliography of the Most Important Books in the English Language Relating to the Art and History of Engraving and the Collection of Prints*, London 1912, p. 79.

7. The important collection of 11,000 bookplates which Maurice formed with his brother Max (d. 1911) was presented to the Department of Prints and Drawings by their sister-in-law in 1932.

8. See Colvin's letter of 6 July 1924 to Campbell Dodgson in the Department of Prints and Drawings Letter Book.

9. See the correspondence of 5–9 July 1930 between Campbell Dodgson and Ian Malcolm in the Departmental Letter Book for 1930–3. The depression in prices between 1930 and 1932 led Dodgson to recommend a temporary halt in the disposal of British Museum duplicates at the Leipzig sales.

10. Lugt 2773.

11. Lugt 2770. Rudolf von Gutmann was an industrialist who amassed an outstanding collection between the wars of prints by the early German masters, and by Rembrandt and Ostade.

12. In an article for the *Jahrbuch des Kgl. Kunstsammlungen* 28, pp. 21–33.

13. See Departmental Letter Book, May 1909.

14. *The Saturday Review*, 28 May 1927.

15. See Ruth Fine, *Lessing J. Rosenwald. Tribute to a Collector*, National Gallery of Art, Washington DC 1982, p. 47. Hind's typescript and his original manuscript are now in the Library of Congress.

16. Lugt 1488.

17. Report dated 1 November 1950.

18. The situation was further complicated by the fact that Colnaghi's had only obtained the foreign currency with which to buy the Lichtenstein Collection on the undertaking they would then sell the prints abroad.

19. 'Excerpts from an interview with Hyatt Mayor' conducted by Paul Cummings in 1968, in *A. Hyatt Mayor. Selected Writings and a Bibliography*, New York 1983, p. 167.

20. Presented by Dr G. H. Fowler and Miss F. L. Cannan respectively.

21. Information on departmental acquisitions was published in the *British Museum Quarterly*, which appeared from 1926 to 1973.

22. Entry for 27 March 1856 in *The English Notebooks*, ed. Randall Stewart, London 1941, p. 294.

23. Aphorism 39, 1915 from 'Die 100 Aphorismen. Das zweite Gesicht' in *Franz Marc Schriften*, ed. Klaus Lankheit, Cologne 1978, p. 197.

24. 'Zur Geschichte des Dresdner Kupferstichkabinetts' in *Mitteilungen aus den Sächsischen Kunstsammlungen*, III 1912, pp. 1–12.

25. Departmental Letter Book, 24 October 1911. The French *dépôt légal* was levied only on professional printers and publishers; therefore artists who printed their own editions escaped the net.

26. The case in point was Rolf Nesch, who had emigrated to Norway from Hamburg in 1933. I am indebted to Eivind Otto Hjelle for supplying me with copies of the correspondence from the Nesch estate relating to this issue.

27. See Barry Herbert and Alisdair Hinshelwood, *The Expressionist Revolution in German Art. A catalogue to the 19th and 20th Century German paintings, Drawings, Prints and Sculpture in the Permanent Collection of Leicestershire Museums and Art Gallery*, 1978. Trevor Thomas was instrumental in securing the release of Hans Hess from a British internment camp in order to work for the Leicester Art Gallery, where he eventally became Keeper of Art.

28. See Carey and Griffiths, *The Print in Germany 1880–1933*, 1984, reprinted 1993, pp. 7 and 86.

29. Carey and Griffiths, op. cit. pp. 7–8 and 226.

30. The Department continued to benefit from the Society in return for the payment of an annual subscription, but on a much reduced level. Finally, in 1992, the CAS changed the basis of its operations as it was felt that the national museums no longer needed to use it as a conduit for modern acquisitions.

31. 'Note on some German Woodcuts at the Twenty-One Gallery' originally published in *Blast no. 1*, 1914, and reprinted in *Wyndham Lewis on Art*, ed. Walter Michel and C. J. Fox, London 1969.

32. Antony Griffiths gave a lively account of how the 1984 German print exhibition was put together in 'Acquiring an exhibition', *British Museum Society Bulletin*, November 1984, pp. 14–17.

33. Carey and Griffiths, op. cit. p. 133.

34. Franz Marc, Aphorism 25, in K. Lankheit op. cit. p. 193.

35. Alfred Whitman, 'The Print Room at the British Museum', *The Printseller*, January 1903, p. 16.

91 Charles-Melchior Descourtis (1753–1820) after Frédéric-Jean Schall (1752–1825)

Les Espiègles (Mischiefmakers), c.1798

Illustrated in colour between pages 112 and 113

Etching and engraving printed from four plates.
700 × 431 mm

French printmaking of the second half of the eighteenth century was remarkable for the variety and refinement of new colour-printing techniques developed to enable the faithful translation of drawings, pastels, watercolours and gouaches. Descourtis was one of the most skilful practitioners of a technique of multiple-plate colour-printing which he learnt from Jean-François Janinet (1752–1814), who minutely abraded the surface of his plates so they would retain just enough of the inks to create the effect of subtle washes of colour. This method, known as the *manière-de-lavis*, was more complex than the colour-printing techniques favoured in England at the same time, where artists working with aquatint and stipple-engraving generally confined themselves to a single plate.

The success of colour printmakers like Janinet, Descourtis and Debucourt depended upon a perfection of colouring that harmonised with the elegance of form and expression in the original composition. Descourtis in this instance was working after a cabinet picture by Schall (now in the Louvre) whose work he frequently engraved in the 1790s (the British Museum owns another print of this type by Descourtis after Schall, *The Surprised Lover*, conceived as a pair to *Les Espiègles*); Schall continued to work in much the same vein until his death, suffering no apparent diminution to his clientele during the Revolutionary period. This did, however, have adverse economic consequences for unduly expensive methods of colour-printing which led to the decline of the multiple-plate technique. (See John Ittmann in Victor Carlson and John Ittmann, *Regency to Empire. French Printmaking 1715–1814*, Baltimore Museum of Art and the Minneapolis Institute of Arts 1985, pp. 22–3.)

1925-1-14-43. Purchased from the London dealer Puttick and Simpson for £89.5.0

92 Carl Wilhelm Kolbe (1759–1835)

Youth Playing a Lyre to a Maiden by a Fountain, 1803

Etching. 412 × 530 mm

Martens 95

Kolbe was the most remarkable printmaker of all the German Romantic artists. He drew his inspiration from the oak forests surrounding Dessau, where he spent most of his career, the idyllic poetry and pictures by the Swiss author Salomon Gessner (1730–88), and the work of the seventeenth-century Dutch landscape etchers, such as Anthonie Waterloo (1609–90) and Paul Potter (1625–54). His compositions, however, far surpassed those of his artistic mentors in originality, the most extraordinary works being the twenty-eight etchings of giant vegetation, or *Kräuterblätter* (vegetable sheets) as he termed them, which he made between 1800 and the end of his life (see Antony Griffiths and Frances Carey, *German Printmaking in the Age of Goethe*, British Museum Press 1994, cat. 72). The loveliest of these were the Arcadian scenes executed around the turn of the century, including this example and the elegiac *Auch ich war in Arkadien* (I too was in Arcadia) of nearly identical size.

The British Museum's impression was one of a number of prints by Kolbe purchased from an exhibition organised by the London dealer Christopher Mendez in 1978, which played an important role in establishing the artist's current reputation.

1978-6-24-16. Purchased

92

93 Edvard Munch (1863–1944)
Eifersucht (Jealousy), 1896

Lithograph printed on Japan paper. 457 × 572
Schiefler 58. Signed in pencil

Munch's move to Paris from Berlin in February 1896 enabled him to take advantage of the professional printing facilities there and the lively climate of interest in original printmaking. He stayed until the spring of 1897, creating a prodigious quantity of work and experimenting with techniques like mezzotint and woodcut that he had not tried before, as well as developing his expertise in lithography. *Jealousy* was among the first lithographs Munch had printed by Auguste Clot; he made two versions of the composition, based on a painting of 1894–5 done in Berlin. The larger of these is catalogued here, and was one of the subjects selected for a series of twenty lithographs and five woodcuts entitled *The Mirror*, which Munch intended to reflect a series of paintings he had exhibited in 1895 under the collective heading of *Love*. These were later subsumed within the concept of the 'frieze of life' which was to preoccupy Munch for more than thirty years. *The Mirror* never materialised as a portfolio but the twenty-five prints, including *The Scream*, *Vampire*, *The Kiss*, *Lovers in the Waves* and *Death in the Sickroom*, were exhibited in the Diorama in Christiania (Oslo) upon Munch's return to Norway in 1897. (See Bente Torjusen, 'The Mirror', in *Edvard Munch. Symbol and Images*, National Gallery of Art, Washington, DC 1978, pp. 185–227.)

The figures in *Jealousy* refer to Munch's circle of literary and artistic friends who congregated in Berlin at the wine cellar 'Zum schwarzen Ferkel' (the Black Piglet). The artist has represented himself dallying in the background with one of his female muses, Dagny Juell, whose husband, Stanislaw Przybyszewski, is the brooding figure in the foreground. Juell was murdered in 1901 but Munch reused the motif between 1902 and 1908 to express the violent nature of his relationship with another woman, Tulla Larsen, who had finally rejected him for a younger painter, Arne Kavli.

1979–12–15–18. Purchased

94 František Kupka (1871–1957)
La Voie du Silence (The Way of Silence), 1900–3

Illustrated in colour between pages 112 and 113

Etching and aquatint; 349 × 345 mm
Stamped with the artist's signature

Kupka left Prague for Vienna in 1892, eventually settling in Paris in 1896, where he later became a leading exponent of abstract colour theory. Once in Paris, Kupka was quick to criticise what he now regarded as the unhealthy cultural climate of *fin-de-siècle* Vienna, but his work remained indebted for some time to the metaphysical and theosophical influences he had absorbed during his residence there.

The Way of Silence is one of three subjects which form a series of vividly coloured aquatints existing in several variants under the collective title of *The Voices of Silence*. The other compositions are *The Beginning of Life*, showing an embryo emerging from the spiritual emanation of a lotus flower; another version of *The Way of Silence*; and *Defiance*, an occult image of a massive, brooding, sphinx-like colossus presiding over a barren terrain which directly invokes the first stanza of Edgar Allan Poe's poem *Dreamland* (1844–5). The series as a whole is preoccupied with the enigma of life, expressed in the inscription 'Quam ad causam sumus' (Why are we here) on a pastel related to *The Way of Silence*, while the lonely figure proceeding along the avenue of sphinxes represents the artist himself.

1989–7–22–38. Purchased with funds from the Playfair Bequest

95 Josef Čapek (1887–1945)
Figure called Lelio, 1913

Etching. 347 × 230 mm
Signed, titled and dated in pencil

Josef Čapek, the brother of the famous writer Karel Čapek (1880–1939), was at the centre of Prague's dynamic cultural life in the early decades of the twentieth century, as a painter, printmaker, illustrator, writer, critic and editor. Following a visit to Paris in 1910–11, Čapek developed his own Cubist style in common with a number of Czech artists, designers and architects working between 1910 and 1918; in addition to their contacts abroad, they also had the example in Prague of one of the best collections of Cubist paintings by Picasso and Braque, belonging to the art historian, and future director of the National Gallery, Vincenc Kramář. Čapek's single-sheet prints had previously been executed in woodcut and linocut; in this instance, however, his choice of medium echoes the Cubist drypoints of Picasso and Braque. It was entirely appropriate to the most rigorous of all Čapek's Cubist compositions, based on a painting which is now in the National Gallery in Prague.

By 1918, the date of the foundation of Czechoslovakia, Čapek had begun to focus more on social themes. His social and political awareness remained a constant feature of all aspects of his work until he was arrested after the German occupation of Czechoslovakia, spending the last five years of his life in concentration camps.

1985–11–9–33. Acquired by exchange from the National Gallery in Prague

Figura zraní Lelio   Josef Čapek
                                        1913

96 Edward Wadsworth (1889–1949)
Illustration (Typhoon), 1914/15

Woodcut printed in black on Japan paper. 280 × 255 mm
Signed in pencil and inscribed by the artist with a quotation from Joseph Conrad's short story, *Typhoon*. (1st edn 1902)

Wadsworth was a founding member of the Vorticist movement in London, launched in 1913 under the aegis of Ezra Pound and Wyndham Lewis; their aim was to espouse an uncompromising modernism appropriate to the machine age, which would capture an 'essential movement and activity' as opposed to what they deemed to be 'the tasteful passivity of Picasso'. The movement quickly gained transatlantic recognition in the form of the patronage of the New York lawyer John Quinn, who expressed admiration for Wadsworth's woodcuts when they were shown as part of the Vorticist exhibition at the Penguin Club in New York in 1917.

Wadsworth's work as a printmaker was concentrated within the period 1913 to 1920, when the woodcut became his principal means of expression. His compositions can be largely divided into what his friend and fellow Vorticist Frederick Etchells called 'the elementary architecture' of England's northern industrial towns and villages; those designed in the Aegean where Wadsworth served in Naval Intelligence in 1916–17; the remarkable 'dazzle' ships based on his experiences of supervising the camouflage of allied shipping docked in Liverpool; and a final, apocalyptic group of the blast furnaces from the Black Country of the industrial Midlands.

Typhoon was unusual in being the only woodcut directly linked to a literary source, Conrad's description of the engine-room of a steamship plying the China Seas at the height of a typhoon: 'Painted white they rose high into the dusk of the skylight, sloping like a roof: and the whole lofty space resembled the interior of a monument ... divided at intervals by floors or iron grating, a mass of gloom lingering in the middle, within the columnar stir of machinery ...'. The subject was ideal for a Vorticist composition, prompting one of the most striking images of Wadsworth's career. (See Carey and Griffiths, *Avant-garde British Printmaking 1914–1960*, London 1990, pp. 29–41.)

1924-2-9-143. Presented by the Contemporary Art Society

97 Ernst Ludwig Kirchner (1867–1945)
Portrait of Otto Müller, 1915

Illustrated in colour between pages 112 and 113

Woodcut printed from a single block in black, blue and brown. 363 × 305 mm
Dube 251, fourth state. Signed and annotated 'Probedruck' (proof impression)

Kirchner was the most important of the printmakers associated with the *Brücke*, of which he was a founder member in 1905. He made prints throughout his career (though with less frequency from 1927 onwards), producing a total *oeuvre* of nearly 1,000 woodcuts, more than 650 etchings and drypoints and over 450 lithographs. Otto Müller (1874–1930), who was the subject of this and one other portrait by Kirchner, became Kirchner's close friend and a member of the *Brücke* in 1910. The two prints were made in Berlin between mid-September and mid-December 1915 when Kirchner had been given leave from the army on the grounds of nervous and physical debilitation. As happened on other occasions, his fraught psychological condition gave rise to an astonishing burst of creativity in painting, drawing and printmaking, which embraced some of his most daring experiments with colour woodblock printing. The portrait catalogued here stands halfway between a conventional woodcut and a monotype in so far as it was printed from a single block painted in different colours; it was only at the third state that Kirchner introduced the remarkable features of the cat with the bow in the top right-hand corner and the two 'eyes' in the bottom corners. The Hamburg judge Gustav Schiefler (see cat. 88), who published the first *catalogue raisonné* of Kirchner's prints in 1926 and 1931, owned this particular impression of the very rare fourth state. (See Carey and Griffiths, *The Print in Germany*, reprinted 1993, cat. 80.)

1983-4-16-3. Purchased

98 László Moholy-Nagy (1895–1946)
Construction VI, 1923

Lithograph printed on grey paper. 600 × 440 mm
Signed in pencil

Moholy-Nagy, who passed briefly through Vienna after leaving Hungary in 1919, moved to Berlin in 1920 in search of a livelier cultural milieu. His friendship with the Russian artist El Lissitzky confirmed his interest in Constructivism, for which he became one of the most influential apologists in his capacity as a teacher at the Bauhaus, where he was appointed to run the basic course and the Metal Workshop in 1923. By the mid-1920s he was endeavouring to move away from the fine arts and

96

99

the concept of individually crafted forms, in favour of mechanical means of design and production.

His printmaking was confined to the years 1919–23, consisting largely of small abstract wood-engravings, lino-cuts and a few drypoints. His one engagement with lithography was the elegant series of six *Constructions* of which an example is reproduced here. This portfolio and another Constructivist album, Lissitzky's second *Proun* portfolio, were part of an ambitious print-publishing venture undertaken in 1923 by the Kestner-Gesellschaft, a privately supported society in Hanover founded in 1916 for the advancement of modern art. The artists worked closely with a firm of commercial printers in Hanover, to whom Moholy probably supplied very precise drawings which were then redrawn on the stones under his supervision. The British Museum's copy was previously owned by the artist's widow, Sybil Moholy-Nagy, and is numbered 29 out of the edition of fifty, but it contains one lithograph which does not appear in other sets. (See Krisztina Passuth, *Moholy-Nagy*, London 1985, and Carey and Griffiths, *The Print in Germany*, reprinted 1993, cat. 215–20.)

1983–3–5–56 (6). Purchased

99 Kurt Schwitters (1887–1948)

Untitled, 1923

Lithograph printed in orange. 556 × 445 mm
Signed in pencil and numbered 48/2

'Merz' was Schwitters's unique contribution to the iconoclasm of the avant-garde in Germany after the First World War. He annexed the second syllable of the word 'Kommerz' as in 'Kommerz und Privatbank' (Commercial and Private Bank) to become the collective heading for the whole range of his activities, whether visual or poetic, which achieved their effect through ironic juxtapositions and collages of fragmentary images, words, materials or sounds. In 1923 he embarked upon his most ambitious project, the 'Merzbau', a collaged environment made of random objects and detritus, which he recreated in two other locations as political events impelled him to flee from Germany in 1937, first to Norway and then to England in 1940.

At the same time as his distinctive 'Merz' style emerged in the early 1920s, Schwitters was profoundly influenced by the *De Stijl* movement in Holland and the Constructivists he met in Berlin such as Lissitzky, who encouraged Schwitters's experimentation with typography and design. The *Merzmappe* (Merz portfolio), Schwitters's only portfolio of prints, united many elements of his current preoccupations, the very details of their physical execution reflecting his *collagiste* approach. They were made at a local printing plant in Schwitters's home town of Hanover, where he was accustomed to salvage waste materials for use in his other work. For the lithographs he transferred freshly printed fragments of papers of all kinds – advertisements, cigarette wrappers etc. – directly on to the stones in order to build his compositions. Each of the six lithographs in the series was printed in a different colour (the British Museum owns one other, printed in black) and the portfolio officially published in an edition of fifty, as the third issue under his own *Merz* imprint, in emulation of the Kestner portfolios. Although Schwitters produced no further prints of his own, the fifth issue of *Merz* was a companion portfolio of lithographs entitled 7 *Arpaden* by Hans Arp.

1983–5–21–3. Purchased

100 Stuart Davis (1894–1964)

Sixth Avenue El, 1931

Lithograph. 304 × 455 mm
Cole 16. Numbered 17/25 and signed in pencil

Davis made his first group of eleven lithographs in less than a year in Paris, where he arrived from America in 1928, already a convinced modernist. After he returned to New York in the summer of 1929 he had difficulty adjusting to the abrupt change in the scale and character of his environment, but his next bout of lithography in 1931 resulted in five more prints of much bolder composition than the Parisian subjects. They demonstrated his successful assimilation of the European stylistic influences of synthetic Cubism and Surrealism to a distinctively American subject-matter. The prints were well received at the time when the first two to be publicly shown, *Barber Shop Chord* and *Sixth Avenue El*, were submitted to the Downtown Gallery's American Printmakers' annual exhibition in 1931.

1983–6–25–42. Purchased. The British Museum's impression came from the artist's estate. *Two Figures and El* from the same group made in 1931 was previously purchased in 1979

17/25   Stuart Davis

100

Bibliography of Print Catalogues Cited in Abbreviated Form

BARTSCH Adam von Bartsch, *Le Peintre-Graveur*, 21 vols, Vienna 1803–21

BARTSCH Adam von Bartsch, *Catalogue raisonné de toutes les estampes qui forment l'oeuvre de Rembrandt*, 2 vols, Vienna 1797, revised by Christopher White and Karel G. Boon in vols 18 and 19 of the Hollstein series

BERLIN *Katalog der Ornamentstichsammlung der Staatlichen Kunstbibliothek, Berlin*, 2 vols, Berlin 1936 and 1939

CAMPBELL–WEES M. J. Campbell and J. D. Wees, *John Martin, Visionary Printmaker*, York City Art Gallery 1992

CHALONER SMITH John Chaloner Smith, *British Mezzotinto Portraits*, 4 vols, London 1883–4

CLAYTON Judy Egerton, *Wright of Derby*, Tate Gallery 1990, with a catalogue of prints after Wright's paintings by Timothy Clayton

COLE Sylvan Cole, *Stuart Davis, Graphic Work and Related Paintings* (ed. Jane Myers), New York 1986

DELTEIL Loys Delteil, *Le Peintre-Graveur illustré XVII: Camille Pissarro*, Paris 1923

DODGSON Campbell Dodgson, *Catalogue of Early German and Flemish Woodcuts in the British Museum*, 2 vols, London 1903 and 1911

DODGSON Campbell Dodgson, *Etchings and Drypoints by Muirhead Bone*, London 1909

DUBE A. and W.-D. Dube, *E. L. Kirchner, das graphische Werk*, 2nd edn, 2 vols, Munich 1980

FAGAN Louis Fagan, *A Catalogue Raisonné of the Engraved Work of William Woollett*, London 1885

FIRMIN-DIDOT Ambroise Firmin-Didot, *Les Drevet, Catalogue Raisonné de leur Oeuvre*, Paris 1876

GLOBE Alexander Globe, *Peter Stent, London Print-seller c.1642–1665*, Vancouver 1985

HARRIS J. C. Harris, *Edouard Manet, Graphic Works*, 2nd edn revised by J. M. Smith, San Francisco 1990

HIND A. M. Hind, *Early Italian Engraving*, 7 vols, London 1938 and 1948

HIND A. M. Hind, *Engraving in England in the Sixteenth and Seventeenth Centuries*, 3 vols, Cambridge 1952–64

HOLLSTEIN F. W. H. Hollstein, *Dutch and Flemish Etchings, Engravings and Woodcuts c.1450–1700*, Amsterdam 1949 continuing (43 vols so far published)

HOLLSTEIN F. W. H. Hollstein, *German Etchings, Engravings and Woodcuts c.1400–1700*, Amsterdam 1954 continuing (36 vols so far published)

JANIS Eugenia Parry Janis, *Degas Monotypes, Essay, Catalogue and Checklist*, Fogg Art Museum, Cambridge (Mass.) 1968

KLIPSTEIN August Klipstein, *Käthe Kollwitz, Verzeichnis des graphischen Werkes*, Bern 1955

KORNFELD E. W. Kornfeld, E. Mongan and H. Joachim, *Paul Gauguin, Catalogue Raisonné of his Prints*, Bern 1988

LEHRS Max Lehrs, *Geschichte und kritischer Katalog des deutschen, niederländischen und französischen Kupferstichs im XV Jahrhundert*, 9 vols, Vienna 1908–34

LIEURE J. Lieure, *Jacques Callot*, 5 vols, Paris 1924–7

MARTENS Ulf Martens, *Der Zeichner und Radierer Carl Wilhelm Kolbe*, Berlin 1978

MAUQUOY-HENDRICKX Marie Mauquoy-Hendrickx, *L'Iconographie d'Antoine van Dyck, catalogue raisonné*, 2nd edn, 2 vols, Brussels 1991

MELLERIO André Mellerio, *Odilon Redon*, Paris 1913

PAULSON Ronald Paulson, *Hogarth's Graphic Works*, 3rd edn, 2 vols, London 1989

PENNINGTON Richard Pennington, *Descriptive Catalogue of the etched Works of Wenceslaus Hollar*, Cambridge 1982

RIGGS Timothy A. Riggs, *Hieronymus Cock, Printmaker and Publisher*, New York 1977

ROBERT-DUMESNIL A. P. F. Robert-Dumesnil, *Le Peintre-Graveur Français*, 11 vols, Paris 1835–71

SCHIEFLER Gustav Schiefler, *Verzeichnis des graphischen Werks Edvard Munchs*, 2 vols, Berlin 1907 and 1927

SCHIEFLER–MOSEL Gustav Schiefler, revised by Christel Mosel, *Emil Nolde, das graphische Werk*, 2 vols, Cologne 1966

SCHREIBER Wilhelm Ludwig Schreiber, *Handbuch der Holz und Metallschnitte des XV Jahrhunderts*, 9 vols, Leipzig 1926–30

WITTROCK Wolfgang Wittrock, *Toulouse-Lautrec, the Complete Prints*, 2 vols, London 1985

ZIGROSSER Carl Zigrosser, 'The Etchings of Edward Hopper' in *Prints*, ed. C. Zigrosser, Philadelphia 1962

Appendices

Appendix A

Transcript of the Entries on the Volumes of Prints, Nos 1 to 325, in the Catalogue of Sir Hans Sloane's Library, British Library, Sloane MS 3972B–C

Antony Griffiths

Slips of the pen are occasionally corrected, abbreviations expanded, punctuation added, but errors of spelling or transcription are not corrected. Sloane's numbering of the volumes is in Roman numerals; these are here changed to Arabic. Square brackets after the first number at the beginning of entries denote later renumberings by Scheuchzer or Stack; in the middle of entries they denote omissions or editorial comments. Round brackets in the descriptions denote later additions, almost always by Stack.

NB Scheuchzer's index to the original number sequence of volumes 1 to 622 (drawn up before he had himself renumbered the volumes) is to be found in MS. Sloane 4019, ff. 220–4.

Pr.1 to 74 on pages 809–16, compiled in 1705

Pr.1 [2]
A very large book of prints of severall masters upon severall subjects

Pr.2 [1]
A large book of prints of towns, provinces etc. (with an index by Dr Scheuchzer)

Pr.3 [2]
Another collection of the same (with an index by the same)

Pr.4 [33]
A large book of prints in wood of severall masters (some very rare with an index by Dr Scheuchzer)

Pr.5 [56]
A large book of blew paper with prints of severall masters in wood & copper

Pr.6 [368]
Res memorabiles quae hisce proximis annis in Gallia contigerunt etc. A Paris par Francois Despres

Pr.7 [91]
Medallions du Roy

Pr.8 [151]
Effigies Romanorum Imperatorum. Petri Aquilae. Romae 1681
— Regum Francorum in fol.

Pr.9 [152]
— Romanorum Pontificum
— Regum Hispaniae in fol. Rome

Pr.10 [46]
A book of blew paper of prints cutt in copper
(birds by N. Robert, Barlow and others. Florilegium of Galleo with an index. Observatory of Greenwich Park)

Pr.11 [150]
Flowers
Nic. Robert's Receuil des oyseaux. Paris 1676

Pr.12 [362]
Clement de Jonghe. Landskips
Perelle's landskips
Zeaman's ships
Vauquier's flowerpotts, with blank paper

Pr.13 [347]
Landskips by Vandermeulen
Cheminées par Le Pautre. 1663
Frises par le mesme
Franciscus van Wingaert
Jo. Lutma Compartemente. 1653
Jos. Dinants grotesques
Frises, Polifilo Zancarli. 1636. Visscher exc.
— Brebiette inv. Ciartres exc.
Landskips Antoni Waterlo
— Perelle
— Berghem
Vases, Horatius Scoppa Neap. fec. 1642
Vestiges des antiquités de Rome or Roma antica
(with an index by Dr Scheuchzer)

Pr.14 [439]
Representatio (of a carroussel) of Johan. Friderick de Wurtemburg. 6 Nov. 1609 in fol.

Pr.15 [436; Min. 187]
Petri Schenkii, Hecatompolis etc.

Pr.16 [446]
— Paradysus oculorum

Pr.17 [347]
Conspectus villae Regiae Risvicianae
— urbis Roterodami
— Lutetiae Parisiorum
— Versaliae
— Urbis Hamburgi
— Berolini & Cliviae

Pr.18 [449]
Le Potre inven. & fecit Le Blond excud
— trophées d'armes
— veues, grottes & fontaines
— montans des trophées etc. 1659
— rinceaux differens feuillages etc.
— frises etc.

— lambris
— ornemens des panneaux pour les lambris
— bordures de tableau

Pr.19 [298]
Vases d'Aeneas Vicus
Lepotre. Fontaines & cuvettes
— Autels à l'Italienne
— Vases
Fleurs pour orfevres & graveurs par Vauquier
Constellationes. impf. (with an index by Dr Scheuchzer)

Pr.20 [451]
Adr. Collaerts menses 12
Cielings. Le Potre
Landskips vander Meulen
Embarquemens par Zeaman
Odoardo Fialetti, Scherzi d'amore
Perelle, landskips
L'enfant prodigue. Audran exc.
Mariette
Vandermeulen
Perelle
Gasparo Duche etc. (with an index by Dr Scheuchzer)

Pr.21 [300]
Portraits des hommes illustres no. 189 (with an index by
   Dr Scheuchzer)

Pr.22 [322]
Portraits des hommes illustres. B. Moncornet (with an index)

Pr.23 [297 vid.pag.815 = Pr.65]
Tulpen en andere bloemen by Frederick de Widt
Theatrum florum etc. 1a & 2a pars.
Idem G. Valck exc.
Jeremiae Falck novae & exquisitae florum icones. Hamb. 1662
Frederick de Widt Niewt bloem boeck
J. H. diverses fleurs du printemps dernier 1653.
Idem Gerard Valck
Francois Le Febure, fleurs d'orfevrerie. Amst. 1679
Nic. Visscher Bloempotties in fol. blank paper

Pr.24 [302]
Schendels Eastern habits
Quast's beggars
History pieces of Rembrandts
Chinese figures in red
Dankers trades
Habits of trades à la burlesque by Car. Allard (with an index by
   Dr Scheuchzer)

Pr.25 [353]
Frederick de Widt, perspective
— Opera antiqua Romana
Joan de Ram, veues de Paris
Perelle, veues
Antoni Waterlo
Perelle, variae regiones graphice delineatae. F. de Widt exc.
Abr. Bloemart's views
Jo. de Ram
Melchior Kussell prospect
Zeaman staadts poorten van Amsterdam
— quelques ports de mer (with an index by Dr Scheuchzer)

Pr.26 [455]
Paul Potter inven. Marc. de Bye fec. Nic. Visscher exc., Beasts,
   lyons, wolves, leopards, goats, etc.
Marc. Gerard inven. de Bye fec. etc., bears
Paul Potter inv. Frederick Hendricksen exc. Horses, cowes,
   goates etc.
— M. de Bye f. Visscher exc. Cowes, nos 1,2,3
— F. de Widt exc. 1650. Cowes pyed
with blank paper (with an index by Dr Scheuchzer)

Pr.27 [465]
Josephi Rivera Spanioletti & Jacobi Palmae, tabb. de
   institutionibus praecipuis ad picturam necessariis. Fred.
   de Widt exc.
The 4 seasons. Van Dalen sculps. Visscher exc.
Gribelin's book of ornaments. The Entrées de Callot & odd
   prints, with blank paper (with an index by Dr Scheuchzer)

Pr.28 [458]
Ornemens gravé par Du Cerceau. ex formis Nic. Visscher
Stef. della Bella ornamenti di fregi & fogliami. Fred. de Widt
   exc.
Nieuwe Festonne. Fred. de Widt exc.
Stef. della Bella. Cartouches. F. de Widt exc.
Nicasius Rousseel Grotissen. J. de Ram exc. 1684
J. Le Potre vasi diversi et ornamenti. Idem exc.
— ornemens & panneaux. Jollain exc.
Van Somer cartouches
J. Oliver of mantlings. Lond. 1686
with blank paper (with an index by Dr Scheuchzer)

Pr.29 [523]
Melchior Tavernier Cartouches 1632
Nicasius Roussel, de Grotesco. 1623
Vriese inventor. Jo. Gallaeus exc. Wells & covers
Polydorus de Caravagio in. Jupiter & Ganymede etc.

Pr.30 [625]
Titi Livii historia

Pr.31 [637]
Prints of Callot & other masters vid. (with an index by
   Dr Scheuchzer)

Pr.32 [548]
Ottonis Vaeni amorum emblemata. Ant. 1608 in 4o

Pr.33 [531]
Sigismund Feyrabendts Drawing book. Franc 1580 4o

Pr.34 [581]
Prints of Callot and other masters

Pr.35 [505]
Arms of the nobles of Venice coloured

Pr.36 [573]
Prints of machines

Pr.37 [574]
Emblems etc.

Pr.38 [166]
Prints of the heads of famous men etc. with an index vid. (made
   by Dr Massey & Dr Scheuchzer, some of them very rare)

Pr.39 [168]
Prints of the heads of great men etc. vid. (with an index by
   Dr Scheuchzer)

Pr.40 [167]
Berchem ovium species diversae, Dr Krieg('s insects), Mr Doody
etc. vid (many rare prints with an index by Dr Scheuchzer)

Pr.41 [367]
Callot's entries etc. vid (with an index by Dr Scheuchzer)

Pr.42 [317]
Callot's prints vid (with an index by Dr Scheuchzer)

Pr.43 [318]
Callot's beggars etc. Alb. Durer's passion etc. (with an index)

Pr.44 [319]
Habiti della nobilita di Fiorenza etc. (with an index)

Pr.45 [437]
A book of prints etc. (with an index by Dr Scheuchzer)

Pr.46 [604]
A book of the same (id. by Dr Scheuchzer)

Pr.47 [280]
The cryes of London. P. Tempest exc. fol.

Pr.48 [290]
The Plenipotentiaries of Munster. Aubry exc.
Comitum Gloriae centum icones. Elias Wideman sculpsit in fol.

Pr.49 [537]
Nurenbergisches Berandert- und Unverandert Trachten-Buch

{gap with four book entries}

Pr.50 [142]
Admiranda Romanarum antiquitatum & veteris sculpturae
vestigia etc. delineata a Pietro Sancti Bartolo, notis Jo. Petri
Bellorii. Rom. 1693 in fol. oblongo

Pr.51 [383]
Domenico Parasacchi, principali fontane di Roma 1637
Statue
Palazzi. Ibid. 1638 in fol. oblong. (with an index by
Dr Scheuchzer)

Pr.52 [196]
Antonio Labacco, libro appartenente all'architettura nel qual si
figurano alcuni notabili antiquita de Roma

Pr.53 [248]
Pitture antiche de sepolcro de Nasoni disegnate & intagliate da
Pietro Santi Bartoli & descritte e illustrate da Giov. Pietro
Bellori. Roma 1702 in fol.

Pr.54 [605]
Book of mapps coelestial & terrestriall. 4o obl.

Pr.55 [53; 67]
A book of mapps & plans of severall cities & fortifications in
Flanders by Mr Beaulieu etc., some drawn with a pen. In fol.
(many prints severall of which belong to the Speculum
Romanae Magnificentiae by Lafrery, Duchet etc. with an
index by Dr Scheuchzer)

Pr.56 [90]
And. van Hulle, Pacificatores orbis Christiani sive Monasterii.
Rotterod. 1697 in fol.

Pr.57 [69]
P. du Val, Cartes de Geographie. Paris 1668 in fol.

Pr.58 [369]
Pieter van den Berge, Theatrum Hispaniae. In fol. forma oblonga

Pr.59 [189]
A book of the heads of severall famous men with an index of
them. in fol. (by Dr Massey, several by Hollar etc. It begins
with that of Guido Patin, contains 112 leaves & ends with
Johannes Hallius)

Pr.60 [258]
Marco Boschini, Il regno tutto di Candia 1651. in fol.

Pr.61 [483]
Tobias Stimmer, Newe Kunstlich Figuren biblischer historien.
Basel 1576 in 4o

Pr.62 [596]
Alessandro Fabri, de Habitibus diversarum nationum in 8o.
(additio ad duos superiores Libro de Habitibus diversarum
nationum)

Pr.63 [583]
Petri Vanderbroecht, Metamorphoseon Ovidianarum libb. 15
apud Theodorum Gallaeum Ant.1622 in 8o forma oblonga

Pr.64 [597]
A collection of Hollar's etc. prints in 8o forma oblonga
(viz. Theatrum mulierum Londini 1643, with an index
by Dr Scheuchzer)

Pr.65 [297 = Pr.23]
Verscheyde niewe tulpen en andere bloemen by Frederick
de Widt
— Theatrum florum. Amst. 1690
— niewt bloem-boeck
Jeremiae Falck, Florum Icones. Hamb. 1662
J.H. divers fleurs du printemps dernier 1653
Flowers by Gerard Valck
Fleurs et feuilles pour l'orfevrerie. Amst. 1679 inventé par
Le Fean (?)
Nicolas Visscher, bloempotties in fol.
(with an index by Dr Scheuchzer)

Pr.66 [457]
Stadthuys van Amsterdam etc. fol. 14
— The same in severall views
— The same
— views of Amsterdam
— views of ruines
Prints of heads Nicol. de Br. etc
Chinese customs
Rope dancers

Pr.67 [509]
John Dunstalls Geometricall figures
— book of houses
Rope dancers by Bellange
Comedians by the same
(with an index by Dr Scheuchzer)

Pr.68 [472]
Livres de fleurs par Vauquer impf.
Flowers & flowerpotts by severall masters impf.
(with an index by Dr Scheuchzer)

Pr.69 [557]
Io. Belleri omnium gentium habitus cum Io. Sluperii epigramm.
Ant. 1572 in 8o.

Pr.70 [609]
Emblemata impf. in 4o

Pr.71 [610]
Iodoci Amani Gynaecaeum sive Theatrum mulierum cum
octostichis Francisci Modii. Francof. apud Sigismundum
Feyrabendium 1586 in 4o

Pr.72 [628]
Avium vivae icones in aes incisae & editae ab Adriano Collardo
in 4o

Pr.73 [546]
Flowers by Adrian. Collard. sine tit. 4o
Franc. Barlow diversae avium species excud. Guil. Faithorne
1658 in 4o
Henri Le Roy, Jardin des sauterelles & papillons etc. in 4o
(Hollar etc.)
Insects impf. in 4o
(with an index by Dr Scheuchzer)

C Pr.74 [621]
Divers veues de ports de mer d'Italie & autres lieus. Silvestre
sculps. Mariette excud.
Diverse vedute di porte di mare intagliate da Israel Silvestre 1648
Veues (?) Stef. della Bella fec. Ciartres exc. in 4o (with an index
by Dr Scheuchzer)

Pr.75 to 98 on pages 918–20, compiled in 1707

Pr.75 [560]
New Model-buch. Strasb. 1596
Scutcheons in 8o (& needle work)

Pr.76 [600]
Nic. de Bruin, Animalia Quadrupeda
Severall small pieces of Callot &c (with an index by
Dr Scheuchzer)

Pr.77 [662; 664; Pr.Or.67]
Libellus precum & psalmorum certis temporibus recitandorum.
Sinice

Pr.78 [663; Pr.Or.68; bound with the four following items]
Part of a Chinese book

Pr.79
A Chinese book an ane Almanack

Pr.80
A description of the island Puto in Chinese

Pr.81
Part of a Chinese book

Pr.82
Brevis relatio eorum quae spectant ad declarationem
Sinarum Imperatoris Kam Hi circa coeli, Cumfucii, &
avorum cultum datum anno 1700. Accedunt primatum
doctissimorumque virorum & antiquissimae traditionis
testimonia, opera P.P.Soc.Jesu Pekini pro evangelii
propagatione laborantium.

Pr.83 [662; Pr.Or.3]
A Chinese common prayer book

Pr.84 [650; 693]
Vigo or Spanish cards

Pr.85 [563]
Prints for goldsmiths work

Pr.86 [556]
The Apostles &c by Callot
— in black wood
Beggars by Brower
— by — (with an index by Dr Scheuchzer)

Pr.87 [181]
Maps, views, etc. of sevll. parts of England by Hollar, Tempest,
Lodge etc (with an index by Dr Scheuchzer)

Pr.88 [13; Min. 53, vid.pag. 2517]
Maps, views, etc. (many in vellum, the rest on paper all drawn,
or painted; the first page is intitled den 30 Maii Anno 1619
folio magno)

Pr.89
Prints, views etc. of Hollar

Pr.90 [78]
Claude Francois Menestrier, Description du colonne historiée de
Constantinople dressée à l'honeur du Theodose le Jeune gravé
par Jerome Vallet

Pr.91 [134]
Davidis Tenieres, Theatrum Pictorium etc. Ant. 1684 in fol.

Pr.92 [339]
Jehan Cousin, Livre de Perspective. Paris 1560 in fol.

Pr.93 [183]
Caval. Lorenzo Sirigatti, La Pratica de prospettiva. Ven. 1596
in fol.

Pr.94 [442]
Jo. Sadler, Boni et mali scientia
Histories of the Bible by Golzius, Stradanus, Cock etc. No. 152
(with an index by Dr Scheuchzer)

Pr.95 [453]
Guil. Bavern, Bellissimum Ovidii Theatrum. Nor. 1688 in 4o
form. oblong.

Pr.96 [265]
Imagines Comitum Hollandiae et effigies. Gerardi a Velsen
in fol.

Pr.97 [456]
Prints of the Bible. Germanice, by P. van Borcht
Pr.98 Io. Bapt. de Cavaleriis. Ant. Statuae urbis Romae. in fol.

Pr.99 to 125 on pages 926–8, compiled in 1707

C Pr.99 [75]
A large book of choice old & new prints on severall subjects by
severall masters gathered by Mr Courten (with an index by
Dr Scheuchzer)

C Pr.100 [36]
A collection of extraordinary prints of Marc Antoine &c
(Alb. Durer, Giles Pence & the Petite Masters) in a portfeuille
[crossed out] (with an index by Dr Scheuchzer)

C Pr.101 [242]
Shells (crossed out) Views etc. by Hollar etc. (with an index
by Dr Scheuchzer)

C Pr.102 [401]
Jo. Bapt. de Cavalleriis, Ecclesiae Anglicanae trophaea sive
sanctorum martyrum qui in Anglia mortem subierunt
passiones. Romae 1608 in 4o

C Pr.103 [543]
Lister de Cochleis etc. in 4o (in three vols. 2 oblong with mss notes of Mr Petiver and the author)

C Pr.104 [613]
Tempest's horses in 4o

C Pr.105 [180]
Lister de cochleis etc in fol. 1685

C Pr.106 [181]
— exoticis etc. ib. 1685 in fol.

C Pr.107 [182]
— cochitis ib. 1688 in fol. in red ink

C Pr.108 [183]
— conchis veneris etc. nott. mss. some in blew paper

C Pr.109 Monsters 6.
Leonis Strozze sistrum Aegyptiacum. Fowlers proposall for a medall on the death of Q. Mary. Julus Americanus Plumier. Scolopendra Americana Plumier. A box found in Sommersetshire. Cutts of Camden's coines. Nummi antiqui Suecui. Proof plate of Dr Leigh's hist of Lancashire. Dr Krieg's insects from Maryland grav'd by himselfe. Plates of Mr Petiver's. A plate of Greek medalls.

Cw Pr.110
Severall pieces of the old masters on copper. George Pentz, Virgilius Solis, Hisbins, Aldegrave, Binx, Theodore de Bry, Albert Durer

Cb Pr.111 [39]
Pourtraits (with an index by Dr Scheuchzer)

Cw Pr.112
Many pieces of Callot, Stefano della Bella, Rembrant

Cb Pr.113
Severall pieces of the old & best masters George Pentz, Stefanus de l'Aune, Lucas van Leyden, Tempesta, Aldegrave, Albert Durer

C Pr.114
Maps & cities

Cb Pr.115
Best prints of ancient masters for Mr Courten's own book, Marc Antoine, Albert Durer, Sadler. Copys of different masters, very good

Cb Pr.116
Callot, Stephano della bella, Elsheimer, Bloemart, Sylvestre, Vandermeulen, Baudin, Mellan, Edelinck, Perrier, Rembrant, Poilly

Cb Pr.117
Naturall things of Hollar, Stradanus, Robert, Barlow

Cw Pr.118
Miscellaneous prints, Rossi, Bloemaert, pieces of devotion, Hollar, Rembrant, Ostade, Tempesta's mutuae ferarum pugnae, Silvestre, Tempesta proelia vet. test., Callot, Goltzius seasons

Cb Pr.119
Things done in wood

Cb Pr.120
Landskips of Silvestre, Perelle, Montaigne, mezzotinto prints, Hollar

Pr.121
Views of Rome, Some prints of Duboys taken of the prints

Pr.121 [188;835]
Giacomo Barozzo da Vignola, Regola delli cinque ordini d'Architettura, in fol. (con nuova et ultima aggiunta delle porte d'architettura di Michel Angelo Buonaroti, da Mich. Angelo Vaccario. Roma appresso Gio. Batt. de Rossi)

Pr.122 [73]
Large views of Rome etc. (with an index by Dr Scheuchzer)

Pr.123 [813]
Methode de dresser les chevaux par Guillaume Duc de Newcastle. Anvers 1658 in fol.

Pr.124
Praecipua Romae templa. Colignon formis. Romae 1650 in fol.

Pr.125 [123]
Palazzi di Roma da Pietro Ferrerio. Rom. in fol.

Pr.126 to 158 on pages 989–91, compiled in 1708

Pr.126 [121]
Afbeelding van tstadthuys van Amsterdam door Jacob van Campen. Amst. 1661 in fol.

Pr.127 [165]
Prima & 2a pars effigierum et ornamentorum amplissimae curiae Amstelodamensis etc. per Artum Quellinum (& Hubertus Quellinus) ib. 1655 in fol.

Pr.128 [140]
Icones principum virorum doctorum etc. ab Antonio van Dyck etc. Ant. in fol.

Pr.129 [343]
A collection of old miscellany prints in fol. (with an index by Dr Scheuchzer)

Pr.130 [400]
Tombs [crossed out], altars, chimnys etc. in fol. (P. Collo invent. Ant Le Merlier incidit. Livre d'architecture d'autels, et de cheminées etc. invent. et dessiné par Barbet etc. Paris 1641)

Pr.131 [409]
Animali piu curiosi del mondo da Antonio Tempesta in 4o

Pr.132
Tragi herbarium. 1a pars illuminated in 4o

Pr.133 [545]
Lobel's icones illuminated by Mrs Power in 4o

Pr.134 [568]
Nederlandtsch Caertboek door Abraham Goos. Amst. 1625 in 8o

Pr.135 [500]
Le cabinet des enigmes des dieux deesses et heros, in 4o

Pr.136 [582]
Divinarum nuptiarum conventa et acta ab Arnoldo Fritachio enarrata et a Philippo Gallaeo edita. Ant. 1580 in 4o

Pr.137 [526]
Belgiae pacificatorum vera delineatio. Hag. Com. 1608 in 4o (Henericus Hondius)

Pr.138 [538]
Icones historiarum veteris Testamenti per Hans Holben. Ludg. 1547 in 8o

Pr.139 [133]
Gallerie de Farneze par Le Blond fol.
Arcus L. Septimii Severi anaglypha cum explicatione Josephi
 Mariae Suaresii. Rom. 1676 in fol.
Tempest's Apostles
Ruinarum varii prospectus etc Phil. Gallaeus

Pr.140 [651; Pr.Or.31 ad 40]
Historia Naturalis Sinarum quatuor Geri foliis ac sex et triginta
 tomis comprehensa, ex Imperiali Bibliotheca ut ipsa
 compactio ostendit deprompta. (They are neatly bound in
 blew silk, ornamented with white and the cases are of the
 same. Continet decem volumina)

Pr.141 [652; Pr.Or.41–49]
Quadrupeds (birds, insects etc in nine vols)

Pr.142 [653; Pr.Or.50–58]
Trees etc (in nine vols)

Pr.143 [654; Pr.Or.59–66]
Trees and plants (in 8 vols)

Pr.144 [655; Pr.Or.121]
Genus omne literarum Sinicarum (an potius Japonicarum?)
 tum antiquarum tum recentium tum ordinariarum tum
 extraordinariarum. Tom 1 in fol.

Pr.145–6 [656–7; Pr.Or.122, 123]
Tom.2,3

Pr.147 [658; Pr.Or.4]
Calendarium (Sinense ann. 42 Kam Hu quod incipit Febr. 16
 excusum Nankini, folio bound in silk with a silk case
 orange col.)

Pr.148 [659; Pr.Or.1]
Calendarium populare in idioma Tartaricam Manchu versum
 (ann. 37 Imperantis Kam Hu fol.)

Pr.149 [660; Pr.Or.2]
Ephemerides (et planetarum Chinensium Ann. 37 Kam Hu fol.)

Pr.150 [661; Pr.Or.74]
Desideratissimis fratribus Tunkinensibus & Cochin Chinensibus

Pr.151 [611]
Horae in usum Sarum. Paris 1498 in 8o with cutts printed on
 parchment

Pr.152 [643]
Jo. Posthii Tetrasticha in Ovidii Metam lib. xv quibus
 accesserunt Virgilii Solis fig. elegantissimae. Francof. 1563
 in 4o forma oblonga

Pr.153 [464]
Ottonis Veenii Batavorum cum Romanis bellum Ant. 1612 in 4o
 forma oblonga

Pr.154 [294]
Heads of great men etc. collected in fol. (with an index)

Pr.155 [485]
Beasts and hunting pieces of Jost Amman with Latin and Dutch
 verses by John Feyrabend. Franc. 1592 in 4o

Pr.156 [528]
Beasts and fowl by Jost Aman & Hans Bocksperger & George
 Schallern by Sigismund Feyrabend Germanice. Francof. 1579
 in 4o

Pr.157 [501]
Jost Aman cutts for the 4 Evangelists & Acts of the Apostles.
 Francof. 1587 German & Latine. John Feyrabendt in 4o

Pr.158 [507]
Alberti Dureri, icones sacrae in 4o

Pr.159 to 185 on pages 1016–8, compiled in 1709

Pr.159 [237]
Hieronymi Natalis, annotationes & meditationes in Missam etc.
 Ant. 1607 in fol.
— Evangelicae historiae imagines, Martin de Vos inventor,
 Hieronymus Wierix fecit. ib. 1596 in fol.

Pr.160 [241]
A drawing book. Abraham Bloemart inventor, Frederic
 Bloemart fec. et excud. pl. 120 in fol.

Pr.161 [272]
Alexander Brown's drawing book, pagg. 38 in fol. A. de Jode
 sculp. etc.

Pr.162 [440]
Vita, passio et resurrectio Jesu Christi variis iconibus a
 celeberrimo pictore Martino de Vos ab Adriano Collart
 nunc primum in aes incisis, in fol. forma oblonga.
Heemskerk, Martin Daniel 10p. in fol.

Pr.163 [315]
Baziloologia or the effigies of the English kings from the
 conquest to 1618 in fol.

Pr.164 [430]
Effigies Imperatorum domus Austriacae delineatae per Johannem
 Meyssens & aeri insculptae per filium suum Cornelis
 Meyssens, in fol. p. 14
— portraits des souverains princes et ducs de Brabant. Petr.
 de Jode etc. fol. 54
— des forestiers et comtes de Flandres 47
— des Comtes de Hollande 1662. 39 (with an index by
 Dr Scheuchzer)

Pr.165 [433]
Vita passio etc. Jesu Christi etc. Martin de Vos inven. Anton
 Wierix sculp. p. 22
Henrici Hondii Pictorum Germaniae inferioris effigies, 69
Dragons etc. p. 5 in fol. (with an index by Dr Scheuchzer)

Pr.166 [431]
De artificiali perspectiva. Tulls 1565 in fol.

Pr.167 [626]
A book of beasts. Joos de Bosscher excud. p. 12 in 4o forma
 oblonga
— of 4 birds

Pr.168 [549]
Neuwe Biblische figuren van Johan Bocksperger & Jost Aman.
 Franc. by Feyrabendt 1564 in forma oblonga

Pr.169 [498]
Juan de Yciar Ortographia practica. Saragosa 1550 in 4o

Pr.170 [571]
Raphaelis Schiaminossi de Burgo Sti Sepulchri, Quindecim
 mysteria rosarii beatae Mariae Virginis. Romae 1609 in 4o
 forma oblonga

Pr.171 [601]
Alciato, metali fatiche etc. di Giovanni Marquale in 8o

Pr.172 [599]
De Witts beasts 28
— doggs and catts 12 in 8o forma oblonga (with an index
    by Dr Scheuchzer)

Pr.173 [622]
Tobiae Stimmeri, novae sacrorum bibliorum figurae.
    Strasb. 1590 in 8o

Pr.174 [569]
Theodori Gallaei, magni patriarchae Josephi vita in 8o

Pr.175 [585]
HSB Biblicae historiae in 12o cum Apocalypsi

Pr.176 [645; 661]
Figurae biblicae. Wood 1551 in 12o

Pr.177 [427]
La passion de Nostre Seigneur Jesus Christ, taillé en cuivre par
    Martin Schoen en 12 tableaux in 4o

Pr.178 [154]
Carlo Fontana Tempio Vaticano e sua origine con gli edificii piu
    conspicui antichi et moderni fatti dentro e fuori di esso etc.
    Roma 1694 in fol.

Pr.179 [83]
Sr de la Colombiere, Hommes illustres et grands capitaines
    Francois qui sont peints dans la Galerie du Palais Royale
    dessinés et gravés par Heince et Bignon. Par. 1690 in fol.
    (the first edition is in 1655, Portraits des hommes illustres
    francais qui sont peints dans la galerie du Palais Cardinal
    de Richelieu etc.)

Pr.180 [161]
Galerie du Duc de Parme peinte a Rome dans le palais Farneze
    par Anibal Carache gravée par Jean Bapt. et Franc. de Poilly
    in fol.

Pr.181 [113]
Jo.Petri Bellori, Veteres Arcus Augustorum triumphis insignes
    etc. Rom. 1690 in fol.

Pr.182 [125]
David Loggan, Cantabrigia illustrata in fol.

Pr.183 [137–8]
Andrea Pozzo, Prospettiva di pittori e architetti. Rom. 1693 in
    fol. Latino & Italico idiomate. Parte prima. Parte secunda.
    Rom. 1700 fol.

Pr.184 [361]
Vita, passio et resurrectio Jesu Christi variis iconibus a Martino
    de Vos expressa ab Adriano Collart incis. in fol. forma
    oblonga

Pr.185 [194]
de la Serre, histoire de l'entrée de la Reine Mere dans les
    provinces unies des pays bas. Lond. 1639 in fol. vid. 1666

Pr.186 to 204 on pages 1066–7, compiled in 1709

Pr.186 [199]
Laurentii Begeri, Hercules Ethnicorum 1705 in fol.

Pr.187 [345]
Medicaea Hospes sive publica gratulatio etc. Casparis Barlaei.
    Amst. 1639 in fol.

Pr.188 [234]
Jo. Bochii, profectio et inauguratio Alberti et Isabellae Austriae
    Archiducum etc. Ant. 1602 in fol.

Pr.189 [391]
Jacobi Lauri, antiquae urbis splendor etc. Rom. 1612 in fol.
    forma oblonga

Pr.190 [271]
Udalrici Pinder, Passio Domini nostri Jesu Christi, Nor. 1508 in
    fol.

Pr.191 [520]
Passio Christi ab Alberto Durero effigiata AB Waesbergen excud.
    in 4o forma oblonga

Pr.192 [579]
Raccolta di le piu illustre et famose citta di tutto il mondo.
    Fra Valero sculps. 4o forma oblonga

Pr.193 [624]
Milagros por il beatificacion del Joan de la Cruz. 2a parte in 8o

Pr.194 [614]
Elogidia praecipuorum virorum virtutes instantia. Upsal. 1631
    in 8o

Pr.195 [41]
A collection of old prints of some of the best masters, on
    imperiall paper covered with Russia leather in fol. very large
    (with an index)

Pr.196 [42]
A collection of prints etched etc of the Caraches etc. in fol. on
    imperiall paper in Russia leather (with an index)

Pr.197 [1]
A collection of very large prints on imperiall paper bound in
    Russia leather in a very large folio

Pr.198 [192]
A collection of miscellaneous prints in fol. (with an index by
    Dr Scheuchzer)

Pr.199 [404]
A collection of miscellaneous old prints (by Albert Durer &
    Lucas van Leyden etc) gathered by Jacobus Colius Ortelianus
    1599 in fol. (without an index)

Pr.200 [981]
A small collection of miscellaneous prints in fol. (without an
    index)

Pr.201 [991]
A collection of small prints of the old masters in fol. (without an
    index)

Pr.202 [395]
A collection of miscellaneous prints old and new in fol. (without
    an index)

Pr.203 [112]
A collection of ancient & modern miscellaneous prints in a large
    fol. (with an index by Dr Scheuchzer)

Pr.204 [24]
A collection of large prints ancient and modern in a large volume
    in fol. (with an index at the latter end by Dr Scheuchzer)

Pr.205 to 213 on page 1071 (runs on from above after three folios of manuscripts), compiled in 1709

Pr.205 [379]
Panoplia Theodori Gallaei, with many other prints of Theodore & Cornelius Gallaeus, Martin Heemskerk etc. in an oblong fol. (without an index)

Pr.206 [333]
A book of heads of severall famous persons on blew paper in fol. (with an index by Dr Scheuchzer)

Pr.207 [37]
A book of prints of severall old masters as Lucas van Leyden, Albert Durer, Martin Schoneus etc. with some of Tempesta etc. in Russia leather in fol. (with an index at the latter end by Dr Scheuchzer)

Pr.208 [43]
A book of prints of severall masters viz.the Sadelers, Goltzius, Callot, Wierx, della Bella etc. on Imperiall paper bound in Russia leather in fol. (with an index by the same)

Pr.209 [40]
A book of prints of severall masters as Augustine Venetien, the Gallaei etc. on Imperiall paper bound in Russia leather in fol. (with an index by Dr Scheuchzer)

Pr.210 [239]
Aesops Fables in Dutch & severall miscellany-prints pasted on paper in fol. (without an index)

Pr.211 [111]
A collection of large prints of severall modern masters in an oblong folio

Pr.212 [236]
A collection of severall prints of severall masters on blew paper in fol. (without an index)

Pr.213 [5]
A collection of severall large prints on a large oblong folio of brown paper

(on a separate slip of paper bound into the catalogue in Stack's hand: 'Pr.5 in this volume are many of various subjects by many masters ancient & modern some of which are rarely to be met with, at the latter end is an index')

Pr.214 to 219, on page 1089, compiled in 1709/1710

Pr.214 [3]
Mich. Rup. Besleri, Uteri muliebris fabrica etc. Norib. 1641 in fol.

Pr.215
Pacificatoris orbis Christiani, sive icones principum etc. qui Monasterii etc. Roterod. 1698 in fol.

Pr.216 [203 & 203*]
Relation du voyage de sa Majesté Britannique en Hollande etc. par Roman de Hogue. à la Haye 1692 in fol.

Pr.217 [353]
Der Turckish Schau-Platz. Hamb. 1685 in fol.

Pr.218 [607]
Cesare Vecelio, Habiti antichi et moderni di tutto il mondo. Ven. 1589 in 8o

Pr.219 [636]
Dance de la Mort
Historiae veteris testamenti etc. Lugd. 1539 in 8o

Pr.220 to 225 on pages 1094–5, compiled in 1710

Pr.220 [143]
Pietro Ferrerio, Palazzi di Roma. fol. (libro primo)

Pr.221 [144]
Bapt. Falda, Palazzi di Rome fol. (libro secundo)

Pr.222 [139]
Gio. Batt. Montano, Architettura etc in fol.

Pr.223 [357]
Romanae magnitudinis monumenta etc. (cura, sumptibus ac typis Dominici de Rubeis. Romae 1699 folio oblato)

Pr.224
Speculum nostrae salutis etc. den Spiegel onser behoudenisse in fol. Harlemi. (the late Lord Pembroke had it of Sir Hans)

Pr.225 [632]
Jo. Bapt. de Cavalleriis, Pontificum Romanorum effigies etc. Rome in 8o

Pr.226–8 on page 1099, compiled in 1710

Pr.226 [118]
Bernardino Genga, anatomia per uso et intelligenza del disegno etc. data in luce da Domenico de Rossi. 1691 in fol.

Pr.227 [965, vid.pag.1676]
Effigies of the painters etc. 1694 in fol.

Pr.228 [393]
Daniel King's cathedrall & conventual churches of England. 1656 in fol.

Pr.229–325 on pages 1162–5, compiled in 1711

(From here onwards the entries are no longer in Sloane's hand, but in that of a clerk with untidy writing with poor command of languages. The missing numbers are supplied by earlier entries renumbered).

Pr.229 [55]
Seren. Principis Ferdinandi Hispaniarum Infantis S. R. Cardinalis triumphalis Introitus in Flandriae Metropolim Gandarum Auctore Guglielmo Becano. Antverpiae 1636 in fol. larg.

Pr.230 [157]
L'Entré Triomphante de leurs Majestez Louis XIV Roy de France et de Navarre et de Marie Therese d'Autriche son epouse dans la ville de Paris [....]. A Paris 1662 in fol.

Pr.231 [338]
Sentimens des plus habiles peintres sur la practique de la peinture et sculpture [....] par Henri Testelin peintre du Roi. A Paris 1696 in fol.

Pr.232 [842]
Les proportions du corps humain mesurées sur les plus belles figures de l'antiquité. P. Urbin inv. & Girard Audran sculpsit. A Paris 1683 fol.

Pr.233 [365]
Pompa funebris Alberti Pii Archiducis Austriae [....] veris imaginibus expressa a Jacobo Franquart, eiusdem principis morientis vitae scriptore E. Puteano. Bruxelliae 1623 in fol.

Pr.235 [191]
Virorum illustrium, viz. Philosoph. Medicorum, Pictorum, sculptorum etc. effigies in no. 63 fol. (with an index by Dr Scheuchzer)

Pr.236 [364]
Sacrae Historiae acta a Raphaele Urbin in Vaticanis Xystis ad picturae miraculum expressa Nicholaus Chapron Gallus a se delineata et incisa DDD Romae 1649 in fol.

Pr.237 [224]
Principum et illustrium quorundam virorum qui in Europa alibique terrarum qua fama qua eruditione celebres fuerunt, verae imagines. Ludg. Bat. apud Petrum vander Aa in fol.

Pr.238 [245]
Portraits des plus illustres Papes, Empereurs, Rois, Princes, Grands Capitains et autres personnes renommés au nombre d'environ six cent [. . . .] en 28 belles planches avec des courtes explications par le sieur Constance della Riviere.
L. Batavorum apud Petrum vander Aa in fol.

Pr.251 [262]
Devises pour les tapisseries du Roy ou sont representez les quatre elemens et les quatre saisons de l'annee, Gallice et Germanice

Pr.252 [276]
Signorum veterum icones in fol. Joanne Episcopio auct.

Pr.265 [376]
The representation of a carrousel by Martin Klotzel in Dutch 1695

Pr.266 [397]
Ovidii Metam. lib. 1 per Klottzium Juten (crossed out and replaced by) Hubertum Goltzium

Pr.272 [416]
La pyrotechnie de Hanzelet Lorrain [. . . .] 1630

Pr.291 [507]
Alberti Dureri icones sacrae in historiam salutis humanae per redemptorem nostrum Jesum Christum dei et Mariae filium in 4o sine anno et loco impressionis

Pr.293 [529]
The figures of various sorts of cupps in 4o by CAP [monogram]

Pr.308 [635]
Le tableau de la croix representée dans les ceremonies de la St Messe, ensemble le tresor de la devotion aux souffrances Nre S.J.C., le tout enrichi de belles figures. A Par. chez F. Marot etc 1651 in 8o

Pr.312 [589]
L'Immaculiée Communion deliniée, Chant des vierges illustres hymne chante ma langue a haut voix le mystere du corps glorieux. 1629 Antwerp in 12o In Dutch and in French. (Bound with) Conte Instrucye end onderwijs [. . . .] ghemaeckt by Meester Cornelius vander Heyden, 1545

Pr.313 [587]
A book of patterns for goldsmiths in 8o

Pr.315 [337]
Cognitione de muscoli del corpo humano per il dissegno opera di Carlo Cesio, Arnoldo van Westerhout formis Romae 1697 in fol.

Pr.316 [438]
Iconographia magni patris Aurelii Augustini Hipponensis episcopi [. . . .] S. A. Bolswert sculpsit et excudit Antwerpiae 1624 in fol.

Pr.317 [358]
Il nuovo teatro delle fabbriche et edificii in prospettiva di Roma moderna sotto il felice pontificato di N. S. Papa Alessandro VII date in luce da Gio. Giacomo Rossi alla pace libro primo, 2o et 3o, con priv. del summo pont.

Pr.318 [381]
Parerga atque ornamenta ex Raphaelis sancti prototypis a Joanne Nannio Utinensi, in Vaticani Palatii Xystis partim opere plastico partim coloribus expressa ad veterum ornamentorum et picturarum qua extabant in ruinis domus imperat. Titi elegantiam. Typis Jo. Jacob de Rubeis Romae. Petrus Sanctus Bartolus delin. incidit in fol.

Pr.319 [202]
Vita S. Antonii Abbatis [. . . .] Antonius Tempesta fecit Romae in fol.

Pr.320 [10]
La Gallerie du Palais du Luxembourg peintée par Rubens dessinée par les Sr Nattier et gravée par les plus illustres graveurs du tempe dedié au Roy. A Paris 1710 in fol.

Pr.321 [86]
Receuil des meilleurs desseins de Raimond la Fage gravé par cinq des plus habiles graveurs et mie en lumiere par les soins de vander Bruggen. Se vend chez Gerard Valck in fol.

Pr.322 [141]
Barberinae Aulae Fornix Romae Eq. Petri Beretini Cortonensis picturis admirandus cuius spirantes imagines et monochromata in hisce delineamentis ad similitudinem adumbrata Urbani VIII Pont. Maximi virtutes exprimunt in fol (Galeria dipinta nel palazzi del Principe Panfilio da Pietro Berettini da Cortona, intagliata da Carlo Cesio vero originale. Si vendono da Gio. Jacomo Rossi in Roma all pace al insegna di Parigi cum priv. S.P.)

Pr.323 [100]
Insignium Romae Templorum prospectus exterior. interioresque a celebrioribus architectis inventis nunc tandem suis cum plantis ac mensuris a Jo. Jacobo de Rubeis Romano suis typis in lucem editi ad aedem pacis com privilegio summi ponteficis 1684 in fol.

Pr.324 [145]
Li Giardini Roma con le loro piante alzante e vedute in prospettiva disegnate e intagliate da Gio. Battista Falda nuovamente dati alle stampe e cura di Gio. Giacomo de Rossi alla Pace all'insegna di Parigi in Rom. con priv. del S. Pont. in fol.

Pr.325 [179]
Argomento della Galleria Farnese dipinta da Annibale Carracci disegnata et intagliata da Carlo Cesio nel quale spiegansi e riduconsi allegoricamente alla moralita, le favole poetiche in essa representate in Roma 1657 in fol.

Appendix B
List of Sloane Volumes that can be Identified in the Department of Prints and Drawings
Antony Griffiths

The following list is a first attempt to give an idea of how much Sloane material survives in more or less its original form in the Department of Prints and Drawings. It is incomplete, and some elements may be inaccurate, but it forms the basis for future additions and corrections. It is arranged in seven columns.

1 Current P&D pressmark
2 Short description of the work
3 Number assigned on arrival in Sloane's collection
4 New number assigned *c.*1711
5 Scheuchzer renumbering *c.*1726
6 Stack renumbering *c.*1734
7 Page number of the entry for the volume in Sloane's library catalogue

Numbers in brackets are no longer written in the book, but can be supplied from the catalogue

1	2	3	4	5	6	7
156a2	Abraham Bloemaert, Drawing Book	(Pr160)	(Pr241)			1016
156a9	Stradanus and Heemskerk, Acta Apostolorum	Pr803			Pr363	3007
157a4	Minne-Kunst, Minne-Dichten …, Amsterdam (Voskuyl) 1622	r1846				
157a7	Jan Galle, Vita S. Josephi	(Pr821)			(Pr656)	3008
157a13	C. Plantin & P. Galle, Divinarum nuptiarum conventa, 1580	Pr136		Pr582		989
157a14	Jan Hagels Companie, F. de Witt exc.	(R126)	(Pr286)	(Pr592)		682
157b7	Avium vivae icones, per Adrian Collaert, T. Galle ed.	Q274	Pr384	Pr459		
157b7	Henri Le Roy, Muscarum scarabeorum figurae	Q275				
157b16	J. Peeters & R. de Hooghe, prints on the Austro-Turkish war	(?P189)	(?Pr264)	(?Pr285)		230
157b21	A. Collaert, Stent, Hoefnagel, sets of fish etc. (with manuscript annotations by Petiver)	Pr513		Pr460		1951
157b23	Bestaande in Regeringe Konsten … ABC, Haarlem 1695	Pr429		Pr508		1418
157b25	Diversae avium species, I de Ram exc.	h69	Pr381	Pr512		1273
	N. Visscher, Piscium vivae icones inv. A. Collaert, 1634		Pr331?			
	N. de Bruyn, Libellus varia genera piscium complectens					
	D. I. Hoefnagel, Diversae insectarum volatilium icones		Pr381			
157b36	De kleyne wonderlijcke Werelt, Amsterdam 1649	C795				
157b40	M. Bril, Topographia variarum regionum, 1652 idem, Topographia etc. inc. a Simon Frisio, 1651	Pr734			Pr1060	2590
157b41	C. Allard, Toutes sortes d'oiseaux, Leyden (vander Aa)	Pr777			Pr1059	2868
157b45	Ornemens de oiseaux par Hans Liefrinck, 1631	Pr736			Pr1107	2591
157c28	F. de Widt, A. Bloemart Nieut Teecken Boeck Nicolaus Guillelmus Lotharingus, Florae (F. Widt) Michel Sweerts, Diversae facies in usum iuvenum, 1656 P. van Somer, Figurae variae, London	N119	Pr273	Pr487		437
157c33	A. Collaert, Florilegium, T. Galle ed. (plus Henri Le Roy, Jardin des sauterelles, now kept as loose sheets)	(Pr73, part)		(Pr546)		816
157*a22	Twerk compleet van Adrian van Ostade	(Pr757)			(Pr1033)	2793
157*a36	Goltzius, Metamorphoses of Ovid	Pr266		Pr397		1162
157*a37	M. Bril, Topographia variarum regionum, 1614	Pr733			Pr355	2590

1	2	3	4	5	6	7
157*a38	A. Tempesta, Sacra bella … Antwerp, P. de Jode	Pr490		Pr373		1808
157*a39	H. van Cleve & T. Galle, Ruinarum varii prospectus	(Pr833, part)			(Pr942)	3059
158c25	Series of 148 etchings on the French civil wars	(?Pr729)			(?Pr1044)	2572
158c26	Liber figurarum in quibus obsidiones in Belgio Duce de Alba gubernante describuntur	H476	Pr220	Pr241	Pr377	1094
158c27	Collection de plusieurs dessins touchant l'expedition du Roi Charles à Tunis	Pr545		Pr378		2029
159b2	G. de Jode, Thesaurus veteris et novi testamenti, 1585	Pr341		Pr384	Min186	1179
159d12	Icones Livianae, per Ph. Lonicerum, Frankfurt 1573	Pr382		Pr550		1273
159*a8	M. Merian, Novae regionum … delineationes, 1624 (plus other sets bound at end)	Pr600		Pr513		2293
159*a15	J.W. Baur, Underschidliche Prospecten, eng. M. Kusell,1681	Pr830			Pr659	3059
159*a16	J.W. Baur, Illustrations to Ovid's Metamorphoses	(Pr367)		(Pr642)		1201
159*a17	L. Sandrart, Illustrations to Ovid's Metamorphoses	Pr359		Pr452		1194
159*b4	Hogenberg, Pompae funebris … Friderici II, 1592	Pr616		Pr389		2364
160a1	Historische Bilder-Bibel, J.W. Krausser, Augsburg 1702	(Pr450)				1483
160a4	Statuae pontis Pragensis, Aug. Neurautter 1715	Pr745			Pr610	2729
160d7	Halbung und Kronung Anna Jonannowa … von Russland 1731	Pr857/8			Pr893	3114
161a18	Callot, Les miseres et les malheurs de la guerre, 1633	Pr366		Pr461		1201
161a21	Callot, La vie de l'enfant prodigue, 1635	W604	Pr294	Pr575		470
161a24	Views of places in suburbs of Paris with sets of letters; outline figures	Pr770			Pr658	2868
161a25	Carousel fait sur l'Arne pour le mariage du Grand Duc, Paris (Filloeul)					
161a29	Albert Flamen, Poissons de mer plus eight other sets	(Pr343)		Pr522		1179
161a30	Jacques Stella, Les jeux et plaisirs de l'enfance, 1657	Pr835			Pr1110	3059
161b3	Le Vergier dyon, Paris c.1500	A1081				
161b13	Baron d'Eisenberg, Description du Manège Moderne, 1727	Pr822			Pr354	3008
161*b3	Receuil des meilleurs desseins de Raymond La Fage	Pr321		Pr86		1162
161*b24	Set of plant engravings by Bosse et al.	(Pr622)		(Pr20)		2394
161*b25	second volume of the same	Pr622		Pr20		2394
162a25	J. Le Moyne, La clef du champs	Min269				
163a18	T. van Thulden, Les travaux d'Ulysse, Paris 1640	(Pr333)		(Pr388)		1173
163b9	Carlo Cesio, Argomento della Galleria Farnese, 1657	Pr325		Pr179		1165
163b10	Iulii Casseri, De vocis auditusq. organis, Ferrara 1600	A698				
163c2	Life of St John Baptist after Andrea del Sarto, 1618					
163*a35	A. Tempesta, Icones venantium species, Eg. Jansz. sc.	Pr1172				3799
163*a36	O. Fialetti, Drawing book, Venice 1608	d209	Pr304	Pr580		128
163*a37	R. Schiaminossi, 15 mysteria Rosarii BVM, Rome 1609	Pr170		Pr571		1016
163*a39	Gregorii Jordani, Prophetiae 14 tabulis expressa, 1622	Pr813			Pr644	3008
163*a48	Guercino, Drawing book by O. Gatti, Rossi ed. 1619	Pr475		Pr639		1840
163*a56	Julio Bonasone, Amori sdegni e gielosie di Giunone	Pr737			Pr1120	2591
165a1	Pacata Hibernia, Ireland appeased and reduced, 1633	H331				
165a2	F. Sandford, The interment of the Duke of Albemarle, 1670	(Pr484)		(Pr147)		1793

1	2	3	4	5	6	7
165c2	T. Baston, 22 prints of ships of … Royal Navy, 1721	(?)		(Pr772)		3059
166*d21	Hollar, Animalium, ferarum & bestiarum … (with other sets in an album, but only a fragment of Sloane's original)	(H66)			(Pr462)	673
168*a18	Enea Vico, Vases (with sets by Le Pautre, Vauquer and de Gheyn)	Pr19		Pr298		810*
168*b26	Vredeman de Vries, Panoplia seu armamentarium, T. Galle					
169a2	Album amicorum habitibus mulierum …, Louvain 1609	Pr738			Pr652	2591
169a3	A. Fabri, Costume book dedicated to Battista Dotto	Pr62		Pr596		815
169b11	Callot, La noblesse; Les gueux					
169b12	Bellange inv. Rope dancers (with Dunstall sets)	Pr67		Pr509		816
169b14	Seb. Le Clerc, set of figures	Pr379		Pr372		1273
170*a10	Lauron/Tempest, Cryes of London					
174c31	Lafrery, Speculum Romanae Magnificentiae	(Pr761)				3373
175c6	Views of ancient Rome, Amsterdam, P. Schenk					
175c7	F. de Widt after J. van der Velde, Dutch castles					
	P. Schenk, Views in Amsterdam and other cities					
175*a1	P. Schenk, Admirandum quadruplex spectaculum, J. van Call	(Pr455)		(Pr525)		1484
175*a4	Israel Silvestre, various French views	G55	Pr256	Pr521		424
175*a8	'Plans of severall places in Europe', vol.I	163				
175*a9	vol.II	270				
175*b29	Views of Rome, Rossi reusing Lafrery plates	(?Pr762)				3373
208a15	John Taylor, A brief remembrance of all the English monarchs, London 1622	R2005				
209a15	Icones Professorum Leidenensium	n25	Pr512	Pr479		634
210*c1	Compton Holland, Basiliologia, London 1618	(Pr163)		(Pr315)		1016
294*	Battles of Alexander after Le Brun	Pr722				3371

Volumes now disbound and plates mounted or kept loose; many were formerly given the pressmark 2AA*a.

1	2	3	4	5	6	7
13	Ducerceau grotesques, Michel Le Blon and other blackwork	(?Pr85)		(?Pr563)		919
29	PRK blackwork; Vauquer; Le Pautre; Mignot	(?Pr313)				1162
52	P. Schenk; Le Pautre; Valck; Le Juge, metalwork designs	(Pr867)			(Pr1108)	3237
72	Master CAP set of cups	(Pr293)		(Pr529)		1162
73	Jean Toutin, copies by F. Witt					
74	Pierre Bourdon, 3 sets of Essaies de gravure	(Pr913)			(Pr1104)	3374
	John Payne, Flowers, fruits, beasts, birds	(?Pr380)		(?Pr462)		1273
	Hollar, Shells	(Pr820)			(Pr653)	3008
	Friezes of Zancarli and vases of Scoppa	(Pr13)		(Pr347)		810*
	van Somer, Cartouches	(Pr28,part)		(Pr458)		812

Appendix C
The Print Collection of William Courten, Sloane MS 3961

Antony Griffiths

William Courten (1642–1702) was the fourth in a family that had been one of the wealthiest in Tudor and Jacobean England, but had lost most of its fortune during the Civil War. Much of William's energies during his life were taken up in lawsuits trying to recover assets. He spent most of his early life on the Continent, especially in Montpellier where he probably first met Sloane. He returned to England in about 1684, and took rooms in Middle Temple. He devoted his time to his very wide-ranging collection, which was much visited and reckoned to be one of the finest in the country. (See the accounts in Edward Edwards, *Lives of the Founders of the British Museum*, London 1870, pp. 249–73; and A. MacGregor, ed., *Sir Hans Sloane*, London 1994, *passim* and especially p. 22.)

In 1702 William Courten bequeathed his entire collection to Hans Sloane (see p. 23). Included in the bequest were his manuscripts, of which several volumes are now bound among the Sloane papers in the British Library. Most of Sloane 3961 contains bound sheets relating to his print collection, and a summary of these sheets, as well as sample extracts from them, is given here. They seem to have been made at a time when Courten was thinking of selling his prints, perhaps in order to raise money to expand other parts of his collection. Certainly other sheets in the volume that list his acquisitions for his collection between 1688 and 1699 include very few prints. Courten spent twenty-five years on the Continent until his return in 1684, and it is likely that he assembled much of his print collection there. There is no reason to think that Courten was a dealer. He did however act as an adviser and agent, and both this manuscript and Sloane 3962 contain many papers relating to his collecting books and medals on behalf of Lord Coleraine.

The importance of these pages for the print historian is considerable. They are the earliest catalogue of a British print collection that not only gives a precise enough description to allow most of the items to be identified, but also gives a valuation. Other sources, such as auction catalogues, are hopelessly inadequate for this period. Although many sheets of the catalogue are missing, those that remain not only allow us to reconstruct much of the collection, but also show what prints then had the highest valuations. Courten had two main principles of classification: first by engraver, and secondly (for his large collection of portrait prints) by sitter. When a print by a selected engraver (such as Hollar) was a portrait, the portrait series usually took priority.

The list of engravers produces a few surprises: already in 1687, only eighteen years after Rembrandt's death, Courten had a separate list of his etchings, with twenty-two prints listed under his name, plus a few more scattered in the portraits. His list of Dürer contains a first-class collection of engravings, but does not include a single woodcut. Woodcuts, like mezzotints, were listed together on a separate sheet, as a collection by technique, not engraver. Only a dozen or so woodcuts were listed in all, and only three Dürers were among them. Prints by Dürer and Lucas van Leyden were valuable, but Dürer more so. The top price for a Lucas (the *Crucifixion*) is 10s, whereas several Dürers make this price. One, the *Adam and Eve*, is exceptionally valued at £2. But the valuations for prints by Marcantonio and his associates (Agostino Veneziano, Marco da Ravenna, as well as Bonasone) are regularly between £1 and £4, showing that the classic works of the Italian High Renaissance had an unassailable prestige.

Much other incidental information of interest will be found in the lists. Courten collected copies as well as originals, and the valuations given to the copies is sometimes significant. He also notes counterproofs (he uses the term 'counterpreuves'), which also bear significant valuations. Clearly both types of print played an accepted and recognised role in print collections of the period. The lists also allow us to find the names of some of the people that he worked with, such as Gibson, Bateman, Talman, Baker, Floyd, Tempest, Thomson and Huckle. Only a few of these are known to existing scholarship, and the rest await further research. Courten's most interesting associate was Adrian Beverland, who valued and swapped his Marcantonios against some valuable gold medals, and purchased a number of other prints at various times (see p. 26).

The Courten papers are all in his own handwriting. Parts are written in his code, which consists of a simple substitution of symbols for letters. A partial key to it is given in Sl. 4019 f. 79 and in the transcripts that follow the code is silently transliterated. Prices are in pre-decimal British currency: twelve pence = one shilling, twenty shillings = one pound. (Courten also had a price code, which I cannot understand; since he gives valuations not in code in the right column, I can only imagine that this code refers to the price that he paid.) The sheets in the volume have been bound in a very illogical order, and the following synopsis of the pages relating to his print collection is arranged by the contents, not the pagination. The pages fall into three main groups: (A) those listing the best prints in his collection that he wanted to keep, or was intending to sell, (B) those on his collection of portrait prints, and (C) those listing his purchases of all kinds of material (mostly natural history) for his collection from 1688 to his death.

Synopsis (certain pages or entries of particular interest are transcribed)

A: [Lists of prints, except portraits. Unless otherwise stated, sheets are headed 'My best stamps that are out of my books catalogued in May (or June) 1687'.]

f. 25 Sold out of my large books 1687

[a list of prints, mostly bundles, some individually specified, sold to Gibson, Cromer, Bateman, Talman (on 17 August 1693), Baker (September 1693), Sir Godfrey Copley (November 1693), Beverland and Lord P.(?Pembroke)]

ff. 29r–30v Stamps in one of my large bookes to part with 4th April 1687 B.no. 3, Best prints

[a long list of 387 prints, totalling £24 2s. with titles and engravers and prices, with names of purchasers of some items added later, including Gibson, Beverland and Lord P.]

f. 53 April 1693 [Lists of purchases of objects of various types from Conyers and Bagford]

f. 54 August 1694 Sold out of my large booke with ferret ribands

1 King of France by Poilly.   0-6
9 November 1695 sold Mr Watts
1 Virgin Mary & our Saviour van Dyck inv.
   Pontius sculpsit.   0-6
1 Hollar's Magdalene.   1-6

f. 78 Notes of various prints after Poussin given out to
Mr Norris 29 September 1694, apparently on consignment
for sale

f. 10 Prints B. f. Mr Beverland, the 3rd of June 1700
[this and the following pages relate to an exchange of prints
('trucking') for medals; the marked valuations are stated as
having been supplied by Beverland]

No. 3 Christus in nubibus, trucked for La Grande   4.0.0
         Reine
No. 6 Bacchus cum sileno, trucked for the Duke of
         Brunswick, R Aequat   1.10.0
No. 7 Bacchus in vindemiario, trucked for Barnevelt   1.13.0
No. 11 Proelium Raphaelis, trucked for Grotius   1.13.0
No. 12 Imperator Traianus, trucked for Innocent the
         12th AU [aurum]
No. 13 Venus et Cupido, trucked for Innocent the 12th 4.0.0
No. 14 Galatea maior, trucked for the D. of Brunswick 2.2.0
No. 20 S. Laurentius Bacchi Bandinelli, trucked for
         Carolus 2nd R nullum numen abest   3.3.0
No. 21 Cosmetae Bonasono Psyche, trucked for a
         medal of L. M. R. Aeternitas Imperii   15.0
No. 22 Nereides Bonason, trucked for
         Carolus 2nd R. nullum numen   1.0.0
No. 25 Nymphae Bonason, trucked for the Duke of
         Brunswick   1.1.6
No. 26 Equites A.V., trucked for Aeternitas Imperii   3.0.0
for the portfeuille the Padouans Bassianus & cavineus
the medal of Cardinal Mazarin Firmando Firmior haeret,
a small medal of Livius Odeschalchi R soror   1.10.0
Total £28.5.6

f. 80 The selling prices [in same pen as above; this list adds the
names of the engravers: Marcantonio, Marco da Ravenna,
Agostino Veneziano and Bonasone]

No. 3 Christus in nubibus MA   2-10-0
  6 Bacchus cum Sileno MA   1-7-0
  7 Bacchus in vindemiario MA   1-8-0
 10 Proelium Raphaelis S. Ravenna   1-10-0
 13 Venus et Cupido MA   2-3-0
 14 Galatea Maior MA   2-0-0
 20 S. Laurentius Bacchi Bandinelli MA 3-3-0
 21 Cosmata Bonasono Psyche   0-12-0
 22 Nereides Bonasone   0-10-0
 25 Nymphae Bonason   0-15-0
 26 Equites AV   3-3-0
Portfeuille   1-1-6
Total £20.2.6

f. 87 [The same list as on f. 80, but with lowered prices, totalling
£13 13s.]

f. 123 The names of several masters that I keepe [a list of names
of engravers, numbered to 74]

f. 180 A catalogue of my prints that are bound August 1687

[this was never completed, and contains only one item]

1 Barlows Birds in painted paper   3-0
f. 111 Things done in wood to keepe
2 pourtraits NK VSichem sculp.   1-6
1 Rhinocerus Albert Durer   0-9
4 upon blew paper by Golzius, 3 landskipps   2-3
                         1 woman   1-6
12 moneths NK 1 landskip HWG   1-6
2 of Albert Durer St Jerosme & the beheading of
   St John Golzius
Judith with Holifernes head   3-6

f. 112 My best stamps Durer, May 1687
    [50 entries, all engravings, total   10-9-0]
Adulterium   6-0
Mellanchollya   6-0
The portrait of Erasmus   10-0
Cardinal Albert Archbishop of Mainz the lesser 10-0
Cardinal Albert the larger   3-0
Melancthon's effigies   5-0
Bilibaldi Pirkeymheri effigies   3-6
The volta santa & a madona   5-0
St Hubert   5-0
St Jerosme   7-0
A country man and country woman a dancing   1-6
A man a scolding at his wife   1-0
The bag piper   2-0
A man and his wife going to market with fowle and eggs 1-6
The 3 conspirators Swisses   2-6
Albert Durer's portrait d. by himself   5-0
Pandora with her box   10-0
Alberts songe   10-0
A woman caryed away by a sea god   5-0
4 naked women; the Trojan horse   8-0
Alberts Adam & Eve   2-0-0
The passion, 17 pieces   15-0
The 5 apostles of Albert Durer   5-0
A man and a woman walking, death standing behind
   the tree   2-0
Another Trojan horse   3-0
The coate of arms with the death's head   1-0
A Turk on horseback & 5 persons on foot   0-6
The madona sitting by a hedge   1-6
The V. giving suck   1-0
The hermite   3-0
A man drawing a bow & a woman siting feeding a stag 1-6
A man with colours in his hand   1-6
A man riding whip & spur   1-0
A woman a horseback & a man walking with a halberd
   by her   1-0
St George   1-0
St Christopher   1-0
The V. under a tree with our saviour in her armes 1-6
A woman riding upon a goat   1-6
2 angells sounding trumpetts   0-6
Friderick Duke of Saxony   5-0
A coate of armes having the cock for the crest 3-0
St George on horseback   1-0
A madona under a tree with a peare in her hand 2-6

A madona siting on a cushion	1-6
Damianus a Goes picture	1-6
The V. giving suck under a hedge	1-6
Judah & Thamar	1-6
The woman giving suck under a rock naked	1-0
The madona with a monkey	1-0
The V. M. & our saviour & St Joseph drawing water out of a well	2-0

f. 113 Lucas van Leyden: 44 entries, total £4-9-6

[including as the two most expensive (the rest being mostly 1s to 2s)]

A large piece of our Saviours being led to be crucified	10-0
A shepheard with cows & a woman with a pale of milk	8-0

f. 114 Aldegrever: 38 entries, total £4-0-0

[these are all 6d or 1s each]

f. 115 Jacob Binck: 18 entries for 18-0

f. 116 Master IB: 7 items total 8-9

f. 117 Stephanus de Laune: 12 sets, total £2-7-2

[including] 5 ovall ornements	1-8
1 counterpreuves oval	0-4

f. 118 HSB Hisbins [Beham]: [43 entries, total £2-9-11]

f. 119 HSP [also Beham]: [10 entries, total 4-10]

f. 120 Virgilius Solis: [5 entries, total 7-5]

[including] 8 pieces a dance, imperfect	0-8

f. 121 J. T. de Bry: [5 entries, total 13-0]

f. 124 Della Bella: [33 entries, total £4-1-8]

f. 125 Rembrandt, Goudt, Bartolomei: my best stamps that are out of my books catalogued in May 1687

4 pieces beggars	2-6
3 portraits	2-3
1 Abraham sending away Hagar	1-0
1 our Saviour driving the merchants out of the Temple	1-0
2 small heads of Rt	1-0
1 piece St Jerosme	0-6
1 piece of severall personages an old man holds a child	0-6
2 pieces of the windmill Rt; a cascade Bartolomei	1-0
1 large counterpreuve of the beggars	0-6
1 beggar a small piece	0-1
2 mens heads	0-8
1 womans head	0-4
1 the rat catcher	0-9
1 head of Castiliones	0-6

f. 129 [another sheet gives further prices for Rembrandts, among a list of prints given on consignment to a Mr Letts to sell. These items do not come from the Rembrandt sheet, but were extracted from the lists of portraits]:

Wtenborgardus	2-6
Joannes Lutma aurifex	1-6
Rhimbrants wife	0-9
Mahomet Rimbrant	
Swalmius	1-6

1 N.K. [not known]	0-6
Abraham & Hagar	0-6

f. 126 [another sheet with a more summary listing of Rembrandt etchings, with prices]

f. 165 Callot: [213 prints for about £14] [see fig. 4 on p. 25]

[including] the Battaglia nel fiume d'Arno	10-0

f. 168 Perelle: [40 entries mostly series]

f. 169 Sold out of the landskips of Perelle. May 1689

f. 170 My best stamps of Hollar's catalogued May 1687 in a parchment bound book

1 Embassy to China	1-0
37 cutts of shells, rare	18-6
12 insects	6-0
2 pieces with muffs	1-1
2 St Mary Over, Piazza in Covent Garden	1-0
1 The Tower	0-6
6 pieces of Tangier	3-0
3 different prospects of Elizabeth Castle in Jarsay, Nasbach neare the Rhin	1-0
2 pieces Strasburgh & the bridge	0-6
2 pieces Ingelstadt & the covered bridge at Strasburgh	
2 other small pieces, landskips	0-4
2 other small landskips, Eslingen & a bridge by Strasburgh	0-4
4 small German landskips	1-0
1 landskip with a windmill	0-4
1 small piece of satires & nymphs a dancing	0-2
4 sea pieces	2-0
2 pieces of the manner of sitting at dinner on the day of princes investiture	1-0
1 urne	0-4
1 piece a person delivering a letter Uriah	0-2
1 portrait of Henry van der Borcht Hollar fecit	0-6
2 pieces of the burning of London & the plan of it	3-0
1 map of Berkshire	1-6
1 view of Richmond	0-6
13 insects Hoffnagel del. Vischer sculpsit	3-3

f. 171 George Pentz: [25 entries, total £1 7s 3d. The most expensive are 1-0 each]

f. 172 G. P. George Pentz [blank sheet with only this heading: annotated by Sloane 'Pr.CXIII' and '&c' added after Pentz]

f. 174 Mezzo tinto to keepe

1 a man playing upon a lute a woman on a flute Van Somer fecit	1-3
1 a man drinking a woman a smoking FBV	1-0
1 the Quakers meeting I. Beckett	0-6
1 a chirurgion dressing a man L VB F	0-9
1 a man a smoking & a woman with a glasse in her hand IB ex.	0-6
1 a counterpreuve LVBF	0-6
1 2 men one with a stick the other with pan of coales in his hand VB	0-6
1 small landskip a sheapherd playing on a flute with his dog by him	0-6
1 the beare Mrs Simons	1-0

f. 175 Tempesta: [24 entries, mostly sets, at up to 10-0 each]

f. 176 The best copys of different mrs [masters] catalogued June 1687

Copys of different mrs [masters] verry good: [13 entries including]

1 copy of Albert Durer's horse by Wierix	1-0
St Cecilia coppy after M. Anthony	2-6
Bataglia del Re Testi et del Re Tinti copy after Callot	0-6
The milkmaid after L. van Leyden	1-0

f. 179 Monsters to keepe

Female children joyned together	0-4
Monstri integri et dissecti effigies	0-3
Eigentlicke etc.	0-3
A hogg with 2 leggs on its back. A. Durer fecit	0-6
A bearded bunch of grapes. J. ab Heyden sculp.	0-4
Description d'un enfant prodigieux veu à Naples 1682	0-3

B: [Sheets listing the portrait print collection, headed with categories of sitter. Each sheet has in the main column the sitter's name, followed by that of the engraver, and in the right column a valuation.]

f. 8 Painters, statuarys, gravers, architects etc.

[including]:

Joannes Lutma aurifex Rhinbrant	1-0
Titian and his mistress Vandyck	1-6

f. 9 Sold from the above [six prints to Mr Tolman (Talman) in August 1693]

f. 178 [A list of the names of 50 artists dated January 1702, and annotated 'Painters for Mr Wren' and 'Layed aside for Mr Wren'. The total price comes to £2 5s 6d. Since Christopher Wren had long been knighted, this was perhaps his son.]

f. 131 Poets to keepe

f. 132 Emperours, Kings and Electors

f. 133 English ladys

f. 134 F.[?oreign] ladys

f. 135 Officers

f. 136 Sea Commanders

f. 137 Ladys [all English]

f. 138 Actores

f. 139 Massanello [and two other portraits]

f. 140 Generalls

f. 141 Sold out of the Generalls

f. 142 Bishops & Abbats etc.

f. 143 Cardinalls

f. 144 Popes

f. 145 Musicians

f. 146 Women N.K. [not known, i.e. unidentified]

f. 147 Sold out of the women N.K.

f. 148 Sts & R. Ldys [Saints and Roman ladies]

f. 149 Bishops & Clergy men

f. 150 Ordres Religieux

f. 151 Hommes de lettres

f. 152 Sold out of the Hommes de lettres

f. 153 Persons of the long robe [i.e. lawyers]

f. 154 Persons of the long robe, of those sold

f. 155 Ministers of state

f. 156 Embassadors

f. 157 Nobility of Scotland

f. 158 Gentry of England

f. 159 Nobility of England

f. 160 Nobility of England, of those sold

f. 161 Kings of England

f. 162 Princesses

f. 163 Sold out of my Princesses

f. 164 Princes

f. 181 Nobility of F. P. [France, Portraits]

f. 182 Sovereign Princes

f. 184 Princes of As[ia], Af[rica] & Am[erica]

f. 185 Prints that I N. K. [i.e. the sitter, profession or engraver is unknown]

C: [Sheets headed 'Things bought', followed by the months covered]

f. 26 September 1688 to January 1689

f. 33 October 1688 to January 1689 [continuation of the above]
[includes] the Duchess of Albemarle's picture in mezzotinto by William Sherwin 1s;
severall prints of Mr Simon's bought of his daughter 9/6d.

f. 31 February to April 1689 [including many medals]

f. 27 May to December 1689

[includes] one large snaile shell green & mother of pearl given by Mr Mariette [presumably the great French print dealer], purchases of Mr Tempest [Pierce Tempest], 5 prints for 4-0; of Mr Floyd at Salisbury Exchange, 9 stamps for 13-6; of Mr Thompson [Richard Thomson] at the Sun in Bedfordberry 18th May, 3 prints for 7-6; of Mr Baker 1 print of Cochin's Saul going to Damascus 1-0; of the same, 4 pieces of Albanus graven by Baudet at 5-0 each, and one piece of devotion by Regnesson for 1-6; and of Mr Huckle 6 prints for 11-0

f. 39　January to April 1690

f. 36　May to August 1690

f. 37　September to December 1690

[includes] purchases from Mr Floyd of many natural history specimens, as well as of 2 cutts, 1 of Inigo Jones Villamena fecit for 0-3, and Mr Le Fevre, Mre des Requetes Troy pinxit Vermeulen sculp. 1-0

f. 34　September to December 1690

[includes] Mr Gibbons his head in mezzotinto Kneller pinxit Smith fecit 1-6

f. 48　January to December 1692

f. 56　January 1697 to January 1698

f. 59　January 1698 to January 1699 [mostly medals]

Appendix D
Transcript of the Catalogue of the Drawings and Prints in the Cracherode Collection
Antony Griffiths

This is taken from a small vellum-bound book with blank leaves. These bear a watermark of Britannia in an oval with the manufacturer's name J. Grove and the date 1802. Books of this kind were often supplied for use in the British Museum at the beginning of the nineteenth century (this information comes from Christopher Date). On the front cover are the initials WB and the date 1804. The initials probably stand for the Rev. William Beloe, although the handwriting is not his. Given the number of basic mistakes, it was probably compiled by a clerk working from notes supplied to him. Written on the flyleaf in pencil in the hand of William Alexander is 'General Catalogue of Prints in the Museum Collection'.

DRAWINGS

1st Portfolio

Drawings

1st division

Cipriani. One from the Oedipus col.
Three Ixion
One Hercules with the lion
One from the Antique
One Cain and Abel
Four additional
Hussey, two, red chalk
Holbein, two. Portrait of Bp. Fisher & a design for a vase

IInd

Gaspar Possino, one

Two, N. Poussin, Adoration of the Shepherds and boys with butterflies
One additional

IIIrd

Seven by Claude, and one, a ship, by R. Tasso

IVth

Four, Borgogne. Conversion of St Paul &
Three P. Panini, St Paul at Athens, and two of ruins

Vth

Twelve. Salv. Rosa. Two Banditti &c &c

VIth

Five Luca Cangiagio and Five B. Castiglione

VIIth

One, D. Campagnola, Three Fr. Bolognese

VIIIth

One Lud. Caracci
Two Agost. Caracci
Nine Annibale, one engraved by Pond
Two Domenichino, one a landscape
Three F. Mola
Two Franceschini
S. da Pesaro, one

IXth

Twelve, Guercino, six landscapes

Xth

One, P. de Cortona
One, Ca. Beglione
Three, Romanelli, one engraved by Pond
One N. Berettoni
One C. Maratt. Carlo Ochiali, engraved by Pond

XIth

Two, P. Farinati
One, Palma il Giovani
One, Pordenone
Three Titian, one engraved by Zucchi

XIIth

Eighteen, Parmegiano

XIIIth

One, Baroccio (a head)
Three, Correggio

XIVth

Two, Fra Bartolomeo
One, Dan. de Volterra
One, Taddeo Zucchero
One, Fred. Zucchero
Two, Fred. Zucchero, Portraits of Q. Elizabeth and the Earl of Leicester

xvth

Baccio Bandinelli, one
L. Cigoli. one engr. by Bartolozzi

xvith

One, Cav. Giuseppe apresso Michelagnolo
Nine M. Agnolo
Three Battista Franco

xviith

Fourteen, Giulio Romano, from the Antique etc.

xviiith

Two, Pierino del Vaga, one engraved by Ryland
Two, P. del Vaga. Vases
Two, Polidoro. (one el suo ritratto)
One, Livia Agresti de Forli

xixth

Five. Raffaelle. Pen drawings
A view of Bologna, by de Pris
A view of Sicily, by Cozens

Drawings. iind Portef.

ist Division

One Rubens
Four Vandyke
Fourteen Rembrandt
Four A. van Ostade
One Doomer

iind

Six Hollar
Eight Rademaker
Two Klotz
One De Haen
One W. Schellinx
Three uncertain

iiird

Three P. Brill
One Thier
Three Backhuysen
Two Cats
Two Coopse
One Van Uden
Three Vandeveld
One Vitringa
One R. Savery
One J. Fyt
One Ridinger
Three F. Ruysdaal
One Corn. Zaft-Level
Two du Pré
One van Drielst
One F. Sneyders
Three ?

ivth

Two Asselyn
One Rosa de Tivoli
One Melchior
Three N. Berghem
Two J. Both
Four Gainsborough
One Hobbima
Two P. Molyn
Two A. Storck
One Vanderdoes
One J. Van Huysum
One Vander Meer
Three Waterloo
One Wynants
One A. v. Vede
Two Suannavelt
One Chateleyn
Two Albert Cuyp
One Vertue, Portrait of Lady Jane Grey

vth

Two Taverner
One Underwood, View of Deans Yard
Three Roberts, Views of Oxford
One P. Sandby, Camp in St James Park, 1781
One Westal

vith

One Guido
Two Baldassar Peruzzi
One Van Kessell
Three Il Bolognese
One Ciro Ferri
One P. Testa
One Aureliano Milani
One Patel
Two Bartolozzi

viith

Anonymous

PRINTS

A: Martin Schoen, Israel van Mechlin, Albert Durer

B: Marc Antonio

C: Do

D: Prints from ancient Masters, viz:
Giotto, Sandro Boticelli, Ant. Pollagoli, L. da Vinci,
Fra. Bartolomeo, And. Salaino, B. Franco, Il Rosso, F. Vanni,
D. Beccafumi, M. Angelo, M. Rota, B. Bandinelli, Brownini,
A. del Sarto, Luca Penni, F. Salviati, G. Vasari, Georg. Giovanni,
F. de ...

CASE II

E: 1   Julio Romano, Polidoro, Giulio Clovio, Aquila, Fer. di
Mantua, And. Camassei, L. da S. Gemeniano, V. Strada, M. Rota,
C. Maratt, And. Sacchi

2   Fr. Francia, L. da Vinci, B. Beccafumi, And. del Sarto,
M. Angelo, P. del Vaga, B. Franco, F. Salviati, D. de Volterra,
Fr. Vanni, R. Manetti, V. Salimbeni, P. de Cortona, C. Ferri,
G. Gemignani, P. Testa, G. B. Mercati, St. della Bella

3   Giov. Lanfranco, Fr. Bolognese, Car. Cignani,
M. A. Franchesini

F: 1   Correggio

2   Primaticcio, N. del Abata

3   Lud. Lana, Guercino, Schidone, Baroccio

4   C. Procacino, Ch. Storer, M. A. Caraggio, And. Solario

5   Etchings and engravings from the French School
Laur. de la Hyrt, Le Sueur, Bourdon, L. Boullogne,
L. Bourguignon, A. Coypel

G: Etchings

1   Aquila, Luca Cangiagio, B. Castelli, Spagnolet, Biscaino
[annotated 'very fine and almost complete'], F. Amato,
Castigliogne, Lu. Giordano

2   Titian, Muziano, Bassano, Tintoret, P. Veronese, P. Farinati

3   Dom. & Jul. Campagnola, B. Montagna, Pordedone, Palma,
Bat. del Moro, Pasq. Ottino, Carpioni, Car. Saracino,
F. Bencoviet, Ant. Balestra

H: Prints and Etchings after Parmegiano

I: Salvator Rosa

K: Rembrandt. History

L: Rembrandt. Landscapes

CASE III

M: 1   Engraved Prints after A. Mantegna, Correggio,
Parmigiano, Primaticcio, L. Sabattini, N. del Abata, Pellegrino
Tibaldi, Luca Cangiagio

2   Giulio Romano, Polidoro, F. Baroccio, G. Clovio,
A. Pomerancio, B. Passani, P. del Vaga, L. A. del Forti,
T. Zucchero, Raffalle da Reggio

N: Lud. Carracci, Agost. Caracci, An. Caracci, Guido

O: 1   Agostino Caracci, Annibale Caracci, Dominichino,
F. Bolognese, P. de Cortona, Borgognone, F. Laura, Zuccarelli,
Gabbiani

2   Asselin, Berghem, Both, P. de Lauri al Bambaccio, Cuyp,
Hobima, Ruysdael, D. Teniers, A. Vandervelde, Vander Veens,
Wynants, Waterloo, Wouverman

P: 1   Rubens, J. Jordaens, A. Both, Fuller, A. Brower, Callot,
Ostade, Cuyp, Teniers, Breugel, Van Joyen

2   Goltzius, Ailsheimer

3   H. Gentileschi, P. de Cortona, Carlo Dolci

4   Albano, Dominichino, S. da Pesaro, Elisabett Sirani, Tiarini,
P. F. Mola, D. Maria Canutis, C. Cignani

Q: 1   Titian, Domenico Campagnola, Gioseppa Porta (Salviati),
Andrea Schiavone, G. Bassan, Tintoret, P. Veronese, P. Farinati,
Mutiano

2   L. Bernini, D. Feti, An. Sacchi, Ciro Ferri, F. Laura, Carlo
Maratti

3   Spagnolet, Schidone, M. A. de Caravaggio, Lanfranco,
Guercino, L. Giordano

R: 1   Etchings by unknown Masters

2   Do

3   Do

4   Do

5   Andrew Mantegna &c

6   Michael Angelo

7   Domenichino, E. Fialetti

8   A. Carracci, Guido, Dominichino, L. Pasinelli

S: 1   Le Valentin, S. Bourdon, Le Seur, Le Brun, Ant. Coypel

2   Engravings on wood from various Masters

CASE IV

Aa: Works of Raphael. 2 vols

Bb: G. Poussin, N. Poussin

Cc: Rubens. Landscapes

Dd: Rubens. Sacred History, Vandyck, Murillio

Ee: 1   Vandyck. Portraits by P. V. Gunst

2   Rubens, Vandyck, Jordaens, Berghem, Ostade, C. de Visscher

3   Diepenbeke, Jordaens, Sighens

Ff: N. Poussin's Scripture Pieces

Gg: A. Caracci (Etchings)

CASE V

Hh: Claude Lorraine

Ii: Etchings

1   Albani, Guido, S. de Pesaro, Sirani, Passeretti, Algardi,
Garberi

2   Caracci, Guido

Kk: Etchings

1   L. Caracci, Guido, Sirani

2   A. Caracci, Guido, Sirani

3   A. Caracci, Guido

Ll: Woollett, Hall

Mm: 1   Agostino Veneziano, Marco da Ravenna

2   Giulio Bonasoni

Nn: Miscellaneous prints not classed

Oo: Portlan[d] Vase, Antiquities, Drawings

CASE VI

Pp: Views in India

Qq: Bartolozzi's Works. 2 vol

Rr: 1   Holbein's Passion of our Saviour by Mechel

2   Etchings from Parmegiano

3   Antiquities

4   Do

5   Mezzotinto Prints

6   Miscellaneous Do

7   Views of Oxford, Rookers Views, Satirical Prints

CASE VII

I   English Portraits from Henry 8 to George 2

II   Do

III   English Portraits by Holbein, Oliver, &c

IV   English Portraits Miscellaneous

V   Do Lely, Kneller &c

VI   Do Kneller, Dahl &c

VII   Do Jansen, Merevelt &c

VIII   Vandyck English

IX   Do Foreign

X   Do Do

CASE VIII

I   French Portraits

II   Portraits of the Interregnum

III   Julio Romano 2v.

IV   Leon. da Vinci & others by Chamberlain

V   Coloured Prints from Raphael

VI   Dassiers Medals

VII   Luxembourg Gallery

VIII   Miscellaneous Portraits, Foreign

IX   Do English

PS

–   English portraits are marked off in Bromleys Catalogue of Engraved British Portraits [now Desk E 3]

–   Vandyck's Portraits are catalogued in an octavo red book [lost]

–   Foreign Portraits the same [lost]

–   Prints from Rubens and his disciples are marked off in Basans Catalogue [BL 680 a.20–22]

–   Visscher's prints the same

–   Rembrandt's works, and those of his disciples are marked off in Gersant's French Catalogue [Annotated in pencil by W. Alexander 'These have also been marked in Dalby's catalogue WA'] [BL 683 c.27–28]

–   Marc Antonio and the works of his disciples are marked off in Heinekins Dictionnaire des Artistes [BL 679 d.12]

–   Various other prints the same

–   Julio Bonasoni's Prints are marked off in Cumberland's catalogue [BL 674 b.9]

–   [added in pencil by W. Alexander: 'Hollars works contained in 3 vols are marked off (though perhaps not completely) in Vertue's catalogue; but such prints by him as are inserted in the collection of portraits are not included: these by way of distinction should be marked with red ink']

Appendix E
Documents on Robert Dighton's Thefts, 1806
Antony Griffiths

These documents have been transcribed from the series of 'Original Papers' in the Central Archives of the British Museum, II pp. 802–44, with various additions from the minutes of the General Meeting of the Trustees.

21 June 1806. At a meeting. Present: the Speaker, Sir Joseph Banks, Mr Rose, Mr Sloane

Mr Planta was called in and stated as follows:

Mr Woodburn, a printseller in St Martin's Lane came to me on Wednesday the 18th inst. and desired to look at Mr Cracherode's collection to find a certain print there, called Rembrandt's Coach Landscape. Mr Beloe not being in the bay, and being myself engaged I gave my key to Mr Ellis (the assistant librarian in that Department) and desired him to shew that particular portfolio. Mr Ellis informed me that the print could not be found in its place, and that Mr Woodburn declared to him that he had seven prints of Albert Durer, on the back of which there was some appearance of Mr Cracherode's mark, and that Mr Woodburn informed Mr Ellis he had purchased these prints of a Mr Dighton.

I went to Mr Woodburn on Friday 20th and saw the prints and have great reason to suspect they were part of Mr Cracherode's collection.

Mr Samuel Woodburn, printseller in St Martin's Lane was called in. He produced the seven prints of Albert Durer and the Coach Landscape and stated as follows:

About six weeks ago I bought the Coach Landscape of Mr Dighton and gave him 12 guineas for it. Being told there was a reason to think it might be a copy I brought it to the Museum on the 18th inst. to compare it with two which I had heard were in Mr Cracherode's collection. I found neither of the two there, but only a coloured one.

NB on the face of the print now produced there is a mark said to be of Sir Edward Astley and on the back of it several names and dates, and six marks of its having been pasted on paper.

Narrative continued: About a month ago I bought the seven Albert Durer's with other prints in one lot of Mr Davis, a printseller, who lives at a perfumer's in the Haymarket, next door or next but one to Broderips. Mr Davis valued the Albert Durer to me at 2 guineas.

NB Four of these appear to have written marks and dates on the back which are imperfectly erased whereof the dates are still distinguishable.

Narrative continued: Mr Davis said he bought these Albert Durer's all at the same time together with others which had on them the mark of Mr Dighton. I had seen Mr Dighton about a fortnight before and he said he should have something to shew me and would call when he had. In consequence of his having called, I went to him on the occasion above mentioned.

About six months ago I went to Mr Dighton to compare a print of Rembrandt called the Goldweigher; and on that occasion he showed me a large collection of Rembrandt's prints, some of them of very considerable value, two worth £40 a piece; amongst these was the Burgomaster Six. The account he gave me was that on the death of his father, who was a collector, his prints were divided between his sister and himself, and in dividing them alternately, the print of the Burgomaster Six came to his sister; that the principal part of his collection came at the same time and manner; and the sort of story was that on his sister's death, from her or her husband this print came to him. This was about six months ago.

The same day, after having been at Mr Dighton's, I met Mr de Claussen, and on conversing with him, he told me that he knew Mr Cracherode's collection at the Museum, and was sure that the prints at Dighton's were taken from thence, for that Dighton wishing to be better informed about prints had on Mr de Claussen's advice come to the Museum – and either at that or a subsequent time, Mr de Claussen told me that Dighton had said he could get admission having acquaintance with Mr Beloe.

NB Mr Thane in Spur Street was principally employed in making the collection of Mr Cracherode's prints, and Mr Philipe of Warwick Street sold the Burgomaster Six to Mr Cracherode.

Mr Beloe was then called in and stated as follows:

Last night at about 5 o'clock I was for the first time informed by Mr Planta that there was a loss of some of the prints of the Cracherode collection, and [that they] were on sale among the collectors and traced to Mr Dighton.

In answer to a question he said: I never saw Mr Dighton till he was brought here by Mr Caley about twelve months ago. He brought him to me to see the Rembrandt prints; he saw them then; I shewed them to him. Mr Caley recommended Mr Dighton to me as a gentleman who was his friend. Mr Caley did not stay long. Mr Dighton stayed a considerable time. I was with him the whole time. I believe nothing was shown him but the Rembrandt prints. He probably might stay an hour or more. He then asked me at what times he might find me and have an opportunity of looking at these prints. I told him my days of attendance at the Museum were Monday and Tuesday, when he would be certain of finding me, but as a friend of Mr Caley, I should be glad to accommodate him. About a fortnight or three weeks later after he came again. I think he came alone. He again saw the Rembrandt prints. I put them on the stand for prints, and continued in the room at my desk. He came six or seven times afterwards, probably more, and generally stayed an hour or an hour and a half. I made a point of it religiously never to leave him alone unless I was accidentally called out to give a ticket or for some such purpose of Museum business, and if I was detained I desired Mr Ellis or one of the messengers to attend. Being disgusted with his manner of examining the prints, I sent him a penny post letter to say he must

not come again till a catalogue was made. I did not suspect at this time that he had made an improper use of the leave given him. I did not at any time examine the portfolio with that view after he had had the inspection.

There is a general catalogue of the prints and drawings, but none specifying each print or drawing individually. Mr Dighton has not been here several months, I should conceive not since the end of February.

The particulars which dissatisfied me in his conduct were that I thought he did not examine the prints as a gentleman or connoisseur, but huddled them backwards and forwards.

Whenever I have observed these prints or any of them loose I have sent down the particular print to Mr Elliott to fasten them.

There are two portfolios of Rembrandt prints. Mr Dighton never had the use of more than one at a time. Occasionally Mr Dighton asked me for the works of other masters, but I do not recollect his having those of Albert Durer. I am not however sure he might not.

NB Mr Conant attended at the Museum, and the above minutes were read to him. He took an affidavit in consequence, and then went to Mr Dighton's and brought away, with his consent, his portfolio and the box described.

28 June 1806: papers put before the adjourned Committee:

Read by Mr Conant: No.2

There is no proof that the collection as contained in Mr Cracherode's catalogue came entire to the Museum, and the prints have not since been so arranged or compared with any lists as to be identified in the hands of the Museum by the Librarians.

About two years ago it happened at different times that two dealers, (more conversant in connoisseur prints than any other men in Europe perhaps) inspected the prints in the Museum, and had before sold many of the prints to Mr Cracherode, and so far that there is any proof that the prints discovered to have been missing and found now in the hands of a person suspected to have stolen them are the same prints that were in the Museum, that proof must come from them. And their evidence is annexed, namely Mr Philipe and Mr Claussen, who since the prints were missed have been desired to examine the prints at the Museum, and so far as their memory goes think that prints they severally saw two years ago to the value of £300 or £400 are now missing.

Dighton, a printseller, who for eighteen months preceding the last six had frequent access to the collection under the ordinary admission of a student, and was suspected to be the thief.

A magistrate was applied to who got possession of Dighton's portfolio; and in that found near one hundred prints (£300 in value), the same to all appearance as those deficient in the Museum, and many of them so extremely scarce as to render it in the opinion of connoisseurs next to impossible that the same assemblage of scarce prints could have arisen in two places. Dighton has also sold considerable parcels of curious prints which are also such as are lost by the Museum. So that when the whole come to be traced, it will probably be seen that the whole deficiency of the Museum has passed through his hands. But as is above stated, there will be no decisive proof except the memory of the gentlemen above mentioned that similar prints ever reached the Museum, although they are mentioned in Mr Cracherode's catalogue; and by their memory only two of those seen in the

Museum have specific marks to identify them: namely the specks arising from damp on one, and the yellow tint on another.

Evidence of Mr Claussen, print collector, Fitchfield Street (as taken by Mr Conant). No. 3, read 28 June

No. 34 Great Coppenol: Saw the portrait of the Great Coppenol at the Museum. It is now missing. There were two, one of them a proof which remains. This he believes to be the other, but he cannot identify it, excepting that it is on India paper which is unusual.

No. 31 Dutch Barn. Saw this at the Museum two years ago. Has no doubt but it is the same; remembers particularly the spots upon it which are occasioned by damp, and he particularly took notice of them considering it as a blemish. It had Sir Edward Astley's mark on it which still remains. There is an erasure on the back which is disguised by writing over it in pencil '1744 and a name'.

Angel and Shepherds. Well remembers seeing it in the Museum – now missing. Knows this to be the same he saw, from a peculiar yellow tint in the sky under the angel, owing to a damage repaired by rubbing, which he particularly noticed at the Museum and now well recollects. He had seen the same print at Mr Barnard's sale, and did not purchase it on account of this damage. Mr Barnard's mark appears to have been erased but some traces of it remain, though very obscure.

Hundred Guilder Print. There were two in the Museum, one with a margin, the other without. The latter remains. This print he is persuaded is the other, both on account of the margin, and from the excellency of the impression which he particularly noticed when he saw it at the Museum; and such an impression is scarce in the extreme. He saw writing on the back of this print, and there now are evident traces of erasure in the same part, but does not recollect the subject of the writing.

Burgomaster Six. There were two; one is missing. This is a proof, and he is sure he saw a proof there, which is known by the name being omitted and also by some inverted figures which were afterwards corrected in the later prints. The reason for thinking this to be the proof that was in the Museum is that no other proof has been known in England, and from the extreme beauty of the impression which he particularly noticed at the Museum and was similar to this.

Coach Print. Vide his account of this, in the other paper of Mr Philipe's evidence.

This gentleman speaks to many other prints in a similar way, but none so nearly to identify the particular print to have been in the Museum. He was more observant of the particular marks, blemishes and qualities of the prints in the Museum, being employed in writing a critical catalogue of rare prints.

No. 3a: continuation of Mr Claussin's evidence dated 28 June

Mr de Claussen is engaged in preparing a catalogue of the prints of the different masters, and with a view to this he visited the Museum with General Turner about two years ago. He was there only once. He is well acquainted with Dighton who used always to show him his collections and seemed to lay great stress on Mr de Claussen's opinion of them. At the time of Mr Geddies sale, which was after Mr de Claussen had been at the Museum, he mentioned to Mr Dighton Rembrandt's collection there, and D.

said he would go to see them. Since this time, Mr Dighton has mentioned his having some curious prints, but has never shewn them to Mr de Claussen. Mr Dighton has sold some Rembrandts, which were not choice prints since he had the fine collection. Mr de Claussen has lately examined the portfolios at the Museum, and finds several missing. He judges the value of those missing might be £400. Mr Philipe says Mr Geddies sale was in May 1804.

Evidence of Mr Philipe, print collector, Golden Square, respecting prints supposed to belong to the Museum found in the portfolios of G. Dighton. No. 4 28 June

Coach Print. Saw two of the genuine prints on one leaf in the Museum. They were both doubled down, which he remarked to the Librarian. Believes they were both on India paper [in margin in pencil 'but doubtful']. One of them only now remains in the Museum. Has no doubt but this is the other, but recollects it only by the general appearance, and from a remarkable difference which he observed between the two prints: viz. one of them having the barn more darkly shaded than the other. The dark one remains. This is lighter and similar to that which is now missing. [in margin in pencil: 'not clear in his recollection about this, but chiefly led to it by Mr Claussen's account']

Mr Claussen also well recollects the two prints on one leaf in the Museum, and particularly took notice of the light upon the barn on the print that is missing; and from this peculiarity is much inclined to believe this to be the same print.

The Large Presentation in the Temple. Well remembers this to have been in Mr Cracherode's collection, having sold it to him, and is the more certain of its identity from it having still on it the mark of his correspondent in Holland from whom he bought it. But he has no recollection of having seen it in the Museum.

[added in another hand] Mr Philipe went to the Museum with a Mr Haring (now abroad) to point out the beauties in the prints. He has lately looked over the portfolio at the Museum, and thinks many are gone.

Evidence of Mr Thane, printseller, Spur Street. No. 5, read 28 June

Collected prints for Mr Cracherode, and conversant in his collection. Well knew his marks and the particular qualities of the individual prints, and has no doubt but the principal part of these prints were in that collection. But the marks by which he could have known them are so erased or mutilated that there is not a single print he could identify. Though from the large portion of the prints missing from the Museum being found together here; from the extreme scarcity of some of the prints and the beauty of the impressions so remarkable in Mr Cracherode's collection, he has no doubt in his own mind but that these are the same. He has seen the collection since they were in the Museum, but his observation there was not such as enables him to identify any particular print as having been there.

28 June 1806: Minutes of Adjourned Committee. Present: the Speaker of the House of Commons [and eight other names]

Mr Conant attended and read the paper (no. 2), the evidence of Mr Claussen was read (no. 3); he was afterwards called in.

He stated that he never saw the prints at the Museum but once, and that was in company with General Turner, but when he went it was for the purpose of correcting a general catalogue he was making of the prints in the different collections. This was a little before the time of Dr Giddies sale. Mr Dighton was always in the habit of shewing Mr de Claussen his prints, and seemed to lay great stress on the approbation of Mr Claussen and not to be satisfied otherwise. Mr de Claussen mentioned to Dighton at Dr Giddies sale the Rembrandts at the Museum, and Dighton said he would go and see them. Mr de Claussen has lately looked over the portfolio and thinks that the prints missing may be worth £400.

Mr Philipe's evidence was also read (no. 4), and he was called in.

Dr Giddies sale was in May 1804. He knew the Cracherode collection; once saw them at the Museum, he noticed the principal prints – not by marks – does not recollect seeing the Presentation in the Temple – only one he can speak to with certainty – there is a mark on the back. Recollects the Coach Landscape; has seen it at Cracherode's; cannot identify it. Had Barnard's collection two years, an erasure is on the back. Barnard generally put his mark on the top, J.B. Has looked over the collection carefully at the Museum. Thinks many gone, rather thinks he saw the Presentation here since Dr Giddies sale; thinks it was in the winter. Mr Herring of Harley Street, a merchant and collector, was with him.

no. 5 Mr Thane's information.

Ordered that the papers relating to this transaction be immediately laid before Mr Garrow and a consultation requested at which Mr Conant may be present.

Paper from W. Garrow, Lincoln's Inn

Papers 1 to 6 inclusive contain the evidence which has been taken as to the loss of certain prints from the Museum. Mr Conant who has been so instrumental in obtaining the evidence has been kind enough to say he will attend Mr Garrow and produce the prints, as to the identity of which the strongest part of the evidence goes.

On this evidence your opinion is requested first, whether there is probable ground to expect conviction of Mr Dighton. Secondly whether it is so doubtful as that you would advise the Trustees of the British Museum under the circumstances to avail themselves of any offer on the part of Mr Dighton of a full disclosure and restitution of the things taken, having regard to the situation of the Trustees. And thirdly whether if Mr Dighton should not at once offer a full disclosure, what steps you would advise.

I have carefully considered the evidence stated and have had the advantage of conversing with Mr Conant upon the subject, and I am of opinion that unless Mr Dighton shall do everything that may be required of him to furnish the most complete information of the manner in which the valuable articles deposited in the Museum have been withdrawn from thence and to enable the Trustees to restore them, there is evidence against him abundantly sufficient to justify a prosecution against him for felony. There are however difficulties in the way of convicting from the circumstances of there not being any catalogue of individual prints or any other means by which any of the librarians can ascertain that prints of the description traced to Dighton have been withdrawn from the national collection, or that they ever formed a part of it. Under these circumstances I have no hesitation in saying that in my humble judgement the highly respectable persons who have attended to this case will be well warranted in the discharge of their duty to abstain from prosecuting where ultimate punish-

ment is doubtful, and to make use of this occurrence to introduce such additional guards and regulations as to them in their wisdom may appear to be necessary.

Signed: W. Garrow, Lincoln's Inn, 28 June 1806

[undated report annotated] 'Paper given in by Mr Conant subsequent to Mr Garrow's opinion'

The Report of Nathaniel Conant Esq., one of his Majesty's Justices of the Peace for the County of Middlesex, who saith that in consequence of having found so great a number of the prints supposed to have been purloined from the Museum in the possession of Dighton, and having discovered many others which had been disposed of by him to several dealers and collectors, he examined Dighton respecting the same, when he expressed a willingness to make an open confession of the whole transaction, which Mr Conant (considering that the extent of the depredations could not otherwise easily be discovered, or the identity of the prints that had been disposed of ascertained, all the marks having been artfully erased) permitted him to do; at the same time giving him distinctly to understand that he must not consider himself as entitled thereby to any favour from the Trustees further than that the light thrown upon the business by his own discoveries should not be brought in evidence against him, in case he made a fair and full disclosure.

Dighton then made the following disclosure, viz:

I was first at the Museum in the year 1794 [sic], being introduced by Mr Calley to Mr Beloe. When we first arrived, Mr Beloe was not there, but a gentleman in attendance gave me out a portfolio, and Mr Beloe soon after arrived. Mr Calley told Mr Beloe who I was, and I said I wished to improve myself in my profession by the sight of scarce prints, which at that time was my real object. I went again in about a week. Mr Beloe was very obliging to me, and said I might see the prints whenever I wished, and I went frequently. Soon afterwards I had an opportunity of offering to take the portraits of some of the family, and Mr Beloe and his daughter were both drawn by me, which having received so much civility I did gratis. My acquaintance with Mr Beloe increased, and my admissions were facilitated.

The prints were slightly pasted in the portfolio and easily got off, many were quite loose, which I mentioned to Mr Beloe and advised them to be pasted at the corners which was done. It occurred to me that several prints were absent from their places, because I understood Mr Cracherode's Rembrandts were very complete, and I could not find among them some that were scarce, particularly the Bull Landscape, and Regnier Hensloo with the margin.

I was altogether at the Museum more than a dozen times. I twice carried with me a portfolio to show Mr Beloe some drawings, and availed myself of that means of conveying prints away. I never found occasion to be particularly guarded in the manner of taking them away; sometimes in my pocket, sometimes in the bosom of my coat, often in a roll in my hand, having occasionally carried with me a print or a drawing rolled up, to which I added others when I came away. At home I put them on paper with margins, and chiefly did so with the most valuable. Having a particular desire to possess Rembrandts, I mounted them on fine paper and kept them in my own collection. I sold the greater number of the rest to Mr Mortimer, to Davis in the Haymarket, and to Mr Woodburn. From Davis I might receive £70, from Mr Mortimer

£100, and about £10 from Mr Woodburn. But I added prints from my own collection, which are not included in this estimate.

I believe the Hundred Guilder print is still in the Museum; that found in my portfolio was bought at Sir Simon Clarke's sale by Mr Claussen for Mr Haring, and I afterwards had it of him in exchange for one I possessed. Mine was bought at King's for a small price, being a very faint impression, but I touched it up afterwards and Mr Haring preferred it to his own. This transaction was before I had access to the Museum. The first of the Museum prints that I sold was in the month of May 1795.

The last time I was at the Museum Mr Beloe mentioned a wish of finding somebody to arrange the prints, and I wrote him a letter to offer my assistance. I soon after received a letter from Mr Beloe to say that he had no intention to do this business immediately, but that some measures were taking respecting the prints, and in the meantime the inspection of them would be suspended, in consequence of which I absented myself.

Upon being interrogated whether he considered himself as receiving any indulgence from the Librarians in the inspection of the prints than was usually allowed, and whether he had any other claim to such indulgence than what arose from the original introduction of Mr Calley, he answered, I have not any claim, but having been always treated with great civility by Mr Beloe, I two or three times sent him presents of fish when I heard he had company, and once of green peas when they were a guinea a quart.

In consequence of this disclosure, a large proportion of the most valuable prints have been recovered over and above those found in Dighton's house, and there is reason to expect that the greater part of the remaining deficiency will be restored. But of this Mr Philipe will be best able to speak when he has gone through the examination of that deficiency.

(signed) N. Conant.

10 July 1806: letter from Philipe to Planta

Sir, After parting from you yesterday I went straight to Mr Conant's, where I found that by the good management of this excellent magistrate, a confession had been obtained from Dighton as to a number of the principal articles by Rembrandt missing in the Museum. They were set apart, and a list is here inclosed.

But upon looking over the remainder which Dighton says are his own, I saw others which I have reason to think belong to Mr Cracherode's collection, and are missing in the Museum. These I separated. And I have set apart another parcel which, though not wanting in the Museum, are I am inclined to believe the prints which did belong to Mr Cracherode, those now found in the Museum, or a part at least, having been substituted by Dighton. The Three Trees landscape for instance is very ordinary at the Museum, while that at Mr Conant's is a jewel of the first water. This is a celebrated print, and certain I am that Mr Cracherode would not have been satisfied with an ordinary impression, when he had opportunities of procuring the best.

It will occur to you that until these matters are cleared up it will be impossible for me to make a satisfactory report on the Rembrandts.

Towards bringing about the wished for settlement, it will be proper to compare the prints in Mr Conant's possession with those in the Museum. But here I confess that I cannot speak to a single item with certainty, though it is possible that something may come out on a strict examination of particulars.

There are other prints by Rembrandt missing at the Museum, not found in Dighton's possession; perhaps they may be found among the prints bought by the different printsellers from D. or his broker Davis.

I think it will be right to quiet the minds of the Trustees as soon as possible respecting the Mark Antonios, which are of more consequence than the Rembrandts, by informing them that only one print of value appears to be missing, though that is a capital one. viz. Paul preaching at Athens. It was purchased by Woodburn of Davis, as I understand, and is the finest impression I ever beheld. I hope it may be recovered. The others not found under their respective numbers in Heinecken are not very material, and may be procured without much difficulty.

I have the honour to be your most obedient humble servant, T. Philipe.

[On a separate paper enclosed is a list of 35 prints by Rembrandt by Gersaint numbers as follows]

27 Rembrandt drawing. 1st proof. D. says the other 2 on the same leaf are his own property.
43 Angel appearing to the shepherds. The unfinished proof.
49 Presentation in the Temple – both impressions
50 Presentation in the Temple – both impressions
51 Similar subject – larger and small plate
56 Flight into Egypt. 1st impression
74 Raising of Lazarus. Before the bonnet
80 The large Three Crosses. The rare one
97 Death of the Virgin, the rare impression
124 Juno, before the crown
133 Onion woman
143 Old man without beard
145 Old man with a large beard
146 Blind man
148 Two Venetian figures
152 This print is on the same leaf with the two in the following number, but is claimed by D. as his own
153 The dog – both impressions
165 Lazarus Klap
167 A beggar
169 Do. with a large beard
197 Woman asleep – two impressions
205 Milk pail landscape, the rare one before the distance. D. claims the other one on the same leaf.
207 The coach landscape
209 A landscape
213 Landscape, irregular form
214 Landscape with a vista, the large proof and another. D. claims the third
215 Landscape – both impressions
217 Large Dutch barn
221 Orchard with a barn
227 Pair landscapes on India paper
251 Portrait of Renier Hanslo. India paper
257 Asselyn with the easel – that with the easel is claimed by D.
260 Portrait of Sylvius
261 Goldweigher – blank face
265 Burgomaster Six – proof

Quere no. 2 Daulby's supplement and 4 ditto

Lot by van Vliet – and two Raising of Lazarus by Lievens.

10 July 1806. Special General Meeting

The evidence on the special enquiry referred to by the Committee on the 26th and 28th June was read, and also Mr Garrow's opinion. Mr Conant attended and read the substance of Mr Dighton's confession, also the evidence of Mr Caley.

The Trustees having considered the evidence respecting the loss of valuable prints belonging to the Museum are of opinion that Mr Beloe is chargeable with negligence in the discharge of his duty relating to the said prints, and that he ought to be removed from his office on account of the same; and he is hereby dismissed accordingly.

RESOLVED that the Secretary notify the vacancy

RESOLVED not to commence any prosecution against Mr Dighton, and that Mr Conant be authorised to use the best means in his power to recover back the property of the Museum.

12 July 1806: General Meeting

A letter from Mr Beloe was read. Ordered that a copy of the resolution referred to in Mr Beloe's letter be sent him, by which it will clearly appear that the only imputation on him was that of negligence in one particular branch of his duty, and that Mr Beloe be acquainted he is at liberty to make any use he pleases of this communication.

21 July 1806: General Meeting

The meeting proceeded on the subject matter of the prints taken away from the Cracherode collection. Mr Conant attended, and desired to deliver back to the Trustees a large number of prints acknowledged as supposed to have been part of the said collection. And thereupon the meeting adverting to the papers referred to in the Committee Book under the dates of 26 and 28 June last, and also to the entry in the book of the General Meeting under the date 10 inst. at which meeting Mr Garrow's opinion was read, and to the resolution made thereupon, requesting Mr Conant to inform them what had passed in consequence of that resolution.

Mr Conant accordingly stated that he had obtained a full disclosure from Mr Dighton of the manner in which the prints had been taken away, and he read his minutes of this confession. He also informed the meeting that he had seen all the persons supposed to have bought the prints taken away from the Museum, and that they had restored all which they bought of Dighton and which they supposed to have belonged to this collection. But if on comparing these with the catalogues in the Museum, any prints not yet restored shall appear to be missing, he (Mr Conant) had taken measures by which they may be traced to the persons supposed to have them, and probably may be recovered. Mr Conant produced the portfolios and left them with Mr Planta to be compared.

In the one containing Rembrandt's prints are

1. those acknowledged by Dighton to have belonged to the Museum

2. those which appear, as far as search has been made, to be missing from the Museum, but which Mr Philipe doubts being the original prints of the collection

3. those prints which Mr Philipe and Mr de Claussen think may be Dighton's own property, and others of which they are doubtful.

In the other portfolio are the prints recovered from Messrs Richardson, Graves, Mortimer, and Woodburn, and others to whom they had been sold.

ORDERED that Mr Planta request Mr Philipe to proceed in the examination of the prints and comparing them with the catalogues.

RESOLVED that this meeting cannot adjourn without expressing the high sense they entertain of the diligence, zeal and sagacity Mr Conant has used in the progress of this business, and how sensible the Trustees are to his activity, by which they have recovered so many valuable articles belonging to the Museum.

RESOLVED that these sentiments be communicated to Mr Conant and that he be requested to continue his best endeavours to recover any articles that may still be missing. Mr Conant was called in and the above resolutions were read to him.

13 December 1806: Philipe's final report on the Museum's losses.

The want of a guide to direct my inquiries into the loss sustained by the Museum has unavoidably protracted the investigation. Mr Cracherode had made no catalogue of his prints, having marked off only a small part on the margins of printed books. I was therefore obliged to have recourse to other means of discovery; and the result has been the recovery of a number of valuable and rare prints, and a confession as to others. But some of these Dighton declares to have been sold to strangers, and they are of course irrecoverable identically; but he promises to replace them by impressions of equal quality and value when they can be procured. Of the remainder discovered to be missing, no account whatever can be obtained as yet, he denying all knowledge of more. It will be perhaps gratifying to the Trustees to be informed that, although there is no likelihood of recovering the whole of the property stolen, yet what has been restored comprises the greater part of the more rare and curious articles.

Of the work (note: Work is a technical term used by print collectors, where the productions of an artist are numerous, and the whole or considerable part thereof assembled together) of *Rembrandt*, above 112 prints have been restored, including the 42 acknowledged at an early stage of the investigation. Between 30 and 40 are still wanting, some of them scarce and valuable, though the greater part are of little consequence and perhaps never collected by Mr Cracherode.

The work of *Marc Antonio*, the most truly valuable in this branch of virtu, and the most difficult to be procured of such quality, has had a narrow escape. One print had been taken away, but is since recovered. Another of no great consequence is supposed to be missing. And the whole of the Italian schools appear in general to have been equally fortunate.

Of the work of *Albert Durer*, which was numerous and remarkably choice, the best articles had been carried away. 19 prints are brought back, and one (Adam and Eve) the most capital, is expected, but the others missing are I fear irrecoverable.

The Dutch school, consisting chiefly of etchings, has been a principal object of pillage. A great part has been recovered, but others, together with the valuable engravings by the Visschers and Suyderhoef, are as yet unaccounted for, nor can any information be at present obtained respecting them.

I expected to have found a work of *Hollar* at the Museum, but do not observe that Mr Cracherode had formed one. The prints of this artist are very numerous, but, excepting portraits (of which there are many by him in that general and extensive class of prints in the Museum) and a few articles of topography, I discovered very few specimens. Some of the best had been taken away and are since recovered, but it cannot yet be ascertained what is missing.

The class of *portraits*, the richest in the collection, abounding in the most curious and rare articles, has not it is believed experienced any considerable defalcation, seven have been restored, some of them scarce. But as the numerous portefolios in which they are placed appear to be very full, I thought it would not answer any valuable purpose to enter into a minute examination of them at present, as I suppose they will soon undergo a complete arrangement, when it may perhaps appear whether or not more have been stolen.

On examining the portfolio containing the works of *Woollet* and *Strange*, I was sorry to find that this interesting class of British art had not escaped material diminution, a number of beautiful proofs and etchings having been carried away. The greater part has now been restored, but several others, having been unfortunately disposed of to strangers, are identically irrecoverable.

List of prints returned to the Museum, exclusive of the Rembrandts and disciples found in the box brought by Mr Conant from Dighton's house.

NB the prices annexed are what Dighton says he paid for redeeming them.

2 portraits by Rembrandt, no. 8 of the catalogue	1.1.0
3 heads by F. Bol, disciple of Rembrandt (philosopher reading, ditto meditating, ditto in a chair)	2.0.0
1 Marc Antonio (St Paul at Athens)	1.1.0
2 Last Judgement, Martin Rota (after Michelangelo, one a proof)	15.0.0
2 St John in the wilderness by Goupy (after Salvator Rosa, proof and lettered impression)	1.6.0
1 Prodigal by Ravenet (after Salvator Rosa, proof)	1.1.0
2 Silence, Hainzelmann (after An.Carracci, one a curious proof)	4.14.6

Albert Durer

1 St Hubert	5.5.0
1 Fortune (rather Pandora)	4.4.0
2 Melancholia and copy	4.4.0
1 Satyr and woman etc.	3.3.0
1 Erasmus	1.11.6
2 Horses	1.1.0
3 different (Small Nativity, Madonna with the monkey, and St Anthony)	2.3.6
2 St Jerome in his chamber and copy	6.6.0
7 different. St George and dragon etc.	2.2.0
1 Death's horse	3.13.6

Beside the capital print of Adam and Eve, a most brilliant impression in the hands of Mr Graves, and expected to be recovered, its supposed value is £21.

Dutch School. Etchings.

The work of Karel Du Jardin	31.10.0
2 by Ruysdael, proofs	10.10.0
4 by ditto, one a proof	2.12.6

NB the remaining three which compleats the set was found in the Museum.

2 sheep by van der Meer, and cattle by van Noorde after P. de Laer	3.3.0
1 cows by A. van de Velde	2.12.6

2 St Anthony, the large plate, and an old man's head (these two are returned, but not mentioned in Dighton's list)

Sundries by Berchem, Waterloo, Cuyp and others, part of those now redeemed from Mr Mortimer, valued at about	42.0.0

Dutch School. Engravings.

– C. de Visscher after:

2 Peter de Laer, robbery etc.	2.12.6
1 the large kiln	4.4.0
1 man on horseback	2.2.0

– J. de Visscher after:

1 Ostade, Haspelaer	2.12.6
1 Wouwermans, Menage	4.4.0
2 Berchems uprights, the other two found in the Museum	1.11.6
1 Suyderhoef after Berchem, not a proof	2.2.0
1 Incantation, J. van de Velde	1.11.6
1 White cow going to market by ditto	3.3.0
1 Goltzius's boy and dog	6.16.6
1 Landscape, Byrne after Both, proof	1.11.6
A Tabagie by J. de Visscher	4.4.0

Flemish School.

2 Watering place, Browne after Rubens, proof & etching	4.14.6
1 Last Supper, Soutman after L. da Vinci	5.5.0

NB it is engraved from the drawing of Rubens

Hollar.

1 His portrait, proof	3.3.0
2 St Francis, large and small after Brouwer	3.3.0
6 muffs	3.3.0
1 landscape from Teniers	1.11.6
5 small views of London	3.3.0

NB the view of Richmond mentioned in the list and marked at £2.2.0 was not seen among the returns

1 Hanging Hare	15.0
1 Stadt house of Antwerp	2.2.0
1 large view of Albury	9.9.0

1 the cup after Andrea Mantegna   3.13.6

2 cat's head & small cathedral (Strasburg)   1.1.0

5 of lyons etc.   1.5.0

2 large landschape from Bruegel (in the box)

4 Seasons, lengthways   3.3.0

1 large merry making, Bruegel (in box)

Woollet.

1 etching of the fishery   3.13.6

1 ditto, Celadon & Amelia   2.12.6

1 ditto, Penn's Treaty by Hall   1.11.6

1 ditto, Woollet after An. Carracci   2.2.0

He confesses to have disposed of the following to strangers and cannot recover them, they are all finished proofs.

Solitude after Wilson

Rural Cot[tage] after Smith

Spanish Pointer after Stubbs

Pair jocund peasants &c after Du Sart

Landschape after Annibal Carracci

Strange.

3 offspring of love after Guido, etching, proof and letters   6.16.6

2 King Charles with the horse after Vandyck, etching and finished proof

2 Queen Henrietta Maria, ditto, ditto   25.0.0

2 Magdalen after Guido, half length, etching & proof   2.12.6

2 Magdalen and Cleopatra, proofs whole lengths   8.8.0

1 Lagmedon detected after S. Rosa, proof   4.4.0

1 Venus attired by the Graces, etching   1.6.0

And Dighton acknowledges to have sold to strangers, and cannot recover, the following:

2 Abraham & Hagar and companion after Guercino

2 other proofs, of which he does not recollect the subjects.

Bartolozzi.

The diploma of the Royal Academy, etching and proof &c.   29.8.0

Lord Thurlow, proof (quere)   4.4.0

ditto, etching   3.3.0

Clytie after An. Carracci, letters £3.13.6, proof £6.6.0   9.9.0

3 Madonna & Child, finished & unfinished proof, and letters   3.3.0

3 Lady & Child, etching, proof & letters   3.3.0

1 sleeping cupid after Guido   0.10.6

2 proofs after Guercino & a lettered impression ditto

1 Venus and Adonis after ditto, proof (Dighton's list says 5, but only 4 produced)   1.18.6

2 Empress of Russia, proofs, one of them unfinished   2.6.0

1 Silence after Carracci, lettered impression   1.1.0

Portraits.

Richard Allestry by Loggan

Lancelot Andrews by Vaughan

Thomas Attwood by Marshall (rare)

Richard, Lord Buckhurst, Earl of Dorset, Passe and copy

Edward Cocker, Gaywood

ditto in an oval of palms

Thomas Coventry, oval, before the address

A lady's head, Teniers (not Mary Lemon)   (total) 9.19.6

Varia.

6 views by Rooker, one a proof   4.0.0

5 etchings S. Bourdon, one a proof

Landschape, mezzotinto, Earlom, proof (Hobbema)   2.12.6

Besides the above, the following, not mentioned, in the list are returned:

20 small Gobbi & title, Callot

5 small landschapes, della Bella

2 others, ditto

2 landschapes Waterloo, not good and certainly not in Mr Cracherode's collection

1 soldiers plundering peasants after Rubens

7 etchings, Castiglione

All of trifling value

The collection of *Bartolozzi*'s works in the Museum has not yet been examined. In fact there appears no means to ascertain what prints by this master were in Mr Cracherode's possession; nor would it have been now discovered that any had been taken away, but for the return of those specified in the inclosed list.

Not being able to prosecute the enquiry any further at present for want of information, I must now conclude with a short statement of the value of the prints returned referring to the inclosed for particulars.

The value of the Rembrandts recovered, according to the prices they would fetch at present, may be about £400.

The value of the various articles restored, which Dighton declares to have paid for their redemption £375.

The value of the prints which he has sold to strangers and can only replace when he can procure them, viz. Woollets and Stranges, about £45.

Besides the Adam and Eve by Durer not yet obtained back from Mr Graves, about £21.

I have the honour to be with respect, Sir, your faithful and obedient servant, T. Philipe. Golden Square, 13 December 1806.

Appendix F

Documents on Thomas Philipe's Rearrangement of the Print Collection between 1806 and 1810

Antony Griffiths

These documents have been transcribed from the series of 'Original Papers' in the Central Archives of the British Museum, II pp. 829–45, with various additions from the minutes of the General Meetings and Committee Meetings of the Trustees. A connected document from the Hardwicke Papers in the British Library is transcribed at the end.

3 July 1806: Trustees Committee

In answer to certain questions which were proposed by Mr Planta to Mr Philipe viz.

1. What mode he recommends as the best for catalogues of the prints etc. in the Museum.

2. Whether he can undertake and upon what terms and within what time, considering the present materials for such a catalogue.

3. What mode he recommends for exhibiting the prints etc. as most convenient to the persons desirous of viewing them and most secure for the Museum.

Mr Philipe's letter to Mr Planta was read suggesting the mode of arrangement and catalogue of the prints, and offering his services. Thanks were ordered.

RESOLVED that Mr Philipe's proposal be taken into consideration when the Special Enquiry now on foot shall have been concluded.

RESOLVED that Mr Planta be desired to obtain an answer from Mr Philipe to the second question as to the terms and time.

[Appended: letter from Mr Philipe dated 3 July 1806]

When the prints taken away are recovered, the first thing to be done is to arrange them methodically and to draw up a catalogue raisonné which is particularly necessary on account of the variations in many of the prints. And as they are intended for the permanent use of the public they ought to be pasted on thick paper, and bound up in volumes. Where it is of consequence to compleat the work of any master, blank leaves or else guards may be left in the volumes for inserting the prints missing, when they can be procured of fine quality.

Every print should be marked with a stamp denoting it to be the property of the British Museum and with another stamp in commemoration of the Donor and these stamps should be as small as possible, since it is necessary for the security of the prints that they should be impressed on the front. But some attention is necessary in placing the stamps, that the effect of the prints may not thereby be injured.

It may be proper to pay attention to the material used for marking which ought to be proof if possible against even chemical preparations.

The numerous unexplored volumes in the Museum ought to be examined for materials to render the principal works more compleat – and their contents may be otherways usefully arranged.

When the most capital and interesting works are compleated as far as the materials will permit, they may be bound up in volumes and exhibited on stated days to a limited number of visitors by tickets to be delivered at the porter's lodge. The practice at the Cabinet du Roi at Paris was to permit no person to touch a portfolio unless he had a seat at the table, by which means and some portion of vigilance in the Keepers, it became impossible to extract anything from the portfolios. But in this respect it will be easy for the Trustees to settle regulations.

I suppose that the drawings collected by Mr Cracherode are likeways in the Museum. These may be arranged and catalogued apart, bound up and marked as the prints.

If the Trustees have no person in view more able to carry this plan into effect, I am willing to undertake and bestow my cordial attention to it. I have been conversant in the subject full fifty years, first as an amateur in the early part of my life, and afterwards, when obliged by the loss of hearing to relinquish the profession I was bred to, as a dealer, in which quality I have carried on business to a considerable extent for near 40 years with every possible opportunity of experience. I have the honour to be your most obedient servant.

Thomas Philipe, Golden Square, 3 July 1806.

12 July 1806: letter to Trustees from Mr Philipe

I have considered the questions put to me respecting the arrangement of the prints and drawings in the British Museum, and putting them into a state for being laid before the public. Also the time that will be necessary for the purpose, and the charge that I would make for my trouble. An answer to the two first points I conceive I have anticipated in my former letter. And as to the time necessary for carrying the proposed plan into effect, I now think upon reflection that it will not be necessary to draw up a catalogue of the prints at all, at least for the present, and that it will be sufficient to verify them with the printed books, and to number them accordingly: viz. the Rembrandts with Daulby's catalogue, and the Marc Antonios with the list in Heinecken's Dictionnaire des Artistes; for which a very few days will be sufficient.

But I have no idea what time it will take to arrange the contents of the numerous volumes of unexplored prints in the Museum (I mean those that are not in sets nor considered as books) since I do not know the quantity. But as my proposition is by no means dictated by avarice but by an ambition to put the whole collection into a state for fulfilling the purposes of the Institution, and of course the intention of the donors, I certainly would not waste a moment uselessly. Nor do I think that a catalogue of these will be necessary at present. And I presume to flatter myself that my terms will vindicate me from any suspicion of protraction.

I was once employed in arranging an extensive collection of prints and drawings, the proprietor of which proposed a guinea per day, with further advantage both immediate and prospective, and I accepted his offer. I should therefore hope that a guinea a day, viz. from 9 or so in the morning to 3 pm. will not be considered an extravagant demand, especially as the occupation is laborious, and which I would not be able to continue more than three days in the week. The catalogues being out of the question, the main purpose may be soon accomplished. I have the honour to be with respect, your faithful humble servant ...
12 July 1806

15 July 1806: Trustees Committee

A letter was read from Mr Philipe stating the terms on which he is willing to make a catalogue of the prints and drawings. Resolved that the consideration of this be postponed as proposed at the meeting of 3 inst.

13 December 1806: General Meeting of Trustees

Mr Philipe's letter on the subject of the prints and drawings, specifying the number which have been restored, and which are still missing was read. The consideration of Mr Philipe's proposal respecting a catalogue of the prints and drawings was postponed.

20 December 1806: Extraordinary General Meeting

Mr Philipe was called in and gave a plan for arranging the prints and drawings and exhibiting them.
RESOLVED that Mr Philipe be directed to make a catalogue of the prints and drawings and mark them as proposed by him, and that he be paid for so doing at the rate of one guinea a day according to his own terms specified in his letter.
RESOLVED that the Marquis of Stafford, the Earl of Hardwicke, Sir Joseph Banks, Sir George Cornewall, Mr Rose, Mr Sloane and Mr Annesley be a Sub-Committee to superintend and direct Mr Philipe from time to time as they shall think proper.

[appended: Thomas Philipe's plan for the arrangement of the collection]

PLAN

The prints to be (in general) arranged according to the schools of painting, beginning with that reputed the most ancient, viz the Florentine.

But the most eminent engravers, viz Marc Antonio, Agostino Carracci, etc. may be excepted from this rule, their works being of the greatest importance. They engraved after painters of different schools.

The works of each painter to be classed according to the subjects, in one uniform manner for which there is an approved rule.

When the whole collection is arranged, by incorporating all the good prints in the Museum, they should be stamped and pasted by one side and by the opposite corners upon strong paper, bound up in portfolios, equally avoiding lavishment and crowding.

In foreign institutions two or three days in the week are allotted for public exhibition, three hours on each day without limitation as to the number of persons admitted provided they are of respectable appearance. No one however is permitted to touch a portfolio unless he occupies a seat at the table. The number of persons viewing at once and the presence of a servant to hand the portfolios as they are called for will prevent the possibility of dilapidation. It may however be found proper to admit by ticket only to prevent the room from being crowded.

A catalogue raisonné may be drawn up either before or after the prints are placed in the portfolios. And this may be done either in alphabetical order referring to the portfolio and leaf in which the article described is to be found, or chronologically, each school separate, with a general index.

A similar plan may be adopted in regard to the drawings.

14 February 1807: General Meeting of Trustees

The report of the Sub-Committee on the prints and drawings was read.

RESOLVED that the said Sub-Committee be requested to proceed in the manner proposed in their report. And that [they] be at liberty to select such books or prints as they may think proper to class with the engravings.

28 February 1807: Extraordinary General Meeting of Trustees

RESOLVED that the collections of engravings be transferred from the Department of Printed Books to the Department of Manuscripts, distinguishing each collection by proper marks and preserving the same together whole and entire.

[A Sub-Committee was also set up to revise the regulations, so that they] may enable artists to have the most convenient access to the original drawings and engravings in the Manuscript Department, and at the same time provide effectually for the securing of these collections

13 February 1808: General Meeting of Trustees

Mr Saunders to report on the best method of fitting up the two rooms in the new building appropriated for the engravings and drawings, and for the coins and medals, so as best to secure their arrangement and preservation.

13 February 1808: Trustees Committee

Mr Philipe's bill respecting the recovery of the prints and attendance on the Sub-Committee mounting to £154.9.0 having been laid before the Trustees and approved, a draft was made for the same on the General Fund

27 February 1808: Trustees Committee

[The Sub-Committee on regulations for admission recommends that access to the collection of prints and drawings should be on Wednesdays from 10 to 4, but be closed in August and September]

14 May 1808: General Meeting of Trustees

[A visitation of the new building shows that] the rooms intended for the drawings and engravings and the coins and medals are in a state fit to receive the same when presses and cabinets have been prepared.

11 June 1808: Trustees Committee

[The appointment of William Alexander as Assistant Librarian is confirmed]

11 February 1809: Trustees Committee

Mr Philipe's report respecting his progress on the print arrangement was read, and his charge of £75 12s allowed

[appended: letter of Thomas Philipe of 10 February 1809]

In compliance with the desire of the Committee to state the progress made in the arrangement of the prints in the course of last year, I beg to say that the works deemed most material to be first taken into consideration, viz. Rembrandts, Marc Antonios, and Hollars were finished and bound up in 8 volumes.

The next object pointed out by the Committee was the arrangement of the British portraits, which could not be entered upon the preceding year. They are very numerous and were found in a confused state, crowded into a small number of portfolios besides a great many dispersed in other volumes. Their arrangement therefore, owing to a want of proper conveniency and other untoward circumstances which could not be obviated, became rather an arduous task, and occupied an unexpectedly long time. They were however arranged in the course of last year down to the reign of Queen Anne, and partly pasted partly placed in volumes prepared for them, occupying 14 volumes – making with the works above specified a total of 22 volumes compleated in the course of last year.

I beg to assure the Committee that not being actuated by any interested motives of delay, I am anxious to bring the arrangement to a conclusion as speedily as possible, and with the greatest respect, I have the honour to be their faithful and obedient servant

Thomas Philipe

PS My account for last year's attendance and labour is for 72 days: £75.12.0

13 January 1810: Trustees Committee

[Payment of £106.16.0 authorised to Philipe for his print arrangement]

10 February 1810: Trustees Committee

The Marquis of Stafford reported from the Sub-Committee on the arrangement of the prints that the Committee expected the arrangement would be compleated in a few weeks and he delivered a letter from Mr Philipe on the subject.
RESOLVED that it be referred to the Print Committee to report what number of books have been removed into the Print Room in order that Mr Saunders may make an estimate of the presses which they will occupy.

[appended: letter from Thomas Philipe dated 9 February 1810]

In compliance with the desire of the Committee to report the progress of arrangement of the prints etc. in the British Museum, I have the honour respectfully to state that it is now so far advanced that only a few weeks more will be necessary to its completion. That they are classed, as far as circumstances would admit, according to the respective schools of painting, and pasted into portfolios provided for the purpose; of which 83 volumes are finished and delivered into the hands of Mr Alexander, after being stamped and marked as far as they are known with the initials of their respective donors. And that there are nine more volumes arranged to be pasted in; besides six volumes of original drawings which are placed in volumes to be pasted in. I have the honour to be, with the greatest respect, the Committee's faithful and obedient servant. Thomas Philipe

9 June 1810: Trustees Committee

[Mr Saunders gives estimate of £175 for a book case over the presses in the Print Room: the case is ordered to be made]

12 January 1811: Trustees Committee

[Payment of £151.1.0 authorised to Philipe for his print arrangement]

9 March 1811: Trustees Committee

The Sub-Committee for selecting the duplicate prints reported that they have so far finished their examination that the sale catalogue may be proceeded with. Ordered that Mr Philipe prepare a catalogue of the duplicate prints for sale.

13 July 1811: Trustees Committee

[Philipe paid £49.10.0 for attendance and £19.5.0 for portfolios]

ADDENDUM

Thomas Philipe's draft account of his arrangement of the prints in the British Museum, undated but prepared in 1808 or 1809 (British Library, Hardwicke Papers, Add.MS.36269, ff. 184–92)

The plan proposed for arranging the prints in the British Museum has been strictly adhered to. It is the simplest, and it is conceived will be found the best to answer its intention. The whole mass is divided into the different schools of painting, and a chronological order will be observed in each.

The first in precedence is the Florentine, and there are prints in the Museum after the following masters:[1]
– Giotto, Leonardo da Vinci, Michael Angelo Buonarota, Andrea del Sarto, Fra Bartolomeo, Daniel da Volterra, Baccio Bandinelli, Rosso, Francesco Salviati, Bronzino, Pierino del Vaga, Vasari, Luca Penni, Giovanni da San Giovanni, Della Bella, Ant. Tempesta,[2] Carlo Dolci, Bramantino & San Gallo (architects), and others.

– Among the engravers after these painters are:
Marc Antonio, from Michael Angelo and Baccio Bandinelli; G. Edelinck from L. da Vinci; Martin Rota from Michael Angelo.

– Marc Antonio the engraver will be more particularly noticed in another place, as it is settled to bind up his works separately. And the other engravers from the Florentine painters may be specified in an index to each volume, or in a general index to all the artists, both painters and engravers in the Museum, including those in books of prints or galleries.

– The Florentine school will make 2 or 3 volumes.

School of Siena is sometimes joined to that of Florence.

– Simone Memmi, Francesco Vanni, Domenico Beccafumi detto Micarino, Ventura Salimbeni, Balthasar Peruzzi

– Among the engravers after the painters of this school is Ag. Carracci, by whom we have the great Praesepe or Wisemens Offering after Balthasar Peruzzi

Roman School

– Raphael Sanzio (2 vols), Julio Romano, Polidoro da Caravaggio, Luca Penni, the Mantuani, Taddeo & Frederico Zuccaro, Barocci (etched), Don Julio Clovio, Pomerancio (Circignano), Martin Rota (a Dalmatian engraved from his own designs as well as after Raphael etc.), Borgognone (Giac. Cortese, etched), Cortone (P. Berettoni da), Cyro Ferri, Gio. Francesco Romanelli, Andrea Camassei, Michael Angelo Caravaggio, Andrea Sacchi, Domenico Feti, Filippo Lauri, Cav. Lorenzo Bernini, Horazio Gentileschi, Mercati, Vespasian Strada (etched), Cherubin Alberti (etched & engraved), Livio Agresti, Raphael Scaminossi (etched), Horatio Borgiani (etched), Cav. Jos. d'Arpino, Carlo Maratti (etched), Francesco Villamena (etched), Benedetto Luti, Francesco Mocchi, Geminani (etched), Fabricio Chiari, Domenico Cerini.

– The principal engravers from paintings and designs of the Roman school are Marc Antonio, from Raphael, G. Edelinck from ditto, Fr. Poilly, Cornelius Bloemart, Chereau, Dorigny, Strange, Bartolozzi, etc. and a great many others who will be mentioned in the index.

[1] There are in the Museum early specimens of engraving by the Florentines, some supposed by Maso Finiguerra to whom the discovery of printing from copper-plates is ascribed, and Baccio Baldini, engraved after Sandro Botticelli, and there are some curious specimens of engraving ascribed to him among Mr Cracherode's prints. Antonio Pollaiuolo engraved a print of his own composition.

[2] Della Bella etched the principal part of his own designs; he is not known to have been a painter. Ant. Tempesta ditto. The works of each of these two artists will make a separate volume.

NB The Roman school, besides the works of Raphael, will form at least 2 volumes.

– In the Roman school may be placed the works of Nicolo Poussin and Gaspar (Duché) Poussin (etched), as they spent the great part of their lives at Rome. But their works in the Museum are sufficiently numerous to form of each a volume. The prints after them are for the most part well engraved by Gerard Audran, Edelinck, Poilly, Strange, Morghen etc.

Lombard Schools

PARMA

Correggio, Parmeggiano (etched many prints), Lanfranco (etched), B. Schedoni (etched 2 pieces), Sisto Badalocchio (etched).

– Agostino Carracci, Francesco Spierre, Duchange, Strange and others have engraved after Correggio, and the etchings of Parmeggiano are numerous in the Museum.

BOLOGNA

Lorenzo Sabadini, Lodovico, Anibal, Agostino, Antonio Carracci (etched and engraved).

– These will form two volumes, and it is recommended to place the whole of Agostino's engravings etc. together, though some of them are engraved after the masters of other schools.
Disciples of the Carracci. Guido and his scholars: Simone Cantarini da Pesaro, Gio. Andrea Sirani and his daughter Elizabetta.

– Guido and his disciples will form at least one volume.
Albano (besides the Verospi), Guercino (besides Bartolozzi), Domenichino (besides the sets usually engraved), Procaccini (Camillo, Ercole, Julio Cesare, Carlo Antonio), Primaticcio (with Rosso at Fontainebleau).

– These will form a volume.

Disciples of the Carracci continued:

Julio Campi (? if Bolognese), Pellegrino Tibaldi, Passarotti (Bartolomeo, etched), O. Fialetti, Lorenzo Pasinelli, Francesco Brizio, D. M. Canuti, Gio. Francesco Grimaldi, Algardi, Giacomo Ligozzi, Lodovico Lana, Lorenzo Garbieri, Gio. Bapt. Mola (etched), Alessandro Tiarini, Marc Antonio Franceschini, Flaminio Torre, Giov. Luigi Valesio, Sassoferrato, Francesco Francia, Mitelli etc.

– The above will form one volume.

Marc Antonio, the celebrated engraver. Besides what he has engraved after the works of his master Francesco Francia, who was a painter and designer, as well as an engraver and goldsmith, he has transmitted to us the most perfect representation of the genius of Raphael and Michael Angelo that we possess. His works in

the Museum are numerous, and nearly compleat, and will form 2 volumes. On account of the manifest inaccuracy of Heineken's catalogue, it is judged best to depart from his mode of arrangement, and to adopt the plan which will be generally followed through the whole arrangement of the prints, as the easiest for finding any subject required, but the pages of Heineken will be referred to. M. Antonio not only copied some of the works of his tramontaine contemporaries Albert Duerer, but an older German master Schoen, and as it is upon record that he corrected the drawing of Baccio Bandinelli's Martyrdom of St Lawrence, there is room to suppose that he was the author of many of the designs which he engraved.

His disciples Agostino Veneziano, Marc da Ravenna and Julio Bonasone will form another volume. Heineken has given catalogues of all these in his Dictionnaire but that of Julio Bonasone is the most imperfect. Mr G. Cumberland has given one more extensive, but not quite perfect. In the catalogue to be drawn up, reference will be given to both. The contemporaries of M.A. may be added, as those in the Museum are not numerous.

MILAN AND BRESCIA

Jerome Mutiano, Andrea Solario, Hippolito Scarsellino.

– These may be bound up with the school of Parma.

Venetian School

will make one volume. There are separate works of Titan, Tintoret etc

Bellini, Titian, Giorgione, Tintoretto, Bassano, Palma, Julio Carpione, Paolo Farinati, Baptista Franco, Julio Sanuto, Domenico & Julio Campagnola, Benedetto Mantegna, Pordenone, Baptista del Moro, Pasqualinus (Roman), Balestra, Boscovich Fred. Siciliano, Diamantini, Zuccarelli (? if Venetian or Florentine), And. Schiavone of Dalmatia (his etchings with those of Parmeggiano, his family name is Meldolla), Carlo Saraceni, ?N. Grassi, Pietro Rotari.

Neapolitan School

Salvator Rosa (makes a volume), Pompeo Aquilano, Luca Giordano, Spagnolet, Horatius Scoppa, Io. Buranus (one print etched by him).
These will make a volume, many of the prints are etched by the artists themselves.

Genoese School

Bart. Biscaino (a fine collection of his etchings), Benedetto Castiglione (ditto), Luca Cangiagio, Paggi

Will make a volume

Claude Lorraine may be placed in the Roman School; there is a very fine collection of his etchings. The Liber Veritatis may remain as a book and the fine engravings after him will form a volume with the etchings.

German School

A considerable collection of the ancient masters prior to the time of Albert Durer.

Martin Schoen, Israhel van Meck etc., some at the same time with dates and unknown marks and others anonymous. They will form a volume, and will be particularly described.

Albert Durer, one volume.

The contemporaries of Albert and the Little Masters will make another volume and the more recent Germans a third.

Flemish School

Masters prior to and contemporary with Rubens will form one volume

Rubens two volumes

Vandyck, historical and whole length portraits by Gunst, proofs, with the addition of other disciples of Rubens may make one volume. Teniers, van Uden etc. may be included

Vandyck's foreign portraits will occupy 2 volumes as there are numerous variations

Dutch School

Lucas van Leyden (engraver), Henry Goltzius, Saenredam, Cornelius van Harlem, Abraham Bloemart, Count Goudt, Nolpe, Cornelis Bloemart, Muller, Matham, Poelemburgh: one volume

Rembrandt's etchings, two volumes

Prints after Rembrandt and disciples of Rembrandt's, one volume

Bamboccio, Berchem, Both, Dusart, Dujardin (Carel), Ostade, Ruysdael, Stoop, Swanevelt, van Uden, Adr. van der Velde, Corn. & J. de Visscher, Waterloo, Wouwermans: one or two volumes

Suyderhoef, and portraits by him and other Dutch artists may require a volume

The English School

is rather of recent date, and what prints of consequence we possess are chiefly by foreign artists. The loose topography is not of considerable extent, though it contains many interesting artists, and including Hollar's prints of this description it will perhaps require two volumes. Hollar's other works (not including portraits) may form another volume.

Strange's proofs are proposed to be kept separate for their better preservation, and likewise Woollet's.

But the most valuable part of the English School is the class of portraits. Mr Cracherode appears to have intended an arrangement according to the periods of Bromley, but had only begun.

On entering upon the arrangement of this class we found the leaves onto which they were placed so much crowded, and the periods so much dispersed (the mezzotintos being in a portfolio apart, and the English portraits of Vandyck mixed with the other portraits of that master) that it was judged proper to leave them for the present, until by getting some of the works already arranged bound up and removed, we can obtain room for stowing the periods away as they are compleated.

For this purpose we have begun with the works of Marc Antonio, and as the operation of stamping and marking is performed without difficulty, it may perhaps be better to proceed with the other masters, until we obtain room for finishing the arrangement of the portraits.

French School

Le Brun, Coypel, Jouvenet, etc. may form one volume
and the views by Silvestre and Perelle another

The portraits of the French school are pretty numerous, but it will be easy to arrange them. They are principally by Cars after Le Brun, Rigaud etc. Drevet, Edelinck, Masson, de Troy, Nanteuil, Pitau, van Schuppen, Wille etc.

I beg now to mention that one uniform rule will be observed in placing the subjects by each master:

1. his portrait
2. other portraits
3. Scripture subjects in their order
4. sacred subjects
5. Saints
6. profane history
7. fable and fancy subjects
8. landscapes
9. sets of prints

A table of contents may be given to each volume, and when the whole work is compleated an alphabetical list of the painters and engravers will be given, distinguishing the professions by a difference of type, and the eminent artists of each profession by a further difference; and a catalogue raisonné for the use of the library will be made out at the same time.

I cannot conclude this memorandum without returning my sincere thanks to the Committee for the kind indulgence I have experienced from them during the course of the arrangement, of which I am the more sensible from the need I stood of it, when in consequence of the great want of conveniency, and the peculiarity of circumstances, I found myself somewhat embarrassed. And I beg to assure them that I entertain a grateful sense of their disposition to assist me.

65 days have been employed in the arrangement

Appendix G
Henry Josi's Two Papers on the Classification and Cataloguing of the Print Collection, 1840
Antony Griffiths

7 April 1840

Mr Henry Josi begs respectfully to deliver his opinion in accordance with the wishes expressed by the Trustees as to a rearrangement and classification of the collection. The state of the prints at present in the portfolios will in a short period render it imperative to remount, clean etc. a great portion of the collection. The Museum collection of prints is chiefly used by two different classes of persons, whose objects are totally different from each other. The first are those who come to the Museum for purposes of research, to identify pictures by different masters, or young painters who come for the purpose of studying the compositions of the Old Masters. And it is very important that a collection should exist as perfect as it is possible to make it of the prints engraved after the principal masters, and each master and school to be kept separate and distinct.

The other class of visitors are those who being principally collectors, connoisseurs, engravers, require to see the work of the engraver, and all that he has done, without reference much to the master he has engraved after.

In regard to the first class of visitors Mr Josi begs to say that coming merely to hunt out a subject, the continual reference and rapid turning of the leaves by them causes a great wear of the prints. These persons naturally care little about the beauty of impression, earliness of state or intrinsic value of the prints, beyond the subject it represents, and it is a pity to place valuable prints in these books where the commonest impressions will sufficiently answer every purpose required.

The second class of visitors come to compare the work of the engraver. These include the collectors, connoisseurs, and the numerous body of engravers. With these it is an object of deep interest to place the plate from its earliest beginning in the etching by the various degrees of advancement, to its perfection. This class naturally examines the print with a critical eye, and are fully apprised of the value and necessity of careful handling. Thus a national collection must naturally in some measure divide itself. Still this division should be made with caution and prudence, distinguishing between those masters whose works are worthy of being preserved separate, and many who are not.

As regards interference with the arrangements of the collections presented to the Museum, Mr Josi begs to state that the various collections have long since been amalgamated with each other, so that no inconvenience could arise from carefully and gradually separating the collection in two tranches. On the contrary it is the most beneficial plan for preserving prints, and accords with the arrangement of all public museums. Since the robbery, nearly the whole collection has been remounted, in a manner that will surely cause the destruction of a great portion of prints in the course of a very few years, many being pasted face to face in old wrinkled portfolios, the continued friction of which is fast wearing them out. Mr Josi begs also to state that the collection in the PR has from the commencement been partially arranged on both plans. For instance the works of Marc Antonio, Bonasone, Hollar, Bartolozzi etc. have been kept separate as engravers, while many of their common impressions are dispersed in the portfolios after masters.

Mr Josi would also recommend the Trustees to allow him to enlarge the collection by increasing the works of our English school of engraving, in which branch of art the PR is deficient, and the first demand made by foreign and country visitors is to see the British school of engraving.

8 May 1840

In obedience to the minute made by the Trustees at their last meeting, Mr Josi has the honour to report more fully upon the present and the proposed arrangement of the collection in the PR.

The prints which are at present classed after the engraver by whom they are executed are:

1. All etchings by masters who have been chiefly distinguished for their paintings or designs. This class includes all the masters mentioned by Bartsch, and whose etchings are to be found in the PR. The exceptions are few, and might easily be withdrawn from the portfolios in which they are now found.

2. The works of the following engravers: Marc Antonio, Bonasone, Durer, Callot, della Bella, Hollar, Woollett, Visscher, Schmidt, Bartolozzi, de Marcenay, and Hogarth. To these Mr Josi would propose to add immediately the works of eminent engravers, whenever the collection furnishes sufficient specimens of a master to form a respectable number for a separate portfolio. These masters would be limited for the present to Strange, Sharp, Heath, Morghen, Edelinck, Drevet, Audran.

It would be desirable, however, to increase this list as the collections are enlarged, and opportunities [arise] of acquiring complete sets of the works of distinguished engravers. The whole number of engravers would then amount to 50 or 60 names.

This would constitute the primary arrangement of the collections. The arrangement after painters and their schools would be subordinate, so that in case of the PR possessing duplicates, the finer impressions would be assigned to the engraver's portfolio, the inferior impression to that of the painter or designer.

To the principle thus laid down there are, however, two or three exceptions to be made. The prints after Rubens and van Dyck, both on account of the importance of the master and of some peculiarities attached to their works, are in all public collections kept by themselves, and Mr Josi would propose in respect to prints after these masters to make this the primary arrangement. The portfolios of prints after Correggio in like manner being particularly complete, and the prints having been selected with extraordinary judgement and care, should on that account be kept intact or rendered more perfect by insertion of the finest impressions, whenever an opportunity may offer.

In consideration of the general and almost national interest attached to a collection of portraits arranged after Granger, and also of the circumstances that the particular collection belonging to the Trustees was bequeathed to them nearly in its present state by that distinguished benefactor to the Museum, Mr Cracherode (note: the arrangement after Granger in the Museum collection was one of the works effected immediately after Dighton's robbery by the Trustees themselves), Mr Josi would propose that this collection should be considered of primary consequence, so that the finest impressions should be added to it rather than to the portfolios of the engravers and painters.

Mr Josi's proposition, if adopted by the Trustees, would still leave the great bulk of the prints arranged in the manner they now are after painters and their schools, and in all cases where a painter has an eminent reputation. Mr Josi would beg to suggest the expediency of endeavouring to supply the place of any prints transferred to the engraver portfolios by the purchase of inferior impressions. Mr Josi begs, however, explicitly to state his opinion that in a national collection, these duplicate impressions ought to be proofs in a fine state of preservation, and though not of that rarity and value which belongs to the impressions taken in the progress of the plate, or immediately on its completion, yet of sufficient vigour and distinctness to give an adequate idea of the merits of the painter, both as regards form and shadow.

Appendix H
Purchases by John Sheepshanks and Sales from his Collection

Martin Royalton-Kisch

The sources of Sheepshanks's collection can to some degree be reconstructed, although many important gaps in our knowledge remain. Chiefly he seems to have acquired prints from the following, most of them being specifically mentioned as sources in the documents in the British Museum archives quoted in the main part of the essay. But it has not proven possible to discover any details of the prints he acquired from the Vindé collection (mentioned in Josi's report to the Trustees as a source; see 2 below), the Josi collection (mentioned by Dominic Colnaghi in his letter to Hawkins) and some other sources discussed below:

1. Count Moritz von Fries. A list of Sheepshanks's purchases made at his sale of 1824 is included at I below. According to Lugt (L.2903), von Fries had a library of 16,000 volumes and owned 300 paintings, 100,000 prints and drawings, and collections of coins and medals, sculpture and minerals. (He was also the dedicatee of Beethoven's seventh symphony.) Von Fries's curator from 1797 was Franz Rechberger (1771–1841), who later directed the Albertina, and some prints from von Fries's collection bear his mark (L.2133). Sheepshanks knew Rechberger: in a letter to Sheepshanks in the family archive from Lengel in Vienna, dated 15 March 1836, Lengel sends Rechberger's regards. Lugt records that von Fries's Rembrandt and Rembrandt school prints were sold to Brondgeest in 1824, presumably for Verstolk. De Claussin bought the rarest and most expensive Berchems and Woodburn purchased the series of Potter's horses for fl.1010 (in fact for Sheepshanks, see below). The Rijksmuseum's Print Room benefited to the tune of fl.6,000-worth of acquisitions at the sale, and Sheepshanks spent the same amount.

2. Charles-Gilbert, Vicomte Morel de Vindé (1759–1842; for his mark see L.2520). He inherited his grandfather's collection (that of Paignon-Dijonval, 1708–92) but greatly added to it. In 1816, he sold 6,000 drawings and 60,000 prints to Woodburn. Sheepshanks's acquisitions from this source presumably came through Woodburn at a later date.

3. Chevalier Ignace-Joseph de Claussin (1766–1844; see L.485). He sold prints only to a few preferred recipients, and it has not proved possible to document Sheepshanks's acquisitions from this source, following the lead given by William Smith and Henry Josi (see p.67). Claussin's collection was not large but it was choice, and Sheepshanks was one of the few beneficiaries of Claussin's disposals prior to the sale of his collection in 1844 (see L.485). The dealer Thane's copy of the Annesley sale, 6 June 1809, lot 105, was later annotated by William Smith to state that a proof by Berchem unrecorded by Bartsch (his nos 41–8 printed from an undivided plate), bought at the sale by Claussin, was later acquired from Claussin by Sheepshanks. The print is in the Museum, reg. no.S.3980.

4. Many of Sheepshanks's prints have on the versos a graphite inscription stating that they came from the sale of the dealer Jean Yver, which took place in Amsterdam, 25 etc. March 1816.

5. Hurst & Robinson, dealers, probably supplied Sheepshanks

with prints. In his letter to William Gott of 4 December 1826 in the possession of his descendants, Sheepshanks writes 'if you wanted anything from the stock of the late Hurst and Robinson, I could get it cheap'.

6. Colnaghi (Dominic). Sheepshanks mentions having seen him in a letter to William Gott, 14 January 1828, now in the Brotherton Library, Leeds University. Colnaghi also wrote to the Museum recommending the purchase of the Sheepshanks Collection (quoted in the main essay).

7. General Dowdeswell sale, London, Evans, 11–15 November 1828. For Sheepshanks's purchases at this sale, see II below.

8. Thomas Wilson sale, London, Hessey, 8 March 1830. See III below.

9. Sir Thomas Francis Baring (later Lord Northbrook) sale, London, Christie's, 1831. According to the letter written by Dominic Colnaghi, which is quoted in the main essay, Sheepshanks acquired prints from this source, but it has not proven possible to isolate which lots he acquired.

10. Reginald Pole Carew sale, London, Wheatley's, 13–15 May 1835. See IV below.

I

Purchases from the sale of Count Moritz von Fries, Amsterdam, 21 etc. June 1824. The Department's copy of the catalogue, said by Lugt to be the most completely annotated, gives the initials JS after numerous purchases by Woodburn, as well as by others – Colnaghi, Claussin, Hurst (perhaps Hurst, Robinson & Co., which went out of business in around 1825), Lamberts and de Ruyter. The annotations seem to be in the hand of Henry Smedley, a well-informed dealer and collector of the period (see p.94). A collection of catalogues annotated in his hand was purchased from Lumley's by the Printed Books Department of the British Museum in 1839 (1839–6–7–235 to 371) and subsequently transferred to Prints and Drawings. I am grateful to Max Griffin and Janet Koss, Public Records Office archivists for the British Library, for tracing them in the Library's registers.

The lots marked with Sheepshanks' initials are:

Kunstboek No. 47

No. 1 Nicolaas Berchem. De drinkende Koe, met de Trekletters, de eerste druk (B.1). Bt Woodburn, JS, f. 91.

No. 5* Nicolaas Berchem. Drie rustende Koeijen, met de witte bergen en dito (i.e. voor den naam) B.3. Bt Woodburn, JS, f. 70.

No. 9 Nicolaas Berchem. De man op den Ezel, voor de lucht (B.5). Bt Colnaghi, JS, f. 80.

No. 11 Nicolaas Berchem. Het vervolg van vijf landschappen, met vee, in de hoogte, allereerst en uitmuntende drukken, voor den naam, en dezelve met het adres, benevens overdrukken, bestaande tezamen in 11 stuks, op 6 bladen. (B.8–12) Bt Woodburn, JS, f. 140.

No. 13 Nicolaas Berchem. Zes stuks, het vrouwtje met de melkemmers, eerste drukken, voor den naam op den steen. (B.22–28). Bt Claussin, JS, f. 48. Presumably also purchased the following two lots, listed as purchased by 'Do', being lots 13*, Dezelfde, met het adres (f. 41) and lot 14, Zes stuks, het Schapenboekje, eerste etsdruk, voor het adres (B.29–32, f. 70).

Kunstboek No. 48

No. 1 J. van Ossenbeek. Het werk van dezen Meester, zoo naar zich zelven, als naar verscheiden anderen, te zamen 37 stuks, op 17 bladen. Bt Woodburn, JS, f. 80.

Kunstboek No. 49

No. 1 Abraham Genoels. Het fraaije Werk van dezen Meester bestaat in Landschappen en Hofgezichten, 81 stuks, op 29 bladen, waarbij eenige onbeschrevene. Beschreven bij Bartsch, IV deel, Bl. 323. No. 1–73, ontbreekt allen No. 40. Bt Hurst, JS, f. 50.

No. 2 Franciscus Millet, Het Werk van dien Meester, bestaande in Arcadische Landschappen, 35 stuks, op 21 bladen, waarbij eenige onbeschrevene. (B.v, Bl. 329–348). Bt Colnaghi, JS, f. 38.

No. 5 A. M. de Koker. Acht stuks, verschillende Landschapjes, op 3 bladen. Bt Lamberts, JS, f. 12.

Kunstboek No. 50

No. 1 Pieter Boel. Het zeldzame Werk van Pieter Boel, bestaande in verschillend soort van Gevogelte, benevens den Tijtel en de Zwijnenjagt, te zamen 7 stuks, alsmede 6 stuks, met gevogelte, naar denzelven. Te zamen 14 Stuks, op 7 bladen. (B.IV, bl. 201) bt with:

No. 2 Twee Olifanten, een Leeuw en twee Tijgerkatten, vermoedelijk naar denzelven. Bt Hurst, JS, f. 20 (with no. 1).

No. 8 Gilles Neyts. Vervolg van het Werk van dien Meester, bestaande in 10 stuks, waarvan verscheidene dubbelden, eerste drukken, te samen 15 stuks, op 3 bladen. Bt Woodburn, JS, f. 50.

Kunstboek No. 51

No. 3 N. Maas. Een Landschap, met rustende Jagers, zeer zeldzaam. Bt Woodburn, JS, f. 30.

No. 5 Karel de Moor. Het werk van dien Meester, zoo naar zich zelven, als naar verschillende anderen, zijnde een uitmuntend en zeldzaam exemplaar, benevens het Portret, door Houbraken. Te zamen 15 stuks, op 5 bladen. Bt Woodburn, JS, f. 30.

No. 7 Arnold Houbraken. De Zinnebeelden, in drie deelen, benevens het Portret van van Gool, door J. Houbraken. Te zamen 61 stuks, op 10 bladen. Bt Hurst, JS, f. 5.

No. 8 J. van der Vinne, Een Landschap, naar L. van der Vinne, zeldz. Bt Hurst, with nos 9–11 below, f. 20.

No. 9 J. van der Vinne. Zes stuks, Gezichten te Rome. Bt with no. 8 above, q.v.

No. 10 J. van der Vinne. Gezigten buiten Haarlem, waaronder zeldzamen. Te zamen 14 stuks, op 5 bladen. Bt with no. 8 above, q.v.

No. 15 N. van Haeften. Het werk van dien Meester, bestaande in boeren Gezelschappen en Portretten, benevens het Portret van den Meester zelve. Te zamen 21 stuks, op 9 bladen. Bt Hurst, JS, f. 38.

No. 16 T. Decker, Drie, stuks, Mans- en Vrouwenhoofden. Bt JS, f. 16 with no. 17.

No. 17 Van De Niepoort, Verschillende Historieele Ordonantiën, Binnenhuizen en Hofgezigten. Te zamen 17 stuks, op 6 bladen. Bt with no. 16 above, q.v.

Kunstboek No. 52

No. 1 Warnard van Valckert. Negen Stuks, verschillende Historiëele Ordonantiën, op 4 bladen. Bt Hurst, JS, f. 7.10.

No. 5 Pieter Verbeek. Het Werkje van dien Meester, waaronder eene allerzeldzaamste druk van het Paardje, van achteren te zien. Te samen 8 stuks, op 2 bladen. Bt Woodburn, JS, f. 95.

Kunstboek No. 54

No. 1 G. Bleker. Het zeer zeldzame Werk van dien Meester, uitmuntende van druk, waarbij de ontmoeting van Laban en Rachel, onbekend bij Bartsch, mankeert No. 2. Te zamen 12 stuks, op 7 bladen. (B.IV, 1, 3, 4–14) Bt Colnaghi, JS, f. 125.

No. 8 P. V. H. Acht stuks, met Honden en één dubbelde. Te zamen, 9 stuks, op 2 bladen. (B.IV, 1–8) Bt Hurst, JS, f. 42.

No. 15 A. van Waas. Het zeldzaam Werk van dien Mees, besaande [sic] in 5 stuks op 3 bladen, onbekend bij Bartsch. Bt Hurst, JS, f. 4.

No. 16 Twee stuks, met Boeren Gezelschappen, door J. C. Droogsloot. Bt Hurst, JS, f. 7.

No. 18 Vier en twintig stuks uit de Fabelen van Esopus, onbekend, op 12 bladen. Bt Hurst, JS, f. 26 (with annotation, *Stoop*).

No. 20 Gezigt aan de Haven van Lissabon. Onbeschreven bij Bartsch. Bt Colnaghi, JS, f. 23.

No. 22 Een Vrouwenhoofd. Bt Hurst, JS, with No. 23, f. 4.

No. 23 Zes stuks Landschappen, door R. Adams. Bt with no. 22 above, q.v.

Kunstboek No. 55

No. 8 H. Seghers, Een Landschap en een Riviergezicht. Onbeschreven bij Bartsch. Bt Woodburn, JS, f. 41.

No. 9 Onbekend. Vijf stuks diverse Landschappen. Bt Woodburn, JS, f. 46.

No. 10 J. Laggoor. Vijf stuks Landschappen, zeldzaam. Onbeschreven bij Bartsch, op 2 bladen. Bt Hurst, JS, f. 10.

No. 15 Fredrik Moucheron. Een boomrijk Landschap, allereerste etsdruk, zeer zeldzaam. Bt Woodburn, JS, f. 51.

No. 16 Hetzelfde, nog eens, opgewerkt. Bt Woodburn, JS, f. 30.

No. 18 Frans van Mieris. Drie stuks, eene Vrouw met een citer; een Mans Hoofdje en eene Fabelordonantie. Bt Hurst, JS, f. 45.

No. 21 D. de Braay. De Ruïne van het Kasteel Brederode. Bt Hurst, JS, f. 17.

No. 22 Jan Toorenvliet. Twee stuks, met Honden, zeldzaam. Bt Woodburn, JS, f. 41.

No. 23 Godfried Schalcken. Drie stuks, een Mans- en Vrouwehoofd, benevens de overdrukken, zeldzaam, Bt with nos. 24–26, Hurst, JS, f. 65.

No. 24 Godfried Schalcken. Het Portret van C. van den Broek, proef- en letterdruk, zeldzaam. Bt with no. 23 above, q.v.

No. 25 Godfried Schalcken, Hetzelfde van Cornelis van Beveren, naar S. van Hoogstraten. Bt with no. 23 above, q.v.

No. 26 Godfried Schalcken. Hetzelfde, van G. Douw. Bt with no. 23 above, q.v.

No. 30 Albert Meyering. Het werk van dezen Meester, bestaande in 26 stuks, Landschappen, benevens een Bijprentje, te zamen 27 stuks, op 15 bladen. (B.IV, p. 357, nos. 1–26). Bt Hurst, JS, f. 26.

No. 31 Gerard Hoet. Vier stuks Fabel-Ordonnatiën, op 2 bladen. Bt de Ruyter, JS, f. 3.

No. 32 Johannes Lingelbach [annotated as *A Stork*] Eene Italiaansche Zeehaven, zeldz. en onbeschreven. Bt Woodburn, JS, f. 12.

No. 35 Twee stuks, Landschappen met vee; onbeschreven bij Bartsch. Bt Woodburn, JS, f. 61.

No. 36 A. Begeijn. Een Herder bij eenig vee, zeer zeldzaam. Bt Woodburn, JS, f. 40.

No. 38 Twee stuks, Landschapjes, door J. van Nikkelen. Bt Hurst, JS, with nos 39–40, f. 11.

No. 39 Ruïne van een Italiaansch Gebouw, door C. de Hooch. Bt with no. 38 above, *q.v.*

No. 40 Een Landschap, door denzelven. Bt with no. 38 above, *q.v.*

No. 41 Twee stuks, Landschapjes, door C. van Veen, Bt Hurst, JS, with nos 42–43, f. 6.

No. 42 Een dito, door Thesing. Bt with no. 41 above, *q.v.*

No. 43 Een Schip, door J. van den Avele. Bt with no. 41 above, *q.v.*

Kunstboek No. 56

No. 1 Pieter Quast. Twee mans Hoofden, zijnde Afbeeldsels van Grijsaards. Bt Hurst, JS, with nos 2–3, f. 9.

No. 2 Pieter Molijn, Vier stuks, Landschapjes, met Boerenlieden, Krijgsknechten als andersins, op 2 bladen (B.IV, p. 11, 1–4). Bt with no. 1 above, *q.v.*

No. 3 Jan van Kampen. Eene zeer oude Vrouw, houdende een Boek in hare hand; zeldzaam. Bt with no. 1 above, *q.v.*

No. 8 Moses Uytenbroeck. Het Portret van Moses Uytenbroek, proefdruk, voor het adres. Bt Hurst, JS, f. 120. [This price suggests that Sheepshanks bought nos 8–29, 46 prints by Uytenbroeck, which are not individually marked in the catalogue. Sheepshanks owned some 130 impressions of prints by this artist.]

Kunstboek No. 57

No. 1** Robert van Hoecke. Verschillende Gezigten, met Kampementen en andere Krijgsvoorstellingen, benevens het Portret, te zamen 22 stuks, op 6 bladen. Bt Colnaghi, JS, f. 50.

No. 4. C. Matheus. Vijf Landschapjes, in de breedte, onbeschreven. Bt Woodburn, JS, f. 20, with no. 5.

No. 5 C. Matheus, Een dito, grooter, als boven. Bt with no. 4 above, *q.v.*

No. 10 F. Wouters. Vier stuks, Landschappen, in de breedte, op 2 bladen, benevens het portret, door P. de Jode. Bt Hurst, JS, f. 50.

No. 11 D. Ryckaert. Het Portret, door F. Boutats, een lagchend Mans Hoofd en een Boeren Gezelschap, 3 stuks, op 2 bladen. Bt Woodburn, JS, f. 20.

No. 12 Fouceel. Twee Landschapjes, in de hoogte, zeldzaam. Bt Hurst, JS, f. 5.

No. 16 J. van der Stok. Zeven stuks, Landschappen, in de breedte, op 4 bladen. Bt Hurst, JS, f. 31.

Kunstboek No. 59

No. 3 Albert Cuyp. Een zeer zeldzaam Prentje, met eene Koe en twee Geiten, benevens een zeldzaam Prentje, in de manier van A. Cuyp. [the last words underlined and *Baur proof* noted] Bt Hurst, JS, f. 16.

No. 9 Cornelis Sagtleven. Het Portret van C. Sagtleven, naar A. van Dijck. M. van den Ende Exc. [also] Een Herder, met eenige Schapen in een landschap. Bt Hurst, JS, with nos. 10–12, f. 53.

No. 10 Cornelis Sagtleven. Tien stuks, zijnde een werkje van vijf stuks, met Caricaturen, en een dito, verbeeldende de vijf Zinnen. Bt with no. 9, *q.v.*

No. 11 Cornelis Sagtleven. Twaalf stuks, met Boeren. P. Beerendrecht Exc. Bt with no. 9 above, *q.v.*

No. 12 Cornelis Sagtleven. Twaalf dito, zijnde een Werkje van zes met Honden en Katten, en een dito van zes met verschillend Gevogelte. Bt with no. 9 above, *q.v.*

Nos. 29–34 Jan Almeloveen [...] (B.I, nos. 1–32; nos 21–26 also in duplicate impressions. Nos 33 [Twee Landscapjes, luchtig geëtst] undescribed. No. 34 [Zes stuks Kopijen, naar Almeloveen], copies. All Bt Colnaghi, JS, f. 55.

No. 35 Leendert van der Koogen. Het werk van dien Meester, bestaande in 9 stuks, benevens eene Ordonantie, met twee lieden, op het Verkeerbord spelende, onbeschreven bij Bartsch. Te samen 10 stuks, op 3 bladen. (B.IV, 1–9) Bt Hurst, JS, f. 30.

No. 36 Nic. de Heldt Stokade. Zes stuks van dezen Meester, op 3 bladen, zijnde het Portret, door P. de Jode; Susanna met de boeven; Venus en Adonis; Anth. van Opstal, naar van Dijck, eerste proefdruk, idem voor het adres en idem met het adres. Bt Hurst, JS, f. 25.

Kunstboek No. 60

No. 4 Ludolf Bakhuyzen. De groote Prent, met de Zeehaven, zeldzaam. (B.IV, p. 275, no. 11) Bt Woodburn, JS, with no. 5, f. 400.

No. 5 Het Portret van L. Bakhuizen, door hemzelven geëtst, zeer zeldzaam. B.IV, p. 275, no. 13) Bt with no. 4, *q.v.*

No. 7 Jan Hackaert. Zes Landschappen, op 2 bladen. (B.IV, p. 289, nos. 1–6) Bt Woodburn, JS, f. 40, with no. 8.

No. 8 Vier stuks der bovenstaande; allereerste drukken, op 2 bladen. Bt with no. 7 above, *q.v.*

No. 19 Jan Le Duck. Een liggend Hond, met een Jongen, door of als le Ducq. Bt Woodburn, JS, f. 80.

No. 22 Abraham Hondius. Het Werk van dien Meester, bestaande in verschillend soort van Wildgedierte en Jagten, waaronder zeldzame en onbeschrevene drukken, te zamen met het Portret 12 stuks, op 6 bladen (B.V, p. 318). Bt Hurst, JS, f. 135.

No. 23. Guillaume de Heusch. Het Werk van dien Meester, bestaande in 9 stuks Landschappen, mankeert No. 1, en No. 4 dubbeld. Te zamen 10 stuks, op 5 bladen. (B.I, p. 325, 1–10) Bt Woodburn, JS, f. 270.

No. 24 Guillaume de Heusch. Twee stuks, Landschappen, zeer zeldzaam. Onbekend bij Bartsch. Bt Woodburn, JS, f. 100.

Kunstboek No. 61

No. 9 J. Ruischer. Een boomrijk Landschap; onbeschreven bij Bartsch. Bt Hurst, JS, f. 17.

No. 10 Philip Wouwerman. Een staand Paard, aan een boom gebonden; van de uiterste zeldzaamheid en uitmuntend geconditioneerd, benevens de kopij van A. Bartsch. (B.I, p. 395, no. 4) Een Paard voor eene kreb, luchtig geëtst, en aan dezen Meester toegeschreven. Bt Woodburn, JS, f. 505.

No. 11 Jean Baptiste Weenix. Een staande Os in een Landschap, zeer raar, benevens de Kopij van A. Bartsch. (B.I, p. 393, no. 1) Bt Woodburn, JS, with no. 11* f. 175.

No. 11* Jean Baptiste Weenix. Een zittend Man een Hond streelende; uiterst zeldzaam, mede benevens de Kopij daarvan. (B.I, p. 393, no. 2) Bt with No. 11 above, *q.v.*

No. 12 Jacob van der Does. Eene groep van vijf schapen in een Landschap, uiterst zeldzaam, benevens de Kopij van Bartsch. (B.IV, p. 195). Een Schaapje, bij dezelve onbekend. Bt Hurst, JS, f. 100.

No. 14 Paulus Potter. Dezelfde [i.e. Eenige staande en liggende Koeijen in een Landschap; de groote plaat, B.I, p. 41, no. 14] de groote plaat, allereerste etsdruk; kunnende deze Prent als éénig worden beschouwd. Zie de Aanmerking over dezelve van Bartsch, op. Bl. 54. Bt Woodburn, JS, f. 460.

No. 20 Paulus Potter. De plant Zebucaia, waarbij een zittende Aap, zeldzaam. Bt Hurst, JS, f. 150.

No. 21 Paulus Potter. Het werk met de Paarden, van vijf stuks, waarbij gevoegt is die van het Paard met de korte staart, eerste druk, benevens de vroegere en minder bewerkte drukken van No. 3 en 5, en een dito van No. 4, van de uiterste zeldzaamheid. Heerlijk Exemplaar, te zamen 9 stuks op 5 bladen. (B.I, 9–14). Bt Woodburn, JS, f. 1010.

Kunstboek No. 62.

Inhoudende de kapitale en uitmuntende werken van Adriaan van Ostade, Cornelis Bega en Cornelis Dusart [Ostade, te zamen met de Portretten door Gole, 101 stuks, Bega, 53 stuks, Dusart, benevens eenige door Gole, naar denzelven (…) 47 stuks]. Bt Woodburn, JS, f. 700.

II

General DOWDESWELL sale, London, Evans, 11–15 November 1828.

Lot 70 includes prints by Everdingen; the British Museum Print Room copy (SC.B.2.7[3]) underlines this name in pencil with the annotation in the margin (in Smedley's hand) *Tiffin, JS.*

Lot 90 Views of the Palace of Nonsuch, & c., by Hoefnagle, rare and curious, and Rubens's House at Antwerp, by F. Harrewyn. Bt Tiffin, JS, £1.0.0.

Lot 104 Curious Etchings, by *P. Lovell*, M. Lauron, J. S. Liotard, P. Loutherbourg, *W. Lodge, J. Lambert*, and J. La Guerre, some very scarce. Bt Tiffin, JS, the three names here italicised are underlined in pencil.

Lot 150 Ditto [i.e. Curious mezzotinto Specimens], by J. van Somer, including his own Portrait, and that of *Hubert Le Sueur*, very rare. Bt Tiffin, JS, the name of Le Sueur being underlined in pencil.

Lot 724 Portraits of Sir Anthony Vandyck, by Vanderbruggen, Gaywood, Hollar, & c. Bt Tiffin, JS, £1.2.0.

III

Thomas Wilson Sale, London, Hessey, 8 March 1830.

Lot 3 Temptation of St Anthony, by Wyngaerde; Etchings by Ruysdael, Everdingen, & c. (15 items) Bt Tiffin, JS, 15s.

Lot 8 The Shepherdess, by J. H. Roos (No. 31 of Bartsch), and various, by Berghem, Breemberg, & c. (13 items). Bt Tiffin, JS, 19s.

Lot 12 Marriage Festival, after Ostade, by J. Visscher, before the plate was cut; the Supplicant, by Roddermondt; Topers, by Dusart, first and second states; &c. (7 items). Bt Tiffin, JS, 15s.

Lot 13 Set of eight Views in Holland, by R. Roghman. Bt Tiffin, 10s 6d.

Lot 14 Set of six ditto, by J. Brosterhurst. Bt Tiffin, JS, £2.5.0.

IV

Reginald Pole Carew sale, London, Wheatley's, 13–15 May 1835.

The British Museum Print Room copy (SC.B.2.17[4], purchased from Daniell in 1874) is annotated: *N.B. Nearly all the lots having the name of Molteno attached as purchaser were bought for the Dutch Collectors. Those with the name of Tiffin were bought for Mr Sheepshanks and those with the name of Thane for Mr Esdaile.* Tiffin bought as follows (the individual lots are only described here in full if they are known to have come to the British Museum): Rembrandt etchings in lots 17, 37, 57, 63, 72, 98, 104, 114, and of the 'Copies from the works of Rembrandt':

Lot 123 Heads of Rembrandt, and of various of his fancy Heads of Men. Also of Rembrandt, Lot 131 (annotated as later sold to Maberly by Smith), 140, 145, 152, 165 (annotated as only the 3rd state and a copy), 184, 186–8, 194, 198, 206, 208–9, 224, 226, 234–5. Of the 'Scholars of Rembrandt':

Lot 257 A Lady in a Flat Bonnet and Feathers, an oval; an old Man in a Mezetin Cap, sitting, both by Bol, very fine, (Bt for £15.10.0 and annotated: *Bought with Mr. Sheepshanks Collection of Mr Smith in 1836 by the British Museum*). Also of Rembrandt, lots 271–2, 274–6, 282–4, 296 (annotated as *Bought by Maberly in 1836 of Mr Smith from Mr Sheepshanks' Coll.*), 298, 307, 308, 311, 313–4, 332–4 (332 annotated: *This print was in a very early state and was bought for Lord Aylesford by Mr Woodburn. It is now in the British Museum*), 339, 342, 345. Of the Doubtful Pieces:

Lot 373 The Strolling Musicians (357 of [Daulby's] Supplement), and Solomon on his Knees before an Idol, very rare – not mentioned by Daulby. Bt Tiffin, £4.6.0.

377 The Woman taken in Adultery (No. 350 of Daulby's doubtful Pieces), very scarce, Bt Tiffin, £4.4.0.

378 The Mountebanks at a Fair, a composition of many figures, No. 355 of Daulby's doubtful Pieces, but supposed to be a production of De Vlieger, it is etched with great spirit, and is very scarce. Bt Tiffin, £1.16.0.

V

Sales from Sheepshanks's Collection (all at Sotheby's unless otherwise stated). The sales suggest that Sheepshanks collected some Dutch Old Master paintings as well as works of the types with which he is usually associated:

1888, 5–7 March (with items owned by James B. Allen): included 85 lots 'from the Collection of the late John Sheepshanks, of Rutland Gate'. They include portrait prints (lots 1–9); drawings and prints by modern masters (lots 10–16, including works by or after W. B. Cooke, Wilson, Mulready, Cotman, Gibbon, Gauermann, Constable [proofs of Lucas prints]), Wilkie, a *volume of Drawings by Austrian Artists; presented to Mr. Sheepshanks by the Archduke Charles* (lot 49), J. F. Lewis, and *Engraving from the Pictures of the National Gallery, india paper proofs and etchings, whole bound* (lot 61); the Etching Club's Publications (lots 62–8) and a varied group of drawings (lots 70–85, many by Cooke, others by or attributed to Edridge, Landseer, Canaletto, Fragonard, Hearne, Gainsborough, Rowlandson and Chalon).

1951, 18–19 July, property of Col. A. C. Sheepshanks, lots 270–2: prints from Turner's *Liber Studiorum*, including many first state and proof impressions.

1951, 25 July, property of A. C. Sheepshanks, lots 19–20: 'F. Snyders and J. Jordaens, A Great Still Life' and 'M. Mierevelt, Portrait of Admiral de Ruyter'.

1956, 12 December, property of Col. A. C. Sheepshanks, lots 48–53: eighteenth- to nineteenth-century Dutch paintings and a Patrick Nasmyth.

1969, 27 June, at Christie's, property of Charles Sheepshanks, by descent from John Sheepshanks, lot 84, 'Cornelis Bega, An Alchemist's Shop' (subsequently Bader collection).

Appendix J
Documents on Acquisitions made from William Smith, 1841–50
Antony Griffiths

Offer of the Harding Collection

31 March 1841: Letter from Messrs Smith

Having lately purchased Mr Harding's magnificent collection of engravings, we beg to submit to the notice of the Trustees of the BM a selection from it which in the opinion of every amateur and artist would prove an almost invaluable addition to the National collection. Mr Harding's well-known taste and knowledge of the art, together with the many peculiar advantages he for so many years possessed enabled him to acquire a most unrivalled assemblage of the finest specimens of the art of engraving. And his collection, though by no means numerous, yet is perhaps unrivalled in the beauty and value of impression, and remarkably pure state of the prints it contains. It includes the most select gems from the best collections that have been dispersed during the last twenty years, and the finest specimens of the art which were in the collections of Sir Mark Sykes, the Count de Fries, the Duke of Bucking-

ham, Mr Job Carew, Mr Wilson and of numerous others, are to be found in this collection.

Previous to its dispersal, and when a few days since we purchased it of Mr Harding, and before any amateur had seen it, we carefully selected such prints as we were aware were desirable for the BM; as in the present advanced state of that collection, the opportunities that occur for adding to it are so rare that it is hardly probable that for the next century so numerous, interesting and almost invaluable assembly of the finest works of the best masters could be obtained. In addition, from the increased taste for collecting that now prevails all over the Continent, and from the high prices that are paid abroad for articles of this description, our best etchings and engravings are continually leaving the country, and for some of the prints of Rembrandt and others, now offered, and of which no other impressions are known to exist in any collection, almost unlimited offers have been made by the Dutch collectors. It therefore becomes a matter of some national importance in the way of art to secure at once for the country such treasures, which as many of them are known to be unique, it is totally impossible should ever be again obtained.

The collection commences with a selection of seven fine and interesting specimens of Italian nielli, six of which are not in the rich collection of the Bibliothèque du Roi in Paris. Then follow several of the rare Taroccho Cards, and several of the most celebrated works of Mocetto, B. Montagna, Robetta etc. There are then some engravings by the engraver of the Year 1466, and some of the finest productions of M. Schongauer, J. van Mecken, including complete sets of the Passion of Christ and of the Life of the Virgin by these masters, of which even separate prints are hardly to be obtained at any price. There is also a complete set of the illustrations of the Apocalypse by J. Duvet, called the Master of the Unicorn, in matchless state, of which no similar set is known. Specimens by Bocholt, Master of the Caduceus, L. van Leyden etc. By Berchem there is one etching so excessively rare as to have escaped the researches of Mr Sheepshanks, and of Rembrandt there are 21 etchings nearly the whole of which are unique, and of course highly desirable to the Dutch collectors, for the museums of which country almost innumerable applications have repeatedly been made to Mr Harding for them. There are also some fine proofs by the Visschers, and some matchless impressions of the great French engravers, including the best works of Audran, Drevet etc. The collection of modern artists contains the selected works of the most eminent English and foreign engravers etc.

We send the accurate list containing a description of the state of each print, in which it will be observed no mention of the condition of the prints is made etc. The collection contains 321 prints, and the price we offer them for is £2,300.

Offer of the Woodburn Collection

25 April 1843: letter from Samuel Woodburn to Lord Ashburton

As your Lordship was so good as to promise me to ascertain whether the Trustees of the BM are disposed to add to the collection of prints in that national establishment, I take the liberty of sending to your Lordship a rough draft of my superb collection requesting your Lordship will have the goodness to show it to the next meeting of the Trustees and return it to me in case they should decline them, as I propose offering the collection by advertisement in the newspapers, thinking it probable that by so doing I may be able to keep it in the Kingdom.

Since I had the honour of seeing your Lordship I have taken some trouble to ascertain respecting the price at which I could afford to sell them, and the result is that I find they cost me about £12,000, which sum I should accept with satisfaction if I can keep them in England, although I feel confident that if declined by the BM they will never be able to obtain such a collection (it is in fact impracticable). No doubt many of the articles must already exist in the BM, therefore I propose in case the Trustees agree to the plan to deliver the whole collection and deduct £2,000 for the duplicates, taking always the inferior one in order that the collection in the BM may be worthy of the country.

Your Lordship will perceive that I do not make any offer respecting my collection of drawings, which is certainly one of the most extensive and valuable that exists. My reasons are that if I can place my collection of engravings I am perfectly indifferent about selling the drawings, indeed I should say I would prefer to keep them; however, should the Trustees prefer the drawings to prints I am ready to do with them exactly the same as I offer with the prints, and in that case should be willing to keep the prints, but I find that both collections is rather too much on my hands.

I regret to be obliged to refer to my negotiations with the Trustees and Government, but as I appear never to have been understood, and have suffered so much through false representations, which I well know to have been made to the Trustees, I wish to be as explicit as possible respecting my present offer. It is very probable that an idea will be tried to be instilled into the Trustees that it is not probable that the collection can be so fine as described because it belongs to a merchant who is continually selling, and therefore the finest things must be gone.

I answer to this that the most valuable and curious part of this collection has never before been seen or offered for sale. That can be proved by my producing every curious print I bought at the sale of Sir M. M. Sykes, which can be verified by the catalogue and on the back of the print in his writing.

I beg to apologise for troubling your Lordship on this matter which I must say I feel of great importance both to the arts and to myself. Should your Lordship wish for any further explanation, I shall have great pleasure in waiting on you. I have heard from Lord Belhaven a council has been formed in Edinburgh, but the affair goes slowly. I intend to petition Her Majesty to subscribe a similar sum as that which H.M. William IV sent me without any explanation when I was engaged in my long and arduous task of exhibiting the drawings.

If H.M. is graciously pleased to patronise this plan, it will be a great boon to Scotland.

29 April 1843: memorandum from Samuel Woodburn describing the above collection

Messrs Woodburn are desirous of placing in the BM or any other public repository where they can be ready accessible to artists and amateurs their magnificent collection of engravings, etchings and wood engravings, of which the following is a rough catalogue:

1. Engravings illustrative of the invention of engraving: the most curious articles are as follows. The celebrated Pax by Maso Finiguerra engraved on silver and included in a rich frame surmounted with enamel. This precious work of art is unique in this Kingdom, and no other of similar interest exists, except in the collection at Florence. Also upwards of 30 smaller engravings in

niello on silver of the highest interest. There is only one small specimen of this series in the BM; but the superb specimen of Finiguerra on sulphur which the BM possesses is of the first importance, and illustrates in a remarkable manner the Pax in silver in this collection. Messrs Woodburn possess several specimens on sulphur prior to the discovery of printing on paper, articles of such extreme rarity that the Royal collections in France and Germany do not contain a single specimen.

The class of nielli on paper is the finest and most numerous that exist; one of them was purchased at the sale of Sir M. M. Sykes against the commission of the BM, who bid £300 for it.

The engravings by Baldini, Botticelli, N. da Modena, J. Brixiano, Mocetto and others as described by Bartsch are both numerous and fine in quality, containing among many other interesting articles a set of the Planets differing in work to the set now in the BM and undoubtedly prior to them. The set usually called the 'Giuoco di Tarrocho' consisting of 50 small prints are particularly interesting in this collection; great part of the second set being found. Here are also the maps by Berlingheria, and plates to the 1st edition of Ptolomey are complete. The chief part of these valuable articles are from the collection of Sir M. M. Sykes, to which has been added several valuable articles purchased whenever opportunity offered both in England and on the Continent.

2. The period of Marc Antonio Raimondi is also most valuable and interesting, containing several of the utmost rarity. The most interesting articles are the celebrated Martyrdom of St Lawrence with the two prongs, almost unique. The figure pulling on his stocking from the Cartoon of Pisa, half in outline and half finished, this most curious print is particularly valuable as it shows the method of workmanship of this celebrated engraver, who appears to have been a perfect master of the graver, and to have with one stroke produced the effect which he required; the usual method engravers practice is to re-enter the lines beginning faintly, the value of this singular specimen must become apparent when it is known that it stands alone, no other example exists in any catalogue or collection that has hitherto appeared. The various celebrated prints from Raffaello, which are well known, are in fine states, and the work of this most celebrated engraver is nearly complete.

3. The works of masters who lived at this period are also equally important and numerous; among the most curious is the beautiful head of a female, which formerly was in the collection of Thomas Wilson, and which according to the opinion of the late W.Y. Ottley is engraved by L. da Vinci. This gentleman has written a letter to Mr Wilson stating his belief in this case, which letter is printed in the catalogue of that choice collection; there are also many other articles in this class absolutely unique.

4. The etchings of the Italian school are numerous and fine impressions, many by Parmegiano and Guido, from the collections of Count Fries of Vienna. The wood engravings also contain several articles of great interest, some may be considered unique.

5. The engravings of ancient masters of Germany are most numerous and choice, several unknown to Bartsch who formed his catalogue from the finest collections on the Continent. The number by the Master of 1466 exceed one hundred, and contain one specimen dated 1464, which is the earliest date hitherto known, consequently it is of the first interest. This department contains so large a portion of the splendid collection made by the Count Fries that there are probably upwards of 200 engravings

which are the identical ones described by Bartsch and which are probably unique; particularly the celebrated set of engraved playing-cards described at length in that work. The entire work by the Hopfers are here and is that from which Bartsch made his catalogue. The work of J. van Meck, Schongauer and others are numerous and fine. There are also in this class several of the finest works of Hollar, and other masters of a later period.

6. The etchings and engravings by Flemish and Dutch masters are most numerous and choice, consisting of a very fine set of the etchings by Rembrandt several of great beauty, and some in states that are absolutely unique being unfinished and touched in black chalk by this great master. The Waterloo are also very fine, containing some proofs before they are finished with the graver. The Ostade, Ruysdael etc. are both numerous and choice. The Flemish school contains some unique engravings half finished after Rubens by the best engravers of the school. There are also specimens by C. Visscher etc.

7. The collection of portraits contains numerous articles of the first importance, particularly among the class that illustrates Granger's 'Biographical History of England'. Notwithstanding this class is particularly strong in the BM from the legacies of Sir H. Sloane, Cracherode, and others, yet many valuable articles are wanting which this collection can furnish. The most curious are James I in Parliament surrounded by the arms of all the nobility by R. Elstrake, Margaret Smith by Faithorne, proof before any writing, also most of the fine and valuable works of Faithorne and Pass, some of which are unique. The collection of portraits of foreigners are very numerous and include a superb collection of the works of Nanteuil, some unfinished and in remarkable states.

8. The most extensive portion remain to describe. They consist of numerous articles in every class particularly of such schools and masters that are not described in printed catalogues, such as a most extensive collection of mezzotints, including the rare prints by Counts Siegen and Furstenberg, Prince Rupert etc.

Offer of the Early German Collection

9 October 1844: letter from Messrs Smith

We beg to submit to the notice of the Trustees of the BM a collection of prints we have recently purchased, which exceeds both in interest and importance every other that has as yet passed through our hands. It consists of the works of the early German engravers and is particularly rich in those of the 15th century, indeed far exceeding in number and consequence every other collection whether public or private in Europe.

To prove this, it will be sufficient to mention that of the excessively rare works of the Master of 1466 and of his period: the Munich collection contains about 80 prints, the Imperial library at Vienna 51, the Archduke Charles's collection at Vienna 83; the Dresden collection 105; that of Berlin 44; of Amsterdam 10; of Paris about 70; of the BM 17; while this collection contains the most extraordinary number of 154. Of such extreme rarity are these prints that during the last 50 years rarely more than 5 or 6 have been found in any collection that has been sold in England, and the only Continental sale in which any number occurred was that of the Count de Fries, the greatest portion of which is now included in this collection. Of the other early masters, such as van Bocholt, Martin Schongauer, Israel van Mecken, Wenceslaus of

Olmütz, Mair, Le Maître de la Navette etc. the number it contains is proportionally extraordinary.

Forming objects of the highest importance for the studies of painters on glass, goldsmiths, carvers in ivory and wood, designers of ornamental metal work, and the large class of artists employed in architectural decoration generally, these prints have always been most eagerly sought after, and more especially during the last few years, when the public taste not only of England but of the whole of Europe has been so much directed to these objects. In the course of our business we have had occasionally opportunities of meeting with small collections or detached prints of this description, which have been immediately purchased from us for the before mentioned purposes, principally by foreign artists and dealers, and particularly by those of Paris, where a publication of very mediocre copies from such of these prints as were attainable for that purpose has met with a most extensive sale.

Under these circumstances, and for the additional reason that the British Museum is excessively deficient in prints of this school, we consider it an object of some national importance that this collection should be secured for the country. If this opportunity be now lost, it can never occur again. Many of the prints, particularly those of the earlier period, are unique, and are the identical prints from which Bartsch took his descriptions when they were in Count Fries's and other German collections, and some further idea may be formed of the interest of this wonderful collection, when we mention that nearly one fourth of the prints contained in it are of such excessive rarity as never to have been seen by Bartsch. The purchase of it would at once place the BM in the same high position with regard to the German school as the purchase of the Sheepshanks collection placed it with regard to the Dutch and Flemish, that of being the first in Europe.

We purchased this collection from Mr Coningham, about two months since, and have since made very considerable additions to it. During the time it has been in our possession it has been freely open for the inspection of artists and amateurs, by numbers of whom it has been seen and admired. It now contains 1,807 prints and the price we ask for it is £3,000.

It being impossible on account of the number of prints to give anything like a detailed catalogue of it, we forward a list of the number of the works of each master, specifying those described by or unknown to Bartsch, and we shall be most happy to attend any meeting of the Trustees of the BM, in order to submit the prints to their inspection, to give any further explanation that may be required, and to show the extraordinary value of this collection to the country.

We are Sir, your most obedient humble servants

Wm and G. Smith

[there follows three pages of transcript of the list, which gives the name of each engraver, followed by the number of items in the collection described by Bartsch, the number not so described, and the total number of prints offered]

Offer of the Early Italian Collection

8 May 1845: letter from Messrs Smith

We beg to offer to the consideration of the Trustees of the British Museum a collection far surpassing in interest and importance any that has ever passed through our hands. It consists, almost entirely, of the works of the Italian designers and engravers of the fifteenth century, and contains an extraordinary, and indeed almost incredible, number of the very earliest specimens of these arts. It forms an admirable and perfect series illustrative of the art of engraving from what may fairly be called its discovery by Maso Finiguerra, to the period when Marc Antonio in Italy, and Albert Durer in Germany, brought it at once to perfection.

The objects of which this wonderful collection is composed have been acquired from many sources, but the principal and most important of them were formerly in the possession of Signor Storck of Milan. That gentleman, one of the most ardent amateurs that ever existed, began to form his collection at a time when greater facilities existed for procuring specimens of early art than can ever again occur. At the latter end of the last and the beginning of the present century, owing to the troubles in Italy consequent upon the French revolution, a vast number of churches, convents and the palaces of noble and ancient families were destroyed, and their contents dispersed. For such places, it is well known, the finest works of art were originally executed, and, up to this period, had been carefully and religiously preserved. Signor Storck's agents secured for him, regardless of price, everything it was possible to obtain, and by degrees his collection became of the greatest importance.

Unfortunately his circumstances became embarrassed, and he was compelled to deposit the whole of his treasures with the Bankers Carli of Milan as a security for a large sum of money advanced by them. Failing to redeem them, these bankers sold them in 1818 to Mr Woodburn, by whom they were brought over to England and sold in one lot to Sir Mark Sykes, who already possessed a considerable number of curiosities of the same description. At the sale of this gentleman's property in 1824, Mr Woodburn repurchased many of the most important articles, and nearly all the others were secured by that distinguished amateur Mr Wilson, whose collection afterwards coming into Mr Woodburn's hands, they were reunited and thus formed the foundation of the magnificent collection now under notice. The dispersal of the collections of Count Fries, Mr Lloyd, the late Duke of Buckingham, and many others (of perhaps not equal consequence) enabled Mr Woodburn to make an enormous number of invaluable additions, and he continued so doing up to the period of his selling it to Mr Coningham in 1843. That gentleman also added considerably to it, and we bought it from him early in March last. We then had by us many very curious articles of this description, and having fortunately obtained during a recent visit to Paris others of no less consequence, by the addition of these we have been enabled to bring it to its present state of perfection.

The collection commences with the extraordinary number of 103 silver plates engraved by the most celebrated workers in niello of the fifteenth century. Among these is the celebrated Pax, an undoubted work by Maso Finiguerra, the inventor of the art of taking impressions from metallic plates, which even at Sir Mark Sykes's sale in 1824 produced no less than 300 guineas. It is unnecessary for us to expatiate either on the beauty or value of this exquisite work as it is well known not only from repeatedly printed descriptions but from two copies, one of which was engraved for the collection of facsimiles of unique engravings published under the superintendence of Mr Ottley, and the other for Mr Duchesne's 'Essai sur les Nielles'. We shall merely mention that the only other indisputable work by this artist is the Pax still preserved in the church of San Giovanni at Florence, for which it

was executed in the year 1452, and in the church records of that year is an entry of a payment to him of 66 florins of gold for it. From this latter, two sulphurs which will be hereafter mentioned, and at least four impressions on paper are known. From the one in this collection, no impression either on sulphur or paper exists, and on a careful examination and comparison it will be evident that it is a much earlier specimen of the art than that in the church of San Giovanni. Besides this wonderful specimen, there are many others in this collection of most extraordinary interest and beauty, among which are some that have also with great reason been attributed to the hand of Finiguerra, and one undoubted specimen by that most interesting artist Francia. The whole of the collections of Europe both public and private combined would not form an assemblage equal in number and importance to this now under consideration, and this is amply proved by the fact mentioned by Duchesne that altogether 165 silver plates only are known. The Paris collection contains no genuine specimen, and the British Museum possesses only three, the most important of which, a silver cup recently purchased, though of great curiosity, is of Flemish workmanship and not of a very early date. They have always been of excessive rarity, and Vasari, in the first edition of his Lives of the Painters published in 1550, states that many of them had been melted down and sold in consequence of the necessities of the City in time of war.

The silver plates are followed by fifteen impressions on sulphur which are objects of perhaps even greater curiosity and interest. They are evidently the identical works mentioned by Vasari (see his life of Pollaiuolo) as being also by Maso Finiguerra, and at his time likewise deposited in the church of San Giovanni. They were afterwards removed from there, and were used as decorations to a shrine or small altar in the chapel of the convent of the Camaldoli at Florence, and were so placed when Lanzi published the first edition of his 'Storia Pittorica' in 1789. [Carpenter's annotation: Lanzi says 'some which are attributed to him in possession of the Fathers of Camaldoli are not ascertained to be his.'] Passing through Signor Storck's hands they formed a portion of Sir Mark Sykes's collection, at the sale of which they produced the very inadequate sum of £338. In the British Museum are only two specimens of this art, one of which, a portion of the same series as the preceding, was bought for £70 at the same sale, and for the other, which it should be observed is by no means in good condition, 25 guineas were paid some time since to the late Duke of Buckingham. A duplicate of the latter is in the Durazzo collection at Genoa, and there are the two impressions in sulphur from the San Giovanni Pax before alluded to. Of the fifteen contained in this collection, neither the silver plates nor any impressions on paper are known. No public collection on the Continent contains even a single specimen, and only 24 altogether are known. Should the British Museum purchase this collection, it will then contain seventeen. Of the others, one as just mentioned is in the Durazzo collection, and the remaining six are all in the collections of private amateurs in England.

Following the progress of the art, our collection next includes 63 impressions on paper from works of the same description as the preceding. Among them is the unique impression of another magnificent Pax also by Maso Finiguerra, the plate of which has unfortunately not reached us. It is of most superb execution, and from the very imperfect manner in which it is printed, there is good reason for supposing that, if not absolutely the first, it may be at any rate one of the very earliest impressions ever rubbed off a silver plate. It was originally purchased by Mr Ottley at Rome, and was sold by him to Sir Mark Sykes for 150 guineas. At the sale of that gentleman's collection, it was purchased by Mr Woodburn against an agent employed by the French Government for 300 guineas. [Carpenter's note: Mr Smedley was the last bidder against Mr Woodburn for the Museum.] Mr Ottley who considered it the most remarkable and interesting specimen in his collection had a facsimile of it engraved as an important illustration to his 'Enquiry'. It has been asserted that a duplicate impression is in the Bibliothèque du Roi in Paris, but a recent examination has enabled us to ascertain beyond a doubt that the one deposited there is nothing more than a rather unskilfully executed ancient copy. The volume of nielli in the Paris collection is stated to contain 65 impressions, but eight of these are not genuine. The British Museum already contains 40, nearly all of which have been purchased during the last few years, and the addition of this collection will form a number unequalled both in interest and value. Besides this magnificent impression, our collection includes many of the finest works of Pellegrini da Cesio and other ancient niellatore, and one most exquisite design that has justly been considered by Duchesne and other authors to be an early work of Marc Antonio Raimondi. They are without exception in a most astonishingly perfect state of preservation.

Having now arrived at the period when the art of printing was invented, our collection contains nearly 650 specimens of the works of the earliest engravers, of a large proportion of which no other impressions are known. This portion commences with a magnificent print representing our Saviour led to execution, which there is every reason for supposing was engraved by Maso Finiguerra himself. It is unique, and is well known to every amateur by the admirable copy introduced into the before mentioned series of facsimiles. A German connoisseur of great celebrity and acknowledged judgement who saw this print when in Mr Coningham's possession considered it the most interesting and valuable specimen of engraving in the world. It was formerly in Mr Lloyd's collection, at the sale of which nearly thirty years ago, when works of art of every description did not produce a third of their present prices, it sold for upwards of £50. Passing over a number of prints of the greatest curiosity, we would beg to point attention to a series of representations of the seven planets ascribed to Baldini, though from what we are about to mention it is possible that they may be of even earlier date. It is well known that the British Museum possesses a set of similar subjects, hitherto considered the most curious prints in the world, and which when in Dr Monro's collection were described by Strutt in his 'Dictionary of Engravers', in which copies of two of the pieces are introduced. Now a very slight comparison will convince even an unpractised observer that these are nothing more than rude copies of the beautiful prints contained in this collection, which are evidently drawn and engraved by an artist of consummate taste and feeling. But the comparison leads to a still more curious discovery. The British Museum set commences with a calendar giving the period of the saints' days etc from 1465 to 1517, of which if there ever existed an original it has not reached us. Now our set being evidently the original, it follows that they must have been engraved at a somewhat earlier period, and this at once settles the disputed fact as to the priority of the German over the Italian school, as no engravings of the former are known of an earlier date than 1466. No other set of these interesting prints in a pure and genuine state is known to exist, indeed the only other impres-

sions in any state are those in the Paris collection which are most coarsely retouched all over. A still more interesting circumstance is the fact that our set contains two repetitions of these subjects in earlier states of the plates. This set was obtained by Mr Wilson from the Fries collection, but as the early Italian portion was not sold by public sale, we have no means of ascertaining the exact price he paid for them.

It will be of course impossible to attempt a description of all the extraordinary works of art included in this collection. We may however mention that it contains a complete series of the Tarocchi cards in matchless state, and a great proportion of a second series of the same subjects which Bartsch very absurdly considers the original prints. A magnificent engraving of a portrait of a young female by the hand of Leonardo da Vinci is also of the highest interest, as independent of its extreme beauty it is the only impression known, and was bought by Mr Wilson at the Sykes sale for £64. That gentleman had a facsimile of it engraved as a frontispiece to his privately circulated catalogue, justly considering it as the most extraordinary gem of his truly wonderful collection. A complete series of the vignettes to Dante with some variations of states, of the plates to Ptolomey's and other early geographical works, and of the Monte Santo di Dio are also included in our collection. It also contains many specimens, and in some instances nearly complete works of Pollaiuolo, Fogolino, Mocetto, Andrea Mantegna, Nicoletto da Modena, Zoan Andrea, the Di Brescias, Benedetto Montagna, the rare master of the Monogram P.P., the Campagnolas, Robetta, and other not less interesting artists, including a vast number of prints that have escaped the researches of Bartsch, Ottley and Duchesne. Besides these, there are a few Italian bronzes and medals illustrative in some measure of the art of engraving, and which though of no particular value we include in the collection because we wish to offer it exactly as we purchased it.

The collection consists of 848 articles and we send an accurate list of every object contained in it. The difference in the numbers of the list and that above specified arises from the fact that on account of additions since it was first commenced, a few of the number are repeated. The price we ask for it is £5,000, a sum we are firmly persuaded very much below what it is worth, but as we purchased the collection at a very reasonable price, we are willing to sell it as a whole accordingly. Some idea may be formed of the market value of articles of this description when we mention that for twenty articles alone, all of which are included in this collection, nearly £1,300 were paid at the sale of Sir Mark Sykes. It is well known that the price of all fine works of art has very greatly advanced since that period, and if now sold they would realise a much more considerable sum. So great is the rarity of the silver nielli that during the more than twenty years that have elapsed since the sale of Sir Mark Sykes's collection scarcely a single genuine specimen has been brought to public or private sale.

It will be observed that we have not given any account of the merit and utility of this collection for the purposes of artistic study, or of its infinite value to all parties engaged in the various arts connected with decorative design. We have considered it unnecessary to do so, because the Italian school is universally known and acknowledged, on account of its accuracy of outline and beauty of form, to be especially adapted for such purposes, and these works of art form the finest studies in the world for the young artist. We shall merely observe that the articles that compose our collection are in an admirable and astonishing state of preservation, and generally most brilliant impressions.

We would beg most earnestly and respectfully to impress upon the Trustees of the British Museum the necessity of adding this magnificent assemblage to the national collection. The purchase of it will at once terminate and complete the series of the works of the early masters, and it will be positively the last time that any large sum will be required for these purposes. This will at once be evident when it is considered that the Museum contains the most complete collections in Europe of the Flemish, Dutch and German schools. Now the only one remaining is that of Italy, and we do hope that the only opportunity that can ever occur of securing a near perfect collection, more than half the articles contained in which are absolutely unique, will not be missed. From what we have stated before, it is perfectly evident that if this collection is broken up and dispersed among the public and private collections throughout Europe, no time and no cost however considerable would be able to collect together another of a tithe of the interest or number. As an additional reason we may mention that the British Museum contains no collection of this kind at all, as besides the three silver plates, the two sulphurs and the forty impressions on paper of nielli, it possesses very little more than one hundred prints by the early Italian masters, a large proportion of which are in such wretched state, both as to impression and condition, as to be totally worthless.

Letter concerning the Verstolk Sale

26 February 1847: letter from Messrs Smith to Carpenter

As it is probable that in the course of a few months the collection of prints formed by the late Baron Verstolk van Soelen will be sold by auction at Amsterdam, and as a vast amount of most interesting objects not contained in the magnificent collection under your care is included in it, I take the liberty of soliciting your attention to the following observations. I do so with the greater confidence, because I am aware that you are at all times ready and anxious to attend to such suggestions as may tend towards enriching and improving it. One of my principal reasons is that access to Baron Verstolk's collection having been at all times exceedingly difficult, few people are acquainted with what it really contains, and I believe that with the exception of my brother and myself nobody in England has had an opportunity of carefully examining it. This for reasons with which you are well acquainted, but which it is not now necessary to mention, we had ample means of doing in the early part of last year.

My present observations will necessarily be confined to such portions of this collection as are wanting in that of the British Museum, and these are so numerous that I fear they will extend to a somewhat inconvenient length. The great value and interest of it are, as you are no doubt aware, principally centred in the works of the Dutch and Flemish artists, chiefly of the seventeenth century, and they are certainly more complete than those ever assembled by any private collector with the exception of Mr Sheepshanks; it contains, however, as will be hereafter seen, the works of many masters which that gentleman had never attended to, but which nevertheless in the history and study of art are of the very highest importance. As Rembrandt is in both these views of the first consequence, I shall commence by a statement of a few of his grandest works which the dispersal of this collection will enable the

Museum to add to its already matchless series, which is now, I do not hesitate to assert, far superior to any other.

1. First in consequence is the portrait of Rembrandt holding a sabre, the entire plate, of which only four impressions are known: one in the Bibliothèque Royale in Paris, one at Amsterdam, one formerly in Lord Aylesford's collection, and now in that of Mr Holford who purchased it lately from Mr Woodburn for between £300 and £400; and this, by far the finest, which was formerly Baron Denon's and Mr Wilson's.

2. The portrait of Rembrandt drawing, the first state

3. Rembrandt in a hat (7), the first and second states

4. Head resembling Rembrandt (8), the uncut plate (purchased at the Carew sale for £23.12.6)

5. The large resurrection of Lazarus, first state, probably unique

6. St Jerome, in Rembrandt's dark manner, first state

7. The rat killer (126), from Carew's collection £59.17.0

8. A little Polish figure (142), Carew's £53.11.0

9. Two beggars coming from behind a bank, first state

10. Six's bridge, first state, unique, from the Baring and Revil collections

11. The same print, second state, one hat covered

12. The coach landscape, in an early unique state

13. Village with a square tower, first state

14. Landscape with an orchard and barn (227), the large plate, Carew's £41.9.6

15. Landscape with a canal and boat (236), Carew's £32.11.0

16. Landscape with two fishermen (255)

17. Portrait of Ephraim Bonus, first state with the black ring, excessively rare. The only other impression in this country was recently sold to Mr Holford from Lord Aylesford's collection for 300 guineas

18. Wtenbogardus the Dutch minister, an early unique state worked upon by Rembrandt himself

19. Van Tolling the advocate, an early unique state

20. An old man with a beard (297)

21. A Morisco, the large plate

Besides these there is an enormous quantity of prints by Rembrandt, either not at all in the Museum collection, or in different and in many instances unique and undescribed states. Among the works of his pupils Bol, Livens, van Vliet, and of the artists of his school, are many that would cover the blank spaces left for them in your volumes.

Of the masters described by Bartsch in the first, second, fourth and fifth volumes of his Peintre-Graveur, rich as Mr Sheepshanks' collection was, there is scarcely one to whose works additions of consequence might not be made from the Verstolk series. A few only of these I shall specify. By Berghem there is a unique impression of his most considerable print, the cow in the water, no.1 of Bartsch, much earlier than that described by him. The four oblong prints of cattle are also in unfinished states, not as far as I am aware to be found in any other collection. There is also an undescribed print by him of three sheeps' heads on one plate; a complete set of the milkpail's proofs, and many others of the greatest interest. Among the works of Ostade are many that would prove invaluable additions, and the same may be said of Potter, van de Velde, Both, Ruisdael, Everdingen, Swanevelt, Waterloo, de Heusch and Naiwincx, by the latter of which are his complete works, sixteen etchings, proofs, the only set known, purchased at the sale of the late Mr Seguier for more than £70. Mr Sheepshanks' collection was limited to the works of those artists either mentioned by Bartsch or of the same period, but Baron Verstolk has continued the series down to the present day, where the Museum is entirely deficient. It is unnecessary for me to mention how desirable it would be to add this series, which I think may be effected at a comparatively inconsiderable cost.

The third volume of Bartsch contains descriptions of the works of Goltzius, Matham, Saenredam and Muller, all admirable designers and engravers, but those works, not coming under the class of etchings, were not contained in Mr Sheepshanks' collection, and scarcely any of them are in the Museum. Baron Verstolk purchased the whole of these at the Fries sale, and during the more than twenty years that have elapsed since, has added considerably to them, thus making them the most complete in Europe. These will probably be sold in works, I mean the prints by each master in one lot, and should undoubtedly be secured. He also possessed a magnificent series of the works of Cornelius Visscher, from which many desirable and unique prints may be obtained. Besides these he had complete collections of the works of Suyderhoef, Bloemart, the Sadelers, and an enormous number of equally interesting masters, which though of no great money value, are highly important as works of art.

You will observe that I have so far only mentioned the Dutch and Flemish schools. Of the early Italian and German, the Verstolk collection contains no specimens, with the exception of some fine prints by Marc Antonio already in the Museum, a fine collection of the works of Albert Durer, most of which are also in the Museum, and nearly complete works of Lucas Cranach and Grun, which would be admirable acquisitions. There are also a few prints by Lucas van Leyden, only one of which you want, namely the Uylenspiegel, a print of excessive rarity, which was purchased at the Duke of Buckingham's sale. Besides these, there is a large quantity of prints by the little German masters described in the eighth and ninth volumes of Bartsch, many of which you should secure.

Another and exceedingly interesting portion of the Verstolk collection is that containing the works of the great French engravers of the seventeenth century. These are more complete than are to be found in any other collection. Here the Museum is lamentably deficient, though it does contain a few fine prints of this class. But I think that such an occasion of purchasing the works of Nanteuil, Edelinck, Drevet, van Schuppen, Masson, Balechou and a host of other engravers of equal importance should not be neglected. Besides these there is a magnificent and nearly complete series of the productions of that interesting artist Callot, originally commenced by Mr Wilson, to which have since been added those of the Duke of Buckingham and Mr Rossi of Marseilles.

The last part of this magnificent collection to which I shall allude is one of very great consequence to the British Museum. It is that comprising the works of the greatest engravers from about 1750 to nearly the present day. Of these the Museum possesses a superb series of Raffaelle Morghen's prints, but of other great

engravers such as Longhi, Muller, Desnoyers, Garavaglia, Anderloni, Forster, Toschi and others, it has only specimens, and those in no great number. They are here nearly complete and in an infinite variety of states. The works of Wille are also extraordinary both in number and quality, and I should not be wrong in stating that four fifths of them will be found to be wanting in your collection. The English school is also very rich, particularly in a class of prints now become exceedingly rare, I mean those by MacArdell, Earlom, Houston, J. R. Smith, and other mezzotint engravers which have never yet been surpassed. Of the earlier school, a very large proportion of the best works of Wenceslaus Hollar will be found, many of which are unique, and as he may be reckoned amongst our own engravers, they are peculiarly interesting.

I shall conclude by stating that nearly every print purchased by Baron Verstolk is in the most perfect condition. Possessing almost unlimited means, and great taste, he invariably desired those parties who supplied him with prints to send nothing for his inspection in which any faults could be found either as to impression or condition. I sincerely hope, though such a course will be directly contrary to my own interest, that you will be able to persuade the Trustees of the British Museum not to allow this opportunity of making such considerable and valuable additions to the print department to escape. Such a one can never again occur, and you may remember while we were in Holland together about a month before Baron Verstolk's death, it was then asserted that in case of such an event his collection would go to the Museum at the Hague. Another strong reason may be mentioned, that no inconsiderable portion of these prints have been allowed to be taken from this country, and if not now secured they will probably find their way into other national collections, from which there will necessarily be no possibility of obtaining them. I must beg you to observe that these are only a few hints, very roughly thrown together, and that I shall be most happy to give you any further information you may be desirous of having.

I remain Dear Sir, your faithful servant, Wm Smith

Letter concerning Smith's purchase of Woodburn's Stock

3 May 1847: letter from Carpenter to Forshall

I think it right to acquaint you with the fact of Messrs Smith of Lisle St having purchased the whole of Messrs Woodburn's stock of prints, including the fine collection of the works of Rembrandt made by Lord Aylesford save the 13 selected by Mr Holford. I looked over a considerable portion last Friday, and find that with the exception of the 'Ephraim Bonus' with the black ring, the Sabre print and two others (which were selected by Mr Holford) the Museum have here the opportunity of obtaining almost every attainable print of the master, and amongst them two or three from the Denon collection, which are perfectly unique.

The Aylesford collection I believe has always been considered by collectors on the whole as the finest as regards condition and extent in the world.

The purchase having been completed by Messrs Smith in the course of Thursday last, they had not had time to price the prints; besides which I had not the time to make myself sufficiently acquainted with what the Museum is actually in want of. Consequently I could not draw up a satisfactory report.

20 May 1847: letter from Smith to Forshall, the Museum Secretary, offers

(Summary only)

1. 266 Aylesford Rembrandts at £3,317

2. 29 prints by early Italian and German engravers £386

3. 16 prints by Faithorne, including portrait of Oliver Cromwell standing between the pillars £135

4. a collection of 503 portraits £1,116

5. a collection of 384 by Hollar £180

6. a collection of 605 works of Primaticcio and the school of Fontainebleau, from the Fries collection with some later additions £120

7. a collection of 2,063 works of Parmigianino and Meldolla formed by Richard Ford £350

The total number of prints is 3,865 and the price is £5,604

20 May 1847: Carpenter's report to the Trustees recommending the purchase of the above from Woodburn's stock:

Mr C. has the honour to report to the Trustees that he has been occupied for some days in looking over an extensive collection of prints recently purchased from Messrs Woodburn by Messrs Smith of Lisle St. A careful selection has been made from it of all such rarities as the BM are not already possessed of, which it is the intention of Messrs Smith to offer to the Trustees.

The most important feature is the well known collection formed by Lord Aylesford of the etchings by Rembrandt. In it are 200 which the Museum does not possess; some 30 of these are unique, or in states not described in any of the printed catalogues of this artist's etchings. The opportunity is therefore afforded of rendering the national collection complete with some eight or nine exceptions and four of these may be supplied from the Verstolk collection.

Judging however from the very high prices at which the drawings by Rembrandt sold at the Baron's sale at Amsterdam in March, it may fairly be presumed that the etchings of the master will sell in the same proportion. Should this prove the case, there will be little opportunity of obtaining so large a quantity as the Museum is in want of, but at a price far exceeding that at which they are offered by Messrs Smith, which is £3,317. It therefore becomes a question whether it may not be more desirable to purchase the selection from Lord Aylesford's collection, not on this account solely, but because some thirty will be obtained which are not in any other collection. Indeed the larger portion of those now offered are only to be found in national collections, and it may be added that they are all in the finest possible condition.

Another very interesting portion, perhaps the most so in a national point of view is a collection of about 500 of the rarest and finest engraved portraits of the English series, ranging from Elizabeth I to Charles II by Delaram, the Pass's, Marshall, Hollar, Faithorne, etc. The price named for them is £1,106.13.6. They are with few exceptions prints of high price as will be seen on consulting the catalogues of Sir M. M. Sykes's and Mr Ord. Mr Woodburn himself having paid no less a sum than £545.18.6 for 17 of the identical prints now offered for purchase.

Sixteen Faithorne's have also been selected which nearly complete the splendid series of that master's works in the Museum. The price named for them is £135. Two of these are of excessive rarity, 'Oliver Cromwell between the pillars' and a proof of 'Margaret Smith'. Of this latter only one other impression is known which is in the Bibliothèque Nationale in Paris. For these prints Mr Woodburn paid £96.12.0.

The collection of portraits now in the Museum consists with few exceptions of the collection made by Mr Cracherode to illustrate Granger's History of England and is consequently very limited. Mr C takes the liberty of laying before the Trustees such volumes of that work as contain the enumeration of the several series to which the portraits now offered belong. In them are marked off all the prints already in the Museum which will enable the Trustees at once to see how deficient the collection is in this truly national department.

The collection of Hollar's works now in the Museum is a fine one and contains many of the rarest and most expensive prints. It still wants many to render it complete. 374 have therefore been selected not being in the collection, and to them are added nine drawings, one of them being very interesting as representing the judges sitting in an open court at Westminster Hall. The price named for the prints and drawings is £180.

29 rare and curious prints by early Italian and German masters. are inserted in the list at the price of £186. One of them the Martyrdom of St Lawrence by Marc Antonio in an early state, is of such extreme rarity that only one other has at any time been brought forward for public sale, and that was in the course of last year in Paris in the Debois collection. It had been very much repaired but was purchased by a French amateur at the large price of 2,600 francs. The one now offered is in a very fine state.

There is also a most extensive and curious collection of the prints engraved after the designs of Rosso Rossi, Primaticcio etc. known as the school of Fontainebleau, amounting to 605, only 274 being described by Bartsch. These, at the price named for the whole, average about 4/- each.

Messrs Smith have also put down the collection of prints by and after Parmegiano and his school. It is the finest and most extensive ever brought together, and contains many of rare occurrence. It was formed by Mr Ford, and was offered for sale some years ago by that gentleman to the Trustees at the price of £600. It contains 2,063 specimens, and is now offered at £350, which does not average 3/6 per print.

Mr Carpenter thinks the purchase of the whole most desirable at the price named, but he respectfully begs to say that he looks on the acquisition of the Rembrandts, and the series of English portraits to be so important that every effort should be made to secure them to the Museum.

Index

This is a selective index of names, organisations and a very few subjects. It omits the names of most artists who are merely mentioned with little or no information being given about them. But it does aim at fairly comprehensive coverage of the names of collectors and dealers.